MASTERING

British politics

Palgrave Master Series

Accounting	Human Resource Management
Accounting Skills	Information Technology
Advanced English Language	International Trade
Advanced Pure Mathematics	Internet
Arabic	Java
Arabic Grammar	Language of Literature
Arabic Script	Management Skills
Basic Management	Marketing Management
Biology	Mathematics
British Politics	Microsoft Office
Business Communication	Microsoft Windows, Novell
Business Environment	NetWare and UNIX
C Programming	Modern British History
C++ Programming	Modern European History
Chemistry	Modern German History 1864–1990
COBOL Programming	Modern United States History
Communication	Modern World History
Computing	Networks
Counselling Skills	Novels of Jane Austen
Counselling Theory	Organisational Behaviour
Customer Relations	Pascal and Delphi Programming
Database Design	Personal Finance
Delphi Programming	Philosophy
Desktop Publishing	Physics
e-Business	Poetry
Economic and Social History	Practical Criticism
Economics	Psychology
Electrical Engineering	Public Relations
Electronics	Shakespeare
Employee Development	Social Welfare
English Grammar	Sociology
English Language	Spanish
English Literature	Statistics
Fashion Buying and Merchandising	Strategic Management
Management	Systems Analysis and Design
Fashion Marketing	Team Leadership
Fashion Styling	Theology
Financial Management	Twentieth-Century Russian History
Geography	Visual Basic
Global Information Systems	World Religions
Globalization of Business	

www.palgravemasterseries.com

Macmillan Master Series
Series Standing Order ISBN 0-333-69343-4
(outside North America only)

You can receive future titles in this series as they are published by
placing a standing order. Please contact your bookseller or, in case
of difficulty, write to us at the address below with your name and
address, the title of the series and the ISBN quoted above.

Customer Services Department, Macmillan Distribution Ltd
Houndmills, Basingstoke, Hampshire RG21 6XS, England

MASTERING

British politics

fifth edition

f. n. forman
and
n. d. j. baldwin

First edition 1985
Second edition 1991
Third edition 1996
Fourth edition 1997
Fifth edition 2007

Published by
PALGRAVE MACMILLAN
Houndmills, Basingstoke, Hampshire RG21 6XS and
175 Fifth Avenue, New York, N.Y. 10010
Companies and representatives throughout the world

PALGRAVE MACMILLAN is the global academic imprint of the
Palgrave Macmillan division of St. Martin's Press, LLC and of Palgrave
Publishers Ltd. Macmillan® is a registered trademark in the United
States, United Kingdom and other countries. Palgrave is a registered
trademark in the European Union and other countries.

ISBN-13: 978-0-230-00012-4
ISBN-10: 0-230-00012-6

The book is printed on paper suitable for recycling and made
from fully managed and sustained forest sources. Logging, pulping
and manufacturing processes are expected to conform to the
environmental regulations of the country of origin.

A catalogue record for this book is available from the British Library.

A catalog record for this book is available from the Library of
Congress.

10   9   8   7   6   5   4   3   2   1
16   15   14   13   12   11   10   09   08   07

Printed and bound in Great Britain by
Creative Print & Design (Wales), Ebbw Vale

To our parents

Contents

list of figures

preface

This book is a general introduction to the British system of government and politics. It is an attempt to convey clear information about every significant aspect of the subject and to facilitate an understanding of the British political system and contemporary British politics.

Since the fourth edition of this book was published in 1999, a great deal of consequence has happened in British politics. Perhaps most significant has been the theme of 'modernisation' which became the hallmark of New Labour in office. It only really got into its stride in 1999, since the first two years of the first Blair Administration saw the Labour Government deliberately adhering to the spending plans of the previous Conservative Government.

However, the theme of modernisation proved to be so elastic and politically useful that it has been stretched to cover almost any aspect of Government policy. Thus the constitutional reform agenda of devolution, human rights and the rest was sold to Parliament and the country as one manifestation of modernisation, while the new delivery agenda in the public services was presented as another form of modernisation, particularly from 2001 when the then Prime Minister, Tony Blair, publicly attached his personal prestige to the idea.

Another large and influential theme evident in British politics during the first decade of the twenty-first century has been the accelerating erosion of the power and influence of a medium-sized nation state such as the United Kingdom. We noted this in the Preface to the fourth edition, but it is a theme which has assumed extra significance with the rise of China, India and, probably, Brazil in the economic power stakes by dint of their dynamic and young populations and their increasing significance in the global supply and consumption chain.

What this means for political scientists is that national political institutions are challenged from above and below, their jurisdiction is challenged from within and without, and their traditional competences are challenged by new power centres to be found principally in the global media and financial markets. The result is that it is becoming harder to write about 'British politics' as an authentic and recognisably distinct area of study or social experience and people living in these islands, as elsewhere, are increasingly seeing themselves as individuals rooted essentially in their immediate localities, but identifying also with wider communities of geography, ethnicity and religious faith.

A third theme which has dominated political and public discussion since '9/11' and '7/7' is undoubtedly 'the war against terror' and the war in Iraq and its tragic aftermath when British armed forces were committed to operate alongside American and other national units to be part of a so-called 'coalition of the willing'. The political and legal significance of these developments is not hard to discern, since, among other things, it has affected the balance in British society between individual human rights and public security. It also brought into sharp focus the issue of public trust (or the lack of it) in a British system of central Government which is still encrusted with opportunities for the Executive to exercise its power even in the face of widespread public opposition. The resulting damage to public trust in government has been stark and may take a long time to heal. Consequently, the restoration of trust will need to be an objective of any future Administration.

For this edition of the book the practical consequences of these real-world developments are apparent in the wide array of constitutional changes that have taken place in the UK, in the increasing internationalisation of government and politics, and in the policies that have been implemented in the spheres of both state security and individual human rights. The structure of the book reflects this – with new chapters having been added, while throughout the book these developments and their consequences are outlined and explained.

Of course, not everything has changed in the eight years or so since the last edition of this book. Britain and its political system are still recognisably the same as they were in the 1990s and before. Yet the three large themes mentioned in this preface have all left a noticeable mark on the ways in which 'we do politics' in Britain and we are inclined to believe that there is now a new political paradigm characterised by the decline of traditional ideologies and the rise of transient celebrity in their place. We hope it will be apparent to those who use this book, whether they are familiar with the material or come to it with a fresh mind, that British politics are an endlessly fascinating subject which repays close study by experts and laymen alike.

Any insights achieved in this edition – and earlier editions – owe a great deal to those with whom we have discussed these subjects over many years. Any errors of fact or opinion are entirely our own responsibility.

F. N. FORMAN
N. D. J. BALDWIN
London and Wroxton
June 2007

acknowledgements

The authors and publishers wish to thank the following for permission to use copyright material: The Controller of HMSO and the Queen's Printer for Scotland for Crown copyright material reproduced under Class Licence No. CO1W0000276; Guardian News & Media Ltd for research data from 'Main National Newspapers in Britain', *The Guardian*, 11 September 2006, copyright © Guardian News & Media Ltd 2006; Ipsos MORI for Figure 4.2 from 'Profile of the Electorate 1979–2005' (amended); Tim O'Donovan for Figure 9.2 from his letter to *The Times*, 1 January 2007; Michael Rush for Figure 11.2 adapted from Michael Rush, 'Parliament: Pay and Resources' included in N. D. J. Baldwin (ed.) *Parliament in the 21st Century* (London: Politico's, 2005).

Every effort has been made to trace all the copyright-holders, but if any have been inadvertently overlooked the publishers will be pleased to make the necessary arrangement at the first opportunity.

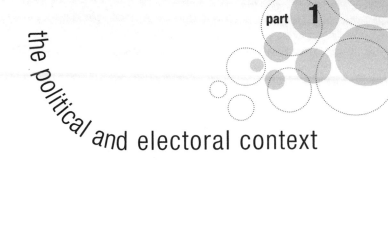

the political and electoral context

part 1

chapter 1

British political culture: an exceptional polity?

The term 'political culture' is taken to mean the historical, cultural and attitudinal setting within which British political institutions have to function.[1] It is possible to identify a number of key characteristics which influence both the process and the outcome of politics in Britain.

1.1 key characteristics

The key characteristics of British political culture can be stated quite simply, but they need to be qualified and refined if they are to be useful to students of British politics. It has often been said that politics in Britain are influenced by the evolutionary adaptability of its political institutions, the notable continuity of its history, the concept of Parliamentary sovereignty, the unitary nature of the state, the underlying cohesion of the society and the degree of political agreement on fundamental issues. Traditionally, there has been considerable moderation in the policies pursued by successive Governments and this has been matched by a considerable degree of public detachment from the process of politics, except on occasions when political crises or closely fought elections heighten media and public interest.

General statements of this kind have often been made and sometimes in a rather complacent tone. Yet it would be unwise to accept them at face value and it is better to examine the extent to which they accord with political conditions today.

evolutionary adaptability

In Saxon times kings were guided by the 'Witan' or 'Witenagemot', an assembly of the most important men – lay and ecclesiastical – in the kingdom. The membership was not static and consisted of those individuals whom the King chose to summon to the three or four meetings held annually. As Ronald Butt put it, 'his natural advisers were the elders; the men of strength, standing, influence, experience and knowledge.'[2] Those present included the chief officers of the Royal Household and others who held high state office, the 'Earldormen' who represented central Government in the shires, Bishops and other senior churchmen, and the principal men who held land directly from the King. The functions of the Witan were ill-defined, but included 'discovering and declaring' the law, in other words being a consultative and law-consenting assembly. In addition, the Witan sat as the King's Supreme Court of Justice. Its actual power was inversely proportional to that of the King at any given time. Together the King and the Witan were the highest authority in the nation.

A new stage in the development of the nation's political institutions was ushered in when Duke William of Normandy defeated Harold, the Saxon claimant to the throne, at the battle of Hastings in 1066. William the Conqueror (as he came to be known) launched a series of campaigns which, in the fullness of time, left him in undisputed control of the country. It was William's claim that he had succeeded to the throne through inheritance. As a result he laid claim to an element of continuity and sought to maintain many of the laws of his Saxon predecessors. At the same time, however, he brought with him from Normandy a new approach to government, namely the feudal system, whereby the greater part of the country was governed by tenants-in-chief, or barons, who held their land directly from the King on condition that they defended the conquered territory for the King. By the time of the Domesday survey of 1085–86, only about eight per cent of the land remained in English hands; indeed, of the tenants-in-chief only two appear to have been English.

The Norman barons assembled in the Court of their sovereign to regulate the affairs of their tenancies, settle disputes between each other and organise the military subjection of the conquered lands. The tenants-in-chief thus assembled – both lay and ecclesiastical – became known as the Magnum Concilium or Great Council. This gathering assisted the King in determining state policy, supervised the work of public administration, acted as the highest Court of Justice, and made or modified the laws of the land. It met only three or four times a year, and then only for a matter of days at a time. For this reason there grew up the Curia Regis or 'Court of the King' – an inner circle of the Great Council – whose function it was to assist the sovereign on a day-to-day basis during the long periods when the Great Council was not assembled.

This system of government worked well for a while, but towards the end of the twelfth century tensions between the King and his 'great men' began to increase. Matters were brought to a head by the abuse of autocratic power by King John. Consequently the barons seized an opportunity in 1215, when the King's position was weakened by war and misrule, to force him to sign a Magna Carta or Great Charter, setting out some clear principles and safeguards against further abuse of power by the Monarch. The intention of the barons was not to create a new system of government, but rather to ensure better government under the existing system. The agreement foreshadowed three of the main principles upon which the development of Parliament was later to be based, namely that:

- The King himself was subject to the law
- The King could only make law and levy taxation with the consent of the governed
- The King's subjects did not owe the King absolute or unconditional obedience.[3]

In short, it asserted the limited nature of kingship – the principle of conditional or 'constitutional' Monarchy which was to be the mainspring of Parliamentary action against the Crown in the seventeenth century.

Within three months of the King's seal being affixed to Magna Carta, however, the concordat which it was supposed to symbolise broke down. John died in October 1216 to be succeeded by Henry III, then a boy of nine. Henry occupied the throne for the next 56 years during which time politics were dominated by the struggle between the Crown and the barons. The relationship between the King and the barons deteriorated eventually to the point of armed conflict in which the barons under Simon de Montfort were victorious. In 1265 de Montfort convened a Parliament (literally a 'talking gathering') which was attended not only by the barons, clergy and knights of the shires, but also by two burgesses from each of the boroughs known to be supportive of the baronial cause. This occasion has since been widely recognised as the real beginning of Parliament at Westminster, and it is the recognition of this date which allows the British Parliament to claim that it is one of the oldest Parliaments in the world.

During the decades and centuries which followed, the holding of 'Parliaments' containing representatives of the counties and towns became the accepted custom and practice and 'Parliament' itself became a feature of the governmental system. At no time was Parliament definitively established, it merely evolved as a consultative forum for the King and the politically important sections of his realm. By about 1485 – the beginning of the Tudor period – it may be said that the institutional foundations of Britain's constitutional Monarchy had been laid.

The Tudor Monarchs found that there was political advantage for them in having their national policies – such as Henry VIII's break with the Catholic Church or Elizabeth I's determination to oppose the Spanish kings – supported and endorsed by the people's representatives in Acts of Parliament. For this reason no Tudor Monarch sought to dispense with Parliament and each member of the dynasty in turn put its support to good use. However, sessions of Parliament were infrequent and brief. Even during the 45-year reign of Elizabeth I, when Parliament counted for more than had previously been the case, the two Houses (Lords and Commons) were in session on average for little more than three weeks a year. During this period, the House of Lords became predominantly a secular body, while the House of Commons increased in size by more than a third to about 300 members. By the end of the sixteenth century Parliament had become second only to the Monarch as a power in the land.

Constitutional tensions came to the fore under the Stuarts, especially James I and Charles I, who laid claim to the 'divine right of kings' and sought to reduce or deny the privileges acquired by Parliament under the Tudors. The mounting disagreements between Crown and Parliament eventually led to the Civil War (1642–49), the triumph of the Parliamentary forces, the execution of Charles I and the abolition of the Monarchy itself. For the next few years the country was ruled by Oliver Cromwell in what was called a Protectorate. It was not until after Cromwell's death in 1658 that the Monarchy was restored, Charles II reclaiming the throne for the Stuarts in 1660. However, the relationship between the Monarch and Parliament was not a great deal better than before the Civil War and matters worsened under James II as he sought to reassert the divine right of kings. The eventual result was that Parliament and people combined against the King who fled the country in 1688 and was replaced by William of Orange (from Holland) and his English wife Mary – daughter of James II – in 1689. This peaceful transfer of constitutional power from one Monarch to another – but actually from the Monarchy to Parliament – has been described by Whig historians as 'the Glorious Revolution'. The new constitutional settlement was given statutory recognition in the 1689 Bill of Rights. The 'pretended power' of the Crown to suspend or dispense laws, or to govern without the consent of Parliament was declared illegal, as was the levying of taxation by Royal prerogative without the authority of Parliament. The 1689 Bill of Rights and the 1701 Act of Settlement confirmed the victory of Parliament in the struggle against the Crown. Constitutional Monarchy was developed in place of the unfettered rights of Kings and Queens, and Parliamentary supremacy in the government of the country was well and truly established.

From the beginning of the Hanoverian dynasty in 1714, the role of the Monarch was reduced still further. George I (1714–1727) was a German, speaking no English and knowing nothing of English ideas and ways. George II (1727–1760), although more interested in his adopted land, lacked the ability to make himself felt in government affairs. In these circumstances the powers which their predecessors had so jealously sought to preserve fell into disuse or into the hands of the English aristocracy who effectively ran the country throughout the eighteenth century. George III (1760–1820), perhaps more English than Hanoverian, tried to recapture the Royal position that had been lost. His influence on Government and politics was far greater than that of his two predecessors to the extent that in 1780 the House of Commons felt driven to declare that the 'influence of the Crown has increased, is increasing, and ought to be diminished'.[4]

After the resignation of Lord North as Prime Minister in 1782, the tide turned back in favour of Parliament, and, during the last decades of his reign, the King was discredited by madness. By then a satisfactory way of running the Government without the active participation of the Monarch had been developed. This fact, soon to be buttressed by successive extensions of the franchise in the nineteenth century, meant that no Monarch could turn back the clock.

There has been notable continuity in the history of the British Isles and the country is one of the oldest nation states in Europe. Although there have also been some notable discontinuities in Britain's national history, such as the Civil War and the Cromwellian Interregnum in the mid-seventeenth century, the country has not been invaded successfully against the popular will since 1066 and the only successful revolution since the Civil War was the political coup of 1688–89 when James II fled the throne and William of Orange and his wife Mary were invited by Parliament from Holland to take his place. This historical continuity applies, to a greater or lesser extent, to all parts of the United Kingdom.

Wales was the first part of the British Isles to be politically joined to England by Edward I and other warrior kings in the fourteenth century. The link was later reinforced and personified by the victory of Henry Tudor, a Welsh warlord, at the battle of Bosworth Field in 1485 and subsequently ratified by Act of Parliament in 1536 at the behest of his son, Henry VIII.

The monarchical bond with *Scotland* was first established in 1603 when James VI of Scotland succeeded Elizabeth I of England and so became James I of England. The constitutional bond was later sealed by the Act of Union in 1707 which abolished the Scottish Parliament and incorporated Scottish representatives into the British Parliament at Westminster.

The troubled relationship between *Ireland* and England can be traced back at least to the Anglo-Norman invasion of Ireland in 1169–71. For centuries thereafter Ireland and England were periodically at loggerheads and it was the fate of the Irish people to be intermittently subdued and then ignored by the British. Eventually, Britain and Ireland were constitutionally united by the Act of Union in 1800. This was by no means a stable political settlement and the mainly Catholic Irish resented their treatment at the hands of the mainly Protestant British, some of whose kith and kin had been firmly settled in Ulster since the seventeenth century. Notwithstanding several unsuccessful attempts by Gladstone to legislate for Irish Home Rule in the second half of the nineteenth century, the constitutional link with Britain was challenged by the Irish nationalist uprising in 1916 and subsequently ruptured by the partition of Ireland in 1921–22 and the creation of Northern Ireland from six counties in Ulster as the last remaining part of the United Kingdom on the island of Ireland.

The result of this long and chequered history in the British Isles is that four different nationalities now coexist in what is known officially as 'the United Kingdom of Great Britain and Northern Ireland'. However, it will be convenient for the rest of this book to use the more colloquial term 'Britain' when referring to the country as a whole. Figure 1.1 is a map of the British Isles showing the boundaries of England, Wales, Scotland and Northern Ireland.

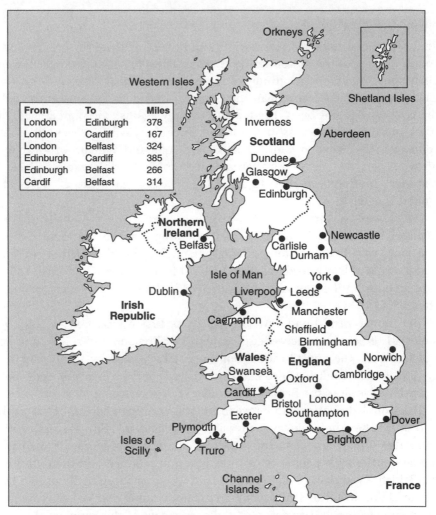

From	To	Miles
London	Edinburgh	378
London	Cardiff	167
London	Belfast	324
Edinburgh	Cardiff	385
Edinburgh	Belfast	266
Cardif	Belfast	314

figure **1.1**   **map of the British Isles showing the boundaries of England, Wales, Scotland and Northern Ireland**

parliamentary sovereignty

Unlike the situation in the United States or Germany, where there are codified federal constitutions which define the legal rights and duties of the various levels of government, in Britain it is Parliament which is legally and constitutionally supreme (except in those matters covered by European Treaties to which this country has agreed where European law prevails over national law – although only at the behest of Parliament) and its writ runs throughout the United Kingdom. Of course (as we shall see in Chapters 18 and 21), the law of the land is interpreted and sometimes modified by judicial decisions of the British Courts and, increasingly, by the European Court of Justice as well. Yet in Britain it is still a basic constitutional principle that no institution is, or should be, on a par with, let alone above, Parliament and it is this which, historically, has given force to the idea that Britain is a Parliamentary democracy.

One important consequence of Britain's national history is that the British people live in a unitary state – possibly the most unitary state in the entire European Union (see Chapter 21). This means essentially that the laws passed by Parliament at Westminster apply normally to the entire country and in most respects it is correct to say that the country is governed from London.

This statement, however, does have to be qualified to take account not only of Britain's membership of the European Union, but also the devolution of powers to Scotland and Wales and the potential for greater self-government in Northern Ireland on the assumption that the 'peace process' can be renewed and the devolved Assembly at Stormont can not only be restored but function normally over a period of time (see Chapter 16). There is also an embryonic structure for regional government/administration in England as well as a clear – albeit recently much altered – structure of local government in Britain whose elected members can claim a degree of democratic legitimacy and whose appointed officials still carry considerable burdens of responsibility for many national services delivered locally. Yet (as we shall see in Chapter 17) the powers and functions of local government are determined by the decisions of central Government in Whitehall acting through legislation passed by Parliament at Westminster.

One of the defining characteristics of the United Kingdom today is that there are probably more self-conscious national (or sometimes nationalist) differences between the major nations (or tribes) than there were during most of the twentieth century when the social effects of two world wars and a number of important Left–Right ideological cleavages contributed to a degree of British national cohesion which was not seen either before or after that period. The reasons for this development are complicated and contentious, but it seems plausible that the effects of rising prosperity coupled with growing disenchantment with the two main parties served (in various measure) to release or fan national or nationalist aspirations in Wales, Scotland and Northern Ireland.

In *Wales*, a small minority of the Welsh are Welsh speaking and for many decades have been attracted to the cause of *Plaid Cymru*, the Welsh Nationalist Party, particularly at times when the powerful Welsh Labour Party was thought to have let them down. A limited measure of devolution for Wales was introduced into the Westminster Parliament by the Callaghan Administration in the late 1970s, but it failed to take effect in 1979 when only 12 per cent of the Welsh electorate – only 20.3 per cent of those voting – supported the policy in a referendum. However, the Blair Administration handled the issue more deftly after its victory at the 1997 General Election and a modest degree of devolution was introduced in the Wales Act 1998 which had narrowly won the approval of the Welsh people in a Welsh referendum held *before* the legislation was put to the Westminster Parliament. Since that time there has been a Welsh National Assembly with a modest – although increasing – range of devolved powers which has served to give

	England	Wales	Scotland	Northern Ireland
Supranational	The European Union (78 UK MEPs)			
	64 MEPs	4 MEPs	7 MEPs	3 MEPs
	The Council of the Isles			
				North–South Ministerial Council
National	The Government of the United Kingdom			
	The House of Lords (approx. 750)			
	The House of Commons (646 MPs)			
	529 MPs	40 MPs	59 MPs	18 MPs
Devolved	9 Government Offices of the Regions 9 Regional Development Agencies Regional Chambers	**Assembly** Leader Executive 60 Members	**Parliament** First Minister Cabinet 129 Members	**Assembly** First Minister Deputy Minister Executive Committee 108 Members
Local	*England (Excluding London)* 34 County Councils 46 Unitary Councils 9 Directly elected mayors 36 Metropolitan District Councils 238 Non-Metropolitan District Councils 10,000 (Approx) Parish Councils *London* **Greater London Authority** Directly elected Mayor 25 Member Assembly 32 Borough Councils 3 Directly elected mayors The Corporation of the City of London	22 Single-tier Authorities 700 Community Councils	29 Single-tier Authorities 3 Unitary Island Councils 1150 (approx) Community Councils	26 District Councils

figure **1.2**   **the structure of government in the United Kingdom** respectable prominence to the cause of Welsh nationalism in all parts of the Principality.

In *Scotland*, a larger minority of the Scots identify with the cause of Scottish nationalism and some of these have consistently voted for the Scottish National Party (SNP) ever since it began to encounter electoral success at by-elections in the 1960s and 1970s. In order to head off the threat of an independent Scotland within the European Union (by then well established SNP policy), the Labour and Liberal Democrat parties in Scotland (in alliance with other non-party opinion formers) combined to campaign for a more ambitious programme of devolution for Scotland which was embodied successfully in the Scotland Act 1998 – once again after taking the precaution of getting an affirmative vote in a Scottish referendum *before* the legislation was put to the Westminster Parliament.[5] Since 1999 there has been a Scottish Parliament once again with a fairly extensive range of devolved powers, establishing devolution as a viable halfway house between unitary government for the UK and independence for Scotland. The extent to which it is a viable half-way house, let alone a means to head off the Nationalist threat, was brought into sharp foicus with the emergence of the SNP as the largest single party and its leader, Alex Salmond, becoming First Minister following the 2007 Scottish Parliamentary Election.

In *Northern Ireland*, political circumstances and popular attitudes are more peculiar and have been difficult for outsiders to understand or explain. Political allegiances have been divided on religious and constitutional lines for centuries according to the contrasting attitudes of the Protestant/Unionist/Loyalist and Catholic/Nationalist/Republican communities towards the idea of eventual Irish reunification. The hard- line Protestant/Unionist/Loyalists wrap themselves in the Union Jack, but might prefer to have self-government for their part of Ireland largely free from Westminster control as they were from 1922 to 1972, when they governed themselves from Stormont Castle in Belfast. The hard-line Catholic/ Nationalist/Republicans, who support Sinn Fein (the political wing of the Irish Republican movement in the North), have been prepared to use both the bomb and the ballot box in their long struggle for reunification with the rest of Ireland.

Since the end of 1993 the British and Irish Governments have worked together in their joint efforts to advance what has been described as the 'peace process' in Northern Ireland. This initiative by the two Governments was originally prompted by exploratory talks between John Hume, the then leader of the Social Democratic and Labour Party, and Gerry Adams, leader of Sinn Fein. It was publicly formalised in the Downing Street Declaration signed on 15th December 1993 by the two Prime Ministers, John Major for the UK Government and Albert Reynolds for the Irish Government. It was later carried forward by paramilitary ceasefires announced by the Irish Republican Army (IRA) and the Unionist paramilitaries in August and September 1994. With many alarms and excursions along the way, agreement between all the parties was eventually reached in Belfast on Good Friday 1998, thus paving the way for the establishment of a devolved Assembly based upon proportional representation and parity of esteem between the two main communities in Northern Ireland.

The path towards permanent peace and reconciliation in Northern Ireland has been far from smooth and relations between the two communities have been blighted by waves of mistrust and mutual recrimination. The moderate Ulster Unionists – then led by David Trimble – agreed to form a power-sharing devolved Administration with the Sinn Fein leaders, Gerry Adams and Martin McGuinness, but the democratic credentials of the latter have been frequently undermined by the recalcitrance of the IRA who agreed only to limited and non-transparent forms of weapons de-commissioning and hesitated over recognising the police and the court system in Northern Ireland. This, in turn, had the long-term effect of undermining and all but eliminating the pro-Agreement Ulster Unionists and bringing the anti-Agreement Democratic Unionists, led by the Reverend Ian Paisley, to the forefront and into contention as possible partners in a potential coalition Government. Indeed this Administration of polar opposites came into being in 2007 and we wait to see if it can be a firm foundation for viable government.

Due allowance must, therefore, be made for all these nationalist and centrifugal forces in the United Kingdom. The nationalist forces have driven forward the process of devolution in Scotland and Wales, and they could have done the same thing in Northern Ireland if it had not been for the ideology of the IRA which for so long rejected the idea of laying down its arms before the strategic goal of Irish reunification had been achieved. The growth of cultural diversity in the UK has been equally influential, especially in the great cities and conurbations of England, so much so that the previously homogeneous English are now conspicuously less confident about their ability to defend any historic connection between their ethnicity and their nationality.

social cohesion and cultural diversity

For centuries there has been considerable social cohesion in Britain. This has meant that in many respects the great majority of the British people lived recognisably similar lives and held a range of common attitudes based upon a body of received ideas and a good deal of common experience. They purchased goods and services designed for a mass market, they used common public services such as education, health and transport, they earned their living in a number of broadly recognisable ways, they spent their leisure time in a range of familiar pursuits, and they shared broadly similar aspirations for themselves and their families. Above all, they were subjected every day to many similar influences derived from mass advertising and the mass media which contributed in a variety of ways to the creation of a shared national experience. In short, the emphasis was on homogeneity.

More recently, however, there has been a material shift away from such a position with some important variations being apparent which seem to have grown in significance over recent years and which have served to offset the traditional concept of cohesion. For example, while in the country as a whole ethnic minorities make up less than 10 per cent of the entire population, there are parts of the large cities and conurbations – for example, London, Bradford and Leicester – where people from ethnic minorities account for more than 20 per cent and sometimes as much as 40 per cent of the local population.[6] These demographic developments, fuelled by the growth of global immigration, both legal and illegal, have led some from within the Moslem community, for example, to call for the establishment of legal and constitutional arrangements designed to give them a distinct identity and a significant degree of cultural, religious and social self-government within the United Kingdom.

In all parts of the country British society still divides on class lines, although many of the traditional class distinctions based upon the occupation of the head of household have been rendered increasingly meaningless by changes in the labour market and in the balance of economic power and responsibilities within families.[7]

From one point of view it seems that, as people in all classes become more similar in their ways of life and materialist aspirations, the tendency towards social uniformity could increase. Yet from another point of view this looks unlikely whenever there is a widening of the disparities of income and wealth between the poorest and the richest sections of society.[8] Indeed, current social developments in Britain and elsewhere suggest that there remains a significant gulf between the experience and prospects of the well-off majority and that of various disadvantaged minorities, such as the young unemployed, the excluded elderly or certain ill-educated groups whose lives can be both frustrating and demoralising.

Much depends upon the extent to which common economic and social aspirations are fulfilled or thwarted by the distribution of the available opportunities between different individuals, social groups and parts of the country. It will also depend upon the extent to which chauvinist or racist attitudes are stoked up or dampened down when the authorities have to deal with an increasingly diverse society.

deference and its decline

Until the early 1960s the British were recognised as deferential people and this characteristic is still to be found among those of older generations today. However, in British society at large deference is no longer a defining characteristic, because class divisions have been challenged and underprivileged members of society are no longer prepared simply to accept their lot and then defer to those with greater income and wealth, opportunity and privilege.

The decline of deference has been a gradual process provoked first by satirical challenges to the Establishment and members of the ruling elite in the 1960s and 1970s and later extended by Thatcherite Conservatives who stimulated an iconoclastic individualism among those who were increasingly attracted to the merits of free markets and who subscribed to a version of 'the devil take the hindmost' in the 1980s. The growth of economic opportunities during this period contributed to widespread public expectations that people could achieve anything if they worked really hard, especially if they were lucky enough to buy their own council house at a subsidised price or become part of the growing army of 'popular capitalists' who emerged in response to successive privatisations of state assets releasing shares in profitable public utilities at discounted prices.

This democratisation of economic opportunities stimulated individualistic attitudes among many who had previously subscribed to collectivist causes and produced much more upward social mobility than had been the case during the first half of the twentieth century. By the time that Margaret Thatcher was toppled by her own party in 1990, it is fair to say that British society, and hence British politics, had changed significantly. For example, trade union representation of what used to be called 'the working class' had been reduced by half, the state industrial sector had been reduced by two-thirds, and civil service numbers had been cut by nearly 300,000 thus contributing to the slimming of the state. By 1997 when New Labour came to power, the younger generation, who had had their formative experience of politics under the rule of free-market Conservatives, were more than happy to reject the social stereotypes of their parents and grandparents and in the process to challenge the more traditional elements who sought to 'put them in their place'. Indeed, Lord (Norman) Tebbit famously observed after the Tories suffered their tidal defeat in 1997 that the real achievement of Thatcherism had been to make it safe for the country to elect a Labour Government.

New Labour arrived in office committed to remove the hereditary peers from the House of Lords and with a markedly unsentimental, even utilitarian, attitude towards the Monarchy which, in any case, had been through a very bad patch in the 1990s as a result, amongst other things, of the marital problems of the younger Royals. For these and other reasons deference as an appropriate social attitude was well and truly discredited and the British people seemed ready to embark upon a more egalitarian future.

the dominance of party politics

Party commitment and partisan politics have long been the most potent and noticeable characteristics in the British political system. British government is party government – government by and through national, organised, disciplined political parties. Typically this means government by a single 'umbrella' party which has managed to win the previous General Election by winning a larger number of seats in the House of Commons than any of its competitors for office. Party loyalty plays a vital part in determining the ways in which the party in office actually carries out the duties of Government and manages to preserve a majority in the House of Commons to sustain itself in office.

Traditionally, British politics has usually been associated with two-party politics. This is based upon the simple idea that the two strongest parties typically compete to gain or retain political power, while the others are significant only at the margin or in atypical political circumstances. Thus there were the Whigs and the Tories in the seventeenth and eighteenth centuries, the Liberals and Conservatives in the nineteenth century and Labour and the

Conservatives in the twentieth century. Yet what this simple binary model tends to overlook is that there have been periods of flux in British party politics and that, during these periods, multiparty politics has been the norm with three, four or more parties all competing for decisive influence upon the British body politic. Thus Irish Nationalists in the nineteenth century, Communists and Fascists in the 1920s and 1930s, Liberals and Nationalists in the 1970s, the Alliance in the 1980s and Liberal Democrats, Scottish Nationalists and Welsh Nationalists in more recent times have all wielded important political influence, notwithstanding the fact that either the Labour party or the Conservative party has been the governing party with a secure overall majority in Parliament for the vast majority of the time since the 1920s.

It was a convenient part of this conventional analysis that for most of the twentieth century the binary division into two main parties coincided with the ideological division between Left-Labour and Right-Conservative. Yet this crude linear analysis was in many ways as misleading as it was revealing, since there have been times when MPs on the Left of the Conservative party were more progressive and MPs on the Right of the Labour party were more reactionary than some of their counterparts across the floor of the House. Indeed, contemporary ideological positioning in British politics is much more complicated and subtle than the traditional Left–Right model will ever allow and the true picture is better represented by a matrix which positions politicians in any one of four quadrants (see Figure 1.3).

Thus Old Labour tended to be hostile to market forces and so favoured extensive state intervention in the working of the economy, yet it was dubious about heavy-handed legislative intervention to influence the behaviour and the values or ordinary people, as long as their private behaviour did not damage others. On the other hand, New Labour seems to be much more relaxed about

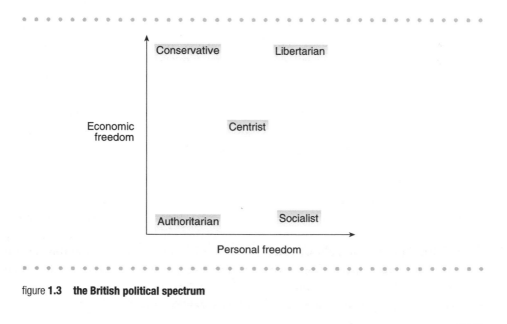

figure **1.3** **the British political spectrum**

the working of market forces and to be quite prepared to promote equality of opportunity and multiculturalism via exhortation and legislation. The contemporary Conservative party, on the other hand, does not appear to have made up its collective mind whether to be authoritarian or libertarian in social policy, although since the time of Margaret Thatcher it has been generally well disposed towards liberal market economics in nearly all circumstances. As for the Liberal Democrats, the party seeks to balance the values of liberty, equality and community – managing, according to its critics, to face both ways on most social issues – while promoting an approach to the economy which centres on the idea of state intervention in order to address clear instances of market failure. In short, party political fortunes are fluid and all three main parties have become markedly more pragmatic as they compete strenuously for the middle ground of British public opinion.

modernisation and policy consensus

Since the mid 1990s modernisation has been one of the most potent political buzzwords in British politics and it has begun to form the basis of a new political consensus which embraces most, although not all, elements of the three main parties. Indeed, ever since the Second World War periods of policy consensus have tended to follow periods of political polarisation. This was true of the era of 'Butskellism' from 1951 to 1964 which followed the post-war Labour Government of 1945–51; and it has been true of the era of 'modernisation' since 1997 which followed the polarisation of 1970 to 1990 when Edward Heath, Harold Wilson and Jim Callaghan led successive Administrations driven by competing Left or Right ideologies and the even more notable period of polarisation when Margaret Thatcher was Prime Minister from 1979 to 1990. In this schematic scenario, the discerning reader will have noticed that there were also two historical interludes (1964–70 and 1990–97) when Administrations led by Harold Wilson and John Major respectively seemed unwilling or unable to present themselves as full-blooded radicals or determined consolidators.

Be that as it may, the era of 'Butskellism' posed the Keynesian question: which of the two main parties could present itself as the most credible manager of mixed economy capitalism; while against the background of the 'Thatcherite revolution' the Blairite period seemed to focus on the post-Keynesian question: which of the three main parties could present itself as the most competent and credible pilot of the ship of state through the storms and shoals of global capitalism?

Since 1997, under the leadership of Tony Blair and Gordon Brown, modernisation has proved to be an elastic and sometimes elusive policy theme. To begin with, it seemed to be a presentational slogan to support the appealing electoral claims of New Labour. Then, in an act of filial piety to the memory of John Smith – the Labour Leader who died in 1994 – it became the central justification for a spate of legislation to engender institutional and constitutional reform, whether of Government and the Civil Service or Parliament and the rules of engagement under which politicians compete for power. Then, with the help of supportive intellectuals, such as Will Hutton or Anthony Giddens, it metamorphosed into 'stakeholder democracy' or the 'Third Way' – the latter being presented essentially as a matter of triangulation between Old Labour and Thatcherite Conservatism. More recently, it became the rubric for policies designed to improve the public services by introducing some market forces.

Underlying all manifestations of contemporary modernisation is the realisation that most national policies in the modern world have to be grounded in pragmatic business realities if they are to be fit for the overriding purposes of being able to compete and prosper in the contemporary global economy. Part of this hinges upon the widespread understanding that high-quality education and skills and the use of science and technology are the basis of modern employability and of any nation's ability to compete against the likes of China and India and, in the future perhaps, the likes of Brazil, Russia and Indonesia. There is also a virtually universal recognition of the need for fundamental welfare reform to bring the social overheads of a nation into line with what its economy can sustainably support. In short, we are seeing in Britain, the rest of 'old Europe' and throughout the industrial and post-industrial world the concept emerging (and being increasingly accepted) of the state as enabler, investor, tax raiser and regulator, but less and less as direct provider of public goods and services.

It may seem to be the case, at least rhetorically, that 'we are all modernisers now'. Yet this does not prevent many people from being sceptical about the characteristics of New Labour modernisation nor does it mean that this particular form of policy consensus has obliterated all debate and divisions both within and between the parties. For example, Britain's relationship with the rest of the European Union remains a potential source of turbulence and trouble in the ranks of both the Conservative and Labour parties, not least over the issues of a European Constitution and whether or not Britain should phase out the pound sterling and adopt the euro as part of a deliberate move to full participation in Economic and Monetary Union (see Chapter 21).

procedural consensus

For many years, even centuries, it was assumed and frequently stated that British politics were characterised by procedural consensus – that is, widespread agreement upon *how* politics should be conducted as opposed to what the political issues should be at any time.

This reflected general agreement within the political class on the desirability of using traditional Parliamentary channels for the discussion and approval of political change. This has meant that it is customary to regard General Election results as decisive mandates not only for the winning party but also for each elected MP, regardless of whether or not the winning party as a whole or individual candidates achieve an overall majority of the votes cast – be it in the nation at large or in an individual constituency. It has also entailed broad acceptance of the view that it is undesirable to make far reaching constitutional changes in the United Kingdom, affecting any or all of the established political procedures, unless these are backed by decisive all-party support in both Houses of Parliament.

These traditional assumptions have come under sustained assault: during Margaret Thatcher's Administrations – for example in legislation to control (emasculate) Labour-run local government; when John Major was Prime Minister and was determined to push through Parliamentary ratification of the 1992 Treaty of Maastricht in the face of determined and deeply divisive opposition from vociferous elements in his own party; and they have come under further assault from the far reaching constitutional reforms introduced by successive Blair Administrations, especially in the 1997–2001 Parliament (see Chapter 2). What this underlines is that, as long as Britain continues without a codified constitution, constitutional arrangements are heavily dependent upon established custom and practice in the political sphere and the self-restraint of all Governments.

Yet, as we have seen in recent years, this traditional approach is always vulnerable to the actions of a powerful Government which is determined to push through extensive constitutional changes of its own design and occasionally change the rules of the political game in ways which bring disproportionate benefit to those in office at the time. For example, the various initiatives to 'modernise' Parliamentary proceedings in the Commons since 1997 have led to a weakening of the elected chamber in relation to the Executive as Government Bills have been 'programmed' (timetabled), the Parliamentary week has been abbreviated and a 'parallel chamber' has been developed in the Grand Committee Room off Westminster Hall in which MPs can 'let off steam' without much discernible political effect. Only the House of Lords – partially reformed but overwhelmingly appointed – has seemed able to mount serious institutional challenges to the Executive, while the media, some non-governmental organisations and a few determined members of the public have found ways to embarrass or challenge the Government.

1.2 other significant features

There are a number of other significant features in British political culture which are worth mentioning in this chapter. Some are most closely associated with the period from 1945 to 1979 when the rules of the political game seemed reassuringly stable, even if there were times of considerable economic, social and political turbulence – such as the Suez Crisis in 1956, the Three Day Week in 1974 and the so-called Winter of Discontent in 1979. Others have arisen from new challenges to the system, some of which are connected with the impact of social diversity and multiculturalism and some of which are related to the growth of political alienation in various parts of society, notably the young, the immigrant communities and a section of the white working class. All of these influences have served to reduce the traditional cohesion of British society.

the caution of Governments

Most British Governments since the Second World War have behaved rather cautiously, but there have been a few notable exceptions. For example, the Attlee Administration from 1945 to 1951 was radical in establishing the foundations of the British welfare state and in its nationalisation of many of the 'commanding heights' of the British economy. The Thatcher Administration from 1979 to 1990 was widely considered to have been equally radical in a free market direction with its extensive privatisation and systematic attempts to curb the trade unions and shrink the size of the state. Yet for the rest of the 60-year span moderation in policy and caution in office were the habitual hallmarks of British central Government.

There are some pretty straightforward reasons for this general phenomenon. Firstly, the influence of the party in Government is typically offset by the varied, and sometimes mutually cancelling, influence of a vast number of interest groups and non-governmental organisations which have access to the policy and decision making process and which usually manage to prevent any party in office from being over-zealous or radical. Secondly, successive opinion polls, focus groups and other methods of taking the political temperature of the British people all tend to suggest that the vast majority of the public greatly prefer a style of politics based upon an atmosphere of constructive cooperation rather than destructive conflict and are more than likely to cast their votes at elections – or be put off voting altogether – under the influence of such a general preference.

A third and even more fundamental reason for political caution and restraint is that the economic and political realities of the modern world impose such cautious behaviour upon all national Governments, no matter how partisan and radical the political rhetoric may be. In the complex conditions of the interdependent world in which we live and with the obvious constraints of having to compete both in the European Union and in the global economy, every Government soon discovers that it can wield relatively little autonomous power, except at the margin of events and in limited circumstances for a short period of time until others catch up with any temporary advantage which may have been established. Both within the domestic national jurisdiction and in the complicated networks in which we have to operate abroad there are so many other influential participants in the economic and political process that any Government has to be very realistic in setting the political goals which it puts before the electorate. It is in this sense of impaired capacity for taking truly independent action that any modern Government is wise to be cautious and restrained in what it attempts to do.

public detachment from party politics

It has been said of British political culture that the British people are normally relatively detached from the process of party politics, put a high value on the maintenance of political stability and are not usually keen to face up to the need for radical change, especially if it would affect them directly.[9] This view is reflected in the typically low turnout at local elections and recently – especially in 2001 and 2005 – at General Elections as well. Indeed, in some quarters of society not merely detachment from but actual disenchantment with and alienation from might be a more appropriate term to describe the attitude of the young and the socially disaffected towards the party-political process.

Public detachment from party politics seems to be linked to a popular preference for privacy and a quiet life, which find expression not in joining political parties but rather in various social institutions from pubs to local amenity groups to sports and hobby clubs which absorb so much of the spare time and energy of many British people. In these circumstances the idea of active and continuous participation in the process of party politics appeals to no more than small and apparently shrinking minorities of the population, although the willingness to defend or promote particular causes has become a defining characteristic of the modern, media-influenced democracy in Britain.

Nonetheless, British people tend to join a myriad of voluntary organisations according to individual taste and experience. Indeed, the British are some of the foremost 'joiners' in the advanced countries of the world. Whether individuals are members of the National Trust or the Royal Society for the Protection of Birds, the Consumers' Association or the Countryside Alliance, the Animal Liberation Front or Amnesty International, they find themselves deeply involved in the process of politics from time to time, even if it is only in connection with a single issue on a narrow front (see Chapter 6). The most likely explanation for this apparent contradiction is that whereas most ordinary citizens have given up on the political parties as satisfactory agents for change and do not really trust the assurances of any Government – or indeed any politician – they are often strongly motivated to combine with other like-minded members of the public in well-organised and often well-financed groups to try to safeguard the interests of rural communities or stop the war in Iraq or prevent the expansion of Stansted Airport – to mention just three notable examples. Equally paradoxical perhaps is that this mistrust and even active dislike of all Governments does not prevent many of the same people from lobbying Government and other public agencies for material advantages or redress of grievances.

In these circumstances the idea of a conscious political culture in Britain has to be reconsidered. It is certainly a concept which still has meaning for practising politicians, interest group activists, academic experts within the policy-making community and those in the burgeoning media sector who often seem to act as the real opposition to the Government of the day. Yet for the rest of British society politics and engagement with political issues are, at best, outlets for popular passion and energy on an intermittent and somewhat unpredictable basis and, at worst, little more than opportunities for unrepresentative and unelected groups to define the public interest.

Although Britain joined the European Community in 1973, it has only been comparatively recently that Britain's membership (of what is now the European Union – see Chapter 21) has begun significantly to influence not only how things are done, but what can (and cannot) be done. The main milestones along this path of Europeanisation have been: the Single European Act in 1986, the Treaty of Maastricht in 1992, the Treaty of Amsterdam in 1997, the Treaty of Nice in 2001 and, most recently, moves towards establishing a Constitution for Europe.[10]

Having come this far towards the realisation of the European project, it is clear that – short of a British decision to renegotiate the terms of its membership or, conceivably, to withdraw from the European Union – more and more aspects of British politics, procedure and political culture are likely to be influenced by its membership of the Union. The process of ever-closer European integration has been driven as much by private sector interests as by national politicians and officials in all the member states. As a result most business people, tourists, young people and many others who hail from other parts of the world take the opportunities and the constraints of the European Union very much for granted. The European Union is thus a community of interests as well as a political community and a community of law. Its practical requirements, its philosophical principles and its symbolic aspirations all contribute to the context within which British political life is conducted.

The practical requirements of European Union membership are typified by the plethora of European legal instruments in the making of which Britain has a say, but which she is legally obliged to implement under the terms of the European Treaties by which she is voluntarily bound. They are reinforced every day by the cumulative process of private-sector integration between firms, individuals and other economic entities in the Single European Market.

The philosophical principles are typified by the European jurisprudential doctrines of 'conferral', 'subsidiarity' and 'proportionality':

- *Conferral* requires the EU to act only within the limits of the competences conferred upon it by the member states and that all competences not conferred upon it in the Constitution remain with the member states
- *Subsidiarity* requires that in areas which do not fall within the exclusive competence of the EU, it shall act only if and insofar as the objectives of the proposed action cannot be sufficiently achieved by the member states but can rather, by reason of the scale or effects of the proposed action, be better achieved at EU level
- *Proportionality* requires that the content and form of EU action shall not exceed what is necessary to achieve the objectives of the Constitution.

The symbolic aspirations of the European Union have subtly changed since the time of the Treaty of Rome in 1957 when the six member states dedicated themselves to the creation of 'an ever closer union of the European peoples'. The comparable objectives set out in the Preamble to the Treaty establishing a Constitution for Europe in 2004 by the 25 member states are that 'while remaining proud of their national identities and history, the peoples of Europe are determined to transcend their former divisions and, united ever more closely, to forge a common destiny'. 'Ever closer union' is an objective for nation-builders; 'to forge a common destiny' is an aspiration for those who are uncertain about their chances of doing so.

As for the global context of British political culture, this is something which most authors of a textbook on British politics would not have thought it necessary to mention until perhaps the final decade of the twentieth century, but which is now an essential part of the intellectual framework for such an endeavour. 'Globalisation' has become a much used term to describe the processes by which a global economy has emerged in the last decade or so. Its meaning has tended to be polarised between those of a liberal market inclination who celebrate its benefits and those of a statist inclination who focus upon its costs and threats. Whichever thesis proves to be correct, it is undeniable that the room for manoeuvre of national Governments and Parliaments, and all the organisations which depend upon them, has been considerably circumscribed by globalisation which is a force that has social and cultural, as well as economic and political, dimensions.

In Britain's case, the development of an increasingly global economy offers new opportunities for the most adventurous and entrepreneurial of her citizens to exploit niches in much larger markets which extend way beyond even the 500 million plus potential consumers in the enlarged European Union. It forces more and more people 'to think global and act local', as the familiar slogan goes, and what is true for individuals and firms applies equally to national institutions and their various clienteles. Modern mass media, financial markets and multinational companies deploying mobile capital and exploiting the energies of increasingly mobile workers all serve to reduce the power and attractions of national jurisdictions, unless the authorities which govern the latter take the trouble to make their business regimes and their regulatory arrangements more attractive by becoming more flexible and accommodating. Giant economic and political entities, such as China and India, are emerging as potential rivals for the European Union and the United States, so it must be rational to conclude that the implications for Britain are at least as significant if not more so.

Some argue that in a world of emerging transcontinental giants, Britain would be wise to dig itself ever more deeply into the European Union. Others favour a destiny for Britain in a close alliance with the United States. Still others argue that Britain could be a successful niche player in the global market, prospering as Norway and Switzerland appear to have done.[11] The point of these few paragraphs is not to lay down the law as to which would be the better path to take; it is simply to draw attention to the significance for Britain and nearly all the other states in the global community of the newly enlarged context within which all national systems have to operate.

1.4 conclusion

When we consider British political culture, the main requirement is to distinguish between the cluster of dated myths and stereotypes which still appear in some accounts and the changing economic, political and social realities which should qualify or replace such traditional notions. For example, when the British economy was growing strongly in the mid 1980s and many individuals were able to enrich themselves significantly at the expense of the public purse, there was little evidence of the values of civic culture which had been identified and admired by American academics visiting Britain in the 1950s and 1960s. Equally, when the British economy experienced a period of unprecedented continuous growth (most of it under a Labour Government) from the mid 1990s to the middle of the first decade of the twenty-first century, there was little evidence of the collectivism and social solidarity which had characterised the Labour Party ever since its inception at the turn of the nineteenth and twentieth centuries. In both these cases it seems that political reality turned out to be rather different to conventional expectations. Doubtless similar surprises will be in store in the future.

SUGGESTED QUESTIONS

1   What are the key characteristics of British political culture and how have these been influenced by Britain's membership of the European Union?
2   Is the nature of British society conducive to the practice of democratic politics?
3   How have changes within British society over the last 30 years affected British political culture?

the evolving constitution

There is no single, universally agreed, definition as to what a nation's constitution should comprise. Some have what can be called a narrow view or definition, namely, a single, written, codified document.[1] Others have a broader view or definition, namely, 'the set of laws, rules and practices that create the basic institutions of the state, and its component and related parts, and stipulate the powers of those institutions and the relationship between the different institutions and between those institutions and the individual'.[2] In seeking some common ground, perhaps we could say that it is a body of fundamental principles, rules and conventions according to which a state (or other organisation) is governed. According to this definition, Britain certainly has a constitution. Yet it is notably different from the constitutions of most other democratic countries, principally because it has not been codified as one basic constitutional document – it is part unwritten, and part written but uncodified – and has relied essentially upon the flexible doctrine of Parliamentary supremacy underpinned by an acceptance of 'the rule of law'.

2.1 key characteristics

Although the key characteristics of the British constitution can be stated quite simply, they contain some potent paradoxes and internal contradictions. This is mainly because it is an *evolutionary* constitution – rather than a *revolutionary* constitution;[3] indeed, it can be described as an evolving constitution which is changing and developing all the time. At one time certain characteristics may be particularly significant, at another time other characteristics take on more significance, and so on. This makes it an interesting subject to study, but one which is hard to describe in a definitive way. Nonetheless, what can be regarded as the basic components of the British constitution are highlighted in Figure 2.1

no codification

The British constitution is unusual, as already mentioned, in that it has not been consolidated at any time into a single codified constitutional document. This

Statute Law (Acts of Parliament)
Conventions (established custom and practice)
Common Law (case law)
Prerogative Powers
European Union Law
Works of Authority

underpinned by the principles of:

The Sovereignty of Parliament
The Rule of Law (the rights of individuals)
Constitutional Monarchy
Unitary–Union–State
Membership of the European Union

figure **2.1 basic components of the British constitution**

makes it distinctive and very different not only from the American constitution but also from those on the Continent of Europe and in many Commonwealth countries which were granted their constitutional independence by Britain. Indeed, of all the democratic countries in the world, only Israel is strictly comparable to Britain in having no consolidated document codifying the ways in which its political institutions are supposed to function and setting out the basic rights and duties of its citizens.[4]

Yet in the absence of a single basic constitutional text, it should not be assumed that Britain has no constitutional documents from which the nature of Britain's constitutional arrangements can be deduced. For example, *Magna Carta*, which was signed by King John at the behest of the leading barons in 1215, is perhaps Britain's best known constitutional document. In 61 clauses it provided a clear statement of feudal laws and customs designed to limit the potentially tyrannical powers of the King and set out the rights of his subjects.

Many other documents of equal or greater constitutional significance have been drawn up since then, most of them by Parliament and some of them by the Courts contributing to the body of common law. *The Bill of Rights* in 1689 put the stamp of Parliamentary approval on the succession of William and Mary to the throne deserted by James II and extended the powers of Parliament at the expense of the Crown. In this respect it was the foundation of Britain's constitutional Monarchy. *The Act of Settlement* in 1701 was described in its preamble as 'an Act for the further limitation of the Crown and the better securing of the rights and liberties of the subject'. *The Act of Union with Scotland* in 1707 declared in Article 3 that 'the United Kingdom of Great Britain be represented by one and the same Parliament to be styled the Parliament of Great Britain'. *The Act of Union with Ireland* in 1800 brought about the formation of the United Kingdom of Great Britain and Ireland, later to be amended to 'Northern Ireland' following the partition of Ireland in 1921. As can readily be seen, all of the above measures were principally concerned with regulating relations between the Monarchy and Parliament and delineating the expanding boundaries of the United Kingdom.

The Reform Act of 1832 was the first of a series of statutes designed to extend the franchise and so give more people the right to vote at Parliamentary elections. *The Ballot Act* of 1872 introduced secret ballots for all elections to Parliament and all contested municipal elections. *The Local Government Act* of 1888 established elected County Councils for the first time in new administrative counties. *The Parliament Act* of 1911 (later amended by the *Parliament Act* of 1949) regulated and rebalanced the relations between the two Houses of Parliament by clipping the wings of the peers in the House of Lords and confirming the legislative superiority of the elected chamber, the House of Commons. *The Redistribution of Seats Act* of 1944 established independent Parliamentary Boundary Commissions to demarcate constituency boundaries on a fair and regular basis taking account of population growth and movements. *The Representation of the People Act* of 1969 lowered the minimum voting age from 21 to 18. *The European Parliamentary Elections Act* of 1978 provided within the United Kingdom for direct elections to the European Parliament every five years.

It is worth noting that the steady stream of constitutional legislation illustrated above was reduced to something more like a trickle during the 18 years that the Conservatives were in office from 1979 to 1997, unless you count the many pieces of legislation during that period designed to reform and even emasculate Labour- controlled local government. This merely emphasises the point that constitutional reform has long appealed more to those on the progressive side of British politics than those on the conservative side – a general proposition which has been powerfully borne out since the Labour Party came into office in 1997. Thus in the 1997–2001 Parliament at least 14 measures of significant constitutional reform found their way onto the Statute Book, ranging from the *Scotland Act* and the *Human Rights Act* in 1998 to the *Local Government Act* and the *Political Parties, Elections and Referendums Act* in 2000.

In general terms, with the exception of Magna Carta and the Bill of Rights, all the examples of constitutional reform given in this section are drawn from **statute law** – in other words, Acts of Parliament. This emphasises the overriding importance of Parliament in Britain's constitutional arrangements. There are, however, many other documentary sources, including **common law** or **case law** arising from judicial proceedings, which have contributed to Britain's constitutional arrangements by setting out the rights, duties and legal limitations which subsequently British subjects and citizens have come to take for granted and which are underpinned by an acceptance of the concept of the rule of law – namely, a belief that all are equal before the law, that no one is above the law and that no one can be made to suffer in body or goods without 'due process' of law. Specific examples of case law would include *Bushell's Case* of 1670 in which Lord Chief Justice Vaughan established the independence of juries. In *Sommersett's Case* of 1772, Lord Mansfield recognised the freedom of a former slave from the American colonies on the grounds of his residence in England and argued that slavery was 'so odious that nothing can be suffered to support it but positive law'. In *Beatty v. Gillbanks* of 1882, Justice Field established the principle that a man may not be convicted for a lawful act, even if he knows that it may cause another man to commit an unlawful act. Much more recently, in *Pepper v. Hart* in 1993, the Law Lords chose to follow the continental European practice of referring to the purposive context of legislation (in this case the *Hansard* record of what was said by Ministers when a Finance Bill was going through Parliament) in order to arrive at a better judicial construction of legislation under dispute.

Other sources of guidance on Britain's constitutional arrangements would be **works of authority**, including *Erskine May*, the classic and frequently updated reference book written by successive Clerks of the House of Commons on the procedures and privileges of Parliament; and certain learned works written by eminent constitutional authorities, such as Blackstone in the eighteenth century, Bagehot in the nineteenth century and Jennings in the twentieth century.[5]

importance of political conventions

A second key characteristic of the British constitution is the importance of **conventions** – in other words, established custom and practice. The conventions which have been so powerful in their influence upon constitutional developments in Britain are the product of organic growth over the centuries. They include, for example, the convention that the Monarch should send first for the leader of the largest single party in the House of Commons when it is necessary to form a new Government following a General Election or the fall of a Prime Minister from office; and the convention that Ministers are responsible and can be held to account by Parliament for what does or does not happen in their Departments during the period between General Elections.

This helps to explain why certain principles not declared in law – such as the Royal prerogative or Ministerial responsibility – have developed so fully over the years. It is also one of the reasons why many Governments have been rather reluctant to initiate deliberate constitutional reform which might very likely have the effect of curbing their discretionary power. Another point which bears upon this conundrum is that traditionally it has been considered desirable to secure all-party agreement to far reaching changes in Britain's constitutional arrangements, yet in practice this desideratum has rarely been fulfilled. Hence there is a paradoxical quality in Britain's constitutional arrangements which can best be understood only after close study of the way in which its political institutions have evolved over the centuries rather than by reference to any basic constitutional document. This is why we refer to Britain's evolving constitution – to its inherent evolutionary adaptability – which reflects the more general development of British politics and society over the centuries.

A third key characteristic of the British constitution is its considerable flexibility. This has derived partly from the absence of neat constitutional formulae consolidated into a single, authoritative constitutional document – in contrast, for example, with the codified constitution of the Fifth Republic in France. However, it is also because, unlike the position elsewhere where constitutional revision requires special majorities or procedures, in Britain no Parliament can bind its successors and any Parliament can undo the legislation of its predecessors. Consequently, it is difficult (if not impossible) to achieve formal methods of constitutional limitation in Britain.

Since Britain joined the European Economic Community (as the European Union was then called) in 1973, the fabled flexibility of British constitutional arrangements has been gradually eroded by the cumulative impact of European law. Increasingly the legal proposals of the European Commission, when they become law for the whole of the European Union and the rulings of the European Court of Justice upon disputed matters brought before the Court, determine and codify aspects of British law in those areas covered by the European Treaties to which Britain is a party and by which Britain is bound. Of course, there are exceptions in those areas from which British Governments have negotiated an 'opt-out', as is the case with European Economic and Monetary Union which affects British economic and monetary conditions but does not yet legally bind Britain or oblige the British Parliament to legislate for Britain's adoption of the euro in place of the pound. In general terms, however, British constitutional and legal arrangements are beginning to resemble those on the Continent of Europe as year by year British law and its practices come more and more to be made through the collective institutions of the European Union with Parliament at Westminster increasingly acting as a national agent for supranational authorities at the European Union level.

It is, therefore, apparent from even a cursory study of the subject that the traditional flexibility of Britain's constitutional arrangements has stemmed from the way in which the theoretically absolute and unlimited power of Parliament (in effect the governing party with a working majority in the House of Commons) has been severely modified and limited in practice by the weight of political tradition and precedent, the influence of well-established constitutional conventions, and the firmly rooted commitment to the rule of law. All these traditional and practical constraints upon the theoretical supremacy of Parliament have been joined by the invasive influence of European law as a function of Britain's membership of the European Union. Together they qualify the traditional precepts and contribute decisively to the evolution of the British constitution.

2.2 views of the constitution

For schematic purposes we can say that there are really three different views of the constitution in Britain. There is the *classic liberal view*, which is based upon a certain nostalgia for the period in the mid-nineteenth century when the House of Commons really did hold sway over the Executive. There is the *governmental view*, which is based upon the assumption that the Executive is answerable not so much to Parliament as to the electorate at periodic General Elections. Then there is the empirical view, which seeks to take account both of the weakness of Parliament in relation to the Executive and of the Government of the day in relation to all the limiting forces in the real world both within Britain and abroad.

classic liberal view

Of the various interpretations of the British constitution which have been put forward over the years, perhaps the most traditional is the classic liberal view which is associated with the writings of Walter Bagehot and A.V. Dicey in the mid-nineteenth century.[6] This view holds that the House of Commons is the supreme political institution with the power to make and unmake Governments, pass any laws and resolve the great political issues of the day. It accords only subsidiary constitutional significance to the Monarchy and the House of Lords. It takes little account of political parties, pressure groups, the Civil Service, the media or public opinion. It is shown in diagrammatic form in Figure 2.2

As R.H.S. Crossman pointed out, such a view could only have been valid for the period before any significant extension of the franchise, before the establishment of national, organised, disciplined political parties and before the development of an impartial and meritocratic civil service.[7]

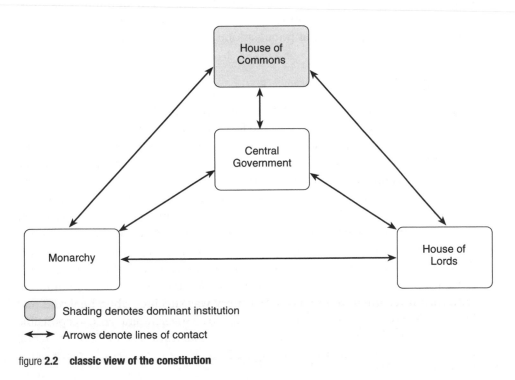

Shading denotes dominant institution

Arrows denote lines of contact

figure **2.2   classic view of the constitution**

Consequently, this classic liberal view was relevant only during a brief era from 1832 to 1867 when the House of Commons really was supreme. During that atypical period no fewer than ten Administrations fell because the House of Commons withdrew its support from them. However, by about 1885 the main constitutional principles propounded by Bagehot and Dicey were already being eroded or overtaken by new political realities which became steadily more apparent during the last quarter of the nineteenth century. For example, the institutional supremacy of Parliament acting as 'the grand inquest of the nation' was gradually overcome by the growing power of the political parties as they sought to appeal to a growing electorate which was extended in successive Reform Bills. The rule of law, which Dicey had identified as a fundamental principle of the constitution, was not necessarily the paramount consideration for all participants in the political process, at any rate for the disadvantaged sections of the community which often appealed to superior notions of natural justice. The importance of political conventions meant little to all those who were outside the charmed circle of Parliamentary politics.

In modern conditions students of the British constitution need to make sense of a much more complex and bureaucratic form of democracy in which Parliamentary supremacy is only one important principle among many. The classic liberal view, although still regarded with respect and firmly established among the received ideas of British politics, is no longer particularly instructive as a guide to the contemporary scene. It has been rendered rather obsolete by the enormously increased scope of modern Government and by the power of political parties, interest groups, the media and public opinion. This elitist Parliamentary model of the nineteenth century has had to give way to the claims of a more pluralist and populist kind of democracy at the beginning of the twenty-first century.

governmental view

Another well-known interpretation of the British constitution is the governmental view. This holds that the former power of the Monarch has been passed not so much to Parliament as to the Prime Minister and Cabinet, who are subject usually to nothing stronger than criticism in Parliament before they face periodic confirmation or rejection by the mass electorate at General Elections. It is a view traditionally associated with the writings of L.S. Amery and Herbert Morrison.[8] It maintains that the Government of the day has a clear responsibility to govern and that the essential form of political accountability is the political contract between the governing party and the electorate. Accordingly, the role of the Opposition and indeed of all back-bench MPs is to act essentially as filters or megaphones for the public in its interaction with the Government of the day. L.S. Amery was succinct when he wrote that 'the combination of responsible leadership by Government with responsible criticism in Parliament is the essence of our constitution.'[9] The Governmental view is shown diagrammatically in Figure 2.3.

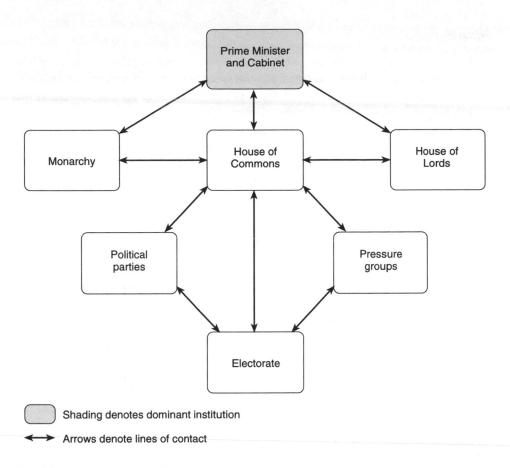

Prime Minister
and Cabinet

Monarchy

House of
Commons

House of
Lords

Political
parties

Pressure
groups

Electorate

Shading denotes dominant institution

Arrows denote lines of contact

figure **2.3** **governmental view of the constitution**

Although this view, too, has to be qualified if we are to form an accurate impression of the way in which the British constitution really works, it has more validity and topical relevance than the classic liberal view, which is now characterised by a certain sentimentality towards a vanished era of truly Parliamentary government. In the administrative and legislative spheres at any rate, modern British Governments have had virtually unlimited power, provided they have had a reliable working majority in the House of Commons and as long as they have been careful to keep their Parliamentary supporters united behind them. Under the terms of the 1911 Parliament Act a Government can retain this power for a maximum of five years before it is obliged to seek a fresh mandate from the electorate. In view of the notable imbalance of political resources between Government and Opposition, there has always been some truth in Lord Hailsham's allegation that the British political system is 'an elective dictatorship' tempered only by the minimal restraints of constitutional conventions and the governing party's normal desire to get re-elected.[10]

More accurate still in modern conditions is the empirical view of the constitution, which emphasises both the weakness of Parliament in relation to the Government of the day and the weakness of the Executive in relation to interest groups, the media, public opinion and other actors on the national and international scene. It emphasises the way in which a deliberate extension of constitutional power can lead to a decline in effective power, no matter how great a Government's Parliamentary majority or the political momentum behind the party in office. This is essentially because, if a Government becomes overextended in its ambitions or overloaded in its commitments, it is likely to encounter so many real-world obstacles and to create so many political enemies that it will be unable to achieve its objectives.

Indeed, a dispassionate reading of British constitutional history leads to the important conclusion that the most abiding political problem has been to gain and retain public consent for the actions of any Government. Stage by stage from the thirteenth century to the present time, Governments in Britain, whether led by the Monarch or by a Prime Minister in Parliament, have had to cede and share power with the other great interests in the land – and nowadays increasingly with their partners in the European Union and other actors on the world stage. Effective government has only been possible with the consent, or at least the tacit acquiescence, of those most directly affected by it or involved with it. Against this background it makes sense to regard successive British Governments as stable rather than strong, and to avoid confusing the concentration of responsibility with the concentration of power. Today public opinion, the influence of the media and the growth of European law are all examples of the powerful forces which condition and limit the exercise of power by any British Government. For a diagrammatic representation of this view see Figure 2.4.

Thus the contemporary British constitution is based upon two key paradoxes. The first is the limited power of a theoretically supreme Parliament. This reflects the fact that, while Parliament is perfectly capable of passing any law, it is in practice able only to criticise and intermittently control the Government of the day. Thus Tony Blair was able to commit British troops to an American-led war in Iraq in 2003—4, despite the largest public demonstrations in modern times, because the Conservative Opposition in Parliament was split and outnumbered and enough of the Government's own backbenchers fell into line. It also has something to do with the growing political power and legal competence of the European Union, which has tended to reduce the independent power of national Governments in those areas of policy covered by the European Treaties and hence the power of national Parliaments which claim to control their Governments.

The second key paradox is the limited power of the allegedly powerful Executive, which reflects the fact that, while a Government with a working majority in the House of Commons can invariably get its way in Whitehall and

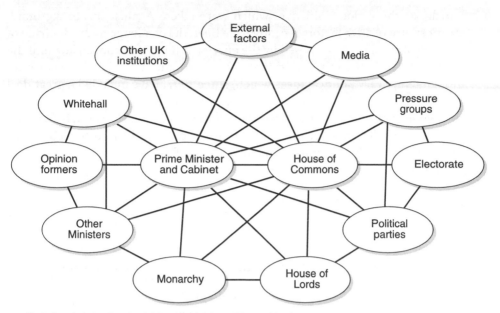

note: No dominant institution. Everything influences and is influenced by everything else.

figure **2.4   empirical view of the constitution**

Westminster, little of value is actually achieved if its freedom of manoeuvre is unduly circumscribed by administrative constraints, enforcement difficulties, interest group or general public resistance, media influence or the limits of European law. The complicated network of informal checks and balances means that the evolving constitution continues to develop organically, but provides few formal safeguards against the arbitrary exercise of executive power.

Formal limitation of the power of any British Government is now more often sought and found in the rulings of the European Court of Justice or the European Court of Human Rights than in any of the traditional mechanisms available at Westminster – although it should be added that since 1999 a largely appointed House of Lords, in which the Labour Government has had no overall numerical majority, has proved to be the most reliable Parliamentary mechanism for persuading the Government to think again on many controversial aspects of its legislation. On the other hand, informal constraints upon the power of all national Governments are to be observed most clearly these days in the capacity of global financial markets to discipline any national authorities which lose credibility in the eyes of global investors, and in the considerable influence of global media corporations.

2.3 pressures for change

Over the years constitutional changes have occurred piecemeal, even haphazardly, in response to the needs of public policy or the dictates of political necessity. No coherent pattern emerged and there was no real attempt to coordinate the various initiatives which were taken. Against this background, the most provocative factors recently have been the challenge to the doctrine of Parliamentary supremacy posed by the encroachment of European law, and the persistent gap between received ideas about Britain's uncodified constitution and contemporary political ideas which, since 1997, have included a great deal of New Labour modernisation with constitutional consequences.

We shall examine each of these matters in due course. However, before that we must consider some of the implications of the trend towards plebiscitary democracy, namely the more frequent use of referenda within the system of Parliamentary government in Britain.

the trend towards plebiscitary democracy

Since the 1970s it has proved more difficult than it used to be to secure public approval, or even acquiescence, for some of the most controversial changes proposed by various Governments in the ways in which we govern ourselves in the British Isles. In narrow political terms, this has usually been because the governing party has been internally divided on the controversial matters at issue. In a wider social and institutional context, it has reflected the decline of popular deference towards the governing elite in all parties and hence the inability of Government and Parliament together to summon up the necessary authority to speak decisively on behalf of the people. The solution, often reluctantly embraced, to these problems of political authority has been to introduce national or regional referenda as devices for final settlement of controversies which were deemed incapable of resolution in any other way.[11]

For these purposes 'referenda' can be defined as a system of decision making by which a question is submitted to the direct vote of the whole electorate (within what is deemed to be the relevant territory). The words in brackets add some unavoidable complexity to what would otherwise be a simple definition, for reasons which will be made clear when we discuss some particular instances below. Any such device sits uneasily with Britain's tradition of Parliamentary government and problems can arise if the result of such referenda simply turns into a vote for or against the Government of the day. Nonetheless, its use on a number of notable occasions testifies to the flexibility of Britain's constitutional arrangements.

In 1973 a referendum took place within Northern Ireland on the constitutional position of Northern Ireland, namely, whether Northern Ireland was to remain part of the United Kingdom or be joined with the Republic of Ireland. On a 58.6 per cent turnout 98.9 per cent voted for Northern Ireland to remain part of the United Kingdom. Having said that, however, the fact that the referendum was boycotted by the Catholic/Nationalist/Republican population in Northern Ireland rather undermined the effectiveness of the use of referenda – certainly at that time – as a way to assist in finding a solution to the problems involved.

In 1975 Britain's membership of the European Economic Community on the terms 'renegotiated' by the Wilson Government was put to the British people for decision in a UK-wide referendum. This was partly because the Labour Government was so deeply divided on the issue that it was unable to reach a collective decision binding the entire Cabinet and partly because it was hoped that this would settle the issue, which divided both the Labour and Conservative parties, once and for all. It proved to be an ingenious device for preventing the disintegration of the Wilson Cabinet, but incapable of permanently settling the issue of Britain's membership.

In 1979 the legislation which had been proposed by the Callaghan Administration in 1977 and passed (with difficulty) by both Houses of Parliament in 1978 for the devolution of certain legislative powers to Scotland and Wales respectively was put to separate referenda in each of those parts of the United Kingdom, because this had been one of the concessions that the Government had had to make to critics on its own backbenches when the legislation was being debated in the Commons. Specifically, a backbench amendment had been carried which stated that, unless at least 40 per cent of those entitled to vote in each relevant part of the country supported the policy with an affirmative vote in a referendum, the provisions of the legislation would not be put into effect. This proved to be a sufficient obstacle to the implementation of the legislation, since in neither Scotland nor Wales did as many as 40 per cent of those entitled to vote support the proposition.[12]

These cases were seen by a growing number of people both inside and outside Parliament as valid precedents for the use of referenda on other issues, especially when the position taken by a majority in the House of Commons has been strongly opposed by an irreconcilable minority in the governing party (as was the case on the controversial issue of Britain's evolving membership of the European Union) or has been apparently at odds with the view held by a clear majority of British public opinion (on the emotive issue of capital punishment, for example). Thus when Parliament was in the process of ratifying the 1992 Maastricht Treaty, Margaret Thatcher and other 'Eurosceptics' both inside and outside Parliament argued vehemently for the matter to be put to a nationwide referendum and only narrowly failed to win an amendment to this effect when the relevant legislation was going through the House of Commons.

By the time that Labour came to power in 1997, Tony Blair and his Cabinet had clearly learned the lessons of the previous two decades about how to handle the referendum dimension of the most vexed constitutional issues. In deciding in the autumn of 1997 to give conditional approval for the idea of replacing the pound sterling with the euro at some stage in the future (an issue which raises for many people constitutional questions to do with national sovereignty), Gordon Brown and Tony Blair were equally clear that such a step would only be taken with the explicit approval of Parliament *and people* in a national referendum. This was also – ultimately – the stance taken in regard to the European Constitution, Tony Blair announcing in April 2004 that there would be a UK referendum on this – although in the aftermath of referendum rejections in both France and Holland the Government announced that they were shelving such plans.

In deciding in the first session of the 1997–2001 Parliament to press ahead with renewed efforts to devolve legislative powers to Scotland, Wales, Northern Ireland and Greater London respectively, Tony Blair and his senior colleagues sought to avoid the mistakes of their Labour Ministerial predecessors by holding referenda on the principle of this policy in each case *before* the relevant legislation was put to Parliament for its consideration, thus making it effectively impossible for diehard critics to destroy the policy as their backbench predecessors had done in the 1970s. This approach proved successful and was instrumental in bringing about substantial devolution to Scotland, lesser devolution to Wales, problematic devolution or power sharing to Northern Ireland and a directly elected Mayor and Assembly for Greater London. Only later, in 2004, did the second Blair Administration suffer a setback with this tactic, when the flagship scheme for devolution to the regions of England was heavily defeated in a regional referendum in the North East in which the regional electorate seemed to resent the idea of adding yet another layer of government without the prospect of any obvious material benefits.[13]

Now that the use of referenda seems to have become an established feature of the constitutional arrangements in Britain, it is worth pausing to reflect upon the issues which this raises and the effects which it is likely to have upon the political process. The most important issue raised by any referendum is whether it is intended by the Government of the day to preserve or overcome the position taken by Parliament on the public policy issue concerned. A referendum held *after* Parliament has approved a certain Executive decision – sometimes referred to as a post-legislative or confirmatory referendum – is likely to be regarded by the Government of the day as welcome confirmation if it wins or merely advisory if it loses. On the other hand, a referendum held *before* Parliament has been asked to approve a certain course of action – sometimes referred to as a pre-legislative or precautionary referendum – is likely to be regarded by the Government of the day as a convenient way of overcoming or at least minimising opposition to its preferred policy and in those circumstances the result is effectively binding upon Parliament and the nation as a whole. If such a referendum were lost, the likelihood is that, despite the wishes of the Government, it would not be able to proceed. In such circumstances the only thing that can trump the result of a referendum is the contrary result of another referendum on the same subject with the same question and the same electorate.

A second important issue is who should be allowed to initiate a referendum and thus have the capacity to influence its timing. In Britain at present only the Government of the day supported by a working majority in the House of Commons has this right: it is effectively a matter of Executive privilege. This is in marked contrast to the practice in Italy, for example, where this initiative can be exercised by the people using petitions, or in the United States, for example, where write-in campaigns may succeed in getting propositions for votes put on the ballot at state elections.

There are other more detailed issues, too, connected with the wider and more frequent use of referenda. Who should be able to formulate the question or questions? Who should make up the appropriate electorate? Who should decide whether the result should be subject to predetermined qualifications, as was the case with devolution to Scotland and Wales in 1979? Who should monitor and regulate the conduct of the political argument or the raising and spending of money by either side in a referendum campaign? Fortunately, as a result of another important piece of constitutional legislation – the Political Parties, Elections and Referendums Act 2000 – there is now an adequate answer to these ticklish points and that is the statutorily independent Electoral Commission which has at least made it clear that it will 'advise' Ministers on the intelligibility and inherent fairness of the questions posed in any referendum, even if some of the other matters mentioned are still in the hands of the Government of the day.

As for the long-term effects of future referenda which may be held in parts of or right across the United Kingdom, it is possible to identify both negative and positive factors. On the negative side, it seems likely that more frequent recourse to referenda will contribute to the further diminution of Parliament as an institution and to the consequent growth of plebiscitary democracy. Moreover, the nature of debate during referendum campaigns can provide opportunities for demagogues and unscrupulous media figures to sensationalise and distort the discussion in ways which may well lead to perverse public verdicts. On the positive side, any well conducted and well regulated referendum campaigns should provide valuable opportunities for members of the public to engage more deeply than usual in the discussion of difficult political issues and to give sensible thought to important political questions before making any decisions. It will also offer a means of resolving – in the short term if not in the long term – difficult constitutional issues which, it seems, can no longer be authoritatively settled by the political class on its own acting within its traditional political institutions.

the encroachment of European law

The challenge to British Parliamentary supremacy posed by the encroachment of European law is an issue with the most far-reaching constitutional implications. It has been highlighted by those in all parties (including notably the UK Independence Party (UKIP)) who have opposed British membership of the European Union, or at any rate Britain's deeper integration into the Union, just as it has tended to be played down by the diminishing number who have favoured Britain's full participation at every stage of the European adventure. Now that Britain has been a member of the European Community/Union for more than 30 years, few people argue seriously for British withdrawal. Yet a number of politicians in all parties (especially the UKIP and some in the Conservative Party) have argued for a radical redefinition of Britain's involvement with the European Union, including repatriation of some supranational powers (the common fisheries policy, for example) to the member states.

On the assumption that Britain remains within the European Union and that a Treaty establishing a Constitution for Europe is ratified by all 27 member states, the likelihood is that European integration will be both broadened and deepened in certain specific areas of policy – fiscal policy, defence policy and foreign policy – from which it has been largely excluded before. However, some argued that the Treaty signed in Rome on 29th October 2004 was actually something of a minor triumph for the British Government and those other Governments which, for one reason or another, had become sceptical of or resistant to the remorseless drive towards more supranational competences for the European institutions. Such Governments fought successfully for a greater access to and role within the European decision making process for national Parliaments and managed to insist that for decisions on a proposal from the European Commission before the Council of Ministers there would not only need to be a majority of member states (14 out of 27) in favour but also at least 255 votes out of the possible 345 cast in favour. In addition the votes in favour would have to represent at least 62 per cent of the total population of the EU member states.

From the very beginning of the European project in 1950, the relationship of the member states with the European institutions has been a matter of somewhat mysterious doctrine, almost the secular equivalent of a religion. In this case the dominant ideas have been those of *supranationality* and the *acquis communautaire*.[14] For decades until the Maastricht Treaty in 1992 and, more recently, the second Rome Treaty in 2004 there has been little serious Governmental resistance to these central articles of faith – other than intermittently from the British, Danish and Swedish Governments. However, Article I-11 of the Constitutional Treaty declared that the limits of EU competences are governed by the principle of conferral (i.e. the member states conferring some of their national powers upon the supranational EU institutions) and the use of EU competences is governed by the principles of *subsidiarity* and *proportionality*.[15] This suggests, at least at face value, that the 2004 European Constitutional Treaty (if it, or something like it, fails to be ratified by all the member states) may turn out to be a high-water mark for European integration, at leastfor a while.

digital democracy

The internet has created new forms of political communication, and web movements have the potential to transform the power relationship between Government and society. Indeed, there are those who believe that this process has already begun, that real power is but a mouse click away. Hence the excitement generated by the level of response to the online petition on road pricing on the Downing Street website early in 2007. In the words of Gordon Brown the debate is about how to respond to the 'explosive power of citizens, consumers and bloggers. The new focus on the environment is the result of that. The Make Poverty History campaign was the result of that. Citizens are flexing their muscles'.[16] For the Conservatives, George Osborne has noted 'people are taking matters into their own hands through their blogs and online networks. They are organising campaigns and building coalitions. They are the masters now'.[17]

Certainly the internet is a way to spread information, argument and debate and it has drawn many individuals into political debate who would not have participated in more traditional forms of involvement (such as attending a meeting or writing to a newspaper). Nonetheless, it is important to note that a significant proportion of the population is completely missing from this 'brave new world', for just under 14 million households (57 per cent) have internet access, which means that 43 per cent do not and that proportion consists – disproportionately – of the poor and the elderly. There is also a geographic bias in that while 66 per cent of households in the south-east of England use the internet this is so for only 48 per cent of households in Scotland.[18] It is also necessary to be aware of the fact that the vast majority of people who use the internet do so for non-political reasons such as keeping in touch with family or friends and for shopping. The politically active internet community is very small. The important question is the extent to which we move towards a more direct democracy – a permanent 'online' referendum.

political issues with constitutional consequences

Successive Conservative Administrations under Margaret Thatcher between 1979 and 1990 pushed through Parliament a wide range of legislation which, while not deliberately designed to bring about constitutional change, had some significant constitutional implications.[19] Most of this legislation was designed to emasculate local government and culminated in the ill-fated Community Charge or Poll Tax introduced into Scotland in 1989 and into England and Wales in 1990, which was subsequently scrapped by the first Major Administration and replaced with the less unpopular Council Tax (1990–92).

Against the background of this conflict over the structure and financing of local government, those elements of the political class which were drawn from Opposition ranks in Scotland took the lead in a multiparty and non-party campaign dramatised by a Constitutional Convention held in Edinburgh in March 1989 to press for devolved government in Scotland – a move that was also partly a response to strong pressure for Scottish independence from the Scottish National Party. At about the same time a UK-wide campaign for constitutional change got underway under the banner of Charter 88 designed principally to strengthen local (Labour-controlled) institutions against the power of the (Conservative-controlled) central institutions at UK level.[20]

During the second Major Administration following the somewhat unexpected Conservative victory at the 1992 General Election, two other matters came to the fore which had significant constitutional consequences: Britain's relations with the European Union and the future of Northern Ireland. In the case of the European Union, the Conservative Government had huge difficulties in persuading some of its own backbenchers to ratify the 1992 Maastricht Treaty and John Major's modest majority in the House of Commons was frequently threatened by the Euro-sceptic Maastricht rebels. The main issues were the opt-out from the Social Chapter, which attracted Conservative support but Opposition criticism, and the freedom of choice successfully negotiated in relation to Britain's possible future adoption of the Euro, which attracted mistrust and misgiving on the Conservative benches but stronger support elsewhere in the House of Commons. Both issues were to have consequences for Britain's constitutional arrangements after Labour regained power at the 1997 General Election.

In the case of *Northern Ireland*, a set of political problems, which had appeared virtually insoluble since the beginning of 'the troubles' in the late 1960s, began to move in a more hopeful direction during John Major's second Administration in the mid 1990s. The first breakthrough came in the form of the Downing Street Declaration of 15th December 1993, which was a joint initiative by John Major and Albert Reynolds on behalf of the British and Irish Governments to restart the 'peace process' in Northern Ireland. This led to exploratory talks both between each of the Governments and between representatives of the two sectarian communities in Northern Ireland, namely the Protestant/Unionist/Loyalist community and the Catholic/Nationalist/Republican community. This bore fruit with the announcement of a complete ceasefire by the IRA in August 1994 and talks about talks at official level on the main political and security issues. These developments served to give possible solutions to the intractable 'Irish question', renewed prominence in British politics and, after many false starts, paved the way for the Good Friday Agreement in the spring of 1998. It is fair to say that on the Northern Ireland issue Tony Blair reaped the benefits of the patient spade-work done by his Conservative predecessor at 10 Downing Street.

The 1998 Good Friday (or Belfast) Agreement laid the foundations for a new Northern Ireland Assembly and power-sharing Executive which was designed to encourage parity of esteem between the two communities in Northern Ireland and to buttress the political settlement with a web of international guarantees provided by London, Dublin and the American Administration in Washington DC. The latter sought successfully to discourage the Irish-American community from funding the IRA and to encourage a more positive approach towards much needed foreign investment in Northern Ireland. Since then the path of devolution and power sharing in Northern Ireland has been problematic, to say the least, with Sinn Fein gradually establishing political ascendancy over the more moderate Social Democratic and Labour Party on the Nationalist side and the Democratic Unionist Party gradually supplanting their more moderate rivals, the Ulster Unionists, as the leading political force on the Unionist side. The net result, following the 2005 General Election, was that Northern Irish politics was more polarised than it had been for some time and the country was temporarily without a functioning devolved Assembly and once again living under British direct rule (the default position of Northern Irish politics since 1972).

Modernisation under New Labour since 1997 has, to a large extent, taken the form of introducing new constitutional arrangements which affect the way Britain is governed, whether in macro or micro terms, from the supranational to the subnational level. Significant constitutional reform measures were introduced in the 1997–2001 Parliament, including in 1998 the devolution legislation for Scotland, Wales and Northern Ireland, respectively; the Human Rights Act; the Bank of England Act, giving operational independence to the Bank; the European Parliament Elections Act; the Registration of Political Parties Act; and the Greater London Authority Referendum Act. In 1999 the House of Lords Act removed the automatic right of the hereditary peers to be members; while in 2000 the Freedom of Information Act, the Local Government Act and the Political Parties, Elections and Referendums Act all reached the Statute Book. The 2001–05 Parliament saw the creation of a specific Department for Constitutional Affairs. A good deal of the initial spate of constitutional legislation was based upon Tony Blair's desire to honour the political legacy of John Smith, his predecessor as Leader of the Labour Party who had died in 1994 and was a true believer in the value of comprehensive constitutional reform.

A second theme running through the constitutional changes that have been made by New Labour was the attempt to restore hygiene and respectability to the British political system after years of what had been termed 'Tory sleaze'. This was largely a matter of making a virtue of necessity by tightening up the rules of the political game, moving from a culture of official secrecy towards freedom of information, adjusting the methods of democratic decision making in an attempt to make elections and referendums cleaner and voting more attractive to the general public, and searching for new ways in which politicians could relate to the people they are supposed to represent. These objectives became tarnished by a number of notable incidents when the Labour party fell below its own high standards, while its claim to deserve the public's respect and trust (if not its active support) was seriously damaged by Tony Blair's perceived dishonesty in some of the arguments he used to justify Britain's commitment to the American cause in Iraq and by the whole 'loans for honours' police inquiry in 2006–07.[21]

A third theme has been the extensive application of the elastic concept of 'modernisation' to the spheres of central and local government by changing the pattern of goals and incentives for civil servants and local government officials alike. Notwithstanding the decentralisation implicit in the Government's policy of devolution, the application of the modernisation theme has entailed a further concentration of power within the central institutions of central Government – 10 Downing Street, H.M. Treasury and the Cabinet Office – in an attempt to ensure 'joined-up' government. As part of this approach Departments and Agencies involved in the functional delivery of New Labour policies have had to dance to the tune of Public Service Agreements (PSAs), off-balance-sheet financial arrangements such as Private Finance Initiatives (PFIs) and Public Private Partnerships (PPPs) and detailed Treasury targets designed to ensure that modernised administrative practices are the precondition for extra public spending sanctioned by the then Chancellor, Gordon Brown. Local authorities have had to apply the doctrine of 'Best Value' in their commissioning of public services from the public, private or voluntary sectors and have found themselves competing for so-called 'earned autonomy' and 'Beacon Council' status if and when they manage to outperform their competitors. All of this may seem to be essentially managerial in character and prosaic in practice; but, as a policy which has been pursued over more than two terms of office, it has brought about cultural change in the thinking, language and practices of thousands of officials at every level of government.[22]

Furthermore, if we keep in mind the fact that the United Kingdom is a democracy in which the Executive, Legislature and Judiciary have all been entwined in the central institutions of Parliament, it is not surprising that New Labour has sought to apply the medicine of modernisation to the House of Commons, the House of Lords and the senior Judiciary as well. Thus the working hours and legislative process in the Commons have been streamlined to the managerial advantage of the Government of the day; the membership of the Lords has been reformed by removing most of the hereditary peers; and the senior Judiciary is being modernised by gradually diversifying its membership and relocating the Law Lords in a separate Supreme Court. In a political system which is still without a codified constitution, these acts of modenisation have potentially far reaching constitutional consequences.

2.4 conclusion

In this chapter we have seen that the timeless characteristics of the evolving constitutional arrangements in Britain are that there is no codification in a single authoritative document, but considerable flexibility which stems chiefly from the doctrine of Parliamentary supremacy. This means that political conventions – established custom and practice – are often the best guide to what will happen in particular political circumstances, although these, too, can be modified or even rendered obsolete by the passage of time.

Schematically, there have been three main views of the constitution, at least two of which still apply in modern conditions. The classic liberal view is a nostalgic retrospective on the mid-nineteenth century, but it still resonates today among those who dislike or despise the characteristics of modern partisan politics. The governmental view is in keeping with the mandate theory of government and consistent with the current trend towards plebiscitary politics. However, it does assume a significant dose of disciplined ideology in each of the main parties and the existence of political circumstances in which people aim to achieve their political objectives via collective institutions such as mass-membership political parties. The empirical view is a catch-all description of modern political reality in which our constitutional arrangements are influenced, buffeted and altered by a whole raft of real world factors ranging from interest groups to the media and from terrorist groups to financial institutions.

Since Britain's constitutional arrangements are dynamic rather static, it is necessary to be aware of the main pressures for change in recent years. The trend towards a plebiscitary democracy has not supplanted the role of Parliament, but it has invested General Elections, referendums and opinion polls of all kinds with much greater influence, especially in the process of arriving at definitive decisions on constitutional issues. The gradual encroachment of European law into the spheres traditionally dominated by statute law and common law has exerted cumulative influence over the ways in which we seek to govern ourselves in the United Kingdom and this trend could become even more significant if the proposed EU constitutional Treaty is ratified by all 27 member states. Finally, there are a range of political issues with constitutional consequences which have been brought to the fore since John Major succeeded Margaret Thatcher as Prime Minister in 1990 – issues which relate principally to alterations in the balance of political power between Whitehall and Westminster on the one hand and the institutions of subnational or supranational government on the other. These initiatives have been portrayed by New Labour as part of the overall drive for 'modernisation', a theme which has been a defining feature of the reforms introduced by three successive Blair Administrations between 1997 and 2007 as well as by Blair's successor, Gordon Brown.

SUGGESTED QUESTIONS

1   What are the key features of the British constitution?
2   Which view of the British constitution accords best with contemporary political circumstances and why?
3   What effect has Britain's membership of the European Union had on Britain's constitutional arrangements?

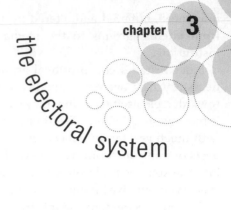

the electoral system

The electoral system in Britain is the product of historical evolution and development. It began to be put on a democratic basis at the time of the Great Reform Act of 1832. This gave the right to vote to an additional half a million individuals who had not previously had it, taking the proportion of the enfranchised adult population to 5 per cent. Subsequent Acts carried forward the process of enfranchisement:

1867   *The Representation of the People Act* – which carried forward the principles of the 1832 legislation, increasing the electorate to number almost 2.5 million (13 per cent of the adult population).

1872   *The Ballot Act* – which introduced the principle of secret or confidential voting.

1883   *The Corrupt and Illegal Practices Act* – which made bribery and other corrupt practices at elections criminal offences.

1884   *The Representation of The People Act* – which extended the franchise to householders and tenants and to all those who occupied land or tenements with an annual value of not less than ten pounds. The main effect of this Act was to give the vote to working men in the counties, taking the total number of voters to 5 million, 25 per cent of the adult population.

1885   *The Redistribution of Seats Act* – which introduced the principle of equal electoral districts – equal in terms of numbers of voters – and to a great extent ensured single-member constituencies.

1918   *The Representation of the People Act* – which did away with virtually all restrictions on adult male suffrage and extended the vote to include 8.5 million women over the age of 30, creating an electorate of over 21 million people, or 75 per cent of the adult population.

1928   *The Representation of the People (Equal Franchise) Act* – which placed women on the same basis as their male counterparts, namely enfranchising virtually all those 21 years of age and over, leading to an electorate of 27 million voters, 99 per cent of the adult population.

1948　*The Representation of the People Act* – which further extended the principle of 'one person, one vote' by abolishing additional votes for university graduates and for those owning business premises and land in constituencies other than those in which they lived.

1969　*The Representation of the People Act* – which reduced the minimum age of voting from 21 to 18.

1985　*The Representation of the People Act* – which extended the right to vote to British citizens resident abroad for a period of up to five years from leaving the country.

1989　*The Representation of the People Act* – which extended the right to vote to British citizens living abroad to a maximum of 20 years since their leaving Britain. This meant a potential electorate of 1.5 million, although only some 23,583 individuals had registered to vote by the time of the 1997 election.

2000　*The Representation of the People Act* – which introduced a new system of electoral registration (a rolling register) and extended the right to vote by post to all electors (apart from Northern Ireland).

2000　*The Political Parties, Elections and Referendums Act* – while providing for the creation of an Electoral Commission to regulate elections and referendums and for the registration of political parties, it also reduced the right to vote for British citizens living abroad from 20 to 15 years.

The result of all these statutes is that there exists in Britain today a system of universal adult suffrage in which all British nationals – as well as citizens of the Irish Republic and of Commonwealth countries resident in the United Kingdom – aged 18 and over have the right to vote (including those British nationals living overseas and those temporarily on holiday abroad), with the exception of:

 ‣ Members of the House of Lords. Hereditary Peers who were excluded from the House of Lords under the provisions of the House of Lords Act 1999 are eligible to vote.
 ‣ Patients detained in psychiatric hospitals as a consequence of criminal behaviour.
 ‣ Sentenced prisoners.
 ‣ Those convicted within the previous 5 years of corrupt or illegal election practices.
 ‣ Those not on the electoral register. Although registration is compulsory, voting is not (unlike, for example, in Australia, Belgium and Luxembourg).

Britain does not operate a system of fixed-term Parliaments with the dates of elections for the House of Commons known in advance. However, according to the Parliament Act of 1911, a Parliament cannot go on longer than five years (unless both Houses of Parliament vote otherwise – as was the case in the two

World Wars between 1914 and 1918 and between 1939 and 1945). Rather, the date for a General Election is set by the Prime Minister of the day. Traditionally, polling day is on a Thursday. The timescale of the 2005 General Election is outlined in Figure 3.1.

5 April: Election date announced.
11 April: Issue of writ for the election. Dissolution of Parliament.
14 April: Nominations commenced.
19 April: Deadlines for:
              ▸ Nominations
              ▸ Withdrawal of candidates
              ▸ Appointment of agents
              ▸ Making objections to nominations
              ▸ Publication of names of candidates
              ▸ Receipt of requests to change or cancel existing postal votes and proxy votes.
26 April: Deadline for postal and proxy vote applications.
27 April: Final Issue of postal/proxy ballot papers. Last day to make alterations to the electoral register.
28 April: First day to apply for replacement (of lost) postal ballot papers.
3 May: Deadline for appointment of polling and counting officers.
4 May: Deadline for issuing of replacement (spoilt or lost) postal ballot papers.
5 May: Polling Day (Hours of poll 7 am to 10 pm).

figure **3.1   the timescale of the 2005 general election**

Traditionally, the four or five weeks of an election campaign are intensely busy for candidates, agents and voluntary helpers. Leaflets must be produced and delivered and envelopes addressed for leaflets being distributed by post. There are meetings to be organised, speeches to be written and made and press releases to be issued. Above all else there are people to contact – via phone, internet and face-to-face; in short there is the task of campaigning in a constituency to gain support from as many people as can be contacted.

Despite the fact that there is some evidence that individual constituency campaigning can have an impact and make a difference,[1] General Election campaigns have come to be dominated by national, as opposed to constituency-based, campaigns. They have in many respects become contests between national parties on national issues, fought out between national party leaders before the television cameras.

3.1 the current system

At the 2005 General Election,[2] 3552 candidates stood for election to the House of Commons (233 more than in 2001), and 44,110,782 people were eligible to vote. The 646 constituencies into which the United Kingdom was divided (13 fewer than in 2001 due to a redistribution of constituencies in Scotland following devolution) varied considerably in both population and geographical area. The electorate in each constituency ranged from, on average, 69,894 in England, through 65,383 in Scotland and 58,085 in Northern Ireland, to 55,836 in Wales. Na h-Eileanan an Iar (the Western Isles) had the smallest electorate (21,576) although it was one of the largest in geographical area (over 2000 square miles), whereas the Isle of Wight with the largest electorate (109,046) was geographically confined to quite a small area (147 square miles). The largest constituency was Ross, Skye and Lochaber covering some 3500 square miles (with an electorate of 50,507); one of the smallest was Kensington and Chelsea covering only 3.6 square miles (with an electorate of 62,662).

Arrangements for elections are the responsibility of the Electoral Commission, an independent body set up by Act of Parliament in 2000. The Commission's responsibilities include:

‣ Registering political parties
‣ Monitoring and publishing significant donations to parties
‣ Regulating expenditure by parties on election campaigns
‣ Reporting on the conduct of elections and referendums
‣ Reviewing electoral law and procedures
‣ Advising the Government on changes in electoral law and practice
‣ Advising those involved on the conduct of elections and referendums
‣ Promoting public awareness of the electoral systems in use
‣ Reviewing electoral boundaries at the local government level.

The review of the number, boundaries and names of constituencies for elections to the House of Commons – as well as for elections at the devolved and European levels – is the responsibility of the Boundary Commissions.[3]

electoral mechanisms

Under the 'first-past-the-post' voting system currently used for Westminster Parliamentary elections, on election day voters go to the polls between 7:00am and 10:00pm to cast their votes in secret by putting 'X' against one name on the ballot paper. Any other mark may produce a 'spoiled vote' which could be judged invalid at the end of the count. The marked ballot papers are folded and deposited by the voters in locked ballot boxes where they remain until the polling stations close. The ballot boxes are then transported to a central point in the constituency (often a Town Hall) where the counting of the votes takes place under the supervision of the Acting Returning Officer (normally the Chief Executive of the local authority concerned). The results are declared at varying times depending on the nature and size of the constituency. In 2005 the first constituency to declare its result was Sunderland South – after just 44 minutes – while the last was Harlow – at 11.31am on Saturday, 7 May.[4]

An experiment in all-postal voting was tried in 2004 for one-third of voters in local and European elections. There were widespread reports of fraud, leading to a series of court cases. In one of them – arising from elections in Birmingham where a combination of postal voting and traditional polling booths had been used – the judge said that the system for postal ballots was 'wide open to abuse' and that he had heard evidence which would 'disgrace a banana republic'.[5] The 2005 General Election was the first since changes to electoral regulations introduced in the Representation of the People Act 2000 entitled voters in England, Scotland and Wales to apply for a postal vote, the result of which saw applications more than quadruple and in some constituencies they rose by almost 500 per cent.[6] However, the election was marred by allegations of postal voting fraud, with allegations of ballot papers being stolen, altered or fraudulently applied for. Following the election the Electoral Commission, in a report on cutting fraud in postal voting, declared that the traditional method of voting in person at polling stations should remain 'the foundation of our voting system', that, over time, voters should be allowed to choose other ways of casting their ballot, such as voting by post or using new technology, but that 'changes to improve the security and reliability of postal voting on demand were essential to secure its future as part of the electoral process' and set out in detail changes which it deemed fundamental to bolster the current system.[7] Following on from this, in the 2005–06 Parliamentary session, the Government secured the passage of the Electoral Administration Act designed to tackle four key areas, namely:

▸ Improving access and engagement for voters
▸ Improving confidence of voters
▸ Extending openness and transparency in party financing
▸ Maintaining professional delivery in elections.[8]

Individuals who are British citizens, or citizens of another Commonwealth country or of the Irish Republic, may stand as candidates for election to the House of Commons, provided that they are not disqualified from so doing. Those not legally entitled to stand include:

▸ Undischarged bankrupts
▸ Individuals sentenced to more than one year's imprisonment (until pardon or completion of sentence)[9]
▸ Certified lunatics
▸ Members of the House of Lords
▸ Ordained clergy in the Church of England, the Church of Scotland, the Church of Ireland and the Roman Catholic Church
▸ Individuals holding offices stipulated in the House of Commons Disqualification Act 1975, including civil servants, senior local government officials, judges, members of the regular armed forces and members of the police service.

The minimum age limit for candidates is 18 – lowered from 21 in 2005. There is no residence requirement, either in the constituency concerned or indeed in the country at large.

In order to be able to stand for Parliament, an individual must be both nominated and seconded and then supported by a further eight individuals whose names appear on the electoral register in the constituency concerned. In addition, candidates must deposit a sum of £500 with the Returning Officer, a sum which is refunded after the election if they obtain more than 5 per cent of the votes cast (1382 candidates, 39 per cent of the total, 'lost their deposits' at the 2005 General Election). Since 1970 candidates have been allowed to put on the ballot papers not only their names (which appear in alphabetical order), but also a description of their party or political position in not more than six words – for example, 'Conservative', 'Labour Party candidate', 'Liberal Democrat', and so on.

Each candidate is restricted by law to a maximum expenditure during the three to five weeks' campaign. For the General Election of 2005 this stood at £7150 plus 7 pence for each name on the register of voters in a county (rural) constituency, and £7150 plus 5 pence for each name on the register of voters in a borough (urban) constituency.[10] In a rural constituency with 76,203 entries on the electoral register this would ensure a maximum expenditure limit of £12,484.21 while in an urban constituency with an electorate of 67,781 this would ensure a maximum expenditure limit of £10,539.05, although most candidates declare expenses of rather less than the legal maxima.[11] In addition, candidates are entitled to post one communication relating to the election to each household in the constituency free of charge, providing it weighs no more than 57 g.

What can be described as the 'serious money' is spent by the political parties nationally on display posters and newspaper advertisements throughout the country. These are not enormous sums for a country with an electorate of more than 44 million.[12] The real explanation is that neither the parties nor the candidates have to spend large sums of money on buying TV time – indeed they are prohibited from doing so – unlike the position in the United States, for example. Indeed, with figures such as these it appears that Parliamentary elections are fought on the cheap in Britain as compared with other democratic countries.[13]

Each candidate has to have a designated agent who is legally responsible for seeing that all aspects of election law are observed and who, in an extreme case, could be sent to prison if found guilty of electoral malpractice by a court. The agent also serves in most cases as the local campaign manager for the candidate, although this is not part of an agent's legal duties. The bulk of the work in every election campaign is done by voluntary workers who are usually subscribing members of the party, but who may simply be sympathisers with the party cause or with the particular candidate.

first-past-the-post

The electoral system used to elect the Westminster Parliament is commonly described as 'first-past-the-post'. This means that in each constituency the

Total expenditure (£)	Conservative	Labour	Lib dem
Payments made	17,731,850	16,864,263	4,243,396
Notional expenditure incurred	120,391	1,075,354	81,178
Unpaid claims	0	0	0
Disputed claims	0	0	0
Total	**17,852,241**	**17,939,617**	**4,324,574**
Number of constituencies contested	627	627	626
Expenditure by type			
A. Party political broadcasts	293,446	470,218	124,871
B. Advertising	8,175,166	5,286,997	1,583,058
C. Unsolicited material to electors	4,493,021	2,698,114	1,235,295
D. Manifesto/poarty policy document	98,955	356,640	134,611
E. Market research/canvassing	1,291,846	1,577,017	165,185
F. Media	448,277	375,410	105,793
G. Transport	934,223	2,188,153	663,513
H. Rallies and other events	1,148,218	2,916,969	68,994
I. Overheads & general administration	969,094	,2,070,100	243,254
Total	**17,852,245**	**17,939,618**	**4,324,574**

source: *Election 2005: Campaign Spending*, The Electoral Commission, March 2006.

figure **3.2   party election spending**

candidate with the largest number of votes wins the seat. Usually this has the effect of turning the largest single minority of votes cast in the nation into a clear majority of seats in the House of Commons for the largest single party – for example the largest single proportion of the vote in 2005 – 35.2 per cent (21.6 per cent of the electorate) – was secured by the Labour Party and this delivered 55.0 per cent of the seats in the House of Commons. In this way the system has benefited both the Conservative and Labour parties and discriminated against the political fortunes of all other parties, unless their votes have been geographically concentrated in a particular part of the country.

This pattern of discrimination has been discernible for years in the British electoral system. At the 17 General Elections since the Second World War no party has ever won even half the votes cast, and often far fewer.[14] Yet the winning party has seldom – in fact only once – won fewer than half the seats in the House of Commons. Both the Conservative and Labour parties have benefited from this so-called 'multiplier effect' which can produce a sizeable majority of Parliamentary seats on the basis of a minority of the popular votes cast. For example, the Labour Party enjoyed a positive differential (that is, between the percentage of seats won and votes cast) of 14 per cent in 1945, 11 per cent in October 1974 and almost 20 per cent in 2005; while the Conservative Party enjoyed a positive differential of 8 per cent in 1959, 9 per cent in 1979, and 15 per cent in 1987. On the other hand, the Liberal Party has been the most

	Votes acquired	Seats won	% of seats	% of vote	% of electorate
Labour	9.55 million	355	55.0	35.2	21.6
Conservative	8.77 million	198	30.6	32.3	19.9
Liberal Democxrat	5.98 million	62	9.6	22.1	13.6
Others	2.82 million	31	4.8	10.4	6.4
Total	**27.12 million**	**646**	**100.0**	**100.0**	**61.5**
Non-voters	16.99 million				38.5
Total	**44.11 million**				

figure **3.3**   **the 2005 General Election Result**

notable victim of the system during the period since 1945. From 1945 to 1979, the Liberal share of the popular vote ranged from 2 per cent in 1951 to 19 per cent in February 1974. Yet the system prevented the Liberals from winning more than 2 per cent of the seats in the Commons even in their most successful attempt in February 1974. In the 1983 General Election, this multiplier effect worked even more dramatically against the interests of the Alliance of Liberals and Social Democrats which won 25 per cent of the votes cast but only 3 per cent of the seats in the House of Commons. In 2005 the Liberal Democrats received 22.1 per cent of the vote, securing them 9.6 per cent of the seats.

Figure 3.3 demonstrates the multiplier effect at the 2005 General Election. From this it can be seen that in 2005 it took 26,877 votes to elect a Labour MP, 44,521 votes to elect a Conservative MP and 96,378 votes to elect a Liberal Democrat MP. Plainly, the number of seats won is in no way proportional to the number of votes cast by the electorate. This was brought home particularly clearly in both 1951 and February 1974: in the General Election of 1951, the Labour Party obtained 231,067 more votes (0.8 per cent) than the Conservative Party, but the Conservatives won 26 more seats than Labour. Similarly – although the roles were reversed – in the General Election of February 1974, the Conservative Party secured 225,789 more votes (0.7 per cent) than Labour, but the Labour Party won four more seats than the Conservatives. These results occurred because the votes of one party – the Conservatives in 1951 and Labour in 1974 – happened to be more effectively concentrated in a number of marginal constituencies, thus giving the winning party an edge over the other main party in Parliament. Yet the system has never been arithmetically fair to all parties and it has always had a bias against second or third parties whose votes are not socially or regionally concentrated. Its political merits lie elsewhere, namely in the tendency for most General Elections to produce effective Parliamentary majorities for single-party Governments. This has enabled the electorate to hold the governing party to account for what happens, or fails to happen, during its term of office.

The characteristics of the system used for elections to the House of Commons have led many people to argue strongly for reform and specifically for the introduction of a system based on proportional representation.[15]

Although there is no one type of proportional representation, rather a number of variants of the basic idea, the 'purest' proposal for it is on the basis of a **Single Transferable Vote** in large multimember constituencies. This allows the electorate in each constituency to vote for individual candidates in order of preference. To secure election, a candidate needs to obtain a certain quota of votes (established by dividing the total number of valid votes cast by the number of representatives to be returned for the constituency plus one, and then adding one to this total). Thus in a five-member constituency in which 240,000 votes were cast, the number of votes required for the quota (and hence election) would be 240,000 divided by 6 plus 1 or 40,001 (about 17 per cent of the votes cast):

$$\frac{240,000}{5+1} + 1 = 40,001$$

If five candidates obtain this number of first preference votes, this is the end of the process. If, however, fewer than five reach the quota, a process of transference, or redistribution, takes place. Firstly, the 'excess' votes of the candidates who have gained more votes than the quota are transferred on the basis of second preferences, with the amount by which the votes of such candidates exceed the quota determining the value of the second preference votes. Hence, if a candidate gains 1500 first preference votes and the quota is 1000, a third of the votes has not been used. This candidate's second preference votes are therefore worth one-third of a vote each. As a result, if 600 second preference votes went to candidate 'X', candidate 'X' would be allocated an additional 200 votes to add to his or her total of first preference votes. After the second preference votes of those with more than the quota have been transferred, and if five candidates have not yet obtained the quota, then the candidate with the fewest first preference votes is eliminated and the votes transferred on the basis of second preferences. This process is then continued until enough candidates reach the quota and all seats are filled.

Under this system, every elected candidate could be said to have sufficient votes from the electorate (at least on the basis of second and subsequent preferences) and it would be possible for the voters to vote for individual candidates within the ideological range of any large party. For example, in a safe Labour seat, the electorate might choose one 'Old Labour' and two 'New Labour' from among Labour's ranks as well as one Liberal Democrat and one moderate Conservative. In a safe Conservative constituency the voters might equally choose two hard-line Conservatives, one moderate Conservative, one Liberal Democrat and one New Labour.

This system of proportional representation was recommended by a Speaker's Conference in 1917. It was actually used in some of the multimember university seats between 1918 and 1948; it was advocated by the Kilbrandon Commission in 1973 as part of the proposals for devolved Assemblies in Scotland and Wales; it was introduced for the election of Scottish Councillors by the Local Governance Act 2004, with the result that the 2007 elections were held under STV; and it is currently used in Northern Ireland for elections to the Assembly, the European Parliament and for local government elections. It is also the system used for Parliamentary elections in the Republic of Ireland. It is estimated by many – certainly if current voting habits continued under a reformed system – that the likely outcome of a General Election fought on the basis of the Single Transferable Vote system would be Coalition Government – a Government made up of more than one political party.

Another variant of proportional representation which has been advocated is the **Additional Member System** (AMS). This system is used in the Federal Republic of Germany, where half of the Bundestag (Lower House) members are elected by plurality in single-member constituencies and the other half from party lists drawn up within each Land (state). The voters have two votes each: one for a constituency candidate and one for a regional party list. The former enables the voters to express their first preferences and, if it is in a good area for their party, to secure their first choice for Parliament by direct election. The latter enables the voters to express what amounts to a second preference, usually by voting for the party list of one of the smaller parties in an attempt to ensure that the major opponent of their first preference does not get elected. In other words, they cast their second vote for the party they dislike least in an attempt to exclude the party they dislike most. The system can often improve the Parliamentary prospects for the smaller parties (such as the Free Democrats or the Greens) which might not otherwise have enough concentrated voting strength to get any of their candidates elected on a basis of first-past-the-post. It is also qualified by the so-called 5 per cent threshold which prevents parties with less than 5 per cent of the popular vote or three outright victories on the basis of first-past-the-post from securing any representation at all in the Bundestag. This is also the system that is used for elections to the Scottish Parliament, the Welsh Assembly and the Greater London Assembly.

Yet another variant is based upon the **Two-Ballot System** used in France. This uses single-member constituencies, but requires a candidate to win over half the votes cast in order to be elected on the first ballot. Failure to do this triggers a second ballot in which the result is decided by simple plurality, that is to say first-past-the-post. To go forward to the second ballot (if there is no outright winner on the first ballot), candidates require at least 12.5 per cent of the votes cast in the first ballot. This eliminates a great number of candidates from smaller parties or political splinter groups and automatically clarifies the voters' choice at the second ballot. The great advantage of this system is that it ensures majority support at least for those elected on the first ballot. The most commonly recognised disadvantage is that it is capable of producing polarised distortions which make it possible for a candidate who came third on the first ballot to triumph on the second because some of the supporters of the candidates who came first or second may find the third placed candidate the least unacceptable of the candidates in the second round. In other words, at the first ballot the voters make a positive choice, whereas at the second they eliminate. This system certainly does not avoid the imbalance between votes obtained and seats won associated with the first-past-the-post system – a point underlined by the fact that in the 2002 elections to the French National Assembly, the Centre-Right UMP and its smaller partner the UDF secured 61.8 per cent of the seats on the basis of only 43.5 per cent of the votes cast.

A variation of this is the **Supplementary Vote System** (SV) under which voters mark their first and second choice candidates on the ballot paper. First preferences are counted and if one candidate gets 50 per cent of the vote or more, that person is elected. If no one gets 50 per cent of the vote, all of the candidates, except the two with the highest number of votes, are eliminated and second preferences on the ballot papers of those eliminated candidates are then allocated to those remaining. Whoever has the most votes at the end of this process is declared the winner.

Two other systems should be noted. First, the **Alternative Vote System** (AV) – similar in some respects to the Supplementary Vote System – under which candidates contest single-member constituencies and voters mark the candidates in order of preference. If a candidate secures over half the votes cast, the candidate is elected; but if no candidate in a constituency does so, then the candidate with the fewest votes is eliminated and the votes redistributed according to the preferences indicated. This process continues until the support for a candidate passes the 50 per cent threshold. This system is currently in use for elections to the Lower House in Australia.

Secondly, there is the **National Party List System**. Here the whole country could constitute a single constituency. Each party draws up a list of its candidates and the electorate vote for the party they prefer. Once the votes have been counted, the parties are allocated seats in proportion to the number of votes they obtained. Hence, if a party gets 25 per cent of the vote, it gets 25 per cent of the seats, with individual candidates securing election according to their position on their party's list. This system is currently in use in Israel, Norway, Portugal and Turkey. In Israel it is used in its 'pure' form; the others use variants on the theme, for example by region and using thresholds. Some countries – for example Belgium, Denmark, Finland, the Netherlands, Spain and Sweden – use a variation of this system that enables voters to indicate a preference for candidates on the list. A variation of this system is the **Regional Party List System**, which has been used in Britain for the elections to the European Parliament since 1999.

Despite the fact that the Labour Party had declared a commitment to holding a referendum on the voting system for elections to the House of Commons in their 1997 election Manifesto and notwithstanding the fact that a subsequently established **Independent Commission on the Voting System** – the Jenkins

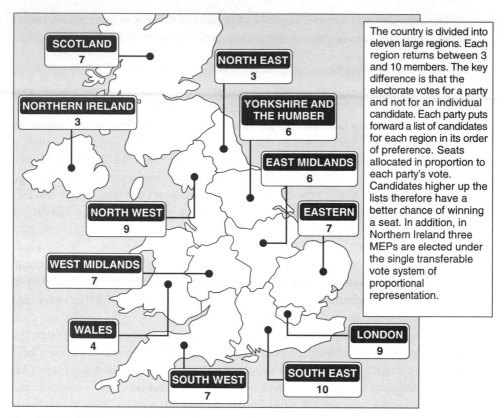

SCOTLAND
7

NORTH EAST
3

NORTHERN IRELAND
3

YORKSHIRE AND
THE HUMBER
6

EAST MIDLANDS
6

NORTH WEST
9

EASTERN
7

WEST MIDLANDS
7

WALES
4

LONDON
9

SOUTH WEST
7

SOUTH EAST
10

The country is divided into eleven large regions. Each region returns between 3 and 10 members. The key difference is that the electorate votes for a party and not for an individual candidate. Each party puts forward a list of candidates for each region in its order of preference. Seats allocated in proportion to each party's vote. Candidates higher up the lists therefore have a better chance of winning a seat. In addition, in Northern Ireland three MEPs are elected under the single transferable vote system of proportional representation.

figure **3.4**   **the UK European election regions: number of MEPs**

Commission[16] – recommended a two-vote mixed system – described as either limited AMS or AV top-up – with the majority of MPs (80–85 per cent) being elected on an individual constituency basis by the alternative vote system and with the remainder elected on a corrective top-up basis using open party lists in local areas, no moves have been made to alter the system for Westminster elections. The issue was one that came very much to the fore in light of the results of the 2005 General Election, an election that was described by the Electoral Reform Society as ' demonstrably unfair' and as 'the worst election in the history of democracy in Britain',[17] and which led *The Independent* to launch a 'Campaign for Democracy' asking individuals to sign a petition calling for a more proportional system so that 'the result of a general election is more representative of their wishes'.[18]

3.2 criteria of assessment

In a celebrated text written many years ago W.J.M. Mackenzie suggested four criteria by which an electoral system could be assessed. These were the quality of those elected, the effectiveness of the legislature, the fairness of the electoral results, and the degree of public confidence inspired.[19] It may still be useful to consider the British electoral system in the light of these four, admittedly rather ideal, criteria.

the quality of those elected

Members of Parliament in Britain are not strictly representative of the general public in that they are usually better educated and financially better off than the electorate as a whole (see Chapter 11). Certainly the House of Commons is far from being a microcosm of the population as a whole – a point which is most clearly evidenced by the fact that only 19.8 per cent (128) of MPs elected in 2005 were women (although this was the highest number ever), even though women comprised 52 per cent of the total electorate at the time; and by the fact that only 2.3 per cent were from minority ethnic groups, even though ethnic minorities comprised 7.9 per cent of the population.

Of course, characteristics such as educational and occupational background are not necessarily signs of quality, and in any case the standard of MPs could always be higher. Yet quality is not really a function of the electoral system. It derives much more from the nature of Parliamentary work, the frustrations of life on the back- benches, the unwillingness of many employers to encourage their employees to stand for Parliament, the increasing intrusion of the media into the private lives of public figures, and the low esteem in which politicians are held by the vast majority of the British people. All these factors discourage many able people from standing for Parliament or even from entering active politics in the first place. Furthermore, in the front-bench-dominated political system that exists in Britain, no more than about 90 MPs are paid members of any Government and no more than about another 90 are involved in the tasks of front-bench Opposition. Thus the vast majority of MPs in the House of Commons at any time are backbenchers who are obliged to busy themselves with other forms of political activity, such as liaising with outside interests or welfare work on behalf of their constituents. This may be appreciated by their constituents and others, but it does not necessarily attract the most talented people into Parliament.

effectiveness of the legislature

There are many shortcomings in the British legislature, but they should not necessarily be attributed to the workings of the electoral system. One of the familiar charges levelled against the British system is that it makes it all too easy for one or other of the parties to win an overall majority in the Commons which can then be used to push through its partisan legislation, often against rather ineffective Parliamentary Opposition and sometimes in defiance of the apparent wishes of the general public. According to this argument, Parliament is actually too effective at churning out partisan, ill-considered legislation and too ineffective at controlling the actions of the Government of the day. If this is so, it is essentially because all MPs not in the Government have little involvement and no responsibility in the formative stages of policy and decision making. It is also because Government backbenchers are inhibited by party loyalty and political self-interest from pursuing continuous public criticism of their own Ministers. Parliamentary control is therefore left largely in the hands of the Opposition, which is usually unable to do more than kick up a fuss about controversial Government decisions or delay the contentious elements in the Government's legislative programme. The system is indeed one in which, although the Opposition has its say, the Government gets its way, at any rate most of the time.

The British people expect their Members of Parliament to be doughty champions of their interests and unabashed spokesmen for their concerns. This is what they expect from an effective legislature. In practice, constituents are often disappointed to discover that the power of party loyalty usually overrides both more parochial and more altruistic considerations when it comes to votes in the House of Commons. The argument for this position is effectively that MPs on the Government side are elected principally to support Government policy as set out in the party Manifesto and other relevant documents and can only rarely defy their party without undermining what is described as 'the mandate theory' of Government (see pp. 000–000). Thus, those opposed to or critical of the Government's programme may well win the argument, but usually lose the vote at the end of debates in Parliament.[20]

fairness of the results

It is here that we enter the area of greatest controversy about the first-past-the-post electoral system. While it enables the electorate to choose what is normally a single-party Government every four or five years at a General Election, it does not produce a House of Commons which is anything like an exact reflection of the votes cast for each party. Essentially, it is a system which enables the largest single minority of voters in the national electorate to bring about the return of single-party Government with an overall majority in the House of Commons. There is, in fact, a threshold of between 35 and 40 per cent of the votes cast above which (especially in marginal seats with three or more candidates) a party has a good chance of capturing seats, but below which it is likely to fail to form the Government.

This situation arises because most General Elections in Britain tend to be contests between at least three parties in which the second- and third-ranking parties frequently split the losing vote between them, thus ensuring that neither has a real chance of defeating the leading party. Obviously there is always the possibility of tactical voting by the supporters of one or other of the losing parties, yet on the whole this has not made much difference to the results (except occasionally at by-elections), since none of the parties can be sure of delivering enough of its supporters to guarantee such an outcome.[21]

In the General Election of February 1974 the third party (the Liberals) received more than six million votes, a little more than half the votes received by either the Conservative or Labour parties, but won only 14 seats in the House of Commons, less than one-twentieth of the seats secured by either the Labour or Conservative parties. At the same time, the party which won the election (Labour) did so with fewer popular votes than the party which came second in terms of Parliamentary seats (the Conservatives). In the 1983 General Election the discrepancy between votes and seats was even more striking: the Conservative Party secured 61 per cent of the seats on 42.4 per cent of the votes cast, the Labour Party got 32 per cent of the seats on 27.6 per cent of the votes cast, while the Alliance of Liberals and Social Democrats, although receiving 25.4 per cent of the popular vote – just 2.2 per cent less than Labour – won only 3.5 per cent of the seats, 28.5 per cent less than Labour.

In the General Election of 2005 Labour won an overall majority of seats – 55.1 per cent – with only 35.2 per cent of the vote: and this with the support of only 21.6 per cent of the electorate. Consequently, the result brought about the election of a Government backed by a solid Parliamentary majority, but which had secured the support of scarcely one in three of those voting and a little over one in five of the total electorate. It also resulted in only one in three MPs having secured majority support from those who voted in their constituencies and not a single MP commanding majority support in their local electorate – that is to say, those entitled to vote. In England more people voted Conservative than voted Labour – 35.7 per cent as opposed to 35.5 per cent – but Labour won more seats: 286 as against 193. As for the Liberal Democrats, despite polling almost 6 million votes (22.1 per cent), they only obtained 62 seats in the House of Commons, 9.6 per cent of the total. The Conservatives polled 32.3 per cent of the vote and received 30.5 per cent of the seats. In Scotland the Conservatives received 15.8 per cent of the vote but won only a single seat (1.6 per cent), whereas the Liberal Democrats received 22.6 per cent of the vote and won 11 seats (18.6 per cent).

Of course, the results could be very different if the potential supporters of parties, those who abstain from voting and those who are deterred from supporting their first preference for fear of casting wasted votes, were all to vote in accordance with their real political preferences. In that case, results could be very different in many parts of the country. Nonetheless, the most sensible conclusion is that fairness is not the prime consideration. The overriding purpose is to elect a Government with a sufficient Parliamentary majority to ensure its authority to govern throughout the period of a normal four or five year Parliament, one that can be held accountable at the subsequent General Election and, in the first-past-the-post system, this usually means single-party Government.

public confidence inspired

It is difficult to produce reliable measures of public confidence in something as abstract as an electoral system. One way of assessing it is to note the degree of popular support for electoral reform as measured by opinion polls. This has consistently proved attractive to representative samples of the electorate as a whole.[22] Exact parallels cannot be drawn with other countries, but it is interesting to note that, when consulted in a referendum in September 1992, the people of New Zealand voted overwhelmingly (84.5 per cent) to end their first-past-the-post electoral system.[23]

Another way of assessing public confidence in the electoral system is through turnout.[24] In the four General Elections in the 1950s turnout averaged 80.5 per cent. In the four elections during the 1970s turnout averaged 74.9 per cent. In 2001, however, turnout fell to 59.4 per cent, only increasing to 61.5 per cent in 2005. The decline in turnout has led some experts to conclude that 'the British people [are] disengaged from electoral politics.'[25]

Another way of assessing public confidence in the electoral system is to log the performance of the two largest parties at successive General Elections. In view of the fact that they have traditionally been associated in the public mind with adherence to the existing electoral system, a high level of support for both of them together could be interpreted as support for the existing rules of the game. Doing this, we find that the proportion of the electorate voting for the Labour and Conservative parties together was as follows:

1951		79%	1979	62%
1955		73%	1983	51%
1959		73%	1987	55%
1964		67%	1992	59%
1966		68%	1997	52%
1970		64%	2001	43%
1974	(Feb)	59%	2005	41%
1974	(Oct)	55%		

figure **3.5**   **proportion of the electorate voting for the Labour and Conservative parties**

In so far as any valid or lasting conclusion can be drawn from this evidence, it seems that the two largest parties and the electoral system with which they are associated have lost much of their popular appeal. Yet another way of measuring the success – or otherwise – of an electoral system is to took at the number of rejected (spoilt) ballot papers that result. To some extent at least this is a measure of whether or not the public understand or are confused by the systems being used. This was highlighted by the 2007 Scottish Parliament elections when voters were asked to cast two different votes, one requiring an 'x' and one requiring numerical ordering, on a single ballot paper (while at the same time having a second ballot paper with an altogether different – and new – system for voting for the local elections). This resulted in a remarkably high number of rejected papers – 141,891 (3.5 per cent of the total) and saw the establishment of an independent review into what was involved.

3.3 the debate about the British electoral system

Supporters of the first-past-the-post system argue that the system works well, pointing out that it has led to stable Governments based on Parliamentary majorities of one party rather than Coalitions, which can be weak and ineffective. Single-party Government is said to mean strong, accountable and responsive Government.

Arguments for FPTP

> ▸ Produces strong, coherent and responsive Government
> ▸ Enhances political accountability
> ▸ Easy to understand and operate
> ▸ Has been tried and tested over many years
> ▸ Enables winning party to deliver its mandate.

Arguments for PR

> ▸ Does not produce a House of Commons which accurately reflects public opinion
> ▸ Is unfair to smaller parties whose votes are not regionally concentrated
> ▸ Results in a single party – with a minority of the popular vote – dominating the House of Commons.

figure **3.6   arguments for and against the first-past-the-post electoral system**

Critics of the present system seek to counter this by pointing out that the system produces the anomalies and unfairness already referred to in this chapter; that it does not produce political stability – witness 1950–51, 1964–66, February and October 1974, and the periods 1976–79 and 1992–97; that if 'strong' Government means a Government that can force through unpopular legislation – such as the Poll Tax or tuition fees – then 'weak' Government, which would have to listen to the views and opinions of others, would be no bad thing; that proportional representation does not necessarily result in weak and unstable Governments – as exemplified by Germany and Sweden; that the first-past-the-post system encourages adversarial politics which is known to be unpopular with the general public; and that it is capable of creating Governments which, despite being supported only by a minority of those who vote, behave like 'elective dictatorships'.

Supporters of the first-past-the-post system argue that electoral reform would lead to a Coalition Government and this would place disproportionate power in the hands of the minor parties. These would then dictate the shape of the Government, exert disproportionate influence on its policy and possibly determine the timing of the subsequent General Election. In short, the tail would wag the dog. To support this assertion, they point to the role of the Free Democrats and the Green Party in Germany – parties which have often struggled to get even 10 per cent of the vote and yet have often been an essential component of post-war German Governments – or to the New Zealand First Party which with only 13 per cent of the vote at the 1996 election determined which of the larger parties formed the Government.

Those who argue for electoral reform respond by asking why this should be a problem if it ensures effective, successful Government. They go on to point out that 'deals' with minor parties are not unknown in the British political system, citing the Lib-Lab Pact of 1977–79 and the Conservative Government's dependence upon the Ulster Unionists at times during 1992–97. In their view, there is nothing inherently wrong with Coalition Governments, since the main political parties are Coalitions in themselves. In other words, the present system is based on intraparty Coalitions, whereas a more proportional system would depend on interparty Coalitions

Those who argue in favour of the current electoral system caution that any reform could lead to a greater visibility for and a consequential rise in support for extremist groups – citing the rise of the Fascist Right in Germany (the DVU) in the 1990s, of Jörg Haider's Freedom Party in Austria in 1999, of Jean-Marie Le Pen's National Front in France and of Pim Fortuyn's party in the Netherlands in 2002.[26]

Advocates of reform respond by observing that those who profess to be worried by the danger of Fascism and the extreme Right would do better to consider introducing formal checks and balances into Britain's constitutional arrangements – such as a formal codified constitution and an entrenched Bill of Rights. They go on to point out that an electoral system based on proportional representation would more accurately reflect the strength or weakness of the various political tendencies in society. It would follow that if racist or extremist sentiment is present in the electorate, it is best to have it channelled through the electoral system.

Supporters of the current electoral arrangements believe that reform would lead to weak Government.[27] To support this, they cite the examples of Italy and New Zealand: Italy where there were 60 Governments in the period 1945–2007 and where the politicians and people finally turned to the first-past-the-post system as a way out of the troubles associated with their previous proportional system; and New Zealand, where more of the people seem to want to return to their old first-past-the-post system than stick with their newer Mixed Member Proportional (MMP) system.[28]

Advocates of reform respond by pointing out that Italy has not adopted the first-past-the-post system entirely, but rather a mixed system in which 75 per cent of members of the Chamber of Deputies are elected by first-past-the-post and the remaining 25 per cent under a proportional system designed to ensure representation for those unlikely to win under pure first-past-the-post. With regard to New Zealand, critics of the current system make the point that what happened there following the introduction of MMP was more a reflection of New Zealand politics and of general political circumstances than of any change in electoral arrangements.

3.4 conclusion

The electoral system used for elections to the House of Commons has come a long way since Queen Victoria confided to her diary that 'it seems to me a defect in our much famed constitution to have to part with an admirable Government … merely on account of the number of votes'.[29] Nowadays, a General Election is usually seen as a public verdict on the record of the party in Government and the competing attractions of the various Opposition parties. Yet the mass electorate is politically sovereign only on condition that it exercises its sovereignty when invited to do so by the Prime Minister of the day and within the limits of political choice offered by the political parties at each General Election.

Modern British politics is essentially about the struggle for power between the political parties. Of course, there has always been some ideology in the political rhetoric and the party manifestos. Yet for most of those who reach the top of the political tree the ideological content has often been little more than a necessary part of the political ritual, the tribute which party leaders and others have had to pay to their more zealous followers and supporters, especially when in Opposition. Some would argue that this changed when Margaret Thatcher was Leader of the Conservative Party from 1975 to 1990. Yet the appeal of political pragmatism usually trumps ideology if the latter is seen as a threat to a party's chances of gaining or retaining power, a fact that is highlighted by the case of Tony Blair and New Labour.

Moreover, the conduct of elections and the Parliamentary results which ensue are seldom more important than the actual behaviour of the parties when elected into Government or when consigned by the voters to Opposition. While free elections on the basis of universal adult suffrage are the essence of the electoral system, it is the quality of party politics between General Elections and the conduct of every Government in office which counts for far more in British Parliamentary democracy.

SUGGESTED QUESTIONS

1   Describe the workings of the electoral system used for elections to the House of Commons.

2   To what extent does the electoral system used to elect members of the House of Commons satisfy the four criteria suggested by W.J.M. Mackenzie?

3   Analyse the arguments for and against a change to proportional representation for elections to the House of Commons.

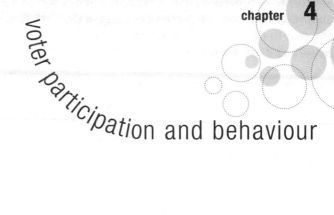

voter participation and behaviour

4.1 two-party politics?

The concept of a two-party politics is not meant to imply that there are *only* two parties but, rather, that only two parties *count*. In short, two parties receive most of the votes, secure most of the representation, alternate in government, govern alone rather than in coalition, and dominate the business of government.

The dominance of two main parties (not always the same two parties) has clear antecedents in British political history and has been encouraged by the electoral system (see Chapter 3). In the late-eighteenth and early nineteenth centuries there was a struggle for power between the Whigs and the Tories. In the late-nineteenth and early twentieth centuries there was a struggle between the Liberals and the Conservatives. During the first few decades of the twentieth century it was uncertain whether or not Labour would displace the Liberals as the main opponent of the Conservatives. However, since the end of the Second World War in 1945 for many people the effective choice at all General Elections has been between the Conservative and Labour parties. Indeed, throughout the 1950s, for example, the average combined vote for these two parties was more than 93 per cent.

However, there have been occasions when the formation of a three-party – or in Wales and especially in Scotland a four-party – system seemed to be imminent. In the early 1970s, for example, there was a revival in the fortunes of both the Liberal Party and the Nationalist parties, with the Liberals taking 19.3 per cent and 18.3 per cent of the national vote in the February and October 1974 General Elections respectively, and the Scottish Nationalists receiving 30.4 per cent of the vote in Scotland and Plaid Cymru 10.8 per cent of the vote in Wales in October 1974. Nevertheless, by 1979 the fortunes of these parties had declined and the two leading parties were again receiving more than 80 per cent of the total vote.

Similarly, in the early 1980s, following the formation of the Alliance between the Liberals and the newly formed Social Democrats, it looked for a time as though the two-party mould of British politics would be broken – combined support for the two main parties declining in the 1983 General Election to 70 per cent. Yet, in the event, this was not the case, the dominance of the two parties reasserting itself, so that by the time of the 1992 General Election the combined vote for the Conservative and Labour parties stood at more than 76 per cent.

In both 1997 and 2001 the Labour and Conservative parties received, combined, 73.9 per cent and 72.4 per cent of the popular vote respectively, less than three-quarters. The Liberal Democrats attracted 16.8 per cent of the vote in 1997 and 18.3 per cent of the vote in 2001, while the Scottish Nationalists received 22.1 per cent and 20.1 per cent of the Scottish vote and Plaid Cymru received 9.9 per cent and 14.3 per cent of the Welsh vote. In 1997 no less than 7.0 per cent of voters cast their ballots for candidates from other than the three main parties, at that time the highest total ever. In 2001, although this figure declined to 6.5 per cent, it was nonetheless above the level recorded at any other previous election. It should also be noted that the traditional two-party model of voting behaviour was undergoing changes in other kinds of elections – local, Parliamentary by-elections, and at the European Parliamentary level – with parties other than the traditional two main parties being increasingly successful.

In the 2005 General Election the combined support for the two traditional parties declined still further to 67.5 per cent of the popular vote and stood at only 41.3 per cent of the registered electorate. Amongst those who voted, the Liberal Democrats attracted the support of 22.1 per cent, the Nationalists 17.7 per cent of the Scottish vote and 12.6 per cent of the Welsh vote, and other candidates 8.2 per cent of the vote – indeed, one feature of the election was to confirm the growing presence of minor parties in British politics. In the House of Commons a total of 10 parties (plus two independents) were represented and a total of 92 MPs (excluding the Speaker) were drawn from parties other than Labour or Conservative, the highest number since 1923. In the light of such results talk was once again of the end of two-party dominance. Whether or not this trend continues, only time – and events – will show. What is clear, however, is that the two-party label has become an over-simplification which obscures almost as much as it reveals about party politics. In short, British politics can no longer be described *simply* and *accurately* as two-party politics.

4.2 voter participation

The lines of political cleavage can be drawn in a number of different ways, according to various criteria. Consequently, it is possible to subdivide the British electorate in a variety of ways. In this section we begin by looking at *party loyalists*, *consumerist voters* (more traditionally referred to as *floating voters*) and *abstainers/non-voters*.

party loyalists

At General Elections since the Second World War the Conservative and Labour parties have been able to count on the loyal support of a significant number of

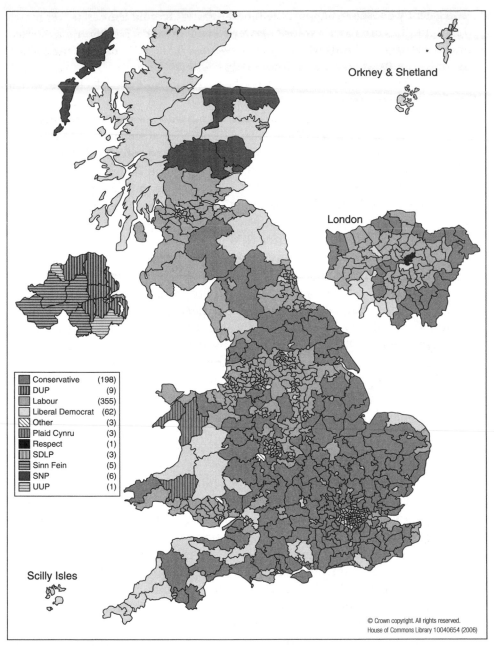

Conservative   (198)
DUP   (9)
Labour   (355)
Liberal Democrat (62)
Other   (3)
Plaid Cynru   (3)
Respect   (1)
SDLP   (3)
Sinn Fein   (5)
SNP   (6)
UUP   (1)

Orkney & Shetland

London

Scilly Isles

© Crown copyright. All rights reserved.
House of Commons Library 10040654 (2006)

figure **4.1** **political map of the United Kingdom 2005 General Election – constituency results**

core voters, individuals who have supported their party almost regardless of the issues or other factors. Estimates have put the number of core voters at between 6.5 million and 7.5 million for each main party. However, recent surveys have indicated that the proportion of the electorate strongly identifying with and consistently voting for one or other of the two main parties has declined.[1] From the mid 1970s there have also been a significant number of voters who have

voter participation and behaviour : **65**

consistently chosen to support the Liberal Party/Liberal Democrats. Estimates have put this core Liberal vote at between 1 million and 1.5 million – a marked increase from the 1960s when it was between 0.5 and 0.75 million and indeed from the 1950s when it was as low as 0.25 million voters.

In Scotland and Wales there have been sections of the electorate which have voted consistently for the Nationalist parties, the Scottish National Party (SNP) and Plaid Cymru (PC). However, it is hard to ascertain how many of these voters can be considered 'core' supporters, since both the SNP and PC have always attracted substantial and varying protest votes and their electoral fortunes have fluctuated accordingly. At the 2005 General Election they collected between them a total of 587,105 votes, only 2.2 per cent of the total vote in the United Kingdom but 17.7 per cent of the total in Scotland and 12.6 per cent of the total in Wales.

The electorate in Northern Ireland (1,148,003 people in 2005) has traditionally been divided along religious lines, with 46 per cent – according to the 2001 census – being Protestant and 40 per cent being Catholic. In addition, 0.3 per cent belonged to other (non-Christian) religions while the remaining 13.7 per cent had no declared religious affiliation. Because of this, more than half have habitually voted for an assortment of Unionist/Loyalist/Protestant candidates (51.5 per cent in 2005), while the votes of most of the rest of the electorate have gone to the Nationalist/Republican/Catholic candidates. The big change in Northern Ireland in recent years has been internal to these general groupings, voters within the Unionist/Loyalist/Protestant community switching from the Ulster Unionist Party (UUP) to the Democratic Unionist Party (DUP), and voters within the Nationalist/Republican/Catholic community switching from the Social Democratic and Labour Party (SDLP) to Sinn Fein, the political wing of the IRA. In 2005 the movement of votes from the UUP to the DUP was stark – in crude terms it amounted to a swing within this section of the community of more than 10 per cent, resulting in the UUP, for long the dominant force in Northern Ireland politics generally and Unionist politics in particular, being all but wiped out, left as they were with only one seat, as apposed to nine for the DUP. The movement within the Nationalist/Republican/Catholic community was less stark, but nonetheless real, with Sinn Fein receiving 24.3 per cent of the vote and five seats, overtaking the SDLP who secured only 17.5 per cent and three seats. In addition there exists the non-sectarian Alliance Party which received an average of a little over 10 per cent of the popular vote – on a range of between 15.3 per cent and 7.6 per cent – in its six 'best' constituencies of the 18 in Northern Ireland in 2005.

fickle – or floating – voters

Voter volatility has varied in number, in proportion and in composition at each General Election since the Second World War but appears to have grown in size over the years. Over the period 1959–79 about half the electorate changed its voting behaviour at least once, if we include moves to and from abstention.[2]

Over one-third of those who voted Labour in 1979 deserted the party in 1983, as did nearly one-quarter of those who voted Conservative, thus effectively determining the outcome of the 1983 election. At the 1987 General Election it was the Alliance of Liberals and Social Democrats which suffered most from this fickle approach to voting, losing nearly one-third of its 1983 vote to other parties or to non-voting. Each of the main parties also suffered from defectors, with the Conservatives losing 23 per cent of their 1983 vote to other parties and abstention and Labour losing 25 per cent in the same way. At the 1992 General Election, of those eligible to vote in both 1987 and 1992, 16 per cent moved from supporting one party to supporting another party and an additional 20 per cent moved to or from abstention.

At the 1997 General Election not only has it been estimated that during the campaign as many as 7.1 million voters changed their minds, but that 23 per cent of those who had voted Conservative in 1992 voted for a different party, as did 7 per cent of the 1992 Labour vote and 31 per cent of the 1992 Liberal Democrat vote. Similarly, it has been estimated that 25 per cent of the electorate decided how to cast their vote in the final week of the campaign – indeed, 11 per cent did so on polling day itself. Of those who ended up voting Liberal Democrat, only 34 per cent had made up their minds to do so before the campaign got underway, against 58 per cent of Conservatives and 65 per cent of Labour voters. By the middle of the campaign the Liberal Democrats had persuaded another 25 per cent of their eventual voters to back them, but as many as 41 per cent of Liberal Democrat voters made up their minds to support the party only in the last week of the campaign; 16 per cent deciding to do so only in the last 24 hours.

At the beginning of the 2005 General Election campaign a MORI poll showed that among the 55 per cent who said that they were 'certain to vote', the Conservatives had a five point lead over Labour, 39 per cent to 34 percent, while among those who were less likely to vote, or certain they would not vote, Labour had a ten point lead. At the outset of both the 1987 and 1997 elections campaigns 25 per cent of those who said they would vote declared that they might change their minds, while at the outset of both the 1992 and 2001 election this was true for 32 per cent and 34 per cent, respectively, of those questioned. However, at the outset of the 2005 campaign, 41 per cent said that although they thought they would vote for a specific, stipulated party, they were doubtful to the point of admitting they might change their mind during the campaign. A disproportionate number of these 'waverers' who said that they might switch came from amongst declared Labour supporters. Similarly, although 74 per cent of declared Conservatives said that they were certain to vote, this was the case for only 57 per cent of declared Labour supporters. If nothing else, the results of the 2005 election indicate a growing trend towards electoral volatility.

It is apparent, therefore, that fickle or floating voters provide the key to electoral victory or defeat at every General Election. These voters in particular determine the electoral fortunes of the minor parties, since without the benefit of desertions from both main parties it would be difficult for them to collect many extra votes. Of course there is always the possibility that a third party can become one of the two leading parties in Parliament, provided it manages to break through a threshold of about 35 per cent of the votes cast, above which it is likely to win a substantial number of seats in the House of Commons but below which it is likely to languish in frustrating Parliamentary weakness. For example, in 1983 the Alliance obtained 25.4 per cent of the vote but secured only 3.5 per cent of the seats in the House of Commons; while the 22.1 per cent of the popular vote won by the Liberal Democrats in 2005 secured only 9.5 per cent of the seats. Nonetheless, it is possible for a third party to make such a breakthrough. After all, it was in just such a manner that the Labour Party gradually displaced the Liberals during the first half of the twentieth century.

In future, the impact of electoral volatility will depend on the net effect of a number of different factors. It is likely that increased volatility will be encouraged by the relative weakening of traditional associations between class and party, the growing tendency for voters to cast their votes instrumentally, the advent of capricious 'consumer' voting, and the unsettling influence of the media on the opinion polls and voting behaviour. On the other hand, volatility could decrease if there were to be a general recognition of the futility of casting votes for smaller parties or a sustained secular trend towards a sea change in voting behaviour of the kind which can occur in Britain every 20 years or so. Any move towards adopting a system of proportional representation could also have a significant impact in this regard. Only time will tell.

abstainers/non-voters

Before considering voter turnout, it should be recognized that such figures are likely to under-record the number of people not voting because they do not take into account those who do not register to vote. It has been estimated that the numbers of unregistered voters may be as high as 15 per cent of the eligible electorate in some constituencies.[3] Reasons for not registering to vote include:

- Alienation from the political system
- Concerns over lack of anonymity
- Concerns over alternative uses of the Register
- Language barriers
- Fear of harassment
- Moving from one location to another
- Administrative inefficiencies.

If political participation is measured simply in terms of the turnout at General Elections, we can see that, since the Second World War, it has fluctuated between a high point of 84 per cent (1950) and a low of 59.4 per cent (2001), with an average of 74.4 per cent over the 17 General Elections involved. In 2001 the proportion of those not voting virtually matched the proportion of those voting for the winning party – 40.6 per cent as opposed to 40.7 per cent, which meant that, for the first time, many more people on the electoral register did not vote than voted for the winning party – 41 per cent as opposed to 24 per cent. The 2001 turnout represented a drop of 12.1 per cent on the turnout in 1997 and was the lowest recorded level of voting participation at a General Election since 1918. Given that many troops were serving overseas at the time of the post-First World War election, it is probably the case that a greater proportion of the electorate abstained in 2001 than in any previous British General Election since the advent of the mass franchise. Turnout in 2005 was only marginally better at 61.3 per cent, despite the ready availability of voting by post. In fact, the proportion not voting surpassed the proportion voting for the victorious party, 38.7 per cent as opposed to 35.2 per cent, and again saw many more people not voting than voting for the winning party – 38.7 per cent as opposed to 21.5 per cent. Indeed, the Labour vote in 2005 – 9.56 million – was the lowest total for any governing party since the 1920s when the electorate was much smaller. These facts, and others, have been interpreted as signs of real alienation from the political process among a growing number of individuals and have led some to the conclusion that the British political class has become seriously disconnected from the public, raising important questions about the effectiveness of British democracy.[4]

Aside from apathy and lack of interest, low turnout can be attributed to a variety of factors, including:

- Inconvenience, namely that voting is too time consuming
- The result being perceived as a foregone conclusion
- A belief that it makes no difference who wins
- The idea that an individual vote can have no real impact on the result
- Disappointment with the Government Party's performance, especially among traditional heartland supporters
- Alternatives to an unpopular Government not being perceived as either attractive or viable
- Parties not being perceived as being very different from each other, reducing the incentive to vote
- Targeted campaigning whereby voters who do not reside in marginal, battleground constituencies feel ignored
- Increasing cynicism about the political process, especially among the young for whom conventional politics has little appeal
- A feeling of detachment from the political process, especially among those who suffer from persistent poverty and social exclusion who, as a result, feel let down by the system.

Since voting in Britain is voluntary, non-voters can have a vital influence on the outcome of an election. For example, it has been estimated that differential non-voting had a significant influence on the results of a number of General

Elections, namely those of 1951, February 1974, October 1974, 1997, 2001 and 2005. It could have a similarly crucial influence on future General Elections.

4.3 factors in voting

A sociological profile of the electorate between 1979 and 2005 is provided in Figure 4.2.

social class

Traditionally one of the most significant cleavages in the British electorate has been based on class factors of one kind or another. Indeed, in 1967 Peter Pulzer observed that 'class is the basis of British party politics; all else is embellishment and detail'.[5] Yet the meaning of social class has changed and its correlation with voting behaviour has changed and diminished accordingly.

At General Elections since the Second World War the Conservative vote has usually consisted of perhaps two-thirds of the total middle-class vote and about one-third of the total working-class vote, according to the broadest definitions. The Labour vote has usually been made up of perhaps one-quarter of the total middle-class vote and more than one-half of the total working-class vote, according to the same broad definitions. The votes for the Liberals/Liberal Democrats have tended to be even less class-based (which has been part of their electoral problem), and there has been no overwhelming class bias in the votes of the Nationalist parties in either Scotland or Wales.

There has always been a significant number of people whose voting behaviour could not easily be explained or predicted on traditional class lines. The most notable example has been that of the working-class Conservatives.[6] Typically, more than one-third of all Conservative votes at General Elections since the Second World War have come from working-class people. In the General Election of 1992 it is estimated that 46 per cent of the total Conservative vote came from within the working-class, with 35 per cent of the working-class casting their votes for Conservative candidates. In view of the bottom-heavy shape of the social structure in Britain at that time, it is evident that the Conservative Party could not have been elected to office if it had not managed to attract a sufficient proportion of the working-class vote.

In general, class-based voting of the traditional kind has weakened steadily in Britain over the years since the 1950s and 1960s, notably within the changing working class. In 1959 Labour's share of the vote of manual workers and their families was 40 per cent larger than its share of the vote of white-collar workers and their families. For a considerable period in the 1970s and 1980s the Labour Party lost working-class votes to the Conservatives. For example, at the 1983 General Election there was a swing from Labour to Conservative of 2 per cent among skilled manual workers and 4 per cent among semi-skilled and unskilled workers.

At the 1987 General Election Labour's fortunes varied between the traditional and the new working class. It did well among the traditional unskilled manual working class, whereas among the new skilled working class Labour lost votes

	Conservative							Labour							Liberal Democrat						
	1979	1983	1987	1992	1997	2001	2005	1979	1983	1987	1992	1997	2001	2005	1979	1983	1987	1992	1997	2001	2005
Total voters	4	44	43	43	31	33	33	38	28	32	35	44	42	36	14	26	23	18	17	19	23
Gender:																					
Male	43	42	43	41	31	32	34	40	30	32	37	44	42	34	13	25	23	18	17	18	22
Female	47	46	43	44	32	31	32	35	26	32	34	44	42	38	15	27	23	18	17	19	23
Age group:																					
18–24	42	42	37	35	27	27	28	41	33	39	38	49	41	38	12	23	22	19	16	24	26
25–34	43	40	39	40	28	24	25	38	29	33	37	49	51	38	15	29	26	18	16	19	27
35–54	46	44	45	43	30			35	27	29	34	45			16	27	24	19	19		
55+	47	47	46	42	36			38	27	31	34	40			13	24	21	17	17		
35–44						28	27						45	41						19	23
45–54						30	31						41	35						24	25
55–64						39	39						37	31						17	22
65+						40	41						39	35						17	18
Occupational category:																					
AB Professional/managerial	61	60	57	56	42	39	37	20	10	14	20	31	30	28	15	28	26	22	21	25	29
C1 Clerical/skilled non-manual (white collar)	52	51	51	52	26	36	37	29	20	21	25	47	38	32	16	27	26	19	19	20	23
C2 Skilled/manual	41	40	40	38	25	29	33	41	32	36	41	54	49	40	15	26	22	17	14	15	19
DE Semi-skilled/unskilled/ pensioners etc.	34	33	30	30	21	24	25	49	41	48	50	61	55	48	13	24	20	15	13	13	18
Other categories:																					
Home owners	53	52	50	49	35	43	44	29	19	23	30	41	32	29	14	28	25	19	17	19	20
Mortgage-payers	N/A	N/A	N/A	47	31	31	31	N/A	N/A	N/A	29	44	42	36	N/A	N/A	N/A	20	18	20	25
Council tenants	27	26	22	24	13	18	16	56	47	56	55	65	60	55	13	24	19	15	15	14	19
Trade Union members	33	31	30	30	18	21	19	51	39	42	47	57	50	46	13	29	26	19	20	19	22

source: Ipsos-MORI/N621. House of Commons Library, Analysis of 2005 British Election Study Dataset.

figure **4.2 profile of the electorate 1979–2005**

to the Conservatives. While on average between 1945 and 1970 62 per cent of all manual workers had voted Labour, by 1983 Labour support from this quarter had fallen to 38 per cent. This represented nothing short of a transformation of working-class voting behaviour and was rightly described by Ivor Crewe as 'the most significant post-war change in the social basis of British politics.'[7]

Labour and the growing middle class

It is worth noting that, even when the Labour Party has fared badly at General Elections, its middle-class voting support has held up rather well. There is no complete explanation for this, although it may partly be explained by Labour's strong support among white-collar workers in the public sector – for example teachers and health service workers. Indeed it is something that was strengthened as New Labour managed to broaden its appeal to encompass more issues of concern to the growing middle-class electorate, such as law and order, the quality of public services, protection of the environment, and greater economic opportunities for women. The 1997, 2001 and 2005 General Election victories provided real evidence of Labour's success in reassuring the middle classes.

Of course, another explanation for this phenomenon is simply that, as the electorate as a whole becomes more middle class, so Labour voters are likely to become more middle class as they move up the economic and social ladder. Even though their improved material circumstances and middle-class life-style might be thought to be more consistent with voting Conservative, such voters remain loyal to their social origins and principles and so vote Labour.

Conservatives and the fragmented working class

It is striking that, in spite of presiding over the two worst economic recessions since the Second World War, namely in 1980–82 and 1990–92, the Conservative Party was able to retain the support of a significant number of working-class voters. In the 1980s this support was critically dependent on the party's ability to maintain a reputation for competence in office, something which was severely dented during the early and mid 1990s and which was a factor in the desertion from the party of large numbers of such voters in the 1997 General Election. Such support also depended on the image of the party in the eyes of the so-called authoritarian working class – that is, those working-class voters who are attracted by whichever party takes the toughest line on issues, such as law and order, immigration and defence. The headway made by Tony Blair and New Labour on these very issues during the mid 1990s and the Conservative party's subsequent loss of the 1997 General Election, showed that it could not afford to take such support for granted.

In 1979 the Conservatives benefited from widespread revulsion at the trade union excesses during the so called 'Winter of Discontent'. In 1983 they benefited from the patriotic appeal of victory in the Falklands and from a divided Opposition. In 1987 they benefited from a rising tide of prosperity and a divided Opposition. In 1992 they benefited from a new leader, the commitment to abolish the Poll Tax, an electorate still reluctant to trust the Labour party, and once again a divided Opposition. They lost in 1997 because their image of integrity in office had been tarnished by sleaze, their reputation for economic competence had been smashed by the fiasco of Black Wednesday, and New Labour was able to portray itself rather more convincingly as the party for those with ambition and drive. In order to have a good chance of winning in the future, the Conservatives will need to regain a good part of the working-class vote which they won in 1979, 1983, 1987 and 1992 but which deserted them in 1997 and which did not return in either 2001 or 2005.

changing sociological perspectives

There are sociological differences in voting behaviour, of which perhaps the most remarkable in recent years has been the cleavage between the *traditional working class* and the *new working class*. As a stereotype, the former group could be described as those who live in Scotland or the North of England, are Council tenants, trade union members and work in the public sector. Equally, the latter group could be described as those who live in the South and East of England, are owner-occupiers, non-trade-union members and work in the private sector, very often in a self-employed capacity.

The decline of traditional class-based voting in Britain could be attributed partly to the changing nature of the working class and partly to the desertion from Labour of the new skilled working class, especially those in this group who were owner-occupiers living in the south of England. A Gallup survey conducted at the time of the 1983 General Election showed that Labour trailed the Conservatives by 22 per cent among working-class owner-occupiers and by 16 per cent among working-class voters living in the south of England.[8] At the 1987 General Election Labour managed once again to achieve a strong position for itself among the traditional working class (especially those who were trade-union members living in Scotland or the north of England), whereas among the new skilled working class it continued to lose support to the Conservatives. By 1992 Labour had recaptured lost ground, but still trailed behind the Conservatives among working-class owner-occupiers (39 per cent to 41 per cent) and among working-class voters in the south of England (38 per cent to 40 per cent).[9] The gradual shrinkage of its traditional support base and the obvious appeal of Thatcherite policies to these groups strengthened the hand of those arguing that Labour had to adapt – modernise – to survive. In short, unless the party could move out from its traditional but shrunken social base it faced persistent defeat. It was from this analysis that 'New Labour' was born.

The 1997 General Election showed that the Labour Party triumphed by maintaining its traditional support base but at the same time extending its appeal to the growing middle class in 'middle England'. In that election Labour increased its share of the vote in each occupational category: 11 per cent among the semi-skilled and unskilled (DE), 13 per cent among skilled workers (C2), 22 per cent among white collar workers (C1), and 11 per cent among the professional and managerial category (AB). In contrast, the

Conservative vote fell in each category: by 9 per cent, 13 per cent, 26 per cent and 14 per cent respectively. Consequently, those constituencies that had swung sharply towards the Conservative Party of Margaret Thatcher – those with a high concentration of clerical and skilled non-manual workers – shifted most strongly towards New Labour. Also of note in this respect is the fact that the swing to Labour among those with mortgages, namely 15 per cent, was higher than among either those who owned their homes outright (11 per cent) or those who were Council tenants (10 per cent), possibly a consequence of the negative equity of the early 1990s and loss of faith in the economic competence of the Conservatives following 'Black Wednesday' (16 September 1992) and the forced withdrawal of the pound sterling from the Exchange Rate Mechanism of the European Monetary System.

Analysis of the results of the 2005 General Election over the results of the 2001 General Election show that the share of the vote among higher social class ABs was 2 per cent lower for both Labour and the Conservatives and 4 per cent higher for the Liberal Democrats. In fact the Liberal Democrats moved ahead of Labour among professionals and managers, with 29 per cent support to Labour's 28 per cent – although the Conservatives secured 37 per cent support from among this category. Skilled non-manual C1s and lower social class DEs moved in line with the national trend, but skilled manual C2s showed a 9 per cent fall in support for Labour and a 4 per cent rise in vote share for both the Conservatives and the Liberal Democrats. Indeed, the Conservatives moved ahead of Labour among white-collar, lower- middle class voters. In addition, of the working class vote lost by Labour, the Conservatives picked up almost a third while the Liberal Democrats were the beneficiaries of most of the rest.

In short, the British electorate no longer divides neatly into two traditional, class-based voting groups, essentially because British society is no longer like that. The voters have become less easy to categorise in sociological terms and less inclined to adhere to their traditional voting allegiances. In such circumstances predictions of voting behaviour along traditional lines on the basis of a simple split between middle class and working class are not going to be accurate in contemporary conditions. Today, greater account has to be taken of the social mobility and the electoral volatility of modern British society. Other factors also have to be taken into account, such as gender, age, ethnicity and geography.

gender

With regard to *gender differences in voting*, the fact that men have been more inclined to vote for the Labour Party and women have been more likely to vote for the Conservative Party, has been a feature of electoral behaviour since both men and women were given the vote in Britain. Indeed, Winston Churchill is said to have remarked that had he known how many women were going to vote Conservative, he would have been more inclined to give them the vote at an earlier stage. Indeed, Labour have traditionally had a clear lead among male voters at General Elections since the Second World War, scoring a notable 19 per cent advantage over the Conservatives in 1945 and 1966. On the other hand, the Conservatives have traditionally had a clear lead among the female voters, scoring an impressive 12 per cent and 13 per cent advantage over Labour in 1951 and 1955 respectively.

However, at the 1979 General Election the Conservatives managed not only to maintain their strength among female voters with a 9 per cent lead over Labour, but since it was such a good result for the Conservatives, they also scored a 5 per cent lead over Labour among male voters.

At the 1983 General Election this trend was reversed and, unusually, the Conservatives drew more of their support from men than from women. This was mainly because the Alliance of Liberals and Social Democrats made such inroads into the female vote, gaining 28 per cent of female support as compared with the 12 per cent achieved by the Liberals on their own in 1979.

At the 1987 General Election although all the parties drew their support about equally from men and women, there was nonetheless a comparative advantage as women were more likely to vote Conservative (43 per cent) than either Labour (32 per cent) or Liberal Democrat (23 per cent).

The gender gap was apparent again in 1992 when 44 per cent of women as opposed to 41 per cent of men voted Conservative. However, a significant development at this time was that although older women – especially pensioners – preferred the Conservative party, younger women actually sided with Labour; indeed, among younger voters generally more women than men voted Labour.

During the 1997 General Election the Labour party made a concerted effort to attract the votes of women, not only by fielding more female candidates than ever before (159, 24.8 per cent) and fielding many of them in targeted winnable seats, but also paying particular attention to differences in women's and men's media preferences and coming forward with a set of policy proposals specifically designed to appeal to women. It was an approach which reaped rich rewards as more women than men moved to support New Labour, 10 per cent as against 7 per cent, with 44 per cent of women voting Labour compared with 32 per cent who voted Conservative.

In 2001 Labour attracted the votes of 42 per cent of both men (down 3 per cent) and women (down 2 per cent), while both the Conservatives and the Liberal Democrats increased their share of both the male and female vote by 1 per cent – to 32 per cent and 33 per cent respectively for the Conservatives and to 18 per cent and 19 per cent for the Liberal Democrats.

In 2005 the female vote provided the mainstay of Labour support for whereas Labour lost 8 per cent of male voters (over 2001) – down from 42 per cent to 34 per cent – they lost only 4 per cent of female voters: 42 per cent down to 38 per cent. The Liberal Democrats gained 4 per cent support from both men and women, to stand at 22 per cent and 23 per cent respectively. In contrast, the Conservatives gained 2 per cent support from men (up to 34 per cent) but lost 1 per cent support from women (down to 32 per cent). Under the leadership of David Cameron a key target for the Conservatives has been to improve its standing in the eyes of women voters.

With regard to *age-related differences in voting behaviour*, Labour has traditionally done particularly well among voters under the age of 30, scoring a 28 per cent lead over the Conservatives in 1945, a 17 per cent lead in 1966 and a 16 per cent lead in October 1974. On the other hand, the Conservatives have traditionally done rather well among those in late middle age (50–64), scoring an 18 per cent lead over Labour in 1951, a 14 per cent lead in 1955 and a 13 per cent lead in 1959. The fortunes of the two main parties in the other age groups (30–49 and 65 plus) have been more evenly balanced. Whereas Labour did well among the 30–49 age group in 1945 and 1966 with leads over the Conservatives of 16 per cent and 13 per cent respectively, the Conservatives did well among those over 65 in 1955, 1970 and February 1974 with leads over Labour of 9 per cent, 9 per cent and 14 per cent respectively. In 1979 Labour was able to retain a small lead of 1 per cent over the Conservatives among the 18–24 age group, notwithstanding the fact that it trailed the Conservatives by 7 per cent among voters of all ages and by 10 per cent among those aged 35 and over. At both General Elections in the 1980s Conservative voting support increased steadily with age, while Labour continued to do well among younger voters – for example in 1987 Labour did best among voters in the 18–24 age group in which it secured the support of 40 per cent. This general pattern was repeated in the 1992 General Election, although the Conservatives gained ground among the 18–29 age group (up 4 per cent over 1987), while Labour made additional headway particularly among those aged 30–44 (up 6 per cent over 1987) and those 65 and over (up 5 per cent over 1987), primarily at the expense of the Liberal Democrats.

In 1997 there was a marked difference in the swing to Labour among different age groups, with those under 30 – already the most pro-Labour – swinging the most (+19 per cent), while Labour's share of the vote among those 65 and over actually fell (–2 per cent). It should also be noted that whereas half of Labour's voters were under 45, this was so of only a third of Conservative voters.

In the election of 2001 although Labour attracted the votes of 41 per cent of 18–24 year olds this was a drop of 8 per cent. Indeed, the only age category that showed an increase (2 per cent) in support for Labour over 1997 was that of 25–34 year olds. For the Conservative Party there were increases of 1, 3 and 4 per cent respectively among the 45–54, 55–64 and 65+ age categories, while the Liberal Democrats showed increases of 2, 3 and 8 per cent respectively among the 35–44, 25–34 and 18–24 age categories.

In the 2005 General Election the Liberal Democrats were particularly successful among those aged 25–34, their share of the vote increasing by 8 per cent to 27 per cent. In contrast, although Labour remained the largest recipient of support from this category, its support from this group fell by 13 per cent.

Although Labour were ahead in all age categories 18–55, the Conservatives were once again the recipient of the largest proportion of support among those aged older than 55; indeed, in a number of constituencies with significant elderly populations, Labour's share of the vote fell sharply.

ethnicity

According to the 2001 census the ethnic population of the United Kingdom stands at 7.9 per cent, a total of 4.6 million individuals. Ethnic differences in voting habits have been evident for some considerable time, with registration and turnout levels lower among communities of black African and Caribbean heritage and highest among certain Asian communities. Having said this, however, it should be noted that some of the lowest turnout figures in recent elections have been recorded in largely white-populated inner city constituencies.

As far as party support is concerned, it has been noted that the Labour party has tended to benefit from the ethnic minority vote and especially from the Afro-Caribbean one. Survey data showed that at the 1992 General Election 79 per cent of ethnic minority voters voted Labour, 10 per cent voted Conservative and 9 per cent voted Liberal Democrat. In 1996/97, survey data showed that 70 per cent of Asian and 86 per cent of black voters intended to vote Labour as opposed to 25 per cent and 8 per cent respectively intending to vote Conservative.[10] Although better-off ethnic minority voters are relatively less likely to vote Conservative than their white counterparts (29 per cent against 43 per cent in 1992), the end of Labour hegemony among ethnic minority voters has been predicted.[30] Indeed, the Commission for Racial Equality calculated that as many as 40 Parliamentary constituencies would not be retained by the Labour Party if Asian, Afro-Caribbean and other ethnic minority voters divided their loyalties in the same proportions as white voters.[11]

In the 2005 General Election Labour's share of the vote fell significantly in those constituencies where there were high proportions of voters of Parkistani, Bangladeshi or Indian ethnicity. Labour's share of the vote also fell in constituencies with high Muslim populations – over 3 per cent more than average.

geography

Elections in Britain have become very diverse geographical affairs with variations in voting behaviour having a major impact on, and important consequences for, British politics. For example, they were a significant factor in the Conservative defeat at the General Election of 1997 and have continued to shape the political map of Britain in the two elections since, namely those of 2001 and 2005. The 1997 election left the Conservative Party for the first time ever without a single MP in Scotland and, for the first time since 1906, without a single MP in Wales. Following the 2005 election the Party had 1 MP in Scotland and 3 in Wales. In 1997, within England, the Conservatives secured

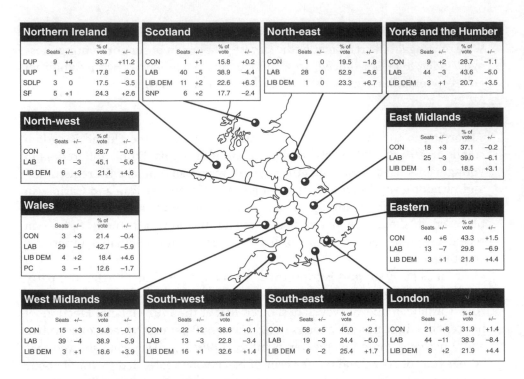

Northern Ireland

	Seats	+/-	% of vote	+/-
DUP	9	+4	33.7	+11.2
UUP	1	-5	17.8	-9.0
SDLP	3	0	17.5	-3.5
SF	5	+1	24.3	+2.6

Scotland

	Seats	+/-	% of vote	+/-
CON	1	+1	15.8	+0.2
LAB	40	-5	38.9	-4.4
LIB DEM	11	+2	22.6	+6.3
SNP	6	+2	17.7	-2.4

North-east

	Seats	+/-	% of vote	+/-
CON	1	0	19.5	-1.8
LAB	28	0	52.9	-6.6
LIB DEM	1	0	23.3	+6.7

Yorks and the Humber

	Seats	+/-	% of vote	+/-
CON	9	+2	28.7	-1.1
LAB	44	-3	43.6	-5.0
LIB DEM	3	+1	20.7	+3.5

North-west

	Seats	+/-	% of vote	+/-
CON	9	0	28.7	-0.6
LAB	61	-3	45.1	-5.6
LIB DEM	6	+3	21.4	+4.6

East Midlands

	Seats	+/-	% of vote	+/-
CON	18	+3	37.1	-0.2
LAB	25	-3	39.0	-6.1
LIB DEM	1	0	18.5	+3.1

Wales

	Seats	+/-	% of vote	+/-
CON	3	+3	21.4	-0.4
LAB	29	-5	42.7	-5.9
LIB DEM	4	+2	18.4	+4.6
PC	3	-1	12.6	-1.7

Eastern

	Seats	+/-	% of vote	+/-
CON	40	+6	43.3	+1.5
LAB	13	-7	29.8	-6.9
LIB DEM	3	+1	21.8	+4.4

West Midlands

	Seats	+/-	% of vote	+/-
CON	15	+3	34.8	-0.1
LAB	39	-4	38.9	-5.9
LIB DEM	3	+1	18.6	+3.9

South-west

	Seats	+/-	% of vote	+/-
CON	22	+2	38.6	+0.1
LAB	13	-3	22.8	-3.4
LIB DEM	16	+1	32.6	+1.4

South-east

	Seats	+/-	% of vote	+/-
CON	58	+5	45.0	+2.1
LAB	19	-3	24.4	-5.0
LIB DEM	6	-2	25.4	+1.7

London

	Seats	+/-	% of vote	+/-
CON	21	+8	31.9	+1.4
LAB	44	-11	38.9	-8.4
LIB DEM	8	+2	21.9	+4.4

figure **4.3**   **how the UK voted in 2005, region by region**

no representation in some of the most populated areas – on Merseyside (16 constituencies), South Yorkshire (15 constituencies), West Yorkshire (23 constituencies) on Tyne and Wear (13 constituencies). Indeed, they won only two out of 28 seats in Greater Manchester, six out of 31 in the West Midlands and two out of 25 in Inner London. In short, in many respects, the Conservative Party was reduced in 1997 to an English rural and suburban rump, securing their lowest Parliamentary representation since 1906. There was some recovery in the intervening period, but not much. Following the 2005 Election, the Party still had no representation on Merseyside (16 constituencies), South Yorkshire (15 constituencies) or Tyne and Wear (13 constituencies), only one MP from Greater Manchester (28 constituencies), one MP from West Yorkshire (23 constituencies), three from the West Midlands (29 constituencies), and four from Inner London (25 constituencies).

The most significant regional factor which damaged the Conservatives in 1997 and from which they have yet to recover was that the swing against them was greater in those areas where they had secured strong support in the Thatcher years, namely the South-East and the Midlands. In 2005 their regional support – excluding Northern Ireland – ranged from a high of 45 per cent in the South-East to a low of 16 per cent in Scotland. In contrast, the regional support for the Labour Party in 1997 ranged from a high of 61 per cent in the North to a low of 26 per cent in the South-West; eight years later their support ranged from a high of 50 per cent in the North to a low of 23 per cent in the South-West. In 1997 the highs and lows for the Liberal Democrats stood at 31 per cent (South-West) and 12 per cent (North), while in 2005 these figures stood at 33 per cent (South-West) and 18 per cent (East Midlands and Wales).

Quite what factors will come to the fore to influence gender, age, ethnic and geographical preferences at future General Elections is difficult to predict. It does appear, however, that they are variables that have an increasing impact and add to the complexities of electoral politics in contemporary Britain.

4.4 influences on voting

Traditionally it has been argued that there are three main influences on voting behaviour in Britain[12], namely:

- Political inheritance
- Self-interest
- Performance of the party in office.

Of course, there are other important influences on voting behaviour which cannot be ignored, such as:

- Policy and sentiment
- Image and technique
- Social factors such as occupation, housing tenure and educational attainment
- Neighbourhood or peer-group pressures.

It is therefore necessary to take account of a wide variety of influences if we are to form a complete picture of the influences on voting.

political inheritance

The influence of political inheritance means the political attitudes and loyalties which voters derive from their parents and families. On the basis of surveys conducted in the 1960s Butler and Stokes were able to show a high correlation (typically over 75 per cent) between the voting behaviour of one generation and the next within family households.[13] This was not surprising at the time, in view of the well-established fact that the opinions of young people on most issues, whether political or not, tended to accord with those of their parents. Indeed there is still considerable inertia in the party-political loyalties of many voters at General Elections, which in most cases reflects the voting habits derived from family inheritance and social surroundings. This can be seen most clearly in the few remaining tight-knit communities, such as the valleys in South Wales, where there is still effectively a one-party voting tradition (in this case for the Labour Party) in spite of the fact that modern social and geographical mobility has begun to erode it at the edges.[14]

The key point at recent General Elections has been that it has not always been possible for either of the main parties to turn such traditional loyalties fully into a level of voting support commensurate with their party identifiers in opinion polls. For example, at the 1997 General Election, despite the fact that opinion polls throughout the campaign put Labour support on average between 50 and 51 per cent, in fact only 44.4 per cent of those who voted actually supported Labour candidates, a figure that was the equivalent to only 30.9 per cent of the electorate.[15] Equally, evidence from the 2005 General Election shows that in securing only 35.2 per cent of the vote, just 21.5 per cent of the electorate, the Labour Party had a significant problem in mobilising some of its traditional support from within its heartlands to come out and vote.[16] This is because the strength of voter commitment to either of the two main parties has become more attenuated over the years as a result of the long-run decline in party-political allegiance and participation in Britain as in all other advanced societies. Indeed, this social development has undermined and diminished the natural, traditional levels of support for the two main parties so that, for example, although between 1945 and 1970 the – combined – two-party vote stood at an average of 90 per cent, since then it has been approximately 75 per cent; indeed, it stood at 67.5 per cent in 2005.

self-interest

The influence of self-interest derives very largely from the personal experience, favourable or unfavourable, consistent or contradictory, of millions of individual voters. For example, there is a fortunate minority of people in Britain who are born into well-off families, benefit from a good education, and secure high-paying jobs. In the majority of cases such people have tended to vote Conservative. Equally, there is a large section of the public (typically several million) for whom life is a constant struggle against adverse material conditions. Their lives are characterised by financial insecurity, dependence on the state and its agencies, and impoverished expectations. In the majority of cases such people have tended to vote Labour, if they have decided to vote at all.

Certainly the majority of those in the AB-professional group and those categorised as C1-white collar who traditionally voted Conservative are likely to have done so principally for reasons of self-interest, although they often describe their reasons for voting in terms of their conception of the national interest – 'what is good for me is good for Britain'. On this point, and as previously stated, the fact that Conservative support from within these two groups fell so sharply at the 1997 General Election (and had not recovered in either 2001 or 2005) can, at least in part, be accounted for by the loss of faith in the economic competence of the Conservatives following Black Wednesday in 1992 and the efforts made by New Labour to broaden their electoral appeal.

Here it is worth noting that one of the objectives of New Labour was to appeal to these sections of the voting public. The modernisers in the party believed that unless the party moved to the ground largely defined by Margaret

Thatcher they would not – could not – win an election. 'Thatcher's people', the professionals and the new middle class – as well as aspirational members of the working class – would never be attracted to a party which appeared to be more interested in the poor and disadvantaged than those who wanted to 'get on'. It was for this reason that Tony Blair replaced the traditional values associated with 'old' Labour – those of redistribution and public ownership – with those of equal opportunity, enterprise and the market, albeit tempered with social justice and responsibility. The 1997 General Election result underlined the validity of this adventurous decision while the 2001 and 2005 results reinforced the validity of this approach.

On the point of self-interest, it should also be noted that the Liberal Democrats now find part of their social base among the well-educated middle class – hence, in making their 2005 Manifesto pledge to fund the abolition of all university tuition fees from a new 50 per cent rate of income tax, they were playing to their natural supporters. This suggests that self-interest is not always a dominant influence on voting behaviour – people do not *necessarily* vote in accordance with their financial interests. Undoubtedly other factors, such as ideology and altruism, apathy and disillusion, play an important part as well.

government performance

The performance of the party in office might seem to be an influence on voting behaviour too obvious to be worth stating, if it were not for the fact that it emphasises the importance of the growing tendency for many people to vote *instrumentally*. This is the technical term to describe what happens when voters effectively strike a bargain with the politicians, whereby they reward the party in office with re-election or punish it with electoral defeat according to their assessment of its period in Government.[17]

This is certainly a view of voting behaviour which is widely held by practising politicians in Britain. It is also supported by the well-established axiom that parties in Government are more likely to *lose* an election than parties in Opposition are to win one. Hence, the Labour Government of James Callaghan 'lost' the 1979 General Election as a result of public hostility to the economic situation and the apparent power of the trade unions, culminating in the 'Winter of Discontent'. However, it is unlikely that there would then have been a change if there had not been an 'acceptable' alternative: the Conservative Party under Margaret Thatcher. Similarly, the lack of an acceptable alternative was one of the reasons why it was possible for the Conservative Party to suffer a decline in its share of the votes cast between 1979 (44.9 per cent), 1983 (43.5 per cent), 1987 (42.3 per cent) and 1992 (41.9 per cent) and still win each election convincingly.

By 1997, however, it was John Major's misfortune to be the leader of a deeply divided party with no real sense of direction, seemingly bereft of new ideas and tarnished by sleaze and public boredom.

Conversely, it was Tony Blair's good fortune to be the leader of a party chastened by long years in Opposition and at last hungry for power, disciplined in its behaviour, efficient in its operations, focused in its goal, furnished with new ideas and a sense of direction, and to find himself in that position at the very time large numbers of voters were looking for an acceptable alternative to the discredited Tories.

In 2005 Labour was elected for the third consecutive term despite the fact that their vote of 9.56 million was 1.17 million fewer than in 2001 and nearly 4 million fewer than in 1997. They won because opposition to them was fragmented and because neither the Conservative Party nor the Liberal Democrats were seen by enough people as a viable alternative Government – the Conservatives may have reinforced their core vote, but they failed to reach out beyond it, while although the Liberal Democrats advanced they did not break through.

policy and sentiment: instrumental or expressive voting

There was a time in the late 1950s and early 1960s when some observers proclaimed the end of ideology in Britain and other advanced Western countries.[18] More recently, however, ideology and policy considerations have become once again a significant influence on voting behaviour. This is consistent with the evidence for so-called *instrumental voting*, whereby voters assess the policies, attitudes and images of the various parties and then cast their votes in the light of their own preferences.

From the late 1970s and throughout the 1980s it seems that the positions taken by the different parties on the main issues of policy had a significant effect on voting behaviour at General Elections. This was brought about partly by the continuing fragmentation of the traditional working class, which created a rootless, upwardly mobile group whose voting behaviour was particularly susceptible to instrumental appeals from the politicians to their particular interests. It was also a reflection of the increasing sophistication of all those voters who regarded their decisions at General Elections as really another form of consumer choice. For such people, as long as there appeared to be an attractive political product on offer, a significant number of them measured its claims against not only their own policy preferences but also their assessment of their own interests. In such a political beauty contest between the parties, the voters' perceptions of political issues and of their own interests in relation to party policies have a significant effect on election results.

On the other hand, there is considerable evidence in support of the so-called *expressive interpretation of voting* – that is to say, the tendency of many in the electorate to vote in accordance with the norms and values of the principal social group to which they belong. According to this theory of voting behaviour, many of the preferences which are expressed in opinion polls by reference to voter predilections for particular party policies are actually little more than rationalisations of more basic interests, or a cover for a dominant social identification. In other words, if voting behaviour is determined principally by social identity, then one need only look at the changing class proportions within society to be able to forecast likely outcomes.

policy-based voting

In recent years policy and sentiment have been increasingly important influences on voting behaviour in Britain. As the voters have become more volatile and instrumental in their attitudes, such factors have begun to weigh at least as heavily as traditional social allegiances.[19]

Sarlvik and Crewe have shown that more than two-thirds of the votes for the three national parties at the 1979 General Election could have been predicted correctly on the basis of the view held by the voters on certain salient policy issues; and the correlation was over 90 per cent for Conservative and Labour voters.[20] They argued that this was a reflection of the fact that over the period 1964–79 there had been a dramatic decline in the level of popular support for three key Labour policies – further nationalisation, the reinforcement of trade-union power, and higher tax-financed spending on the Welfare State. These policies, which had commanded majority support (at any rate among those voters who identified with the Labour Party) in 1964, received less than 25 per cent support among Labour voters in 1979. Labour had therefore lost a great deal of its earlier policy-based appeal.

Yet nothing remains exactly the same in this area of analysis. After a period in the 1970s and 1980s when many of Labour's most salient policies were not popular with the electorate (for example the commitment to higher direct taxation or support for unilateral nuclear disarmament), the party emerged from a period of comprehensive policy review with a range of more moderate and pragmatic – and as a result acceptable – policies.

This should remind us that voters are less inclined than they used to be to vote in accordance with traditional class or family loyalties, and more inclined to vote in the light of which party most closely reflects their own interests and policy preferences. Indeed, evidence adduced by Sarlvik and Crewe suggested that voters' opinions on the policies and performances of each party are twice as likely to explain their voting behaviour as all their social and economic characteristics taken together.[21] A Gallup survey conducted for the BBC at the time of the 1983 General Election also showed that, when the voters preferred the policies of one party but the leader of another, they decided in favour of the former by about four to one, a tendency which on that occasion worked principally to the advantage of the Conservatives.[22]

Yet in weighing the influence of policy on voting behaviour, it is important to distinguish between those policies which the voters, when questioned by opinion pollsters, may consider to be the best in the abstract or for the sake of the country, and those for which they actually vote in the privacy of the polling booth. At the 1987 General Election the Labour Party would have won if the voters had cast their votes in accordance with their proclaimed altruistic policy preferences as expressed in answer to opinion polls at the time. The same thing was true at the 1992 General Election. For example, when Gallup asked the question 'Of all the urgent problems facing the country at the present time, when you decided which way to vote, which two issues did you personally consider most important?', 41 per cent of respondents mentioned health, 36 per cent mentioned unemployment, and 23 per cent mentioned education – all issues on which the Labour Party enjoyed a lead as the best party – yet the Conservatives still won the election quite comfortably.[23] Evidently, altruism does not necessarily translate into voting behaviour when the voters are choosing a Government at a General Election. The explanation for this has been provided by Ivor Crewe, who has pointed out that, when answering opinion pollsters, the voters respond altruistically and in the abstract, whereas when actually voting they tend to think much more instrumentally of their personal and family interests.[24]

capricious sentiment

Hilde Himmelweit and others have shown that, 'although in practice both consistency (that is, party loyalty) and ideological thinking (that is, policy considerations) influence the decision to vote, each election is like a new shopping expedition in a situation where new as well as familiar goods are on offer'.[25] This means that evidence from General Elections can be interpreted and explained by using a consumer model of voting behaviour. Of course, a great deal depends on how the voters feel during the period just before and during an election campaign and on whether the public eventually decides to vote for positive or negative reasons or indeed to vote at all.

At the 1997 General Election, for example, when voters were asked which party they trusted most to take the right decision about the economy, Labour were placed ahead of the Conservatives by 44 per cent to 42 per cent; a stark contrast to the position in 1992 when the Conservatives had led Labour on the issue by 53 per cent to 33 per cent. Equally on the issue of income tax, traditionally one of the Conservative Party's strongest and which they had led Labour by 24 per cent in 1992 (55 per cent to 31 per cent), in 1997 Labour were ahead of the Conservatives – by 8 per cent – on this as well (44 per cent to 36 per cent).[26]

Although the 2001 General Election was one in which Labour were judged best on issues deemed important by many voters, this was certainly not the case at the time of the 2005 election when the Conservatives and the Liberal Democrats were in a position to challenge Labour on issues that many people thought had been mishandled or neglected and when the Government's – and especially the Prime Minister's – approval rating had plummeted in the wake of the war in Iraq. Indeed, for many the 2005 election was dominated by the issue of the war in Iraq and it was argued that this was a – if not the – critical reason as to why core Labour supporters deserted the party in such large numbers. The available research provides a mixed picture,[27] but what one can say for sure is that attitudes and opinions over British involvement in the war in Iraq certainly played a part in the decline in the Labour vote, the increase in the level of support for the Liberal Democrats and the level of support registered for the Respect Unity Coalition and various anti-war independent candidates.

image and technique

Party images and campaign techniques are some of the other significant influences on voting behaviour in this age of modern mass media. They have been identified by the political communications specialists of all the parties as crucial to electoral success in the modern age.

party images

These are formed in the public mind largely by the party leaders themselves – for example Lloyd George as the Welsh Wizard, Winston Churchill as the British Bulldog, Stanley Baldwin as the quintessential English country gentleman, Harold Macmillan as 'Super Mac', James Callaghan as 'jovial gentleman Jim', Margaret Thatcher as the 'Iron Lady'. More recently, we have seen the association of classlessness and geniality with John Major and vision and modernity with Tony Blair. Party images are also formed by the performance and behaviour of the parties whether in Government or Opposition. The party leaders and their media advisers work hard to preserve or improve their respective images. Indeed, the presentation of policy, if not policy itself, is usually influenced by professional assessments of the image it is likely to convey. Above all, the parties are careful to try to foster an image of unity in their own ranks and of disunity in the ranks of their opponents, since the appearance of disunity is invariably damaging to the electoral prospects of any party.

Party images are formed incrementally, even subliminally, over many years by what the parties do or fail to do when in Government and by the way they behave when in Opposition. For example, the Conservative Party undoubtedly benefited at both the 1983 and 1987 General Elections from Margaret Thatcher's acknowledged experience in high office and her resolute public image as someone who stuck to her guns when the going got tough – for instance at the time of the Falklands crisis in 1982, and during the long miners strike in 1984/85. On the other hand this same image undoubtedly damaged her in relation to both the Community Charge and Europe, leading to her removal from office in 1990. Equally, during the late 1970s and well into the 1980s the Labour Party suffered in the eyes of many people from a poor image which was the product of unconvincing leadership, party in-fighting and internecine ideological struggles. During the 1987 General Election the Labour Party strove very hard and quite effectively to present the party leader, Neil Kinnock, in a favourable and 'presidential' light, impressing many media professionals and party workers in the process; but even this was not enough to counter an adverse public image that had taken years to crystallise.

However, by the time of the 1997 General Election when the reputation of the Conservatives for economic competence had collapsed (a direct result of 'Black Wednesday' in September 1992 when the pound was forced out of the

Exchange Rate Mechanism of the European Monetary System), New Labour was seen as having 'modernised'; it constituted a sea-change in public perceptions. An aspect of this was seen in the images of the parties as being either united or divided: only 16 per cent of voters believed that the Conservative Party was united – indeed, 93 per cent of Conservative defectors described the party as divided. Conversely, 66 per cent of voters described Labour as united, a figure which rose to 83 per cent among New Labour converts.[28]

In both the 2001 and 2005 General Elections, with a strong economy, low inflation and low unemployment, Labour were seen as the party of sound economic stewardship. By 2005 it was on other matters that the Party was vulnerable, namely the war in Iraq and the issue of public trust in Tony Blair.

campaign techniques

These can also have an important influence on voting behaviour, especially since many voters do not make up their minds until the final stages of a campaign. The parties therefore make every effort during a campaign to get as much good media coverage as possible and to present both their leaders and their policies in the most favourable light. Yet, in spite of these often expensive efforts, the actual conduct of a campaign seldom makes a decisive difference to the electoral outcome. For example, in the 1992 General Election campaign the Conservatives had some success with their vivid posters (put up on 4500 sites) and newspaper advertising drawing attention to what they described as 'Labour's Double Whammy' – namely, higher taxes and higher prices – and asserting that the average voter would pay over £1000 a year more in tax under a Labour Government. Indeed, Labour campaign strategists in 1997 were determined to learn the lessons of the 1992 campaign and not to make the same mistakes again, namely failing to counter the accusations over tax and being unprepared for the late swing away from the party. Hence the Labour pledged not to raise marginal rates of income tax in the lifetime of the following Parliament and to accept Conservative public spending limits for two years, all in a convincing effort to 'square' the national press.

The 1997 Labour campaign demonstrated the importance of being able to respond rapidly to the arguments of the other parties, of having a clear and straightforward message and the importance of discipline and being able to stay 'on message' – what critics describe as 'message', 'control' and 'spin'. However, this approach, repeated in 2001 and 2005, has – if not caused then certainly reinforced – what has been called a sense of disengagement from the whole process. Another aspect of this is the fact that political leaders rarely, if ever, come face-to-face with the electorate, save for those carefully selected by the 'handlers' and campaign managers.

More than ever before, and perhaps above all else, the 2005 General Election campaign demonstrated the increasing importance of technology – emails, direct-mailing and recorded phone messages – in targeting voters. Most particularly, both the Labour and Conservative campaigns utilised commercially available computer programs in order to identify voters by collating information ranging from their postcodes through reading habits to shopping preferences – systems apparently able to predict not merely an individual's propensity to vote but also which party they would support with an accuracy of 70per cent.[29] Indeed, the campaign techniques used were very different from those used in previous general elections – as was observed: 'The crack troops were not voluntary party activists … but the paid mercenaries of professional telephone canvassing.'[30] Another factor of note – although one that was not unrelated – was that in many parts of the country the campaign itself was invisible, only really taking place in a small number of marginal constituencies where all the resources of the parties were concentrated. One consequence of this was that, in certain respects at least, the campaign was a collection of individual, locally based campaigns, albeit ones directed from the national level.

In the case of the minor parties, which in normal times do not get much media attention, effective campaign techniques can be more significant in drawing helpful attention both to their leaders and to their policies – as was shown by the positive impact of the Liberal Democrat Leader, Charles Kennedy, in both 2001 and 2005.

the candidates

In normal circumstances party has a much greater pull than does the personality of individual candidates, party image nationally has a greater impact on the result in an individual constituency than the local activity of any candidate, and national issues tend to take precedence over local ones.

Consequently, conventional wisdom has held to the view that individual candidates are unlikely to count for more than possibly 500–1000 votes. This may not seem very much, but it could have a decisive impact on a result in a marginal constituency. However, the significance of candidates can have a greater impact on the result than the conventional wisdom allows. This is particularly so in by-elections, as was apparent for example in the Dunfirmline and West Fife by-election in February 2006 in which the Liberal Democrat candidate, Willie Rennie, overturned a Labour majority of 11,562 to take the seat with a majority of 1800. Other examples would include the cases of Wallace Lawler at Birmingham Ladywood (1969), Cyril Smith at Rochdale (1972), Dick Taverne at Lincoln (1973) and Peter Tatchell at Bermondsey (1983). Nonetheless, circumstances can arise which result in individual candidates having a significant impact at the time of a General Election as well, a factor that was underlined by the contests between Martin Bell and Neil Hamilton in Tatton (1997), Dr Richard Taylor and David Lock in Wyre Forest (2001), George Galloway and Oona King in Bethnal Green and Bow (2005), and Peter Law and Maggie Jones in Blaenau Gwent (2005).

other influences on voting

In one of the most authoritative studies of voting behaviour in Britain, Heath, Jowell and Curtice demonstrated the advantages of drawing multidimensional maps of the electorate.[31] Using this technique, it is possible to take full account of all the various cleavages in the electorate and go beyond the familiar criteria of social class and electoral geography. A contemporary list of variables should include the influence of neighbourhood, occupation, housing tenure, share ownership, educational attainment, gender and ethnic identity.

In short, there is a wide variety of influences on voting behaviour in Britain. The traditional influences – that is, political inheritance, self-interest and the performance of the party in office – are still of fundamental importance. Yet the more ephemeral influences (for instance, policy and sentiment, image and technique) have made themselves increasingly felt in recent years and have assumed a growing importance as the voters have shown more volatility in their voting behaviour and as General Election campaigns have become more presidential both in style and in content. The use of modern techniques emphasises the manipulative aspects of modern party politics and reminds us of the influence of the mass media. Yet in spite of such new developments, it is clear that British electoral politics have not been completely Americanised, not least because of the tight legal limits on the amount which each Parliamentary candidate may spend on election expenses during the rather brief General Election campaigns in Britain, and the fact that it is impossible for the parties under British electoral law to purchase broadcasting time on the electronic media.

Certainly, there are a number of continuing uncertainties which are likely to have a significant influence on the outcome of future General Elections in Britain:

- Will voters be more or less concerned with issues of policy?
- Will a substantial part of the middle class continue to vote Labour or Liberal Democrat?
- Will the Conservative vote increase among the new working class?
- Will men and women come to have less differentiated political leanings?
- Will ethnic minority voters continue to divide their loyalties differently from their white counterparts?
- Will the electorate become more or less volatile in its voting behaviour?
- Will the Liberal Democrats, Nationalists and other parties as well as independents continue to attract sizeable levels of support, or will they suffer significant defections?
- Will voting turnout at General Elections grow or decline?
- To what extent will there be further signs of political alienation?
- What effects will flow from any changes in methods of voting or in the electoral system?

4.5 conclusion

It can be said that the main influences on voter participation and behaviour in Britain are political inheritance, self-interest and the performance of the party in office. Nevertheless these are often subjective influences which can depend on the conclusions which individual voters draw from their own experience and observation of the political scene. From a more objective point of view, it seems clear that social class, gender, ethnicity, economic occupation, housing tenure, educational attainment and geographical location are among the most important influences on the way people cast their votes at General Elections. Furthermore, the electorate does not cast its votes in a vacuum. They go to the polls (or decide not to bother) after weeks and months of verbal bombardment by the politicians and the media as well as assiduous attention from the opinion pollsters. All these various forces help to form the views of the voters, whose voting behaviour has become more volatile and even capricious in consequence.

Many years ago Jean Blondel wrote that 'the simple division between working and middle class ... contributes to the clearest cleavage in British political attitudes and voting behaviour.'[32] Although there is still some truth in this statement today, equally it no longer tells us all we need to know about voting behaviour in contemporary Britain. Voters are changing, not least of all because the traditional working class has become significantly smaller while the middle class has grown, in each case as a function of changing patterns of employment. Voters were once tied to parties through long-established almost tribal identies, shared among family, friends, neighbours and colleagues. Such traditional loyalties have weakened considerably in recent years, with class losing the pre-eminence it once had as the sole explanation of political allegiance. Today, voters are much more inclined to shift support from one party to another with voting itself being seen as something of a lifestyle choice – it having been observed that 'We are no longer organized into tribal party camps, weighed down by civic duty to vote whenever asked. Instead we are "shop-around" voters, picking and choosing from whichever parties, or candidates, we like and increasingly exercising the none-of-the-above option.'[33]

Tactical electioneering must also be part of the picture, with parties increasingly concentrating their resources not simply on target seats but on target voters, customising their message, utilising direct mailing on specialist issues, personal contact through the use of national call centres and new forms of making contact and getting a message across such as emails and text messaging as well as the use of DVDs and CD Roms. This has itself reinforced a more organic, less traditional, less deferential, approach to voting. Consequently, whatever happens in the minds of the voters, it is well to remember that there are few, if any, certainties in voter participation and behaviour.

SUGGESTED QUESTIONS

1   What are the main divisions in the British electorate?
2   What are the most significant influences on voting behaviour in Britain?
3   To what extent is social class still a factor in determining the outcome of elections in Britain?

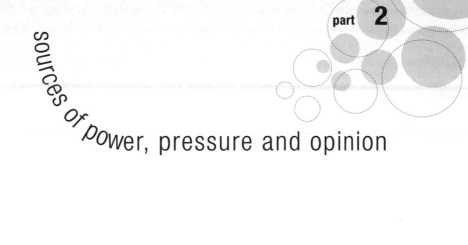

part **2**

sources of power, pressure and opinion

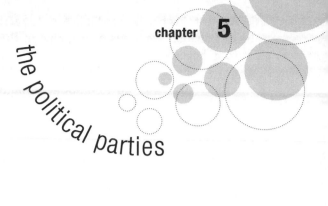

the political parties

In Britain there is a system of party government – government by and through political parties. Parties are at the very centre of the system: national, organised, disciplined political parties. The rise of parties changed the nature of elections, altered the relationship between Members of Parliament and their constituents, determined the position of Prime Minister and Cabinet and transformed the House of Commons. As a result political parties have had a dominant influence upon the whole nature of the British political system.

5.1 origins and development

Although groups identified as either Whigs or Tories could be found in Parliament as early as the seventeenth century, parties in the modern sense only appeared in the nineteenth century as a direct consequence of Parliamentary reform. Due to successive extensions of the franchise (see Chapter 3), factions or groups within the House of Commons were increasingly obliged to organise outside Parliament in an attempt to secure the necessary voter support at elections.

The 1832 Reform Act led to the creation of a number of 'societies' whose function it was to arrange for the registration of voters sympathetic to their cause. The Tories established a central organisation to coordinate their efforts in this regard in 1832, and were followed two years later by the Whigs. However, it was the consequences of the 1867 Representation of the People Act which triggered the creation of parties in their modern form. The 1867 Act created a larger electorate, too large to deal with effectively in the traditional ways of personal influence, bribery, intimidation, and so on. Consequently, national party organisations were created in a way through which widespread electoral support could be mobilised – seeking to secure the election of 'our' party and the defeat of 'their' party, with politics becoming a matter of 'us' against 'them'. Thus the National Union of Conservative Associations was established in 1867 and the National Liberal Federation ten years later. The age of nationally organised and relatively disciplined political parties had arrived in Britain.

Against this background it is easy to see that British politics is party politics. In this chapter we focus principally on the Labour and Conservative parties, as they have been the two most significant political forces in Britain, at any rate since the Second World War. Beyond them we shall look at other parties, whether those with an aspiration throughout Britain – such as the Liberal Democrats – or those with a more geographically limited vocation, such as the nationalist parties in Scotland and Wales, as well as consider briefly the parties in Northern Ireland and the fringe parties in the rest of the United Kingdom – the Greens, UKIP, the British National Party and so on.

At the outset it is worth trying to offer a common **definition** which can be applied to every political party to a greater or lesser extent. In the eighteenth century Edmund Burke defined a political party as 'a body of men united for promoting by their joint endeavours the national interest upon some particular principle in which they are all agreed.'[1] Today, however, there are difficulties with such a definition, not least because it places such an emphasis on agreements freely entered into between relatively independent individuals – an emphasis which no longer reflects the realities of modern British politics. Political parties in Britain, as elsewhere in the democratic world, are nowadays more like organised coalitions, each containing a wide spectrum of ideology, principle, opinion and belief. As a result, a rather better definition of a political party in modern conditions might be: '**an organised and relatively disciplined group of people who freely combine to advance a set of political attitudes or beliefs with a view to translating them via success at elections into administrative decisions or legislative actions**.' In other words, all parties try to influence and a few aspire to win the democratic power of Government.

5.2 functions and activity

The political parties in Britain perform a range of political functions. Essentially these can be reduced to one primary function and a number of subsidiary functions, all of which contribute to the working of the British political system.

primary function

The primary function of the main political parties in Britain, as Robert McKenzie made clear, is to sustain competing teams of potential leaders in the House of Commons in order that the electorate as a whole may choose between them at periodic General Elections.[2] Indeed, any attempt by the parties to play a more prominent role in their own right would cut across the chain of responsibility from Cabinet to Parliament to electorate which is fundamental to the British system of Parliamentary democracy. In the British political system constitutional power resides essentially with the Prime Minister and Cabinet, supported by a working majority in the House of Commons. In these circumstances the supreme function of the parties is the gaining and retaining of public consent for the exercise of such power.

All political parties perform similar subsidiary functions which vary in importance depending on the particular circumstances of the time:

First, they encourage public interest and participation in the process of politics. In other words, they provide permanent structures within which individuals and groups can act, if they wish to play a part in politics at the local, national or European levels.

Second, they reflect, moderate and direct into constitutional channels the views and interests of a wide range of sectional groups. Of course, pressure groups have a powerful independent existence in their own right within the political system. Yet the existence of parties enables and encourages all sectional groups to act in a constitutional manner and leads them to pay more attention to Parliament than might otherwise be the case.

Third, they provide legitimate frameworks for the ventilation, discussion and criticism of political issues.

Fourth, and by no means least important, they exist to build up membership, raise money, select candidates and organise political campaigns at local, national and European levels. The key to all of this activity is money and consequently all of the political parties put considerable effort into fundraising.

income

Traditionally the Labour Party was heavily reliant on the financial support of affiliated trade unions, support which provided 92 per cent of the party's income in the 1960s. As a direct result of a conscious effort to move away from a position of financial dependence on the unions, this declined to 66 per cent in 1992, 40 per cent in 1997 and 35 per cent in 2001. By the end of 2006 it was estimated to account for 26 per cent of the total. In addition to money from the unions, income comes from small donations, mainly from party members, from large donors – a source that all but dried up after 2005 – and from other activities such as the sale of policy papers and so on.

In the Conservative Party a great share of the income was traditionally provided by industry and commerce, a source which accounted for 60 per cent of its income in the 1970s. In the late 1990s, however, this figure had declined to about 20 per cent. Aside from this, income is derived from donations from members and supporters, from the fundraising efforts of the voluntary workers in Constituency Associations and from miscellaneous party activities.

The Liberal Democrats seek to raise money both locally and nationally in broadly similar ways, except for the fact that they do not receive official trade union support and their support from business has always been limited.

membership

One of the developments in British political life has been a decline in the membership of political parties. For example, the Conservative Party claimed a membership of 2.8 million in 1953, a figure which had fallen to just under 1.5 million in 1979 and 253,600 in 2005 (although only 198,844 (78 per cent) voted in the leadership election. Similarly, although the Labour Party claimed over one million members in 1953, this had declined to 405,238 in early 1998, and stood at 248,294 by the end of 2002; a figure that had declined still further by 2005. Similarly, although the Liberal Democrats claimed a membership of 100,000 in 1998, in March 2006 the official membership stood at 73,000 – although only 52,036 (71 per cent) recorded a vote at the time of the leadership election). In 2004, amongst the minor parties, it was claimed that the Scottish Nationalists had 16,122 members, Plaid Cymru had 8750 members and the Greens had some 6000 members.

campaigning expenditure

As far as the costs of political activity are concerned – as outlined in Chapter 3 – the 2005 General Election campaign cost the parties over £42 million across the UK, with the Labour and Conservative parites alone accounting for 84 per cent of the total.

Since the publication of the Houghton Report in 1976, there has been the additional possibility for the Opposition parties to receive financial support from public funds in proportion to the votes which they secured at the previous General Election.[3] In the year following the 2005 General Election the Conservative Party received £4.2 million of public money to support their opposition work in Parliament and the Liberal Democrats received £1.5 million.

Throughout the 1990s there was mounting disquiet on the whole matter of party funding following a series of allegations and revelations concerning donations made to the Conservative Party.[4] The disquiet continued following the 1997 election when it became public knowledge that a gift of £1 million to the Labour Party had been made by the head of Formula 1 motor racing,

Income (£m)

	2001	2002	2003	2004	2005
Labour	35.5	21.2	26.9	29.3	35.3
Conservative	23.3	9.9	13.6	20.0	24.2
Liberal democrats	5.0	3.7	4.1	5.1	8.6

Expenditure (£m)

	2001	2002	2003	2004	2005
Labour	35.5	21.2	26.9	29.3	35.3
Conservative	23.3	9.9	13.6	20.0	24.2
Liberal democrats	5.0	3.7	4.1	5.1	8.6

source: House of Commons Constitutional Affairs Select Committee First Report Session 2006–07, 'The Founding of Political Parties in the UK', HC 163, (13 December 2006).

figure **5.1** **annual income and expenditure for the three main parties, 2001–2005**

Bernie Ecclestone, with resulting allegations that the money had influenced the Labour Government's decision to seek an exemption for Formula 1 from a European tobacco advertising ban, an action that had been contrary to their previously stated policy on the matter.

Having been elected on a pledge to 'clean up' British politics and to ensure that the way political parties were funded was open and transparent, the Government asked the Committee on Standards in Public Life to consider how the funding of political parties should be regulated and reformed. The Report from the Committee made 100 recommendations.[5] In response the Government issued a White Paper[6] and subsequently introduced legislation which reached the statute book as the **Registration of Political Parties Act 1998**.[7]

Subsequent legislation – the **Political Parties Elections and Referendums Act 2000**[8] – banned certain donations to political parties, ensured that all other large donations were made public and introduced a regulatory body – the **Electoral Commission** [9] – to 'police' what was involved. However, by seeking transparency rather than rejecting political donations, the Government encouraged the press to focus on business donations and contracts awarded, favours received or honours granted; and public trust in the whole system declined. In the wake of the 'loans for peerages affair' in 2006–07, public trust declined still further.

Against the backdrop of high-profile scandals, it has become harder for parties to raise money. Consequently, there have been renewed calls for the introduction of state funding for political parties (see Figure 5.2) although the general public does not seem to favour this in opinion polls..

activity at the national level

Party members are involved at the national level in **choosing the Party Leader.** Labour members have a share in the electoral college which chooses the Party Leader, while in the Liberal Democrats and – since 1998 – in the Conservative Party the leader is essentially elected on the basis of one member one vote. Similarly, in all the political parties, it is now accepted that ordinary party members should have some **real influence on the process of policy making**.

activity at the constituency level

The Labour, Conservative and Liberal Democrat parties have all sought to ensure and maintain political activity in each of the Parliamentary constituencies throughout Great Britain. Nevertheless, all three parties have tended to focus their resources and concentrate their efforts rather more directly than this statement might suggest. In particular, the Liberal Democrats have concentrated their efforts and resources in relatively few constituencies where they already have local support and where their electoral prospects appear to be quite good – an approach which reaped rich rewards in the 1997 and 2001 General Elections in particular. Constituency organisations vary in size from a

Arguments in favour:

1   It would 'purify' the political process. If there were state funding on a substantial scale, the parties would no longer be reliant upon large donors and, consequently, would be immune – and would be seen to be immune – from any temptation to grant them privileged access to top politicians or unwarranted influence over policy, contracts or honours.

2   It would enable parties to perform their essential functions more fully and effectively. Parties are caught in a vice between falling incomes from traditional sources and the rising costs of campaigning and the demand for more sophisticatod policy research. Without state funding we might see the development of either 'a slum democracy', in which the parties would be poorly staffed and unable to prepare themselves adequately for the task of running the country, or 'a sleaze democracy', in which the parties were forced into an unhealthy reliance on funding from private individuals.

3   It would signal to the public that political parties are valuable, indeed essential, institutions in a democratic country.

4   It could be used as a means of increasing the involvement of private individuals in the political parties and in the financing of them. A system of 'matching funds' under which citizens are encouraged to give money to the parties in the knowledge that their individual contributions will be wholly or partly matched by the state or, alternatively, in which the parties themselves are given an incentive to raise money in the knowledge that whatever they raise will be wholly or partially matched by the state.

Arguments against

1   Taxpayers should not be compelled to contribute to the support of political parties with whose outlook and policies they strongly disagree.

2   It could cause the party system to ossify, with the existing parties handsomely supported out of the public purse but with new parties finding that they had to struggle to break in.

3   If political parties were to become reliant on state ftinding, they might be tempted to abandon their efforts to raise money at the grassroots. Fund-raising is one of the most common activities in which local party members engage; if they did not have to engage in it, they might become less active in the party overall.

4   State funding would almost inevitably be channelled through party headquarters; as a result, the power of party headquarters vis-à-vis the grassroots might be considerably increased.

5   State funding would make parties, in effect, part of the state. Instead of representing the citizens vis-à-vis the state, the parties would be tempted to represent the state vis-à-vis the citizens; they would, in effect, have been 'captured' by the state. At the very least, there would be the danger that that would become the public perception.

6   The public are opposed to the idea of state fimding.

7   The needs of political parties are not the greatest priority in terms of public expenditure.

source: Based upon 'The Funding of Political Parties in the United Kingdom', the Fifth Report of the Committee on Standards in Public Life, Cm 4057-I, October 1998, pp. 90–92.

figure **5.2   state funding for political parties: the arguments** mere handful of members in areas where parties are weak to as many as several thousand in the strongest areas of the large parties. In all cases they exist to serve the campaigning and fundraising purposes of the parties and to enable them to contest local, Parliamentary and European elections.

In the *Conservative Party* the key constituency bodies are the Executive Councils of perhaps 30 to 80 members, composed partly of Association Officers, but mostly of representatives of the various wards or branches in the constituency. In the Labour Party the key constituency bodies are the General Management Committees, which are composed in the same sort of way, but which are often somewhat smaller.

financial support at the constituency level

Constituency parties in Britain try to remain solvent and operational throughout the time between General Elections. They are assisted in doing this by the need to contest local and European elections at regular intervals and occasionally Parliamentary by-elections as well. Yet they rely for their continued existence on individual and corporate subscriptions and donations made possible by the voluntary efforts and fund-raising activities of the party workers.

In the *Labour Party*, although trade union sponsorship of MPs was discontinued in 1995, some constituency organisations receive financial support from local trade union branches through what are known as 'Constituency Plan Agreements'. The bulk of the money is raised from membership subscriptions, donations and various forms of fundraising activity. In the *Conservative Party*, a considerable portion of the income at constituency level comes from local business and commercial interests, although the bulk of the money is raised from individual subscriptions and voluntary fund-raising activities of all kinds. The *Liberal Democrats* have sought to maintain similar activities at constituency level in order to perform similar political functions.

membership at the constituency level

Political parties can grow and prosper only if their grassroots are vigorous and healthy. Traditionally active Local Associations were the necessary foundations on which a national party existed and flourished, with a party seeking to have one in each Parliamentary constituency. Today, although still important, their importance has been reduced for three reasons: first, because the parties all operate national, centralised membership schemes; second, because campaigning resources tend to be concentrated in a small number of marginal constituencies; and, third, because the parties use modern technologically based campaigning techniques – telephone canvassing, recorded phone messages, emails, direct-mailing and the like – to target key swing voters.

It is difficult to generalise about the membership of political parties since a wide variety of people become involved in politics at the local level at one time or another. What can be said is that, in each party, active members at the constituency level come from many different walks of life. They tend to hold political views which are more zealous and uncompromising than those of the electorate in general. Indeed, if this were not the case, it is unlikely that many of them would be sufficiently motivated to join their chosen political party in the first place or to remain as a paid-up member.

With regard to **membership of the Labour Party**, recent research has sought to make a distinction between 'old Labour' – those who joined the party before 1994 – and 'new Labour' – those who joined the party after 1994. From the data provided we can see that new Labour members are younger, although they still rank overall as middle-aged. Amongst new Labour 25 per cent are aged 35 or below, compared with 12 per cent for old Labour; the average age of new Labour members is 48 compared to 54 amongst old Labour. As far as gender is concerned, 63 per cent of new Labour members are male and 37 per cent are female, compared with 60 per cent and 40 per cent respectively amongst old Labour members. The party – old and new – tends to be middle class with 60 per cent of new Labour members and 67 per cent of old Labour members coming from among the white-collar professional salariat, with a high proportion of individuals working in the public sector among both new and old members. Only 2 per cent of both new and old Labour members are classified as small businesspeople. A total of 38 per cent of old Labour members belong to a trade union, compared with only 29 per cent of new Labour members. As far as education is concerned, 30 per cent of new Labour and 37 per cent of old Labour are graduates. New Labour members are more strongly in favour of the free market than old Labour (32 per cent as opposed to 23 per cent), are more inclined to believe in the incentive effects of low rates of income tax (30 per cent as opposed to 21 per cent), are more inclined to be 'tough' on law and order issues (between 58 and 61 per cent compared with figures between 46 and 51 per cent) and are rather more sanguine on the matter of private education (only 21 per cent definitely wanting to abolish it compared with 31 per cent of old Labour members). In short, new Labour members are more conservative than old Labour members. They are also less likely to be active within the party – 43 per cent less active than old Labour members – and less partisan – with only 38 per cent of new Labour members as opposed to 58 per cent of old Labour members describing themselves as 'very strong' Labour and with 9 per cent as opposed to 4 per cent describing themselves as 'not very strong' Labour.[10]

With regard to **Conservative Party membership**, the available data shows that the 'typical' Conservative member is retired, middle class, Protestant and white, with 49 per cent being female and 51 per cent being male. The average age of members had been found to be 62, while 43 per cent are aged 66 or over. Only 5 per cent of its membership is below the age of 35 and only 1 per cent is aged 25 or less. Indeed, failure to appeal to a younger generation was a significant problem facing David Cameron when he became leader in 2005. It is a failure underlined by the fact that in 2005 there were fewer than 12,000 Young Conservatives – Conservative Future – compared with 160,000 in 1949. Two-thirds of Conservatives see themselves as belonging to a particular class, with 75 per cent of these describing themselves as middle class. In total

8 per cent fall into the category of traditional working-class manual workers. Only 29 per cent of members are still in work, the remainder being classified as retired. Of those in work more than half are part of the salariat, with teachers forming the largest single group, then financial service workers, and with marketing and public relations executives as well as central- and local-government administrative workers forming sizeable groups. Typists, clerks and so on – what can be termed routine white collar workers – account for 18 per cent of the membership and proprietors of small businesses a further 13 per cent. In all, 70 per cent of members own stocks and shares. Aside from this, the available material shows that 99 per cent of the membership is white and 1 per cent Asian. Over 75 per cent are Protestant, with 10 per cent being Catholic. Only 12 per cent have a university degree and 31 per cent have no educational qualifications at all. Surveys of Conservative members show that 40 per cent are not active members and that, amongst the 60 per cent who are active, 20 per cent are 'very active' and 80 per cent are 'active to some degree'.[11]

Detailed information on the membership of the Liberal Democrat Party is not so readily available. What is known, however, is that the male/female ratio amongst the membership is 51:49 and that 2 per cent of the membership is under 25 years of age, 15 per cent are aged 25–40, 33 per cent are aged 41–55, 31 per cent are aged 56–70 and 19 per cent are over the age of 70. It can also be said that members tend to be drawn from a wider cross-section of the population and include many people who are not so closely identified with obvious class interests as well as some who have not previously been active in party politics at all. By defining 'activists' as those who hold office within the party, or who are elected as local authority Councillors, some 10 per cent of the party's membership is active. However, such a narrow definition clearly very seriously underestimates those who have some level of activity in the party. Survey evidence has shown that over 70 per cent of members define themselves as being active in some way.

In the final analysis, however, no generalisations about party membership are really satisfactory, not least of all because the figures for membership are very fluid. For example, in 2001, despite gaining (or 'reactivating') more than 17,000 members, some 50,000 members of the Labour Party, a significant proportion of the total, failed to renew their membership. All that can be said with any certainty is that the trends over the years have been characterised by a steady erosion of active support for each of the two main parties and by significantly changing social composition in each case. As far as membership is concerned, the numbers who join have fallen sharply from the high point of the 1950s. It is also noticeable that over the period since the early 1970s the Conservative Party has become less dominated at constituency level by traditional middle-class people, while the Labour Party in the constituencies has become less the party of the working class and the trade unions than it was before. Such social changes at constituency level have had an important effect on the character of each of the parties in Parliament.

In so far as members of constituency parties exercise effective political power, they do so mainly through their right to select and, occasionally, deselect Parliamentary candidates (as well as those for local and devolved institutions and the European Parliament). In view of the fact that roughly two-thirds of all the seats in the Commons have been considered 'safe' for one or other of the two main parties, the power to select and deselect the candidate has often amounted to the ability to determine the choice of the MP in many parts of the country. This is the real foundation of political power at constituency level and it has had to be taken very seriously by MPs and candidates alike.

In each of the main parties the candidates for Parliament chosen by the 'selectorates' have tended to be rather different both from the groups which select them and from the electorate as a whole. There has been a tendency over the years for social convergence between the Parliamentary candidates of the two main parties. This has often meant the selection of middle-aged, middle-class white men with families in preference to women, blue-collar workers or people from the ethnic minorities.

However, in more recent times it has become increasingly necessary to qualify this overall description. In the *Conservative Party* there is nowadays a wider variety of candidates for Parliament. Although the privileged origins of some Conservative aspirants remain very noticeable, there has also been a growing number of self-made men and women who have managed to fight their way into Parliament. In the *Labour Party* the changes have been even more dramatic in recent years. Nowadays many more Labour candidates have been selected from the ranks of white-collar and public-sector occupations to the exclusion of many of the more traditional types from the old-fashioned working class. In the late 1970s and early 1980s there was a marked shift towards more radical attitudes in constituency Labour parties which put a greater emphasis on the selection of candidates who were eager (or at least prepared) to carry out the wishes of the party activists. However, from the middle 1980s the Labour leadership began to take a greater interest in candidate selection, especially at by-elections which attracted more than the usual amount of national media attention. In addition, in the run-up to the 1997 General Election, the party, through the use of all-women shortlists, ensured that 24.8 per cent of all Labour candidates were women.

The position has been rather different as far as the *Liberal Democrats* are concerned. Traditionally the Liberal Party attracted men and women of broadly liberal outlook who wished to see the liberal point of view translated into public policy. However, it did not lay great insistence on strict adherence to party orthodoxy. This approach has continued in the Liberal Democrats, although it has been tempered by a degree of hard-nosed political realism and a willingness to follow the line laid down by the leadership, both of which characteristics were brought to the party from the former SDP. More recently it has been reinforced by the intake of a growing number of able and ambitious individuals into the Parliamentary Party. Under the leadership of Sir Menzies Campbell a 'gender balance' task force was established with a view to securing the selection of more women as candidates in winnable seats.

While the nature and strength of a candidate's commitment to party ideology seems to have become more important in determining an individual's progress in all parties, it is no longer usually the case that the wealth or family connections of an aspiring candidate have much bearing on the chances of success at constituency level (although it must be said that there have been a few husband-and-wife or other family combinations in the House of Commons). Since the late 1940s all parties have set low limits on the personal donations which candidates or MPs may make to their constituency parties, so it is no longer possible to purchase a nomination, as it used to be, at any rate in the Conservative Party before the Second World War. Yet some candidates still have a better chance of success than others, especially at by-elections, when the parties wish to take no unnecessary chances, and in the competition for the safest seats.

In the *Labour Party* candidates seeking selection have to be nominated by at least one branch of the constituency party. At the national level there is a list of approved Parliamentary candidates which is kept at party headquarters in London following endorsement of the names by the NEC. Nonetheless some candidates who emerge as 'local favourites' of their constituency parties do not appear on the national list, but nevertheless are usually endorsed by the NEC if they are selected. In exceptional cases the modern Labour Party has actually limited the range of local choice or even imposed a candidate on the local party in order to avoid the selection of a candidate believed to be detrimental to the party's chances. Between 1993 and 1996 (when an Industrial Tribunal ruled the process to be illegal) positive discrimination in favour of women was exercised in candidate selection, a move designed to ensure that more women would be elected to Parliament.

In the *Conservative Party* there is also a list of approved Parliamentary candidates which is kept centrally at party headquarters in London. In order to get on this list aspirants have to go through a complicated process of written submissions and personal interviews, as well as a subsequent assessment process. In some cases these stages can prove more difficult than the later appearance before Constituency Selection Committees. Traditionally each Constituency Association has had the unfettered right to select anyone it liked, even if the person concerned was not on the centrally approved list of Parliamentary candidates at the time, or indeed was deemed unacceptable to the national Party leadership. This fact came sharply into the spotlight at the time of the 1997 General Election when the Beckenham Association reselected Piers Merchant – despite allegations in the press that he had had an affair with a 17-year-old nightclub hostess – and the Tatton Association reselected Neil Hamilton – despite his being at the centre of the 'cash-for-questions' row

– notwithstanding the fact that the national Party made it known to the local Associations concerned that they would prefer these two candidates *not* to be reselected, because of the adverse national impact such selections would have. Consequently, reforms intended to strengthen the centre – such as the creation of the Ethics and Integrity Committee with power to suspend and even expel miscreants – have been made. To the extent that at the beginning of the 2005 election the then Conservative leader, Michael Howard, banned Howard Flight – a sitting MP – from being a Conservative candidate after he had been reported to say that the party had secret plans to cut public spending .

In the *Liberal Democrats* responsibility for the shortlisting of candidates rests with the executive committee of the local party or a shortlisting subcommittee appointed by it. All candidates must be on the party's list of approved candidates, a process which involves a series of oral and written interviews, tests and submissions. Unless a sitting MP or previous candidate is reselected, the process involves drawing up a shortlist incorporating a specified number of candidates which, subject to there being a sufficient number of applicants, must include at least one member of each sex. Each member of the party in the constituency has a vote in the process and the choice of candidate is determined by proportional representation.

5.3 principles and organisation

Since the Second World War it has been the Labour and Conservative Parties which have dominated the British political scene. They have brought to British politics two distinct ideological traditions within which their respective political principles have been advanced in the light of circumstances prevailing at the time.

These two distinct ideological traditions have been reflected in matters of national party organization and, consequently, there has traditionally been a notable contrast between the Conservative Party, which was created from the centre and the top down, and the Labour Party which was created from the grass roots up. The Conservative organisation was originally intended to act as the handmaid of the Parliamentary Party, whereas the Labour organisation was conceived as the servant of the National Executive Committee and ultimately the annual Party Conference. Such contrasting origins and traditions have left their mark on the way in which each of the main parties is organised today. Having said this, however, it should be pointed out that Neil Kinnock, who led the Labour Party between 1983 and 1992, made significant organisational changes in the Labour Party which brought it more under the sway of the Parliamentary leadership, changes which both his successors, John Smith and Tony Blair, took ever further. Similarly, William Hague, Conservative leader between 1997 and 2001, set off on a course of radical structural reform of a party organisation essentially unchanged since its inception in 1867, changes which were built upon by his successors, Iain Duncan Smith, Michael Howard and David Cameron.

the Labour Party – principles

From the outset, and certainly ever since the party constitution was adopted in 1918, the Labour tradition was based on a commitment to the ideology of Socialism. Yet from the beginning the importance of ideology was balanced to some extent by the more pragmatic outlook of the Fabians and Christian Socialists. It was also tempered by trade-union scepticism towards some Socialist principles. Nevertheless, as Samuel Beer observed, 'if the implication of sudden and violent change is extracted ... it is correct to say that the meaning of Socialism to the Labour Party was a commitment to ultimate social revolution.'[12] To the Labour Party this always meant more than a commitment to the public ownership of the means of production, distribution and exchange, as laid down originally in Clause IV of the party constitution. It also meant a commitment to a form of moral collectivism which drew on the reserves of fellowship and fraternity traditionally associated with the trade union movement.

The Socialist tradition continued in the modern Labour Party. For example, the October 1974 Labour Manifesto contained a clear commitment to 'an irreversible shift in the balance of wealth and power' in favour of working people. The fact that the Labour Party, when in office, has not always acted in a particularly Socialist way has merely engendered disillusion and recrimination among its more zealous members. It was for this reason that the Party swung markedly to the Left following defeat at the 1979 General Election.

However, following further electoral defeats at both the 1987 and 1992 General Elections, 'modernisers' in the party realised that in order to have a chance of defeating the Conservatives in future, it was necessary to modernise both the party's internal structures and its policies. In attempting to achieve these objectives, they followed three courses of action. *Firstly*, they introduced a wider franchise for the selection and reselection of party candidates in order to stop small groups of hardline activists dominating the process and to make constituency parties more representative of ordinary Labour supporters and the party more attractive to the voters. *Secondly*, they restructured the National Executive Committee (NEC) to give the Shadow Cabinet and the PLP more power and the NEC and the Party Conference less power for similar reasons. *Thirdly*, they initiated a wide ranging policy review designed to produce a set of modern policies for the 1990s which would improve Labour's chances of returning to office.

The Policy Review was overwhelmingly endorsed at the 1989 Labour Conference. Having dropped the Socialist policies which were perceived as having made Labour unelectable, the leader, Neil Kinnock, felt able to declare that the party was 'fit for Government'. Undoubtedly the party was more united than it had been for many years and it had become a more formidable contender for power than it had been for a considerable time. Although the Policy Review did not offer a completely new definition of Labour's ideological principles for the 1990s, it did convey to the British electorate the symbolically important fact that the party had modernised its stance and abandoned old-fashioned Socialism.

Following yet another defeat for the Labour Party at the 1992 General Election, Neil Kinnock resigned as Leader and John Smith was elected in his place. The new Leader, who was also a 'moderniser', immediately decided to build on the reforms of his predecessor by pledging to abolish trade-union block votes within the Labour movement and to introduce the principle of 'one member one vote' into the party's own decision making. After a fierce and often passionate debate at the 1993 Labour Conference, delegates voted in favour of One Member One Vote (OMOV) for the selection of Parliamentary candidates, reform of the system for electing the Leader and Deputy Leader, and the abolition of the union block vote in Party Conference decisions. In short, although the party remained the political voice of the trade unions, the relationship between the two was put upon a modern and politically acceptable basis of individual membership and voluntary participation. By the time of John Smith's untimely death in May 1994 the Labour Party had moved a very long way from the old-fashioned Socialism for which it had stood – at least rhetorically – in the 1970s and early 1980s.

Under the leadership of Tony Blair the process of 'modernisation' continued, to the extent that it seemed possible sometimes that Labour had positioned itself to the right of the Conservatives on particular issues where majority public opinion held such a position. However, Tony Blair was careful to say that Labour's redefinition of its policy had not altered its traditional commitment to social justice. Rather it had balanced that commitment with recognition of the economic and political realities both in Britain and worldwide.

Following a long series of electoral defeats, Labour made a significant shift towards a more moderate and pragmatic policy stance. Successive Labour Leaders sought to maximise the party's chances of returning to power and clearly believed that this could not be achieved on the basis of old-style Socialism. The party's willingness to accept many of the economic and social changes made by the Conservatives during the 1980s was an indication that they recognised that there had been a sea change in the conventional wisdom and assumptions of British politics which it had to accept if it were to persuade the voters of its suitability for Office.

The Labour Party's shift towards pragmatism and moderation was particularly noticeable on some sensitive and important issues, such as trade union reform and wider home ownership; but it became increasingly evident right across the board. For example, mainstream Labour attitudes on public ownership, taxation and consumer rights became more cautious and less doctrinaire than previously, and Tony Blair and John Prescott (his Deputy) were even able to persuade the party to accept a new, more modern definition of Clause IV of the

1918 party constitution, namely one which declared that the party sought to create a community in which power, wealth and opportunity are in the hands of the many not the few, and where rights enjoyed reflect the duties owed. In short, Neil Kinnock, John Smith and Tony Blair all seemed determined to let no ideological shibboleths stand in the way of the return to power of a modern and voter-friendly Labour Party on a modern and pragmatic platform. Indeed throughout the run-up to the 1997 General Election Tony Blair's efforts to make the Labour Party electable continued apace. It was for this reason that he matched the Conservatives with a pledge to hold a referendum on British participation in the European single currency, and why Gordon Brown announced that there would be no increase in the rates of income tax for five years under a Labour Government. Indeed, bearing in mind the effectiveness of the Conservatives' attempts to portray the Labour Party as a 'tax and spend' party in the 1992 election, they went even further by announcing that they would abide by the Conservative Government's spending plans for the first two years of a Labour Government.

In short, the Labour Party – the party for so long committed to the public ownership of the means of production, distribution and exchange – transformed its image, structure and policy in order to reposition itself on the new centre ground of British politics largely defined by Margaret Thatcher. This was supported by a series of organisational changes which gave greater authority to the leader and by a mastery of the techniques of modern media-focused campaigning.

By the time of the 2005 General Election Labour rhetoric focused on economic dynamism and social justice going hand-in-hand and on fostering entrepreneurship, with frequent references to 'partnership' between the public and private sectors of the economy, 'fairness' in taxation and social security arrangements, and 'empowerment' and 'choice' in relation to health and education, with policy focusing on a number of other areas as well:

- The economy, stressing a record of stability, rising prosperity and wider opportunities
- Modernising public services, with particular reference to both education and the NHS
- Tackling crime and anti-social behaviour
- Dealing with immigration and asylum
- Taking tough action to combat international terrorism
- Creating 'a vibrant civil society'.

the Labour Party – organisation

For much of its history the Labour Party organisation was under the control of the General Secretary, who was the senior paid official responsible to the National Executive Committee, which was accountable in its turn to the annual Party Conference. In view of the dual hierarchy in the party, the Leader of

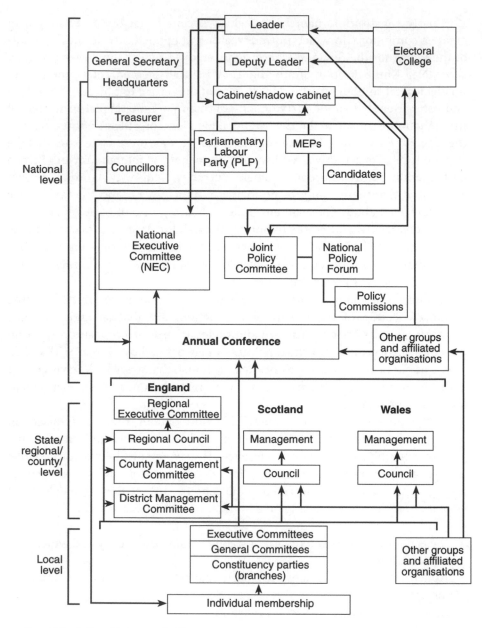

figure **5.3** **Labour Party organisation**

the Party and senior Parliamentary colleagues could be at odds over matters of policy and procedure with prominent members of the National Executive Committee, who were often backbench MPs of a more radical disposition elected to the NEC by the constituency Labour Parties, as was the case during the Labour Governments in the 1970s.

However, under Neil Kinnock's leadership (1983–92) and thereafter under the leadership of both John Smith (1992–94) and Tony Blair (1994–2007), serious efforts were made by the Parliamentary leadership to regain effective control of the NEC and the party organisation which served it. This has meant not only much greater emphasis on attractive presentation of united Labour policy, but also much greater influence from the centre than was formerly the case in the Labour movement. It was for this reason that in 1990 a new policy-making process was established consisting of a Joint Policy Committee – including the Leader, the Shadow Cabinet (the Cabinet when in Government) and the NEC – and a National Policy Forum. It was an attempt to ensure that policies which came before Conference had emerged from an inclusive process of consultation and deliberation; in short, an attempt to find a balance between the aspirations of the party activists and the realities of Government.

The staff at Labour Party headquarters, including the Research Department, are responsible to the General Secretary and perform a range of support functions. The Party Chairman used to hold office for one year only and was usually the member of the NEC with the longest continuous membership of that body and had responsibility to the party as a whole rather than to the Leader of the Party. Under Tony Blair's leadership, however, the position has become one at the disposal of the leader.

The Labour Party Conference has traditionally been a powerful gathering. Its claim to a real political role was based on the fact that it is constitutionally and formally the policy-making body of the party, while the party in Parliament is theoretically little more than the Parliamentary arm of the entire Labour movement. The Conference is presided over by the Chairman of the Party, who is assisted by a Conference Arrangements Committee composed of representatives of all the main sections of the Labour movement. In the past the Conference was dominated by the block votes of the trade unions. For example, the Transport and General Workers Union had a block vote of about 1.2 million and the Amalgamated Engineering Union had one of about 840,000 votes. By comparison, neither the smaller trade unions nor the constituency parties had much voting power at Conference, although they could make their influence felt with extra militancy. The Conference was composed of mandated delegations which were expected to vote in accordance with the decisions previously taken by the organisations which they represented. However, in 1993 the union block vote was abolished with union delegates thenceforth being free to vote independently and with the proportion of union votes falling to 50 per cent of the total. Labour Members of Parliament can attend Conference, but unless they are members of the NEC, they do not usually play a prominent part in the proceedings.

The NEC has traditionally been a powerful body which has claimed to act in the name of the entire Labour movement between annual Conferences. It includes representatives of the affiliated trade unions, the constituency parties, the Women's Section, the Youth Movement, other affiliated Socialist societies, together with automatic representation for the Leader, the Deputy Leader, the General Secretary and the Party Treasurer. It acts in the name of the Conference and carries on the business of the party from one year to the next. It has also had a constitutional claim to a major role in party policy making and to participation with the Cabinet or Shadow Cabinet in the preparation of the Party Manifesto – both somewhat diluted following the creation of the Joint Policy Committee and the National Policy Forum and the use of membership plebiscites. In the past there has been the possibility of tension between it and the leadership of the Parliamentary Party. In recent years, however, under the leadership and reforms of Tony Blair, such tensions have been largely 'managed' out of existence.

In the House of Commons the Parliamentary Labour Party is led by the Leader. When the party is in Opposition, the leader chairs the Parliamentary Committee (Shadow Cabinet) which is the executive committee of the party in Parliament in those circumstances. Constitutionally the position is slightly different when the party is in Government as the leader is Prime Minister and his most senior colleagues are members of the Cabinet. Since 1970 the weekly meetings of the entire PLP have been chaired by an elected Chairman who is usually a senior backbencher. Backbenchers involve themselves with various subject groups, depending on their particular policy or constituency interests. In both cases, however, they have relatively little formative influence over the process of policy making.

In Opposition, the members of the PLP vote every year for those of their colleagues who aspire to places in the Shadow Cabinet. The top 15 are elected and the Leader is then free to distribute the portfolios between them. The junior Shadow spokesmen are appointed by the Leader according to the usual criteria of political clout, personal merit and regional or ideological balance. In Government, the Party Leader is, of course, Prime Minister and therefore free to allocate the real Ministerial responsibilities as appropriate, subject to the usual political considerations of ideological and regional balance within the party. However, in particular response to pressure in the early 1980s – when the Hard Left of the party urged that members of a Labour Cabinet should be elected by the PLP rather than appointed by the Prime Minister of the day – provision is now made for all the elected members of the Shadow Cabinet to become members of the Cabinet automatically when the party moves into Government, although not necessarily in the Ministerial posts which they had been shadowing.

From 1922 to 1980 the Leader of the Party was elected exclusively by the PLP. However, in 1981 this power was entrusted to an electoral college in which the three main sections of the Labour movement were represented. Following changes in 1993 the college votes have been divided into thirds with individual party members accounting for one-third, Labour MPs and MEPs accounting for one-third, and trade union members (plus the members of other affiliated organisations) all voting individually accounting for the remaining one-third. Candidates for the leadership must be MPs and their nominations must be supported by at least one-eighth of the PLP.

the Conservative Party – principles

The Conservative tradition stresses the importance of strong Government, in the sense that Conservatives believe that a Government should act with determination and self-confidence based on the democratic legitimacy which it derives from its Parliamentary majority in the House of Commons. Conservatives have traditionally been suspicious of political ideology of an imperative or all embracing kind, although during Margaret Thatcher's period as Leader (1975–90) many observers doubted the validity of such a proposition. In the opinion of Samuel Beer, the ideas of independent authority for the Executive, class rule by those deemed best equipped to govern, pragmatic decisions of a non-ideological character and strong determined Government were all discernible in Conservative political thought for a long time.[13]

Even though a conscious political ideology does not seem to belong in the Conservative tradition, the party appeared much more ideological in the 1980s – certainly in its free-market rhetoric and occasionally in its actions. This reflected the influence of what was then called the New Right on Conservative thinking. Pressure groups outside Parliament, such as the Institute of Economic Affairs and the Adam Smith Institute, and factions within Parliament, such as the self-styled No Turning Back Group of radical Conservative backbenchers, combined to push the party's policy and decision making in a markedly more right-wing direction and to give extra political impetus to the Thatcherite revolution.

The party has also traditionally made a point, even a fetish, of trying to preserve party unity (or at least the appearance of unity), since it is well aware of the political disadvantages of obvious disunity. Indeed, loyalty to the leader and the consequent image of unity was at one time said to be the Party's 'secret weapon'. Nevertheless, this did not prevent the conduct of a bitter (though often coded) argument between the Thatcherites and the non-Thatcherites about the pace and scale of supply-side reform (such as privatisation), nor did it prevent frequent outbreaks of internecine strife within the party about the nature and extent of Britain's commitment to the future development of the European Union – particularly with regard to a single European currency – during the 1990s. The former argument was largely resolved in favour of the Thatcherites, since most of the prominent 'Wets' were sacked or had retired from the Cabinet by the end of the 1980s and the rest of the party came to recognise the force of three successive General Election victories under the leadership of Margaret Thatcher. With regard to the latter argument, it was one of the factors that led to the removal of Margaret Thatcher as party leader and Prime Minister in 1990, and proved to be the most disruptive issue for the party during the leadership of John Major (1990–97). In Opposition, under the leadership of William Hague, Iain Duncan Smith and Michael Howard, it was apparent that the fault lines in the party on the issue of Europe had not gone away. In the wake of the French and Dutch votes against the European Constitution, the leadership of David Cameron has been helped by the fact that the issue has been pushed down the political agenda.

During Margaret Thatcher's period as leader of the party (1975–90), the emphasis in Conservative rhetoric was put on the paramount importance of individual attitudes and behaviour in response to material incentives and legislative penalties. Leading party spokesmen were at pains to emphasise the comparatively limited role of the state and other public agencies, but equally to stress that the law should be clearly defined and strongly enforced in those areas in which state power could legitimately be exercised. There were also sustained attempts to reward individual success and to penalise failure, whether in education, work or life in general. Above all, the Conservatives sought to persuade people not to look to the Government for salvation, but to take responsibility for themselves and their families.

Under John Major a more emollient style of leadership and a less exclusive approach to politics was apparent. Nonetheless, there was considerable continuity of policy, especially in respect of the party's commitments to sound money, reducing the size of the public sector and concentrating social security on those who needed it most. Under Major the Conservatives presented a less ideological and more pragmatic profile. The slogans and ideas most closely associated with Major's period as Prime Minister included:

- His declared wish to create 'a nation at ease with itself'
- The concept of 'the Citizens Charter' designed to make the providers of public services more responsive to the needs and expectations of citizens as customers and consumers
- The aspiration that Britain should be 'at the heart of Europe' (but without any commitment to further integration)
- A rather counterproductive call to get 'back to basics' in such areas as education and law and order.

John Major's critics in the media and in his own party accused him of having insufficient political conviction and failing to demonstrate real leadership qualities. In these respects unfavourable contrasts were drawn with his predecessor, notwithstanding the fact that he was chosen to succeed Margaret Thatcher in 1990 very largely because he was different in style and character.

Following its massive electoral defeat in 1997 and subsequent defeats in 2001 and 2005, the Conservative Party under David Cameron – its fifth leader in nine years – describes itself as a modern, compassionate party with enduring values which believes in trusting people, sharing responsibility, championing freedom and supporting the institutions and culture that is shared as 'one nation'. In 2006, in a new statement of aims and values, *Built to Last*, the party declared that:

- A successful Britain must be able to compete with the world, consequently they would put economic stability and fiscal responsibility first, coming before tax cuts. Only over time would it be possible to share the proceeds of growth between public services and lower taxes
- 'There is such a thing as society', but that it is not the same thing as the state. The right test for policies is how they help the most disadvantaged in society, not the rich. Consequently, they declared that they would stand up for the victims of state failure and ensure that social justice and equal opportunity are achieved by empowering people and communities.

- The quality of life matters, as well as rising living standards. As such they pledged to enhance the environment by seeking a long-term cross-party consensus on sustainable development and climate change and pledged to support the choices that women make about their work and home lives.
- Public services – including the NHS and education – should be provided for everyone, guaranteed by the state but not necessarily run by the state.
- Making poverty history was a moral obligation and, as such, a pledge was given to fight for free and fair trade, increase international aid and press for further debt relief.
- Strong defence was to be ensured, as was the effective enforcement of laws that balance liberty and safety.
- 'We understand the limitations of government, but are not limited in our aspirations for government. We believe in the role of government as a force for good. It can and should support aspirations such as home ownership, saving for a pension, and starting a business. It should support families and marriage, and those who care for others. And it should support the shared experiences that bring us together – such as sport, the arts and culture.'
- 'We believe that government should be closer to the people, not further away. We want to see more local democracy, instead of more centralisation and we want to make the devolved institutions in Scotland and Wales work. Communities should have more say over their own futures.'[14]

the Conservative Party – organisation

Following the 1997 General Election defeat and subsequent organisational reforms designed to renew the party initiated under the leadership of William Hague, the three separate and distinct pillars of the old party – the Parliamentary Party, the voluntary party and the professional party (Central Office) – were drawn together in a single structure. Consequently, today the Conservative Party is managed by a single governing body – the Board – under a single constitution (watched over by a Constitutional College) with a national membership and provision for direct membership involvement and participation. Indeed, the reforms themselves were put to a postal ballot of all members in 1998, receiving approval by 110,165 votes to 4425; a margin of 96.1 per cent to 3.9 per cent. See Figure 5.4 for a diagram of Conservative Party organization.

The idea behind the creation of the Board was that of unity; to create for the first time a single, unified Party. It is for this reason that the Board is the supreme decision-making body in all matters relating to Party organisation and management. It comprises the Chairman of the Party – who chairs its meetings – a Deputy Chairman, the Treasurer, the Leader of the Party in the House of Lords and a senior member of the professional staff – all of whom are appointed by the Party Leader – as well as the Chairman of the 1922 Committee, the President and Chairman of the National Convention, three members elected from the National Convention, an elected representative of

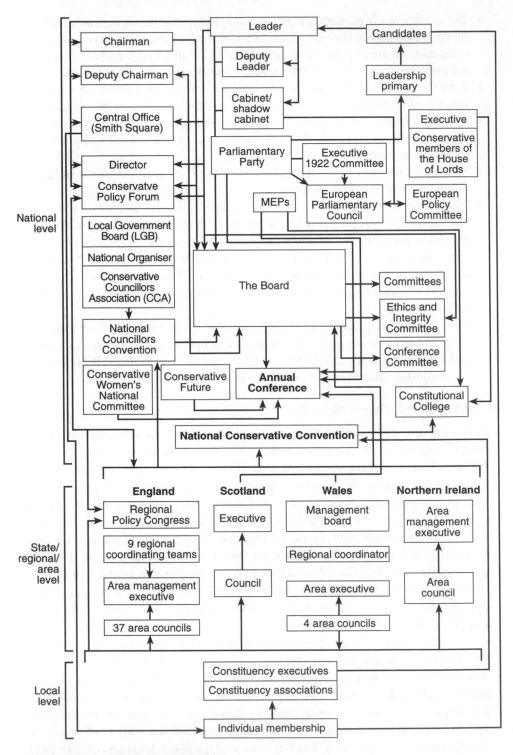

figure **5.4** **Conservative Party organisation**

the Party in Scotland, the Welsh Coordinating Chairman and the Chairman of the Association of Conservative Councillors. An additional member can be appointed by the Party Leader, subject to the endorsement of the Board, and one by the Board subject to the approval of the Party Leader.

Another guiding principle of the Hague reforms was that of decentralisation. Consequently, Constituency Associations remain an important focus, and the role of Constituency Chairman has been enhanced. Above the constituency is the area level with Area Councils and Area Executives, the principal link between the Board and Constituency Associations. However, there is also a Regional level providing for coordination of activity and policy formulation. Important in all of this has been the establishment of the National Conservative Convention to provide a focus for the views of party members and to act as a link between the leadership and the membership. The annual Party Conference continues to be the main party gathering of the year.

Another important principle said to underpin the Hague reforms was that of democracy; in short, giving power to the membership of the party. Consequently, the membership was asked to endorse William Hague as Leader, vote on the principles of Party reform, vote on policy concerning the Single European Currency and vote on the 'Built to Last' statement of its aims and values. In addition they have been given greater involvement in the selection of candidates and the vote in leadership elections. A part of this approach has also been to provide for greater involvement by the membership in the development of policy. As a result the Conservative Policy Forum (CPF) has been established to provide for the involvement of party members – via Regional Policy congresses and regular surveys – in discussing and formulating policy proposals. The CPF itself has been given considerable input into the annual Party Conference agenda.

Also important in the Hague reforms were the principles of integrity and openness. The party knew that it had been damaged by the accusations of sleaze in the run-up to and during the 1997 General Election. Consequently, an Ethics and Integrity Committee was established to investigate instances of misconduct referred to it by the Party Leader or the Board and any action it stipulates must be implemented by the Board. As far as openness is concerned the Party began to publish the names of its major donors and refused to accept foreign donations prior to either of these being required by law.

In the House of Commons the party is organised within a framework capped by the 1922 Committee, which was named after a famous meeting of Conservative backbenchers held at the Carlton Club in that year. The Committee is led by its chairman, who is a senior backbencher elected annually by backbench colleagues. It has an influential Executive Committee made up of other senior backbenchers also elected annually by their colleagues. Under its auspices there is a considerable substructure of Party backbench committees each covering an area of policy – for example finance, industry, agriculture, employment, environment, education, defence, foreign affairs and so on – and each with a slate of officers elected annually by their colleagues. In the House of Lords the Party is more loosely organised in the Committee of Conservative and Unionist Peers.

When the party is in Government, such committees can have an influence on policy via the subtle process of *the politics of anticipated reaction*, that is, when Ministers adjust their intended actions in the light of expected or actual responses from the relevant backbench committees. When the Party is in Opposition, such committees are probably more influential and they are certainly busier, since the various Shadow spokesmen are appointed to chair the relevant committees and their fellow officers from the backbenches can have considerable influence on the process of party policy making. In Opposition there has also been a so-called Business Committee which is made up of the officers of the 1922 Committee and the officers of all the various backbench committees under one rubric. This has served as a broader institutional link between the Shadow Cabinet and the various backbench subject committees.

As for the position of the Party Leader, before 1965 such a person was said to 'emerge' from a process of informal soundings and consultations within all sections of the Party, but principally in the Commons. Between 1965 and 1998 the choice of Party Leader resulted from a process of election by all members of the Parliamentary Party in the Commons, who were expected to consult each other informally and take account of the views of the party in the Lords, the European Parliament and the country as well. Such elections could take place every year in the autumn. Yet, as long as the Leader maintained the confidence of senior colleagues and the Parliamentary Party as a whole, the contest was merely an annual formality with only one nomination.

Margaret Thatcher secured the leadership in 1975 by challenging the then Leader, Edward Heath, while the party was in Opposition. She remained unchallenged until 1989 when the backbencher Sir Anthony Meyer challenged her unsuccessfully. The following year, 1990, Michael Heseltine challenged her and, although obtaining only 152 votes to her 204 on the first ballot, secured enough support under the rules to ensure a second ballot, thus undermining her position to such an extent that she withdrew from the contest. On the second ballot – which allowed new candidates to enter the contest – John Major came top of the poll with 185 votes and secured the leadership because the other candidates did not press their rights to initiate a third ballot, even though he had not achieved a large enough margin of victory to rule it out. In 1995 John Major himself resigned as Party Leader, challenging critics to 'put up or shut up'. This brought forth a challenge from John Redwood; but Major secured re-election on the first ballot.

Following the election of William Hague as Party Leader in 1997, both the rules for initiating and the mechanism for conducting a leadership election were changed. First, the Party Leader can only be removed following a vote of no-confidence by a majority of Conservative MPs. Second, the Party Leader is to be elected by the entire party membership on the basis of one-member-one-vote following a primary election among Conservative MPs to select a shortlist of candidates to place before the entire party membership. In 2001

Iain Duncan Smith was elected under this system, although when he stood down – as a result of a vote of no-confidence among his MPs – there was no election as there was only one candidate, Michael Howard. Despite attempts to alter the system, it was this system through which David Cameron was elected leader towards the end of 2005.

main party contrasts

The traditional organisation of each of the main parties reflected the contrast between the traditionally democratic aspirations of the Labour Party and the traditionally hierarchical principles of the Conservative Party. In the former case, this meant that the origins of party decisions were often blurred and the implementation occasionally challenged by some of those involved. In the latter case, it meant that party decisions were normally taken expeditiously and implemented without undue debate or difficulty. In short, the Labour Party often seemed temperamentally and organisationally averse to firm leadership from the top whereas the Conservative Party tended to be more amenable to it. Nonetheless it has been observed that in the Blair-led Labour Party and the post-Thatcher Conservative Party these traditional views are no longer accurate; indeed, some might say that the defining characteristics of the two parties have been reversed.

The problem for Labour was that it had been difficult adequately to control a party which served a movement which had aspired to be both ideological and democratic, although the ideology of democratic Socialism held that there was no conflict between these two characteristics. The problems of the Conservatives have been more subtle, but just as real on occasions. In spite of their autocratic style and tradition, the management of the party has been by no means trouble-free. For example, exposure to a hostile Party Conference could be an unpleasant and tricky ordeal for even the most senior and experienced politician, as was seen over decolonisation in the 1950s, Rhodesia in the 1960s, law and order in the 1980s and Europe in the 1990s.

In the Labour Party power has traditionally been diffuse, certainly from the adoption of the party constitution in 1918, since it was shared between the PLP on the one hand and the affiliated trade unions and constituency parties on the other. This uneasy alliance has been balanced sometimes in favour of the extra-Parliamentary elements and sometimes in favour of the PLP. In the 1970s and early 1980s great efforts were made by the constituency parties to seize a larger share of power and to strengthen the NEC against the PLP. Power has tended to reside with the Parliamentary leadership more when the party has been in Government and less when it has been in Opposition. A great deal has depended on the inclinations and ambitions of the leading figures in the movement at different times. Yet, as has been shown in the case of Tony Blair, if a Labour Leader is determined to assert authority, this can certainly be done.

In the Conservative Party effective power has traditionally been wielded mainly by the Leader and to a lesser extent by the other senior Parliamentary figures, in Government or Opposition. The senior figures in the hierarchy of the National Union were soothed with knighthoods rather than seriously consulted on matters of policy and on the whole the voluntary side of the party knew its place in the scheme of things. Yet even a powerful Conservative Leader could not afford to ignore party opinion, since the activists could put pressure on backbenchers who then felt obliged to lobby Ministers when in Government or Shadow spokesmen when in Opposition. Indeed, Conservative Leaders have been more vulnerable than their Labour counterparts to political 'assassination' when they fail to win General Elections or are directly involved in other events politically calamitous for their party.

the Liberal Democrats – principles

The Liberal Democrats were formally launched on 3 March 1988, under the slogan 'The New Choice – The Best Future', born out of the decision by the old Liberal Party and the Social Democratic Party (SDP) to merge their two separate parties – previously cooperating as the Alliance – into a single entity. Under their leader, Paddy Ashdown, the party sought to establish a distinctive political profile. In doing so, it identified four pillars of policy:

‣ Investing in the future by allocating more public funds to education, health and the nation's technological base
‣ Modernising and defending democracy by developing a new concept of citizenship
‣ Developing a more ambitious environmental policy
‣ Laying great stress on Britain's international vocation and responsibilities.

Within its new concept of citizenship, the party was strongly committed to:

‣ The achievement of a fairer voting system
‣ Devolution of power to Assemblies in Scotland, Wales and the regions of England
‣ Greater power for individuals through the introduction of employee councils at their place of work
‣ The introduction of legislation guaranteeing freedom of information
‣ A new Bill of Rights.

Above all, they advocated a less divisive and more decentralised approach to solving the continuing problems of British politics within the context of the European Union, to which they showed more commitment than either of the two main parties.

Having abandoned not only their original strategy of replacing Labour as the Centre-Left alternative to the Conservative Party, but also their subsequent stance of equal distance between the two main parties, the Liberal Democrats entered the 1997 General Election in the hope that it would produce a Parliament in which no single party had a majority but where they would be left holding the balance. Although they saw their share of the national vote go down slightly on their 1992 figure, the focused nature of their campaign strategy – targeting some 50 constituencies – enabled them to increase their Parliamentary representation from 20 to 46 MPs, giving them their best result in 70 years. Nonetheless, with an overall Labour majority of 178 they were further from holding the balance of power than before.

In June 1999 Paddy Ashdown stood down as leader to be replaced by Charles Kennedy. He set about refashioning the party as a fully independent political force, uncoupling it from Labour and forming distinctive policies on taxation, education, the environment and Europe. At the 2001 General Election the party improved its share of the vote and won 52 seats. In the wake of the attacks of 9/11 and the resulting 'war on terrorism', the party decided to oppose the US-led invasion of Iraq in 2003, a decision which saw Charles Kennedy became the unofficial leader of the anti-war movement and the main voice of opposition in the House of Commons. This was seen by many as a principled stand and attracted support from Conservative and Labour voters disaffected by their parties' support for the war. The party was also at the forefront of campaigns to safeguard civil liberties in the face of contentious anti-terrorism legislation. Fighting the 2005 election as 'The Real Alternative', the party won 62 seats, its highest number since the 1920s.

Despite this success, some in the party saw the result as a missed opportunity, and the different strands of opinion in the party – in simplistic terms between economic liberalism and social liberalism – began pulling in different directions. Early in 2006, pressured by a large number of his MPs, Charles Kennedy stood down from the leadership on personal grounds, although the pressures were undoubtedly underpinned and fuelled by the division of opinion on the future direction of the party and the ambition for office of the increasing number of Liberal Democrat MPs. The new leader was Sir Menzies Campbell, pledging to act as a 'bridge to the future'; he promoted young talent and sought to develop a modern, distinctive, forward-looking, liberal agenda. With both Labour and the Conservatives either having moved or apparently seeking to move onto at least some of the ground previously occupied by the Liberal Democrats, the party undoubtedly faces a struggle. Its ability to construct this new distinctive agenda will determine not only the future direction of the party but also its likely prospects for success.

the Liberal Democrats – organisation

The organisation of the Liberal Democrats is federal in nature, in that there are autonomous parties in England, Scotland and Wales, each with its own national offices, staff and conferences. The party in England is further subdivided into 12 regional parties. The Federal Conference, which meets twice a year, is composed of representatives from the constituencies, the Parliamentary Party, associated organisations – such as those representing youth – and the officers of the national organisation. The party's Federal Executive, the Federal Policy

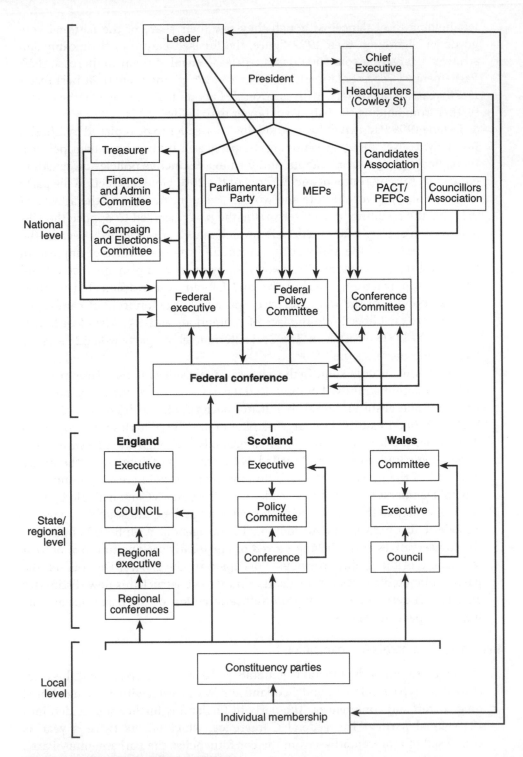

figure **5.5** **Liberal Democrat Party organisation**

Committee and the Federal Conference Committee all report to it. See Figure 5.5 for a diagram of Liberal Democrat Party organisation.

Responsibility for developing and presenting party policy, including the preparation of the General Election Manifesto, is placed on the Federal Policy Committee. This is composed of the Party Leader, the Party President, five representatives of the party in both Houses of Parliament, three representatives from local authority Councillors, two representatives each from the Scottish and Welsh parties, and 13 members elected by the Federal Conference. Responsibility for directing, coordinating and implementing the work of the Federal Party falls to the Federal Executive, a body formed on a similar basis to the Federal Policy Committee. Its tasks include setting up a Finance and Administration Committee to manage the finances and direct the administration of the Federal Party, including its headquarters at 4 Cowley Street, London SW1, and the appointment of a General Secretary. Party headquarters is divided into seven Departments – membership and direct mail, finance, campaigns and elections, policy, Conference, party newspaper, and the General Secretary's Department.

Elections for the position of Leader of the Party are held every two years, unless postponed by a vote of two-thirds of the Federal Executive. Apart from this, an election can be held either at the Leader's own request or following the loss of the Leader's Parliamentary seat, or a vote of no-confidence in the Leader by a majority of Liberal Democrat MPs, or at the request of 75 local parties. Candidates for the leadership have to be an MP, to be proposed and seconded by MPs and to be supported by at least 200 party members in at least 20 local parties or associated organisations. The election of the Leader is carried out on the basis of one member one vote via a postal ballot of the entire party membership.

other parties

the nationalist parties

Formed in 1928 (but under its current name from 1934) and describing itself as a democratic, left-of-centre political party, the *Scottish National Party* (SNP) has been motivated principally by the quest for Scottish independence and has therefore been able to encompass a broad ideological spectrum of opinion on nearly all other issues.

Plaid Cymru, the Welsh Nationalist Party, was founded in 1925 and has an ideology which is based on its determination to preserve the Welsh language and culture as the foundation of a distinctive Welsh identity within the United Kingdom. The party has both a radical and a moderate wing, with the former being in favour of certain forms of direct action in protest against the English dominance of Wales (for instance on the issues of Welsh water for English cities or English second homes in Wales) and the latter seeming more content to use the traditional channels of Parliamentary influence and the opportunities provided by devolution to advance the Welsh nationalist cause.

Northern Ireland parties

Northern Ireland is split between, on the one hand, the Protestant/Unionist/Loyalist community and, on the other, the Catholic/Nationalist/Republican community. The majority Protestant community has been represented at Westminster by the two main factions of the Unionist cause – the *Ulster Unionist Party* (UUP) and the *Democratic Unionist Party* (DUP). The 2005 General Election saw a significant switch within this community, with the DUP receiving more votes than any other party – 33.7 per cent, an increase of 11.2 per cent over 2001 – for the first time at a General Election, gaining four seats from the Ulster Unionists. The vote for the UUP declined by 9 per cent to just 17.8 per cent, and they were left with just one MP. Both the DUP and the UUP stand, to a greater or lesser extent, for continued Protestant supremacy and the maintenance of Northern Ireland as an integral part of the United Kingdom. The minority Catholic community is represented by the *Social Democratic and Labour Party* (SDLP), which has campaigned to improve the economic and social conditions of its supporters and which favours closer links between Northern Ireland and the Irish Republic as a step towards eventual Irish unity by consent, and the much more radical *Sinn Fein*, the political wing of the Irish Republican movement in the north, which campaigns openly for British withdrawal and the establishment of a united Ireland – a policy which from the late 1960s through into the 1990s they sought to achieve by all means at their disposal, including the use of force. In the 2005 General Election *Sinn Fein* supplanted the SDLP as the largest Catholic party with 5 seats and 24.3 per cent of the vote (as opposed to 3 for the SDLP on 17.5 per cent of the vote); indeed, it became the second largest party in Northern Ireland, a position which eventually enabled it to join a power-sharing Administration at Stormont with the DUP.

the fringe parties

There are many fringe parties in British politics, a total of 113 (by no means all) fielding candidates at the 2005 General Election. Indeed, a total of 1666 candidates stood under a minor party (namely, a party other than either Labour, Conservative or Liberal Democrat) or independent label; a total of 1495 if the Scottish and Welsh Nationalists and four main Northern Irish parties are removed from the total. Some wax and wane with bewildering frequency, a tendency that is true particularly among those on the extremes of either the Right or the Left.

On the extreme Right, the *British National Party* (BNP), and the *National Front* are based on a white racialist ideology which is heavily tinged with xenophobia and impatience with the democratic methods of Parliamentary politics. The BNP fielded 119 candidates and polled 192,850 votes in 2005, 0.7 per cent of the total but an average of 4.3 per cent per candidate; 34 of their candidates saved their deposits. On the extreme Left are to be found the *Communist Party of Britain*, the *Revolutionary Communist Party of Britain (Marxist-Leninist)*, and the *Communist Party of Great Britain*. Also on the extreme Left are the

Socialist Labour Party, formed in 1996 as a Socialist alternative to New Labour by Arthur Scargill, the then President of the National Union of Mineworkers; the *Socialist Party of Great Britain*, the *Socialist Alternative*, the *Workers Party*, and the *Workers' Revolutionary Party*. The 2005 General Election also saw the appearance of Respect – *the Unity Coalition*. The most high-profile member was the former Labour MP George Galloway, expelled from the Labour Party as a result of his opposition to the war in Iraq and in particular for comments which had been interpreted as incitement for British troops to mutiny. George Galloway himself stood and won in the constituency of Bethnal Green and Bow, securing 35.9 per cent of the vote, while Respect candidates came second in three other constituencies; in all, nine of the 26 Respect candidates saved their deposits.

In the 2005 General Election the largest number of fringe party candidates – 496 – belonged to the *United Kingdom Independence Party* (UKIP), the Euro-hostile party seeking UK withdrawal from the European Union. In the European Parliamentary Elections of 2004 the party had secured 16.1 per cent of the vote and 12 MEPs and approached the 2005 election with high hopes. However, infighting undoubtedly did little to help their cause and at the General Election UKIP only polled 618,000 votes, 2.3 per cent of the total (although placing them fourth of all parties contesting the election). This was an average of 2.8 per cent of the vote in the constituencies contested – with a high of 9.6 per cent – and the party saved 37 deposits. The influence of UKIP was seen by some to have been in the seats they blocked, rather than making any gains themselves – it being estimated that they may have prevented the Conservatives from winning as many as 27 seats.[15] Nonetheless, it is difficult to confirm such an assertion, not least because, according to polls and indeed UKIP itself, the party draws its support from across the political spectrum, not simply from those who had previously voted Conservative. However, some recent evidence suggests that the Conservatives are losing activists to UKIP.[16]

In a different category altogether there is the *Green Party*, which stands for an ecological approach to all political issues. Formed as the People's Party in 1973, it became the Ecology Party in 1975 and changed to its current name in 1985. It reached considerable prominence in the late 1980s, riding the wave of a buoyant popular environmentalism which swept across Europe at the time. Indeed, in the 1989 elections to the European Parliament it secured 14.5 per cent of the votes cast (20 per cent in the south-east of England), coming second in six seats out of 78 in Britain and third in 61. However, because of internal disputes and structural weaknesses, the re-emergence of the Liberal Democrats, the effects of the recession and the fact that the other parties sought to display their own 'green' credentials, the party proved unable to build on this performance, and in the 1992 General Election its average share of the vote in the 253 seats which it contested was only 1.3 per cent. In 1997, fielding only 95 candidates and advocating policies to withdraw from the European Union, scrap nuclear weapons and take the railways back into public ownership, it secured 0.2 per cent of the vote, an average of 673 votes per candidate. However, the party then underwent something of a resurgence which resulted in them securing the election of seven members of the Scottish Parliament in 2003, two members of the European Parliament in 2004 and two members of the Greater London Assembly. In the 2005 General Election, fielding 183 candidates, they won 283,084 votes, 1.0 per cent of the total and their highest ever; an average of 3.4 per cent in contested seats. Their 'best performance' was third place in Brighton Pavillion with 21.9 per cent of the vote.

Perhaps the most remarkable individual result of the 2005 General Election was that of Peter Law in Blaenau Gwent. As a result of an internal Labour party dispute over the imposition of all-women shortlists, Labour's safest seat in Wales fell to Peter Law on a swing of 58.2 per cent; a Labour majority of 19,313 becoming an Independent majority of 9121.[17] Also significant was the retention of Wyre Forest by the Independent Kidderminster Hospital and Health Concern candidate, Dr Richard Taylor. Having captured the seat in 2001 he retained the seat with a majority of 5250, despite an adverse swing of 13.9 per cent.

Apart from the victories of George Galloway, Peter Law and Dr Richard Taylor the performance of another candidate can be mentioned, namely that of Reg Keys who, standing as an independent in Tony Blair's Sedgefield constituency in protest at the death of his son Tom in Iraq, came fourth with 4252 votes, 10.2 per cent.

The 2005 General Election also saw candidates stand under a variety of eccentric labels including the *Monster Raving Loony Party*, the *Rock 'N' Roll Loony Party*, the *Church of the Militant Elvis Party*, and others – all individuals who have sought to get involved simply for the fun of it and who have undoubtedly added a touch of colour to British elections.

5.4 conclusion

Political parties are central to the British political system. Indeed, it involves a system of government by and through political parties. Having said this, however, there are a number of factors which have already caused difficulties for the political parties and which could in the future further undermine their position. The factors include:

- Declining membership of political parties
- Declining popular attachment to political parties
- The myriad of other opportunities for political activity and public participation in which, non-political interests increasingly participate
- The weakening of links between pressure groups and political parties
- The increasing de-alignment of newspapers with a particular political party
- The growing importance of the media as political actors in their own right.

A final point to note would be that political parties are less self-contained and self-reliant than before, in campaigning and contesting elections, but dependent on a growing army of communications and public relations experts.

The maintenance of party discipline is a very important factor in determining a party's chances at General Elections. Quite simply, a party divided within itself is unlikely to win as Labour found to its cost in the 1980s and the Conservatives learned from 1997 to 2005.

In Government, the tasks of the victorious party are three-fold:

- To ensure that the policies on which it was elected are translated into administrative decisions or legislation as appropriate
- To ensure that the Government's measures are supported and carried through whenever there are key votes in Parliament
- To explain and defend Government policy through the media and in direct contacts with the public.

In Opposition, the task of the defeated parties is essentially to criticise and oppose the Government of the day, and to elaborate alternative policies and political stances which can be put before the electorate in the run-up to the following General Election. In this context it is important to note that the second largest party in the House of Commons becomes the *official Opposition* and thus shares with the Governing party the responsibilities of conducting Parliamentary proceedings in an effective and business-like manner, which normally allows the Government of the day to get its way in the end while allowing the Opposition full opportunities to play its constitutional roles of criticism, scrutiny and occasionally delay.

While the Labour and Conservative parties differ quite considerably in their history, ideology and constituency membership, they are more similar in many other respects than some accounts have suggested. When in Opposition, each Party has tended to use distinctive political language and to develop a distinctive political style in order to differentiate itself from the party in Government and often from its own record or behaviour in previous times. When in Government, each party has traditionally behaved in a broadly responsible and moderate way and each has pursued policies which belonged within the framework of the consensus of the time.

From the early 1970s a number of significant developments in each of the main parties led them both to depart quite markedly from their previous adherence to the post-war consensus. The Labour Party began to change significantly when in Opposition from 1970 to 1974, as those on the Left of the Party began to denigrate the Labour Government of 1964 to 1970 for its failure to be sufficiently Socialist. The Conservative Party began to change when in Opposition from 1974 to 1979 as Margaret Thatcher and her supporters began to redefine the purposes and priorities of Conservatism in contradistinction to the policies pursued during the second half of the 1970–74 Conservative Government. As a consequence of these movements of opinion, the ideological gap between the two parties became wider during most of the 1970s and 1980s.

The position began to change yet again in the late 1980s. One result of winning three General Elections in a row was to make the Conservative Party increasingly radical and self-confident in its Thatcherite beliefs. On the other hand, another consequence of this chain of Conservative victories was to force the Labour Party under successive Leaders to reconsider and revise many of its previously Socialist policies in a determined and conscious attempt to make its appeal more credible to the mass electorate. In fact, in many respects, politicians in all of the mainstream parties had come to accept the essential tenets of the Thatcherite agenda to the extent that a new Thatcherite consensus had emerged. Indeed, Labour's victory in the 1997 election was, in a bizarre, even perverse, way, evidence of the success of Conservatives under Margaret Thatcher in the 1980s. In no small measure her assault on the post-war consensus and her three electoral victories in a row laid the basis for a new bi-partisan consensus and made her the midwife to New Labour.

As for the future, much will depend on exactly how firmly embedded the post-Thatcher/Blairite consensus really is. Much will depend on the extent to which Gordon Brown seeks to distance himself from his predecessor. Similarly, much will depend on whether David Cameron can match the experience and authority of Gordon Brown. Much will also depend on events and influences outside the control of politicians, such as the workings of global markets and the practices of global media. Indeed, a durable conclusion is not possible, since in party politics the journey matters at least as much as the destination.

SUGGESTED QUESTIONS

1   What are the principal functions of political parties in the British political system?
2   'British politics is party politics.' What factors lie behind such a view?
3   Where does real power lie in the Conservative and Labour parties?

pressure groups

6.1 some definitions

In the British context pressure groups have been defined variously as:

- 'Organised groups possessing both formal structure and real common interests in so far as they influence the decisions of public bodies'[1]
- 'Any organised group which attempts to influence Government'[2]
- 'Organisations ... trying to influence the policy of public bodies in their own chosen direction, though never themselves prepared to undertake the direct Government of the country'[3]
- 'An association of individuals joined together by a common interest, belief, activity or purpose that seeks to achieve its objectives, further its interests and enhance its status in relation to other groups, by gaining the approval and co-operation of authority in the form of favourable policies, legislation and conditions'.[4]

Thus a pressure group is any group in society which, through political or other action, seeks to achieve changes which it regards as desirable or to prevent changes which it regards as undesirable.

The expression 'pressure group' is a comprehensive term which subsumes both sectional interest groups and more widely based attitudinal cause groups. The former are usually well-established groups advocating or defending a vested interest. The latter can be ephemeral organisations which may decline or disappear when their goals have been achieved, although in modern times they have played an increasingly influential and continuous role in the political process. However, the term presupposes that all pressure groups are promotional in the sense that they seek to promote their various objectives in the most effective possible ways. It also implies that they are irresponsible in the strict sense that they are not democratically accountable to the general public. It is the political parties which have to accept that form of responsibility and which are vulnerable to the verdict of the electorate at every General Election, and at other elections to a lesser extent as well.

6.2 classification of groups

When looking at pressure groups, it is necessary to make a preliminary distinction between Interest Groups and Cause Groups. The former are usually defensive in their functions and often closely involved with the institutions of central Government. The latter usually begin as institutional outsiders, but some of them attain a degree of prominence which virtually requires their views to be taken into account. In practice there is considerable overlap between the two types of group and some find a place in both categories.

interest groups

Interest groups are those whose basis of association is a common interest, usually economic or social. Put simply, they exist to defend and advance the interests of their members. The best example of such a group would be a trade union, an employers' association or a professional body. As far as trade unions are concerned, there are a large number of these bodies in Britain including, for example:

- UNISON – membership 1,317,000
- UNITE – formed in 2007 following the merging of the TGWU (Transport and General Workers Union) and AMICUS (Manufacturing, technical and Skilled Persons Union) – with a membership of 1,977,325
- GMB (a general union) – membership 575,370.

Collectively, such unions come together in the TUC (Trades Union Congress), the umbrella body for 62 trade unions, with a combined membership in 2006 of nearly 6.5 million.[5]

With regard to employers' organisations, there is the CBI (Confederation of British Industry), which exists primarily to ensure that Governments understand the intentions, needs and problems of British business. With a membership of some 200,000 UK-based businesses, including approximately 85 per cent of the FTSE 100 companies and nearly half of the FTSE 350, it is the leading 'voice' of business in Britain. Rivals to the CBI include the British Chambers of Commerce and the Institute of Directors, and there are many trade associations which speak for different sectors of British industry and commerce. Mention should also be made of the NFU (National Farmers' Union), the largest farming organisation in the UK, representing around three-quarters of the full time commercial farmers of England and Wales.

With regard to professional associations, prominent examples would include the Royal College of Nursing, the Law Society and the Institute of Chartered Accountants, to name but a few. A vast array of other groups are also classified as 'interest groups', such as the Society of Authors, the Royal British Legion, the Association of Licensed Taxi Drivers, the Scotch Whisky Association and the AA (Automobile Association).

cause groups

Cause groups are those which seek to achieve objectives based on a common cause, shared attitude or belief, rather than common economic or social interests. The activities of such groups involve the promotion of particular causes. For example, there are groups dedicated to the cause of environmental protection:

» Friends of the Earth – with 101,802 financial supporters
» Greenpeace – with 221,000 members
» The Campaign to Protect Rural England – with 59,000 members and supporters

to civil rights:

» Liberty – with just over 9000 members
» The Howard League for Penal Reform – with 2351 members

to political reform:

» The Electoral Reform Society – about 2000 members
» Charter 88/Unlock Democracy – with 3850 members

to social protection:

» The Child Poverty Action Group (CPAG) – with 3500 members
» MIND – the National Association for Mental Health – with 6700 people actively involved and a further 121,000 involved through MIND's broader networks, including local associations
» The National Society for the Prevention of Cruelty to Children (NSPCC) – with 4.2 million supporters

or animal welfare groups:

» The Royal Society for the Prevention of Cruelty to Animals, (RSPCA) – with 36,170 adult members and 35,194 junior members
» The League Against Cruel Sports – with 35,000 members and supporters
» The Royal Society for the Protection of Birds – with over a million members, including nearly 150,000 youth members.[6]

There are also a wide range of cause groups which campaign on what have been called 'moral' causes, such as those arguing for or against abortion, for or against gay rights, for or against smoking, and for or against extended licensing (drinking) hours.

Mention should also be made of 'NIMBY' – Not In My Back Yard – groups. These are groups which oppose particular developments – such as new power stations, motorways or airport extensions – because of the adverse effects on their own quality of life at local level.

From this it is apparent that pressure groups differ widely. They can be international, national or local, large or small, permanent or temporary, proactive or reactive, rich or poor, powerful or weak, successful or unsuccessful, or any combination of these.

6.3 main functions

In the contemporary British context pressure groups have a number of main functions.

They act as intermediaries between the Government and the public. This is a role which has become more important as the scope and complexity of politics have increased and as it has become more difficult for the political parties on their own to perform all the representative functions. This means that they act as spokesmen and negotiators on behalf of clearly defined sectional interests – for example, the National Farmers' Union on behalf of farmers, or the British Medical Association on behalf of doctors. It also means that they help all Governments to develop and implement their policies by entering into detailed consultations on proposals for administrative action or legislation and subsequently by delivering a measure of public consent to the output of the policy and decision making process.

They act as opponents and critics of Government, especially when the interests of those whom they claim to represent are threatened by Government policy. For example, the British Medical Association was in the forefront of the campaign to resist the Conservative Government's reforms of the National Health Service in the late 1980s and early 1990s; the Bar Council and the Law Society lobbied heavily against some of the Major Government's proposals for reform of the legal profession. Similarly, the Fuel Lobby pressured the Blair Government on several occasions to reduce the tax on fuel for farmers and hauliers, while in 2007 the anti-road-pricing campaign pressured the Blair Administration not to introduce road-pricing. Some people might argue that, in behaving like this, pressure groups are duplicating or even usurping the role of the political parties. Yet that would be an outdated point of view in a modern, pluralist democracy. As Robert McKenzie pointed out long ago, 'the voters undertake to do far more than select their elected representatives; they also insist on their right to advise, cajole and warn them regarding the policies which they should adopt and they do this for the most part through the pressure group system.'[7]

They have acted as extensions or agents of Government. This is a role which has grown in importance whenever the tendency towards corporatism has grown in British society.[8] For example, the British Medical Association had a number of expert and advisory functions under the auspices of the 1946 National Health Service Act. The National Farmers' Union had a number of analogous functions under the auspices of the 1947 and 1957 Agriculture Acts. The Law Society is responsible for administering the system of state-financed legal aid. Perhaps the most familiar example of corporatism, especially under Labour Governments during the 1960s and 1970s, has been the prominent role played by the TUC and the CBI, both as economic interest groups and as virtually obligatory partners with Government in nearly all matters to do with the management of the economy and often much else as well. In addition, there are occasions when the Government makes grants to a pressure group so that it can provide a particular service. For example, Relate, the national marriage guidance organisation, has been the recipient of grants for the advice centres it runs.

They have acted occasionally as substitutes for or outright opponents of Government itself. This is a rare occurrence in British politics and it is not a role which even the most powerful groups are keen to play, since it can so easily engender a serious and lasting public backlash. If it happens, it is usually the result of either a breakdown of Government authority in certain areas of policy or the deliberate implementation of some form of syndicalism.[9] To some extent the former conditions applied in certain circumstances during the serious trade union disruption of essential public services which took place during the 'Winter of Discontent' in 1979. The latter conditions applied on a local scale during the time of the Meriden Co-operative in the late 1970s, when the workers themselves took over and ran their own motorcycle factory for a while until market forces and Japanese competition got the better of them.

They act as publicists and purveyors of information in order to promote a particular point of view or defend a particular standpoint. For example, during the 1980s the Campaign for Nuclear Disarmament was very active in the cause of unilateral nuclear disarmament. It sought to do this by organising public meetings, mass demonstrations and other carefully planned media events, as well as by producing a wide range of campaign material and propaganda. Equally, environmental groups, such as Friends of the Earth or Greenpeace, have used similar techniques in their successful campaigns for environmental improvement, for example the use of returnable bottles, the preservation of rare animal species or the abandonment of the fast-breeder reactor programme in Britain. The Child Poverty Action Group is an unabashed user of publicity as a battering ram for change. As one of its early directors made clear, 'our main aim is to shift Government, not to chat with civil servants – coverage in the media is our strategy.'[10] Equally, from its formation in 1966, the housing group Shelter showed itself to be a most effective publicist of the dreadful housing conditions in which many millions lived and the need for substantial improvement. More recently animal welfare groups such as Compassion in World Farming, have used publicity to considerable advantage in their campaign against the live animal export trade.

In nearly all cases the most successful techniques involve staging media events to attract publicity and then further steps to capitalise on the public attention thus gained by advancing persuasive arguments in suitable supporting material. The publicity techniques may involve an unlikely combination of endorsement by show-business personalities and follow-up with detailed and well-researched arguments. An example would be Bob Geldof and the Live

Eight concerts held in 2005 in ten cities, including London, Philadelphia, Paris, Berlin, Johannesburg, Rome and Moscow, that were designed to put pressure on the G8 leaders to tackle global poverty. Sometimes those concerned even go so far as to undertake difficult or dangerous stunts in order to capture media attention; for example, the Greenpeace campaigns to save whales and seals by sailing small boats into the hunting areas in order to disrupt the activities to which they objected and their occupation of the Brent Spar oil-storage installation in 1995 as part of a campaign to prevent it being dumped in the Atlantic. The media coverage achieved for campaigns of this kind is not an end in itself, but rather a means of getting such issues onto the political agenda and of putting pressure on politicians and others to take appropriate action.

6.4 organisation and power

Pressure groups in Britain are organised in almost as many ways as there are different groups. The pattern of organisation which evolves and the degree of power which can be exerted depend on a number of different factors:

nature and scope of membership

When the interests of the membership are material and immediate, a group will usually reflect them and concentrate most of its resources on defending them by whatever means are available. For example, for many years until the coal dispute of 1984–85, the National Union of Mineworkers (NUM) proved its ability to exploit both the strength of its organisation and the concentration of its interest as a way of gaining substantial material rewards for its members. The result was that the miners managed to stay consistently at or near the top of the industrial earnings league and all Governments treated them with wary respect. On the other hand, when the interests of the membership are diffuse and varied, it is usually more difficult for a group to exert direct and immediate influence on behalf of its members. For example, the Consumers' Association, which has some 503,475 subscribing members, has been more successful in raising the profile of consumer interests and consumer rights in general than in defending the position of individual consumers. Nevertheless, the high-quality and well -publicised research done by organisations of this kind can have a considerable impact on firms and on Government.

The power of a group also depends to a considerable extent on both the coverage and the cohesion of its membership. If a group has a clear identity and purpose and if it manages to attract into its membership a high proportion of those eligible to join, it can be said to have a good coverage and is likely to be effective in defence of its members' interests. On the other hand, if a group seeks to represent a wide range of interests, it is likely to have little natural cohesion and be less effective in defence of its members' interests.

loyalty of the rank and file

The degree of loyalty shown by the rank and file towards their leaders and spokesmen is another aspect of the relative power or weakness of any pressure group. Certainly such loyalty cannot be taken for granted in an age of greatly diminished deference. However, in most circumstances, the leaders of a pressure group have more scope for initiative if they are in the job for life and not subject to periodic recall or re-election, an advantage traditionally enjoyed by several prominent trade union leaders. It is also the case that the leadership enjoys more latitude if the material interests of the rank and file are not directly threatened by any policy initiatives.

When the activities of pressure group leaders seem likely to prejudice the interests of the ordinary members, the rank and file are quite likely to reject the lead which is given. For example, Arthur Scargill, as President of the NUM, was opposed by a majority of his own members when he was precipitate in seeking their endorsement for a political campaign of industrial action against the 1979–83 Conservative Government and succeeded only in splitting his union. In 1979 the NUM, with a membership of 372,122, was widely regarded as providing the 'shock troops' of the Labour movement. However, by 2005 it could claim only 3042 members, a fall of 99.2 per cent. Although much of this decline has been due to broader factors, such as technological changes in the fuel economy and the competitiveness of the British coal industry, it is undoubtedly the case that the style and policies of Arthur Scargill contributed to the union's downfall in the 1980s.

political leverage

The power of pressure groups also depends on the degree of political leverage which they can exert. If a group is in a position to exert significant leverage, it can be truly formidable. Such leverage can take the form of an ability to deny to the rest of society the provision of goods or services which the community cannot easily do without and which others are not able immediately to supply. For example, power station workers or air traffic controllers can be in such a position, as can computer operators in the Civil Service or safety workers in the water industry. Currency speculators and company treasurers can also wield financial power in the money markets which amounts to a form of highly effective political leverage. In 1989 the brewing industry showed its ability to sway the then Conservative Government, partly through its ability to exploit a clever and hard-hitting advertising campaign, partly through an adroit use of political contacts, and partly because many Conservative backbenchers realised the significant part it played in providing financial support for the party.[11]

Political leverage on its own may not be sufficient for the attainment of a pressure group's objectives without the support of other attributes of group power, such as Civil Service contacts, the ability to use the media effectively and financial clout. Yet it can achieve a great deal in a complex, modern society in which such groups can sometimes be in a position to hold the rest of the community to ransom. Only very rarely does it consist in the ability to create completely new balances of power in society which allow one particular group or interest to coerce the rest. On such occasions the Government of the day may have to use the full powers of the modern state – for instance, a massive police presence or even military units – in order to counter one brand of ruthlessness with another. No system of democratic Government can afford to tolerate, still less allow itself to be defeated by, groups using violence or coercion – such as some elements within the animal rights lobby.

Certainly some groups have used campaigns of civil disobedience as a way to achieve their aims. The suffragettes were an early example. More recently there has been:

- The wide-scale campaign for the non-payment of the Poll Tax
- The high-profile activity engaged in by some of those from the Fathers For Justice campaign
- The campaigns waged by animal rights activists against Oxford University in an attempt to stop the expansion of its vivisection capabilities
- The activity of DAN (Disabled People's Direct Action Network) which has fought hard in recent years to change the nature of disability activism – such as lying on the pavement outside Downing Street in pools of blood-red paint.

Other groups have become involved in direct action which has involved violence. Examples of this would include:

- The picket-line violence at Grunwick in 1977, at Warrington in 1983, at Wapping in 1987 and during the miners' strike in 1984–85
- The inner city riots of the early 1980s, the Poll Tax riot in Trafalgar Square in 1990 and the riot against the Criminal Justice and Public Order Bill in 1994
- The direct action campaigns against the Newbury bypass, the Exeter–Honiton A30 extension scheme, the Twyford Down cutting and the Manchester Airport extension in the mid-to-late 1990s
- The activities of some animal rights activists protesting against Huntingdon Life Sciences in 2004 and 2005, including firebomb and ammonia attacks on staff
- The damage done by those protesting against genetically modified crops in 2004 and 2005.

It is perhaps worth noting that in most cases the use of civil disobedience is effective in advancing the interests of the groups concerned, whereas degeneration into violence is invariably counterproductive and alienates general public opinion.

Civil Service contacts

The strength and frequency of contacts with the Civil Service is another aspect of the power and influence of pressure groups. As J.J. Richardson and

A.G. Jordan have pointed out, 'it is the relationships involved in committees, the policy community of Departments and groups, the practices of co-option and the consensual state which account better for policy outcomes than examinations of party stances, Manifestos or Parliamentary influence'.[12] On the whole, established groups prefer to have a continuous, quiet influence on the process of government rather than an intermittent and noisy impact based on the use of media publicity and the staging of public demonstrations. Widely publicised campaigns are often a last resort for groups, which normally succeed in keeping in close touch with civil servants and the rest of the policy-making community. They use their reliable and frequent contacts with Whitehall and the expertise of their own professional staff to influence Ministerial decisions and the detailed content of legislation. In most cases resorting to widely publicised campaigns is almost an admission of failure.

A number of groups secure official representation on advisory committees established within the orbits of Whitehall Departments and in this way are able to influence and monitor detailed aspects of policy making. This gives them extra status and recognition in Whitehall, rights of access to Ministers when the need arises and opportunities for consultation and influence not available to others outside the charmed circle of customary consultative arrangements in central Government. Since 1997 New Labour 'modernisation' has provided extra opportunities for trusted and respected pressure groups to influence the policy and decision making process at formative stages – whether during the procedures of formal consultation or when Parliamentary committees and others are considering draft legislation.

publicity value

The publicity value of the causes espoused by different groups is another factor which influences the success or failure of such organisations. For example, in 1998 the Countryside Alliance with a well orchestrated and highly vociferous campaign of posters, protests and mass meetings raised the profile of a whole range of rural concerns, placing countryside issues firmly on the political agenda. Equally, in the early 1980s, the Campaign for Lead-Free Air (CLEAR) was able to make considerable headway towards achieving its goal as a result of the publicity arising first from the leaking of a letter from the Government's Chief Medical Officer to the effect that lead in petrol was permanently reducing the IQ of many children, and then from the report of the Royal Commission on Environmental Pollution which called for the banning of lead in petrol, embarrassing Ministers into action.

On the other hand, the publicity secured by the Campaign for Nuclear Disarmament in the early 1980s had little effect on public policy at the time, other than to harden the resolve of the then Conservative Government to oppose such a policy. In general, the publicity gained by a group for its cause depends on the spirit of the times as much as its technical skill in using the media to its own advantage.

financial power

The mere possession of wealth and financial power by pressure groups cannot buy success in British politics, although it obviously helps to pay the bills and to finance the necessary publicity. Not even the most lavishly funded campaigns achieve their objectives simply because they can out-spend their opponents – as the billionaire Sir James Goldsmith found in 1997 when he spent £20 million but failed in his efforts to secure a referendum on Britain's future in the European Union. This reflects the way in which the British party system can shield politicians from the full force of group pressures and it is also a tribute to the skills of the British Civil Service in protecting Ministers.

In Britain there have been few occasions when the spending of large sums of money has bought success for a pressure group – unlike in the United States where 'money talks' via Political Action Committees and other devices designed to influence national politicians. For example, there is no conclusive evidence that the expensive 'Mr Cube' campaign of Tate & Lyle and other sugar producers against the proposed nationalisation of the sugar refining industry in the late 1940s had a decisive influence on the subsequent decision of the Labour Government not to proceed with such a policy. Similarly, there is no conclusive evidence that the fact that the 'Keep Britain In' campaign outspent the 'National Referendum Campaign' (those campaigning for British withdrawal) by ten-to-one had a decisive effect on the way in which the British people voted in the 1975 Referendum on Britain's membership of the European Community. However, the large donations from Bernie Ecclestone and other business people to Labour Party funds since 1997 caused many people to question whether this traditional position still obtained.[13]

influence upon voting

As for the power of pressure groups to deliver votes at elections, British history has shown that the pull of party consistently triumphs over the pull of groups. Ever since the emergence of recognisably modern political parties during the last quarter of the nineteenth century, the nature of the Westminster first-past-the-post electoral system and the influence of strong party discipline has left all groups with a poor chance of striking effective political bargains with individual Members of Parliament or Parliamentary candidates. Yet certain influential groups can exercise considerable influence on the parties, especially when the latter are in Opposition and unshielded by cautious official advice.

Unlike the situation in the United States, individual politicians in Britain do not have to construct precarious platforms of electoral support by seeking to appeal directly to powerful interest or cause groups in their constituencies. If their party has been in office, they tend to concentrate on presenting its record in the most favourable light. If their party has been in Opposition, they tend to demonstrate how bad things have been under the stewardship of their opponents and how they could do much better if given the chance. Yet this is not to say that it is sensible or prudent for politicians to ignore pressure of groups which are active or influential in their own constituencies.

Of course, there remains the special case of trade-union influence on the Labour Party.[14] This stems from the fact that the creation of the Labour Party at the end of the nineteenth century was largely the work of the trade unions and ever since then trade-union influence within the wider movement was often significant and occasionally decisive. The connection has been one of the defining links in British politics, although the strength of the connection and the influence derived from it has waxed and waned in recent years.

6.5 channels of influence

There are many channels of influence open to pressure groups through which they can try to achieve their objectives. These channels relate very closely to the various institutional structures through which political decisions are taken and to the nature of the British political system itself. As a result, groups in Britain attempt to exert influence through five basic channels, namely:

- Directly on public opinion via use of the media and advertising
- Indirectly via the choice of candidates for public office
- Directly via financial contributions to party funds
- Frequently via pressure during the legislative process
- Continuously via expert and technical representations to civil servants.

Pressure groups attempt to influence public opinion through all the media of mass communication and all the techniques of advertising and public relations. The purpose of such pressure is either to persuade the public to act directly or to mobilise them politically and so achieve effective influence on Whitehall and Westminster – for example, the RSPCA campaign to persuade shoppers not to buy products from companies that did not meet the animal protection group's criteria for 'cruelty-free' animal testing or the organized anti-road-pricing online petition on the issue in 2007. Obtaining favourable publicity and gaining public sympathy may not be enough to ensure a satisfactory solution to the problem identified. For example, in the late 1960s the National Campaign for the Homeless (Shelter) produced publicity of considerable persuasive power which aroused widespread public concern for the homeless, but action by Government to eradicate the problems identified did not follow immediately. Indeed, official figures in December 2004 showed that the number of homeless households living in temporary accommodation had reached an all-time high.

Groups seek to exert influence on the selection of candidates for public office. The most obvious example in this respect is provided by 'constituency plan agreements' between trade unions and certain constituency Labour parties, whereby some trade union financial support goes towards constituency activities in return for which a trade union secures representation on the General Management Committee of a Constituency Labour Party. This was the system devised to replace direct trade- union sponsorship of Labour MPs, a practice which was discontinued in 1995. Some other groups encourage their members, if already involved in a political party, to participate in candidate selection in an attempt to ensure that candidates well disposed to their objectives are selected. Examples of this practice can be found in the groups on either side of the argument over blood sports and country pursuits. The effect, however, is usually only marginal, since it is such an indirect and uncertain method.

It should also be pointed out that some groups put forward their own candidates at elections. The most obvious case in point would be the 547 candidates standing for the Referendum Party – a single-issue party whose goal was to bring about a referendum on the issue of Britain's membership of the European Union – at the 1997 General Election. In 2001 and 2005 the group campaigning to keep Kidderminster Hospital open won and held the parliamentary constituency of Wyre Forrest. A number of groups, ranging from the 'Build Duddon and Morecambe Bridges' and the 'Croydon Pensioners Alliance' to the 'Removal of Tetramasts in Cornwall' and the 'Save Bristol North Baths Party', all fielded candidates in the 2005 General Election.

Groups make financial contributions to political parties in the hope that their money will buy some political influence. The most familiar example is provided by the open and well-established financial support by many trade unions to the Labour Party. Yet in more recent times greater media and public attention has been paid to the more opaque financial support from certain companies, entrepreneurs and commercial interests to the Conservative and Labour Parties. These donations have constituted a sizeable part of the party's national income – estimates vary, but suggest a figure of at least 50 per cent. The interesting question is whether and, if so, to what extent such financial support really succeeded in buying effective influence. It is worth noting, for example, that when in 1991 British Airways, a long-term contributor to the Conservative Party, announced that it would no longer do so because of the Government's alleged failure to defend the BA interest in international negotiations on air routes and landing slots at Heathrow, Ministers paid no obvious heed to such pressure. Equally, in 1998, when it was revealed that the head of Formula 1 motor racing, Bernie Ecclestone, had donated £1 million to the Labour Party allegedly to influence the Government's decision to grant an exemption for Formula 1 from a European tobacco advertising ban, although the allegations were strenuously denied, the money was nonetheless returned.[15]

Pressure groups seek to exert influence upon legislation during its passage through both Houses of Parliament. They attempt to influence MPs and Peers in a variety of ways. They may, for example, deluge Members of either House with letters from the public urging their point of view or arrange for a mass lobby of Parliament which entails large numbers of people seeking to present their views directly to MPs and Peers at Westminster. They can prepare detailed briefs for Parliamentary debates, a tactic used to good effect, for example, by the Haemophilia Society in 1987 when it persuaded a large number of MPs to press the Government to provide special financial help to the 1200 haemophiliacs who had become HIV positive as a result of receiving contaminated blood and plasma in the course of NHS treatment. Many groups maintain close contacts with individual MPs and Peers, either directly or through the growing band of professional lobbyists. This practice can both advance the interests of the groups concerned and provide useful information and advice for Members of both Houses of Parliament, especially those in Opposition, who do not normally have the benefit of much reputable advice.[16]

Groups frequently make expert and technical representations to civil servants and so contribute influentially to the policy and decision making process. As the tasks of modern Government have become more technical and complex, the necessity for close liaison between the Whitehall machine and a myriad of pressure groups has increased. The resulting relationship is a two-way affair: pressure groups seek information on decisions which may affect their areas of interest and try to ensure advantageous decisions, while civil servants on behalf of their political masters seek data and expert advice as well as the cooperation of groups in the implementation of policy. Since 1997 under Labour these contacts have become more systematic in the context of regular consultations with influential stakeholders, who are systematically consulted on proposed legislation and potential regulations.

All these different channels of influence for pressure groups are not, of course, mutually exclusive. Very often a group will be engaged, for example, in discussions with a Government Department about a particular legislative proposal, while at the same time trying to influence MPs and Peers in a variety of different ways.

6.6 involvement in policy and decision making

Since the British political system is pluralist, liberal and democratic, it affords many opportunities for the involvement of pressure groups in the policy and decision-making process.[17] Indeed, it is impossible fully to describe political activity in Whitehall and Westminster without giving an account of the significant part played by pressure groups. They have become desirable participants in the process of official consultation and as such they contribute to the achievement of public consent for the acts of Government. Their involvement in the policy and decision-making process is shown diagrammatically in Figure 6.1.

policy germination

At the initial stage of policy germination the main role of pressure groups is to identify problems and to get issues onto the political agenda. For example, the Institute of Economic Affairs can claim much of the credit for getting the policy of privatisation onto the political agenda of the Conservative Government in the 1980s while the group Migration Watch UK, established in 2001, undoubtedly helped to get the issue of immigration on the mainstream political agenda.

In playing their part at this early stage of the policy and decision-making process, pressure groups depend very heavily on their ability to excite the interest of the media. Without such media assistance many of the campaigns

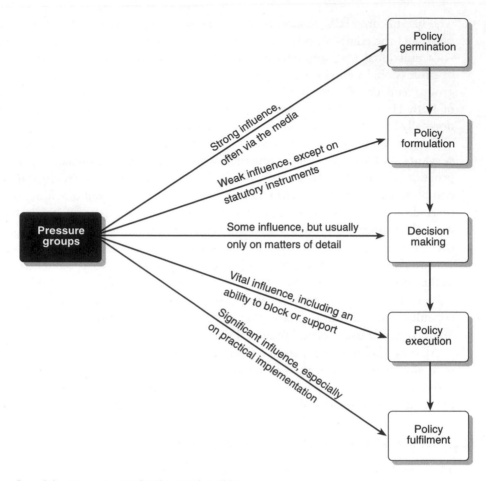

Strong influence, often via the media

Weak influence, except on statutory instruments

Some influence, but usually only on matters of detail

Vital influence, including an ability to block or support

Significant influence, especially on practical implementation

Pressure groups

Policy germination

Policy formulation

Decision making

Policy execution

Policy fulfilment

figure **6.1** **pressure group involvement in politics**

would never get off the ground at all. For example, in the 1980s and 1990s, Friends of the Earth, Greenpeace and other environmental pressure groups had a significant influence on the pace and direction of various 'green' initiatives, not only at national level but also at the European and wider international levels as well.

Pressure groups also need to persuade powerful politicians of the good sense and timeliness of their cause. For example, the proponents of employee share ownership, such as Job Ownership Ltd, worked hard and continuously during the 1980s and early 1990s to persuade the Conservative Government to given further legislative backing and tax relief to their cause.

The introduction in 1997 of a Pre-Budget Report setting out areas for consultation has provided groups with a greater opportunity to influence the Government's income and expenditure plans than ever before. In 1998 the Chancellor, Gordon Brown, spelled out in advance the areas in which he sought input from pressure groups and members of the public – such as tax and benefit reform, measures to promote investment and the closing of tax loopholes – and he received some 1500 submissions from the TUC, CBI, AA, RAC, the Brewers and Licensed Retailers Association, the Royal Society for Protection of Birds and the Engineering Employers' Federation and many others.

When pressure groups wish to get issues onto the political agenda, the most effective approach is usually to persuade officials in the relevant Whitehall Department of the importance of their particular problem or interest and then to follow up with expert and detailed advice on how it might be tackled in ways which would be congruent with the principles of the Government of the day.

The other principal way of achieving such an objective is for a group to get on a common wavelength with leading figures in the governing party and then provide them with new ideas which can be presented as a logical development of their existing policies. For example, the Institute for Economic Affairs and the Centre for Policy Studies managed to play the role of intellectual pathfinders for the free- market policies of the Conservatives in the 1980s and the Institute for Public Policy Research was influential upon the development of New Labour's policies in the 1990s.

policy formulation

Pressure groups can also have influence at the stage of policy formulation. When a political party is in Opposition, policy formulation is mainly the work of its leading personalities, who are assisted by officials from the party organisation. When a party is in Government, it is mainly the work of civil servants and Special Advisers in the Departments concerned working under the leadership and guidance of senior Ministers. Yet in each case those who formulate policy may well consult pressure groups, provided the latter can be trusted to preserve the necessary confidentiality and are able to supply timely advice or information.

The role of groups can be especially significant when policy needs to be turned into new legislation. For example, the Constitution Unit had a very real influence on the way in which the constitutional reform agenda of the 1997 Labour Government was implemented. More generally, the systematic consultation of stakeholders in a given policy area is now a standard part of the policy-making process for the Labour Government.

decision making

In a strict sense pressure groups have no direct involvement at the decision-making stage of the policy process, since this is essentially a matter for elected politicians. Yet even such a clear-cut statement does not fully reflect the various ways in which political decisions are actually taken. For example, many Ministerial decisions are taken by civil servants acting in the name of Ministers, notably in the detailed and complex area of delegated legislation. Groups with the necessary expertise and access to officials can have an influential role in this aspect of decision making. Examples could be found in the close and frequent contacts between the Law Society and the Department for Constitutional Affairs of the Local Authority Associations and the Department for Communities and Local

Government. However, the influence of all groups can vary over time, depending upon the priority attached to consultation taken by the Government of the day.

Since the introduction of new legislation is also a form of decision making, pressure groups can play an influential part at this stage of the process as well. For example, the Committee of Vice-Chancellors and Principals (now Universities UK) waged an effective and successful campaign in 1993–94 to persuade Ministers at the Department for Education to modify their legislative proposals for the reform of student unions. Similarly, the Finance Bills which pass through the House of Commons every year and which contain legislative changes of considerable importance can be influenced in matters of detail by pressure groups with interests to defend or causes to advance. For example, the Institute of Chartered Accountants and other professional bodies were instrumental in persuading Treasury Ministers to drop a clause from the 1994 Finance Bill concerning Inland Revenue rights of access to confidential papers in the possession of accountants and other financial advisers, pending further detailed consultations with the interested bodies concerned to refine and improve the measure. More recent examples would include the role played by think tanks such as the Institute for Public Policy Research in persuading the Number 10 Policy Unit and the Treasury of the attractions of Public–Private Partnerships, as well as the role played by Liberty – the human rights and civil liberties organization – in persuading the House of Lords to resist aspects of the Government's anti-terrorist legislation.

policy execution

The real test of effective power for all modern Governments is how well they manage to execute and deliver their policies. Ministerial decisions or Acts of Parliament are not worth very much if they cannot be successfully put into practice. In this the role of pressure groups can be vital, since their active cooperation or passive acquiescence is often a condition of the satisfactory execution of policy. For example, in 2005 and 2006 the critical response of the Association of Chief Police Officers to the Government's proposals to reorganise the 43 local forces in England and Wales forced the Government to back down. Similar examples could be given of the Prison Officers' Association in relation to offender management or the BMA and the Royal Colleges in relation to NHS reform.

Acquiescence in Government policy by the relevant practitioners is an important condition for successful policy execution. One of the main tasks of Ministers is to assess the limits of what is 'politically possible' in a given situation at a given time. In making such assessments, the cooperation of the relevant interest groups is a distinct advantage and their non-cooperation a serious liability in the execution and implementation of policy.

policy fulfilment

A similar point can be made about the final stage of policy fulfilment. Few policies can be brought to fruition without the active cooperation or at least the passive acquiescence of the groups most directly affected. Ministers and civil servants commit serious mistakes if they are ever tempted to equate the political process solely with what happens in Whitehall and Westminster. In modern political conditions there are many external factors which can influence the success or failure of a given policy. For example, the world-wide commodity price explosion of 1972–73 damaged the counter-inflation policies of the 1970–74 Conservative Government. Similarly, in September 1992 the Conservative Government proved unable to sustain its monetary policy in the face of a tidal wave of sterling being sold on the foreign exchanges, and was forced to suspend British membership of the Exchange Rate Mechanism of the European Monetary System by the power of market forces. Equally, the agenda and focus of the Labour Government of Tony Blair was undoubtedly altered following the terrorist attack on the twin towers on 11 September 2001.

Such examples extend the scope of the present discussion beyond the sphere of national politics. Yet it is undeniable that political issues have to be considered in a much wider context if we are to take full account of all the limitations on the autonomy of national Governments.

Politicians in office may sometimes believe that they are the undisputed masters of the political scene. Yet they would do well to remember that in modern political conditions they need the cooperation of interest groups and the support of other external influences if they are to have a reasonable chance of political success.

6.7 conclusion

The effectiveness of a pressure group does not depend only on its size, its privileged contacts or its financial resources. It depends also on a wide variety of internal and external factors. Internal factors include unity of purpose, leadership quality and organisational competence. External factors include the nature of the political environment, the strength of competing groups and the attitudes of the media and the general public. Politicians try to take all such factors into account when deciding the weight and significance to be accorded to particular groups.

In Britain involvement in pressure groups, particularly cause groups, has burgeoned in the past 35 years, not least because of increasing public disillusion with established political parties. As active participation in party politics has continued its long-term decline, this has been matched by an impressive growth in pressure group participation. For example, Friends of the Earth increased its membership from 1000 in 1971 to 101,802 in 2005, while the membership – over 3 million – of the National Trust (not primarily a pressure group but an organization that can at times act as one) is more than ten times larger than either the Labour or the Conservative parties. In these circumstances there are reasons for regarding the activities of pressure groups as broadly beneficial and other reasons for regarding them as rather harmful to the British political system.

On the positive side, the following points can be made about pressure groups:

- They can provide the Government of the day with expert information and advice which would not necessarily be available from other sources
- They can provide frameworks for public participation in the political process between General Elections, especially for those who are unwilling or unable to channel their energies through one or other of the political parties
- They help to focus public attention on issues which may not be ripe for decision, but which need nevertheless to be placed on the political agenda
- They can provide a form of institutional ratification and public consent for the actions of Government which goes beyond Parliamentary approval.

On the negative side, the following points can be made:

- They tend to give too much weight in the political process to the concurrent majority – that is, the various sectional groups in Britain's pluralist society – to the detriment of the Parliamentary majority, that is, the part of the electorate which voted for the winning party at the preceding General Election
- They can become accomplices in a system of government which is based on exclusive, metropolitan circles of policy and decision making and which may exclude others with a legitimate interest in the outcome
- They can reinforce tendencies towards corporatism which can be at odds with British Parliamentary democracy
- Their demands can add greatly not just to the volume of work but also to the difficulty of achieving decisions in the general interest.

Pressure groups undoubtedly inject considerable vitality into contemporary politics, provide their members with access to and influence on the political system, and the general public with information, advice and ideas which might not be forthcoming from the political parties. Without the activities of pressure groups, aided and abetted by the media, the political process would be heavily stacked in favour of the Government of the day and this would not be good for the health of British democracy.

In conclusion, it is necessary to assess the role of pressure groups in parallel with an assessment of the political parties. Both categories of institution play vital roles of mediation and representation which contribute to the working of the political system. Whereas pressure groups are not democratically accountable in the way that political parties have to be, they do share common aspirations to reflect and defend the views and interests of their members. In this way they bring a measure of public consent to the working of the political process and help to endow it with a measure of legitimacy which might otherwise be absent. On the other hand, they have been seen by some as 'serpents' which can prevent political decisions being taken in the general public interest. Either way, they are among the most significant sources of power, pressure and opinion in the British political system.

1   What are the main functions of pressure groups in British politics?
2   Which factors make some pressure groups more powerful than others?
3   At what stages in the political process do pressure groups exert their most effective influence?

the media

In considering the media in Britain, we are concerned with more than neutral channels of communication. We are examining some of the most influential participants in the political system, even though they have no formally recognised place in British constitutional arrangements. We live in a mass-media age which is characterised by the widespread use and abuse of the various channels of communication for a broad range of political and other purposes. Politicians need the media more than ever and seek every opportunity to get their messages across to the public. Equally, those who own or work for the media are not shy to exert a real influence on the political process in Britain and many other democratic countries.

7.1 the current situation

The current situation in all parts of the media is particularly dynamic and seemingly always in a state of flux. The following account can, therefore, only provide a snapshot of the situation taken at a particular time and the information provided should be seen in that light. In the press, some publications come and go, some change their ownership, and nearly all have to adapt or modify what they offer in response to technological change or market pressures. The trend towards multimedia companies under multinational ownership has been growing with the result that it is almost a misnomer to refer any longer to 'the British media'. In the electronic media, national boundaries and jurisdictions mean less and less and the emergence of huge multinational media corporations with a global reach, such as News Corporation, Worldcom, Bertelsmann, the BBC, CNN and Al Jazeera, means that people in Britain and elsewhere are living in what Marshall McLuhan described many years ago as 'a global village' connected by bewildering networks of media communications including nowadays the internet, many intranets and the World Wide Web. The effects of these technological developments upon politics and culture in Britain and other countries have yet to be fully understood.

The current situation in the British press is that there are five national daily newspapers of quality, nine of a populist variety, five Sunday national newspapers of quality, and seven of a populist variety. There is only one significant London-wide newspaper, the *Evening Standard*, but there are a number of viable 'free newspapers' financed from the proceeds of advertising – for example, *The Metro* – and some local newspapers in other parts of the country which are commercially viable – for example, the *Western Morning News*, the *Yorkshire Post*, the *Manchester Evening News*, and the *Glasgow Herald*.

The Sunday national newspapers are fewer in number than the national dailies, but in some cases their circulation is more substantial because people are more inclined to buy a newspaper when they have more time to read it. The five broadsheet Sunday newspapers have pretensions to quality, whereas the seven tabloid Sundays pride themselves on being hard hitting and sensational in their treatment of any story. They tend to follow leads given earlier in the week by their daily counterparts, but they also try to achieve lurid scoops of their own which usually set out to embarrass celebrities in the sporting, entertainment or political worlds. The political influence of all parts of the national press is considerable, because many politicians go in fear of being exposed or opposed by any of the mass-circulation newspapers. However, some consolation can be derived from the fact that with their different political standpoints national newspapers often cancel each other out on any salient political issue.

There are a number of weekly journals which give prominence to political issues – for example, the *Economist*, the *Spectator*, and the *New Statesman*. There are also a number of more academic or intellectual periodicals which specialise in political issues, such as *Prospect*, the *Political Quarterly*, and *Parliamentary Affairs*. Mention should also be made of the Communist daily newspaper, the *Morning Star*, satirical and anti-Establishment periodicals, such as *Private Eye*, and the publications of the political fringe, such as *Militant* and *Socialist Worker* on the far Left and *Spearhead* on the far Right. There is, therefore, a wide variety of political points of view expressed in the British press, although it is worth noting that some of the most widely read publications are not really political at all – for example, the *Radio Times*, *Woman's Own* and *Hello Magazine*.

Until the 1980s a common denominator of nearly all the British national press was the difficulty of making a profit. This was largely due to old-fashioned management practices and chronic labour relations and it brought in its wake increasing concentration of ownership as titles were forced to amalgamate or close. When the national newspapers were based in Fleet Street in the centre of London, virtually every attempt by management to introduce new technology and ways of working was fiercely resisted by the powerful print unions. It was only after a new breed of much tougher newspaper owners had founded or bought some of the titles, such as Eddy Shah with *Today* and Rupert Murdoch with the *Sun*, that things began to change in a radical way. A number of bitter industrial disputes were fought between the traditional print unions and the new owners when the latter set out to break the trade-union stranglehold by moving their production facilities to lower-cost locations in the East End of London and by introducing new technology which enabled journalists to write and produce their own copy with only a minimum requirement for traditional printers' skills. These bitter struggles exemplified both the ingrained resistance to change which had characterised the industry in the past and the inevitability of such change once a determined employer, such as Rupert Murdoch, decided to break ranks with the traditional newspaper proprietors and bust the mutually destructive arrangements between employers and trade unions in the newspaper industry.

Since that time there has been a climate of fierce commercial competition in the newspaper market which has enabled those proprietors with the deepest purse, such as Rupert Murdoch, Richard Sullivan and the Berkeley brothers, to put greater competitive pressures on their weaker rivals. This has led to price wars, free offers and an increasingly strident and sensationalist tone in all the national newspapers – with the possible exceptions of *The Independent* and the *Financial Times* which have each tried to stay a little above the depths of the commercial struggle. Against this background it is not surprising that fewer than ten multinational companies own all the mass-circulation newspapers in Britain and that one tycoon – Rupert Murdoch – controls a huge multimedia empire worldwide and owns about one third of the British national press. A table showing the national newspapers with their ownership, political leanings and circulation figures is set out in Figure 7.1.

the electronic media

In *television* the situation is that there are a growing number of terrestrial channels (at least 16 at the time of writing) which seek to provide a national service covering the entire country. In the tax-funded broadcasting sector, there are four main BBC TV channels:

- BBC 1 is the basic foundation channel that has always sought a broad appeal to everyone in the country based upon the original Reithian purpose which was 'to educate, inform and entertain'
- BBC 2 is a more highbrow channel catering for more focused audience interests, but which also carries a lot of sport, music, and programmes dealing with science and nature
- BBC 3 offers a mixture of comedy, panel games, 'human interest' stories and films
- BBC 4 offers a varied mixture of current affairs, history, drama, comedy, animal programmes and repeats of popular TV series from earlier times.

There are also two children's channels (CBBC and CBeebies) and two specialist channels for those interested in politics and current affairs (BBC News 24 and BBC Parliament).

Title	Foundation date	Ownership Group/Chairman	Political leaning	Average daily circulation (April 2007)	Market share (%)
Quality dailies:					
The Times	1788	News International Newspapers (News Corporation – (Rupert Murdoch)	Right wing Euro-Sceptic	629,157	5.7
The Guardian	1821	Guardian Newspapers Ltd	New Labour	370,934	3.4
Daily Telegraph	1855	Telegraph Media Group Ltd (Press Holdings Ltd – Aidan and Howard Barclay)	Conservative	898,817	8.2
Financial Times	1888	Financial Times Ltd (Pearson plc)	Business European	452,930	4.1
The Independent	1986	Independent Newspapers (UK) Ltd	Centre Left	249,536	2.2
Tabloid/Red-top Dailies:					
The Daily Mail	1896	Associated Newspapers Ltd (Daily Mail & General Trust plc – Viscount Rothermere)	Thatcherite Conservative	2,300,420	20.9
Daily Express	1900	Express Newspapers (Northern & Shell Group – Richard Desmond)	Thatcherite Conservative	760,086	6.9
Daily Mirror	1903	Trinity Mirror plc	Labour	1,537,143	13.9
The Sun	1969	News International Newspapers (News Corporation Ltd – Rupert Murdoch)	Chauvinist Populist	3,047,527	27.7
Daily Star	1978	Express Newspapers (Northern & Shell Group – Richard Desmond)	Thatcherite Conservative	770,313	7.0
Broadsheet Sundays:					
The Observer	1791	Guardian Newspapers Ltd	Centre Left	463,128	4.2
The Sunday Times	1822	News International Newspapers (News Corporation Ltd – Rupert Murdoch)	Radical Conservative Republican	1,231,153	11.1
The Sunday Telegraph	1961	Telegraph Media Group Ltd. (Press Holdings Ltd – Aidan and Howard Barclay)	Conservative Euro-Sceptic	666,905	6.0
Independent on Sunday	1990	Independent Newspapers (UK) Ltd	Centre Left	244,809	2.2
Tabloid/Red-top Sundays:					
News of the World	1843	News International Newspapers (News Corporation Ltd – Rupert Murdoch)	Chauvinist Populist	3,282,263	29.6
The People	1881	Trinity Mirror plc	Labour	721,667	6.5
Sunday Express	1918	Express Newspapers (Northern & Shell Group – Richard Desmond)	Thatcherite Conservative	739,298	6.7
Sunday Mirror	1963	Trinity Mirror plc	Labour	1,463,970	13.93
The Mail on Sunday	1982	Associated Newspapers Ltd (Daily Mail & General Trust plc – Viscount Rothermere)	Thatcherite Conservative	2,285,632	15.50

source of circulation figures: The Audit Bureau of Circulatons Ltd..

figure **7.1** **main national newspapers in Britain**

In the commercially funded ('independent') broadcasting sector, there are four main ITV channels financed by sponsorship and advertising:

- ITV 1 is the basic 'independent' channel which since the early 1950s has sought to match the breadth and the universal character of BBC 1
- ITV 2 specialises in soap operas, chat shows, popular films and other forms of popular entertainment
- ITV 3 focuses upon popular drama, more soap operas, popular series, films and game shows
- ITV 4 focuses upon science fiction, chat shows, American drama imports, some 'reality TV' and comedy programmes.

In addition, *Channel Four*, *More 4* and *More 4+1* offer a wide variety of programmes ranging from cult American cartoons and other US imports to chat shows, game shows and property programmes, and from unusual documentaries to a regular news programme which attracts the attention of up-market viewers; while channel Five specialises in old movies, reality TV shows and late night sport.

The BBC still makes and broadcasts much of its own material within a vertically integrated broadcasting organisation which employs thousands of journalists, technicians and programme makers. However, as the market outlets for broadcast material expand, this situation is changing and more of the material is provided under contract by independent programme makers. The BBC is still largely financed from the proceeds of an annual licence fee which is levied by law on all who own a television (set at £131.50 for 2006–07; increasing to £151.50 by 2012). The question for the politicians – and the BBC – is can this form of funding survive when digital, cable, satellite and other forms of 'narrowcasting' massively replace the traditional technology of broadcasting.

In contrast, independent (commercial) television is financed by the proceeds of sponsorship and advertising which is carried during and between its programmes. Despite having 50 per cent of all advertising revenue, ITV has been losing market share to other channels, particularly cable and satellite stations. In addition its financial position was further weakened by the collapse of its ITV Digital venture. The response was merger – for example of the Carlton Communications Group and Grenada – in an attempt to save at least £50m a year through avoiding duplication.

The broadcast output of ITV is produced by 15 regional programme companies, each with an exclusive franchise for a geographical part of the country for an agreed contractual period (typically ten years). News is gathered for the commercial TV broadcasters by *Independent Television News* (ITN), the world's largest independent news organisation. It was founded in 1955 by the independent production companies, but it is now owned by four corporate shareholders – ITV plc, Daily Mail & General Trust, Reuters and United Business Media – and produces a wide range of news and factual programme material for television, radio and a variety of other media customers around the world.

In addition, British Sky Broadcasting (BSkyB) owns and operates 11 channels, including Sky One, Sky News, Sky Travel, the Sky Sports channels and the Sky Movies channels and is the operator of the UK's largest digital television platform, Sky digital, cumulatively offering almost 400 channels providing a choice of films, news, entertainment and sports channels and interactive services (for example allowing subscribers to send emails, shop on screen, play games, select their own camera angles, gamble and manage their finances all via their television).

The BBC is run by a Director General and a senior management team who are answerable to an independent Trust. The BBC Trust consists of a Chairman, ViceChairman and ten members, appointed by the Government of the day. It was an arrangement which developed as a result of the fallout from the report of the Hutton Inquiry[1] and came into being at the beginning of 2007. The purpose and role of the Trust is to work on behalf of licence fee payers, ensuring the BBC provides high quality output and good value for all UK citizens, and to protect itsindependence.

By contrast, the management of independent television companies is responsive to a range of commercial pressures in the market place, such as advertisers, sponsors and competing multimedia companies, and subject to arm's length regulation by the Office of Communications (Ofcom).

Ofcom was established under the Communications Act 2003 as the regulator for the UK communications industries with responsibilities across television, radio, telecommunications and wireless communications services. It has taken over the responsibilities of all other regulators in this sector of the economy with the exception of the BBC Trust. The specific duties of Ofcom fall into six areas:

- Ensuring the optimal use of the electromagnetic spectrum
- Ensuring that a wide range of electronic communications services is available throughout the UK
- Ensuring a wide range of TV and radio services of high quality and wide appeal
- Maintaining plurality in the provision of broadcasting
- Providing adequate protection for audiences against offensive or harmful material
- Providing adequate protection for audiences against unfairness or the infringement of privacy.

As was pointed out in an Ofcom report analysing the overall communications market, consumers are beginning to take control of communications and gaining greater access to improved on-demand, interactive and multichannel services.[2] Platform convergence and fierce competition between service providers means that there are now over 350 TV channels available to UK audiences with the fastest growth coming in digital TV and broadband telephony channels. All four main UK broadcasters have plans for further platform diversification with new digital channels and more use of interactive broadband. Among the satellite companies, BSkyB and Freeview have been the most successful in increasing market share, while cable TV providers, such as Telewest, have experienced less dramatic growth. The growth of digital terrestrial TV to about 6 million subscribers has been significant, but its coverage is likely to remain at about 75 per cent of the potential market until analogue TV is withdrawn in 2010. Its market prospects are also limited somewhat compared to cable and satellite platforms by the lesser degree of interactivity which it can offer to subscribers.

In tax-financed *national radio*, the BBC has eleven national channels. *Radio 1* provides mostly popular music and interactive talk shows and is aimed very much at a young audience. *Radio 2* provides middle-of-the-road music programmes and light entertainment of one kind or another. *Radio 3* caters for minority interests of a more highbrow nature (notably classical music, jazz, opera, drama and the arts) and traditionally has provided ball-by-ball commentaries on cricket Test matches. *Radio 4* (broadcast on two channels (FM and long wave) and branded as 'intelligent speech') provides most of the regular news, information and analysis of current affairs and the arts, as well as some high-quality drama and other popular entertainment. *Radio Five* is divided between Five Live (mostly sport) and Sports Extra (more sport). In addition there are 1Xtra BBC (new black music), BBC 6 Music, BBC 7 (comedy and drama), BBC Asian Network and the BBC World Service, which is designed to serve English language listeners around the world and broadcasts to more than 150 countries and many different audiences in more than 40 languages.

In tax-financed *local radio*, the BBC has 49 regional radio services, including two in Northern Ireland, five in Scotland, two in Wales, 38 in England and two in the Channel Islands. All these stations broadcast a mixture of news, popular music, chat shows, phone-in programmes, 'reality radio', magazine programmes and other material of local or even parochial interest. Many would argue that local radio has been a healthy development which has boosted a sense of community and local consciousness in parts of the country where previously these things were rather lacking.

Commercial radio has grown at a similar pace over the years. In 2004 there were only three national commercial stations – Classic FM, TalkSPORT and Virgin 1215 – but by the beginning of 2006 there were 277 independent local radio stations using analogue technology, one national digital multiplex carrying 8 radio services and 46 local digital multiplexes carrying some 300 local radio services. The broadcasting formula and the range of programme content are much the same in the commercial sector as in the tax-financed sector of national and local radio. The essential difference is to be found in the methods of financing with commercial radio (like commercial television) being financed from the proceeds of advertising and sponsorship carried on air between and during the programmes.

The problems of the press are both internal and external. For the purposes of this chapter, we shall be concerned mainly with the way in which the activity of the press and some of its working methods cause disquiet, even hostility, among politicians and public alike. Most people in Britain are glad that there is a free press; but, if there is a common thread of public criticism, it is invariably that the press is too 'free' in the sense that it may have become too powerful, too invasive and too destructive of peoples' privacy. This was an argument which came to the fore in 1997 in the aftermath of the death of Diana, Princess of Wales, and it has flared up from time to time ever since. On the other hand, newspaper proprietors, editors and journalists are usually more concerned to defend the rights and political independence of what has been termed the 'Fourth Estate' against what they are inclined to see as over-mighty Ministers and draconian laws. In this age-old struggle between the press and its prominent critics, there has been a good deal of hypocrisy and double standards on both sides. This has made it hard to get at the truth of the matter. Nevertheless the following section attempts to cover the salient issues and perennial problems.

influence and bias

All the national newspapers have political reporters and commentators who usually take distinctive lines on the political issues of the day. In the populist or tabloid newspapers, however, the main purposes are to attract and entertain the readers and maintain or boost the circulation, so that advertisers do not take their custom elsewhere and profits can be increased. The result of these commercial imperatives is that the coverage of political issues is usually not very extensive and certainly not very subtle. Instead the emphasis is put upon presenting news and opinion in stark, sensational and eye-catching ways with the use of dramatic photographs, screaming headlines and vivid language.[3]

As a general rule, the influence of the populist press seems to vary inversely with the knowledge or interest of its readers. For example, *The Daily Mirror*, which has consistently supported the Labour party at General Elections since the war, seems to have had a significant influence upon its readers only to the extent of persuading them to remain loyal to their traditional Labour allegiance. Equally, when *The Sun*, which had previously supported the Conservative party, gave strong and unequivocal support to New Labour in 1997, this appears to have influenced the voting behaviour of some of its readers at that election, although there were other factors which probably had a greater influence upon those who switched their votes away from the Conservatives to whichever party seemed best placed to dislodge incumbent Conservative MPs. On the psephological evidence of many elections it seems that newspapers can have a significant *reinforcing* effect upon some people's voting behaviour (especially at high profile by-elections), but are unlikely to change the voting behaviour of the public on any significant scale. This fits in with the cynical, but probably correct, theory that newspaper proprietors and editors are usually more interested in the commercial performance of their businesses than in direct political influence upon their readers. However, this is not to say that the print media – like their counterparts in the electronic media – do not relish the idea of influencing the fate of Ministers in Government, even if it is only a matter of demolishing the reputation of someone who, a little while before, they may have been busy building up.

The reality seems to be that the relatively frivolous nature of the populist press and the relative ignorance or lack of sustained interest in politics among their readers may increase the modest amount of political influence which they can wield if their editors decide to pull out all the stops in favour of a given political party or political cause or against a particular policy or leading politician. Yet in most instances most of the time few readers of the populist press pay much attention to the political line taken by the newspaper which they habitually read and the political influence of such organs seems to have been exaggerated by journalists and politicians alike. Furthermore, most academic research on this subject seems to suggest that newspapers have no measurable effect upon the way in which their readers vote.[4] Most readers of the populist press are demonstrably more interested in the sport, scandal and celebrity voyeurism which dominate so many pages. The editors and proprietors clearly know what sells newspapers and invariably allocate their column inches accordingly.

The quality national newspapers devote much more space to political reporting and commentary, and certainly they aspire to influence the political process in their chosen directions. However, their influence is often of a subtle and indirect kind in that they seek to persuade the politicians and civil servants involved in the policy- and decision-making process, together with the wide variety of interest groups and other opinion formers who are involved directly or indirectly, permanently or spasmodically, in British politics. Thus well known commentators, such as Andrew Rawnsley in *The Observer*, Peter Riddell in *The Times* or Jonathan Friedland in *The Guardian*, can have real influence from time to time upon the evolving political debate. Similarly, leading articles, political features and interviews, and even letters to the editor, in such newspapers are taken seriously and often carry weight in Whitehall and Westminster. Such contributions are rather like a house notice board for the political class and the policy community and they can have a significant political impact in view of the elitist and metropolitan character of much political opinion formation in Britain.

Many on the Left of British politics argued in the past that there was a persistent bias in the national press in favour of the Conservatives and a right-wing political agenda. It certainly used to be true in the 1980s that *The Daily Mirror* and the *Sunday Mirror* were normally the only national newspapers which consistently supported the Labour party as a matter of editorial policy. All the other national newspapers could be categorised essentially as either broadly in favour of the post-war consensus (mixed economy and active welfare state) – for example, *The Guardian* or *The Observer* – or in favour of the Conservative agenda of the 1980s (low taxes and a smaller state) – for example, the *Daily Express* or the *Sunday Telegraph*. However, these traditional alignments were undermined and extensively altered by the political shambles into which the Conservatives plunged in the 1990s and the success of Tony Blair and Gordon Brown in remodelling the Labour party into 'New Labour' at about the same time.

privacy and public interest

One of the strongest political and public concerns about the press in Britain is the way in which it is seen to invade people's privacy and make some lives miserable as a result of various forms of media intrusion – whether listening into mobile phone calls or accessing mobile phone records, telephone tapping, bugging with concealed or directional microphones, computer 'hacking', photography with telephoto lenses or intimidatory 'door-stepping' of people in the news. Although such concerns are often voiced by or on behalf of politicians, it is a problem which can afflict many other people as well, including members of the Royal Family, television personalities, sports stars and a whole range of other 'celebrities' some of whom seem to be famous simply for being famous. More worryingly, it can also afflict members of the general public from time to time – the so-called 'innocent by-standers' – if and when they are involved in some particularly newsworthy or ghoulish event, such as the death of a child, a massive win on the National Lottery, the loss of a loved one in a terrorist outrage or some other personal tragedy. In nearly every case self-righteous editors and investigative journalists seek to justify their actions by claiming that the public has 'a right to know' and that their journalistic intrusion is 'in the public interest'. Sometimes this may, indeed, be true; but more often than not the real explanation is that sensational journalism boosts the circulation of the newspapers which go in for it and hence increases both the future advertising revenue and the profits of the media corporations which stand to benefit.

There is no denying the fact that significant numbers of the public are 'interested' in such squalid journalism, since the circulation figures of the newspapers concerned invariably increase dramatically when they serialise a lurid political memoir or publish the transcript of sensational revelations about members of the Royal Family. Nor is there much doubt that many prominent figures in public life benefit – at least financially – from selling their stories to the press, in much the same way as less prominent people do when they succumb to the lure of cheque-book journalism.

It is more questionable, however, whether the publication of what interests or titillates the newspaper-buying public is always and necessarily 'in the public interest', since such vivid and sensational journalism manifestly damaged the Royal Family in the 1990s and did not exactly assist either John Major or Tony Blair to govern the country with confidence at a time when a seemingly steady stream of political colleagues were exposed by the media in compromising circumstances.

Those who hold a brief for the Fourth Estate will invariably say that members of the Government and all those in public life deserve all they get when their indiscretions or their wrong doings or their double standards are exposed by the media. Yet there was not always such open warfare between journalists and those in public life, as can be seen from the discreet way in which many journalists and editors declined to report or publish all that they knew to be true of Edward VIII, David Lloyd George or Harold Macmillan. The inescapable conclusion is that the press, like the public, has become totally non-deferential to politicians and others in public life; and that the competitive pressures upon all editors 'to publish and be damned' are now compelling in a world of intense media competition in which any newspaper which acts 'responsibly' by withholding a sensational story (once it has been able to confirm the facts) will almost certainly lose ground commercially to its rivals which are not so fastidious.

The question has often arisen, therefore, as to what – if anything – can or should be done about these problems. In April 1989 the then Conservative Government charged Sir David Calcutt with the difficult task of examining all the issues and making recommendations on 'what measures (whether legislative or otherwise) were needed to give further protection to individual privacy from the activities of the press and to improve recourse against the press for the individual (ordinary) citizen, taking account of existing remedies including the law on defamation and breach of confidence.'[5] In an attempt to pre-empt the Calcutt Report, the newspaper editors agreed a Code of Practice and appointed in-house ombudsmen to consider readers' complaints. In the event Sir David Calcutt's committee decided to give the press one last chance to put its own house in order and urged that a new Press Complaints Commission be established to oversee this form of self-regulation, warning that if it did not perform adequately it should be replaced by a Tribunal with statutory powers to back a new Code of Practice.[6]

The Press Complaints Commission (PCC) came into being in January 1991 and soon claimed that it was proving itself to be effective.[7] However, the following year brought forth a series of sensational press stories about the private lives of a number of national political figures – stories which had been obtained in some cases with the use of bugging devices and other unethical, possibly illegal, methods. There was also almost hysterical press and public attention paid to the behaviour of some members of the Royal Family which reached such a crescendo in coverage of the failing marriage of the Prince and Princess of Wales that the Queen herself was motivated to observe in her Christmas Message to Britain and the Commonwealth that she and her family had been through an 'annus horribilis' (awful year). Although the chairman of the PCC described much of the press coverage as 'an odious exhibition of journalists dabbling their fingers in the stuff of other people's souls,'[8] the resulting lack of any action to restrain the press made the PCC look completely ineffectual.

The Minister with responsibility for media issues at the time, David Mellor, warned that the newspapers were 'drinking in the last chance saloon' and in July

1992 he asked Sir David Calcutt to conduct another inquiry specifically into press self-regulation. Sir David produced his second report in 1993 in which he called for a compulsory system of press controls to be operated by an official Press Tribunal.[9] After a considerable lapse of time and following a barrage of press hostility to the Report's recommendations, the Government rejected the proposals for statutory regulation, confirming instead the familiar principle of self-regulation.[10]

The vexed relationship between the press and those most prominent in public life took another turn following the death of Princess Diana in a car accident in Paris at the end of August 1997. Lord Wakeham, who had become chairman of the PCC in 1995, initiated a review of the rules covering the behaviour of 'paparazzi' photographers, but to many this seemed hardly a sufficient response to the argument that the hounding by the press had in some way contributed to Princess Diana's tragic death. By the end of September 1997 Lord Wakeham had put forward a number of amendments to the voluntary Press Code which were designed to ensure greater protection of individual privacy. These included proposals:

- To ban the publication of photographs obtained illegally or through persistent pursuit or stalking
- To tackle the problem of deeply intimidating media scrums
- To strengthen the protection of children
- To introduce a wider definition of 'private property'
- To define 'private life' in much wider terms as an area of people's lives into which the press should not intrude without the justification of 'overriding public interest'.

The proposals were accepted by the PCC Code Committee in December 1997 and came into effect in January 1998.

Although the incoming Labour Government in 1997 had no plans to legislate to protect privacy, it did bring forward legislation to incorporate the European Convention on Human Rights into domestic law. Article 8 of the Convention establishes a right to respect for private and family life, people's homes and their correspondence. The Human Rights Act 1998[11] brought this principle into effect within the UK, but it still left unresolved a number of consequential questions in relation to privacy:

- Can there ever be an effective right to privacy in the modern world when so much personal information is available to the authorities and to the public?
- If so, who can claim such a right and to what extent?
- How best can redress be provided for those who can establish that their privacy has been intolerably invaded?

It would seem to be common ground that everyone should be able to expect a high degree of privacy about those aspects of their lives of which public disclosure would be severely prejudicial to their interests – for example, someone's medical notes or tax return. On the other hand, those who *choose* to enter public life or who accept a position of high responsibility (and visibility) cannot reasonably expect the same level of privacy, at any rate in connection with their public duties. Furthermore, if people in the public eye choose to sound off on issues of personal morality or integrity and, even more, if they choose to legislate for the exemplary behaviour of others, they should not be surprised if this provokes the media and others to explore their personal lives and background for evidence of double standards between their public pronouncements and their private practices.

The challenge in this area of public policy is to draw a convincing distinction between those in public life and everyone else and perhaps a further line for those in public life between the public and private aspects of their lives – including what David Cameron, the Conservative leader, has referred to as 'a private past'. In practice, the latter distinction has proved almost impossible to achieve and sustain because any journalist worth his salt will proclaim 'the freedom of the press', claim a 'right to free speech', and will tend to argue that a revelation drawn from the private life of someone in public office or in the public eye necessarily has a bearing upon either that person's fitness to hold public office or the public's ability to put their trust in the person concerned. In such testing circumstances those actively engaged in public life and, regrettably, often their families too are regarded as fair game by the media whenever any newsworthy information is uncovered about them. It is therefore difficult to see how there could be a watertight and fully enforceable statutory right to privacy covering all aspects of people's lives and certainly not for those who have chosen to be in public life.

As for the quest for appropriate means of redress for people whose privacy has been intolerably invaded, the consensus of political opinion in all parties still seems to fight shy of any system of statutory press controls. The essence of the problem is that any effective and complete right to privacy would entail a substantial curtailment of press and media freedom, whereas any qualified right to privacy would have loopholes through which a determined editor or producer could navigate.

secrecy and censorship

Another important characteristic of the British press is that it has been more inhibited than its counterparts in other Western countries (notably the United States) by the traditional secrecy of British Government and the traditionally restrictive attitudes in Whitehall towards the unauthorised disclosure of official information. Such secretive habits were established years ago and can be traced back at least to the Official Secrets Act 1911 which, in Section 2, was meant to deter public servants (including Ministers) from communicating and journalists or others from receiving any official information whose disclosure had not been authorised – that is to say deliberately released by Ministers or by civil servants acting on their behalf.

There has been a certain Alice in Wonderland quality about this aspect of the law which for years allowed Ministers to authorise their own indiscretions (if it suited their political purposes), but which equally allowed the system to come down like a ton of bricks on any unfortunate participant in the policy- and decision-making process who was caught disseminating or receiving information that Ministers wished to be kept secret. Over many years the effect of this legislation was to discredit the whole idea of official secrecy in the eyes of most people without removing the need for occasional, often farcical, prosecutions. This bred an understandably cynical attitude among all journalists and even some public servants.

Pressures for reform built up over the decades and there was a widespread welcome for a new Official Secrets Bill which was introduced by the then Conservative Government in November 1988 and duly became the Official Secrets Act 1989.[12] This was designed to remove the 'catch-all' provisions in Section 2 of the 1911 Act and replace them with provisions which restricted the application of the criminal law to specific categories of official information – such as defence of the realm, security and intelligence, international relations, law and order, and the interception of communications (phone tapping or letter opening). However, it soon became obvious that the effect of the new law upon the press and the rest of the media was actually more restrictive, although less capricious, than the discredited law which it had replaced. It was therefore hard to argue that much, if anything, had been achieved for the cause of journalistic freedom.

The Major Administration tinkered with the legislative framework for the security services (MI5 and MI6) and produced the Security Service Act 1996 which, together with the powers that had been provided in the Interception of Communications Act 1995, effectively gave MI5 carte blanche to develop a new and wider role for itself in the post-Cold War world against every conceivable activity which could be construed as subversive to the interests of the state. In this climate journalists felt more, rather than less, oppressed than they had felt before under the previous legal dispensation.

Official secrecy and covert operations against perceived enemies of the state have not declined under a Labour Government since 1997. Indeed, the cumulative effects of global terrorism since the attack on the Twin Towers in New York on 11th September 2001 – including in Bali, Madrid, Amman, New Delhi, Baghdad and those of 7th July 2005 in London – have produced a backdrop of hugely enhanced security concerns against which liberal ideals of free speech and free association with unpopular causes have been very hard for journalists and others to maintain.

Occasional attempts have been made – such as the Regulation of Investigatory Powers Act 2000 (RIPA 2000) – to enhance the supervision of aspects of the work of the security services which report confidentially to the Prime Minister, the Home Secretary and the Foreign Secretary; and a Parliamentary Select Committee has been established for more general political oversight. Yet none of these measures has changed the fundamental imbalance between the state and the citizens which, in current, sometimes hysterical, circumstances, puts the security interests of the former before the declared rights of the latter, even when they have the statutory backing of the Human Rights Act 1998 (HRA 1998). Section 7 of this act gave the citizen the right to bring proceedings in a special Tribunal against any actual or proposed unlawful act by the security services, the armed forces or the police which could be shown to damage his human rights under the Convention. Sections 65 to 70 of the RIPA 2000 provided for the declaratory powers of the Tribunal which, in the event of a discovery of officially authorised wrongdoing, has a duty to report its findings to the Prime Minister. Thus at the end of a long and elaborate process, the issue returns to the Prime Minister and the Government in whose name and at whose behest the security and intelligence services conduct their murky operations in the first place.

Restrictive attitudes have also been reflected in the libel and copyright laws in Britain and this has had the effect of inhibiting some forms of aggressive and fearless reporting, especially when the person or company under media scrutiny has the wealth and the self-confidence to use the laws to the full. These laws confer extensive powers of prior restraint, and hence effective censorship, upon those who wish to prevent publication or broadcast of any material which their lawyers advise may be libellous or defamatory by the simple expedient of obtaining a High Court injunction to stop it. They also permit plaintiffs to go to Court to obtain 'justice' in libel cases and, if successful in their suits, to secure orders for damages which have been known to reach half a million pounds or more.[13] While there is an obvious need for people to be able to protect themselves from libel or defamation by the media, or even from intolerable invasion of privacy, it is generally unsatisfactory that only the rich, the powerful and the well connected seem able to avail themselves of the protection of the law in this way, while the rest of the population is neither adequately protected from journalistic excesses nor sufficiently compensated by journalistic vigilance on behalf of the public good.

freedom of information and data protection

The media have an obvious interest in freedom of information, since this should make many aspects of their job easier – especially the gathering of accurate information on subjects to which only privileged access was previously granted. They have less of an interest in data protection, which is primarily a safeguard for the citizen to prevent sensitive personal information (for example, medical records or tax returns) from being made available to people who should have no right to see it. Yet the two subjects have often been considered together and it is no coincidence that, when the office of Information Commissioner was established under the Freedom of Information Act 2000, it was amalgamated with the office of Data Protection Registrar. There had been a limited Data Protection Act under a Conservative Government in 1984. However, the more extensive Data Protection Act 1998 was passed under a Labour Government which needed to ensure that Britain came into compliance with an earlier European Directive on the subject.

The Freedom of Information Act 2000 'went live' in January 2005 and during the first few months of its operation it was the media, often egged on by various pressure groups, which tended to make the most use of the new rights of access under the legislation. Yet although there has been a presumption in favour of disclosure in the Act and in the 'case law' which has gradually emerged from the Office of the Information Commissioner, the media and others have sometimes been frustrated by the practices in certain parts of Whitehall where the old instincts in favour of official secrecy seem to have survived. Furthermore, the permitted exemptions in the legislation, which are both category-based and contents-based, were considered by many campaigners to be too broad (for example, in relation to commercial confidentiality) or downright undesirable (for example, in relation to the formulation and development of Government policy). Ministers have stood their ground in defence of these exemptions – for example, in resisting the full publication of the Attorney General's advice to the Cabinet on the legality or otherwise of British participation in the war in Iraq – and senior civil servants in some Departments (for example, the Ministry of Defence, the Foreign Office, the Home Office and the Treasury) have been very keen to preserve the complete confidentiality of their policy advice to Ministers as one of the foundations for a truly impartial civil service.

Journalists and all those involved in the media usually side in this debate with the evangelists for 'open government'; while pressure groups and other campaigning networks usually give strong support to 'the public's right to know' (by which they often mean their right to satisfy their own curiosity or to advance their cause by securing timely access to information which their opponents would not want disclosed). Yet good government would be much more difficult if literally everything were out in the open and privacy campaigners would definitely not be happy if official information were too freely exchanged and everyone's private life were open to permanent and transparent scrutiny by bureaucrats, busybodies and salacious media. So in a well-ordered society an appropriate balance has to be struck and all those who feel strongly on either side of these well-rehearsed arguments must be prepared to compromise.

the role of the Lobby

The final piece in this very British jigsaw is the role of the Lobby in Westminster and Whitehall. This reflects the long established paradox that whereas there has been much emphasis upon secrecy and censorship in the formal and legal arrangements of British government, in practice a great deal of information has been made available to the press and the rest of the media on what are called 'Lobby terms'.[14] This practice involves supplying accredited Lobby journalists (that is to say those entitled to frequent the Members' Lobby and other restricted parts of the Houses of Parliament) with privileged and unattributable information and comment on the strict understanding that there is no disclosure of sources or direct attribution of comments. Over the years this practice has spread beyond the precincts of Parliament to every part of Whitehall, so that every Department and especially 10 Downing Street, as well as many Government Agencies have contacts with journalists who are the privileged recipients of official information and advice. Indeed, most Ministers, nearly all Special Advisers and some officials see it as an important part of their jobs to keep at least a few journalists well informed about what is happening or about to happen in their spheres of responsibility. Equally, the journalists concerned find it convenient to take advantage of this form of news management by Government and, to a lesser extent, by members of the Opposition, since it ensures a steady supply of news, gossip and opinion without which political journalism might be a very dull affair.

The Lobby system has advantages for both the providers and the recipients of such privileged information. For Ministers and officials it can be an effective way of defusing potentially difficult issues through judicious and timely leaks, so that when the facts are formally released, much of their adverse publicity impact has been removed. The system is also used to fly kites for possible policy initiatives in order to get some idea of how they might be received by press and public alike. Occasionally, it is even used to pursue through the media policy arguments or personality conflicts which are taking place behind closed doors in Westminster or Whitehall. For journalists and media people the system is a blessing for those of a lazy or cautious disposition and in some cases it can flatter the vanity of those who like to believe they are 'in the loop' with the movers and shakers in Government.

Over the years, however, there have been growing doubts as to whether the Lobby system is really worthwhile and indeed desirable. Some national newspapers (notably *The Independent* and *The Guardian*) have challenged it on a point of principle, because it so obviously conflicts with their well-established preference for open government. More significant perhaps is the fact that under Tony Blair's leadership there has been a deliberate move towards releasing information on the record whether via the Prime Minister's Official Spokesman or the Prime Minister himself in his monthly press conferences and even more frequent public statements and comments on everything under the sun. These developments, which were partly a response to the adverse public reaction to 'spin' by Government 'spin doctors' and news managers, would appear to have established a new convention which is most unlikely to be scrapped by any future Government in an age of websites, bloggers and instant, universal dissemination of news and views. Doubtless the Lobby will continue in existence in some more attenuated form, because it is still convenient for some journalists and politicians who, for their own different reasons, still wish to operate from time to time behind a veil of anonymity.

The problems of the electronic media are technological, political and ideological. They are *technological* in the sense that new media technologies are being developed and brought to market all the time quite independently of what Ministers in Government and other politicians in Parliament may wish to see happen or may wish to avoid. For example, in the technological sphere there is nowadays a great deal of 'platform convergence' (as it is described in media jargon) which means effectively that the once separate technologies of television, computers and telephony are becoming more and more interoperative with the result that the previous limitations imposed by broadcasting spectrum scarcity no longer apply and a much wider range of programmes and services are being made available locally, nationally and globally; and many of these services, such as digital radio and television, offer superior sound or visual quality for millions of customers. This means that the range of programme content is likely to be continuously widened and methods of payment are likely to focus increasingly upon customers paying only for the services they want via some form of subscription, although it may also mean that, on average, the quality of the output will suffer as media firms compete for the highest ratings and the largest audiences.

Political problems are arising because, with the growth of global media companies and the 'dumbing down' of media content, national Governments and other national media regulators are becoming less able than they used to be to limit corporate concentration in the media sector of the global economy and to insist upon high standards of taste and decency, still less to safeguard the singularity of any national culture. Eloquent concern has been expressed in many quarters about the need to safeguard quality, to prevent media-driven 'cultural pollution' and to work out new regulatory arrangements at global level which can match the global reach of the new converging technologies and the global structure of the largest media companies. So far at least, the global multimedia companies seem to be winning and national authorities, even when they try to coordinate their efforts as they do via the Council of Europe, seem to be losing.

The problems are *ideological* in the sense that previous Conservative Administrations in Britain before 1997 seemed convinced that 'the growth of (media) choice means that a rigid regulatory structure neither can nor should be perpetuated.'[15] The Labour Government which assumed the reins of political power in 1997 turned out to share its predecessor's preference for so-called 'light touch regulation' of the expanding media sector. This may have had something to do with Tony Blair's obvious determination to do nothing which would alienate Rupert Murdoch, the head of News Corporation, but in general it reflected a desire to continue with a policy of minimal political interference in the technologically dynamic media sector in which many British firms seemed to have some comparative advantage. Total revenues in the UK communications market were £56 billion in 2004, of which retail revenues (payments by customers) were £47 billion, accounting for about 4 per cent of UK GDP. With the natural advantage of the English language and the business-driven advantage of a booming media, telecommunications and computer sector, Britain seems particularly well placed to come a respectable second to the United States in this part of the global economic future.

the power and influence of television

The power of television has affected many aspects of British life and in the political sphere notably the style and nature of political debate. As Anthony Smith has observed, 'television has become a well from which society draws many of its common allusions (and illusions too) and an important source of social reference points'.[16] This means that in considering the power and influence of television, we need to look not so much at its impact upon voting behaviour – which appears to have been minimal – as its capacity to influence the way in which the political debate is conducted and to set the political agenda both between elections and during election campaigns.

In essence, television treats political issues and politicians as if they were simply another source of public entertainment and politics as a whole as a rather bizarre spectator sport. This has encouraged the tendency for politicians to perform before the people rather than reason with them. The respectable argument for this tendency is that it serves to grab and hold (if only briefly) the attention of what would otherwise be an uninterested and cynical public. Yet while it may produce a fleeting public awareness of some political issues and a few political personalities, it does not necessarily raise the level of public understanding and may often produce a bias against it.[17]

In so far as television has a discernible effect upon political allegiance in Britain, it seems to have been one of reinforcement rather than conversion, although early studies of this subject seemed also to suggest that the direct effects on voting behaviour were rather slight either way.[18] However, with the notable increase in voter volatility since the mid 1970s, the growth of multiparty politics since the mid 1980s and the low level of overall voter participation in 2001 and 2005, it is plausible to argue that the impact of television on party fortunes – and especially party leader image – has become greater than it was when the conventional wisdom on these matters was established nearly fifty years ago.

In more recent times there has been something approaching saturation coverage of General Election campaigns on television, although much of this has revolved around attempts by the competing parties to capture and set the media agenda for the day via their morning press conferences and other photo opportunities. This may appeal to the instincts of leading politicians, but there is evidence that it puts off the bulk of the apolitical British public. For example, during the 1987 campaign Gallup found that 69 per cent of its sample expected there to be too much political coverage on television, while another opinion poll in the same campaign found that 27 per cent thought there should be no election coverage at all.[19] After the 1992 election the consensus view of the experts was that while television coverage may have shaped the rhythm and pattern of the campaign, it had much less influence upon the final outcome; except that in so far as the campaign had a presidential quality to it, the Conservatives clearly 'won' with John Major who had more Governmental credibility than Neil Kinnock was ever likely to achieve.[20]

In the 1997 campaign, although the television coverage was greater and more detailed than before, it did not appear to be decisive. Indeed, it was arguable that previous television coverage of all the troubles that the Conservatives had experienced in Government – from 'Black Wednesday' to the many manifestations of 'sleaze' – and of the transformation of the Labour Party into 'New Labour' under Tony Blair and Gordon Brown were more influential upon the election result in 1997 than anything which happened during the actual campaign. In fact, it has been suggested that the TV and media coverage during the campaign was more negative all round than in previous campaigns and that this may have contributed to the relatively low overall voter turnout.[21]

In general terms, the evidence both anecdotal and systematic seems to suggest that one of the most significant effects of television upon British politics has been manifest in the style and methods of political argument and election campaigning rather than in actual voting behaviour. Since the 1964 General Election campaign the parties have been in the habit of holding daily press conferences in the morning during the formal campaign period. This development, amplified by the nightly news bulletins on more and more TV channels, has had the effect of focusing public attention on the party leaders and no more than a few of their senior party colleagues to the detriment of everyone else involved. This emphasis upon a presidential style of campaigning has been increased over the years by the presence of a veritable media circus which travels everywhere with each of the party leaders. It has diminished the role and importance of most Parliamentary candidates, except those in very marginal seats or very special circumstances. It has also diminished still further the impact of public meetings as a form of political campaigning, although once again there are a few exceptions to this rule in isolated constituencies with small cohesive communities.

Equally significant in its effect on British politics has been the tendency for television to personalise, trivialise and sensationalise nearly every political issue. It does this almost unconsciously in that programme producers will tend to prefer staging confrontational interviews with the party leaders rather than with any lesser, and possibly more interesting, political figures. Indeed, the producers cannot really afford to be more high-minded than this, since they are in competition with many other channels of radio and TV and with the quality and populist press. Moreover, it has long been a media habit to translate the antagonistic conventions of the House of Commons into the television and radio studios in the interests of achieving a dramatic effect.

Just as some on the Left of British politics have been concerned about what they see as the anti-Labour bias of the national press, so others in all parties have maintained that television is far from being a neutral or balanced medium of mass communication. According to this argument, the political effect of television is no longer simply to reinforce existing values and preferences in society, but actually to *set the agenda* of British political discussion. In particular, public faith in the impartiality of television news is said to be misplaced on several different grounds. Firstly, complete objectivity can never really be achieved by those who produce and present the programmes, because there is bound to be a degree of arbitrary selection and conscious or unconscious bias which is driven by the 'undeclared criteria and preferences of those who produce and present the programmes'.[22] This point of view was first publicised by the Glasgow Media Group at the University of Strathclyde, but these Left-wing academics have not been alone in their suspicion of television programme makers and have been matched by a swathe of Right-wing opinion which is equally convinced that all programme makers in general, and those who work for the BBC in particular, are out to do them down by innuendo and any other methods which come to hand.

Secondly, the explosion in TV and other media outlets in recent years has put a premium in terms of audience figures on the adoption of a clear *point of view* in order to give an identity and a visibility to any current affairs programme. This may not necessarily be a party political point of view, but it does need to be a clear stance of some kind which can differentiate one programme from another or one presenter from another at a time when otherwise the totality of current affairs output might be little more than a blur in the minds of the diminishing portion of the general public who feel inclined to tune into such programmes at all. Thirdly, with the explosion in TV output, there has necessarily been a *growing segmentation* in the media market place with the result that smaller, but more dedicated, audiences emerge for any single programme and viewers may notice bias less readily than their predecessors did, largely because they are in fundamental agreement with the style and approach of the programmes they choose to watch.

There is a counter-argument which is essentially that political bias on television is completely in the mind of the viewer, just as on radio it is in the mind of the listener.[23] Sceptics, such as Martin Harrison and Alastair Hetherington, have pointed out that everything really depends on the elements of broadcast material selected for this sort of analysis and that in the case of the Glasgow Media Group the academics concerned were doing little more than display their own prejudices. In short, this is an argument which is unlikely to be settled, other than to say that value-free political news and views (from whatever standpoint) are really a contradiction in terms.

During the 1992–97 period most Conservative politicians certainly felt persecuted by the media and became convinced that the real agenda of many

TV producers and other media figures was to hound them out of office. Unsurprisingly, they linked their media critics with the 'spin doctors' of the Labour Opposition led by Peter Mandelson and Alistair Campbell and in many ways they were right to do so, because any Opposition will often try to make common cause with the media and pressure groups against the Government of the day. That is just party politics. Moreover, media professionals both at that time and since could use the argument that they were doing little more than hold up a mirror to some distasteful aspects of political reality or pursuing their vocation as investigative journalists on the lookout for a juicy story. In the final analysis most political reporting and editorialising is a matter of opportunity, taste and judgement rather than clearly delineated right or wrong.

Whatever the correct judgement on these matters, it is worth noting that New Labour learned many useful lessons from the experience of the Conservatives at the hands of a voracious press and media. They learned the value of 'spin' in trying to control the context or framework within which a news story emerged; they learned the value of instant rebuttal which they were able to use very effectively both in Opposition and in Government; and they learned the value of orchestrating party political and Government announcements in such a way that the presentation of news was treated with as much care as the substance in order to maximise the chances of a favourable media response. From 1997 onwards there were many occasions when the balance of power between the media and the New Labour Government seemed to favour the latter and when New Labour Ministers seemed to live a charmed existence. Yet nothing really lasts in these matters and Tony Blair was heavily criticised over his controversial decisions to back President Bush in relation to Iraq and to give the police and security services carte blanche in relation to counter-terrorist measures.[24] The evidence in these instances reminds us that even the most teflon-coated political leaders can find themselves moving from popularity to controversy to ignominy in three easy stages at the hands of the media.[25]

the power of radio

Radio is another powerful, and sometimes underrated, medium which has had its effect upon both politics and society in Britain. For example, the programmes broadcast by the BBC serve, in various ways, to inform, educate and entertain the British people. Taken together, the 11 national channels and the 49 regional services offer a wide range of media output, but one which, taken in the round, has moved some distance from the balance struck in the original Reithian objectives to one which can be described as a blend of 'info-tainment'.

One political effect of the recent and current explosion in the quantity (if not the quality) of radio broadcasting has been to give a real boost to local consciousness in the UK and some colourful local personalities (political and otherwise) have thrived in the atmosphere which has been created. Apart from heavy doses of popular music and other forms of popular entertainment, the radio stations tend to broadcast a large number of chat shows, quiz games and phone-in programmes which provide opportunities for members of the public to air their views and prejudices, while politicians and other public figures have opportunities to demonstrate their activity and concern. Thus local radio has undoubtedly contributed to the vitality of British life and it often provides the most lively forum for local political debate.

In the future, radio in Britain will have further opportunities for development and expansion. The commercial interests will benefit from the relatively light touch regulatory regime of Ofcom, while the BBC networks will continue to be mindful of their public service obligations. With the full take-up of digital radio, spectrum scarcity should become a thing of the past and there will be even more scope (although not necessarily an endlessly growing public appetite) for new community and special interest radio services in hospitals, schools, offices, etc. All of this means that there will be new opportunities for media entrepreneurs to make money, more competition for the BBC which may feel obliged to go further 'down market' in pursuit of a significantly sized audience, and new opportunities for pressure and cause groups to peddle their ideas in a more pluralist and less regulated media environment. Many of these developments may affect the nature and practice of British politics; all of them will have an impact upon the quality of life in Britain.

the impact of new technologies

It is already clear that new technologies have had, and will continue to have, a very significant impact upon the development of the electronic media in Britain. The availability of more radio frequencies, as well as the growth of satellite, cable and digital transmission of television, will make many more increasingly interactive services available to local, regional, national or supranational audiences. The main constraint on the pace and scale of these developments is likely to be the ability to make them all commercially viable in an increasingly crowded media market rather than any serious doubts about their technical feasibility or their political acceptability.

If everything goes well and the new technologies are developed along the benign lines foreseen by their most enthusiastic proponents, we could see the development of a society which was well described by a former Minister for Information Technology in the Thatcher Administration as 'better informed ... more relaxed, less formal, more mobile, less enamoured with structure, more skilled, less ridden with class and social differences, and full of scope for more individuality'.[26] Yet if things go differently and the new technologies are developed overwhelmingly for short term commercial gain and, subsequently perhaps, for socially manipulative purposes either by powerful media corporations or by public authorities at a national or supranational level, then individual freedom could be eroded, social variety could be stifled and totalitarian tendencies could take root along lines predicted in the 1930s by Aldous Huxley and in the 1940s by George Orwell.[27]

As indicated earlier in this chapter, the traditional distinctions between computers, mobile phones and television are disappearing fast and may one day be eliminated altogether in a new kind of 'wireless world'. This would lead to a larger range of home-based educational, business and leisure opportunities – new opportunities for buying and selling from home, a growing variety of consumer services available from home – while pay-as-you-view, subscription television and 'time-shift' technology will see more people not merely deciding what they watch, but when and how they watch it.

It already seems clear that the so-called dot.com economy, which rose into a stock market bubble at the turn of the century, is back in favour with investors and especially large media corporations. Rupert Murdoch of News Corp has eventually demonstrated by his actions that he believes the internet is complementary, even essential, to the future of his corporate empire and other multimedia companies are following suit. A Carnegie Corporation survey showed that 44 per cent of 18–34 year olds get their news from the internet rather than from newspapers; Bill Gates of Microsoft has predicted that the value of internet advertising will soon reach $30 billion globally; and Sir Martin Sorrell of the advertiser WPP reckons that market spending in the new media is likely to be greater than in the old media from now on – hence the rush by media companies to purchase internet companies.[28]

The current giant corporations in cyberspace – such as Google, Yahoo, Amazon, Expedia and E-bay – were among the first to recognise that the commercial impact of the internet would affect every business sector, transform the ways in which business is done, give the comparative advantage to 'early movers', and permanently boost economic productivity in those jurisdictions which embraced these developments with open arms. Thus it is not altogether surprising that Yahoo and Google have overtaken News Corp and the other multimedia giants in market capitalisation and that US productivity grew by 13 per cent between 2001 and 2004, double the average gains for comparable periods during the whole post-war era. Obviously, the media corporations in Britain cannot stand aside from these global developments and it must be expected that over the years ahead the traditional media (newspapers, radio and television) will reach saturation or stagnate, while the new cybermedia will expand and prosper.

It is too soon to tell what will be the full consequences of these new media technologies upon British society and British politics. From one point of view, they might encourage political participation and make instant public referenda as popular as *Big Brother* and other 'reality TV shows' have been. The potential for this was shown by the online petition against road-pricing in 2007. On the other hand, they might entail a frivolous allocation of scarce financial resources, the Balkanisation of British society along unpredictable and unfamiliar lines, and significant damage to the national culture which used to hold people together in the United Kingdom and in other relatively homogeneous societies.

Finally, one suspects that the combined effects of all these media technologies and the business interests which seek to exploit them will include the further erosion of traditional ideas about national sovereignty and cultural identity. In the global media village which has begun to emerge, more and more media content is likely to consist of commodified, Anglophone material, conveying mid-Atlantic mediocrity designed to appeal to the lowest common denominators in the global market place. The implications for public attitudes and behaviour in Britain and elsewhere are potentially very disturbing.

7.4 the media and politics

There is absolutely no doubt that the media have come to play an increasingly important part in the British political system over the last forty or fifty years. Media professionals no longer carry conviction if they claim that all they are doing is to reflect what is happening in British politics and society. Rather they should acknowledge their ability and their inclination to influence the agenda of politics and recognise the tensions which their own priorities can create between themselves and the politicians and between the politicians and the public.

There are essentially five main points which need to be made about the role of the media in contemporary British politics. *Firstly*, it is argued that the media, and especially television, give a distorted impression of politics and political issues, since bad news is usually given priority over good news, sensation over dull normality, disunity over unity, disagreement over agreement and tendentious speculation over solid reporting and analysis. These media tendencies may be most noticeable in the populist press and the coarser TV programmes, but even those who work for the so-called quality media are not shy about copying their cruder colleagues when market considerations point in that direction. The usual excuse is that the imperatives of competition and the need to attract and hold the attention of a fickle and often ignorant public, leave nearly all branches of the media with no option but to behave in this way. Whether or not such explanations are sincerely given, it seems that they will be offered more and more frequently as the liberalisation of the media market proceeds apace.

Such media distortion can take several forms. It may be perceived bias in the reporting of the activities and policies of a political party; it may be the ubiquitous tendency to personalise and sensationalise complicated political issues in the interests of boosting ratings and circulation. Of course, media professionals will reply that such techniques merely reflect political realities which include the creeping presidentialism of initiative and responsibility in political parties, whether in Government or in Opposition, and the tendency of the public to personalise their political likes and dislikes.

Secondly, it is argued by political scientists and others that the media have an impressive capacity to set the agenda of British politics. This is true in broad terms, but it probably takes insufficient account of political 'spin', which is the capacity of politicians and their close aides to present their decisions and the arguments they use to support them in a persuasive and favourable light to the extent that the media and much of the general public come to accept the interpretation put upon events by the prime actors themselves. In this permanent tussle between the media and the politicians to control, or at least influence, the public agenda, the media tend to win when it comes to setting the framework of assumptions and opinions which condition the various responses of the public to political developments, whereas the politicians in office tend to win when it comes to creating facts by taking autonomous decisions, including those which take the media and the public by surprise. The positive results of this competition may be to draw public attention to new or difficult issues which have not been credited with the importance they deserve or to remind the public of some of the intractable issues which have not yet been resolved.

Some people may feel uneasy when faced with this aspect of media power, particularly those who hold the old-fashioned view that it is the political parties rather than anyone else who should be accorded the sole, or principal, right to initiate new polices or set the political agenda. In reality, of course, there will tend to be considerable interplay between the politicians in office and the media, with little expectation that this situation will be seriously modified by the passage of events, however bizarre. This is not because politicians are bereft of good ideas, but rather because in a democratic society they tend to be in responsive rather than proactive mode most of the time.

Thirdly, whenever the party in power at Westminster has a comfortable majority in the House of Commons, people in the media can be tempted to take the view that they have a duty to provide an effective opposition, especially if the politicians on the Opposition benches appear temporarily unwilling or unable to do so. Such a view was widely held in media circles during the 1980s when the Conservatives had comfortable majorities in the House of Commons and the Labour Party seemed preoccupied with trying to sort out its own problems and again after 1997 when the roles of the Labour and Conservative parties in this respect were reversed. In such circumstances there is often a real temptation for those in the media to try to fill the void left by an ineffective and demoralised Opposition.

All Governments, when they become deeply unpopular, are tempted to conclude that the media are to blame for most, if not all, their political difficulties. This was very evident during the time of the second Wilson Administration (1966–70), especially following the mortal blow to Labour's economic credibility inflicted by the 1967 devaluation of sterling. Such attitudes of persecution and paranoia were equally evident during John Major's second Administration (1992–97), especially following 'Black Wednesday' on 16th September 1992 when sterling was forced out of the European Exchange Rate Mechanism and subsequently devalued by 15 per cent. On the other hand, leading figures in the media have had cause from time to time to resent New Labour's 'spin machine' which operated at a very high level of sophistication during New Labour's first two terms of office (1997–2001 and 2001–2005). While there can be no final or definitive assessment of the rights and wrongs of this controversy, most impartial observers would probably agree that it is not healthy for any Parliamentary democracy if the media become effectively the real Opposition to the Government of the day.

Fourthly, it is argued by some of a fastidious disposition that the media in Britain and other modern societies can have a deleterious effect upon the quality of life by encouraging or causing various forms of cultural pollution. This criticism is mounted especially in relation to the possible effects of weakening the regulatory framework within which the media operate and it is reinforced by the evidently lower cultural and aesthetic standards associated with the tabloid press and junk television. For example, it was clear from the 1988 Broadcasting White Paper and subsequent statements made by Conservative Ministers at the Home Office (the Department then responsible for broadcasting policy) that a strong rearguard action was being fought in Whitehall against the more liberalising instincts of 10 Downing Street and the Department of Trade and Industry. Yet the outcome, as far as commercial television was concerned, was clearly favourable to the freer play of market forces and so-called 'light touch regulation'. As the *Financial Times* observed in a critical editorial, 'British broadcasting faces a future in which bottom line considerations will increasingly dictate the contents of programmes.'[29] On the other hand, Channel 4 was shielded to some extent from the full force of commercial competition, and the traditional financial framework of the BBC (based on the annual Licence Fee) was safeguarded until 2002 and has subsequently been safeguarded until 2010.[30]

Notwithstanding these moves to keep the forces of rampant commercialism at bay, there remains a fear in some quarters that the quality and range of British broadcasting will continue to deteriorate during a relatively speedy transition from the former paternalistic duopoly of the BBC and the ITV to a flagrantly free market, multichannel and multiplatform future constrained only by the lightest touch regulation to support education, high quality and good taste. Rapid and extensive technological changes, coupled with increasingly triumphant and universal market forces, seem likely to put the new multimedia entrepreneurs very much in the driving seat and there are growing worries that the few remaining islands of British media quality – such as Radio 3, BBC 2 and Channel 4 – may not survive for very long in their traditional form in a sea of mass-media mediocrity.

Fifthly, strong concern has been expressed in many quarters that heavy concentrations of media ownership have begun to develop, because there have been no really effective ground rules in competition policy at national level to prevent this from happening. In 1989 the then Home Secretary, Douglas Hurd, made it clear to the House of Commons that 'we should regard it as quite unacceptable if British broadcasting were allowed to be dominated by a handful of tycoons or international conglomerates.'[31] The Conservative Government therefore promised effective rules to safeguard diversity of ownership and editorial stance, and Ministers made it clear that excessive cross-media holdings would be prevented. Specifically, it was laid down in subordinate legislation that no single media group would be allowed to own two large television or radio franchises and that no British national newspaper group would be allowed to have more than a 20 per cent stake in any satellite company, terrestrial television or radio franchise.[32]

In the event this dyke against the commercial flood did not hold and a few years later the Broadcasting Act 1996 scrapped many of the earlier restrictions, lowered the regulatory hurdles that had to be surmounted and permitted newspaper groups to own and control commercial television companies for the first time in the United Kingdom, subject only to some rather ineffective 'public-interest' criteria. When Tony Blair and New Labour came to power in 1997, they were as cautious (or pusillanimous) as their Conservative predecessors in their regulatory treatment of multimedia empires and did nothing effective to close the gaping loopholes in the rules against excessive media ownership through which Rupert Murdoch and others had already slipped. To be fair, few knowledgeable observers have ever believed that it would be easy, or even possible, to ensure both high quality and content diversity once the free play of market forces was let rip in the multimedia sector of the economy. Apart from other considerations, it is difficult to argue that regulatory limits should be strictly imposed at national level in Britain when many of the new media technologies can only effectively be regulated at an EU or even global level. In many ways the very idea of national media may become as obsolete as the idea of national capitalism and, if so, everyone will have to adjust their traditional assumptions.

In considering the rapidly evolving relationship between the media and politics, a great deal depends upon the mixture of interest, temperament and ideology which prevails at any time. Ministers in both Conservative and Labour Governments since the late 1980s have argued that by giving scope for greater consumer choice of channels, platforms and media outlets, it is possible to engender greater diversity and commercial opportunity without sacrificing quality, taste or decency. Their critics have stolidly maintained that the consequences of such media liberalisation will include a race to the bottom and a dumbing down of traditional standards without much increase in real consumer choice. Only time will tell which side of the argument is proved right.

7.5 conclusion

We have seen in this chapter how the power and influence of the media in Britain is in one sense greater, but in another sense not so great, as it was in previous times – for example, in the heyday of the twentieth-century press barons Rothermere, Northcliffe and Beaverbrook. Today television, computers and mobile telephony vie for technological, and hence market, dominance and are gearing themselves up to exert an even stronger influence upon the content and style of British politics. Yet it must also be recognised that proprietors and shareholders in the media are usually more interested in commercial success than in political influence and merely accept the latter when it turns out to be a real by-product of their corporate power or journalistic success. Newspapers, in particular, are beginning to look a little like an endangered species, although they may well find some financial relief in a growing online and subscription-based readership which may gradually replace some of the income they have derived from selling hard copies.

Certainly television has had an unsettling and pervasive influence upon politics in Britain and many other societies. For most politicians it has acted like a lamp to moths and in many cases radio and television studios have challenged Parliamentary forums as the main battlegrounds of politics. This has been seriously disturbing to the extent that television has been known to achieve an aura of impartiality and authority derived from its often graphic portrayal of real events in real time. 'The camera cannot lie', people are wont to say. Yet anyone who has studied these matters knows that the angles and prejudices of TV editors and producers can be decisive in creating one predominant impression rather than another in the public mind.

On the other side of the argument, it is worth underlining the fact that radio and television have provided increased scope for two-way communication between opinion formers and decision takers on the one hand and members of the public on the other. This reflects not only changes in media practices, but also the autonomous emergence of a much less deferential and more participatory democracy – although not registered perhaps in terms of turnout at recent General Elections. Yet this contribution from the modern electronic media will tend to disappoint if the commercial exploitation of the new technologies simply creates more air time for mediocre programme content. The existing tendencies towards triviality and sensationalism seem unlikely to disappear, since they are not even generally acknowledged by media professionals. In these circumstances it is up to the media themselves to demonstrate that the new technologies and commercial opportunities can be exploited in ways which enhance, rather than degrade, the quality of life and the vitality of British democracy.

With these considerations in mind, it is possible to summarise the overall contribution of the media to the British political system as:

▸ The encouragement of a greater awareness of political issues among the general public
▸ The influencing of the political agenda through media selection of the issues and personalities which are thought to be worth dramatising at any time.

It can be argued that these two roles of the media are particularly important for the myriad interest groups which compete fiercely for political attention and public sympathy in an era in which traditional ideologies are no longer the most significant organising principles of British politics.

Of course, the influence of the media extends well beyond the sphere of party politics, since it has a demonstrable effect on the values, assumptions, attitudes and behaviour of millions of people in British society. For example, the media have contributed to the materialism of modern society by reinforcing the widely held assumption that individual status should be measured principally in financial terms. They have influenced public attitudes towards Government and its Agencies by raising public expectations that problems exposed or discussed in the media will be swiftly addressed and effectively dealt with. The media have also raised the levels of public awareness and prompted official responses to many of the problems and injustices of the modern world – for example, famine, environmental degradation or abuses of human rights – and thus can be a force for good on a much wider scale.

In short, while the media have undoubtedly made it more difficult for Governments to govern by highlighting the flaws and shortcomings in many aspects of public policy and the politicians responsible for it, and by encouraging levels of public expectations which no Governments have been able to satisfy, they have also communicated a great deal of useful information and opinion to the general public and occasionally raised the levels of public consciousness in ways which have strengthened British democracy. In reaching any conclusions on the political role of the media in Britain or any comparable country, it is as well to remember that in a free society the media are more likely to be critics than buttresses of those in power and in a pluralist, liberal democracy it is right that this should be so.

SUGGESTED QUESTIONS

1 How influential is the British press?
2 In what ways do radio and television influence the practices of British politics?
3 What have been the implications of new media and communication technologies on British politics?

public opinion

The term 'public opinion' has no generally accepted fixed and definite meaning. Certainly the diversity that exists reflects the different views taken at different times by different people, depending upon the society in which they lived and the political outlook which they had. For example:

- Jeremy Bentham (1748–1832) defined it as 'a system of law emanating from the body of the people'[1]
- Robert Peel (1788–1850) defined it as 'that great compound of folly, weakness, prejudice, wrong feeling, right feeling, obstinacy and newspaper paragraphs'[2]
- Oscar Wilde (1854–1900) described it as 'an attempt to organise the ignorance of the community and to elevate it to the dignity of physical force'[3]
- Dean Inge (1860–1954) saw it as 'a vulgar, impertinent, anonymous tyrant'[4]
- Nicolas Sebastien Chamfort (1741–1794) asked simply 'How many fools does it take to make a public?'[5]
- William Hazlitt (1778–1830) observed that 'there is not a more mean, stupid, dastardly, pitiless, selfish, spiteful, envious, ungrateful animal than the public'[6]
- A.V. Dicey (1835–1922) declared public opinion to be 'a mere abstraction', and 'not a power which has any independent existence', defining it simply as 'a general term for the beliefs held by a number of human beings',[7] and more particularly as 'the wishes and ideas as to legislation held by the majority of those citizens who have ... taken an effective part in public life'[8]
- V.O. Key (1908–1963) was perhaps more realistic when he defined it as 'those opinions of private persons which Governments find it prudent to heed'.[9]

In Britain in the nineteenth century public opinion was usually considered to be synonymous with the views of the relatively small number of people who had the right to vote and so had opportunities for political influence, at least at election time. Nowadays it is generally accepted that public opinion includes the views and prejudices of all adults, no matter how shallow or fitful or indeed non-existent their involvement in politics may be.

On those matters which impinge on the concerns, interests or emotions of the public it is likely that enough individuals will react in the same way for their collective private opinions to constitute a manifestation of public opinion. As a result, public opinion is collectively expressed. Thus, for the purposes of this chapter, public opinion is defined as *the sum of opinions held on social, economic and political issues by the general public*, although it does comprise many different components which vary from issue to issue and from time to time. The composition of public opinion is therefore more akin to a mosaic than to a well-defined diagram. It is nevertheless possible to show the flow of public opinion in diagrammatic form:

8.1 the formation of opinion

inheritance and experience

Expert studies have shown that public opinion is formed from a myriad of private opinions, whether personal or group opinions. Such private opinions are often formed quite early in life, usually when people first become aware of political issues. They tend to be derived principally from family influence and personal experience, with the pressures from school, work, friends and neighbours all playing a part.

In the 1960s Butler and Stokes demonstrated the strength of *family influence* as a factor in voting behaviour.[10] Although the growth of electoral volatility from the 1970s onwards indicated that its significance had declined, young people today still derive many of their attitudes and opinions from their parents, and family influence remains one of the more constant factors in the development of every young generation. Of course, there have always been young people who reject the attitudes and opinions of their parents, either as part of a transient adolescent rebellion or as a function of economic and social mobility. Yet on the whole family influence still plays a major part in the formation of public opinion.

As for the influence of *personal experience*, it is obvious that this has a significant impact on the formation of individual opinions. Few people form their opinions on political issues on a basis of detached or altruistic reflection, since this is a luxury which is usually available only to those whose material circumstances and educational background allow them to adopt such a Platonic stance. For most people individual opinions are formed in the light of the fortune or misfortune which they experience during the course of their lives, whether at home, at work or at leisure. Indeed, it has been argued that it is the formative experience of young adults which has the most lasting influence on their opinions later in life. This is known as 'the cohort theory' of opinion formation. A cautious conclusion would be that formative experience remains

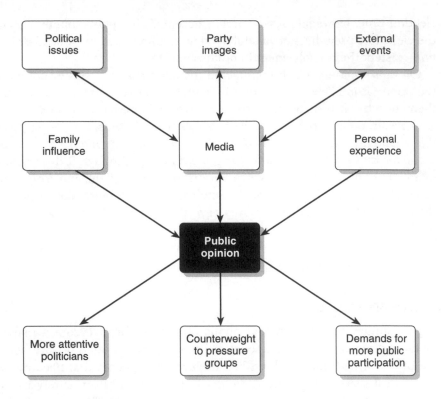

figure **8.1**   **the flow of public opinion**

important as an influence upon the formation of opinion, but that the pace and scale of economic and social change in the modern world has generated a volatility of opinion which makes public attitudes more contingent and provisional.

issues and images

Opinions are also formed by individual responses to political issues and party images. Traditionally the psephological evidence seemed to suggest that people tend to reconcile their political opinions with their party allegiances, rather than the other way around. In the 1950s and 1960s neither policy nor ideology seemed to mean very much to the average British citizen whose political opinions and voting behaviour appeared to be largely unaffected by such considerations. Yet evidence drawn from the 1970s and 1980s suggests that *political issues* do have an impact on the formation of public opinion and hence on voting behaviour. For example, Ivor Crewe concluded that 'it was issues, not organisation or personalities, that won the [1979] election for the Conservatives.'[11] Indeed even those who voted Labour on that occasion often preferred Conservative policies, although evidently not enough to persuade them to align their votes with their policy preferences. For much of the 1980s the nature and extent of trade-union power was one of the major issues in the political debate and on the whole its salience worked in favour of the Conservatives who were seen to adopt a consistently tougher stance in relation to the trade unions. The same might be said of the issue of nuclear weapons on which the Labour leadership had, perhaps reluctantly, to concede points to the Conservative position. In 2003–05 it was very apparent that both the anti-Iraq War stance and the stance taken in opposition to university tuition fees taken by the Liberal Democrats increased the party's popularity, certainly amongst some members of the public.

Yet, in considering the influence of political issues upon opinion, we need to distinguish between the bread-and-butter issues of daily life (such as inflation, jobs, health, education and pensions), together with issues of war and peace (certainly at times of conflict) upon which most people have strongly held views which influence their voting behaviour, and the more esoteric issues of policy (for example, the control of money supply or theories of nuclear deterrence) upon which some people hold opinions, but which tend not to interest the vast majority. In considering the influence of issues in the latter category, it is as well not to exaggerate the importance of the views held by the general public.

Among the more ephemeral considerations which influence the formation of public opinion, *the images* of the parties and especially of their leaders constitute another important factor in modern political conditions. For example, for decades the Conservative Party managed to secure and preserve a reputation for competence in Government which led many people to support it even when it might not have appeared particularly warm or sympathetic to most of the general public. This reputation suffered severe damage when Britain was forced to leave the European Exchange Rate Mechanism of the European Monetary System in September 1992. This, along with internal divisions over European policy and a growing image of 'sleaze', contributed to three successive election defeats and four changes of leader in eight years.

On the other hand, the Labour Party has traditionally had an image of understanding and concern for ordinary people which has helped it to retain the voting loyalties of a large part of the electorate. This achievement was partly a reflection of the positive personal image of several of its leaders – such as Clement Attlee, Hugh Gaitskell, and Harold Wilson – but mainly a tribute to the image of the Party as the Parliamentary vanguard of the entire Labour movement at a time when the latter had authenticity, fraternity and solidarity. From the middle 1970s, however, Labour had more trouble with its image, particularly during the brief period of Michael Foot's leadership in the early 1980s, and it required all the media and presentational skills of Labour image-makers to attempt to recreate and present a positive, modern image for the party. This was eventually achieved by the 'modernising' of New Labour under the leadership of Tony Blair and the party was swept into office in 1997 on a tide of popular approval which was not significantly dissipated by the time of the General Elections of 2001 and 2005.

Notwithstanding the wonders that the image-makers and spin doctors can perform, it should be borne in mind that it is the performance and credibility of the Government of the day which is likely to be decisive in the battle for the hearts and minds of the British people and which mainly determines the outcome of General Elections. In Britain, as in other democratic countries, Governments tend to lose elections rather than Opposition parties to win them.

the influence of the media

As we saw in Chapter 7, perhaps the most influential factor in the formation of public opinion in Britain today is the power of the media to reflect, explain or distort the most important political issues and personalities at any time. For example, during the 1980s and into the early 1990s most of the tabloid press conducted a ruthless and single-minded campaign to portray the Labour Party as completely beholden to the trade unions and the trade unions as stereotypically mindless and militant. Such a campaign would not have been so credible to the general public if certain trade union leaders – for example, Arthur Scargill of the National Union of Mineworkers (NUM) – had not played into the hands of the media by behaving in a manner which might have been calculated to lend credence to their caricatures. Yet undeniably the public image of the so-called 'loony Left', whether identified with some of the trade unions or some of the local Councillors up and down the country, was heavily influenced by columns and pictures in *The Sun*, the *News of the World*, the *Mail on Sunday*, the *Express* and other such newspapers. Conversely, these same newspapers and others like them consistently indulged in sycophancy towards Margaret Thatcher in a crude and sustained attempt, one must suppose, to keep the Conservatives in office. By contrast, following the 1992 General Election most of these same newspapers turned viciously against John Major, criticising him mercilessly for what they alleged were his failures of leadership. Following the Conservatives' loss of the 1997 General Election, a number of observers and commentators were quick to attribute the outcome at least in part to the switch of the so-called 'Tory press' into the camp of Tony Blair and 'New Labour'.

As for radio and television, the part which the electronic media play in the formation of public opinion is agreed to be more insidious, even manipulative. It consists essentially of helping to set the political agenda by influencing the relative salience of different political issues as they waft in and out of the public's consciousness. It is not so much that influential programmes, like *Today*, *Channel 4 News* or *Newsnight*, consciously set out to tell the general public what to think about a given politician or political issue; rather they set the framework of values, assumptions and information within which the public has to make up its own mind. In a world in which real public interest in politics is desultory and attention spans are short, this form of media influence is obviously both ephemeral and unpredictable. Indeed it may well be that the influence of the media is greater via mass entertainment programmes, such as *EastEnders*, *Coronation Street* or *Big Brother*, than it is via the more serious programmes which are specifically designed to inform and educate the public.

Indeed, it was perhaps not all that surprising that the 2006 series of *Celebrity Big Brother* included a Member of Parliament, George Galloway, amongst the housemates.

Another example of media influence would include the saturation coverage of the relationship between the then Home Secretary, David Blunkett, and his former lover Mrs Kimberly Quinn, not least, the revelation that Mrs Quinn's nanny's visa application had been 'fast-tracked' by the Immigration and Nationality Department of the Home Office, which undoubtedly contributed to his resignation at the end of 2004. Another example would be the resignation of Charles Kennedy as leader of the Liberal Democrats early in 2006. It was only after it became apparent that ITN were to run anonymous allegations that Charles Kennedy was undergoing treatment for a drink problem that he confirmed that he did indeed have such a problem and was receiving treatment for it. Within a matter of days he stepped down as leader.

In any event we cannot review the various factors which influence the formation of public opinion in Britain today without laying great stress on the role of the media.

8.2 the sources of opinion

Public opinion is an amorphous and infinitely malleable concept. Like information on the electronic superhighway, it will pass on by without being picked up unless the proper receiving apparatus is available, switched on and tuned in. The opinions of the public are communicated to politicians in a variety of ways, although it is perhaps more accurate to say that politicians perceive public opinion from a number of different sources. The following are the main ones.

General Elections

Political leaders are continually conscious of the fact that their performance is constantly subjected to evaluation by the public. They are also acutely aware that whether or not they hold office ultimately depends on the judgement of the public as expressed at a General Election. The significance of this reality was attested by the political demise of Margaret Thatcher and her replacement by John Major when the Conservative party wanted to improve its chances of winning the 1992 General Election and so remain the party of Government. For politicians in both Government and Opposition nothing concentrates the mind more than the prospect of defeat at the next General Election.

Also important in this context is the **mandate theory** of Government. The idea is that at the time of a General Election each political party publishes its Manifesto outlining what it proposes to do and what policies it will pursue, if it were to form the Government. The assumption is that the voters will read the various manifestos and make up their minds on how to cast their votes based on their assessment of and support for the policies outlined. This process is then presumed to grant to the newly elected Government the legitimate authority to implement the policies concerned.

A problem arises, however, if the mandate theory is taken to its logical conclusion, namely that a Government can *only* introduce measures that have been placed before the electorate at the previous General Election. It is for this reason that Governments have tended to adopt a rather more wide-ranging definition of what is entailed, namely that the role of the electorate is to choose a Government not a Government's policies. Hence a Government obtains a general mandate to govern for a maximum period of five years at a time before it has to resubmit itself and its policies for public approval at the next General Election.

Finally, there are doubts about the ability of the electoral system to reflect accurately the wishes of the voters. For example, in the 1951 General Election more people voted Labour than voted Conservative, yet the result produced a Conservative Government. Similarly, in the General Election of February 1974, more people voted Conservative than voted Labour, but the result brought the Labour Party to power. Indeed, no Government elected since 1935 has secured a majority of those entitled to vote or even of those who did vote and yet, with only one exception (February 1974), every Government secured a majority of seats in the House of Commons. In 2005 Labour secured a Parliamentary majority of 67 seats (55 per cent of the seats) with only 35 per cent of the popular vote and only 22 per cent of those eligible to vote. Thus the results of General Elections need to be interpreted with caution, even when the winning party appears to dominate the House of Commons.

by-elections

If in the period between General Elections a Member of Parliament dies or resigns, a by-election is held in order to fill the resulting vacancy. By-elections have become ways in which the popularity, or otherwise, of the Government of the day is put to the test. They are invariably fought on national issues and their results are often interpreted as reflecting public opinion as a whole. This is so even though most constituencies are far from perfect samples of public opinion in the country at large, the number of people casting a vote is likely to be no more than 45,000–55,000, there may be special factors surrounding one or other of the candidates, or local issues which are decisive in determining the way people vote.

Whether or not by-elections are an accurate reflection of public opinion, politicians certainly take them seriously. For example, in October 1933 a by-election occurred in East Fulham, a seat that had been held by the Conservatives in 1931 with a majority of 14,521. It was captured by the Labour candidate on an appeasement platform with a majority of 4840, a massive switch of votes in just two years. The Prime Minister, Stanley Baldwin, took the result as evidence of a pacifist wave sweeping the country and this undoubtedly influenced his whole approach to the issue of rearmament.[12] Similarly, the Orpington by-election in March 1962, which saw a Conservative majority over Labour of 14,760 turned into a Liberal majority of 7855, provided a shock to the then Prime Minister, Harold Macmillan. When this was followed by another by-election defeat for the Conservatives at North-East Leicester, Harold Macmillan responded by carrying through an extensive Cabinet reshuffle – the so-called 'night of the long knives' – in which he dismissed a third of his cabinet.[13] On the other hand, there is the case of the Hull North by-election which took place early in 1966 and produced an increased majority for the Labour Party in office. This was undoubtedly an important factor in persuading the then Prime Minister, Harold Wilson, to call a General Election which gave the Government a considerably enhanced majority. More recently there is the example of the Brent East by-election of September 2003 when, on a swing of 29 per cent from Labour and 15 per cent from the Conservatives, the Liberal Democrats, harnessing a backlash against the war in Iraq and the unpopularity of a Conservative party led by Iain Duncan Smith, came from third place to capture the seat. This result was one of the factors that led to the removal of Iain Duncan Smith as Conservative leader the following month.

European and local elections

Just as the results of by-elections can be misleading snapshots of public opinion, so too can be the results of European and local elections, which often tend to be fought on national issues. For example, the local elections of May 1990 were widely portrayed as a referendum on the performance of the Conservative Government in general and Margaret Thatcher in particular. In the event, the results were cleverly presented by Kenneth Baker, then Conservative Party Chairman, as nothing like as bad as expected or predicted because of Conservative victories in Wandsworth and Westminster.

Similarly, the elections for the European Parliament in June 1994 came after a series of electoral setbacks for the Conservative Party all of which put considerable pressure on the leadership of the Prime Minister, John Major. The expectation in some quarters was of electoral annihilation for the Conservatives. As things turned out, the results were not as bad as originally feared and the backbench pressure on John Major was reduced, albeit temporarily.

referenda

Britain has only had one *national* referendum. It was held in June 1975 on the issue of whether or not the country should remain in the European Economic Community and, on a turnout of 65 per cent, it produced a majority of almost two to one in favour of Britain's continued membership of the EEC.[14] There have, however, been eight *regional* referenda – two in Northern Ireland (1973 and 1998), two each in Scotland and Wales (1979 and 1997) one in London (1998) and one in the North East of England (2004).[15] Since mid 2001 there have also been a number (30) of local referenda on the issue of directly elected mayors.

The reasons for holding these referenda owed little to the idea that the people ought to be consulted because of the importance of the issues involved. Rather they were the result in 1975 of deep and irreconcilable divisions within the governing Labour party and in 1979 of the Parliamentary circumstances in which a minority Labour Government was seeking to legislate on an issue which divided its own backbenchers. Similarly, the Northern Ireland referendum of 1973 could only be understood in the light of the troubled circumstances prevailing in the province at the time. However, it was a rather different matter in the various referenda of 1997 and 1998. These were held in Scotland, Wales and London with a view to confirming popular support and to strengthening the legitimacy of the proposals concerned and so speeding their passage through Parliament. With regard to the Northern Ireland referendum, this was deemed necessary to show that the future of the province was being determined with the consent of the people. The regional referendum in the north-east of England was held because the Government believed it to be the region where the policy of establishing regional assemblies had the most support. However, anti-regional assembly campaigners argued that any such new tier of government would be an expensive talking shop with little real power, and it was this argument that won the day with the general public.

The Labour Government which first came into office in 1997 had stated its intention to hold two national referenda, one on the electoral system used for elections to the House of Commons and one on whether or not Britain should join the single European currency, while in 2004 Tony Blair had announced that there would be a referendum on the European Constitution. To date, none of these intentions has been put into effect, although for rather different reasons – namely because successive landslide majorities have made Labour less inclined to see any merits in electoral reform, because Tony Blair and Gordon Brown were not confident of winning on the issue of a single currency, and because the whole issue of a European Constitution was 'put on ice' following the rejection of the Constitutional Treaty in referenda in both France and the Netherlands.

giving people more say over their own lives

Finally, it is necessary to mention a number of initiatives during the 1980s which extended the principle of consultation through the use of local votes in a number of areas. For example, the Housing Act 1988 provided for Council tenants to 'choose' a landlord by allowing them to vote to transfer to a Housing Association, Housing Trust or private landlord. Similarly, the Education Act 1988 provided for schools to 'opt out' of Local Authority control via an affirmative vote amongst parents. The Thatcher Government also introduced a series of measures of trade-union reform, among which the Trade Union Act 1984 stipulated that trade unions should hold secret ballots before taking industrial action. Similarly, under the Local Government Act 2000 local authorities were given the power to organize local referenda on whether or not to have directly elected mayors: 30 such referenda have taken place with 11 voting in favour of directly elected mayors and the rest voting against.

public opinion polls

Public opinion polls are a means by which an attempt is made to measure the attitudes, behaviour, beliefs, intentions and opinions of the public. Political opinion polls are primarily concerned with voting intentions and opinions relating to current issues and personalities. Their purpose is to enable conclusions to be drawn about the opinions and intentions of the public as a whole by extrapolating from small, though representative, samples. As a result they have emerged as a means by which the sometimes incoherent opinions of the public are formulated and then communicated to those involved in the political process.

Opinion polls have undoubtedly contributed to Government action or inaction in some cases. For example, they were a significant factor in the debate concerning abortion law reform in the mid 1960s. A series of opinion polls was commissioned by the Abortion Law Reform Association and the findings were used to demonstrate to the Government and to Parliament that public opinion had shifted to the side of reform. Similarly, it is apparent that Government activity in important areas of policy has been influenced by opinion polls. For example, opinion poll findings which demonstrated the unpopularity of the Poll Tax were influential in persuading the Conservative Government under Margaret Thatcher to modify the impact of the tax in ways designed to reduce, if only marginally, its adverse impact.[16]

Overall it can be said that although politicians pay close attention to opinion polls, the action which they take is not necessarily based on them. The clearest case in which public opinion, as revealed by opinion polls, has been conspicuously and continuously ignored is on the issue of capital punishment. To begin with, in 1965 the death penalty was abolished provisionally for a five-year period by a free vote in the House of Commons – a decision taken in the face of considerable public opposition evidenced by overwhelming opinion poll majorities of 80 per cent or more in favour of its retention.[17] Despite the fact that every poll taken since that time has revealed a large, if declining, majority of the population in favour of restoring the death penalty, Parliament has repeatedly and clearly voted against such a step. More recently the Labour Government legislated to outlaw fox hunting in 2005, despite opinion poll evidence showing that 59 per cent of the public were opposed to such a move.[18]

focus groups and people's panels

During their years in Opposition (1979–97) the Labour Party began to use focus groups – small representative groups of people – to test reaction to existing or suggested policy. These market research techniques were seen by many as important contributions to the modernisation of Labour policy and hence the party's eventual return to power. In office the Government sought to carry the idea forward, setting up a 5000 strong 'People's Panel' reflecting representative samples of the population to ensure that all the various groups were included. This enabled the organizers to assess public attitudes to the Government, what it did and the services it offered. This testing of public opinion has been done in a number of ways:

- General surveys conducted over the telephone
- Small focus groups
- Larger 'citizens' juries', where those selected spend several days in discussion and answer detailed questions.

One criticism of this approach is that it bypasses open, public consultation in favour of a more closed process dominated by market research analysts, pollsters and 'spin doctors'. Another argument is that it is the job of politicians to give a lead and not simply to follow the results of such soundings.

surveys and enquiries

At the turn of the century a number of social enquiries into living conditions which involved extensive house-to-house surveys – such as Charles Booth's *Life and Labour of the People of London* (1897) and Seebohm Rowntree's *Poverty: A Study of Town Life* – had a significant impact on the climate of political opinion at the time and provided much factual support for the drive towards social reform and public welfare. Lord Scarman's *Report into the Brixton Disorders of 10–12 April 1981* owed a lot to the oral evidence provided by more than 50 witnesses, including police officers, journalists, members of the emergency services and residents of the area who had witnessed the course of events, as well as the written evidence from 284 organisations and individuals and some 450 letters from members of the public.[19] Described by the *Daily Mirror* as 'one of the great social documents of our time', it influenced the subsequent political debate on the inner cities, the police and the ethnic minorities. The same could be said of the Report of the Archbishop of Canterbury's Commission on Urban Priority Areas (*Faith in the City*, 1985), which drew extensively on evidence taken by the Commission all over the country.[20]

As the range of Government activity has become greater and the role of Government correspondingly larger, so the requirement for information has grown, both to estimate social needs and to monitor the effects of Government action. Fundamental to this process is the census carried out every ten years, the most recent in 2001. In addition, the Office for National Statistics carries out surveys and research on a regular and continuing basis which provides essential factual information for policy makers in Government. The Family Expenditure Survey and the International Passenger Survey are both examples of this work. Individual Government Departments are also involved in gathering data. For example, the Department for Transport carries out extensive and detailed analysis of the numbers of people who cross the English Channel.[21] We should also mention in this context the public opinion research done for large-scale planning inquiries, such as those which examined proposals for a third London Airport, the Sizewell B nuclear power station, and the Channel Tunnel Rail Link. All of these investigations were intended to contribute to the quality of policy making.

In addition it is now standard practice for the views of the public to be sought as part of a process of general consultation during the policy-making process. For example, in 1997 the Government sought to test public opinion on the matter of women serving as front-line troops in the army, while in 1998 the Human Genetics Advisory Commission (HGAC) and the Human Fertilisation and Embryology Authority (HFEA) published a document which asked a series of questions on the matter of therapeutic cloning and invited responses from the public on this morally difficult issue.[22] More generally, within the context of modernization, systematic consultation of so-called 'stateholders' has become an essential element of a modernized process for preparing Ministerial decisions and Government legislation.

direct contacts between MPs and the public

There are a variety of opportunities available to Members of Parliament directly to ascertain the views of the public. First, there are the letters, emails and phone calls which MPs receive both from their constituents and more widely from the general public. A typical MP now receives more than 150 such communications a week, receiving in one day the amount of correspondence which would have been received in one week in the 1960s.[23]

Second, Members of Parliament are lobbied with increasing frequency by sometimes very large delegations which turn up at the Palace of Westminster or at their constituency offices demanding to see their MP and put their case. Third, nearly all MPs hold what are described as 'surgeries' or 'advice bureaux' in their constituencies either once a week or twice a month. These provide yet another source of information on public attitudes, although because of their self-selecting characteristics, such aggrieved constituents may not be representative of the broader swathe of public opinion.

organised groups

Pressure groups have been considered in Chapter 6, so it is sufficient here simply to point out that individuals can and do join with others of a like mind in an attempt to get a particular opinion or set of opinions across to politicians of all parties and to the Government of the day and, by so doing, seek to secure political action consistent with those opinions. On the other hand, it is worth noting the cautionary advice offered by Jack Straw when Home Secretary in 1998 that 'elected politicians should be ever wary of the dangers of becoming the agents of sectional interests and of ignoring the concerns of those who elect them. One need only look at how unsuccessful the Labour Party was throughout the 1980s to see that.'[24]

political parties

Political parties were considered in Chapter 5, so we need merely point out here that individuals can join the political party whose broad ideological approach most closely matches their own and then work within its structures in an attempt to influence party policy and, by extension, public policy as well.

the media

Although the subject of the media was covered in Chapter 7, it is nonetheless necessary to make two further points in this chapter. First, although the media exert great influence on public opinion, it is often a transient and unreliable influence. Moreover, political news and opinion is usually only a fairly small part of total media output and often reflects not much more than the views and prejudices of the journalists and editors or producers concerned.

Second, there is the issue of the extent to which the media are acting as neutral channels of communication between the Government and the governed, or seeking to lead, form and even distort public opinion. It is argued by some that the only political reality is that created by the media, since it is the media which assess what people think and then broadcast their conclusions to others. However, active politicians and their followers contend that they have to deal with the problems caused by media distortions, including public misconceptions. The truth is that there is no final answer to this dispute and nearly everything depends upon an individual's own point of view and personal experience.

8.3 the effects of opinion

more deferential politicians

Public opinion in Britain has a variety of political effects. It is arguable that one effect has been to make most politicians more deferential to the wishes of the electorate. While this tendency may seem to have reached its zenith in the time of Harold Wilson, who as Leader of the Labour Party (1963–76) paid assiduous attention to opinion polls and other psephological data (such as by-election and local election results), it has remained significant at all times, especially when General Elections are imminent. Certainly it has been true in the negative sense that leading politicians both in and out of office usually take considerable care not to put forward policies or take positions which seem destined to encounter powerful opposition from public opinion. Even the redoubtable Margaret Thatcher, who more than any other leader sought to do what she believed to be right regardless of the political consequences, adjusted Conservative policy on some occasions in order to take account of the public responses which might have been expected if she and her Ministerial colleagues had pressed ahead with certain radical policies in an unaltered form.[25]

It has been true in a positive sense as well. For example, it was the public response to the Dunblane shooting in 1995 that led the Government of the day to introduce tough gun-control legislation and the Labour Opposition of the time to pledge to introduce a complete ban on all handguns in civilian use – a pledge they later fulfilled when in Government. Similarly, in 2000 when the Labour Chancellor, Gordon Brown, was committed to raising fuel taxes, the opposition of the People's Fuel Lobby took the Government by surprise and forced the Chancellor to freeze the level of fuel taxes. More recently, the anti-road pricing online petition in 2007 was seen as firing a warning shot across the Government's bows against such a policy.

This draws attention to the elusive and controversial concept of *political impossibility* which has played such an important part in so many political calculations by leading politicians over the years. In essence it can be defined as the influence on political decision makers of anticipated public reaction. Some have argued that this is a harmful influence on politics, since it can prevent the adoption of radical policies which may be justified as an appropriate response to many of Britain's deep-seated national problems. Others have argued that it is a beneficial influence, since it can be seen as a contribution to British national cohesion, especially during difficult periods of disappointment and relative decline when a less sensitive political approach could prove very damaging. The argument is really between those who regard the conservatism of British public opinion as something of a saving grace, since it constitutes a significant obstacle to the ambitions of the zealots in each main party, and those who see it as a tragedy, since it has often constituted a virtually insuperable barrier to radical action. If the overriding priority is to guard against radical change, then the former view ought to be commended; if it is to make radical change, then the latter view ought to prevail. In any event the outcome is likely to depend on the personal temperament of the leading politicians who have to carry the responsibility of Government.

Under Margaret Thatcher's leadership in the 1980s the Conservative Government tended to press for what it believed to be right almost regardless of the political consequences. Under John Major's leadership in the 1990s the approach was less ideological and more pragmatic in a way strangely reminiscent of Harold Wilson's period as Prime Minister. John Major's supporters justified his pragmatism on two principal grounds. First, he had been elected leader of his party in 1990 precisely because he was *not* Margaret Thatcher, and, second, he had to give his highest priority to holding his party together – something which was made more difficult after the 1992 General Election when the Conservative majority in the Commons was reduced to a small fraction of the majority that Margaret Thatcher had enjoyed.

Both in Opposition and in Government, Tony Blair was highly sensitive to public opinion and he sought – with the notable exception of the Iraq War – to be in tune with the views of the general public. Indeed he observed that: 'Supposing you are running Marks & Spencer or Sainsbury ... you will be continually trying to work out whether your consumers are satisfied with the product that they are getting. I don't think there is anything wrong with Government trying to do that in the same way.'[26]

a counterweight to pressure groups

Another important effect of public opinion has been the way in which it has provided a useful counterweight to the influence of pressure groups in the British political system. As noted in Chapter 6, there have been times when it has been very difficult for any Government to resist the claims of certain powerful interest groups, such as the National Union of Mineworkers in the 1970s or the British Medical Association in the late 1980s, without appealing over the heads of the group concerned to the general public. This is essentially what Edward Heath sought to do when he called a General Election in February 1974 on the issue of 'who governs?'. It is also what the 1979–83 Conservative Government sought to do when it introduced legislation to provide for secret ballots in trade-union affairs. In each case the intention of Ministers was to appeal over the heads of obstructive interest groups to the wider public in an effort to fulfil their political purposes. Of course, the success of this tactic depends on the power of the opposing interest group and the degree of public sympathy or support which it can generate for its cause. For example, the NUT's campaign against the Conservative Government's determination to introduce national curriculum assessment in the 1990s depended on the credibility of its propaganda, the willingness of its members to remain solidly behind the union line and the sympathy of parents.

Whenever politicians invoke the views of the wider public in support of their cause, it is usually a sign that they have been obstructed or opposed by a small but powerful group which seeks to set its sectional interest above that of the general community. This has been as true when Labour Ministers in the 1970s complained about the pernicious influence of the City of London as when Conservative Ministers in the 1980s criticised the abuse of trade-union power. In each case they sought to defend the principle that general public opinion has more inherent legitimacy than any sectional group. Yet every political system also needs safeguards against the tyranny of the majority (or even of a minority of the electorate exploiting a Parliamentary majority), since in most societies there have been times when majority opinion has been unfair or unenlightened and defeated minorities have needed protection against it. Thus a balance has to be struck which allows fair opportunities for both majority and minority opinion, while retaining a democratic presumption in favour of the former.

the influence of opinion polls

Yet another effect of public opinion has been to give considerable credence to political opinion polls. Such polls have become the most systematic expression of public opinion between General Elections. When sensibly interpreted, they can provide a useful navigational aid for politicians, whether in Government or Opposition. The systematic analysis of opinion poll data has enabled the parties to identify key target groups of voters – for instance, the wives of blue-collar workers in the case of the Conservative Party, or the public sector salariat in the case of the Labour Party – and then to concentrate and organise their efforts with particular target groups in mind.

Opinion polls also guide the Prime Minister of the day in making the decision about when to call a General Election and they can affect the morale of party activists if the findings are very good or very bad for a particular party or its leader.[27] While opinion polls are not normally decisive in determining policy or decision making, it is understandable that they influence both the development and the presentation of policy. On the other hand, there is a widely held view that local and European elections are a better guide to the public mood.

Special considerations apply to the role of opinion polls during election campaigns. Some experts have argued that the polls produce a bandwagon effect which assists the party that seems to be winning. Others have argued for the backlash effect which leads doubting voters to rally to the party that appears to be the underdog. One thing seems certain, however, and that is that opinion polls can have a more powerful effect on the result at by-elections than at General Elections, since they can signal to floating voters which is the best vehicle for effective tactical voting.[28]

the increasing use of referenda

Still another effect of public opinion is visible in the way in which the growing self-confidence and declining deference of the general public has led to periodic demands for national referenda. These demands have arisen on a variety of political issues, notably those which demonstrate that Parliamentary opinion is out of tune with public opinion, for example on the emotive issue of capital punishment. Of course, national referenda have not been a defining characteristic of the constitutional arrangements in Britain and most MPs in all parties have been keen to see that this remains the position. Yet there is an increasing tendency for politicians to offer national referenda on certain issues which split their own parties and on which there is no actual consensus – for example, the adoption of the euro or a possible switch to PR for Westminster elections.

The referenda on Britain's membership of the European Community in 1975, on devolution to Scotland and Wales in 1979 and 1997, on a Mayor and Assembly for London in 1998 and on an elected assembly for the North East region are all examples of the expediency of this device. The stated reason for holding referenda in these cases was that they were issues of constitutional importance which did not lend themselves to ordinary Parliamentary decision making. However, this does not explain why there was no referendum on the 1992 Maastricht Treaty, an issue which undoubtedly involved constitutional change. The actual reasons for holding referenda in 1975 and 1979 owed more to the party political and Parliamentary circumstances of the times; those of 1997, 1998 and 2004 owed more to the problem of consent, but grew out of the experience of these earlier examples.

Despite the fact that the Labour Government which came into office in 1997 promised referenda on the electoral system for Westminster, on joining the single European currency and later on the European Constitution, the holding of referenda are exceptions to the general rule that Britain is still a Parliamentary rather than a plebiscitary democracy. On the other hand, as such precedents have been set, it may prove increasingly difficult for Ministers to resist future demands for referenda on a wide range of political issues, especially when majority opinion in the House of Commons is seen to be out of tune with the overwhelming opinion of the general public.[29]

the impact of direct action

Finally, mention should be made of the impact of direct action as a powerful form of political communication. At various stages in British history public protest, whether spontaneous or induced, has played an important, sometimes decisive, part in the expression of public opinion. Historical examples would include:

▸ Wat Tyler and the Peasants' Revolt in 1381
▸ The Peterloo Massacre in 1819
▸ The Chartist Movement in the 1840s
▸ The Suffragette demonstrations in the early 1900s
▸ The Invergordon 'mutiny' in 1931
▸ The Jarrow and other unemployment marches in the 1930s
▸ The inner city riots in the summer of 1981
▸ The miners' dispute of 1984–85
▸ The campaign of civil disobedience against the Poll Tax in the late 1980s
▸ The activity of animal welfare protesters against the live animal export trade in 1994–95.

More recent examples would include:

▸ The People's Fuel Lobby in 2000
▸ The mass demonstration against the Iraq War in February 2003
▸ The actions of both pro- and anti-hunt campaigners in 2003–05.

Nowadays lawful public demonstrations are usually organised for publicity purposes by minorities who feel strongly about an issue, but who also feel excluded from the regular channels of influence and representation in society. The fact that some people have recourse to such methods may cast doubt upon the strength of their arguments, but more often it reflects an assessment of the chances of attaining their objectives by more orthodox institutional means, such as Parliamentary pressure or official contacts in Whitehall. For example, the Muslim demonstrations in London against the appearance (in a Danish newspaper) of cartoons depicting the prophet Mohammed illustrated the anger and frustration of some in the Muslim community at the unwillingness of the Government and Parliament to respond to their feelings. Public demonstrations have always been a recognised way of seeking publicity for a grievance or support for a cause, and most are conducted in a peaceful and law-abiding manner. Yet they do not always succeed in influencing political decisions in their chosen direction, since the impact on the general public can be the opposite of what they seek.

8.4 public opinion in context

The question has often been asked about the circumstances in which politicians should follow, lead, educate, cajole or simply ignore public opinion. The issue is certainly not new. Edmund Burke writing to his constituents in 1774 stated what is the classic case for representative government. He said: 'Your representative owes to you not his industry only, but his judgement; and he betrays, instead of serving you, if he sacrifices it to your opinion.'[30] This approach has been cited with approval by MPs over the years when refusing to bow to what they regard as the unreasonable or untutored demands of public opinion – for example, for the restoration of capital punishment. The traditional position can be simply stated – namely that the public is expected at a General Election to choose the party which it wishes to see in Government and then to allow its representatives to get on with the job until the following General Election when the voters can make a further decision whether to grant or withdraw an electoral mandate to the party in office.

The alternative view is one derived from the philosophy of Jean-Jacques Rousseau who declared that: 'the deputies of the people are not and cannot be their representatives, they can only be their commissioners, and as such they are not qualified to conclude anything definitely. No act of theirs can be a law, unless it has been ratified by the people in person; and without their ratification nothing is a law.'[31] This view (often described as 'direct democracy') has never gained much support in Britain, not least because it clearly conflicts with the concept of Parliamentary democracy. Yet it seems likely to gain ground in the future given that the British people have become less deferential to leaders and appear keener to take their own decisions.

Traditional discussion of the part that public opinion ought to play in the formation of public policy tends to assume that members of the public have worthwhile opinions to communicate. Such an assumption, however, is not necessarily borne out by experience. It should also be recognised that the relationship between public opinion and decision making is two-way and no simple causal relationship is apparent. Public opinion seldom moves in a single direction without setting up contradictory and countervailing forces. Nor does it exist in a vacuum. Rather it is an integral part of any political system and promotes the politics of anticipated reaction.

Public opinion is only likely to have a positive effect if channelled or exploited by politicians, pressure groups or the media. It is more often a factor of constraint, setting limits to what is acceptable in a pluralist society rather than providing new opportunities for action by decision makers or opinion formers.

For this reason the art of governing in a Parliamentary democracy entails the ability to calculate when too many people will say 'no', but before they have an opportunity to do so.

There has been both consensus and controversy in British politics since the Second World War. Generally, Governments have relied on at least the tacit acquiescence, if not the positive consent, of the various groups and interests with which they have to deal; and on the whole they have preferred discussion, compromise and agreement to the imposition of partisan policy on unwilling institutions, groups or interests.

The 1945–51 Labour Government under Clement Attlee established the post-war consensus under which Britain was governed for more than a quarter of a century thereafter. There were six main elements in this consensus:

- A mixed economy with extensive state intervention, including a large industrial public sector
- A commitment to full employment
- An extensive welfare state – with provisions 'from the cradle to the grave'
- Progressive taxation with high marginal rates and a commitment to buoyant public expenditure
- Acceptance of the trade unions as legitimate economic and social partners in the process of Government
- A belief in the goal of a fairer and more equal society.

Although this consensus was modified or extended by successive Governments of both parties, there was no substantial or sustained challenge to it until the mid 1970s.[32] In these circumstances the political argument was largely confined to disputes about the best way to manage the mixed economy and to distribute the fruits of economic growth. Admittedly, there were some deep divisions of opinion about some issues, notably in the sphere of foreign policy. For example, the Suez expedition in 1956, the process of decolonisation in the late 1950s and early 1960s, and Britain's relationship with the European Community all caused serious dissension between and within the main parties. Yet such arguments took place against a background of basic agreement on socio-economic issues of fundamental importance.

This political consensus was challenged during the latter part of the 1960s and finally undermined by powerful events in the 1970s:

- Inflation began to soar as a consequence of volatile exchange rates and the quadrupling of oil prices triggered by OPEC
- As the recession went deeper, unemployment rose and the public finances plunged into debt
- Uunder the new policy of monetarism imposed by the IMF in 1976, Keynesian remedies began to be seen as part of the problem rather than the solution

▸ Both the Labour Government and the Conservative Government which followed it in 1979 were obliged to manage or even lower public expectations to fit the new realities.

In such circumstances the Labour Party moved to the Left and the Conservative Party to the Right, thus producing the political polarisation of the 1980s which had not been seen in Britain since the 1930s.

From 1979 to 1990 three successive Thatcher Administrations effectively demolished much of the post-war concensus. As Norman Tebbit, one of Margaret Thatcher's closest allies, explained at the time: 'our task is to establish the new political consensus within which our opponents, too, must work'.[33] The commitment to full employment was abandoned, the battle against inflation was given priority, the role and responsibilities of the state were deliberately reduced, and the power of the trade unions was curbed. In the process public attitudes and perceptions were changed, leading to a greater sense of economic realism, more respect for market forces and greater acceptance that people should not look to Government for solutions to every problem. By the end of the 1980s the result was the establishment of a new 'common ground', one with which the Government's opponents were obliged to come to terms. Among the political casualties were the old Labour Party, which lost a considerable part of its support to the newly formed 'Alliance' of Liberals and Social Democrats, and the so-called 'Wets' within the Conservative Party who had sought, but failed, to uphold the principles of the post-war consensus.

On becoming Leader of the Labour Party in 1994 Tony Blair was convinced that it was necessary to the future success of his party to demonstrate that it accepted much of the Thatcherite consensus. This involved adopting centre-Right positions on key issues, such as taxation and public spending, the role of markets, the powers of trade unions, privatisation and law and order. In short it involved the acceptance of at least some of the tenets of the Thatcherite legacy. The resulting policy revolution within the Labour Party was implemented with considerable skill and efficiency and reaped the rewards of a resounding victory at the General Election of 1997 and re-election in both 2001 and 2005.

However, nothing ever stands still in British politics, so we should not be surprised to notice that the new middle ground seems to be occupied by all three main parties which acknowledge the new, post-Thatcherite/Blairite consensus. The guiding principles seem to include a readiness to accept most of the implications of living in a market economy, offset in Labour's case by an urge to intervene and to redistribute some income and wealth via a 'fairer' tax and social security system; in the Conservative case by a wish to regulate the liberalised economy no more than strictly necessary and to concentrate social provision principally upon those who really need it; and in the Liberal Democrat case by the concept of empowering the individual through the creation of a contractual relationship between tax payer and Government, by seeking to change the relationship between Whitehall and Town Hall; and by focusing particularly on civil liberties.

Differences between the Left and the Right are not the only significant cleavages in British public opinion. There is also the important gap which exists between informed opinion and mass opinion.

Informed opinion may be defined as opinion held by the minority of people who are 'in the know' about political issues and whose views are usually, but not always, the result of a recognisably rational process of thought. Typically it is the opinion of politicians at Westminster, civil servants in Whitehall, political journalists, pressure group spokesmen and those prominent in some other walks of life, such as public corporations, local government, medicine, education, the law, the church and the City. In view of the metropolitan character of British political opinion, it often derives disproportionately from interacting London elites, although it can also be influenced by ephemeral intellectual trends which often originate in the universities and in so-called 'think tanks', such as the Institute for Economic Affairs, the Institute for Public Policy Research, Demos and the Social Market Foundation. It is therefore essentially the opinion of the current Establishment and its licensed critics.[34]

Mass opinion, on the other hand, is often little more than ignorant sentiment, although it is usually based on significant attitudes, beliefs and ideas which are rooted in popular experience. This means that it has often to be conjured up before it can be said to exist. As V.O. Key observed, 'public opinion does not emerge like a cyclone and push obstacles before it; rather it develops under leadership.'[35] The extent of public ignorance about the basic facts of politics contributes to this situation and has been a matter of record for some time. For example, in 1964 almost a quarter of a representative sample did not know that the coal industry had been nationalised for nearly 20 years. In 1971 another opinion poll showed that only 13 per cent of those questioned could name the six member states of the European Community at a time when the British Government was engaged in widely publicised negotiations for British entry. In 1978 only 46 per cent of those questioned in a national poll could give the name of their MP and a poll in 1979 showed that 77 per cent of those questioned did not know what was meant by the acronym NATO – 30 years after the foundation of the North Atlantic Treaty Organization.

The high level of public ignorance of the facts of politics has persisted ever since especially among younger people. For example, a MORI 'state of the nation' poll for the Joseph Rowntree Reform Trust in 1995 revealed that 53 per cent of women and 35 per cent of men were prepared to admit that they 'know nothing or had never heard' of proportional representation; that 54 per cent of women and 34 per cent of men were equally ignorant of the European Union; and that 43 per cent of women and 29 per cent of men knew absolutely nothing about the House of Lords. In 1998 in a survey of young people aged 16–24 commissioned by the British Youth Council, 10 per cent of respondents were unable to name the Prime Minister, 60 per cent were unable to name the Leader of the Conservative Party, 85 per cent were unable to name the Home

Secretary and 97 per cent were unable to name the Health Secretary. In 2004 a MORI poll showed that only 13 per cent of people asked could name an MEP representing their region while 82 per cent said that they did not have enough information on the issues involved to make a considered decision on the European Constitution. In 2005 an ICM poll of first-time voters found 20 per cent not voting because of 'not knowing enough about it'.

Bearing in mind the amount of political communication which takes place, it is perhaps a little difficult to understand why such a degree of public ignorance and apathy has persisted. The explanation could be that those politicians and others who have something to say are not saying it with sufficient clarity or repetition. It could be that the channels of communication in the mass media are defective for this purpose. It could even be that the public is perfectly able to hear, but not really prepared to listen because of a widespread mood of cynicism and even alienation from the whole process of party politics. Simple observation would suggest that politicians and other opinion formers try hard to impart a great deal of fact and opinion to the general public, perhaps even too much for easy assimilation. It would also suggest that the media, and especially television, are more pervasive and influential than ever before. Yet it is equally clear that this large amount of communication does not necessarily produce a well-informed or enlightened public.

In short, mass opinion on most political issues consists of a large component of ignorance, a considerable lack of interest, a high degree of cynicism, a certain amount of prejudice, an assortment of received ideas, a smattering of popular mythology, a dose of wishful thinking and considerable rationalisation of personal experience. If this appears to be something of a caricature, then it must be said that there is not much evidence from opinion polls or other systematic sources to disprove it. It seems to be the political reality in Britain and other democracies and it will probably continue to be the case until such time as a more positive and less cynical political culture develops.

8.5 conclusion

Governments are undoubtedly influenced by public opinion. However, the extent to which they choose to pay attention to it depends on how vital it is in the resolution of a particular issue. The extent to which a Government follows public opinion will also depend on how it interprets the views of informed opinion. The opinions expressed from these quarters often carry more weight than mass opinion. It is evident that all those involved in political decision making have to take full account of public opinion. Where they differ is over their definitions of public opinion, how it should be measured and assessed and the significance to be attached to what they find out. The conclusion must be that public opinion in Britain influences, but is not necessarily a determinant of, what happens in British politics.

Whatever shape it takes or force it demonstrates, public opinion in Britain can be regarded as a source of political legitimacy, a counterweight to the influence of pressure groups, a form of political intelligence and occasionally even a 'Court of Appeal' in matters of strong public concern or great importance. Yet its true value is limited by the fact that, in complex issues of national policy, it is usually not based on sufficient knowledge or experience and is often more of an echo than an inspiration for the positions taken by leading politicians and other opinion formers. It is undoubtedly a dynamic factor in the working of the British political system, since it involves a constant and continuous process of two-way communication between the politicians and the people.

Political leadership will always have a major part to play in the formation of public opinion. Yet, if such leadership is to be really effective, it will have to make itself felt beyond the limited confines of Whitehall and Westminster. Metropolitan elites will need to leave the corridors of power and make more frequent contact with the general public in all parts of the country. In any event all opinion-formers will need to have a clearer idea of what they want to say and how best to say it. The key people in the media will need to offer more political news and views and to present such material in balanced and responsible ways. Schools and other institutions of learning will need to put more emphasis on political literacy in all its forms. Yet, even assuming a reasonable degree of success with all these endeavours, the politicians will still have to keep their fingers crossed and hope that the British people really want to play an active part in the nation's pluralist political process.

SUGGESTED QUESTIONS

1   How is public opinion formed and influenced in Britain?
2   What are the ways in which public opinion is brought to the attention of politicians in Britain?
3   What are the effects of public opinion on British Government and politics?

part **3**

parliament

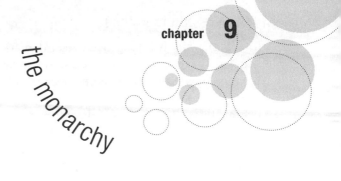

There was a time – certainly the late 1970s (1977 was Queen Elizabeth II's Silver Jubilee) and the early 1980s (1981 saw the wedding of Prince Charles to Lady Diana Spencer) – when the institution of Monarchy was sure of itself, widely admired and overwhelmingly popular; in short, it stood unchallenged at the apex of British society. The fact that the Monarch was a constituent part of the British system of government tended to be glossed over, even ignored altogether. Indeed, part of the success of constitutional monarchy in Britain has been that as it ceased to be politically significant it grew in popular acclaim. However, any golden age did not last as the personal lives of members of the Royal Family became temporarily dysfunctional in the early 1990s, reaching a crescendo in the immediate aftermath of the death of Diana, Princess of Wales, in 1997. As a result of these events the institution of Monarchy and the role of the Royal Family in Britain came to be politically and publicly questioned as they had not been since the brief reign of Edward VIII in 1936.

In Britain continuity and change have gone hand-in-hand. Continuity has been the dominant feature of British constitutional development, yet this has not meant the absence of change as age-old institutions have evolved and adapted to fulfil purposes often very different from those for which they were originally created. Nowhere is this more true than in the case of the Monarchy.

In formal terms the Monarchy is one of the institutions of Parliament. With a Queen on the throne every Government is 'Her Majesty's Government', the Opposition is 'Her Majesty's Loyal Opposition' and the Monarch still has an important, if largely formal, part to play in Britain's constitutional arrangements. It is the Queen who opens each new session of Parliament, who reads 'the Queen's Speech' from the throne on such occasions,and who gives her Royal Assent to Bills, without which they could not become Acts of Parliament and hence the law of the land.

The Monarchy has long been regarded as one of the 'dignified' rather than 'efficient' parts of the constitution, to use Walter Bagehot's nineteenth-century terminology. As a result the powers which the Monarch possesses today are more theoretical than real. They are based upon convention and residual Royal prerogatives, the residue of discretionary or arbitrary authority legally left in the hands of the Monarch but actually exercised by the Government of the day. Such power can only be used within the confines of well-established custom and practice. If such conventions were ever broken by the Monarch, it would discredit and possibly do fatal damage to the institution of the Monarchy itself. If the Monarch were to exercise constitutional power without reference to the views and preferences of the Prime Minister of the day, it could provoke a constitutional crisis.

Today the residual powers and functions of the Monarchy essentially fall under two broad headings which can be termed the *political* and the *symbolic*. The self-restraint exercised by the Monarch in the political sphere has bolstered the appeal of the Monarchy in the symbolic sphere.

political functions

the choice of Prime Minister

Whereas George III chose and dismissed Prime Ministers almost at will, the last Monarch to choose a Prime Minister without advice was Queen Victoria in 1894, and today Elizabeth II is 'free' to choose as Prime Minister only the elected leader of the party which commands majority support in the House of Commons. It would only be in the exceptional circumstances of a so-called 'hung Parliament' – that is, one in which no single party has an overall majority in the Commons – that the Monarch could be faced with alternatives, either calling upon the leader of the largest single party to form a minority Government or possibly looking for a senior political figure with a better chance of forming a Government which could command the support of a majority in the Commons.

During the first 20 years following the Second World War, however, the position was more shaded, at any rate in relation to the choice of Conservative Prime Ministers. In January 1957, when Anthony Eden became too ill to continue as Prime Minister after the debacle of the Suez expedition, the Queen took advice from Sir Winston Churchill and the Marquess of Salisbury before inviting Harold Macmillan to form a new Government. In October 1963, when Harold Macmillan became seriously ill and a successor had to be found for the position of Prime Minister, the Queen again took advice – this time from Harold Macmillan himself, who was in hospital – before inviting Lord Home to form a new Government. In both cases a new leader of the Conservative Party was said to have 'emerged' from the process of informal soundings which characterised the decision making of the party in those days. On the last occasion, the behaviour of the so-called 'magic circle' was strongly criticised by Iain Macleod and Enoch Powell, who subsequently both refused to serve in the Administration of Sir Alec Douglas-Home (the style to which Lord Home reverted after renouncing his peerage in order to sit in the Commons as Prime Minister).

Since 1965 in the case of the Conservative Party, 1935 in the case of the Liberal/Liberal Democrat Party and 1922 in the case of the Labour Party, there have been systematic arrangements to ensure that a new leader is elected to succeed one who retires or dies. The result is that the role of the Queen is now confined to choosing as Prime Minister whoever has already been elected as leader of the governing party – hence Gordon Brown became Prime Minister in 2007 with his (unopposed) election as leader of the Labour Party following Tony Blair's decision to stand down. Of course, when there is a clear change of Government following a decisive result in a General Election, the Queen sends for the leader of the victorious party and invites that individual to form a new Government – hence Tony Blair was sent for in May 1997.

There has always been the possibility of a more significant role for the Monarch at a time of national crisis or when a General Election has produced a 'hung Parliament'. An example of the first eventuality occurred in 1931 when George V was instrumental in encouraging the formation of the National Government under Ramsay MacDonald in order to get through the Commons the deflationary economic measures which had not been acceptable to a significant part of the Parliamentary Labour Party when it had been in power on its own.[1] Another example occurred in 1940, when George VI had some influence on the choice of Winston Churchill to succeed Neville Chamberlain as Prime Minister after the latter had been discredited by the significant number of abstentions within the Conservative Parliamentary Party at the end of a crucial debate of confidence on the conduct of the war.[2]

An example of the second eventuality occurred in February 1974 when it seemed possible for a while that the Queen could have been drawn into party political controversy by Edward Heath's attempt to retain power for the Conservatives by offering a pact (and seats in his Cabinet) to the Liberals after his party had been defeated at the General Election. As things turned out, it proved impossible for the then Liberal leader, Jeremy Thorpe, to persuade his party to do such a deal with the Conservatives. Thus a few days later Harold Wilson was duly invited by the Queen to form a minority Labour Government.[3]

Certainly the scenario of a hung Parliament – the prospects of which would increase if a proportional voting system were to be adopted for Westminster elections – is one which could give rise to the Monarch being involved in some very awkward decisions which could have very far-reaching political consequences. In such a situation the Monarch would be expected to send initially for the leader of the largest single party in the Commons who would then have to see whether a minority Government could be formed or whether some sort of understanding with one or more of the other parties was possible. Either course would be quite plausible and it would only be in the unlikely event of complete Parliamentary deadlock that the Monarch might be advised to send for another party leader or leading political figure to form a viable Government – rather than agree to a dissolution very soon after the previous General Election. Whatever happened, the Monarch might be obliged to play a significant, even decisive, role in the process of Government formation. This is not something which either the Monarch or the Monarch's advisers would relish, since it might well cast doubt on the traditional impartiality of the Monarchy in party political matters. Nonetheless, the possibility remains that the Monarch might have to exercise the discretion which constitutionally rests in the Monarch's hands, if there seemed to be no alternative.

dissolution of Parliament

It is now a well-established convention that the Monarch can only dissolve Parliament at the request of the Prime Minister in office within the five-year maximum life span of a Parliament. It is necessary to go back to the reign of Queen Anne to find the last example of a Monarch exercising the Royal prerogative to dissolve Parliament in an independent way. Even in 1913, when it was argued by some that George V might have been within his constitutional rights to have dissolved Parliament in order to give the electorate a chance to pronounce upon the Liberal Government's Bill for Irish Home Rule, A.V. Dicey, the eminent constitutional expert, was not prepared to recommend such a step to the King for fear that it would compromise the neutral constitutional position of the Monarchy.

Since that time various views have been advanced about the power of dissolution. One view, which was advocated by some after the very close General Election result in 1950, holds that if the Prime Minister in office is not prepared to recommend a dissolution in circumstances where it might be considered in the national interest to have one, then the Monarch is entitled to seek other leading figures in the Commons who might be prepared to recommend such a course. In the event such a view did not prevail in 1950 and it has not prevailed ever since. The Monarch is therefore bound by the established view and obliged to accept only the advice of the Prime Minister in office.

There may be a valid distinction, however, between the Monarch's constitutional right *to refuse* a dissolution on the grounds that it would lead to a premature and unnecessary General Election and the now unsustainable claim by any Monarch *to impose* a dissolution against the wishes of the Prime Minister in office. As far as the right to refuse a dissolution is concerned, no such request has been refused since the middle of the nineteenth century, although dissolutions have been refused more recently by Governors-General acting on behalf of the Monarch in Commonwealth countries. As for the right to impose a dissolution upon the Government of the day – in essence the dismissal of the Government – no British Government has been dismissed by the Monarch since George III dismissed the Fox–North Coalition under the titular leadership of the Duke of Portland in 1783.

There is another way in which the Monarch could become involved in controversy surrounding a dissolution. This would be if the Monarch suggested a dissolution – and hence a General Election – before agreeing to a request from the Government to exercise the Royal prerogative. This was the position in 1910 under both Edward VII and George V with regard to Herbert Asquith's request to create enough new Liberal peers to ensure the passage of the Parliament Bill in the House of Lords. On that occasion, two successive Monarchs made it clear that they would not feel justified in creating new peers until the electorate had a chance to express its views on the issue in a General Election.[4] In practice, of course, the exercise of any such form of royal initiative today would run the serious risk of totally discrediting the whole idea of constitutional Monarchy in Britain. It would involve the Monarchy in apparently taking sides in the political battle and that would destroy one of its vital assets, namely political impartiality.

Notwithstanding the conventional wisdom on this matter, there are some conceivable circumstances in which a Monarch might be justified in exercising the Royal prerogative of dissolution in defiance of the wishes of the Prime Minister in office. For example, if it became clear in the course of a 'hung Parliament' that a minority Government had outlived its usefulness and was simply standing in the way of a timely General Election which might produce a clearer Parliamentary result, those who advise the Palace on constitutional issues might be prepared to emphasise the arguments for such a dissolution. Such a course of action might also have to be considered if the Government broke the most basic of electoral rules, namely the five-year maximum life-span of a Parliament, without the necessary all-party support for doing so, as existed, exceptionally, during both World Wars.[5]

Another possibility is that an unpopular Prime Minister might carry out a threat to call a General Election in mid Parliament rather than agree under pressure from senior Cabinet colleagues either to change policy or even to resign as Prime Minister. In such circumstances established political conventions would support the position of the Prime Minister, even if there appeared to be sufficient support in the governing party for a change of policy or a new Prime Minister or both. Whatever might be the private views of the Monarch and the Monarch's advisers, it seems clear that they would be obliged to grant the wish of the Prime Minister in office, however unpopular that might be with most of the governing party. It would therefore be for the governing party to sort out its own problems of policy and personality rather than for the Monarch to intervene in the dispute. It must be stressed, however, that these are all hypothetical circumstances which would be most unlikely to arise in modern political conditions.

If the Monarch did proceed along these lines, it is likely that no more than a pyrrhic victory would be won, since such steps would almost certainly lead to a 'Monarch versus the people' clash at the ensuing General Election. This would probably be won by the aggrieved political party and might put in jeopardy the very continuation of Britain's constitutional Monarchy. Indeed, the exercise of Royal prerogative by the Governor-General in Australia in 1975 – when Sir John Kerr dismissed Gough Whitlam's Labour Government – was undoubtedly an important factor behind the rise of Republican sentiment in that country. The practical conclusion is that the Monarch in Britain today has no sensible alternative to accepting the advice of the Prime Minister in office, whatever might appear to be the arguments for doing otherwise.

assent to legislation

Royal assent to legislation is another aspect of the Monarch's prerogative which has become purely formal over the years. In the seventeenth century Charles II managed to postpone or quash Bills of which he disapproved by the simple expedient of mislaying them. Queen Anne was the last British Monarch to veto legislation outright when in 1707 she withheld assent from the Scottish Militia Bill. George III certainly encouraged the House of Lords to reject the India Bill in 1783, while George IV managed to delay legislation on Catholic emancipation by letting it be known that he was not happy with the idea. Queen Victoria was the last Monarch seriously to consider withholding assent, although there is some evidence that in 1913 George V toyed with the idea of refusing assent to the Government of Ireland Bill which was then being put through Parliament under the Parliament Act of 1911.

During Elizabeth II's Silver Jubilee speech to Parliament on 4 May 1977 – at a time when the question of legislating for devolution to Scotland and Wales was very firmly on the political agenda – the Queen declared: 'I cannot forget that I was crowned Queen of the United Kingdom of Great Britain and Northern Ireland. Perhaps this Jubilee is a time to remind ourselves of the benefits which union has conferred, at home and in our international dealings, on the inhabitants of all parts of this United Kingdom.'[6] Some took these words to be a warning shot fired across the bow of those politicians who sought in any way to weaken the unity of the Kingdom. However, this theory was never put to the test, since the devolution legislation received royal assent in the normal way in 1978. Thus the granting of Royal Assent has become a mere formality. Any attempt to make it otherwise would prompt a constitutional crisis and, consequently, all involved would go to great lengths to avoid any such eventuality.

creation of peers

The Monarch has the power to create new peers and in certain cases it is believed that the Palace still has some influence over the final selection from the various names proposed. Certainly there was a time when the use of this particular Royal prerogative was formidable indeed. For example, in 1711–12 Queen Anne, on the advice of her Ministers, created 12 new peers precisely to ensure ratification by the House of Lords of the Treaty of Utrecht. In 1831 William IV's threat (at the instigation of his Whig Prime Minister, Lord Grey) to create new peers helped to ensure the passage of the first Reform Bill against fierce Tory opposition. In 1911 the willingness of George V to create as many as 400 new Liberal peers (discreetly made known by the Prime Minister, Herbert

Asquith) caused the hereditary majority of Conservatives in the Upper House to give way to the Liberal majority in the House of Commons over what was to become the 1911 Parliament Act.[7]

Whereas in the past Monarchs took a keen interest in the creation of peers, in contemporary circumstances the creation of new peers by the Monarch has become little more than a constitutional formality. Appointments to the peerage are normally made twice a year when the names of the newly created peers appear in the Honours Lists. The appointments are made on the basis of advice given and coordinated by the Prime Minister in office. Nominations can be made by political parties, by the Appointments Commission – a non-statutory advisory non-departmental public body that makes recommendations for non-party-political peers – and members of the public. Suggestions are discreetly sifted and assessed by a small unit of civil servants attached to 10 Downing Street and by the Appointments Commission before the Prime Minister of the day makes the formal recommendations.

From 1964, life peerages were the usual order of the day, mainly because successive Prime Ministers felt generally disinclined to recommend the creation of hereditary peerages. Yet this was no more than a convention and as such it was capable of modification.[8] However, with the passage of the 1999 House of Lords Act and the consequent removal of the right to membership of the House of Lords for all but a residual group of 92 hereditary peers, there is now a separation, at least to some extent, of the peerage and automatic membership of the House of Lords. It is possible that further reform may lead to a complete separation.

granting of honours

The Monarch is also formally involved in the granting of honours, both civilian and military, to those whom it is customary for the nation to recognise and reward in this way. As with the creation of peerages, this usually happens twice a year when the Honours Lists are published. However, there can be special investitures to recognise special events: for example, the honours awarded to those whose acts of conspicuous gallantry had been recognised during the 1982 Falklands campaign, the 1990–91 Gulf War and following the invasion of Iraq in 2003. In nearly all cases the system is a popular and effective way of recording public recognition for those who have made notable contributions to the well-being of British society and who have shone in various walks of life. It also adds lustre to the institution of Monarchy and provides regular opportunities for rewarding service to the community.[9]

Nearly all such honours are awarded by the Monarch on the formal recommendation of the Prime Minister who, in turn, is advised by a small Civil Service unit attached to 10 Downing Street. Once again this unit sifts and assesses a wide range of recommendations made by MPs and others. Even so, a few honours have remained in the personal gift of the Monarch – for example, the Order of the Garter, the Order of the Thistle, the Order of Merit and the Royal Victorian Order. Usually these awards have no political significance, but are simply a way of signifying the Monarch's personal recognition of an outstanding person, such as Mother Theresa, the Catholic nun who worked for the hungry and the destitute in Calcutta until her death in 1997 and who was awarded the Order of Merit by the Queen on her visit to India in 1983, or Nelson Mandela, the first President of post-apartheid South Africa, who was awarded the Order of Merit by the Queen during her state visit to that country in 1995. Very occasionally such awards do have political significance, albeit marginally, as was the case in 1990 when the Queen awarded Margaret Thatcher the Order of Merit, following her resignation as Prime Minister, and Denis Thatcher an hereditary Baronetcy in recognition of his role in support of his wife; or in 1998 when the Queen invested Emperor Akihito of Japan with the Order of the Garter during a state visit to Britain, despite the hostility from former prisoners of war of the Japanese who have been seeking a full apology and financial compensation.

public appointments

The Monarch plays a formal role in a vast range of public appointments, since all important posts in the Civil Service, the police, the judiciary, the BBC and the Church of England are filled in the name of the Monarch, not to mention, of course, the Ministerial appointments in every Government. Once again such appointments are usually made on the basis of advice given or coordinated by the Prime Minister, often with the help of the small Civil Service unit attached to 10 Downing Street which processes the recommendations from all quarters. Senior appointments in the Diplomatic Service are made on the advice of the Foreign Secretary, in the Armed Services on the advice of the Defence Secretary and in the police on the advice of the Home Secretary. In short, senior Ministers effectively have considerable power of public patronage which they exercise in the name of the Monarch and every Prime Minister takes a close personal interest in all the main appointments.

In these circumstances it is not surprising perhaps that concern has been expressed from time to time about the nature and scope of such political patronage, which is Royal in name but Ministerial in fact.[10] Concern arises over the apparent lack of public scrutiny or subsequent democratic accountability for such public appointments, not to mention the implications for public expenditure in the wide range of public bodies to which such people are appointed. The problem is compounded in the eyes of many observers when such public appointments appear to be made on party-political criteria – for example, when a prominent businessman has donated generously to the governing party. Yet this kind of political patronage has not led the critics to attack the Monarchy, since it is well understood that the Monarch is merely acting as a dignified rubber stamp for appointments which are nearly always not within her control.

quasi-judicial functions

mercy and pardon

The prerogatives of mercy and pardon are still vested in the Monarch, who is entitled to exercise them on the advice of the Home Secretary of the day. Yet since the House of Commons voted in 1965 to abolish the death penalty on a provisional basis, and since that decision has subsequently been confirmed in successive free votes over the years, it now seems that this particular aspect of the Royal prerogative has fallen into disuse. Pardons are granted only after conviction and sentence in rare cases when there is some special reason why a sentence should not be carried out or a conviction should be quashed – for example, a discovery that the evidence on which a conviction was based is actually false. Thus the exercise of this aspect of the Royal prerogative has been both formal and rare.

prerogative powers

In Britain the Government of the day enjoys not merely powers derived from Parliament but also those that it exercises in the name of the Crown, namely what are known as **the powers of the Royal prerogative**. This enables a Government to act in a variety of ways without requiring the prior and formal approval of Parliament. In such cases the Monarch is acting as a splendid and dignified veil for decisions which are actually taken by Ministers in the Government of the day.

In the conduct of foreign policy the *Royal prerogative to conclude treaties* enables Ministers to reach legally binding agreements with other Governments or international organisations without having to secure the *prior* approval of Parliament. For example, the 1972 Treaty of Accession which took Britain into the European Community was signed by Edward Heath as Prime Minister in Brussels without the Government having had to secure the specific prior approval of Parliament at Westminster. The same procedure applied to the 1986 Single European Act and the 1992 Treaty of Maastricht, both of which involved initiatives taken by Ministers in the name of the Crown which had the effect of committing the United Kingdom to certain highly controversial courses of action before Parliament had an opportunity to give a formal opinion. Unlike the position in the United States, where treaties negotiated by the Administration have to secure the 'advice and consent' of the Senate *before* they can become American law, or the position in the European Union where the European Parliament has to give its formal opinion *before* the Council of Ministers and the Commission can conclude a new European treaty in the name of the European Union, the position in Britain is that only if treaties have legislative consequences in the United Kingdom does the Government have to involve Parliament. Even then, this need only be done *after* a treaty has been signed by a Minister on behalf of the Crown.

A declaration of war is made officially in the name of the Monarch, although in the nuclear age such formalities would be of little real interest if time were very short. In the event of a war which directly affected Britain, it would be for the Prime Minister and a few senior colleagues and military advisers to take all the key decisions. The Monarch would merely be kept informed as and when appropriate. In the case of the 1982 Falklands conflict, Britain did **not** declare war on Argentina, since there were compelling technical and legal reasons for not doing so in the light of British diplomatic efforts at the United Nations and elsewhere. Although the Queen was not therefore required to sign a declaration of war, she was kept informed by the Prime Minister at every stage of the conflict.

Colonial constitutions have been promulgated or changed in the name of the Monarch. For example, the constitution of Zimbabwe, which British Ministers under Lord Carrington had negotiated with the representatives of all the Rhodesian parties at Lancaster House in 1979–80, was eventually promulgated in the name of the Queen and later given statutory authority in the Zimbabwe Independence Act of 1980.

The creation of public corporations is also done in the name of the Monarch through the granting of Royal Charters to the bodies concerned. For example, the BBC became a public corporation by Royal Charter in 1926. The various 'new towns', such as Milton Keynes, which were built over the years since the Second World War, were established in a similar way.

A Prime Minister can also *create, abolish or merge Departments of Government* by Royal prerogative – as was evidenced under Tony Blair in 2007 when the Home Office was reorganised and a new *Justice* Department was set up to take over some of its responsibilities as well as replacing the Department for Constitutional Affairs (which had itself been newly created in 2003). It was also evidenced under Gordon Brown when forming his first Cabinet – in 2007 – when he created new Departments for *Children, Schools and Families* and *Innovation, Universities and Skills* as well as one for *Business, Enterprise and Regulatory Reform* in place of the old Departments for Education and Skills and Trade and Industry.

The significant growth of so-called QUANGOs (Quasi-Autonomous Non-Governmental Organisations) under Governments has been another aspect of central Government activity facilitated by the use of the Royal prerogative. This has simplified the procedures for public appointments made by Ministers, but it has also assisted the 'patronage state' to grow without undue hindrance from Parliament or other elected bodies and, consequently, has been the subject of some criticism.[11] Indeed, the use of the powers of the Royal prerogative can be extremely controversial as Margaret Thatcher and her Government found out when they used it to remove the right of trade-union membership from employees at GCHQ, the Government's Communications Headquarters at Cheltenham, in 1984. This right was restored by the Labour Government which was returned to power in 1997, again by exercising the powers of the Royal prerogative. Alleged misuse of the Royal prerogative was also one of the questions raised during the Scott Inquiry into the Conservative Government's handling of the 'Arms to Iraq' affair over the period 1984–90.[12] Similar questions were raised out of the Labour Government's decision to participate in the invasion of Iraq in 2003 – indeed, in 2005 the House of Lords Select Committee on the Constitution announced that it would conduct an inquiry on 'The use of the royal prerogative power by Government to deploy the UK's armed forces'.[13]

unpublicised functions

Within the political sphere the Monarch also performs some unpublicised functions, the most notable of which are the regular and confidential conversations with the Prime Minister of the day. On such occasions the Monarch enjoys what Walter Bagehot once described as 'the right to be consulted, the right to encourage and the right to warn'.[14] In modern circumstances these rights are exercised during private meetings every week at Buckingham Palace (when the Monarch is in residence) and once a year for a weekend in the late summer when the Monarch is resident at Balmoral in Scotland.

Queen Elizabeth II's experience of the affairs of state is unrivalled in modern times, since in more than 50 years on the throne she has been served by 11 different Prime Ministers and 21 different Governments. She came to the throne in 1952 when Winston Churchill was Prime Minister, President Truman occupied the White House and Stalin still ruled in the Kremlin. She has the undisputed right to see all state papers and in consequence she is almost certainly better informed about key political developments than virtually anyone else in Britain. Her private advice to all Prime Ministers must be invaluable in view of the length and variety of her experience of matters of state. Indeed one former Prime Minister apparently accepted the analogy of paying a weekly visit to a psychiatrist and admitted that he could say things to the Queen that he could not say even to his closest political colleagues.[15]

The functions of the Monarchy are summarised in Figure 9.1.

Political functions
Choice of Prime Minister
Dissolution of Parliament
Royal Assent to Bills
Creation of peers
Granting of Honours
Public appointments

Formal functions
Conclusion of treaties
Declaration of war
Introduction or amendment of colonial constitutions
Establishment of public corporations
Creation/abolition of Government Departments

Symbolic functions
State Opening of Parliament
Head of the Commonwealth
State visits abroad
Entertaining foreign heads of state in UK
Patronage of good causes
Visits to all parts of UK
Military ceremonial
Religious ceremonial

Unpublicised functions
Personal contacts with the Prime Minister
Confidential advice to the Goveroment

Quasi-judicial functions
Prerogative of mercy
Prerogative of pardon

figure **9.1 functions of the monarchy**

symbolic functions

The Monarch and other members of the Royal Family play an important symbolic role in many different ways. For example, Queen Elizabeth II and Prince Philip have made frequent state visits to countries in all parts of the world. The Queen has also played an important role at successive Commonwealth

	Official visits, opening ceremonies and other engagements	Receptions, lunches, dinners and banquets	Other engagements, including investitures, meetings attended and audiences given	Total number of engagements in the United Kingdom	Engagements while abroad an official tours	Total
Queen Elizabeth II	92	69	219	380	45	425
Duke of Edinburgh	134	150	69	353	53	406
Prince of Wales	164	104	159	427	73	500
Dichess of Cornwall	110	46	6	162	50	212
Duke of York	101	71	40	212	234	446
Earl of Wessex	107	82	34	223	195	418
Countess of Wessex	113	43	26	182	53	235
The Princess Royal	305	102	84	491	104	595
Duke of Gloucester	145	36	31	212	26	238
Duchess of Gloucester	74	17	18	109	18	127
Duke of Kent	138	45	18	201	28	229
Princess Alexandra	69	31	25	125	–	125
Total	1552	796	729	3077	879	3956

note: In addition, Prince William carried out 13 engagements and Prince Harry carried out 6.
source: Tim O'Donovan, The Times, 1 January 2007.

figure **9.2** **the Royal Family's working year: 2006**

Conferences and in entertaining foreign Heads of State or Government when they visit Britain. In all such activities the Monarch and other members of the Royal Family are serving the national interest, as defined by the Government of the day. As far as the Monarch's travels are concerned, Royal trips abroad are judged to be good for British foreign policy and for the promotion of British trade. Furthermore, the making or withholding of a Royal visit can be used by the British Government as a way of indicating approval or disapproval of political regimes in other countries. In more than 54 years the Queen has undertaken over 250 official overseas visits to 128 different countries.

In relation to the Commonwealth, Queen Elizabeth II plays a significant role as titular head of this free association of 53 nations (in 16 of which she is Head of State) and she is known to attach particular personal importance to it. This has involved her and other members of the Royal Family in travelling tens of thousands of miles to different parts of the world to see and be seen by many thousands of people. It has also led her to attach considerable personal importance to her annual Christmas broadcasts to the people of the United Kingdom and the Commonwealth.

Within Britain the Monarch and other members of the Royal Family are involved, by custom and tradition, in various forms of public ceremonial designed to raise the morale or reinforce the unity of the British people. For example, the Queen usually leads the nation in paying respect to the dead of two world wars, and other conflicts in which the British armed services have been involved, at the Cenotaph in Whitehall on Remembrance Sunday every year. In the same way, the Queen and The Duke of Edinburgh attended the Memorial Service that took place in St. Paul's Cathedral in November 2005 for the victims of 7 July (2005) London Bombings. The Queen and other members of the Royal Family also pay conspicuous visits to all parts of the United Kingdom, including notably those where the people have suffered from natural disaster (as when hundreds of school children were killed by a coal-tip landslide at Aberfan in 1966) or been involved in serious social unrest (as in the inner city areas of London, Bristol and Liverpool after the 1981 riots).

The Monarch and other members of the Royal Family visit many parts of the United Kingdom each year – almost 4000 such visits in 2006 – with official functions often featuring prominently during such visits, including opening new buildings, visiting businesses, schools, hospitals, hostels for the homeless, local community schemes, military units and other organisations. They are also involved in the promotion of good causes and make an important contribution to the work and activities of a large number of charities. The Queen and other members of the Royal Family are patrons of over 3200 charities and have close associations with a wide range of charitable organisations covering many areas of national life.

In these and many other ways the Monarch and the Royal Family make a valuable contribution to the underlying cohesion and morale of people in the United Kingdom. See Figure 9.2 for a summary of the Royal Family's working year.

9.2 financing the Monarchy

Although any well-researched attempt at a comprehensive cost–benefit analysis of the British Monarchy would almost certainly show that it generates a financial profit for the nation, for many years the annual publication of the Civil List (the grants from taxpayers for the upkeep of the Royal Family) tended to provoke considerable media and public interest – and in some cases criticism – not least because of the Queen's great private wealth and tax-free status at the time. In 1990, in an attempt to defuse these issues an agreement was reached between the Queen and the Government of the day setting an annual sum of £7.9 million for the Civil List to be averaged over the period 1991–2000 for the support of the Queen, with further annual allowances totalling £1.88 million net to be paid to the Duke of Edinburgh, the Duke of York, the Queen Mother, Princess Margaret, the Princess Royal and other active members of the Royal Family. The income of the Prince of Wales and his two sons, Princes William and Harry, is derived from rent and other revenues of the Duchy of Cornwall and so he was not part of this settlement.[16] In addition, the costs of maintaining the Royal residences (except for Balmoral and Sandringham), the Royal Flight and the Royal Yacht *Britannia* were to continue to be met from public funds.

Royal Public Finances: Year to 31st March 2006

	£m	£m
The Queen's Civil List[1]		11.2
Parliamentary Annuities[2]		0.4
Grants-in-Aid[3]		
Property Services	14.3	
Communication and Information	0.5	
Royal Travel	5.5	
Total		20.3
Expenditure met directly by Government Departments and the Crown Estate		
Adiminstration of honours	0.5	
Equerries, orderlies and other support	0.9	
Maintenance of the Palace of Holyroodhouse	1.9	
State visits to and by The Queen and liaison with the Diplomatic Corps	1.1	
Ceremonial occasions	0.4	
Maintenance of the Home Park at Windsor Castle	0.6	
Other	0.1	
Total		5.5
Grand Total		37.4

notes:

1 The Civil List is the funding provided by Parliament, on a 10 yearly cycle, to meet the central staff costs and running expenses of Her Majesty's official Household.

2 The Parliamentary Annuity was paid to The Duke of Edinburgh to meet official expcnses. Parliamentary Annuities for other Members of the Royal Family are not a cost to the taxpayer as they are reimbursed by The Queen from private sources.

3 Grants-in-aid are provided to the Royal Household annually by the Department for Culture, Media and Sport for Property Services and Communications and Information, and by the Department for Transport for Royal Travel, Property Services meets the cost of property maintenance, and of utilities, telephones and related services at the Occupied Royal Palaces in England. Communications and Information meets the cost of such sciviccs for official royal functions and engagements in England and Scotland. Royal Travel meets the cost of official royal travel by air and rail.

figure **9.3**   **financing the monarchy**

In November 1992, however, it was announced – on the initiative of the Queen herself – that the Monarch would start paying income tax on her private fortune and that she would finance the payments made to members of her family other than herself, her husband and her mother.[17] This unexpected announcement seemed to meet much of the public criticism that had grown up around this issue, as did the announcement in June 1994 – again on the Queen's personal initiative – that the Royal Yacht Britannia would be decommissioned in 1997 and that the Royal Family would in future pay for their private use of the Queen's Flight. In the interest of greater transparency, the Queen agreed in 1998 to allow Parliament's financial watchdog, the National Audit Office, direct access to the finances of the Royal palaces, the Queen's Flight and the Royal Train and authorised the publication of the accounts for Royal travel. In short, the methods of financing the British Monarchy changed very significantly in the 1990s as the Royal Family and the whole institution of Monarchy came under greater scrutiny, media exposure and public criticism. See Figure 9.3 for a summary statement of the financing of the Monarchy.

Traditionally, the Monarchy has been one of the most revered national institutions in Britain. An opinion poll in 1969 demonstrated considerable public support for the Monarchy in that only 13 per cent thought it should be ended, 30 per cent thought it should continue as it was, and 50 per cent thought it should continue but change with the times (7 per cent had no opinion).[18] A similar opinion poll in 1980 showed that the appeal of the Monarchy was derived to a significant extent from the fact that it was usually projected to the people as the 'Royal Family', which 80 per cent of those questioned thought to be 'a marvellous example to everyone of good family life'.[19] The same poll also showed that 90 per cent preferred the idea of Monarchy to a Republic of the French or American type. This was a point emphasised by another poll in 1984 in which 77 per cent of the respondents considered that Britain would be worse off and only 5 per cent thought that Britain would be better off as a Republic.[20]

From the mid 1980s, however, both the respect for and the popularity of the Monarchy declined, with polls showing that those who considered that Britain would be better off without the Monarchy had increased to 13 per cent in 1987, 20 per cent in 1992 and 27 per cent in 1995.[21] By 1996 for the first time the balance of public opinion was that Britain would *not* have a Monarchy in 50 years' time, with a poll showing that only 33 per cent believed that the Monarchy had a long-term future, while 43 per cent believed that it did not.[22]

The institution and its leading personalities were subjected to an unprecedented degree of media scrutiny, disclosure and criticism. In March 1992 it was confirmed that the Duke and Duchess of York were to separate. Equally, there was increasing concern about the marriage of Prince Charles and Princess Diana. Media speculation and public prurience reached fever pitch with the publication of a book by Andrew Morton entitled *Diana: Her True Story*, in which it was claimed that the Princess of Wales was 'trapped in a loveless marriage' and was so unhappy that she had attempted to commit suicide on six occasions. In November 1992, during a Royal visit to South Korea, the awful relationship between the Prince and Princess of Wales became painfully apparent to TV audiences, thus increasing speculation about separation and even divorce for the Royal couple.

Throughout this time some Members of Parliament were agitating for a reduction in the financial privileges enjoyed by the Monarchy. Such agitation reached a peak after a fire destroyed part of Windsor Castle on 20 November 1992 and the Government announced that it would cover all the costs involved in repairs and restoration. On 24 November 1992, in a speech at the Guildhall, the Queen spoke of how the year of her fortieth anniversary on the throne had deteriorated from a celebration to what she termed an '*annus horribilis*' (awful year). She admitted that the Monarchy and other institutions were not above reproach, but suggested that less savage and more constructive criticism would be appreciated. The year ended with the Sun newspaper's premature publication of the Queen's Christmas broadcast, and 1993 began with the Monarch successfully suing the paper for breach of copyright – an action which was settled out of court in the Queen's favour.

Since the mid 1980s, therefore, the gap between myth and reality in public perceptions of the Monarchy has widened and people have been made aware that the Royal Family consists of frail human beings rather than impeccable public symbols. As a result, the moral authority of the Monarchy suffered a serious setback. Some opinion formers, such as Ludovic Kennedy, even argued that the Monarchy had had its day and the time had come for a Republic.[23]

the death of Princess Diana and beyond

The news of the death of Diana, Princess of Wales, in a car crash in Paris at the end of August 1997 stunned the British people as no event had done since the assassination of President Kennedy in 1963. Although at the time she held no official position – following the divorce she was no longer a member of the Royal Family – in life and even more so in death she acquired an iconic significance. The event was a tragedy that touched the hearts of millions of people, and the Prime Minister, Tony Blair, spoke of 'a nation in shock' at the untimely death of 'the People's Princess'.

Public anger was initially directed towards the press, but as officials debated the complexities of protocol for the funeral and the Royal Family sought to deal with the tragedy with traditional stoicism and dignity, the focus of public criticism shifted to the Royal Family itself and their failure to make a sufficient expression of grief over the death.

Grudgingly and gradually the Monarchy began to compromise in the face of media and public pressure. On the day before the funeral the Queen broadcast live to the nation. Then came the funeral itself with the Royal Family standing in the street and bowing their heads as the cortege drove past, the Union flag flying at half-mast over Buckingham Palace, and Earl Spencer's funeral address being applauded by the public gathered outside Westminster Abbey.

The death of the Princess brought pressure on the Royal Family to reinvent itself, to adapt or die. But this had always been the watchword of the British Monarchy: it had continued to exist for so long because of its ability to adapt, to move with the times, to adjust to the demands of the media and the people. Indeed, the events following Diana's death came to be seen not as the beginning of the end for the Monarchy, but simply as one more stage in its evolutionary development. As one observer noted, 'What happened in the end was ... proof of Royalist ardour, not the beginning of the end of the magic',[24] a viewpoint that was later supported by the opinion polls.[25]

By the time of the death of the Queen Mother – at the age of 101 – in March 2002 and the events held in June 2002 to mark the Golden Anniversary of the Queens reign, it had become clear that the institution of Monarchy was more resilient than many had thought in the hysteria which followed Princess Diana's death. In this improved atmosphere it became feasible for Prince Charles to consider marrying his long-time friend Camilla Parker-Bowles – the marriage eventually taking place at Windsor Registry Office in 2005.

the price of de-mystification

It is apparent from developments over many years that public attitudes towards the Royal Family as public figures and the British Monarchy as an institution have become less reliably positive, certainly ever since the media began to give saturation coverage to the personal lives of members of the Royal family. All of this severely tarnished the 'ideal family' image which advisers at Buckingham Palace had earlier sought to present. The result was a combination of prurience and ridicule which led some observers to speculate that Monarchy itself had had its day.

Obviously it has been difficult, particularly for the younger members of the Royal Family, to live anything resembling a 'normal' life when they have had to do so in the glare of unremitting and intrusive media publicity. However, in an age when the traditional 'nuclear family' has become a minority model rather than the social norm and when as many as one in two new marriages are destined to end in divorce, it may be that a more tolerant and indifferent public has sympathized with the Royal Family to a greater extent than before.

When in 1969 Queen Elizabeth II first decided to accept the advice that she should allow the television cameras in to show not only her public face but also her more private and family activities, a fateful decision was made from which it has been difficult to retreat, even though at times she must have been sorely tempted to do so. There was always a risk in this strategy, namely that the greater sense of familiarity would breed, if not contempt, then a larger degree of public cynicism and hence a loss of public respect for the institution of Monarchy. Distance and mystique were previously important – some would say vital – elements in the public appeal of the Monarchy. As Walter Bagehot observed, 'we must not let daylight in on magic'.[26] Now that the media have largely demystified the public image of the Monarchy it will be much more difficult to restore a sense of public deference and reinforce the sense of public respect which is still felt for the Queen herself.

It should always be remembered that on many occasions before in its long history the Monarchy has engendered great controversy and experienced extensive public criticism, and yet has managed to survive such crises. For example, the Prince Regent and William IV were deeply unpopular and heavily ridiculed in the early nineteenth century; Edward VII, as Prince of Wales, was the butt of many jokes and much public ribaldry; and Edward VIII effectively split public opinion down the middle during the Abdication Crisis in 1936 when he chose marriage to an American divorcee, Wallis Simpson, in preference to the throne. It seems that the Monarchy has survived its most recent troubles as well and that the controversies of the 1980s and 1990s are now largely forgotten. The present Queen is not only one of the most respected Monarchs in the world, but also likely to remain on the throne as long or longer than her illustrious predecessor, Queen Victoria. This very longevity and continuity in the person of the Queen herself is likely to stand the institution of Monarchy in good stead for many years to come.

9.4 conclusion

The Monarchy still holds the supreme position at the apex of British society, yet it does so at the expense of its previous claims (before 1837) to wield real political power. Today it serves as a powerful symbol of continuity, tradition and community which is particularly valuable to the nation in difficult or troubled times – as long as the Queen and her advisors judge the public mood correctly.

The Monarchy also provides an excellent example of the many paradoxes which abound in the British political system. It is an inherently conservative institution which can facilitate change. Whatever else may be altered, the Monarchy still appeals to many people as an unchanging and reassuring national symbol. Such seemingly permanent and unchanging institutions can make it easier for people to accept radical change in other areas of their lives. The Monarchy plays an important part in preserving the cohesion of British society and it contributes significantly to the sense of underlying national unity which helps to hold the British people together.

SUGGESTED QUESTIONS

1   What are the functions of the British Monarchy?
2   Does the Monarch have any real power in Britain today?
3   'The Queen reigns but does not rule.' What does this mean?

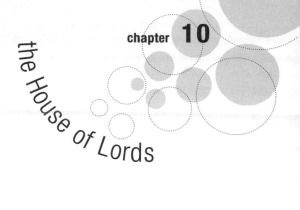

the House of Lords

As has been noted previously, an important – possibly the most important – feature of the British constitution is its capacity gradually to adapt to changing circumstances. In this respect the House of Lords is a microcosm of the British constitution, since throughout its long history it has been able to do just this. In contrast to other Second Chambers elsewhere in the world which have been specifically created with powers and composition clearly defined in basic constitutional documents, the House of Lords is the product of history. It was not created by Founding Fathers or under a Basic Law; it has simply developed and changed organically in the soil of British history. This is not to say that its evolution has been linear or continuous; on the contrary, it has been haphazard, spasmodic and uncertain. Yet it has survived for a very long time and its evolutionary adaptability will probably enable it to survive a good while longer.

10.1 origins and historical development

As the product of evolution rather than deliberate creation, it is not possible to say exactly when the House of Lords originated, for Parliament as a whole had no single genesis. Rather it came into being gradually 'from the medieval Court and Council where Plantagenet kings consulted the great men of the realm to secure support and offer their people justice.'[1] Nonetheless, it is possible to find the deepest roots of the British Parliament in the consultative customs of the Saxon kings who took periodic advice and support from the 'Witan'.

From the late thirteenth century onward there was a gradual and halting alignment of the membership of Parliament into two principal groups: the House of Lords and the House of Commons – the former composed of men who attended in response to individual summons from the Monarch, and the latter of people elected in the Counties and Boroughs who attended in a representative capacity. By 1485 – at the outset of the Tudor period – the institutional foundations of Parliament had been laid. The power of Parliament (especially the Commons) made steady progress throughout the Tudor period, to such an extent that the historic clash in the seventeenth century with the pretensions of the Stuart Monarchy became inevitable. In consequence the nation experienced a Civil War (1642–49), the execution of the King (1649), an interregnum under Oliver Cromwell (1649–58), the restoration of Charles II as King (1660), and the so-called 'Glorious Revolution' (1688–89) before a new constitutional order was firmly established.

As the principle of representative and responsible government developed in the eighteenth century, the power of control over the Executive fell increasingly to the House of Commons rather than the House of Lords. It was to the Commons, not the Lords, that individual Ministers and the Government collectively came to be held responsible. However, the Lords did not meekly accept the constitutional superiority of the Commons, and the leading territorial magnates in the Upper House managed to retain effective control over the Lower House by controlling the processes of election to many seats in the Commons, especially the so-called pocket or rotten boroughs. The personification of this manipulative power in the second half of the eighteenth century was the Duke of Newcastle who, in cooperation with his noble friends and relatives, managed to control up to as many as 100 seats in the House of Commons – enough 'placemen' to ensure that he and his faction either formed or dominated many Administrations.

The Reform Act of 1832, which enlarged the electorate from about three to five per cent of the adult population and which abolished many of the rotten boroughs, deprived the House of Lords of much of the political power which it had enjoyed in the eighteenth century. The Tory peers had strongly opposed it, but in the end were forced to concede to a combination of Liberal reformers in both Houses (led by Earl Grey) and popular pressure from what was called 'the mob' – that is, angry public demonstrations in favour of reform. The Monarch, William IV, also played a significant part on the side of reform by indicating his willingness to create a large number of new peers who, if necessary, could have swamped the die-hard opposition in the Lords. In the event, this threat, along with the other pressures mentioned, was sufficient to get the legislation passed.

The expansion of the suffrage and the development of more modern electoral arrangements between 1832 and 1867 gave the House of Commons a growing claim to genuinely representative credentials. At the same time, the power of the landed interest was in decline in the wake of the growth of the industrial towns and, after the repeal of the Corn Laws in 1845, the enormous impact of free trade on the economy and society. These and other factors brought about a gradual shift of political power away from the House of Lords to the House of Commons – for example, the proportion of peers in the Cabinet declined from about three-quarters to about a third of the total. During these years the House of Lords was able to head off challenges to its legal powers and to the hereditary basis of its membership as long as the peers were content to play second fiddle to the Commons. Indeed, in many ways the leading figures in the Lords were careful not to alienate or challenge their counterparts in the Commons for fear of provoking further instalments of constitutional reform which would have weakened their institutional position still more. As Walter Bagehot explained the position of the Lords in 1867: 'the House has ceased to be one of the latent directors, and has become one of the temporary rejecters and palpable alterers' (of legislation passed by the Commons).[2] He went on to describe the House of Lords as a Chamber with powers of delay and revision, but little else and concluded that: 'its danger is not in assassination, but atrophy; not abolition but decline'.[3]

constitutional crisis and the Parliament Act 1911

It was not long, however, before the validity of Bagehot's observations was challenged, since during the last decades of the nineteenth century and the first decade of the twentieth century there was recurrent conflict between the Tory and Unionist majority in the Lords and the Liberal majority in the House of Commons. This finally came to a head in the constitutional crisis of 1909–11. In 1893 the Conservative and Unionist majority in the Lords had heavily defeated William Gladstone's Liberal attempt at Irish Home Rule. In 1906 the Liberal Education Bill had been very drastically amended by the Lords, and consequently abandoned by the Commons. The Lords had rejected the Land Valuation Bill in 1907, and again in 1908, the Licensing Bill in 1908, and finally (and fatefully) the Liberal Finance Bill of 1909. The quarrel between the two legislative Chambers – a quarrel which in Winston Churchill's words was 'often threatened, often averted, long debated, long delayed, always inevitable' – came to a head at last.[4]

The House of Commons immediately voted to declare the House of Lords' action unconstitutional and a breach of privilege. Parliament was then dissolved. In the ensuing General Election the Liberals were returned to power, although with a much reduced majority. However, when the Parliament Bill to curb the power of the Lords was introduced into the Commons in April 1910, the Liberals were able to count on Labour and Irish Nationalist support. The first consequence of the new Parliamentary arithmetic was that the 1910 Liberal Budget was passed by the Commons and then accepted by the Lords without a vote. However, owing to the death of King Edward VII on 6 May 1910, the Parliament Bill itself was not proceeded with. Following the failure of attempts to negotiate an agreed settlement at a constitutional Conference, the Liberal Government decided that a second General Election should be held in 1910 before it could legitimately proceed with the Bill. The Prime Minister (Herbert Asquith) also obtained a promise from the new King George V that, should the Liberals win the election, he would agree to create enough new Liberal peers to overcome the die-hard Conservative opposition to the Bill in the Lords. The new House of Commons (elected in November 1910) was almost identical in composition with the old, so the Liberals remained in office, reintroduced the Parliament Bill and promptly secured a Parliamentary majority for it in the Commons. This time the Lords gave it a Second Reading, but watered it down in Committee. On its return to the Commons, the Lower House refused to accept most of the amendments proposed by the Lords and promptly returned it to the peers. On 10 August 1911, after considerable behind the scenes activity and argument within the Conservative and Unionist peers, the majority in the Upper House was reluctantly prepared to accept the Bill as it then stood as the lesser of two evils. Consequently, the Lords voted not to insist on their amendments by 131 votes to 114, with some 300 Conservatives abstaining, and the Bill duly became law.[5]

The *1911 Parliament Act* removed the Lords' power to reject Money Bills, while their powers to veto ordinary Public Bills were replaced with a power of delay for a maximum of two years. This meant that if a Bill were approved by the Commons in three successive Sessions, it automatically became law at the end of that time whether or not their Lordships were content. Together with the reduction in the maximum permitted span of a Parliament from seven to five years, this meant that any Bill passed by the Commons in the first two sessions of a five-year Parliament would inevitably become the law of the land if insisted on by a majority in the Commons. Although the Bill curbed the powers of the Lords, the composition of the upper House was not addressed, any more than the whole issue of the appropriate functions for a curtailed second Chamber.

In 1917 a constitutional Conference of 32 distinguished individuals under the chairmanship of Viscount Bryce was set up with the object of finding solutions to the problems of reforming both the powers and the composition of the House of Lords. In its report the following year it proposed that a reformed Upper House should have three-quarters of its members indirectly elected by MPs on a regional basis, while the remaining quarter should be chosen by a joint committee of both Houses. As far as powers were concerned, it proposed that legislation which was the subject of dispute between the two Houses should be submitted to a 'free conference', consisting of a small number of Members from each House who should be given very great power in determining whether or not the legislation should pass and in what form. There was, however, a substantial dissenting minority within the Bryce Commission and this disagreement was sufficient to prevent the Government of the day from acting on its majority recommendations. Even though many other proposals were made between the wars for reforming the House of Lords and the Labour Party Conference became committed to the abolition of the second Chamber, the constitutional position remained unchanged until after the Second World War.

the Parliament Act 1949

In 1945 the victorious Labour Government did not put forward any proposals for reform or abolition of the House of Lords, since it had many other more pressing legislative priorities – such as the creation of the National Health Service, various nationalisation Bills and the legislation to bring about independence for India. Furthermore, the Conservative peers under the leadership of Lord Salisbury adopted a deliberate convention of self-restraint

– the **Salisbury Convention** – under which they did not oppose at Second Reading any legislative measures emanating from the Governing party's Election Manifesto, although they were prepared to press amendments to Labour Bills in the name of 'improving' the legislation. By 1947, however, the mood of the Conservative majority in the Upper House had changed and it became clear that, at any rate in relation to the proposed nationalisation of the iron and steel industries, the Conservative peers were prepared to use their inbuilt majority against such legislation. Faced with this threat from their Conservative opponents in the Lords, Labour Ministers secured approval in the Commons for a further Parliament Bill designed to reduce the delaying power of the Upper House to one year. In spite of efforts to find a compromise between the respective majorities in the two Houses, agreement proved impossible. The Government went ahead without all-party agreement, using provisions of the 1911 Parliament Act to ensure the passage of what was to become the *1949 Parliament Act*. This provided that in the event of the Lords failing to agree to a Bill which has been passed by the Commons and sent to them at least one month before the end of a session, the Bill may, in a subsequent session be presented for royal assent by the Commons alone, without the agreement of the Lords. This, in effect, reduced the period of delay to less than 13 months. To be eligible for this procedure, a Bill has to be passed by the Commons in the following session in exactly the same form that they had passed it in the preceding session. A Bill has also to be given its third reading by the Commons at least one year after it received its second reading in the previous session and at least one month before the end of the second session. Once passed this second time, the Speaker of the House of Commons certifies that the Bill falls within the terms stipulated before it is again presented to the House of Lords. If the Lords fail to agree to the Bill within one month in the form in which it had been sent to them by the Commons, the Bill is presented for royal assent without the agreement of the House of Lords. This Act, however, did nothing to change the composition or the functions of the second Chamber, and when the Labour Party lost office and the Conservative Party returned to power in 1951 the whole issue of comprehensive reform fell out of the reckoning.

minor reforms

A number of minor reforms did, however, take place during the late 1950s and early 1960s. In 1957 daily allowances were introduced for travel to and from and attendance at the House of Lords. In 1958 the *Life Peerages Act* made possible the creation of Life Peers (that is, peerages which cannot be inherited), including peerages for women in their own right. In 1963 the *Peerage Act* enabled female hereditary peers to sit and allowed hereditary peers to renounce their titles – while in no way impinging on the rights of their heirs and successors – in order to make themselves eligible for membership of the House of Commons.[6] In the wake of these minor changes, the right of hereditary peers to sit in the House of Lords remained, as did the rights of the House as a whole to reject subordinate legislation, Private Bills and Bills to confirm provisional Orders. In addition, the minimal delaying power which the Upper House still possessed not only gave the Peers the ability to dislocate considerably the Government's legislative programme, but also, in the final year of a Parliament, to defeat a Government Bill in its entirety.

an attempt at major reform

The 1964 General Election saw the return of a Labour Government, which at the 1966 General Election managed to increase its majority in the Commons to nearly 100. One result of this was the subsequent introduction of the ill-fated *Parliament (No. 2) Bill* in 1968, which involved both a reduction in the total number of peers and an attack on the hereditary principle. The Bill secured a comfortable majority on Second Reading in the House of Commons. However, when it went into Committee on the floor of the House (as is conventional with constitutional measures), it was effectively defeated by a sustained and devastating filibuster by backbenchers on both sides of the Commons led by Enoch Powell and Michael Foot. Such traditionalists in the Commons opposed further reform of the House of Lords mainly on the grounds that a reformed second Chamber was likely to be a strengthened second Chamber, whereas they were determined to preserve the primacy of the House of Commons. In the face of this time-consuming and highly effective opposition, the Wilson Government abandoned the Bill, leaving the Upper House still unreformed in both composition and functions.[7]

New Labour and the House of Lords Act 1999

Despite no shortage of reform proposals – even suggestions of abolition – it was not until the victory of New Labour at the 1997 General Election that the issue again took centre stage. In December 1998 the Government introduced legislation –*the House of Lords Bill* – to remove the right of hereditary peers to sit in the House of Lords. Early the following year a White Paper was published outlining a step-by-step approach to reform.[8] Step one was the removal of the right of hereditary peers to sit and vote in the House of Lords. As far as step two was concerned – a transitional House – the Government declared itself 'minded to accept' the proposal that a small number of hereditary peers be allowed to sit temporarily as members. It also pledged that no one party would be in a position to dominate the transitional House and that steps would be taken to reduce the unfettered power of the Prime Minister to nominate life peers, pledging to establish an independent Appointments Commission to recommend non-political appointments. Step three was the establishment of a Royal Commission – under the chairmanship of the Conservative peer and former Cabinet Minister, Lord Wakeham. The White Paper set out four main options for future composition for the Royal Commission to consider – a nominated chamber, a directly elected chamber, an indirectly elected chamber and a mixed chamber – and charged it to consider reform in the context of devolution, the incorporation of the European Convention of Human Rights into UK law and what were described as 'developing relations' with the European Union. Step four saw the recommendations of the Royal Commission, published in January 2000,[9] being considered by a Joint Committee of both Houses of Parliament to examine in more detail the Parliamentary aspects of the proposed reforms. The final step five was to be legislation to implement the resulting proposals designed to 'renew the House of Lords as a modern, fit and effective second chamber of Parliament for the 21st century'.

During the passage of the Bill through the House of Lords a substantial amendment was passed by 351 votes to 32 allowing a total of 92 hereditary peers to remain as members of the 'transitional House'.[10] In addition, although not part of the amendment, a further ten hereditary peers – six former Leaders of the Lords and four hereditary peers of the first creation – were created life peers. The legislation received Royal Assent as the *House of Lords Act* shortly before the end of the session in November, 1999. The new 'interim' House sat for the first time at the beginning of the 1999–2000 Session.

10.2 composition

In 2006 the membership of the House of Lords was still divided between ecclesiastical and lay members, formally described as 'Lords Spiritual' and 'Lords Temporal'. *The Lords Spiritual* are the senior clergy of the Church of England, namely the Archbishops of Canterbury and York, the Bishops of London, Durham and Winchester, and the 21 most senior among the other diocesan Bishops. They cease to be members of the House when they retire as Bishops and so are the only members who are not members until they die. They sit on the Bishops' bench and do not take a party whip. *The Lords Temporal* are those individuals who have either been awarded a life peerage or who are part of the group of 92 surviving hereditary peers.

life peers

Life peers are those whose title is limited to the lifetime of the title-holder. They fall into two categories: those created under the 1876 *Appellate Jurisdiction Act* and those created under the *1958 Life Peerages Act*. The former Act provided for a limited number of Lords of Appeal in Ordinary (Law Lords) who are appointed to hear and determine judicial appeals. The general category of Law Lords also includes those other peers who have held or are currently holding high judicial office in a superior Court – for example, present and former Lords Chancellor.

In 2004 the Government introduced proposals to abolish the appellate jurisdiction of the House of Lords, establishing a separate Supreme Court in its place, one consequence of which was to be the removal of the Law Lords from the legislature. The proposals became law in 2005 as part of the *Constitutional Reform Act*, although in 2006 all the necessary procedures were not yet in place for this change to have taken place and, consequently, the Law Lords were still members of the House of Lords.

Hereditary peers: House of Lords Act 1999

Party grouping	Life peers 1958 Act Male	1958 Act Female	1876 Act Male	1876 Act Female	Elected by Party/Group* Male	Female	Elected office holders† Male	Female	Appointed Royal Office holders Male	Archbishops/ Bishops Male	Total No	Total %
Conservative	124	33	–	–	39	–	9	–	–	–	205	27.44
Labour	154	53	–	–	2	–	2	–	–	–	211	28.25
Liberal Democrat	52	20	–	–	3	–	2	–	–	–	77	10.31
Crossbench	117	26	25	1	28	1	1	1	2	–	202	27.04
Non-party	–	–	–	–	–	–	–	–	–	2 + 24	26	3.48
Other	7	3	–	–	1	1	–	–	–	–	12	1.61
Members on leave of absense	11	3	–	–	–	–	–	–	–	–	14	1.87
Total No	465	138	25	1	73	2	14	1	2	26	747	
%	62.25	18.47	3.34	0.14	9.77	0.27	1.87	0.14	0.27	3.48		100.00
No	603		26		75		15		2	26	747	
%	80.72		3.48		10.04		2.01		0.27	3.48		100.00
No	629				92							
%	84.20				12.32							

* elected by the party/group concerned
† elected by the whole House

figure **10.1 composition and political affiliation of the Hose of Lords, February 2007**

The 1958 Life Peerages Act enabled distinguished men and women from many walks of life to have peerages conferred on them in recognition of their political or public services to the nation. Such life peers may be former civil servants or diplomats; distinguished soldiers, sailors or airmen who rose to the highest military ranks; successful industrialists or prominent trade union leaders; distinguished scientists or other academics; renowned actors or other leading figures from the world of the arts and the media. In 2006 there were 130 female life peers, an increase compared with earlier times, but still rather a small number and only 21.3 per cent of life peers.

By far the largest single category of life peers is composed of politicians who have previously sat in the House of Commons or been active in local government. In the former case, they tend to have been either retired Ministers or previously eminent backbenchers whom the Prime Minister of the day and the other party leaders wish to reward with a seat in the Lords and whose political skills can be kept in play in the Upper House. In the latter case, they tend to have been distinguished figures from the world of elected local government whose experience in that sphere is seen as an attribute for membership of the Lords.

hereditary peers

Prior to the passage of the 1999 House of Lords Act a clear majority – over 56 per cent – of the membership of the House of Lords were hereditary peers, namely those whose title was held by virtue of inheritance. However, since the passage of the Act only 92 hereditary peers remain as members – 75 party and crossbench members elected by their own party or group, 15 office holders elected by the House and two appointed Royal office holders, the Lord Great Chamberlain, who is the Queen's representative in Parliament, and the Earl Marshal, who is responsible for ceremonies such as the State Opening of Parliament.

On the death of any one of these individuals, membership does not pass to the heir – as it did in the past – but, rather, a new vote takes place amongst the category concerned in order to find a replacement.

political affiliations

In 2006 the Labour party had the largest grouping in the House of Lords, accounting for 28.5 per cent of the total eligible membership, compared to 28.1 per cent for the Conservatives and 10.1 per cent for the Liberal Democrats. In addition, a sizable proportion of the membership, 26.5 per cent, sat as independents on the crossbenches. Amongst the Conservative ranks a sizeable minority were hereditary peers (23.9 per cent) while the Labour contingent was overwhelmingly composed of life peers (98.0 per cent). Amongst Liberal Democrat peers 93.2 per cent were life peers and 6.8 per cent were hereditary members.

Any analysis of the political complexion in the contemporary House of Lords must go hand-in-hand with an awareness of a number of important variables, such as the subject under discussion, the persuasive power of certain individuals, the day of the week and even the hour of the day. From such an analysis, it is apparent that, whatever the situation in the past, today *no single party can be sure of getting its way in the Lords.*

Whatever the party-political balance in the House of Lords may be, it is as well to note that political divisions on party lines in the Upper House are not usually as sharp or bitter as they can be in the Commons. This is apparent in the often relaxed and courteous style of debate in the Lords. Furthermore, most of the speech-making and legislative work is done by perhaps 200 to 275 particularly active peers, although a larger number usually take part in divisions.

10.3 powers and functions

The classic statement of the powers and functions of the second Chamber in the British political system was made in the **Bryce Commission Report** (1918).[11] This report identified four powers and functions, namely:

- *The power of legislative delay* – the ability to delay for about one year the passage of a Bill approved by the Commons
- *The power of legislative scrutiny and revision* – the ability to amend and improve a Bill considered to have been inadequately drafted by the Commons
- The power of well-informed discussion and deliberation – the ability to debate the issues of the day in a better-informed and less partisan way than is often the case in the Commons
- *The power to initiate non-controversial legislation*, thus relieving the Commons of at least some of the legislative burden at the beginning of every session of Parliament.

More recently, the **Wakeham Commission Report on the Reform of the House of Lords** (2000)[12] identified four main **roles** for a reformed second chamber, namely:

- It should bring a range of different perceptions to bear on the development of public policy.
- It should be broadly representative of British society – regional, gender, vocational, ethnic, professional, cultural and religious.
- It should play a vital role as one of the main 'checks and balances' within the British constitution. Its role should be complementary to that of the House of Commons in identifying points of concern and requiring the Government to reconsider or justify its policy intentions. It should have the power to make the House of Commons think again.
- It should provide a voice for the nations and regions of the United Kingdom at the centre of public affairs.

As far as **functions** were concerned, the report stated that a reformed second chamber should have a large role to play in:

- Scrutinising the executive and holding the Government to account
- Scrutinising EU business
- Protecting the constitution
- Scrutinising treaties
- Safeguarding human rights
- Deliberating on issues which arise from devolution and decentralisation
- Examining secondary legislation.

As far as **powers** were concerned, the report stated that a reformed second chamber should:

- Have the power of delay set out in the 1911 and 1949 Parliament Acts
- In effect have the power to veto amendments to the Parliament Acts as it declared that it should no longer be possible to amend the Parliament Acts by using the Parliament Act procedures
- Keep the principles underlying the 'Salisbury Convention'
- Have the power to veto Statutory Instruments turned into a power to delay, one which could be overridden by a positive decision of the House of Commons
- Have the law-making powers of the current House of Lords (in short, that there should be no significant change in the second chambers' law-making powers).

The present activities of the House of Lords can be considered in the light of the powers and functions identified and stipulated in these two influential reports.

legislative scrutiny and revision

The power of legislative scrutiny and revision exercised by the House of Lords has often been regarded as its most important function, especially when dealing with particularly complex or controversial Government Bills. This is mainly because MPs very often make inefficient use of the Parliamentary time available in Standing Committees when they are supposed to scrutinise and debate Bills clause by clause and line by line. The result is that there is often a need for additional legislative revision. This falls on the House of Lords, where many of the necessary amendments and new clauses are introduced by Ministers when the Government has had second thoughts about aspects of its own legislation.

Sometimes this is in response to suggestions made in the House of Commons or to sustained pressure from interest groups which have lobbied for or against aspects of the legislation. Sometimes it is simply a matter of doing in the Lords what should have been done in the Commons, if there had been enough Parliamentary time to do so. Although the close scrutiny of Bills involves a great deal of often painstakingly dull work, it is clear that the House of Lords performs an essential Parliamentary function in this respect. In doing so, it does invaluable work which would otherwise have to be done by the House of Commons or which would simply be left undone to the detriment of the quality of legislation. It also helps to see that the Courts do not have to spend too much of their time subsequently clarifying the original intentions of Parliament via the medium of case law. On the other hand, it is argued by some that when acting as a revising chamber the actions of the House of Lords have sometimes gone rather further than mere 'revision', namely substantially altering Government legislation from the Lower House of which a majority of their Lordships strongly disapprove.

legislative delay

In theory, the power of legislative delay is used by the Lords when they refuse to approve legislation already passed by the Commons. The 1911 Parliament Act laid the foundation for this by enabling the Lords to delay legislation (with the exception of Money Bills) for up to two years. Subsequently the 1949 Parliament Act reduced the delaying period to one year. In practice, since 1911 this power has been used only sparingly, because the members of the Upper House have been well aware of the danger that excessive use of this power could hasten the day when a Government might decide to reform radically or even to abolish the Lords altogether. The only Bills which passed into law under the terms of the 1911 Parliament Act were the *1914 Welsh Church Act*, the *1914 Government of Ireland Act*, and the *1949 Parliament Act*.

Until 1991 no Bills passed into law under the terms of the 1949 Parliament Act. However, the House of Lords did seek to use its constitutional delaying power on two occasions in the mid 1970s when the then Labour Government pressed ahead with highly contentious legislation (namely the *1975 Trade Union and Labour Relations Bill* and the *1976 Aircraft and Shipbuilding Industries Bill*) at a time when it had little or no overall majority in the Commons. In both these cases, the Labour Government called the peers' bluff by reintroducing the legislation a second time under the terms of the Parliament Acts. This proved sufficient to persuade their Lordships to back down and each of these Bills duly became law at the second time of asking.

In 1991 the Conservative Government was obliged to use the Parliament Act to get the *War Crimes Act* onto the statute book, legislation which sought, retrospectively, to create a new criminal offence to enable charges to be brought against alleged perpetrators of atrocities in continental Europe during the Second World War.

Under the Labour Government in office since 1997 the Parliament Act procedures have been used on three occasions. In 1998–99 the Government sought to introduce a closed-list system for elections to the European Parliament (the *European Parliamentary Elections Bill*), but the peers persistently voted against such a change; in 1999–2000 when the Government sought to secure the passage of the *Sexual Offences (Amendment) Bill* which lowered the age of homosexual consent from 18 to 16; and in 2003–04 with the *Hunting Bill* designed to outlaw fox and deer hunting, as well as hare-coursing with dogs in England and Wales.

The moral of the tale is that the majority in the Commons can always get its way in the end if it really wants to do so, although Governments have sometimes been obliged not only to take account of opposition to their legislation in the Lords but also to accept the limited delaying power still available to the Upper House.

initiation of non-partisan legislation

The initiation in the Lords of Bills dealing with subjects of a comparatively non-partisan character is a particularly appropriate procedure when dealing with Government legislation which is both complex and technical, such as Bills on data protection, energy conservation and patent law for example. The reason for introducing such legislation in the Upper House is that such Bills, having been fully discussed and put into shape prior to submission to the House of Commons, may have an easier passage through the Commons than would otherwise be the case. The view often held is that because work on such legislation is dull and politically uncontroversial, members of the House of Lords are better suited to carry it out than members of the House of Commons. It is also pointed out that when such Bills are examined first by the Lords, this can save a considerable amount of legislative time in the Lower House.

deliberative function

The deliberative function of well-informed debate on the great issues of the day is another worthwhile aspect of the activities of the House of Lords. This is because the level of knowledge and the standard of argument in the Upper House is often very high and because the issues are usually approached in a serious and relatively dispassionate way. Indeed, the Lords can often find time to debate important and topical issues which might not get an airing in the more partisan and busy conditions of the Commons. In such debates the Lords can also draw on the great knowledge and experience which is available in their ranks, especially among the life peers who include Fellows of the Royal Society, leading industrialists and others of great intellectual and professional distinction. For example, in a debate to call attention to the role of parents in providing for the needs of the nation's children in the 21st century – held in the House of Lords in March 2003 – there were a total of 20 speakers and included the Chairmen of the Parenting Support Forum and the Youth Justice Board, two former school governors, a consultant paediatrician, a former minister for Education, a practicing youth worker, the president of MENCAP, a former headmistress and the current and former Archbishops of Canterbury. This is therefore one of the ways in which their Lordships can have considerable influence in Whitehall and Westminster and on the climate of informed opinion in the country as well.

The House of Lords is actually quite effective at scrutinising the activities of the Executive in Britain. There are several ways in which their Lordships do this beyond their normal participation in debates and in the legislative process. For example, peers may ask up to four Questions for oral answer each day that the House is sitting, each of which can lead to Supplementary Questions. Unstarred Questions, Private Notice Questions and Questions for Written Answer are also available. In addition, the most important statements of Government policy made in the House of Commons are usually made simultaneously in the House of Lords and on such occasions peers have the opportunity to probe or criticise Ministerial decisions.

In recent years, the House of Lords has also made very good use of its Select Committees which, in some cases, have built up unrivalled reputations for their expert knowledge and the quality of their reports. There are four permanent committees which cover the European Union, Science and Technology, Economic Affairs and the Constitution. Examples of the work carried out in recent years would include investigations into *Pandemic Influenza* (2005) and *Science Teaching in Schools* (2006); *The Economics of Climate Change* (2005) and *Government Policy on the Management of Risk* (2006); and *Devolution: Inter-institutional Relations in the United Kingdom* (2003) and *The Use of the Royal Prerogative Power by the Government to Deploy the UK's Armed Forces* (2005–06). In addition, Lords committees can be set up on an ad hoc basis in order to deal with issues outside the remit of the permanent committees. Examples would include the Religious Affairs Committee established during the 2002–03 session to explore appropriate means of defining and tackling offences of religious intolerance and the BBC Charter Review Committee appointed in 2005 to consider and report on the review of the BBC Charter. In all these ways members of the House of Lords scrutinise the activities of the Executive, sometimes more effectively than their counterparts in the House of Commons.

There are three other forms of scrutiny exercised by the House of Lords most of which are highly technical, but nevertheless important in the overall process of Parliamentary control. These are the careful scrutiny of Private Bills, Secondary Legislation and draft European legislation flowing from the European institutions.

Private Bills (which are Bills to alter the law relating to a particular locality or to confer rights or relieve liabilities from a particular person or category of persons) may be assigned to a committee of five peers for detailed consideration once the legislation has been through the earlier stages of public notification and Second Reading. Such committees have some of the attributes of quasi-judicial proceedings in that the promoters and opponents of Private Bills are usually represented by legal counsel and may call evidence in support of their arguments. Once this committee stage is successfully concluded, the Bill is reported to the House where its subsequent stages are similar to those of a Public Bill.

Secondary Legislation (delegated legislation and statutory instruments) flows from Whitehall Departments under previous primary legislation. The House of Lords' *Delegated Powers and Regulatory Reform Committee* examines all legislation in order to see what delegated powers are proposed and to determine if they are appropriate prior to the legislation going forward for consideration by the whole House. In the 2002–03 session the Committee reported on delegated powers in 57 Bills, making recommendations on 21 of them, almost all of which the Government accepted. The Committee undoubtedly adds to the efficiency and effectiveness of the legislative process and has earned a formidable reputation as an effective watchdog over the use – and potential abuse – of Ministerial power. There is also a *Merits of Statutory Instruments Committee* charged with the task of considering statutory instruments and drawing to the attention of the House those which merit closer attention. For example, if there would be a charge on public funds, or an element of retrospection, or doubts about *ultra vires* – that is, outside the acknowledged legal competence of the Minister and Department concerned.

As for Parliamentary scrutiny of *European legislation* (that is, Directives issued by European institutions), Committees of each of the two Houses of the Westminster Parliament have been in existence since 1974. The House of Lords Select Committee on the European Union more than matches the House of Commons Select Committee on European Scrutiny and is considered by many knowledgeable observers to be unrivalled in its expertise and timely scrutiny of European legislation. The Lords Committee has a membership of 18, but it is able to, and frequently does, co-opt other peers on to its sub-committees of which there are seven, namely:

- *Economic and Financial Affairs* (Subcommittee A)
- *Internal Market* (Subcommittee B)
- *Foreign Affairs, Defence and Development* (Subcommittee C)
- *Environment and Agriculture* (Subcommittee D)
- *Law and Institutions* (Subcommittee E)
- *Home Affairs* (Subcommittee F)
- *Social Policy and Consumer Affairs* (subcommittee G).

Recent reports have included *More Effective Regulation in the EU* (2005), *Completing the Internal Market in Services* (2005–06) and *Economic Migration to the EU* (2005–06), and in 2006 the Committee launched an inquiry into whether the House of Lords could play any further role in ensuring that matters relating to the EU are clearly and objectively explained to the citizen.

Both the Lords' and Commons' committees are continuously involved in the scrutiny of draft European legislation, and both may report to their respective Houses with recommendations that particular legislative proposals should be debated in plenary session.

judicial powers and functions

In 2004 the Government introduced proposals to abolish the appellate jurisdiction of the House of Lords and to establish a separate Supreme Court in its place. The proposals became law in 2005 as part of the Constitutional Reform Act, although in 2006 all the necessary procedures were not in place for this change to have taken place. Consequently, the House of Lords is still the final court of appeal for all civil and criminal cases in the United Kingdom (with the exception of criminal cases in Scottish law).

Theoretically, there is no distinction between the House of Lords in its judicial role as the final court of appeal and in its other activities. In practice, the judicial proceedings are separate from all other proceedings as only the Law Lords participate in hearing appeals, legal sittings are separate from the sittings of the whole House, and the Law Lords may sit in their judicial capacity even after the House has been prorogued or dissolved.

Judgments on appeal to the Law Lords are delivered by members of the Appellate Committee meeting in the Chamber of the Lords, but since 1963 these have taken the form of a written opinion from each individual judge. Usually appeals are heard by a committee of five Law Lords and decisions are reached by a majority. The judgments have great authority and have influenced the development of English law over centuries. Traditionally, the Law Lords regarded themselves as bound by legal precedents established in earlier decisions, but since the mid 1960s they have been prepared occasionally to modify that doctrine by departing from previous decisions when it has appeared right to do so. (See Chapter 18 for more on this subject.)

overall assessment

In spite of its anachronistic image, the House of Lords is still in a position to act as an important constitutional check on the Government of the day and as a safeguard of judicial independence in Britain. This significant role for the Second Chamber derives at least partly from the fact that the consent of the Lords is required before the Lower House can extend the life of an elected Parliament beyond five years (as happened in both world wars); and the fact that senior judges can only be dismissed on an address to the Monarch from *both* Houses of Parliament, thus giving the Lords an effective veto against any serious attempt to muzzle the judiciary.

However, the position of the House of Lords also depends upon its institutional longevity and its association with the role of constitutional Monarchy. The three elements of Parliament's structure need to be considered together. The House of Lords may lack the democratic legitimacy of the House of Commons, but it is capable of wielding political influence as a revising and improving House which contains voices of real expertise and authority.

10.4 the work and influence of the Lords

As far as the work of the House of Lords is concerned, the first thing to be aware of is the fact that a significant proportion of the membership chooses to attend only occasionally. For example, during the 2003–04 Session 17.6 per cent of their Lordships either did not attend or attended on less than 10 per cent of sitting days. In all, 39.8 per cent of those who did attend did so on fewer than half of the sitting days and 38.9 per cent attended on 75 per cent or more of the sitting days.

However, the introduction of life peers, together with the recent removal of all but 92 of the hereditary peers, has gradually caused the style and working methods of the House to alter. This reflects the fact that a large proportion of the life peers that have been appointed are former MPs, leading lights in local government or people with other kinds of party political experience.[13] The peers drawn from these categories have tended to approach their role as members of the House of Lords with a degree of political professionalism not previously demonstrated by the members of the House. Indeed, in most cases those appointed to the upper House on the recommendation of the respective party leaders in the Commons are referred to as 'working peers' to differentiate them from others who are appointed more in recognition of their previous contributions to British national life in spheres which are not necessarily related to party politics. In this respect, the character of the House of Lords has gradually changed and its behaviour has moved closer to that of the House of Commons. The changing nature and scope of work in the House of Lords is shown in Figures 10.2 and 10.3.

It is clear from these tables that the number of peers attending sittings has greatly increased and their Lordships are more deeply involved in Parliamentary business than before. Whereas peers used to participate in Lords' business only from Tuesday to Thursday and between the hours of 4:00 pm and 7:00 pm, the House now sits more often, for longer hours, largely to accommodate the greater volume of legislation and other Parliamentary business. The procedures of the House of Lords have gradually been changed to meet the new requirements. Since the House is a self-regulating institution with relatively few Standing Orders, it has been able to respond quite flexibly to changing needs and requirements.

Throughout the 1979–97 period of determined and sometimes highly ideological Conservative Government, the House of Lords often asserted its

Statistical item	1950–51	1960–61	1970-71	1980–81	1990–91	2001-02	2002–03	2005–06
Average Daily Attendance	86	142	265	296	324	370	362	403
Number of Sitting Days	100	125	153	143	137	200	174	206
Number pf Sitting Hours	294:45	599:00	966:02	919:53	885:52	1295:21	1262:30	1372:44
Average Length of Sitting	2:57	4:47	6:18	6:25	6:28	6:58	7:15	6:39
Sittings after 10 pm	1	5	38	53	42	88	67	54
Friday Sittings	–	–	–	11	9	14	18	14

note: The 1970–71, 2001–02 and 2005–06 sessions were longer than usual because they began after June General Elections.

figure **10.2   sessional statistics 1950–51 to 2005–06**

Type of work	1950–51	1960–61	1970-71	1980–81	1990–91	2001-02	2005–06
Questions for oral answer[a]	119	290	511	537	531	713	743
Quetions for Written Answer	38	73	283	857	1304	5798	7374
Questions for short debate	12	12	39	31	42	81	89
Motions leading to debate	[b]	[b]	46	47	71	111	104
Public Bills introduced							
Government Bills[c]	6	7	11	12	10	12	18
Private Members' Bills	2	2	14	23	8	17	18
Amendments made in the							
House of Lords	*1951–52*	*1962–63*					
Government Bills (Commons)	30	456	558	418	544	1737	1385
PM Bills (Commons)	27	29	15	49	24	0	0
Government (Lords)	75	283	207	940	1012	303	1803
PM Bills (Lords)	0	8	75	53	5	62	18
Total	132	776	855	1460	1585	2102	3206

note: The 1970–71 and 2001–02 sessions were longer than usual because they began after June General Elections.

(a) In 1954 the limit was put up to three per day on any Sitting Day; previously it had been three only on Tuesdays and wednesdays. In 1959 the limit was raised to four per day on any Sitting Day. In 2002 the limit was raised to five per day on Tuesdays and Wednesdays.
(b) Figures are not available.
(c) Excluding Consolidation Bills/Order Confirmation Bills.

figure **10.3**   **the work of the House of Lords 1950–51 to 2005–06**

institutional independence and during that time the peers sought to provide some of the effective scrutiny and opposition which they felt that the House of Commons was unable or unwilling to provide. This resulted in the Lords inflicting 72 defeats on the Government during the *1987–92 Parliament* and 62 defeats during *the 1992–97 Parliament.*[14]

Equally, under New Labour during the *1997–2001 Parliament* the Lords inflicted defeats on the Government for broadly analogous reasons – namely, because the Government of the day had an overwhelming majority in the Commons and relatively few Labour backbenchers were inclined to rebel.[15]

During the *2001–05 Parliament* the Lords persisted with their critical behaviour and sought to amend and improve Government legislation on many occasions.[16]

In the first session of the Parliament elected in 2005, the Lords voted to block the scheme for identity cards until full costs were known, more security was provided for personal data and stricter controls were introduced on those who get access to the information. Similarly, during consideration of the Terrorism Bill, the Lords voted by 270 votes to 144 against plans to create a new offence of glorifying terror; and, by 234 votes to 134, in favour of new safeguards on laws designed to stop the spread of terrorist publications. Peers also changed the Terrorism Bill so as to ensure that police had to ask judges before telling internet providers that web pages related to terrorism should be removed. The Government was also heavily defeated in the Lords over plans to outlaw incitement to religious hatred, peers voting by a majority of 149 to put freedom of speech safeguards into the Racial and Religious Hatred Bill, changes that were subsequently agreed with by the House of Commons against the wishes of the Government.

In all these cases under successive Administrations their Lordships demonstrated considerable self-confidence in playing one of their legitimate roles as a constitutional check on the Government of the day. Since the removal of most of the hereditary peers in 1999, the number of defeats inflicted on the Government in the Lords has been considerable – 18 per cent of divisions in 1999–2000; 32.7 per cent in 2001–02; 38.9 per cent in 2003–03; 36.3 per cent in 2003–04; 55.2 per cent in 2004–05 and 32 per cent in 2005–06 – as the members have gained confidence in challenging the Executive. Nonetheless, it should be pointed out that successive Governments have usually been able to meet the objections raised in the House of Lords with judicious compromise solutions and, when necessary, to use their majority in the Commons to get their way on the big political issues.

10.5 Lords reform and modernisation

For very many years there has been a lively and continuing debate about the future of the House of Lords which has taken place within, between and beyond all parties. Proposals for change have tended to fall into one or more of four broad categories:

- Abolish the House of Lords altogether, creating a unicameral – single chamber – Parliamentary system
- Abolish the House of Lords, but create in its place a new body with different composition, powers and functions
- Change the composition of the House of Lords, but keep its powers and functions as they are
- Reform both the composition and the powers and functions of the House of Lords.

There has certainly been no shortage of proposals – indeed, it often appears that whenever a group of ten interested individuals discuss these matters, there are likely to be at least a dozen different proposals for reform! Set against the backdrop of the many different proposals for reform, there is also, of course, the traditional conservative view (with a small 'c') that the House of Lords should be left as it is. Over the years the Labour Party has wavered between a wish to reform it, a wish to replace it and a wish to abolish it altogether, with many not wanting any reform that would strengthen the Lords in relation to the Commons. Those Conservatives (with a capital 'C') who are interested in this matter have tended to press for reform of the Upper House in order to strengthen and entrench its position in relation to the Commons. The Liberal Democrats have tended to see reform of the House of Lords as part of a new constitutional settlement covering Parliament as a whole and other institutions such as the judiciary.

New Labour: modernization and reform

In its 1997 election Manifesto the Labour party, in a section entitled 'A Modern House of Lords', declared that the House of Lords must be reformed and that as an initial, self-contained reform, the right of hereditary peers to sit and vote in the House of Lords should be ended by statute. It was explained that this was to be the first stage in a process of reform designed to make the House of Lords both more democratic and representative. It went on to state that the legislative power of the House of Lords would remain unaltered. In addition, the system of appointing life peers to the House of Lords would be reviewed, the objective being to ensure that, over time, party appointees as life peers more accurately reflect the proportion of votes cast at the previous General Election. The Manifesto went on to declare a commitment to maintaining an independent cross-bench presence of life peers and that no one political party should seek an overall majority in the House of Lords. The section concluded by saying that a committee of both Houses of Parliament would be appointed to undertake a wide-ranging review of possible further change and then bring forward proposals for reform.

Early in 1999 the Government published a White Paper **Modernising Parliament: Reforming the House of Lords** outlining its step-by-step approach to reform.[17] Step one was the removal of the right of hereditary peers to sit and vote in the House of Lords with legislation to achieve this being introduced during the 1998–99 Session. As step two, the Government declared itself 'minded to accept' the proposal that a small number of hereditary peers be allowed to sit temporarily as members. It also pledged that no one party would be in a position to dominate the transitional House and that steps would be taken to reduce the unfettered power of the Prime Minister to nominate those to be appointed to life peerages, pledging to establish an independent Appointment Commission to recommend non-political appointments. Step three was the creation of a Royal Commission – under the chairmanship of Lord Wakeham – to examine a range of possible alternatives for longer-term reform covering roles and functions as well as composition.[18] On composition the White Paper set out four main options for the Royal Commission to consider: a nominated Chamber, a directly elected Chamber, an indirectly elected Chamber and a mixed Chamber. Step four would see the Royal Commission's recommendations (published in January 2000) being considered by a Joint Committee of both Houses of Parliament to examine in more detail the Parliamentary implications of any proposed reform. Step five would be legislation to implement the resulting proposals.

During the passage of the **House of Lords Bill** in the 1998–99 session, the legislation designed to achieve the removal of the hereditary peers, an amendment was passed allowing a total of 92 hereditary peers to remain as members of the 'transitional House'. It was a compromise that ensured that the legislation reached the statute book, receiving Royal assent shortly before the end of the session. The new 'transitional' or 'interim' House sat for the first time at the beginning of the 1999–2000 session.

In November 2001 the Government published a White Paper entitled **The House of Lords – Completing the Reform**,[19] in which it accepted parts of the Wakeham Report, but rejected others. It proposed a reduction in the number of members over ten years from 700 to 600; the removal of the remaining 92 hereditary peers; a reduction in the number of bishops from 26 to 16; the direct election of 20 per cent (120) of the membership; the appointment of 20 per cent of the independent peers by a new Appointments Commission; and the nomination of 60 per cent of 'working peers' in proportion to the share of the vote received by each of the political parties at the previous general election. Various points were left open for discussion, including the overall balance between elected, nominated and ex-officio members; the balance between political and independent members; whether or not elections for the membership should be linked to European elections or regional elections or held at the same time as elections to the House of Commons; the length of time for which members should be elected – 5, 10 or 15 years; the length of time for which appointed members should serve – 5, 10 or 15; whether or not it would matter if the terms of office differed; what the rules should be for disqualifying members and whether or not these should be statutory procedures or left to the House itself to decide; and finally the payment of members.

The White Paper received widespread criticism from a variety of different standpoints. The Public Administration Select Committee of the House of Commons published a detailed critique in which it recommended a chamber of 350 members with 60 per cent elected and 40 per cent appointed.[20]

In May 2002, in the hope of forging the broadest possible Parliamentary consensus, the Government entrusted the issue to a Joint Committee of both Houses of Parliament. The Committee began by looking at the composition of the Lords and reported in early December recommending that both Houses should vote on seven different options:

- A fully appointed House
- A fully elected House
- 80 per cent appointed/20 per cent elected
- 80 per cent elected/20 per cent appointed
- 60 per cent appointed/40 per cent elected
- 60 per cent elected/40 per cent appointed
- 50 per cent appointed/50 per cent elected.

Early in February 2003, the House of Commons voted to reject each of the seven options,[21] while the House of Lords voted by 335 votes to 110 in favour of an all-appointed House. The Joint Committee then handed the whole matter back to the Government, which in March decided not to pursue the matter further at that stage.[22]

Labour's 2005 Election Manifesto stated that 'as part of the process of modernization, we will remove the remaining hereditary peers and allow a free vote on the composition of the House'. They also pledged to seek agreement on codifying the key conventions of the Lords, to develop alternative forms of scrutiny that would complement rather than replicate those of the Commons, and to introduce legislation to place 'reasonable limits' on the time Bills spend in the Second Chamber, declaring that this would be no longer than 60 sitting days for most Bills.

Early in 2007 the Government brought forward proposals in a White Paper on further reform of the House of Lords.[23] The White Paper declared that the primacy of the Commons over the Lords has to remain and that the Lords should not become a rival but instead complement the Commons. The House of Lords was to retain its role in revising and scrutinising legislation. It was stated that although having some elected members would make the Lords more legitimate it would not give it parity with the Commons. The White Paper suggested that:

- A proportion of members should be elected (via some form of proportional representation, using a partially open list system in the regional constituencies used for the elections to the European Parliament). MPs were to decide on the proportion.
- The remaining 92 hereditary peers would go.
- One third of elected seats would be up for election every five years.
- Elected members would have a single term in office of 15 years. They could not stand for re-election.
- Political parties could pick 60 per cent of appointees, with the remainder being non-political.
- A third of appointed members would be replaced every five years
- Members who were elected could not later be appointed – and vice versa.
- Appointed members could only serve a maximum of 15 years.
- The size of the House be reduced to 540 members
- There should be a lengthy transition period, with no peers being forced to leave and with those who choose to go early being eligible for a retirement package
- There should be no reduction in the number of Anglican bishops and archbishops.

The Government announced that MPs were to be offered a range of seven choices for the make-up of the Lords: all elected; 80 per cent elected and 20 per cent appointed; 60 per cent elected and 40 per cent appointed; 50 per cent elected and 50 per cent appointed; 40 per cent elected and 60 per cent appointed; 20 per cent elected and 80 per cent appointed; all appointed. Peers would then be able to vote on what the Commons had decided.

Nonetheless, the way forward seems strewn with difficulties and we wait to see what, if anything, will happen.

House of Lords' plans for self-modernization

In February 2001 the House of Lords established a Select Committee on the Constitution to examine the constitutional implications of all public Bills and keep under review the operation of the constitution. The Leader's Group on Working Practices set up after the 2001 General Election produced a unanimous report which was approved in May 2002. Its proposals were then taken forward by a Procedure Committee whose recommendations were accepted in July and phased in during the 2002–03 session. The changes included:

- Arrangements for pre-legislative scrutiny for almost all major Bills
- More bills to have a committee stage off the floor of the House
- Automatic carry-over of Bills from one session to the next when pre-legislative scrutiny had taken place
- A change in the working hours so that the House would sit in September and rise on sitting days at 10:00pm
- More time for backbench initiated debates
- More debates on Select Committee Reports
- aAnew ad hoc Select Committee to oversee Finance Bills
- A new Committee to consider the merits of Statutory Instruments.

Taken together, these changes were significant and constituted nothing less than a small revolution in the working practices of the House of Lords.

The announcement in June 2003 by the Prime Minister in the course of a Ministerial reshuffle that the position of Lord Chancellor was to be abolished had important implications for the House of Lords as the Lord Chancellor acted as the Presiding Officer of the House. In December 2005 a House of Lords Select Committee recommended that a 'Lord Speaker' be elected for a renewable five-year term by secret ballot using the alternative vote system. In mid 2006 Baroness Hayman was duly elected first Lord Speaker.

Conservative proposals for Lords' reform

In Opposition following the 1997 General Election, some Conservatives turned their attention to Lords reform. For example, Andrew Tyrie MP argued for a mainly elected Upper House with the same powers of scrutiny and revision as the existing House of Lords,[24] while Nick Kent of the Tory Reform Group advocated a 350-strong Second Chamber made up of about 160 members elected regionally for nine-year terms, about 90 appointed life peers, bishops and other religious leaders, Law Lords and representatives from British territories overseas.[25] In July 1998 William Hague, then Conservative party Leader, announced the establishment of a Constitutional Commission on the House of Lords under the chairmanship of the former Lord Chancellor, Lord Mackay of Clashfern, to consider all options for reform. Reporting the following year, it advocated a predominantly elected chamber.[26] In 2001 the then Conservative leader, Iain Duncan Smith, declared his support for a House with 80 per cent of the members elected, and in 2002 the Conservatives proposed a House of 300 members, 80 per cent of whom were to be elected under the first-past-the-post system from 80 countrywide constituencies and 20 per cent appointed as independent crossbenchers.[27] At the time of the 2005 General Election the Conservative party pledged itself to 'seek cross-party consensus for a substantially elected House of Lords'.

Liberal Democrat proposals for Lords' reform

In the 1997 General Election campaign the Liberal Democrats sought to place the 'modernisation'of what they described as 'Britain's antiquated and ineffective constitution' at the head of their policy priorities. They therefore advocated reform of the House of Lords as part of a new constitutional settlement, including a codified constitution, an entrenched Bill of Rights, Home Rule for Scotland and Wales, regional Assemblies throughout England, and proportional representation for all elections. As far as the Second Chamber was concerned, they advocated transforming the House of Lords into a directly elected Senate with the task of representing the various nations and regions of the UK. Members of this Upper House were to be elected by Single Transferable Vote for fixed terms of six years, with one-third retiring every two years. They would be empowered to delay legislation, with the exception of Money Bills, for up to two years and would have a power of veto over proposed constitutional changes emanating from the Lower House.[28] In the debates on this subject the party advocated a House of 300 members, 80 per cent of whom were to be elected under a proportional system and 20 per cent appointed. At the time of the 2005 General Election the party was advocating 'a predominantly elected second chamber'.

10.6 conclusion

A study of the House of Lords in recent years provides clear evidence that it is not in danger of atrophy or decline; indeed, quite the reverse. The House of Lords has demonstrated a remarkable ability to evolve and adapt to changing circumstances. This stems very largely from its extraordinary character which is derived from the fact that it has been shaped by a small number of Parliamentary statutes and influenced by tradition, custom and practice dating back at least to medieval times.

The House of Lords, as it exists today, is thus the product of a long evolutionary process. It may appear to be a strange institution in that it is hard to believe that anyone would set out to establish a Second Chamber of this kind. Yet its unusual character can be regarded as a strength, because it involves a delicate balance of real effectiveness and curtailed powers which makes a significant contribution to the work of Parliament and the British political system. If it did not exist, it would almost certainly need to be replaced with another Parliamentary institution of comparable purpose and utility which would fit as comfortably into British political culture.

SUGGESTED QUESTIONS

1   Analyse the composition of the contemporary House of Lords.
2   What are the functions of the House of Lords and how well is it able to perform them?
3   What are the implications of directly electing members of the House of Lords?

chapter **11**

the House of Commons

Unlike the Monarchy or the House of Lords, the House of Commons still has real power in the British political system, at any rate on those occasions when it is willing and able to use it. Yet the nature of its power is different from what it was in the nineteenth century when most of the traditional notions about the House were established. The House of Commons of the twenty-first century is neither the Government of the country nor even the principal place where official decisions or legislative proposals are conceived. It is essentially the sounding board for popular representation and redress, one of the stages on which the party battle is fought, the principal forum within which legislation and other decisions of Government are scrutinised, and the framework for Parliamentary control of the Executive – one of the tasks which it shares with the House of Lords.

The essential purposes of the House of Commons have not changed significantly since the last quarter of the nineteenth century. W.I. Jennings described them as being 'to question and debate the policy of the Government and in doing so to bring home ... the unpopularity (or popularity) of a particular line of policy'.[1] L.S. Amery described them as being 'to secure full discussion and ventilation of all matters ... as the condition of giving its assent to Bills ... or its support to Ministers'.[2] Such descriptions are still broadly valid today.

11.1 composition

At the General Election of 2005 a total of 355 Labour Members of Parliament (MPs) were elected, along with 198 Conservatives, 62 Liberal Democrats, 6 Scottish Nationalists, 3 Welsh Nationalists (Plaid Cymru), 9 Democratic Unionists, 1 Ulster Unionist, 3 Social Democratic and Labour, 5 Sinn Fein, 1 Respect, 2 Independents and the Speaker, giving a House of Commons composed of 646 members elected on a uniform national franchise from single-member constituencies with an average of 68,516 electors. The Speaker and three Deputy Speakers are all elected MPs. The current Speaker, Michael Martin, prior to being elected Speaker by MPs, was a Labour MP. The Speaker and the Deputy Speakers – one Labour MP and two Conservative MPs – take no partisan role in the proceedings (unless a vote is tied, in which case they are expected to vote for the *status quo*), since they are responsible in the chair for seeing that the rules of order are maintained. Thus, at the 2005 election the Labour Government secured an overall Parliamentary majority of 66.

MPs as representatives

Members of Parliament can be seen as more or less representative in several different senses. *First*, we can consider the educational and occupational backgrounds of individual MPs and, *second*, we can consider the extent to which the composition of the House of Commons reflects the composition of the electorate as a whole. This information is provided in Figure 11.1.

From this it is evident that British MPs as a whole are still something of an elite in educational and occupational terms, although notably less than some years ago. Of course, much depends on whether one refers to the individuals concerned or to their family backgrounds. If the latter criterion is adopted, the social and class differences between the parties remain significant – a fact which is best explained by the upward social mobility achieved by many people. In general, it is evident that as the middle class has become larger, so, its contingent of MPs has become larger as a reflection of changes in society as a whole. Equally, as the influence of the prestigious public schools and the universities of Oxford and Cambridge has declined there has been an educational and social convergence in the Parliamentary representation of the three main parties. This has, however, greatly diminished the presence of MPs from each end of the social spectrum.

In considering the extent to which the composition of the House of Commons reflects the composition of the electorate as a whole, the most obvious example is that of *women*, who account for 52 per cent of the electorate but only 19.8 per cent (128) of all MPs. In the past this has been largely due to the prejudices of constituency selection committees who have seemed opposed to choosing women as candidates for winnable seats. However, in recent years things have begun to change and there has been a degree of positive discrimination in favour of women candidates. As a result the 2005 election saw the return of more women MPs – mainly on the Labour side – than ever before (one in five). Subsequently, both the Conservatives under David Cameron and the Liberal Democrats under Sir Menzies Campbell have been trying to secure the selection of more female candidates in winnable seats.

Another example of a disproportion between representation at Westminster and in the population as a whole is that of minority ethnic groups – 8 per cent of the total population but only 2 per cent of MPs. Only 15 MPs elected in 2005 were from minority ethnic groups (13 Labour and 2 Conservative) and five of them were elected to Parliament for the first time. Those under 30 years or over 70 years of age are also under-represented in the House of Commons. The 2005 election saw the return of only 3 MPs under the age of 30 and of only 14

MPs elected by party and sex, ethnicity and previous parliamentary experience

| | Sex | | | | Parliamentary experience | | | | |
	Male		Female		Minority ethnique		Immediately pre-election	Previous (retread)	None (new MP)	All
Labour	257	72%	98	28%	13	4%	315	–	40	355
Conservative	181	91%	17	9%	2	1%	143	3	51	198
Liberal Democrat	52	84%	10	16%	–	–	42	–	20	62
SNP	6	100%	–	–	–	–	4	–	2	6
Plaid Cymru	3	100%	–	–	–	–	3	–	–	3
DUP	8	89%	1	11%	–	–	6	1	2	9
UUP	–	–	1	100%	–	–	1	–	–	l
SDLP	3	100%	–	–	–	–	1	–	2	3
Sinn Féin	4	80%	1	20%	–	–	4	–	1	5
Other	4	100%	–	–	–	–	3	–	1	4
All	**518**	**80%**	**128**	**20%**	**15**	**2%**	**522**	**4**	**119**	**646**

note: Minority ethnic data from Operation Black Vote

Education of MPs: main parties

| | | MPs elected | | | | % of MPS | | | |
		Con	Lab	LD	Total	Con	Lab	LD	Total
State School		80	292	38	410	40%	82%	61%	67%
Independent school		118	63	24	205	60%	18%	39%	33%
Of which	Eton	15	1	1	17	8%	0%	2%	3%
	Harrow	0	0	0	0	0%	0%	0%	0%
University		160	226	49	435	81%	64%	79%	71%
Of which	Cambridge	37	18	8	63	19%	5%	13%	10%
	Oxford	49	40	11	100	25%	11%	18%	16%

note: Data published for the three main parties only
source: Kavanagh and Butler, *The British General Election of 2005*. Palgrave 2005, table 10.5

Occupations of MPs: main parties

▶ 118 MPs from the main parties were drawn from business, including 75 Conservatives, 38% of the parliamentary party.

▶ 91 teachers won seats, 73 Labour, 12 Liberal Democrat and 6 Conservative. Teachers accounted for 21% of successful Labour candidates.

▶ 87 professional politicians were elected, 14% of the total, including 60 for Labour.

Average age of MPs elected by party
Age in years on 5 May 2005

Conservative	49
Labour	5
Liberal Democrat	4
Others	51
Total	**51**

source: 'General Election 2005', House of Commons Library Research Paper 05/53, 17 May 2005.

figure **11.1**   **sociological background of MPs**

MPs over the age of 70. Amongst Labour MPs the average age was 52 with only 10 per cent under the age of 40 and with 19 per cent over the age of 60; amongst Conservative MPs the average age was 49, with 17 per cent under the age of 40 and 18 per cent over the age of 60; the Liberal Democrats had the youngest age profile with an average age of 46 and with 31 per cent of their MPs being under the age of 40 and only 10 per cent over the age of 60. On the other hand, there are groups which are over-represented in the House of Commons, notably lawyers, people from public relations and the media. Nevertheless it should be noted that many MPs develop a wide range of interests and expertise during their time in the House and this can turn them into 'virtual representatives' of various categories and interests in the electorate.

frontbenchers

In 2006 paid office-holders in the Government (frontbenchers) accounted for some 90 of the 355 Labour MPs. This figure included 16 Government Whips who facilitate the business in the Commons, but who do not speak in debates or share in the running of Government Departments in the way that other Ministers do. The so-called payroll vote (that is, those who are expected to support the Government on all occasions) is supplemented by some 46 Parliamentary Private Secretaries (PPSs) who sit on the second bench just behind their Ministers and who are expected to be completely loyal to the Government in the same way as the Ministers whom they serve. At the heart of the Government frontbench is the Cabinet which in 2006 had 23 members, of whom 21 sat in the Commons, since only the Secretary of State for Constitutional Affairs and the Leader of the House of Lords sat in the upper House.[3]

On the Opposition side, the front bench is made up of the Shadow Cabinet and other more junior spokesmen who support their more senior colleagues. In 2006 the Conservative Shadow Cabinet consisted of 25 individuals – 23 MPs and 2 from the House of Lords. In addition there were 48 MPs, as well as a number of peers, appointed by the Leader of the Opposition as front-bench spokesmen and 12 Opposition Whips in the House of Commons, led by the Chief Whip. The Liberal Democrats, with 62 MPs following the 2005 General Election, also have a Shadow Cabinet and a team of junior spokesmen, as well as a Chief Whip, a Deputy Whip and a team of four other whips in the House of Commons.

backbenchers

The 400 or so MPs who have no direct involvement either in Government or in the tasks of front-bench Opposition make up the generality of backbenchers. Some are senior, have been in the House a long time, may well have been Ministers at an earlier stage in their careers, and wield a good deal of influence within their parties. A few carry considerable weight in the House as a whole and still attract a larger than normal audience of their colleagues when they speak in debate. However, a large number of backbenchers are relatively junior and have been in the House for only a short period. They try to make their way in politics as well as they can. This means that they are likely to spend a great deal of their time trying to attract the attention and approval of their party Whips by playing an active and helpful part in proceedings in the Chamber, in Westminster Hall and in Committee. Among those elected in 2005, 523 (81 per cent) had been MPs in the previous Parliament (2001–05) and 119 (18 per cent) had no previous Parliamentary experience.[4]

The principal duty of backbenchers when their party is in Government is to support it with their votes in the division lobbies and, to a lesser extent, with their voices during Parliamentary proceedings. When their party is in Opposition, their principal task is to harry the Government on every suitable occasion. Some backbenchers, however, may choose to become rebels within their party, as was the case with those in the Labour Party who rebelled over foundation hospitals, university tuition fees and the war in Iraq during the 2001–05 Parliament and over ID cards and education reforms in the Parliament elected in 2005. However, persistent or serial rebels can come to be seen by the party hierarchy simply as 'mavericks', 'eccentrics' or 'the usual suspects'. Such behaviour is not normally recommended for those who are ambitious for Ministerial office, but there are some formidable exceptions who get taken into Government in an attempt to turn them into team players or, at the very least, to silence them.[5]

The life of a backbencher in the modern House of Commons is usually more fun in Opposition than in Government. This is because, in the former case, there are more opportunities to play a prominent role in the party battle (since by definition there are always fewer MPs on the Opposition benches than on the Government side) and to make a favourable impression on the party leadership. It is also because nothing which is said or done by Opposition backbenchers matters very much and such politicians can therefore enjoy (at least at Westminster, if not in their constituencies where their role is different) the luxury of considerable irresponsibility. When their party is in Government, backbenchers have to tread the much more difficult, narrow path between sycophancy and rebellion. In such conditions they can be forgiven for thinking that all the Whips really want is their presence in the division lobbies at the appointed times to support the Government.

Certainly backbenchers in both main parties have cause to complain about the privileges granted to Privy Councillors (very senior backbenchers nearly all of whom have held Ministerial office at an earlier stage in their careers) and to the spokesmen of minor parties, since both categories are almost certain to be called to speak in debates at favourable times and to catch the Speaker's eye if they wish to intervene at Question Time or following Ministerial Statements. This is mainly a reflection of the seniority principle which influences the pecking order at Westminster and indeed in virtually every other Parliament around the world. Nonetheless, there is also a well-established Westminster convention that the Speaker should try to ensure a hearing not simply for minority points of view but for dissidents within the main parties. Thus backbenchers who intend to abstain or vote against their party (especially if it is in Government) will normally be given a chance to explain their reasons during the course of the relevant debate.

pay and conditions of work

All MPs receive a Parliamentary salary from public funds which is based on recommendations from the independent Senior Salaries Review Body (SSRB) with the final decision being taken by the House of Commons itself. Although members' staff are the employees of MPs, their salaries are paid centrally by the House Authorities according to agreed pay scales and standard contracts as recommended by the SSRB. The staffing allowance is intended to pay for between two and three full-time or equivalent staff. Up to 10 per cent of the sum can be used to fund constituency offices. In addition, certain IT equipment for MPs offices is centrally provided and maintained and an incidental expenses provision is available for other expenses involved in running an office, such as rent and rates. Central funding is also provided for staff training.

MPs are also entitled to free, first-class travel within the United Kingdom as long as they are on Parliamentary or constituency business, and to one free trip a year to the institutions of the European Union or the national Parliament of any other EU state. At Westminster they do not have to pay for telephone calls within the United Kingdom and have the benefit of free, first-class post for written communication with their constituents and others (for example, public bodies) in connection with their constituency duties. For those who travel by car, motorbike, motorcycle or bicycle there are allowances available for travel to and from (and within) their constituencies.[6] Inner London MPs qualify for a London allowance while all other MPs are entitled to claim an Additional Costs Allowance to cover the expenses incurred in staying overnight away from home whilst engaged in Parliamentary activities.

In addition to their Parliamentary salaries, Ministers receive various levels of salary from public funds according to their level in the Government. The Leader of the Opposition, as well as the Opposition Chief Whip, Deputy Chief Whip and Assistant Whip also receive additional salaries from public funds in recognition of their extra Parliamentary responsibilities. The Speaker, the three Deputy Speakers and a number of Select Committee Chairmen also receive additional salaries from public funds. The amounts involved are outlined in Figure 11.2.

Compared with their counterparts in comparable democracies, British Ministers and Members of Parliament do not enjoy very lavish rewards. However, their overall package of pay and allowances is probably as good as the average in many other countries. Ever since MPs began to award themselves significant pay and allowances in 1964, the issue has been controversial and it seems that there is never a right moment for Members of Parliament, Ministers (and indeed peers who can claim daily allowances for their attendance at the

	Date introduced	Provision from 1 November 2006
Salary	1912	£60,277
Staffing Allowance	1969	£87,276 (a)
Incidental expenses provision (IEP) (b)	2001	£20,440
IT equipment (b)		(centrally provided) (c)
Telephone & postage	1969	Free on parliamentary business within the UK
Travel	1924	Free to and from constituency and between home and Westminster, plus some provision for family, car mileage and bicycle allowance.
Subsistence (additional costs allowance)	1972	Allowance when the House is sitting: £22,110 London supplement (inner London MPs): £2712
Pension	(d) 1965	Payable at 65 (60 with reduced benefit) according to length of service; minimum of 4 years' service.
Resettlement grant	1974	Lump sum equivalent to 50–100 per cent of salary, depending on age and service.

notes: (a) Varying according to type of post and whether staff work in London or elsewhere. There is also provision for a contribution equal to ten per cent of each employee's gross salary to fund pensions.

(b) The IEP is intended to cover other expenses e.g. office rental, staff travel.

(c) The provision allows for up to one laptop, four desktop PCs and two printers.

(d) Backdated to 1964.

source: adapted from Michael Rush, 'Parliament: Pay and Resoureces', in N.D.J. Baldwin (ed.) *Parliament in the 21st Century* (London: Politico's, 2005)

figure **11.2   MPs: Pay and allowances**

House of Lords) to increase their remuneration, even if only in line with the cost of living.

The situation had been exacerbated in the middle 1990s by a succession of sensational revelations in the media of MPs allegedly being prepared to take money from outside interests in return for asking Parliamentary Questions, and this opened up a much wider debate about the propriety or otherwise of MPs having paid outside interests in addition to their public duties. All outside interests (both paid and unpaid) are supposed to be declared in the Register of Members' Interests which is kept up to date by a senior Parliamentary clerk and initially the principle of full, voluntary disclosure was thought to be sufficient. However, public and media interest in these matters became much more acute in the middle 1990s, following a succession of sensational revelations, and this led to the establishment of a Committee on Standards in Public Life in 1994.

The following year the House of Commons agreed that MPs could not be advocates for causes in the House if such causes provided them with any personal financial benefit. They also agreed, following recommendations of the Committee, to establish a Parliamentary Commissioner for Standards, an official who can advise MPs on standards of conduct and who is responsible for conducting investigations into alleged breaches of the rules. The Commissioner reports to the House of Commons Select Committee on Standards and Privileges.

It should also be noted that there is financial assistance from public funds – the so-called Short Money – to Opposition parties to assist them in carrying out their Parliamentary activities.[7] These financial arrangements symbolise the longstanding commitment in Britain to the idea of a constitutional Opposition and give financial expression to the traditional term 'Her Majesty's Loyal Opposition'. Indeed, Britain was the first Parliamentary democracy to make such financial arrangements for leading members of the Opposition in recognition of their constitutional duty to oppose the Government of the day.

The conditions of work for MPs have improved dramatically over the last 40 years, not least because some buildings at 1 Parliament Street and 7 Millbank were refurbished for MPs and their personal staff in the late 1980s and early 1990s and a completely new Parliamentary office building – Portcullis House – was opened in 2000, ensuring that there is no longer a shortage of suitably equipped office premises for individual MPs at Westminster. Gone are the days when MPs had to make do with a desk, telephone and filing cabinet in a room shared with their colleagues.

11.2 main functions

In 1867 Walter Bagehot suggested that the House of Commons needed to perform the following functions if it was to do its duty: 'elect a Ministry, legislate, teach the nation, express the nation's will and bring matters to the nation's attention.'[8] If we were to translate his words into modern terms,

we would say that the House of Commons has to provide most of the Ministers in any Government, to scrutinise and pass legislation, to give a lead to public opinion on the great issues of the day, and to seek redress for the grievances and concerns of the general public. There are, of course, other vital functions performed by the modern House of Commons, notably Parliamentary control of the Executive and party political conflict on the Parliamentary stage. Yet the essential functions of the House have not changed very much since the

Representation and redress	The party battle
On behalf of constituents	In the Chamber
On behalf of interest	In Committees
On behalf of causes	In the media
The legislative process	Parliamentary control
First reading	Debates in the Chamber
Second reading	Oral and written questions
Committee stage	Select Committee work
Report stage	Representations to ministers
Third reading	Representations ro agencies

figure **11.3**   **functions of the House of Commons**

time when Walter Bagehot made his authoritative observation. The functions of the Commons are summarised in Figure 11.3.

representation and redress

The oldest function of Members of Parliament is to represent the interests of their constituents and to seek redress for their grievances by the Government of the day. This function, which has been performed ever since the establishment of Parliament in the thirteenth century, is still a vital task for MPs in modern conditions. There are a number of different ways in which it is carried out. These include having a quiet word with a Minister in the division lobby and signing an Early Day Motion with other MPs in order to signal the breadth and depth of support for a particular cause or concern. They also include such techniques as:

▸ Writing a letter to a Minister enclosing documentary evidence of a constituent's complaint
▸ Leading a delegation to lobby a Minister in their office in Whitehall
▸ Putting down a Parliamentary Question for written answer in order to get a Ministerial response on the record in *Hansard*
▸ Putting down a Question for oral answer in order to be able to make a point in a Supplementary Question on the floor of the House
▸ Applying to the Speaker for an Adjournment Debate at the end of the day's Parliamentary proceedings or an Emergency Debate immediately after Oral Questions and any Ministerial Statements.

As must be evident from this brief description, there are many channels of representation available to MPs when performing this aspect of their duties. It is normal for them to begin with one of the lower key methods and to resort to the more dramatic ones only if the former do not have the desired effect. The wide range of possible techniques for publicising the concerns or grievances of their constituents gives backbench MPs a real degree of influence in their representations to Ministers and civil servants.

If MPs did not speak up and intervene on behalf of their constituents when the latter feel frustrated by the bureaucracy of central Government or other public agencies, many people might conclude that Parliamentary democracy was a bit of a sham and withdraw their support for it. Even as things stand, the general public has a pretty cynical attitude towards the role and utility of MPs and it is not usually until people experience a positive response from their own MP that they are prepared to reconsider their habitually low opinion of the political process. On the other hand, when a conscientious MP is able to provide effective help for a constituent, it can make the beneficiary of such political action more likely to appreciate the value of having an MP in the first place. To the extent that MPs exert themselves in this way – and nearly all of them do – it provides at least one recognisable justification for the British Parliamentary system. Indeed, the rise of the constituency role of

MPs has been a significant feature over recent years. An example of this can be seen in the increase that has taken place in constituency correspondence, MPs receiving per day the number of letters that used to be received per week 30 years ago, and this does not take into account the advent of emails and text messages.[9]

the party battle

Another function of Members of Parliament is to act as combatants for their party when it is in Government and critics or opponents of the Government when their party is in Opposition. The party battle, which was particularly polarised in the 1970s and 1980s, has been deplored in many quarters, especially by the minor parties whose interests are not very well catered for in the procedural arrangements at Westminster. However, there are some points to be made in its favour. It encourages the voters to take an interest in national politics between General Elections, to consider at least two sides to every political argument and to pay some attention to topical policy issues. Without the drama of the party battle at Westminster and, of course, in the columns and studios of the media, the political process would lose much of its vitality and the influence of the bureaucracy would increase. While there are those who would welcome such an alternative way of conducting British political life, even they would have to concede that it would probably produce a less accountable and less democratic form of government.

Although in Britain many people pay little or no attention to the processes of politics, there would probably be even less public interest and even more public apathy without the stimulus and often annoyance of the party battle. Evidence over a long period suggests that the degree of success or failure of the Opposition parties in criticising the Government of the day and putting forward their own proposals does have a cumulative effect on public opinion and subsequently on the voting behaviour of at least the more attentive voters. Opposition parties very often fail to get all the publicity which they would like (especially for their own policy proposals), but they are often successful in sowing the seeds of doubt and resentment about the performance of the party in office in the minds of the voters. In this way, more than any other, there tends to be a negative bias in the British party battle. Yet it is hard to see how things could be otherwise as long as the House of Commons retains its present 'winner-takes-all' electoral system.

the legislative process

Another well-recognised, but not always well-understood, function of Members of Parliament is the scrutiny and passage of legislation. It is the function most often mentioned by members of the public when asked to describe the activities of Parliament. Over the years it has absorbed an increasing proportion of Parliamentary time as the scope and complexity of legislation have increased and as the public, especially pressure groups, have made greater demands on Governments of all political persuasions. The legislative process is shown diagrammatically in Figure 11.4.

The legislative process in the Commons begins with **First Reading**. This is the name of the formal stage at which printed copies of a Bill are made available in the Vote Office for all MPs and others who are interested to read and consider. After about two weeks this is followed by **Second Reading** when a wide ranging debate takes place for about six hours on the broad purposes of a Bill and at the end of which a vote is usually taken which shows whether or not the House approves of a Bill in principle. This is the stage of the debate when the senior Minister in charge of a Bill sets out the broad arguments for it, the chief Opposition spokesman sets out the broad arguments against it (unless a Bill is wholly uncontentious in which case detailed criticism and constructive suggestions are more likely to be offered), interested backbenchers on both sides of the House make national or constituency points, and junior Ministers and Opposition spokesmen wind up the debate during the final hour by answering (or sometimes ignoring) the various points made during the course of the debate. At the end of such debates on all Government Bills the votes are whipped, which means that MPs are expected to support the position of their own party, unless they have persuasive reasons for doing otherwise – for example, conscientious objections or overriding constituency reasons.

Assuming that a Bill is approved by the House at Second Reading, it is then referred to a **Standing Committee** 'upstairs' where it is debated in detail and at length by a committee of between 16 and 50 MPs chosen to reflect the party balance in the House as a whole.[10] A typical Standing Committee may be made up of two or more Ministers in charge of the Bill, a Government Whip and perhaps a dozen or more backbenchers on the Government side, ranged against a variety of Opposition MPs who will invariably include two or more Opposition spokesmen and an Opposition Whip as well as a number of interested Opposition backbenchers who between them usually share the burdens of scrutinising or opposing the Bill. The task of a Standing Committee is to debate and scrutinise a Bill clause by clause and line by line. This usually involves members of the Opposition putting down a considerable number of critical or even wrecking amendments, some merely probing but some seeking to alter fundamentally or even destroy the effect of a Bill. The Ministers in charge of a Bill have to answer each separate debate and, if necessary, to persuade their own backbenchers to vote against any amendments unacceptable to the Government, if the Opposition is not prepared to withdraw them at the end of each debate. Once all the debates on amendments and on each clause 'stand part' have been concluded, new clauses can be proposed and debated, provided they fall within the scope of the long title of a Bill.

It used to be the case that unusually complex and controversial Bills had to be timetabled as long as the Government could persuade the House as a whole to vote for a so-called 'guillotine' motion at the end of a three-hour debate in the Chamber, thus ensuring that the proceedings were timetabled for the remainder of the committee stage. This procedural device was supposed to

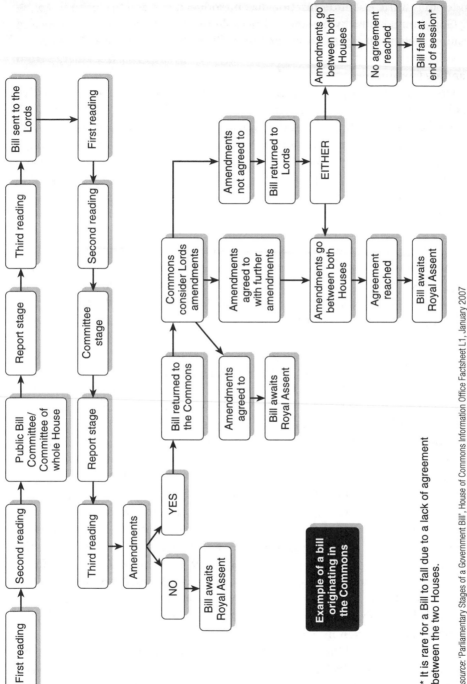

First reading → Second reading → Public Bill Committee/ Committee of whole House → Report stage → Third reading → Bill sent to the Lords

First reading → Second reading → Committee stage → Report stage → Third reading → Amendments

Amendments → YES → Bill returned to the Commons → Commons consider Lords amendments

Amendments → NO → Bill awaits Royal Assent

Commons consider Lords amendments → Amendments agreed to → Bill awaits Royal Assent

Commons consider Lords amendments → Amendments not agreed to → Bill returned to Lords → EITHER

EITHER → Amendments go between both Houses → No agreement reached → Bill falls at end of session*

EITHER → Amendments agreed to with further amendments → Amendments go between both Houses → Agreement reached → Bill awaits Royal Assent

Example of a bill originating in the Commons

* It is rare for a Bill to fall due to a lack of agreement between the two Houses.

source: 'Parliamentary Stages of a Government Bill', House of Commons Information Office Factsheet L1, January 2007

figure **11.4 The Legislative Process**

ensure that all parts of a Bill were discussed, but it was never very satisfactory from the Government's point of view. Since 1997 the Labour Government under the rubric of 'modernisation' has introduced the practice of timetabling all Government Bills by passing a timetable motion at the end of the Second Reading debate designed to ensure that all parts of a Bill are discussed, if only briefly, and Ministers can know in advance when a Bill will emerge from standing Committee.

After an appropriate interval to give time to officials and legislative draftsmen to take account of amendments put forward in Committee, the Bill is then returned to the floor of the House for the Report and Third Reading. These are usually taken on the same day and may last for at least one full day's debate in the Chamber. The **Report** stage is the time when other members of the House as a whole, notably those who did not serve on the Standing Committee, have a chance to speak and vote on any new amendments or new clauses which have been accepted by the Speaker for debate. It is out of order for opponents of a Bill to go over ground already traversed during earlier stages of the legislative process. **Third Reading**, which follows immediately, is usually no more than a fairly brief debate on the general merits or demerits of a Bill as it stands, and provides what is usually a final opportunity for the House as a whole to record its views. The debate is concluded by yet another vote of principle on the Bill in which MPs tend to vote on party lines once again.

By this stage of the legislative process the House of Commons has usually concluded its scrutiny of a Bill, unless subsequently the House of Lords insists on making some substantial amendments which Ministers decide to resist. If this happens the Commons have later to give **further consideration to the Bill as amended by the Lords**. If all the Lords' amendments are acceptable to the Commons (which really means to the Government of the day), the Lower House simply sends a message to the Upper House signifying its agreement. If, however, some of the Lords' amendments are not acceptable to the governing party in the Commons, the Lower House sends a message containing its reasons for disagreement and possibly some counter-amendments of its own. It is then for the Lords to decide whether to persist with their opposition to the Commons or to give way gracefully in the light of the fact that under the constitutional provisions of the 1911 and 1949 Parliament Acts, the House of Commons can ultimately get its way. On nearly all occasions since 1949 – indeed, on all but four occasions when the procedures of the Parliament Acts were involved – the House of Lords has given way to the will of the elected members in the Commons (see Chapter 10).

Once a Bill is out of the Lords, it requires only the formality of Royal Assent. The whole process from First Reading to Royal Assent normally takes between six months and one year. However, it can be speeded up dramatically in cases of emergency – for example, Bills to deal with terrorism or civil disorder which, with the benefit of agreement between the parties, can be put through all stages of the legislative process in 24 hours if necessary.

Parliamentary scrutiny and control

Yet another vital function of Members of Parliament is to scrutinise and seek to control the activities of the Executive. This is probably the most necessary, but also the most difficult, function to be performed by the House in modern conditions, essentially because, unlike in many other comparable countries, there is no formal separation of powers between the Executive and the Legislature in Britain. This means that in Britain the Government of the day – provided it has a secure overall majority in the House of Commons – is more often able to dominate Parliament than Parliament is able to dominate the Government of the day.

Traditionally, it was assumed that Ministers' responsibility to answer the questions and debating points of Members of Parliament constituted adequate and respectable Parliamentary control of the Executive. Yet with the remorseless extension of the perceived responsibilities of Government over the last 65 years, it has become painfully clear that this traditional and complacent assumption does not meet public expectations and needs to be reinforced if central Government and its Agencies are to be properly scrutinised, let alone controlled by the elected representatives of the people. The fundamental problem here is that with typical British ambiguity there is a clash between two different versions of democratic legitimacy – that of the party elected into office at the previous General Election to govern the country for a period of years according to the principles and policies which it put before the electorate, and that of the House of Commons as a whole as the democratic manifestation of the will of the people at any particular time.

In modern times Parliamentarians have sought to square this circle by making increasingly full and effective use of Select Committees. In the House of Commons these are committees reflecting broadly the political balance in the House at any time which are charged by the House as a whole with scrutinizing the activities of the Executive in given policy areas. Originally, they were set up by the House *ad hoc* to look closely into particular issues of public concern – for example, Britain's military shortcomings in the Crimean War. They can also be traced back to the attitudes of William Gladstone and other Parliamentarians in the 1850s who, in their determination to guarantee the probity and efficiency of public expenditure, established the Public Accounts Committee to enable the House as a whole to be satisfied that public money was being correctly and properly spent. Since then the fortunes of Select Committees have waxed and waned. They have tended to be more powerful when the Government of the day has had only a very small majority in the Commons or no majority at all, but considerably less powerful when the Government of the day has had a commanding majority which it could use, if necessary, to steamroller any flickering challenge from Select Committees. Indeed, there has been a school of thought that holds that the correct way to scrutinise and control the Executive is on the floor of the House and that Select Committees are little more than a self-important and time-consuming distraction from what should be the cockpit of Parliamentary control in the Chamber.

It was against this historical background that the incoming Conservative Government in 1979 decided, perhaps somewhat surprisingly, to propose a comprehensive reform of the Select Committee structure which was willingly accepted by most Government backbenchers and certainly by the Opposition parties. Consequently, since then there has been one of these all-party and largely non-partisan Committees for each Departmental area of central Government activity, as well as a number of non-Departmental committees, such as the Public Accounts Committee, which have deeper roots in Parliamentary soil.[11] These Select Committees, each of which is usually composed of between 11 and 16 MPs broadly reflecting the party political balance in the House as a whole, meet regularly (perhaps two days a week when the House is sitting and on other occasions as well) to oversee and investigate their particular areas of Government activity. In the course of their investigations, which can include foreign travel, they can call for persons and papers, and their findings are normally written up in substantial reports produced for the benefit of the whole House. Occasionally, they can have real influence on the course of Parliamentary debate and Government policy.[12]

In normal circumstances Select Committees have no legislative role, so they are not really analogous to the Committees in the United States Congress. However, they are used increasingly as Parliamentary mechanisms for the consideration of Government Bills at a pre-legislative stage.[13] Whatever their shortcomings and weaknesses, they do represent a systematic attempt to improve Parliamentary scrutiny and control of the Executive, a tack which has become all the more necessary as it has been recognised that the traditional forms of Ministerial accountability to the House as a whole do not guarantee the achievement of this important Parliamentary objective.

In recent years the influence and salience of Select Committees has increased in that their public hearings often attract a degree of extra media and public interest. This makes them more formidable interlocutors for Ministers and senior civil servants and a more visible part of Parliamentary accountability. Those who chair such committees can become (or may already be) influential and newsworthy MPs who are often called to speak early in debates on the floor of the House and can be much in demand for media interviews. Yet it would be a mistake to believe that this extra visibility for Select Committees has altered to any real extent the fundamental imbalance of power in the House of Commons between a self-confident Government with a secure Parliamentary majority and the rest of the House, no matter how effective the Opposition may be or how keen MPs may have become to use Select Committees and other Parliamentary procedures more effectively to hold Ministers and the Executive to account.

Experience of clashes between Members of Parliament and the Executive underlines the fact that Parliamentary control of the Executive in Britain is not as effective as its proponents or some members of the general public would like.[14] In the final analysis, Select Committees, and indeed Parliament as a whole, are likely to remain relatively weak when faced with a strong and determined

Government which is confident of its ability to use its voting support on the floor of the House to overcome any challenge. The only circumstances in which this situation might be changed would be if a Government were committed to, or had imposed on it by dint of its minority status in the Commons, extensive Parliamentary reform and the introduction of proportional representation for elections to Westminster.

11.3 the power of the Commons

The tasks of the House of Commons are diffuse, variable and rather difficult to define in a permanent and authoritative way. They are not set out in any definitive document or defined in any Court ruling.

In cases of dispute the most reliable guide is *Erskine May*, the reference book which covers the whole of Parliamentary procedure in the Lower House according to the precedents established over centuries by successive Speakers and codified by successive Clerks of the Commons.[15]

theory and practice

In theory, the House of Commons has very great power in British constitutional arrangements. This could be said to include the power to make and unmake Governments, to topple Prime Ministers, to safeguard the liberties of British subjects, to bring to light and remedy injustices, and even to legislate itself out of existence or the country into a dictatorship.

In practice, the power of the Commons is usually subsumed in the power of the Government of the day, which governs through Parliament as long as it retains the voting support of an overall majority in the House of Commons. It is usually misleading to refer to the powers of the Commons in any way which implies that such powers can be divorced from those of modern single-party Government. In normal Parliamentary conditions, when one of the main parties on its own has an overall majority in the Commons, the power of the House as a representative institution seeking to monitor and control the Government of the day is wielded principally by the Opposition parties in their constant efforts to draw attention to the shortcomings of Government policy and to criticise, delay and occasionally obstruct the progress of Government legislation. There is also an important, if delicate, role for Government backbenchers, both as representatives of those in the electorate who voted for the party in office and as critics of Government policy when they believe it goes against party commitments or falls short of public expectations.

Only on rare occasions in the twentieth century did the power of the House of Commons really make itself felt. One of the most famous examples was in May 1940, when the result of a vital confidence debate on the conduct of the war (when the Chamberlain Government won the vote with a reduced majority, but entirely lost the argument and the mood of the House) led Neville Chamberlain to resign as Prime Minister and so make way for Winston Churchill to succeed him as the country's war-time leader. Another memorable example was in

March 1979 when, at the end of a confidence debate following the so-called 'Winter of Discontent', all the Opposition parties united to defeat what was by then a minority Labour Government and so precipitated the May 1979 General Election which brought to power the Conservatives under Margaret Thatcher.

A recent example of Parliamentary power would be when in 2005 the House of Commons rejected the Government's policy to allow the police to detain terror suspects for up to 90 days without charge. On the whole examples of raw Parliamentary power have been rare in modern times, since on most occasions Governments have been able to count on the voting support and loyalty of their own backbenchers and so ensure not only their survival in office but also the implementation of their policies.

the ability to influence and to embarrass

In most normal circumstances the House of Commons has to rely upon its ability to exert influence – that is, influence on Ministers in the Government, influence on the policies of the Government, and influence on the media and public opinion. Effective influence in the Commons is frequently exercised in a discreet manner *before* the event, whether in party committees, formal delegations or informal conversations. On the other hand, the exercise of overt Parliamentary power is usually confined to the comparatively rare occasions when the authority of a Minister or sometimes of the Government as a whole is in jeopardy or may even have broken down. For example, when it became clear at the beginning of April 1982 that Ministers in the Foreign Office and the Ministry of Defence had lost the confidence of the bulk of the Conservative Parliamentary Party following the Argentinian invasion of the Falkland Islands, Lord Carrington and most of his Ministerial team at the Foreign Office resigned and John Nott at the Ministry of Defence offered his resignation, but which had been refused at the time by Margaret Thatcher because the nation was by then effectively at war with Argentina. In crude and capricious Parliamentary conditions this was a vivid example of the power of the Commons or, more precisely, the influence of Government backbenchers when they are no longer prepared to support a Minister.

Other examples are provided by the cases of Norman Lamont and Harriet Harman. The former, when Chancellor of the Exchequer, came to be seen as increasingly inept and accident prone, especially during the long economic recession of the early 1990s. Conservative MPs were bombarded with demands from their constituents and from the media for a political sacrifice. The situation became even more embarrassing following Black Wednesday on 16 September 1992 when the pound was effectively ejected by the financial markets from the European Exchange Rate Mechanism, a structure to which the Government's entire anti-inflation policy had been anchored. Although Norman Lamont clung onto office for a few more months, his case became hopeless and his fate was eventually sealed. Accordingly, John Major sacked him in May 1993. Harriet Harman, when Secretary of State for Social Security in the 1997–2001 Labour

Government, never recovered her authority after a significant backbench rebellion over cuts in lone parent benefits and the perceived threat of further withdrawal of some disability benefits. As a result, she was dismissed by Tony Blair in his first reshuffle of July 1998, although she returned to Government as Solicitor General in 2001.

A more recent example would be the case of David Blunkett. Having been obliged to resign from the Cabinet in 2004 over allegations that his office had fast-tracked a visa application for the nanny of an individual with whom he was involved in a personal relationship, he had returned to the Cabinet following the General Election of 2005. However, in October 2005 he hit the headlines again as it became known that, during his period out of office before becoming Secretary of State for Work and Pensions, he had taken on a number of directorships, including that of a company marketing DNA testing equipment, an area with considerable potential for securing lucrative Government contracts. Once again Blunkett claimed that he had done nothing wrong and sought to defy the clamour in the press and elsewhere for his resignation. However, following revelations that he had failed to seek the advice of the Independent Advisory Committee on Business Appointments before taking up his paid appointments and that he had been slow to declare certain payments in cash and kind in the register of Members Interests, the support of Labour backbenchers fell away and he felt obliged to resign again on 2 November 2005.

Such cases, and many more besides, exemplify the political truth that when Ministers become a significant liability or embarrassment to their Ministerial colleagues and lose support on the Government back benches, they usually have to resign. In the febrile atmosphere of mass-media politics the vulnerability of errant or fallible Ministers appears to have increased. Certainly such things seem to happen faster and with greater sensationalism these days than was the case even 30 years ago and in this respect, as in many others, the nature of British politics has changed significantly over the years. Nowadays Parliamentary reputations can be built up and then demolished, sometimes with alarming rapidity. The more that some individuals are thrown into the limelight, the more rapidly they seem to become vulnerable to destruction at the hands of the media and their own back-bench 'colleagues'. This was highlighted by the examples of Ron Davies, who resigned as Welsh Secretary in October 1998 following a 'moment of madness' on Clapham Common; Peter Mandelson, who resigned as Secretary of State for Trade and Industry in December 1998 following publication of details concerning a home loan he had obtained from Geoffrey Robinson; Peter Mandelson again in 2001 when he resigned as Northern Ireland Secretary over the Hinduja passport affair; and David Blunkett as previously cited. In all such cases the most decisive criteria for Ministerial survival are the degree of political embarrassment caused to the rest of the Government, the extent to which Government backbenchers are prepared to weather it, and whether the Prime Minister eventually wishes to sacrifice or stand by the Minister in question. Opposition politicians can also play a part in Ministerial downfalls by using their access to publicity to increase the embarrassment already generated. This is highlighted by the examples of Norman Baker in the case of Peter Mandelson and Chris Grayling in the case of David Blunkett.

The reality which lies behind all this is that at nearly every General Election since the Second World War the electorate has voted and the electoral system has worked in such a way as to ensure that one of the main parties has had an overall majority in the Commons large enough to withstand most back-bench rebellions and the political erosion which takes place due to death and retirement during the normal span of a Parliament. In such circumstances the power of the Commons has not normally been manifested in successful attempts to censure Ministers, still less to defeat Governments. Instead it has been exercised through constant back-bench influence on Ministers and the constant interplay between Government striving to get its policy approved and legislation onto the Statute book and Oppositions parties striving to criticise Government action and delay or frustrate its progress.

the impact of radio and television

Since November 1989 the proceedings of the House of Commons, including its Select Committees, have been broadcast on radio and television. The idea had been under discussion in Britain at least since the 1960s and had been promoted by both media and academic interests with growing support from MPs in all parties. For a long time there was nothing more adventurous than a limited experiment, which began in the late 1970s, with live radio transmission of a few particularly newsworthy exchanges or debates in the Chamber. This tended to concentrate on Prime Minister's Questions and a few significant debates or Parliamentary occasions of particular media interest, such as the Chancellor's annual Budget Statement.

The present position is that radio producers use edited extracts from tape recordings of proceedings in the Chamber, Westminster Hall and in Committee 'upstairs' as the raw material for programmes which are usually broadcast after the event, such as the BBC programmes *Today in Parliament* or *The Week in Westminister*. On television, although originally accepted only as an experiment, the House voted on a free vote in July 1990 to make the arrangements permanent and, as well as being able to see edited extracts on the news programmes on the various networks, it is now possible to watch continuous coverage of proceedings on a dedicated Parliamentary Channel.

As to the effects of allowing television cameras into the House of Commons, the proponents of televising the Commons have argued that it brings the proceedings closer to the public and can enhance public understanding and support for the working of British Parliamentary democracy. They have also argued that, if the House had continued to resist the televising of its proceedings, it would have condemned itself to increasing quaintness and irrelevance in the eyes of most people who have become used to being able to watch the leading political figures appear in front of the cameras.

On the other hand, the opponents of televising the Commons argued that it could have the effect of trivialising and sensationalising Parliamentary proceedings, both because the media are usually more interested in the trivial and the sensational than the dull but worthy aspects of what happens and because many MPs are not able to resist the temptation of playing to the gallery of viewers especially on big occasions. The opponents also argued that the imperatives of 'good television' (from the producer's point of view) would predominate over a more restrained approach to portraying Parliamentary proceedings. They have had to admit, however, that their worst fears have not been borne out in practice and that both Parliament and people have emerged relatively unscathed from the experience.

Parliamentary culture at Westminster

The House of Commons used to be described as 'the best club in London', a view that undoubtedly said something about Parliamentary culture in Britain. It is still an atmosphere in which the cut and thrust of the party battle is balanced by a political camaraderie which often makes it easier to form friendships across the floor of the House than with other members on the same side. It is an institution which relies on the assumption that all its Members are 'honourable' and all are equal in terms of democratic legitimacy.

Yet in an institution in which there are supposed to be no second-class members, it is remarkable how some are more equal than others, and how frontbenchers and Privy Councillors seem to get all the best parts. The main explanation is that traditional Parliamentary procedure, much of which dates from the 1880s, assumed that debate and discussion would be conducted largely by the political giants of the day and that the rest would be content with minor roles as spear-carriers or cheer leaders. This established tendency was reinforced by the simple fact that the Chamber itself is rather small (deliberately so) and that no more than about two-thirds of those entitled to be there can possibly find a seat on the green benches when the House is full – for example on Budget Day or during Prime Minister's Question Time. In short, there are only limited opportunities for MPs to shine during prime Parliamentary time at Westminster and most of these are taken by senior Ministers and their 'shadows' on the Opposition front bench.

Another important aspect of Parliamentary culture in the House of Commons is the extent to which the institutionalised, almost ritual, party conflict is organised by the party Whips working through what are known as 'the usual channels'. This phrase is a euphemism for the confidential discussions which take place behind the scenes between the two front benches. Without the benefit of such discussions, which can include the Prime Minister and the Leader of the Opposition on occasions, the whole place would grind to a halt. The House of Commons can only operate satisfactorily by consent and the tacit cooperation between the front benches. The essential deal between the two sides is based on two key assumptions that:

- The Government must 'get its business' (that is, get its legislation passed more or less intact)
- The Opposition must have opportunities to oppose and, within limits, determine what is newsworthy and contentious or what is routine and uncontentious and hence suitable for cooperation between the parties.

The basic idea is that it is the duty of Her Majesty's Loyal Opposition to criticise and oppose the Government of the day, but it is right that this should not extend to preventing the Government from fulfilling its electoral mandate.

A final aspect of Parliamentary culture which is worth mentioning is the fondness of MPs in all parties for informal gatherings of all kinds. The common denominator on such occasions is the desire to exchange political gossip and ideas or to pursue common interests which often cross party lines. The views which emanate from such gatherings are taken forward by the MPs concerned, who usually lose little time in passing on the essence of their discussions to their party whips and, sometimes, to lobby journalists. It is in these ways that some political opinion at Westminster is moulded and developed.

11.4 Parliamentary modernisation

The term 'modernisation' entered the Parliamentary lexicon following the election of New Labour in 1997. Arguments advocating Parliamentary reform were not new – indeed, a series of advances in this regard had been made from the mid 1960s, not least the establishment of Departmental Select Committees in 1979 and changes to sitting times and 'standards' regulation in the 1990s. However, it soon became apparent that the term 'modernisation' could mean different things to different people. To some it meant greater efficiency by simply bringing the procedures of the House of Commons up-to-date with the introduction of new technology and the abandonment of what were seen as anachronistic procedures from a by-gone era. To others it meant including Parliamentary modernization within the ambit of the New Labour project. The Labour Party had modernised itself by removing Clause Four and introducing one-member-one-vote, and were embarking upon modernized policy making designed to improve the delivery of public services. Consequently, the idea of modernizing the House of Commons seemed to be necessary and desirable as well.

Following the General Election of 1997, a Modernisation Committee was established under the chairmanship of the then Leader of the House, Ann Taylor, with a remit to 'consider how the practices and procedures of the House should be modernized'. In its first report the Committee outlined a set of essential criteria which it believed were necessary for the improvement of the legislative process:

- The Government of the day must be assured of getting its legislation through in reasonable time

- The Opposition in particular and Members in general must have a full opportunity to discuss and seek to change provisions to which they attach importance
- All parts of a Bill must be properly considered
- The time and expertise of Members must be used to better effect
- The House as a whole, and its legislative Committees in particular, must be given full and direct information on the meaning and effect of the proposed legislation and full explanations from the Government on the detailed provisions of its Bill
- Throughout the legislative process there must be greater accessibility to the public and legislation should, as far as possible, be readily understandable and in plain English
- The legislative programme needs to be spread as evenly as possible throughout the session in both Houses
- There must be sufficient flexibility in any procedures to cope with emergency legislation
- Monitoring and, if necessary, amending legislation which has come into force should become a vital part of the role of Parliament.[16]

Since 1997 the Modernization Committee has put forward a number of proposals for change, most of which have been adopted by the House of Commons – albeit sometimes on a provisional basis:

- More Government Bills are published in draft and some are subject to pre-legislative scrutiny
- Some public Bills have been carried over from one session to another
- The timetabling or 'programming' of Government Bills following Second Reading has become standard procedure
- The idea of deferred divisions which can be grouped together at more convenient times has been attempted/experimented with
- The establishment of a parallel debating Chamber off Westminster Hall
- The procedures for Parliamentary Questions have been reformed, providing for the electronic tabling of questions, a reduction in the number of days required to table both written and oral questions (thereby allowing them to be more topical), the replacement of Private Notice Questions with 'Urgent Questions' and provision for cross-cutting question sessions in the Grand Committee Room off Westminster Hall, with the possibility of Ministers from several Departments answering questions on a common theme
- The modification of scrutiny procedures for European Union legislation
- Clearer guidance on the core tasks for Select Committees
- Shorter sitting hours for the House as a whole with 'constituency Fridays' when the House does not sit and more frequent short recesses to suit MPs with young children
- Initiatives to improve communication with the media and the general public.

Nonetheless, it has been argued by some that the cumulative effect of all these changes has done little to address what is considered by many to be the trend towards Executive dominance of Parliament. Others have suggested that the changes ought not to be seen in this light but rather as an attempt to bring a greater degree of efficiency to the procedures of the House. For others the focus has been on the 'quality of life' of MPs and their ability to spend time with their families, thereby making a Parliamentary career more attractive to many. Still others have focused on the value of making Parliament more understandable to both the media and the public at large. What is clear is that 'modernisation' is an elusive and elastic term which is interpreted differently by different people at different times. Chaired by the Leader of the House, the Modernisation Committee was never likely to do Parliament many favours in its continuing struggles with the Executive.

11.5 conclusion

The House of Commons has a range of powers and functions which can be formidable or merely nominal, depending on the Parliamentary arithmetic at any time and the mood or inclinations of its 646 MPs. In what might be described as normal circumstances, when the governing party has an effective overall majority, the Government of the day is able to get its way, provided only that it retains the confidence and voting support of its backbenchers. In the rarer circumstances when the result of a General Election has produced a very small majority for the governing party or even a so-called 'hung Parliament' (in which the Government has no overall majority), there can be a serious risk of defeat at the hands of combined Opposition parties. Indeed, even when a Government has a sufficient overall majority, it can still encounter great danger in Parliament if a significant and cohesive group of its own backbenchers are in revolt on a political issue – as Tony Blair and his Ministerial colleagues discovered following the 2005 General Election when the Government was defeated by 322 votes to 291 – with 49 Labour MPs rebelling – on plans to allow the police to detain terror suspects for up to 90 days without charge.

There are many paradoxical aspects of the House of Commons which ought to discourage sweeping generalisations. All that can really be said is that the House carries out its various tasks with varying degrees of efficiency and success. It is reasonably effective as a forum for popular representation and redress. It is best known as a dramatic stage for party-political conflict, especially as it is broadcast to a potentially large audience by radio and television. It is quite good at the detailed scrutiny of legislation (although it still does not make the most efficient use of this time), but almost incapable of modifying legislation against the wishes of the Government of the day unless a large enough group of party rebels are prepared to stick to their guns to the point of defying the party Whips. It is gradually becoming more effective as a mechanism for the scrutiny of the Executive, although in this respect it does not emulate the power and independence of the American Congress, and will not do so as long as there is no formal separation of powers between the Executive and the Legislature in Britain.

In short, while the House of Commons is theoretically supreme in the British political system, in practice it is usually controlled by the Government of the day in tacit collusion with the official Opposition. In other words, the power of all MPs – and especially most backbenchers – is severely limited by the rules and conventions of Britain's 'front-bench constitution'. This position is unlikely to change significantly unless and until there are far-reaching reforms of Britain's Parliamentary and electoral arrangements.

The situation in which Parliament finds itself in twenty-first century Britain is still dependent upon the history, traditions and special circumstances that are to be found within the British body politic. Any analysis illustrates, to one degree or another, the complexity of the relationship between Parliament and the Executive. It is not simply a case of Parliament controlling the Executive or of the Executive controlling Parliament. Even in those instances where the balance of power undoubtedly favours the Executive, it is not a matter of total subordination, as is evident from recent examples.

In conclusion what can be seen is a complex set of relationships involving, in most cases, the capacity to influence rather than determine; the ability to advise rather than to command; the facility to criticise and embarrass but not to obstruct; the ability to scrutinise rather than to initiate; and the desire to ensure that light is shed upon events rather than having things covered by a shroud of secrecy. In short, it is the ability to hold the Executive to account and ensure that it has to explain and justify its actions – or inactions – which is the essential role of the House of Commons.

SUGGESTED QUESTIONS

1 To what extent do Members of Parliament reflect the views and interests of their constituents?

2 How well does the House of Commons perform its main functions?

3 What changes could be made to improve Parliamentary control of the Executive?

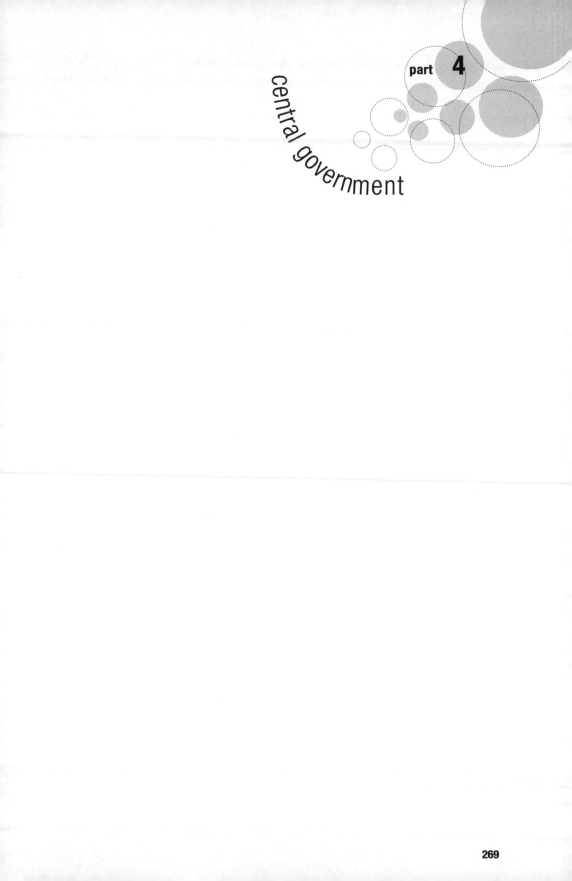

part 4

central government

chapter **12**

Prime Minister and Cabinet

12.1 historical development of the Premiership

The use of the term 'Prime Minister' was no more than a tenuous convention from the time of Robert Walpole (1721–42) to the time when Lord North insisted that his Administration resign *en bloc* in 1782 when he lost favour with King George III. In fact, it is worth noting that the term when used to describe both Harley and Godolphin during the reign of Queen Anne (1702–14) was actually used as a term of abuse; an insult to signify that the politician concerned was seen as being in the pocket of the Monarch and as little more than the Monarch's messenger. Indeed, on a number of occasions during the eighteenth century, the most powerful politician of the time, Lord Chatham, was actually the leading Secretary of State in various Administrations headed by others, such as Lord Pelham or Lord Newcastle. Until the beginning of William Pitt's Administration in 1784, all Prime Ministers were chosen because of their good relationships with the Monarch and they survived in office because of their ability to manage the House of Commons.

The term 'Cabinet' is older in origin and was first used during the reign of Charles II. At that time the King used to summon a few favoured members of his Privy Council for consultations in his private apartments and such courtiers became known as members of his 'Cabinet' after the French word for 'private quarters'. For a time they were also known as the 'Cabal', which was an acronym for the names of those involved – Clifford, Arlington, Buckingham, Ashley and Lauderdale.

The office of Prime Minister and the institution of the Cabinet evolved together throughout the nineteenth century. Until the 1832 Reform Act the Prime Minister and Cabinet were answerable to the Monarch almost as much as they were to Parliament. The extension of the franchise in 1832 meant that the Prime Minister and Cabinet became more answerable to and dependent upon shifting majorities in the House of Commons. Further changes occurred after the 1867 Reform Act as the growing power of nationally organised political parties began to limit the independence of individual MPs. One of the consequences was to accord increased political stature to the main party leaders, such as William Gladstone and Benjamin Disraeli, who alternated as Prime Minister for nearly twenty years. In 1878 the title of 'Prime Minister' was officially recorded in a public document for the first time when Benjamin Disraeli signed the Treaty of Berlin on behalf of the British Government. Another equally important development during this period was the growth of the power of the Cabinet in relation to the House of Commons. Thus by the time of Lord Salisbury's second Administration (1886–92) Britain had moved essentially from Parliamentary Government of the classic type to Cabinet government of the modern type – that is, government *through* Parliament rather than government *by* Parliament.

Statutory recognition of the office of Prime Minister was not formally complete until 1937 when the Ministers of the Crown Act provided the Prime Minister of the day with a salary and a pension from public funds. Yet to this day the powers and responsibilities of the Prime Minister have not been defined in statute. Like the institution of the Cabinet, the office of Prime Minister provides a classic example of the importance of conventions in British constitutional arrangements. Figure 12.1 lists all British Prime Ministers since Sir Robert Walpole.

In theory, the Cabinet constitutes the supreme decision-making body in the British political system. Yet, in practice, the Prime Minister can be more than 'first among equals' in any modern British Government. Nonetheless, both the Prime Minister and the Cabinet are influenced in an imprecise but real way by the shifting views and feelings of their back-bench supporters in the House of Commons; the need to take account of the Opposition's demands which can affect the progress of Government legislative business in Parliament; their relations with party activists, pressure groups and the media; and their assessment of public opinion on any given issue at any given time. All these factors can qualify and refine the power and authority of the Prime Minister and the Cabinet in modern conditions. Indeed, in political terms the most effective sanctions against Prime Ministerial or Cabinet decisions of which people may disapprove is a decisive back-bench revolt in the governing party or the verdict of the electorate at the subsequent General Election.

12.2 Prime Ministerial power

The Prime Minister of the day could be described as the most powerful person in Britain. Certainly the reality of Prime Ministerial power has been recognised for some time by practising politicians and academic observers alike. Yet the nature and extent of such power is a matter of controversy and there are some significant constraints on its exercise, no matter who occupies the premises at 10 Downing Street.

conflicting interpretations

There have been at least two strongly conflicting interpretations of Prime Ministerial power in Britain. On the one hand, Harold Wilson concluded that

Sir Robert Walpole (Whig)	1721–42	George Gordon, 4th Earl of Aberdeen (Coalition)	1852–55
Spencer Compton, Earl of Wilmington (Whig)	1742–43	Henry Temple. 3rd Viscount Palmerston (Lib)	1855–58
Henry Pelham (Whig)	1743–54	Edward Stanley, 14th Earl of Derby (Con)	1858–59
Thomas Pelham-Holles, Duke of Newcastle (Whig)	1754–56	Henry Temple, 3rd Viscount Palmerston (Lib)	1959–65
William Cavendish, 4th Duke of Devonshire (Whig)	1756–57	Earl Russell (Lib)	1865–66
Thomas Pelham-Holles, Duke of Newcastle (Whig)	1757–62	Edward Stanley, 14th Earl of Derby (Con)	1866–68
John Stuart, 3rd Earl of Bute (Tory)	1762–63	Benjamin Disraeli (Con)	1868
George Grenville (Whig)	1763–65	William Ewart Gladstone (Lib)	1868–74
Charles Wentworth, 2nd Marquis of Rockingham (Whig)	1765–66	Benjamin Disraeli, Earl of Beaconsfield (Con)	1874–80
William Pitt, Earl of Chatham (Whig)	1766–68	William Ewart Gladstone (Lib)	1890–95
Augustus Fitzroy, 3rd Duke of Grafton (Whig)	1768-70	Robert Gascoyne-Cecil, 3rd Marquis of Salisbury (Con)	1885
Frederick, Lord North (Tory)	1770–82	William Ewart Gladstone (Lib)	1886
Charles Wentworth, 2nd Marquis of Rockingham (Whig)	1782	Robert Gascoyne-Cecil, 3rd Marquis of Salisbury (Con)	1886–92
William Fitzmaurice, 2nd Earl of Shelburne (Whig)	1782–83	William Ewart Gladstone (Lib)	1892–94
William Cavendish-Bentinck, 3rd Duke of Portland (Coalition)	1783	Archibald Primrose, 5th Earl of Rosebery (Lib)	1894–95
William Pill. the younger (Tory)	1783–1801	Robert Gascoyne-Cecil, 3rd Marquis of Salisbury (Con)	1895–1902
Henry Addington (Tory)	1801–04	Arthur James Balfour (Con)	1902–05
William Pitt, the younger (Tory)	1804–06	Sir Henry Campbell-Bannerman (Lib)	1905–08
William Wyndham, Lord Grenville (Whig)	1806–07	Herbert Henry Asquith (Lib)	1908–16
William Cavendish-Bentinck, 3rd Duke of Portland	1907–09	David Lloyd George (Coalition)	1916–22
Spencer Perceval (Tory)	1809–12	Andrew Bonar Law (Con)	1922–23
Robert Jenkinson, 2nd Earl of Liverpool (Tory)	1812–27	Stanley Baldwin (Con)	1923–24
George Canning (Tory)	1827	Ramsay MacDonald (Lab)	1924
Frederick Robinson, Viscount Goderich (Tory)	1827–28	Stanley Baldwin (Con)	1924–29
Arthur Wellesley, Duke of Wellington (Tory)	1828–30	Ramsay MacDonald (Lab)	1929–31
Charles, 2nd Earl Grey (Whig)	1830–34	Ramsay MacDonald (National)	1931–35
William Lamb, 2nd Viscount Melbourne (Whig)	1834	Stanley Baldwin (National)	1935–37
Sir Robert Peel, 2nd Baronet (Tory)	1834–35	Neville Chamberlain (National)	1937–40
William Lamb, 2nd Viscount Melbourne (Whig)	1835–41	Winston Churchill (Coalition)	1940–45
Sir Robert Peel, 2nd Baronet (Tory)	1841–46	Clement Attlee (Lab)	1945–51
Lord John Russell (Whig)	1846–52	Sir Winston Churchill (Con)	1951–55
Edward Stanley, l4th Earl of Derby (Con)	1852	Sir Anthony Eden (Con)	1955–57
		Harold Macmillan (Con)	1957–63
		Sir Alec Douglas-Home (Con)	1963–64
		Harold Wilson (Lab)	1964–70
		Edward Heath (Con)	1970–74
		Harold Wilson (Lab)	1974–76
		James Callaghan (Lab)	1976–79
		Margaret Thatcher (Con)	1979–90
		John Major (Con)	1990–97
		Tony Blair (Lab)	1997–2007
		Gordon Brown	2007–

figure **12.1** **Prime Ministers since Robert Walpole**

'the predominantly academic verdict of overriding Prime Ministerial power is wrong'.[1] In making this forthright comment, Lord Wilson was probably reflecting on his own experience of having to preside over several Labour Cabinets which contained powerful and determined personalities who did not take kindly to excessive Prime Ministerial leadership. On the other hand, Lord Morley, as long ago as 1889, wrote that 'the flexibility of the Cabinet system allows the Prime Minister to take on himself a power not inferior to that of a dictator, provided always that the House of Commons will stand by him'.[2] This view has had its strong adherents ever since, including at least three Prime Ministers, Sir Anthony Eden (1955–57), Margaret Thatcher (1979–90) and Tony Blair (1997–2007). Perhaps the most common-sense view was expressed by Herbert Asquith (Prime Minister 1908–16) when he wrote in his memoirs that 'the office of Prime Minister is what its holder chooses and is able to make of it'.[3]

The best way of assessing these conflicting interpretations is to examine the various aspects of Prime Ministerial power in order to see which of the two schools of thought is best supported by the evidence of history. The scope of Prime Ministerial powers is outlined in Figure 12.2.

the power of patronage

The Prime Minister of the day has the power of political patronage. This is manifested principally in the power of appointment to and dismissal from Ministerial posts in Government. Having accepted the Royal commission to form a new Government, the party leader concerned can fill the hundred or so Ministerial posts in the Commons and the Lords in the most appropriate ways. Yet for reasons of practical politics there are always a number of senior figures in any party who virtually select themselves for Ministerial office and some others whom it would be imprudent for any Prime Minister to exclude. Other considerations which come into play in the course of Government formation are regional and ideological balance as well as age, political debt and personal loyalty. Thus, although Prime Ministers may appear to have done almost as they liked when making Ministerial appointments, their freedom of manoeuvre has always been limited in practice by common prudence and sensible calculation of their own strength or weakness as well as those of others at any time.

Equally, the Prime Minister can ask for the resignation of any member of the Government at any time on the grounds that the Minister concerned is not up to the job or is too old to continue or the office is needed for someone else. Although the most usual motives for Prime Ministerial dismissal of a senior Minister are to improve the general effectiveness and political balance of the Cabinet, there have been occasions when the Prime Minister of the day has deliberately sought to create a more politically congenial array of senior Ministers. For example, in September 1981 Margaret Thatcher sacked three Cabinet Ministers (Lord Soames, Sir Ian Gilmour, and Mark Carlisle) at least

Patronage

Appoints Government Ministers

Dismisses Government Ministers

Appoints senior civil servants

Dispenses a large number of honours

Appoints to a large number of paid public posts

Within Parliament

▸ Party leader

▸ Appoints Government Ministers

▸ Dismisses Government Ministers

▸ Can dissolve Parliament

Within Party

▸ party leader

▸ power of patronage

▸ Can determine (he date of the General Election

Within Government

▸ Head of Government – sets agenda and priorities

▸ Appoints and dismisses Government Ministers

▸ Determines membership of Cabinet orrinautees

▸ Determines membership of mini-Cabinets/inner-Cabinets

▸ Draws up the Cabinet agenda

▸ Summons Cabinet meetings

▸ Chairs Cabinet discussions

▸ Summarises Cabinet 'conclusions'

▸ Sends 'minutes' (directives) to Ministers

On the national and international stage

▸ Natural focus of publicity

▸ Nation's chief representative in itnernational relations

▸ Controls use of nation's military power, including nuclear weapons

figure **12.2   Prime Ministerial powers**

two of whom she found ideologically uncongenial, and appointed three new ones (Nigel Lawson, Norman Tebbit and Lady Young) at least two of whom were very close to her own brand of Conservatism. John Major, by contrast, was more loath to use his power of dismissal and tended to do so only when the passage of events forced it on him – as was the case, for example, when he sacked Norman Lamont as Chancellor of the Exchequer in May 1993 in a belated attempt to placate public opinion following the forced withdrawal of sterling from the Exchange Rate Mechanism of the European Monetary System in September 1992.

The Prime Minister of the day also has a wider and more general power of political patronage which stems from the right to advise the Monarch on public appointments made in the name of the Crown. This means that a large number of important and influential positions – for example, the Permanent Secretaries of Whitehall Departments, Bishops in the Church of England (albeit on the advice of the Ecclesiastical Appointments Committee), the Governor of the Bank of England, the chairmen of public bodies such as the BBC, and key appointments to a host of other public bodies – all depend to a considerable extent on finding favour with the Prime Minister of the day, although other senior Ministers have a good deal of influence in their own Departmental spheres. In view of the influential nature of many of these positions, these appointments can have great significance. Thus Prime Ministerial patronage, whether exercised positively in favour of some or negatively against others, is a formidable aspect of Prime Ministerial power in Britain.

A strong Prime Minister has the ability to dominate the Government by personally setting its strategic agenda and political priorities. This is done in a number of different ways, all of which are facets of Prime Ministerial power. It is achieved through:

- The Prime Minister's control of the Cabinet agenda
- The right to establish Cabinet committees and to pick their membership
- The right to chair the most important committees and discussions
- The right to summarise the conclusions of Cabinet meetings
- The ability to bypass the 'formal' machinery of the Cabinet altogether through the use of bilateral meetings and informal conversations with individuals or small groups of Ministers and advisers
- The right to have the best available advice from the Civil Service and outside
- The ability to take an overall and non-Departmental view of political issues
- The power of Ministerial appointment and dismissal
- The pre-eminent position in the eyes of the media and the public
- The leadership of the governing party in the House of Commons.

During Margaret Thatcher's long occupancy of 10 Downing Street (1979–90), the power of the Prime Minister within the Government increased very largely at the expense of the Cabinet as a whole. This happened for a number of reasons. It was partly an obvious consequence of Margaret Thatcher having led her party to three consecutive General Election victories. More insidiously, however, it was a consequence of her ability gradually to transform the membership of the Cabinet over a period of years from one which she largely inherited from Edward Heath to one which she could call her own, because all but one of its members (Sir Geoffrey Howe) owed their positions in Cabinet directly to her. It was also a consequence of her marked preference for bilateral meetings with key Ministers as an effective and disciplined way of resolving policy problems rather than having recourse to the more traditional but less controllable methods of Cabinet committees or full Cabinet meetings.

During John Major's period at 10 Downing Street (1990–97), the power of the Prime Minister within the Government was not so obvious. This should not have come as a surprise, partly because he set out to be more collegiate in his approach to leadership than his combative predecessor, but mainly because during his time as Party Leader and Prime Minister the Parliamentary arithmetic was much less comfortable for the Conservatives than at any time when Margaret Thatcher was Prime Minister.

Under Tony Blair a 'presidential' approach to the Premiership was again evident; indeed, perhaps more than ever before. Although Margaret Thatcher was 'presidential' in her personal style and personal approach, Tony Blair from the outset sought to be 'presidential' not merely in style and approach but also institutionally. The emphasis on ensuring that the Prime Minister's objectives were delivered was an important sign of this.

Nonetheless, the extent and nature of Prime Ministerial power within Government can change frequently and sometimes almost without warning – as was the case with John Major's loss of authority following 'Black Wednesday' on 16 September 1992. Such power has been a matter of continuing controversy under all Prime Ministers. In the space of even a few months – let alone a few years – the perception of a given Prime Minister can change dramatically, as even the careers of Winston Churchill, Harold Macmillan and Margaret Thatcher showed so clearly.

Furthermore, the available evidence is often relayed by observers or participants in the process of British politics who are strongly committed for or against a particular Prime Minister, while most academic accounts are largely speculative in view of the unreliable quality of their sources. The honest investigator is left with not much more than a series of impressions of one Prime Minister as compared with another or of the same Prime Minister at different phases of electoral and political fortune. The dilemma is that those who might be reliable and fairly objective witnesses of the drama do not normally gain real first-hand access to the political theatre, whereas those who were privileged to be on stage at the relevant time have not usually been the most reliable witnesses – especially when writing their memoirs some time afterwards. Since no final or definitive conclusions can be drawn, it would be wise to rest on the observation that Prime Ministerial power in Government has varied greatly from one Administration to another and indeed from one time to another during a particular Prime Minister's tenure of the office.

power in Parliament

Most Prime Ministers have usually had formidable power and authority in Parliament. This is partly because the power of appointment to and dismissal from posts in the Government can do so much to determine the political fortunes of MPs in the governing party, and partly a reflection of their leading role in the gladiatorial battles between the parties both in the House and in the media. Clearly the extent and nature of such power has varied from time to time, depending on the personal fortunes of each Prime Minister and the political standing of the governing party at any time. Much also depends on the extent to which the Prime Minister can rely on the loyalty and support of Parliamentary colleagues, the efficiency and subtlety of the Government Whips, and the personal standing of the Prime Minister in the eyes of the media and the general public.

On the whole, Conservative Prime Ministers seem to have been more powerful in relation to their Parliamentary followers than Labour Prime Ministers in relation to theirs, although there have been exceptions to the rule from time to time. The general position reflects the contrasting origins, organisation and instincts of each main party. Whereas the Conservative

Party has been *traditionally* both hierarchical and deferential towards its leader, the Labour Party has tended to be more democratic in its aspirations and egalitarian in its attitude towards the leader. In most cases this has made it easier for Conservative Prime Ministers to preserve their Parliamentary authority than for Labour Prime Ministers to preserve theirs, although the contrast should not be exaggerated. Not only is it true that there have been relatively strong and decisive Labour Prime Ministers – for example, Clement Attlee from 1945 to 1950, Harold Wilson from 1964 to 1967 and Tony Blair between 1997 and 2005 – it is also true that there have been relatively weak and indecisive Conservative Prime Ministers – for example, Sir Anthony Eden from 1955 to 1957, Sir Alec Douglas-Home from 1963 to 1964 and John Major from September 1992 to 1997. It should also be borne in mind that all political relationships in Britain have become much less deferential over the years and that the media have become more powerfully destructive, so it is not surprising that the authority of all modern Prime Ministers is probably not as secure as their illustrious, but less widely criticised predecessors.

In general, all peace-time Prime Ministers in Britain in the modern era have been able to exercise predominant power in Parliament as long as they have retained high standing in the eyes of the media and the public, and have been able to count on the loyal support of the vast majority of their own backbenchers. This last condition of Prime Ministerial power is critical, as was made clear by the circumstances which led to Michael Heseltine's challenge to Margaret Thatcher for the leadership of the Conservative Party in November 1990 and hence the office of Prime Minister. This challenge to a very powerful Prime Minister and her subsequent downfall was the culmination of consistently low opinion poll ratings since July 1989 and a growing belief both in the Cabinet and the rest of the Conservative Parliamentary Party that it would be impossible to win another General Election under her leadership. Indeed, in many ways, the exceptions have been more interesting than the rule. For example, there were several times after the devaluation of the pound in 1967 when

Harold Wilson had to head off the threat of serious revolts against his damaged political authority – a threat which came from those of his Cabinet colleagues who were particularly close to the trade unions and from those who more or less openly resented his leadership or coveted his job. Equally, there were times during John Major's tenure at 10 Downing Street when he was openly defied by some of his Cabinet colleagues and by troublesome backbenchers on issues such as Britain's deeper involvement in European integration and from the so-called 'peace process' in Northern Ireland. Indeed, the sniping at John Major became so damaging in 1994 and 1995 that he felt obliged to resign the leadership of the Conservative Party in June 1995 in order to be able to confront his critics in the party in a subsequent leadership election. Equally, Tony Blair's reduced Parliamentary majority following the 2005 General Election, along with concern among some on the Labour benches about the direction and details of Government policy, made him susceptible to defeat in the House of Commons – defeats actually inflicted on plans to allow police to detain terrorist suspects for up to 90 days without charge and over laws against religious hatred.

party-political power

The Prime Minister of the day can also have great power over the fortunes and destiny of the governing party. In the Conservative Party, this stems from the degree of deference traditionally accorded to the party leader, especially when that person is also Prime Minister – although this is undoubtedly less true nowadays than in the past. In the Labour Party, the party-political dominance of the leader has not traditionally been so clear-cut since power has had to be shared with the Parliamentary Party, affiliated trade unions and constituency parties, all of whom had acknowledged roles to play. The balance of power has been very different under New Labour since 1997 and for long periods Tony Blair was considered to be one of the most presidential of Labour Prime Ministers – even at times when his policy preferences were challenged by some Labour backbenchers.

In the party-political context, the power of any British Prime Minister is probably at its greatest (and certainly most lonely) in the exclusive right of the occupant of the office to select the date for a General Election within the five-year maximum span of a Parliament. The exercise of this aspect of Prime Ministerial power can have lasting effects for good or ill on the political fortunes of the Prime Minister, the party and the destiny of the country. It is a formidable power, as Tony Blair demonstrated in 2001 and 2005, when on each occasion he called an election a year before he had to and successfully contributed to the continuation in office of the Government which he led.

power on the national and international stage

In contemporary political conditions Prime Ministers in Britain have considerable power and prestige on the national and international stage, even allowing for demystified public attitudes and widespread public cynicism. Of course, the symbols and trappings of Prime Ministerial power should not be confused with the substance. Yet they are significant as part of the aura of power which tends to surround all heads of Government in the modern media age. Certainly this particular aspect of power can be strongly reinforced by the attention which the media sometimes devote to nearly every aspect of a Prime Minister's life. It is also dramatised by the need for the Prime Minister of the day to attend frequent summit meetings with counterparts in other countries, all of which serve to elevate the Prime Minister to a political level above other Ministers.

On the other hand, in the cases of Harold Wilson after the 1967 devaluation of the pound, John Major after the 1992 forced departure of sterling from the Exchange Rate Mechanism of the European Monetary System, and Tony Blair as a result of the Iraq war in 2003, the media (and hence public opinion) have shown a marked tendency to turn swiftly against leaders whom they may have admired only a little while before. This may happen because they believe they have genuine cause to reassess the competence or integrity of the Prime Minister or, more cynically, it may be because it suits their commercial purposes to build up even the most senior politicians only to have the pleasure of knocking them down some time later. Either way, these characteristics underline the strong trend towards presidentialism in Britain and other Parliamentary democracies – something which has become more visible than ever in the political presentation and public perception of Tony Blair as a truly 'presidential' Prime Minister.

Needless to say, these aspects of Prime Ministerial power are enhanced every time there is a real international crisis or a requirement for particularly swift or decisive national leadership. This is especially true in time of war, but it is also true in relation to matters of national security in time of peace. For example, it is normally the Prime Minister of the day who has to act decisively in the event of a terrorist outrage, a spy scandal or a major industrial crisis which threatens essential services. Equally in foreign affairs, it is for the Prime Minister to give a clear lead when British national interests are deemed to be threatened – as Sir Anthony Eden did at the time of the Suez crisis in 1956, Margaret Thatcher did at the time of the conflict over the Falkland Islands in 1982, and Tony Blair did in leading Britain's efforts against international terrorism. Similar requirements for Prime Ministerial leadership have applied to the so-called 'peace process' in Northern Ireland and would also apply in the event of Britain having to respond to chemical, biological or nuclear blackmail from a 'rogue state' or a terrorist group.

12.3 Cabinet Government

The Cabinet in modern Britain has been composed of between 19 and 24 senior Ministers who meet formally once a week, every Thursday morning (although not usually in August), for up to an hour, although extra meetings can be arranged as and when the need arises.[4] Meetings take place around the large coffin-shaped table in the Cabinet room at 10 Downing Street. The Cabinet subsumes a large network of committees, both Ministerial and official, and it depends for its efficient operation upon the work of the Cabinet Secretary and a small number of civil servants based in the Cabinet Office.[5] The latter is the administrative nerve-centre of central Government and responsible for recording all Cabinet and Cabinet committee decisions, and then communicating them to those who need to know in the various Departments in Whitehall. The Cabinet Secretariat also has an important role in progress chasing, scheduling meetings, setting agendas, checking that papers are circulated in good time and cover the subject properly, and briefing the chairmen of the committees.

Certain very senior Ministers have a place in every Cabinet – for example, the Chancellor of the Exchequer, the Home Secretary and the Foreign Secretary. Some other Ministers have a place by dint of the area of the country which their Department represents – for example, despite devolution, the Secretaries of

State for Wales, Scotland, and Northern Ireland. Occasionally some important Ministers, such as the Secretary of State for Transport, have been included in the Cabinet at one time and excluded from it at another, depending on the competing claims of other Departments and the personal preferences of the Prime Minister of the day. Occasionally a Minister may belong to the Cabinet but draw no public salary for it, simply because the Prime Minister of the day has decided to breach the upper limit on the permitted number of such positions (currently 23). Traditionally, the Government Chief Whip has not been a formal member of the Cabinet, although the occupant invariably attends all Cabinet meetings. However, under Tony Blair both Ann Taylor and Hillary Armstrong, when Chief Whip, were full members of the Cabinet. It is also quite common for others to attend Cabinet meetings although not to be members themselves – such as the Government Chief Whip in the House of Lords and the Attorney General for example. At the invitation of the Prime Minister other non-Cabinet Ministers may attend and speak at Cabinet meetings when their views are needed, while others attending in a listening role can include the Prime Minister's Parliamentary Private Secretary and the Prime Minister's Press Secretary.

Owing to the size of the Cabinet, there is no question of all its members taking a full part in all the items under discussion. Some members of the Cabinet remain silent because their Department is not involved in the issue under discussion and some may be unavoidably absent on the day in question (which is quite often the case with the Foreign Secretary). In such circumstances the Minister concerned may submit views in writing to the Prime Minister, so that these can be taken into account in any discussion. It is just as well that the Cabinet proceeds in this way, since if every Cabinet Minister spoke on every item of Cabinet business, the agenda would never be covered in the time available. In fact, little discussion takes place in Cabinet these days since issues tend to be discussed in bilateral meetings between the Prime Minister and the relevant Departmental Minister or in the relevant Cabinet Committee.

Cabinet committees are an essential and integral part of Cabinet government. They are usually composed of the relevant Ministers according to the subject under discussion, chaired by the Prime Minister or another senior Cabinet Minister, and are often empowered to take decisions on behalf of the entire Cabinet. It is only in cases of serious disagreement that matters are referred back to the full Cabinet for final resolution. Few substantial issues are considered by full Cabinet which have not already been dealt with either in the bilateral meetings between the Prime Minister and the relevant Departmental Minister or by the relevant Cabinet committee. Thus one of the main purposes of Cabinet committee meetings is to reach decisions which can then be put to full Cabinet simply for formal ratification. When Cabinet committees cannot reach agreement or when the issues under discussion are too important to be settled at a smaller meeting, the whole Cabinet has to argue things out in order to reach conclusions which then bind the entire Government.

Cabinet committees can conveniently be divided between *Standing Committees* - permanent committees that exist on an on-going basis – such as the *Economic Affairs, Productivity and Competitiveness Committee*, the *Domestic Affairs Committee*, the *Defence and Overseas Policy Committee* and the *Legislative Programme Committee* – and *Ad Hoc Committees* – such as (in 2006) *the Animal Rights Activists Committee*, the *Anti-Social Behaviour Committee* and the *Olympic Games Committee* – which remain in being only as long as is necessary to resolve a particular issue.

Senior civil servants and the military Chiefs of Staff are not formally members of the Cabinet or its committees, at any rate in peace-time. Yet the Chief of the Defence Staff regularly attends the Overseas and Defence Policy Committee of the Cabinet, although not formally a member of it. In the broader framework of Cabinet government, junior Ministers play a frequent and useful part in Cabinet committees where they can relieve senior Ministers of many of the burdens of collective decision making. Indeed, junior Ministers are the workhorses of the Cabinet committee system and they can make or mar their reputations when performing this aspect of their Ministerial duties.[6]

It is difficult to consider the idea of Cabinet Government in Britain in a way which separates it from the role of the Prime Minister. Yet there are some important points about Cabinet government and collective responsibility which serve to illustrate some of the limitations on the exercise of Prime Ministerial power. Many years ago Walter Bagehot focused attention on the Cabinet describing it as 'a hyphen which joins, a buckle which fastens the legislative part of the state to the executive part of the state. In its origin it belongs to the one, in its functions it belongs to the other'.[7] In the 1960s John Mackintosh provided a useful framework of analysis when he argued that there were three main tasks of the British Cabinet:[8]

- To take or review the major decisions of central Government
- To consider, though not necessarily at the formative stage, any proposals which might affect the future of the Government
- To ensure that no Departmental interests are overlooked, thus giving the work of Government a measure of unity and coherence.

We shall now consider each of these aspects in turn.

decision making

In theory, the Cabinet is the most important decision-making body in British central Government. It is supposed to play this vital role because there is no other institution so well placed or qualified to meet the need for decisive arbitration at the apex of central Government. After all there is formally no chief executive in British central Government and all executive power is vested by statute in the various Secretaries of State and other Ministerial heads of the Whitehall Departments. Thus whatever the impact of Prime Ministerial power, the Cabinet is supposed to be the most important decision-making body and to give institutional expression to the principle of collective responsibility.

On the other hand, some have argued that in modern times it has invariably been the Prime Minister of the day who has taken all the really important political decisions, albeit usually after discussion with senior Ministerial colleagues. The historical evidence to support this view would include:

- The 1947 decision to develop a British nuclear weapons capability
- The 1956 decision to invade the Suez Canal Zone
- The 1982 decision to send a Task Force to recapture the Falkland Islands
- The 1993 Downing Street Declaration on the future of Northern Ireland
- The 1998 Belfast 'Good Friday' Agreement;
- The 2003 decision to go to war in Iraq
- The 2006 decision to maintain/renew Britain's nuclear weapons capability.

The argument is also borne out when speed of response is an essential factor in Government decision making, as was the case, for example, with the decision in September 1992 to leave the Exchange Rate Mechanism of the European Monetary System. Yet all these essentially Prime Ministerial decisions had to be cleared with a few very senior Ministers and advisers and were subsequently either endorsed or at least accepted by the Cabinet as a whole.

There are several reasons why the Prime Minister of the day usually comes out on top in the decision-making process of British central Government. The main reason is that in every modern Cabinet the Prime Minister has usually been more than first among equals. This is partly for the reasons already given, but also because the Civil Service is accustomed to dealing with Ministers in a hierarchical way. Indeed, it is usually convenient to have a Prime Minister who is regarded as being head and shoulders above the rest of the Cabinet, since this provides a mechanism for resolving the most intractable inter-Departmental disputes.

Nearly every Cabinet in modern times has divided quite conveniently into two layers: a 'first eleven' of very senior Ministers who carry real weight and authority in the Government and a 'second eleven' who, although in charge of Departments and holding Cabinet rank, count for less in any Government. At one time in the early 1950s Winston Churchill sought to formalise this division by nominating a few 'Overlords' from among his most senior Cabinet colleagues to supervise and coordinate the work of clusters of other Cabinet Ministers. The experiment did not really work and was soon abandoned because of Ministerial resentment and jealousy. In the late 1960s Harold Wilson also experimented with the idea of creating an 'inner Cabinet' composed of fewer than half a dozen of Labour's real political heavyweights at that time. Once again the idea did not really work in practice for similar reasons and was soon abandoned. In July 1995 John Major's appointment of Michael Heseltine as 'First Secretary of State' and Deputy Prime Minister provided another example of a move in this direction, as did Tony Blair's appointments of Gordon Brown as Chancellor of the Exchequer with an expanded remit beyond the Treasury and John Prescott as Deputy Prime Minister with a wide remit across the domestic political agenda.

In every Cabinet it is the Prime Minister who usually holds most of the high cards in dealings with Cabinet colleagues. The Prime Minister can determine the membership of Cabinet committees – at least at the margin – by including members who can be relied on to support his own position, although the bulk of the membership of such committees is really determined by the nature and scope of the issues under discussion. The Prime Minister can exploit informal and bilateral meetings with individual Ministers in order to divide and rule any collective opposition within the Cabinet to his preferred policies. Indeed, as long as a political axis is preserved between the Prime Minister and the Chancellor of the Exchequer, there are few, if any, occasions on which the two of them are likely to be defeated by the rest of the Cabinet.

All of these realities are underpinned by the doctrine of collective responsibility. This means that the invidious choice facing any member of the Cabinet (or indeed any other Minister or PPS) who is really unhappy about an aspect of Government policy is either to threaten resignation, with the high risk that such a threat might be called, or to keep quiet and so risk losing political credibility if it is widely known in Westminster and Whitehall that the Minister concerned is at odds with Government policy. On most occasions in modern times Ministers faced with this dilemma have chosen the latter course and remained within the Government. All of this really underlines that it is not sensible for even a powerful Cabinet Minister to threaten resignation unless the Minister concerned is fully prepared to carry out the threat, especially since the evidence shows that few Ministerial resignations have strengthened the position of the individual taking such a step. Indeed, in most cases in modern times it has proved to be a ticket to political obscurity.

To find examples of senior Cabinet Ministers who chose to resign on significant issues of policy from a Labour Government it is customary to refer to the following cases:

‣ Aneurin Bevan, Harold Wilson and John Freeman in 1951 who resigned against the Treasury policy of introducing charges for false teeth and spectacles within the National Health Service
‣ George Brown in 1968 who resigned in a fit of pique against Harold Wilson's continued prevarications on Britain's European policy
‣ Robin Cook who resigned in March 2003 over the Government's failure to secure a clear UN mandate for war in Iraq
‣ Claire Short who resigned in May 2003 over the lack of consultation about post-war reconstruction in Iraq.

In all these cases clashes of personality and the influence of personal ambition were bound up with policy differences of fundamental importance. For example, Aneurin Bevan and Hugh Gaitskell (the Labour Chancellor in 1951) were rivals for the succession to Clement Attlee; George Brown had been defeated by Harold Wilson in the 1963 Labour leadership contest; Robin Cook had been demoted by Tony Blair from Foreign Secretary to Leader of the House of Commons; and it was widely expected that Claire Short would be sacked in the next reshuffle.

Just as interesting and revealing, however, have been the counter-examples of Michael Foot and Tony Benn, two of the leading Left-wingers in the 1974–79 Labour Governments of Harold Wilson and James Callaghan, neither of whom resigned from the Cabinet at any stage, even when faced with the appalling need (from a Socialist point of view) to make deep and immediate cuts in public expenditure at the behest of the International Monetary Fund in the autumn of 1976.[9] One could also cite the example of John Prescott, the personification of Old Labour, who as Deputy Prime Minister under Tony Blair, nonetheless went along with the New Labour project. These cases demonstrate not only the addiction to high office of even previously rebellious individuals, but also the good sense of successive Labour Prime Ministers in keeping some of their potential adversaries inside rather than outside the tent.

To find examples of senior Cabinet Ministers who chose to resign on significant issues of policy from a Conservative Government it is customary to refer to the following cases:

‣ Anthony Eden who resigned in 1938 in opposition to the policy of appeasing Hitler and Mussolini
‣ Peter Thorneycroft who resigned in 1958 because of his inability to carry the Prime Minister and other Cabinet colleagues with him on his policy of public expenditure cuts
‣ Lord Carrington and Ministerial colleagues at the Foreign Office in April 1982 who resigned as a direct and immediate atonement for the policy failure of their Department to foresee or prevent the Argentinian invasion of the Falkland Islands, even though it was widely agreed that the Ministry of Defence was equally culpable
‣ Michael Heseltine's dramatic resignation in January 1986 when he concluded that he was losing his argument in favour of a European future for Westland Helicopters, although he was also exasperated at the way in which Margaret Thatcher had conducted Cabinet government over many years
‣ Nigel Lawson who resigned in 1989 having become increasingly exasperated during his later years as Chancellor with the baleful influence of Sir Alan Walters over Margaret Thatcher, but who had also drifted apart from his powerful neighbour in Downing Street on one of the key issues of economic policy, namely the weight to be given to stability of the exchange rate in the conduct of monetary policy
‣ Most dramatic, and consequential, of all examples was the resignation of Sir Geoffrey Howe as Leader of the House and 'Deputy Prime Minister' in November 1990, an act which gave him the opportunity to make an uncharacteristically electrifying personal statement to the House of Commons indicting Margaret Thatcher for her whole approach to political leadership, especially on European policy, and thus precipitating her downfall.

Given all the constraints and inhibitions of collective responsibility, there has been a tendency in many British Governments for disaffected or unhappy members of the Cabinet to convey their disapproval of certain aspects of Government policy either via private and unattributable conversations with Lobby journalists (see Chapter 7) or in carefully coded public speeches designed to be just within the bounds of collective responsibility, while marking out important differences designed to distance them from the prevailing Government orthodoxy. The use of such techniques can be regarded as a tribute to the durability and elasticity of collective responsibility, but it can also end in tears.

The latitude provided by such techniques was used with impunity by Tony Benn during the period in the 1970s when he was the self-styled Socialist enfant terrible of the Wilson and Callaghan Administrations. It was equally exploited by the leading Tory 'Wets', such as Peter Walker and James Prior, during their surprisingly long Ministerial careers under Margaret Thatcher. In the 1990s, similar techniques were used by some in the Major Cabinet (Michael Portillo, Peter Lilley and John Redwood) who occasionally made coded speeches undermining John Major's policy on Europe, but who were not sacked for doing so. Under Tony Blair the International Development Secretary, Claire Short, was often 'off message', but remained in office until her resignation in 2003. In all such cases behaviour of this kind is only possible as long as the Prime Minister of the day feels unable or disinclined to punish it.

Notwithstanding such drama and difficulty, the Cabinet is still the forum within which the most important decisions of Government are ratified, if not actually taken. It is the body in whose name the Government acts and its ostensible unity is vital to the continuation in office of any Administration. At times it can be a formidable brake on Prime Ministerial power and individual Ministerial initiative alike. Yet in modern British politics it has had a notably varied role, as illustrated by the contrast in its behaviour under Tony Blair, John Major and Margaret Thatcher respectively.

review of key problems

Another vital role of the Cabinet is the review of key problems which can affect the future of the Government and the country. To the outside observer this would appear to be an activity on which any Cabinet worth its salt ought to be engaged. After all, where else but around the Cabinet table should there be serious and timely discussion of such vital subjects as the consequences of global warming, the concept of sustainable development or the difficulties of pursuing radical welfare reform? Yet the truth seems to be that this aspect of the work of the Cabinet has often been neglected in favour of dealing with more urgent, or at least more immediate, political issues.

In recent years the agenda of every regular Cabinet meeting has included an item on the following week's Parliamentary business (when Parliament is sitting), an item which permits the Prime Minister or Foreign Secretary to give a brief report on current international developments or recent international conferences with implications for Britain, and often an item which allows the Chancellor of the Exchequer to report on the state of the economy as indicated by the latest official statistics. Of course, any member of the Cabinet may apply to the Cabinet Secretary to have a particular item included on the agenda of a future meeting, but it is not uncommon for such requests to be turned down or for the matter to be referred to the appropriate Cabinet Committee at the behest of the Prime Minister who is in effective control of the Cabinet agenda. On most occasions when Prime Ministers do this, they are merely acting as good chairmen by seeking to get decisions taken at the appropriate level consistent with the political importance of the issue. However, in the case of a real emergency or if a Cabinet Minister is not prepared to accept the decision of a Cabinet Committee, the Prime Minister will normally ensure that the matter is put immediately on the agenda of the full Cabinet. Any other response would lead to deterioration in the general atmosphere of mutual trust and this would not be in the interest of any Prime Minister, however powerful. In general, therefore, the preparation and timing of Cabinet decisions is very much in the hands of the Prime Minister, which gives the holder of that office a real advantage over his colleagues.

The fact that successive Prime Ministers and senior officials in the Cabinet Office have not always encouraged the Cabinet as a whole to discharge its responsibility for strategic policy review of this kind can be explained in a number of ways. Firstly, it is doubtful whether regular Cabinet meetings are the appropriate occasions on which to attempt this task, since senior Ministers are always very busy and short of time – they have their own Departmental business to manage, the demands of Parliament, constituency and party to which to respond, and a variety of public engagements in Britain and abroad to fulfill (to say nothing of family and private life). Secondly, the Cabinet exists mainly to settle or endorse the big decisions which have already been carefully prepared in Whitehall and which may even have been taken (in effect at any rate) by the Prime Minister and a few senior colleagues in advance of regular Cabinet meetings. In these circumstances it is not surprising that the Cabinet has an unimpressive record in this respect.

Occasionally the Cabinet does engage in intensive and extensive discussions. This happened, for example, in the discussions of the Churchill Cabinet about British withdrawal from Egypt in 1954, in the Macmillan Cabinet about Britain's relationship with the rest of Western Europe in the late 1950s, in the Heath Cabinet about policy towards Northern Ireland in 1972–73, and in the Callaghan Cabinet in 1976 when it was necessary to agree on a package of public expenditure cuts to satisfy the conditions of the IMF loan to Britain. Discussions also take place from time to time in the more informal setting of Chequers (the Prime Minister's official country residence), but these are usually focused on a single theme (for example, the fuel crisis under Tony Blair in September 2000) and do not necessarily involve the entire Cabinet. In general, most regular Cabinet discussions are largely pre-ordained and even a little ritualistic. The Cabinet remains the supreme decision-making body in the British political system, but it has often been a disappointment to those who have looked to it for deep or original discussion of the key political issues of the time. Indeed, soon after Tony Blair became Prime Minister in 1997 it was noted that the Cabinet had largely ceased to function as a forum for meaningful decision making[10] and that Britain was consequently 'as close to having a presidential system as is possible.'[11] In 2004, in the aftermath of the Hutton and Butler Inquiries, it was remarked by one long-time insider that 'Cabinet government of the traditional model has manifestly atrophied over the past seven years, and moreover by deliberate neglect, not accident'. Yet the balance of power between Prime Minister and Cabinet is constantly changing and few dogmatic observations will stand the test of time.

inter-Departmental coordination

The third important role of the Cabinet is to ensure inter-Departmental coordination in the development of Government policy. In the opinion of many well-informed observers this has long been the most notable role of the Cabinet in Britain. It is obviously a vital aspect of Cabinet activity, since it helps to impart a degree of coherence and unity to Government policy and so reinforces the doctrine of collective responsibility. Indeed, it could not really be otherwise, since senior Ministers cannot be expected to be bound by Cabinet decisions affecting their spheres of responsibility if their Departmental interests and political points of view have not been adequately taken into account. Such inter-Departmental coordination helps to guard against the taking of political decisions by one Department which may have unintended or adverse consequences for other Departments. It is also meant to contribute to the administrative efficiency of any Government, in that it can help to avoid both unnecessary duplication in Whitehall and the creation of awkward or damaging gaps in the scope of official action.

Since individual Cabinet Ministers are not always good 'team players' by temperament or calculation, it is necessary to bolster the unity and collegiality of the Cabinet with a number of institutional devices. For example, the Permanent Secretaries of all the various Whitehall Departments have a regular weekly meeting under the chairmanship of the Cabinet Secretary the day before each Cabinet meeting. The Press Officers in all the various Departments are also in frequent contact and work collectively under the overall guidance of 10 Downing Street. The Private Offices of all Cabinet Ministers keep in touch and include an increasingly significant sub-network of Political Advisers, each of whom works directly for a Cabinet Minister. The various units, directorates and offices at 10 Downing Street – under the three main spheres of 'Policy and Government', 'Communications and Strategy' and 'Government and Political Relations' – work exclusively for the Prime Minister of the day and deal principally with policy focus and delivery. All these various Whitehall networks are there to reinforce the coherence of Government policy and the unity of the Government as a whole.

Indeed, it was in order to achieve these twin objectives that, on taking office in 1997, Tony Blair and his key advisers sought to apply in Government the strict and highly centralised controls over policy and its presentation that they had operated so successfully in Opposition. As part of this approach they stipulated that 'all major interviews and media appearances (by Ministers), both print and broadcast, should be agreed with the No. 10 Press Office before any commitments were entered into. The policy content of all major speeches, press releases, and new policy initiatives should be cleared in good time with the No. 10 Private Office; the timing and form of announcements should be cleared with the No. 10 Press Office.'[12] These arrangements led one commentator to write of 'the biggest centralisation of power seen in Whitehall in peacetime.'[13] It was an approach that was intensified in 1998 with the appointment of a Minister for the Cabinet Office with a seat in the Cabinet, a place on several Cabinet committees, direct access to the Prime Minister, and with responsibility for ensuring coherence and central control over all important Government policy and its presentation. The goal was to achieve what Tony Blair refered to as 'joined-up Government'. A *Modernising Government* White Paper was published in March 1999 setting out the basis for change in five key areas: forward-looking policy making, responsive public services, high-quality public services, information age Government and valuing public service.[14] In July 1999 an *Action Plan* was published with the objective of driving forward the commitments contained in the White Paper.[15] January 2000 saw the publication of *Wiring It Up*, a report by the Performance and Innovation Unit on Whitehall's management of cross-cutting policies and services.[16] This was followed in 2001 by changes to both Downing Street and Whitehall designed to ensure delivery.[17]

It is clear that single-party Government in Britain needs to be united Government if the political system is to work satisfactorily. The Cabinet is the main institutional expression of this unity and it is therefore vital that its decision-making procedures should contribute to rather than detract from the essentially collegiate nature of central Government in Britain. Whenever a Cabinet is seriously split on policy – as the Callaghan Cabinet was in 1976 over the IMF demand for public expenditure cuts, or the Thatcher Cabinet was in 1979–81 over the general thrust of economic policy, or the Major Cabinet was in 1992–97 on Britain's approach to further development of the European Union, or the Blair Cabinet was in 2006 over reform of secondary education – the morale and effectiveness of the whole Government suffers. It can also lead to reduced levels of public support for the governing party when the media and the general public perceive that the Cabinet is divided on important issues of policy or personality. It is therefore not surprising that all Prime Ministers strive mightily to avoid such splits and try to deal promptly with them when they occur.

12.4 the changing balance in central Government

Over the years each of the three entities at the centre of British Government (10 Downing Street, the Cabinet Office and the Treasury) – the so-called

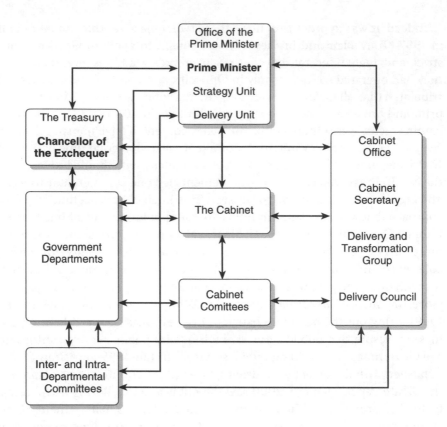

figure **12.3** **the core executive**

core executive – has had a role to play in coordinating the activities of Departments throughout Whitehall and beyond. In this mixture, 10 Downing Street has provided support and advice to Prime Ministers on the whole range of Government business, giving strategic direction to Departments on the basis of the Prime Minister's views and has orchestrated the presentation of Government policy; the Cabinet Office facilitates the collective consideration of issues by Cabinet and Ministerial Committees and has traditionally ensured that Government policies are coordinated throughout the machinery of government; while the Treasury has managed public spending and the levying of taxation. The core executive is shown in diagrammatical form in Figure 12.3

On coming to power in 1997, Tony Blair was determined to focus on the task of developing and coordinating policy across Government Departments – particularly coordinating closer working between 10 Downing Street, the Cabinet Office and the Treasury on long-term policy, preventing bottlenecks arising in the process of policy coordination and removing unnecessary diversions from a focused pursuit of the Government's objectives, delivery of the Government's policies and achievement of the Government's targets. Emphasis was placed upon policy presentation in a clear attempt to ensure that the perceived failings of previous Governments – namely the lack of central direction and frequency of arguments between various Departments – would not be features of the Blair Government.[18] As a result of this new approach, a number of developments have occurred at the heart of central Government.

10 Downing Street

In addition to the formal structure of Cabinet government already described, successive Prime Ministers since Lloyd George (1916–22) have taken steps to have other sources of advice and support available to them at 10 Downing Street. As a result of changes carried out under Tony Blair, there are three key headings – *Policy and Government, Communications and Strategy*, and *Government and Political Relations* – under which a network of individuals and offices operate.[19] The Prime Minister's support structure is outlined in Figure 12.4.

The Policy and Government Unit (in part formally the Private Office) is headed by the Prime Minister's Chief of Staff (under Tony Blair, Jonathan Powell) and incorporates a Principal Private Secretary with additional private secretaries for specific areas of responsibility. The individuals involved are primarily Civil Service high-fliers whose tasks include:

▸ Collating advice for the Prime Minister from within No 10, Whitehall Departments and elsewhere
▸ Conveying the Prime Minister's views and decisions to those involved
▸ Ensuring follow-up on the Prime Minister's decisions
▸ Preparing the Prime Minister's visits, both in the UK and overseas
▸ Preparing the necessary ground for visits by others to the Prime Minister
▸ Dealing with the Prime Minister's correspondence
▸ Managing the Prime Minister's diary
▸ Recording the Prime Minister's meetings and phone conversations.

The Unit also incorporates a Policy Directorate (the Prime Minister's Foreign Policy and European Policy Advisers), a Delivery Unit, a Strategy Unit, an Office of Public Services Reform, an Honours and Appointments Office, and Sections for Parliament, Operations and Administration.

The *Policy Directorate* (previously the Policy Unit) consists of a small group of advisers brought in to serve the Prime Minister and to assist with political tasks. Personnel have varied from Government to Government, depending on the outlook and preferences of the Prime Minister of the day. For example, Harold Wilson and James Callaghan depended quite heavily on Dr Bernard Donoghue, an academic from the London School of Economics; Margaret Thatcher had advice and support from Sir John Hoskyns, a businessman, and Ferdinand Mount, a journalist; John Major depended on the advice and support of Sarah Hogg, a journalist, and Norman Blackwell, a management consultant; Tony Blair relied on Geoff Mulgan of the Young Foundation, Andrew Adonis (later enobled in the House of Lords), Roger Liddle formerly of the SDP, Lord Birt the former Director General of the BBC, and David Miliband formally of

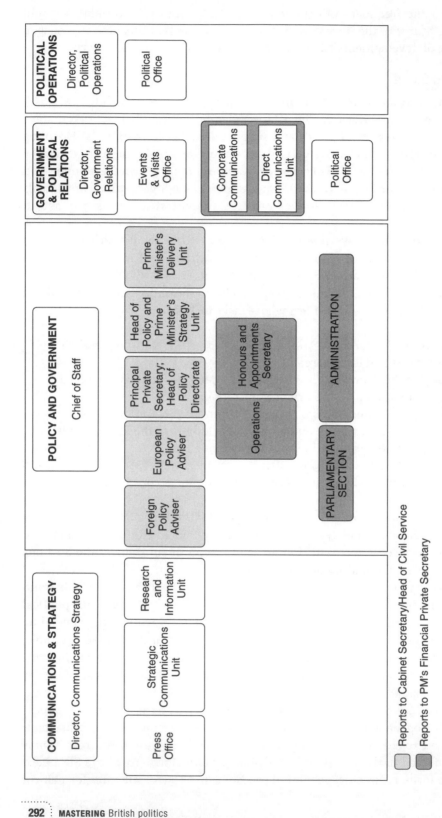

COMMUNICATIONS & STRATEGY
Director, Communications Strategy

- Press Office
- Strategic Communications Unit
- Research and Information Unit

POLICY AND GOVERNMENT
Chief of Staff

- Foreign Policy Adviser
- European Policy Adviser
- Principal Private Secretary; Head of Policy Directorate
- Head of Policy and Prime Minister's Strategy Unit
- Prime Minister's Delivery Unit
- Operations
- Honours and Appointments Secretary
- PARLIAMENTARY SECTION
- ADMINISTRATION

GOVERNMENT & POLITICAL RELATIONS
Director, Government Relations

- Events & Visits Office
- Corporate Communications
- Direct Communications Unit
- Political Office

POLITICAL OPERATIONS
Director, Political Operations

- Political Office

Reports to Cabinet Secretary/Head of Civil Service

Reports to PM's Financial Private Secretary

source: 'The Centre of Government – No. 10, The Cabinet Office and HM treasury', House of Commons Library Research Paper, 05/92, 21 December 2005.

figure 12.4   the No. 10 organisation, April 2004

the Institute for Public Policy Research and later in the Cabinet as Minister for Communities. Whether such advisers were installed in the Policy Unit or worked more informally for the Prime Minister on an ad hoc basis or in a 'kitchen cabinet', their contributions to the policy-making process can be very significant. They often act as speech-writers and help the Prime Minister to develop a distinctive personal agenda, and they can act as political trouble-shooters, when necessary, between conflicting interests in Government.

Prime Minister's have long relied on specialist advice in matters of foreign affairs – for example, Neville Chamberlain had Sir Horace Wilson, Harold Macmillan had both John Wyndham and Philip de Zulueta, while Margaret Thatcher had Sir Anthony Parsons (who had been UK Permanent Representative to the UN from 1979 to 1982), and then Sir Percy Cradock (between 1978 and 1983 Ambassador to China and an authority on the Far East), and she came to rely upon Charles Powell, a former diplomat and then her Private Secretary, during the latter part of her time in office. Tony Blair had a *Foreign Policy Adviser* and a *European Policy Advisor*, roles undertaken by Sir David Manning and Sir Stephen Wall respectively, and then by Sir Nigel Sheinwald and Kim Darroch.

The *Delivery Unit*, established in 2001, is headed by the Prime Minister's Chief Advisor on Delivery (Sir Michael Barber for several years) and has a staff of around 40 people drawn from both the public and private sectors. It is charged with the task of improving public service delivery by working with Departments to help them meet their Public Service Agreement (PSA) targets and deliver desired policy outcomes.

The *Strategy Unit*, which was formed in 2002 from a merger of the Performance and Innovation Unit (PIU) and the Forward Strategy Unit (FSU), is responsible for providing the Prime Minister with strategic advice and policy analysis on the priority issues laid down by him. It reports to the Prime Minister through the Cabinet Secretary. In 2006 it had three specific roles:

▶ To carry out strategy reviews and provide policy advice in accordance with policy priorities
▶ To support Government Departments in developing effective strategies and policies
▶ To conduct occasional strategic audits, and to identify and disseminate positive thinking on emerging issues and challenges for the Government.

The *Office of Public Services Reform* (OPSR), which was created in 2001, aids the Government in its programme of public sector reform and is responsible for carrying forward the reform of public services in accordance with the Prime Minister's four principles of reform:

▶ National standards to ensure that people have high-quality services wherever they live
▶ Devolution to give local leaders the means to deliver these services to local people

- More flexibility in service provision in light of rising public expectations
- Greater customer choice for users of public services.

The *Honours and Appointments Office* – headed by a senior civil servant and staffed by civil servants – deals with the various honours and appointments which fall within the remit of the Prime Minister, but which are essentially non-political, such as appointments within the Church of England.

The *Parliamentary Section* deals with Parliamentary affairs for the Prime Minister, liaising with Government Departments through the Parliamentary Units on matters such as Prime Minister's Questions, Answers to Written Questions and Oral Statements. There are additional Sections dealing with *Operations* and *Administration*.

The Communications and Strategy Unit which came into being in 2001 with certain responsibilities and reporting lines, was adjusted in 2003 following the departure of Alastair Campbell as Tony Blair's Press Secretary/Director of Communications. The Unit is headed by a Director of Communications and Strategy and is divided into three sections, a *Press Office*, a *Strategic Communications Unit* and a *Research and Information Unit*. The *Press Office* handles the Prime Minister's dealings with the media and has become an increasingly important aspect of activity. Currently, the Prime Minister's Official Spokesman (Tom Kelly) briefs the media regularly on the record – unlike in former times when such briefings were usually off the record and on 'Lobby terms'.

The Government and Political Relations Unit, under a Director of Government Relations, is divided between a *Political Office* responsible for dealings between the Prime Minister and the Labour party organization for activity of a party political nature, and the *Events and Visits Office* which is responsible for organizing events hosted by the Prime Minister in his official capacity and for visits, both in the UK and overseas, made by the Prime Minister.

Also to be noted is the Prime Ministers' *Parliamentary Private Secretary* (PPS), a Member of Parliament whose role is to keep the Prime Minister in touch with back-bench opinion in the House of Commons. Ian Gow was particularly effective in this role for Margaret Thatcher during the period 1979–83. John Major as Prime Minister had a PPS from the House of Commons and one from the House of Lords. Tony Blair's PPSs included Bruce Grocott and David Hanson and in 2006 was Keith Hill.

These developments (both cause and effect) together reflect the growing dominance of the Prime Minister – any Prime Minister – with this organizational and institutional backup at their disposal within the contemporary British political framework.

the Cabinet Office

In the process of central Government the Cabinet Office has a vital role to play in ensuring fast and efficient communication of inter-Departmental decisions to all who need to know of them throughout Whitehall. This central secretariat, which consists mainly of Civil Service high-flyers seconded from other Departments, communicates Government decisions in the form of extracts from Cabinet or Cabinet Committee minutes to those parts of the central Government machine which have to act on them. This means that in the first instance such decisions are communicated to the Private Offices of the Ministers involved in the implementation of the policy and then further relayed from there within the respective Departments. Such minutes are drawn up by officials of the Cabinet Office under the overall supervision and direction of the Cabinet Secretary. It is open to the Prime Minister, or indeed any other Cabinet Minister, to see the minutes in draft, to point out errors and then ask for suitable amendments. Yet if this is to be done, it has to be done quickly. Consequently, requests are not frequently made and even less frequently granted. In short, Cabinet Office officials keep a tight and effective grip on this aspect of Cabinet government.

Meetings of the Cabinet and its Committees would not proceed as smoothly as they usually do if it were not for the fact that the Ministerial meetings are prepared and supported by official meetings of senior civil servants from the various Departments concerned. It is this parallel structure of official committees which keeps Government business moving along and makes it possible for the Cabinet and its Committees to dispatch a great deal of Government business in a rather expeditious way. Cabinet Office officials usually chair these official committees which are intended to maximise the areas of potential inter-Departmental agreement and to define, if not minimise, the areas of potential disagreement. Since each Department tends to respect the interests and responsibilities of every other Department and since there is an established pecking order in Whitehall with 10 Downing Street and the Treasury at the top and the smaller or newer Departments at the bottom, the outcome of inter-Departmental discussions at official level often reflects the balance of bureaucratic power in Whitehall. This may facilitate the collective decision-making process, but it can also make for inter-Departmental compromises which may lower the quality or reduce the effectiveness of the decisions actually taken. In other words, a significant political price can be paid for the collegiate conventions of Whitehall government.

The main work of the Cabinet Office is grouped within a number of Secretariats, each of which coves a significant policy area:

- Economic and Domestic affairs
- European Union matters
- Defence and Overseas policy
- Intelligence and Security
- Constitutional reform issues.

There is also a Central Secretariat providing advice to the Head of the Civil Service, Ministers and Departments on such matters as Ministerial responsibility, the structure and organization of Central Government, and standards of propriety and ethics in relation to Ministers, Special Advisers and civil servants.

Cabinet Committees have two main purposes: to relieve the burden on the Cabinet as a whole by dealing with Government business on behalf of the Cabinet; and to support the principle of collective responsibility by ensuring that such decisions are taken only after the issues have been fully considered from all the relevant angles. The main categories of Cabinet Committee activity are: the coordination of complex Government business, such as the legislative programme and the allocation of public expenditure; the discussion of major policy issues which have proved incapable of resolution lower down the tree of collective decision making; and the settlement of disagreements or disputes between Departments. Under Tony Blair's Administrations notable emphasis was put upon public service delivery, cross-cutting issues and joined-up government, all of which involved the Cabinet Office. For example, the work of public service reform, which from 2001 to 2006 was led by the Office of Public Services Reform, was carried forward by the Economic and Domestic Secretariat of the Cabinet Office, the Government Communication Group and the Strategy Unit in their respective spheres. This work was inspired by Tony Blair's four principles of reform: high standards, flexibility, greater choice and delegation of operational activity and responsibility to the local level.

the Treasury

Normally the most powerful Department of Government, under the Chancellorship of Gordon Brown and the Premiership of Tony Blair, the Treasury has become even more powerful, because it has been in the lead on the public service reform agenda of New Labour. To do this it has used the contractual device of Public Service Agreements (PSAs) which require Departments to outline their aims and objectives and then meet performance and value-for-money targets stipulated in detailed operational plans known as Service Delivery Agreements (SDAs). Treasury officials are then responsible for monitoring how Departments perform in the light of such objectives.

The outcome of Cabinet discussions and inter-Departmental discussions at official level is affected by the relative standing and influence of the various Ministers whose Departments are involved at a given time. When the Chancellor of the Exchequer and the Chief Secretary win battles with their Cabinet colleagues over PSAs or public spending, the Treasury becomes even more formidable than usual in its dealings with other Departments. Thus it is usually wise to enlist the support of the Treasury and 10 Downing Street in any important inter-Departmental battle.

12.5 conclusion

Considerable controversy continues to surround the issues raised by the respective roles of the Prime Minister and Cabinet in modern British politics.

There is no consensus of opinion among academic observers or practising politicians, although in Tony Blair's time at 10 Downing Street many people come to see British central Government as increasingly presidential, both presentationally and in terms of institutional balance.

However, in view of the contradictory evidence, some observers agree with John Mackintosh, who wrote that 'British Prime Ministers are in a position of great strength as against their colleagues and within the whole framework of British Government'.[20] Others agree with George Jones who wrote that 'the Prime Minister is the leading figure in the Cabinet whose voice carries most weight, but he is not the all-powerful individual which many have claimed him to be'.[21] Robert Blake probably came to the safest conclusion that 'the powers of the Prime Minister have varied with the personality of the Prime Minister or with the particular political circumstances of his tenure'.[22] On the whole this last view allows for the fact that there have been times when Prime Ministers have carried all before them – for example, in the immediate aftermath of General Election victories or other personal political triumphs – and times when powerful Ministers or the Cabinet collectively have asserted their authority over weak, lazy, sick, politically damaged or discredited Prime Ministers. Indeed, Prime Ministerial power is like a fortress built on sand: it can look impregnable, yet can be washed away by a turn in the tide.

Although we have been looking at two distinct components of the British political system, the fortunes of the Prime Minister and Cabinet are inextricably linked. Whatever their respective roles and capabilities, neither can function satisfactorily without the consent and cooperation of the other. In so far as each is limited in the exercise of political power, the constraints are essentially political rather than constitutional, practical rather than theoretical. It is the other actors in the political process – the political parties, pressure groups, the Civil Service, the media, the markets, foreign Governments and public opinion – which keep both Prime Minister and Cabinet in check. However, in the modern world it is the passage of events, very often in other countries, and the periodic verdict of the British electorate which usually determine their fate.

SUGGESTED QUESTIONS

1   Describe the structure and problems of Cabinet government in Britain.
2   How powerful is the Prime Minister in modern Britain?
3   Does collective responsibility raise or lower the quality of decision making in British central Government?

ministers and departments

Britain is a country with a long tradition of centralised Government. Some of the public offices of central Government have been in existence for centuries. For example, the Exchequer developed in the twelfth century, and the office of Lord President of the Council dates from 1497. Other Departments of central Government are now over 200 years old, with two of the most prestigious having been established in 1782 under George III when both a Department for Foreign Affairs and a Department for Home and Colonial Affairs (now the Home Office) were created.

Since the mid-nineteenth century Departments of central Government have been created, reorganised and dissolved, often as a direct result of the changing political agenda and priorities of Government. For example, a Board of Education was established in 1870 with a Minister directly responsible to Parliament for the whole area of public education; the Board of Agriculture and Fisheries was converted into a Ministry in 1919 after the struggle to feed the nation during the First World War; while an Air Ministry was created in 1937 to organise what at the time was a relatively new arm of warfare. In 1970 a Department of the Environment was established as one of a number of super-Departments designed to secure better coordination in Whitehall, while in 1974 a separate Department of Energy was established as a partial response to the energy crisis of the time. The 1974–79 Labour Government split the super-Departments into several smaller Departments.

The 1979–83 Conservative Government abolished the Civil Service Department and redistributed its functions between the Treasury and the Cabinet Office; the 1983–87 Conservative Government recreated the Department of Trade and Industry, but transferred some of its functions to an enlarged Department of Transport; the 1987–92 Conservative Government split the Department of Health and Social Security into separate Departments of Health and Social Security respectively; the 1992-97 Conservative Government did away with the Department of Energy, redistributing its functions to the Department of Trade and Industry, created a new Department of National Heritage, and in 1995 merged the Department of Employment with the Department for Education. The

Labour Government that came into office in 1997 created a large Department of the Environment, Transport and the Regions, only to reorganise this later to create a distinct Department of Transport, merging Environment with Food and Rural Affairs, while responsibility for the regions and local government was allocated to the Office of the Deputy Prime Minister. In 2003 the Department for Constitutional Affairs was created in order to spearhead Labour's constitutional and judicial reform agenda – only to be replaced by a new Ministry of Justice in 2007. Thus it is apparent that there has been both change and continuity in the organisation of British central Government.

13.1 the structure and work of Departments

Throughout the entire period of Departmental government in Britain there has been only one fundamental examination of the overall structure of central Government. This was carried out by a committee chaired by Lord Haldane which reported to Lloyd George's Government in 1918.[1] The two main recommendations of the report were that Departmental boundaries should be based upon functional criteria (such as health, agriculture or defence), and that the Cabinet should be kept as a compact policy-making body at the apex of central Government. Neither recommendation has been fully implemented over subsequent years. Thus it has been quite common for Departments based on a single function to coexist with some based on a mixture of functions (such as the Home Office) and others based on geography (such as the Scotland Office). Furthermore, Cabinets have had as few as five members (Winston Churchill's War Cabinet in 1940) or as many as 24 members (Harold Wilson's Cabinet in 1975). Following the 2005 General Election the Cabinet was comprised of 23 members, 21 MPs and 2 members of the House of Lords.

Departmental structure

The Departmental structure in Whitehall today consists of 21 Departments – as outlined in Figure 13.1. In political terms the most important are the Treasury, the Foreign Office and the Home Office. Yet in terms of the public spending for which they are responsible, the Department for Work and Pensions, the Department of Health, and the Department for Education and Skills are the most significant. In formal terms there is no Prime Minister's Department, although the staff at 10 Downing Street and in the Cabinet Office provide support for the Prime Minister of the day as if there were such a Department. The Cabinet Office and the Cabinet Secretary advise the Cabinet as a whole, not just the Prime Minister, although many of the Units within it work disproportionately for the Prime Minister.

Apart from the Prime Minister, there are other non-Departmental Ministers – for example, the Lord Privy Seal, the Lord President of the Council and the Chancellor of the Duchy of Lancaster.[2] It is also possible to appoint a Minister 'without Portfolio', a convenient way for the Prime Minister of the day to include

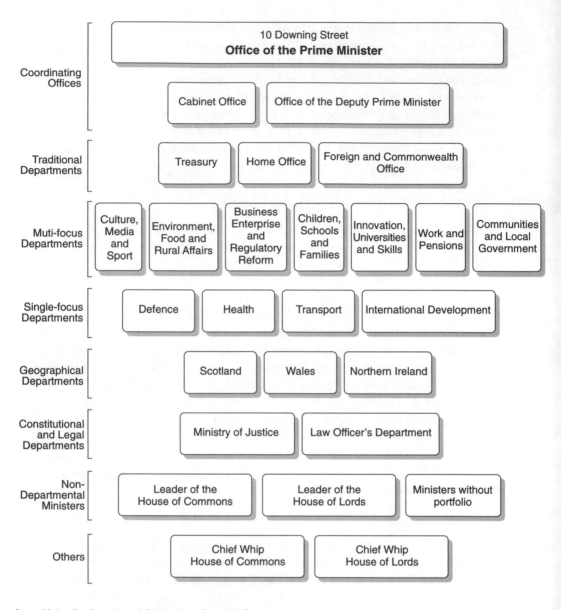

Coordinating Offices	10 Downing Street **Office of the Prime Minister**					
	Cabinet Office	Office of the Deputy Prime Minister				
Traditional Departments	Treasury	Home Office	Foreign and Commonwealth Office			
Muti-focus Departments	Culture, Media and Sport	Environment, Food and Rural Affairs	Business Enterprise and Regulatory Reform	Children, Schools and Families	Innovation, Universities and Skills	Work and Pensions	Communities and Local Government
Single-focus Departments	Defence	Health	Transport	International Development		
Geographical Departments	Scotland	Wales	Northern Ireland			
Constitutional and Legal Departments	Ministry of Justice	Law Officer's Department				
Non-Departmental Ministers	Leader of the House of Commons	Leader of the House of Lords	Ministers without portfolio			
Others	Chief Whip House of Commons	Chief Whip House of Lords				

figure **13.1**   **the departmental structure of central Government**

an individual in the Government whose main responsibility is to liaise with all parts of the governing party in Parliament and the country.

Within each significant Department the normal pattern is for there to be a Secretary of State or Minister of equivalent Cabinet rank as Departmental head, supported by at least one Minister of State at the second level and perhaps two or more Undersecretaries at the third level. There are, however, variations in this pattern which flow mainly from the nature and scope of each Department's responsibilities. The Treasury is distinctive in many ways, not least in having two Cabinet Ministers and normally the backing of the Prime

Minister as well (who is known formally as the First Lord of the Treasury). Nonetheless, there have been occasions when other Departments have been represented by more than one Cabinet Minister. This was the case in the first Cabinet formed by Tony Blair in 1997 when the Deputy Prime Minister, John Prescott, was appointed Secretary of State for the Environment, Transport and the Regions and Gavin Strang was appointed Minister for Transport with a seat in the Cabinet. It was also the case following the 2005 General Election when the Office of the Deputy Prime Minister, John Prescott, had David Miliband as a second Cabinet Minister of Communities and Local Government. It is also possible for two Departments to be represented in Cabinet by a single Minister, as was the case with Transport and Scotland under Alistair Darling and Wales and Northern Ireland under Peter Hain in 2005.

Just as the number and importance of Ministers varies from one Department to another, so the number of civil servants working in each Department also varies considerably. For example, in 2004 the Ministry of Defence employed 75,780 non-industrial civil servants and the Department of Work and Pensions employed 125,170 civil servants, whereas the Treasury only employed 1,030, the Department for Education and Skills employed 5,130, the Department for Culture, Media and Sport employed 730 and the Northern Ireland office employed only 170. The explanation for these wide differences is mainly that some Departments discharge widespread and complicated functions, whereas some do not. Despite such variations, there is nevertheless a recognisably standard structure for any Department in Whitehall. This is shown in Figure 13.2.

central Government functions

It is difficult to generalise about the way in which central Government works in Britain. So much depends on the personality, outlook and experience of the senior Ministers concerned and also on the calibre and performance of the senior civil servants involved, as well as the various Departmental habits and traditions. According to the traditional view propounded by Sir Ivor Jennings, the essential features of British central Government are 'the clear division between politicians and public servants and the close relationship between policy and administration.'[3] This emphasises one of the key paradoxes of British central Government. On the one hand, there is a clear theoretical distinction between the role of Ministers, who are supposed to determine the policy and take all the decisions, and that of civil servants, who are supposed to advise Ministers and see that the business of Government is conducted in conformity with the policy laid down by Ministers and with enduring standards of probity and propriety. On the other hand, there is the practical impossibility in modern British Government of sustaining such a clear distinction. In short, it has become increasingly apparent that the theory that Ministers take the political decisions and civil servants carry them out has long since been overtaken by reality. This fact has certainly been made apparent by the various findings of the 1996 Scott Report, the 1998 Legg Reportand the 2004 Hutton and Butler Reports.[4]

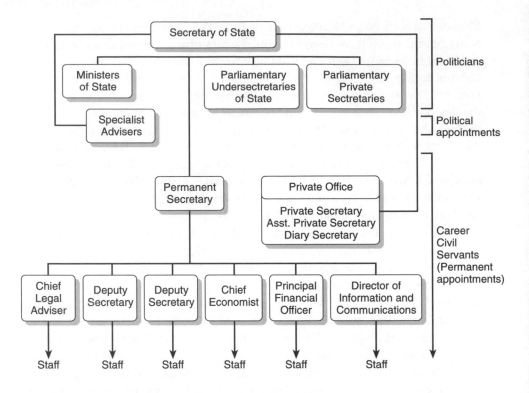

figure **13.2** **Government department: standard structure**

Most Ministers have to work very hard, often for between 12 and 18 hours a day. There are policy discussions to conduct; official papers to be considered and, where possible, approved; Ministerial correspondence to be dealt with; frequent meetings both within their own Departments and bilaterally with other Departments or 10 Downing Street; meetings of the Cabinet or Cabinet Committees to attend; meetings to be held with outside bodies and the representatives of various pressure or interest groups; Parliamentary committees to attend, Parliamentary Questions to be answered, and Parliamentary debates in which to take part; official visits to be made to various parts of the country and abroad; foreign visitors to be welcomed and entertained; journalists and others in the media to be briefed and interviews to be given; meetings of the European Union and other international organisations to attend; constituents and party activists to be kept content as well as constituency work to attend to.

A graphic illustration of the demands of Ministerial life was given by Tony Benn, when describing how he allocated his time in 1977 when he was Secretary of State for Energy.[5] Although some thirty years ago, it is still valid:

▸ Fulfilled 50 public engagements in the constituency, made 12 general speeches in Bristol, held 16 constituency surgeries, and handled more than 1000 personal cases.

- Attended 4 General Management Committee meetings of the Bristol South East Labour Party; attended 20 ward meetings, and 5 Labour Group meetings to discuss policy.
- Attended 12 meetings of the Parliamentary Labour Party, and made 14 speeches to various sub-group meetings of MPs.
- Dealt in Parliament with three Energy Bills, produced 54 Statutory Instruments; presented 33 explanatory memoranda to the House on European Community energy matters; answered 51 oral questions and 171 written questions; had 154 meetings with non-Governmental groups; produced 1821 Ministerial minutes on papers taken home in the official red box; made 133 public appointments to various bodies.
- Attended 42 Cabinet meetings and 106 Cabinet Committee meetings; submitted four Cabinet papers and 45 Cabinet Committee papers; received 1750 Cabinet papers covering the whole range of Government policies.
- Made 19 visits abroad, and received 32 Ministers and Ambassadors from foreign countries.
- In the first half of 1977, presided over the Energy Council of the European Community, which involved taking the chair at six Council meetings and having sundry other official meetings on European energy questions.
- Attended 15 meetings of the Labour Party National Executive Committee and 62 other Labour meetings.
- Made 80 speeches up and down the country, gave 83 radio interviews, 57 television interviews and 34 press conferences, wrote 16 articles, had 30 interviews with individual journalists, and received or answered 1000 letters which did not involve constituency casework or Ministerial responsibilities.

This is a considerable amount of work by any standards, but it is by no means untypical of Ministerial life today. However, any inventory can only provide a superficial and incomplete sketch of the full range of Ministerial activities, since it is impossible to give a definitive description of a working life which is inherently so varied and unpredictable.

In addition to the problems which can be caused by what can be termed 'Ministerial musical chairs'[6] whenever the Prime Minister has a reshuffle, incoming Ministers usually get no time to prepare for their jobs and little or no advice from their predecessors. New Ministers seldom have anything more than superficial knowledge or understanding of their new responsibilities unless they have been promoted from within or are returning to a Department which they already know. The normal assumption is that they will learn on the job with the assistance of their Ministerial colleagues and Civil Service advisers. Indeed, the ability to get to grips with a complex brief in a short period of time is considered to be one of the main qualifications for Ministerial office in Britain.

Civil servants for their part, and notably those in the senior administrative grades, do their best to ensure that Ministers are adequately briefed on all matters with which they have to deal. Yet at the same time they try to see that Ministers are not overburdened with unnecessary paperwork or matters which can be handled by officials. This means that one of the key roles of civil servants, and especially those who work in Ministerial Private Offices, is that of 'gatekeeper' in the information-gathering and decision-making process of central Government. Every day such civil servants have to decide whether to refer matters to Ministers for information or decision or whether to deal with issues themselves within the confines of established Government policy. Although there is a natural tendency for civil servants to err on the side of caution by referring all politically sensitive matters to Ministers, their 'gatekeeper' role gives them considerable influence within central Government and the veil of confidentiality behind which they work makes it hard for the outside observer – and sometimes even Ministers – to evaluate just how satisfactorily they perform their tasks.

Perhaps the most characteristic aspect of activity in Whitehall is the work which is done in the extensive network of *inter-Departmental committees* both by Ministers in Cabinet Committees and bilateral meetings and at official level in the inter-Departmental Committees made up of officials from the Departments concerned. Since many of the issues with which central Government has to deal are too broad and complex to be handled within the sphere of a single Department, the process of inter-Departmental coordination by officials, prior to collective Ministerial decisions, is vital to much of the policy and decision-making process. It puts a considerable burden on the officials involved – especially those in the Cabinet Office – who have to see that the various strands of policy are pulled together. The process of central Government would not work so smoothly without such inter-Departmental coordination by officials.

Another important aspect of the work of British central Government is the frequent and systematic consultation which takes place between officials and various client or pressure groups (stakeholders in New Labour language). Nowadays every Department finds it useful to consult widely with such groups, not so much about which policy to adopt as about the detailed effects and implications of policy already determined by Ministers, and all Departments make it their business to keep in touch with the various interest and cause groups which have a stake in their spheres of Departmental responsibility. Certainly any Government which spurned or neglected such contacts would not only find its tasks more difficult, but also lay itself open to serious criticism in Parliament and in the media.

13.2 the role of Ministers

The role of Ministers in British central Government can be defined as taking the lead in, and making decisions on, matters of policy; and the defence and promotion of that policy in Whitehall, Westminster, Brussels and the world at large. Within their Departments Ministers act essentially as political jurymen who take decisions on the basis of advice supplied to them by their civil servants and others. Of course, Ministers are always free to question, ignore or discard such advice, but this can be unwise. Civil servants do not usually recommend courses of action or inaction which they know would be politically unacceptable to Ministers at the time. Ministers for their part sometimes may not have the time or the inclination to question or reject the policy advice which is put to them. Usually only strong, self-confident and experienced Ministers, or those who are engaged on implementing clearly established party policy, manage to dominate all policy work in their Departments.

Every Government since the Second World War has contained a few senior Ministers who have been able, more often than not, to get their way with officials, with their Ministerial colleagues and with Parliament. This has applied particularly to strong and determined Prime Ministers, yet it has also applied very clearly to some leading Ministers. It is not easy to define the qualities such Ministers have which earn them the accolade of 'political heavyweight', but politicians and pundits alike know one when they see one. Force of character and political judgement undoubtedly play an important part, but so do Ministerial competence and Prime Ministerial backing.

It is evident that the balance of experience and ability can often determine the balance of power between Ministers, between Ministers and their senior civil servants and between Departments. In general terms it is apparent that a variety of factors are involved in successful policy making, notably the following:

- Popular support (certainly the absence of popular dissent)
- A Manifesto commitment (described by Richard Crossman as 'the battering ram of change')
- Prime Ministerial support (or, as a minimum, Prime Ministerial acquiescence)
- Cabinet commitment (certainly the absence of hostility from among the Cabinet 'heavyweights')
- The availability of sufficient time in which to carry things through to fruition
- Favourable circumstances and conditions (such as the absence of other overriding policy priorities and time-consuming emergencies and crises)
- Support amongst senior civil servants (certainly the absence of hostility towards a policy)
- Support among Parliamentary colleagues on the Government back benches (certainly the avoidance if possible of coordinated intra-party dissent)
- Support amongst governing party activists and members (certainly the absence of anything approaching organised opposition)
- Leadership from a determined and politically astute Minister who is effective in the House of Commons.

Ministerial responsibility: individual

Ministers, both *individually* and *collectively*, are constitutionally responsible for their actions. This is not only one of the key conventions of political behaviour in Britain, but also one of the key concepts in the British system of government. Under *the doctrine of individual responsibility* Ministers have a duty accountable to Parliament for the policies, decisions and actions of their Departments. As part of this, Ministers must give accurate and truthful information to Parliament, correcting any inadvertently misleading error at the earliest opportunity. Ministers who knowingly mislead Parliament are expected to offer their resignation. A Minister who no longer enjoys the confidence of Parliament is expected to resign. Ministers in a Department are theoretically responsible for everything which happens or fails to happen within the Department and are held to account by Parliament – and increasingly by the media – for acts of omission as well as commission.

The classic view holds that Ministers are responsible for every act of their civil servants, regardless of whether or not they are fully aware of what is happening in their Departments. The most often cited example of this doctrine was the resignation of the Minister of Agriculture, *Sir Thomas Dugdale*, in the 1954 Crichel Down Affair.[7] Other examples cited usually include the resignation of *James Callaghan* as Chancellor of the Exchequer in November 1967, following the devaluation of sterling[8], and the resignation of *Lord Carrington* and two of his Ministerial colleagues at the Foreign Office in April 1982 in recognition of his Department's failure to foresee and prevent the Argentinian invasion of the Falkland Islands.[9]

Ministerial resignations often result from what can be called political necessity – namely, when there is a perceived need to assuage either party, Commons, media or public opinion or, indeed, any combination of these. Examples in this category would include the resignations of *Leon Brittan* as Secretary of State for Trade and Industry in 1986 over the Westland helicopter affair;[10] the resignations of *Peter Mandelson* as Secretary of State for Trade and Industry and Geoffrey Robinson as Paymaster General in 1998 over an undeclared home loan of £373,000 from the latter to the former; the resignation – again – of *Peter Mandelson* as Secretary of State for Northern Ireland in 2001 over the so-called 'Hinduja passport affair'; the resignation of *Stephen Byers* as Secretary of State for Transport, Local Government and the Regions in 2002 in the aftermath of the so-called 'Jo Moore affair' following months of pressure from the media; the resignation in 2004 of *Beverley Hughes* as Minister of State at the Home Office for having 'unwittingly misled MPs' over the operation of immigration policy; and the resignation in December 2004 of *David Blunkett* as Home Secretary following a string of allegations about his conduct as a Minister, notably that he had used his position as Home Secretary to 'fast track' a visa for his lover's Filipino nanny.

On the other hand, there are a large number of examples of Ministers *not* resigning, even when their policies have failed and their personal reputations have been damaged. For example, *John Davies* did not resign as Secretary of State for Trade and Industry in 1972 after the failure of the Vehicle and General insurance company. *Tony Benn* did not resign as Secretary of State for Industry in 1974 in the wake of the collapse of the Court Line Company. *Norman*

Lamont did not resign as Chancellor of the Exchequer in September 1992 following the forced withdrawal of sterling from the Exchange Rate Mechanism of the European Monetary System. *Michael Howard* did not resign as Home Secretary in April 1995 when the Courts threw out his cost-cutting Crime Injuries Scheme, even though he was accused of abusing power and flouting the will of Parliament. Neither did *William Waldegrave* or *Sir Nicholas Lyell* following criticisms in the Scott Report into the Arms to Iraq affair in 1996. Nor did *Robin Cook* resign as Foreign Secretary despite damning criticisms of his Department contained in a House of Commons Select Committee report into the arms to Sierra Leone affair in 1999. Moreover, Prime Ministers have occasionally challenged the whole concept of Ministerial responsibility – for example, Margaret Thatcher refused to accept either the resignation of *William Whitelaw* as Home Secretary following a widely publicised breach of security at Buckingham Palace in 1982, or that of *James Prior* as Secretary of State for Northern Ireland following a mass escape from the Maze prison in September 1983.[11] John Major stood by *Kenneth Baker*, then Home Secretary, when in July 1991 two Republican prisoners escaped from Brixton Prison; by *Peter Lilley*, then Secretary of State for Trade and Industry, following revelations in July 1991 that his Department had sanctioned the sale of nuclear and chemical material to Iraq until three days after the August 1990 Iraq invasion of Kuwait; and by *Michael Howard* when he did not resign as Home Secretary in 1995 over escapes from Parkhurst prison but dismissed the chief executive of the Prisons Agency instead.

A factor that should be noted, however, is that resigning (or not resigning) at the moment in question, are not the only possible outcomes. It may be that in a subsequent reshuffle at a quieter moment the Minister concerned is moved sideways, demoted or dropped altogether. For example, *Nick Brown*, who as Minister for Agriculture had been the target of considerable criticism from the public and the media about his Departments mishandling of the foot-and-mouth outbreak in 2001, was later demoted to Minister of State at the Department of Work and Pensions and subsequently dropped altogether. It is apparent, therefore, that there are no hard-and-fast rules which determine the application of Ministerial responsibility in all cases and the outcome depends on an unpredictable mixture of precedents and political circumstances. In contemporary conditions the factors which determine whether or not Ministers resign from office seem to depend more on the extent to which they still command the confidence of the Prime Minister, the Chief Whip and Government backbenchers than on any objective assessment of the incompetence or impropriety of the action or inaction for which they may be criticised. In other words, holding on to Ministerial office seems to have taken precedence over principled resignation in the majority of cases.

Nonetheless, it is worth noting that principled resignations do occur. Indeed, an example of this occurred in October 2002 when the then Education Secretary, *Estelle Morris*, resigned after a succession of bruising rows had destroyed her confidence to do the job, declaring: *'I've learned what I'm good at, and also what I'm less good at. I'm good at dealing with the issues and the teaching profession. I'm less good at strategic management of a huge Department and I'm not good at dealing with the media. In recent situations I have not felt I have been as effective as I should be.'* [12] Resigning for 'not being up to the job' is certainly unusual and this case is an interesting addition to the very short list of those Ministers who have resigned from office as a result of failures in policy and delivery.

Resignations also occur as a result of serious policy disagreements within Government. This was the case with the resignations of *Michael Heseltine* in 1986 over the Prime Minister's management of the Westland affair; *Nigel Lawson* in 1989 over the Prime Minister's conduct of economic policy and the role of her special adviser, Sir Alan Walters; *Geoffrey Howe* in 1990 over the Prime Minister's style of leadership on the issue of European cooperation; *Robin Cook* in March 2003 over the Government's failure to secure a clear UN mandate for war in Iraq; and *Clare Short* in May 2003 over what she claimed was a lack of consultation about the post-war reconstruction of Iraq.

Ministerial resignations can also arise for personal reasons – a clash with business interests, lack of career development, declining health, strained family relations, and so on. For example, in June 2003 the then Health Secretary, *Alan Milburn*, resigned from the Cabinet explaining that he was finding it hard to balance the demands of the job with the demands of having a young family, but was subsequently prevailed upon by the Prime Minister to the Cabinet in September 2004 in the run-up to the 2005 General Election. In cases of resignation 'for personal reasons' there can, of course, be a disparity between the officially stated reason and the real underlying reason, since it may be in the best interests of all concerned to mask evidence of personal incompetence or policy disagreement which may have been the real reason for a resignation.

The chain of responsibility in a Department is hierarchical, which means that civil servants and junior Ministers alike report to senior Ministers at the head of their Departments and it is the latter who are supposed to take the ultimate responsibility for their action or inaction. Of course, there have been times when junior Ministers have been so out of sympathy with a particular policy of their Department or the Government as a whole that they have felt bound to resign. This was the case, for example, with *Ian Gow* who resigned as Minister of State at the Treasury in 1985 in protest against the Anglo-Irish Agreement;[13] and with both *John Denman* (Minister of State at the Home Office) and *Lord Hunt of Kings Heath* (Parliamentary Undersecretary at the Department of Health), who resigned in 2003 in protest over Government policy in Iraq. Others have resigned in order to be free to criticise Government policy more generally – as was the case over policy towards Europe which led to the resignation of *David Heathcoat-Amory* as Paymaster General in 1996. Yet on the whole junior Ministers stay at their posts and tender their resignations only if they are obliged to do so in the course of a Ministerial reshuffle or as a result of political pressure arising from some scandal publicised by the media.

In short, it seems that *individual Ministerial responsibility* has been blurred and eroded in modern times by the size and complexity of modern Government. This is because it has been effectively impossible for Ministers to be aware of, let alone control, everything which happens or fails to happen in their Departments. For example, thousands of planning appeals have to be decided every year by the responsible Department, many of them important and nearly all of them complicated and contentious. Yet no Minister can possibly consider all of them personally, so civil servants often take the decisions in the Minister's name. In most cases individual Ministerial responsibility has become little more than a constitutional 'cloak', a convenient fiction for Parliamentary and Civil Service purposes, but a convention which is put strictly into practice on rather few occasions.

Ministerial responsibility: collective

Collective Ministerial responsibility is a reality in modern political conditions, because it reflects the collegiate and usually cohesive nature of single party Government in Britain. It is really a way of expressing the fact that all Ministers and Whips – and, indeed, Parliamentary Private Secretaries too – are bound to support Government policy and are expected to stand by it and speak and vote for it. While politicians cannot really be expected to believe totally in everything which they have to support in public for reasons of party loyalty, those who are covered by collective Ministerial responsibility are expected to support the Government on all occasions. If they feel unable or unwilling to do so, they are supposed to resign or can expect to be dismissed.[14]

It should come as no surprise, however, that the convention of collective responsibility has not always been fully observed. On those, admittedly rare, occasions when Governments have been so split that collective responsibility has been effectively impossible, temporary suspension has become the only effective course. For example, in 1931 there was an open 'agreement to differ' in the National Government on the issue of tariff reform, and in 1975 during the European Referendum campaign Labour Cabinet Ministers were allowed to argue against each other on public platforms. It will be interesting to see if this device is used again during a future Euro-referendum campaign. It should also be noted that individual ministers can be skilled at letting their views be known without stepping formally out of line with Government policy. It is unwise, however, for those covered by collective responsibility to test the boundaries of the permissible too obviously or too often, since in doing so they are quite likely to invite dismissal by the Prime Minister of the day. On the whole, therefore, collective Ministerial responsibility is a reality in British central Government and it needs to be if the process of government is to be reasonably coherent and cohesive.

Parliamentary accountability

The proper constitutional check on the power of the Executive in Britain and the counterpart to Ministerial responsibility is to be found in Ministerial accountability to Parliament. This can be achieved in three ways. None of these is adequate on its own, but taken together there are some safeguards for the public interest between General Elections.

Firstly, there are the opportunities for MPs and Peers to hold Ministers to account during proceedings in both Houses of Parliament at Question Time, following Ministerial statements and during debates. Yet the scope for effective Parliamentary influence in such proceedings is limited by the ability of most competent Ministers to answer points in Parliament without revealing much substantial information, if they do not want to do so. Experience also shows that such proceedings in the Commons can be a rather empty ritual, since any attempt at a strong Parliamentary challenge often gives way to party-political point-scoring.

Secondly, there are opportunities for MPs and peers to probe Ministerial thinking and Government policy during Select Committee investigations and during the committee stage of Government Bills. These have proved to be somewhat more effective mechanisms for Parliamentary influence. Yet, in the former case, the effectiveness of such investigations can be limited by the unwillingness of Governments to act on the recommendations of Select Committees and occasionally even to allow certain witnesses to appear before the Committee at all.[15] In the latter case, legislative scrutiny by the Opposition parties in Standing Committees has to be set against the normal voting power of the Government majority both in Standing Committees and subsequently on the floor of the House at Report and Third Reading. However, the more balanced the arithmetic of support for the parties in the House of Lords and the influence of the Delegated Powers and Regulatory Reform Committee mean that Ministers are often significantly challenged by the more independent minded Second Chamber.

Thirdly, there are the various opportunities for MPs and peers to use their power of publicity to dramatise the errors of Ministers or the shortcomings of Government policy. The principal effect of this form of Parliamentary accountability has been to encourage an attitude of caution on the part of civil servants and to reinforce the tendency for Whitehall Departments to play safe in the conduct of Government business. It is the capricious and unpredictable quality of such Parliamentary accountability which has led both Ministers and officials to treat it with wary respect. This has had a marked influence on attitudes and working practices in Whitehall and may have discouraged bold or imaginative decision making by Ministers.

If we reflect upon the various forms of Parliamentary accountability, we discover that none of them has proved to be particularly effective. The lack of accountability has been most marked in the detailed areas of policy covered by Statutory Instruments, the secondary legislation which is drafted by civil servants in the name of Ministers and lawfully implemented under the authority of existing statutes. In effect, legislation of this type is no longer fully under effective Parliamentary control. Although there is a Joint Committee on Statutory Instruments, a Sifting Committee in the Commons and a Merits

Committee in the Lords, the challenge remains almost unmanageable now that there are more than 2000 Statutory Instruments issued each year. The volume of such secondary legislation and the shortcomings of Parliamentary procedures for dealing with it are such that genuine Parliamentary accountability is almost unattainable.

The other notable area in which Parliamentary accountability has been defective is that of *European Legislation*. Under the 1972 European Communities Act the British Government is obliged to implement automatically the *Regulations* issued by the European Commission, notably in the spheres of agriculture, trade and competition policy, and to find appropriate national means of carrying out the *Directives* which flow from decisions taken by the Council of Ministers. In 1974 both the House of Commons and the House of Lords established Select Committees to sift draft European legislation and to make recommendations as to whether or not the various items contained therein were sufficiently important to merit a debate on the floor of their respective chambers. As things have turned out, such debates (in the House of Commons at any rate) have been brief and comparatively rare. However, in more recent times both Houses have equipped themselves better to deal with European legislation. The Commons has created a European Scrutiny Committee for the examination of EU proposals before Ministers take decisions in their meetings in Brussels and the development of the parallel chamber off Westminster Hall has created further opportunities to debate European legislative proposals. The Lords for its part has developed an elaborate structure of eight European Select Committees (a main Committee and seven Subcommittees) which comprehensively examine European legislative proposals as far 'upstream' as possible and then report their conclusions for possible debate by the House as a whole. These structures of Parliamentary accountability are a great improvement upon the situation which applied in the past.

Special Advisers

Although Special Advisers are technically civil servants they are political appointees installed by Ministers. As a result their position is dependent upon the Minister concerned, in that if a Minister is moved to another Department the Special Adviser may also move and if a Minister is sacked or resigns the Special Adviser – in most cases – also loses his or her position. In July 2006 there were 84 Special Advisers in post, of whom 25 were in No. 10 and 10 in the Treasury. The Foreign and Commonwealth Office had 6 and most other departments had no more than 2 each. Their total cost was £5.9m in 2005–06.

The role of Special Advisers is to give political, presentational and policy advice to Ministers, in effect providing a party-political dimension to the advice provided to a Minister – something that the civil service is not permitted to do.

The Civil Service (Amendment) Order in Council 1997, passed shortly after New Labour came into power, provided that up to three special advisers (in practice, three working for the Prime Minister) could exercise management control over permanent civil servants. In 2004 it was announced that, with the exception of two Special Advisers based in No.10 Downing Street, Special Advisers would not be able to authorise expenditure, exercise line management responsibility over permanent civil servants, or discharge any statutory power.

Following the drawing up of a revised Code of Conduct for Special Advisers in 2005,[1616] Special Advisers have been allowed to 'give assistance [to Ministers] on any aspect of departmental business' rather than simply provide advice. This appeared to give Special Advisers rather more power, although in practice it probably made very little difference.

13.3 the balance of power in central Government

One question which has to be faced by all Governments is whether or not Ministers are really in control of their Departments and therefore able to give political impetus to the Government as a whole. The answer to this question varies from Minister to Minister, from Department to Department and from time to time. In this section we examine some of the problems which make it hard to give a convincing, affirmative answer to this question.

Ministerial workload

One major problem of British central Government is the heavy workload which Ministers have to bear. The size, scope and complexity of some Departments militate against the idea that Ministers can readily dominate or control every aspect of their Department's activities. Yet this is what they are expected to do, notwithstanding the extra requirements imposed upon them by the insatiable demands of the media and the functions of the European Union. In view of the collegiate nature of central Government in Britain, it is a problem with which all Ministers have to cope to a greater or lesser extent.

The privatisation of much of the previously large public sector has been one way of lightening the burden on Ministers. This process occurred between 1979 and 1997 under successive Conservative Governments and by 1997 it had reduced the state industrial sector by about two-thirds. It has continued since then, although on a reduced scale and in somewhat disguised form. Thus the areas of activity for which Ministers are held directly responsible have diminished, even if this does not seem to have reduced the extent to which the general public is apt to blame Ministers for things which go wrong in any aspect of modern life.

One possibility for a further reduction in the range of tasks which Ministers are expected to perform would be to relieve them of their constituency duties as in France or of their responsibilities for the administration of policy as in Sweden. While the former idea is probably a non-starter in Britain, because backbenchers like to ensure that Ministers have to deal with the same constituency problems as themselves, the latter idea has effectively been implemented with the establishment of so many agencies which operate at arm's length from their parent Departments.

Of course, the problems of Ministerial workload are exacerbated by some of the conventions of central Government, notably the assumption that Ministers will consult widely and systematically before taking major decisions or introducing important new legislation. Admittedly, many of these consultations with interest groups and other stakeholders are conducted by civil servants on behalf of Ministers. Yet Ministers still have to lay down the political guidelines for such discussions and in some cases have to take a leading part in them as well.

Departmental policy

Another problem of central Government is the continuously powerful influence of established Departmental policy. This may not make itself felt very much during the first year or two following a General Election, but it can assume considerable importance as time goes by if the political momentum of the party in office begins to falter. This phenomenon was particularly noticeable during the period of the post-war consensus from 1945 to 1973 and especially in the well-established Departments with long traditions and considerable self-confidence, such as the Treasury, the Foreign Office and the Home Office. Yet the outcome of tussels between Ministers and civil servants is never a foregone conclusion. Much depends upon whether Ministers are determined to carry out their policies and impose their authority on the Government as a whole. If they are determined, both the realities of political authority and the conventions of Whitehall should enable them to get their own way. If they are not determined, the underlying strength of Departmental policy may triumph in the end.

The strength of Departmental policy is enhanced by the conditions of Ministerial life, notably the tendency for Prime Ministers to shift Ministers from post to post quite frequently, sometimes simply to assert Prime Ministerial authority. Typically, a Minister may hold office for about two years, although there have been examples of them holding an office for less time than this. The classic case would be that of John Reid in the Governments led by Tony Blair who held nine ministerial posts in the ten years between 1997 and 2007, four of them in less than one year. The situation under Tony Blair was similar for junior Ministers. For example, between 1997 and 2007 there were six asylum Ministers, six Africa Ministers, seven Europe Ministers and nine Ministers for immigration.[17] Hence many are precluded from making anything more than a temporary or marginal impact upon the political issues with which they have to deal. Nonetheless, examples of Ministerial continuity also exist, not least of all the case of Gordon Brown who served as Chancellor of the Exchequer under Tony Blair throughout the ten years of his Premiership.

The enduring strength of Departmental policy is also enhanced by some of the habits of Civil Service life. This is because it has been customary to move civil servants in the higher administrative grades frequently from one job to another either within a single Department or sometimes between Departments. In many instances this means that key personnel may stay in post for only a year or two, with the result that they do not really have time to develop their own contribution to the policy area concerned. Although an able civil servant is very good at coming to grips with new policy areas – one of the professional skills which mark them out as 'high flyers' – the inevitable consequence is that they may have to rely upon Departmental 'experts' and especially upon what is already in Departmental filing cabinets – in other words the accumulated wisdom of established Departmental policy. Such tendencies can only be overcome by sustained political will on the part of Ministers and significant changes in the continuous professional development of civil servants – developments which have been notable features of New Labour's modernization agenda.

the quality of advice

Another problem of central Government is the quality of official information and advice available to Ministers. While such material is a source of strength for Ministers in relation to the Opposition and all backbenchers, it does not necessarily strengthen their position within their own Departments. This is because it is not unusual for politicians who become Ministers to be posted to a Department about which they know little or nothing and which deals with areas of policy of which they have had little or no previous experience.[18] Even when Ministers appoint expert Special Advisers from outside the Civil Service, such outsiders may be 'domesticated' by their Departments and are unlikely on their own to be able to provide their Minister with sufficiently weighty advice to counter the established Departmental view. The result is that, unless Ministers are engaged in the implementation of clear Manifesto commitments or are pushing through other forms of unambiguous party policy, they are obliged to rely on the advice from their Departmental civil servants.

This is an unfortunate state of affairs for two reasons. First, the best answers to many of the most difficult problems of central Government are not necessarily to be found either in the claims of party Manifestos or in the drawers of Departmental filing cabinets. Second, the policy and decision-making process may be deprived of some high-quality information and advice from 'outsiders' who are both expert in their field and independent of Government. Some of this has changed with the tendency for Prime Ministers to hold policy seminars and other 'brainstorming' sessions at Chequers or 10 Downing Street. It has also been modified by the growing tendency among very senior Ministers to establish their own channels of communication with business people and other influential advisers who may or may not have an official position within Whitehall.[19]

13.4 conclusion

Well-qualified observers of British politics and some distinguished practitioners have argued for years about whether or not Ministers are really in control of their Departments. As long ago as the 1850s Lord Palmerston wrote to Queen Victoria: 'Your Majesty will see how greatly such a system [of government] must place in the hands of the subordinate members of public Departments [civil servants] the power of directing the policy and the measures of the Government, because the value, tendency and consequence of a measure frequently depends as much upon the manner in which it was worked out [that is, administered] as the intention and spirit with which it was planned.'[20] This was one of the earliest and most famous statements of the now familiar argument that in the process of government the power to administer can be as important as the power to decide. On the other hand, Herbert Morrison wrote in the 1950s that 'if the Minister in charge [of a Department] knows what he wants and is intelligent in going about it, he can command the understanding, co-operation and support of his civil servants.'[21] This statement from a senior Labour Minister with Departmental experience dating back to before the Second World War could be interpreted as an affirmation of Ministerial dominance in Whitehall. Yet it could also be interpreted as a back-handed compliment to the power of the Civil Service and a warning that Whitehall officials tend to fill any vacuum which may be left by Ministers. Clearly it is necessary to refine the conventional statement that Ministers decide the policy and civil servants simply carry it out. The modern realities are more subtle, and the traditional model takes insufficient account of the complexities of modern Government.

What we see is an *interdependent working relationship between civil servants and Ministers*. Civil servants look to Ministers to be clear about the policy objectives they wish to pursue, to heed advice on the likely consequences and methods of implementation, to be able to carry their Ministerial colleagues with them, and to present a convincing case for the policy to Parliament, the media and the general public. Ministers look to civil servants to be responsive to their political directions, to provide accurate, candid, clear and constructive advice on policy, and to conduct efficient administration of the Department and its Agencies.

In modern conditions it is, of course, possible for Ministers to exercise clear political leadership and there have been many examples of this over the past 30 years or so. Yet the long timescale and great complexity of decision making in Government, and the limited scope for truly autonomous political action, all tend to reduce the impact of Ministerial leadership. The broad conclusion may be that Ministers are in charge of their Departments and of the Government as a whole, but only within the limits set by established administrative conventions and the uncompromising political and economic realities in Britain today.

SUGGESTED QUESTIONS

1   Describe the structure and work of British central Government.
2   The tradition that Ministers take the political decisions and civil servants carry them out has long been overtaken by reality. What factors give rise to such a view and how valid are they?
3   What problems are associated with the administration of British central Government? Are they capable of solution within existing institutions and conventions?

the Civil Service

In this chapter we are concerned mainly with those civil servants who work directly for Ministers, especially those in the Senior Civil Service – a category created in 1996 and consisting of about 3500 people. We are therefore examining the relatively small administrative elite at the heart of British central Government – known in short hand terms as 'Whitehall' after the street in central London in which a number of Government Departments have their headquarters.

14.1 composition

In Britain the standard definition of a civil servant is still based upon the formulation offered by the Tomlin Commission in 1931, namely 'a servant of the Crown employed in a civil capacity who is paid wholly and directly from money voted by Parliament.'[1] In April 2007 there were some 515,650 civil servants (full-time equivalents), a figure well below the high point of more than 740,000 in 1979 when the first Thatcher Administration came to power. A growing proportion (about 16 per cent) of all staff work part-time and a much larger proportion (about 52 per cent) are female, while about 8 per cent are from ethnic minorities and about 4 per cent have some kind of disability. Of the total number of civil servants in 2007, only around 18 per cent work in London (compared with about half in 1967). Indeed, by April 2007 about three-quarters of all civil servants were working for Executive Agencies many of which had their headquarters and most of their operations outside London.

Civil Service numbers are distributed unevenly between various Departments and more than 130 Agencies. The four largest Departments (together with their satellite Agencies) account for about two-thirds of all civil servants, while the three smallest Departments each have fewer than 40 staff on a full-time equivalent basis. The Treasury with just over 1000 civil servants is the most powerful and prestigious Department with the principal tasks of controlling public expenditure and advising the Chancellor of the Exchequer on various aspects of macro- and micro-economic policy. The

Ministry of Defence with over 90,000 civil servants has the tasks of advising the Secretary of State on matters of defence policy and providing civilian control of and support for the armed forces. In terms of personnel, the three largest Departments are Work and Pensions (125,170), Defence (91,430) and HM Revenue & Customs (103,691). In terms of public expenditure incurred, the most significant Departments are Work and Pensions, Health, Education and Skills and Defence.[2]

In a typical Whitehall Department (if there can be said to be such a thing), perhaps half the civil servants are involved in the administrative tasks of central Government (delivery in modern parlance), while the other half perform a range of technical, scientific and support functions for Ministers and for their bureaucratic colleagues. Perhaps 20,000 civil servants are involved in one way or another in contributions to the policy- and decision-making process, although only about 3500 have close and frequent face-to-face contacts with Ministers. It is this small policy-advising elite which over the years has established the conventions of Whitehall and determined much of the traditional character of the British Civil Service.

Beyond the bureaucratic core, there is a bewildering variety of public bodies which exist within the orbit of Whitehall Departments. However, most of these bodies are situated outside London and increasingly outside the South East. The variety of Governmental institutions is best conveyed by a diagram and a schematic representation is offered in Figure 14.1.

What many of these institutions have in common is that they work for central Government and in the name of the Crown, although only a few of them actually involve Royal appointments. The common purposes of nearly all these bodies include policy advice, policy delivery, regulation and oversight. British central Government could not function satisfactorily without most of them, although it would be a brave person who asserted that all of them are vital to the commonweal.

14.2 functions

The Civil Service in Britain today has a wide range of distinct, but interconnected functions. Some of these are traditional and date back at least to the Northcote-Trevelyan Report in 1854, whereas some of them are modern and inspired by the contemporary needs of government in the twenty-first century. The traditional functions include:

• Informing and advising Ministers
• Helping Ministers to formulate policy and make decisions
• Helping Ministers to get legislation through Parliament
• Drafting Ministerial memoranda and correspondence
• Representing Ministers in meetings within Government
• Representing Ministers in meetings with outsiders
• Managing the bureaucracy of central Government.

Prime Minister and Cabinet
- Most decisions taken in one or other of 33 Cabinet Committees and 16 Sub-Committees – to be endorsed later by the full Cabinet
- Other decisions taken in bilateral meetings between the PM and individual Ministers or between a Treasury Minister and Ministers from delivery Departments

Central Departments and Office (PM's Office, Cabinet Office, Treasury)
- Provide the political leadership and coordination of Government policy (PM and Chancellor)
- Supervise public expenditure, taxation, Public Service Agreements and Capability Reviews etc. (HM Treasury)
- Provide the focus and strategic goals for nearly all Administrations at nearly all times (PM and Chancellor)
- Perform coordinating roles in central Government and spread best practice throughout Whitehall (Cabinet Office)

Functional (delivery) Departments and Offices (e.g. Health, Transport, etc.)
- Provide information and policy advice to Ministers
- Provide facts, submissions and defensive briefing
- Support Ministers in preparing and carrying legislation through both Houses of Parliament
- Administer and oversee the early stages of policy delivery, often via executive Agencies
- Share responsibility with Ministers for upholding the integrity and probity of public administration
- Liaise with devolved Administrations, Government Offices for the Regions and local government

Territorial Offices (Scotland, Wales, Northern Ireland)
- Perform many of the same tasks as functional Departments, but intensively than before the development of devolution
- Liaise with the devolved Administrations to ensure UK-wide compatibility of policy and administration
- Represent the UK in dealings with the devolved Administrations and devolved interests in dealings with UK central Government

Legal Departments and Offices (Ministry of Justice, Law Offices, etc.)
- Provide legal advice to the Cabinet and the Government
- Take the lead within central Government on legal and constitutional issues
- Administer the Courts and Tribunals (England and Wales), supervise judicial appointments and conduct of judiciary
- Assist the Judicial Committee in providing appellate jurisdiction for some Overseas Territories and some professional bodies
- Provide final adjudication in the event of any serious disputes occurring between the Government and the devolved Administrations
- Support Ministers attending the Privy Council
- Draft Government Hills (Parliamentary Counsel)

Parliamentary Offices (Commons Leader, Lords leader, Whips)
- Advise the Prime Minister and other Ministers on the likely back-bench reaction to Government initiatives, Bills and other measures in both Houses of Parliament
- Manage Government business in both Houses of Parliament – under the guidance of the Legislative Programme Committee of the Cabinet
- Perform the often delicate and occasionally brutal tasks of maximising Parliamentary support for the Government's measures in both Houses (Whips)
- Support the Leaders of both Houses in their duties in Parliament

Multi-purpose Public Offices (Deputy PM, Minister without Portfolio, etc.)
- Represent the campaigning and electoral interests of the governing party at the top level of central Government
- Promote good triangular relations between Ministers, the Parliamentary Party and the Party in the country
- Act as leading spokesmen in the media for Government policy and its achievements
- Promote the cause of social inclusion
- Oversee the administration of certain Royal Estates in London, Lancashire and Cornwall

Executive Agencies and other public bodies (e.g. Prison Service, DVLA, etc.)
- The specialised focus of such bodies can improve policy delivery

figure **14.1** **schematic representation of governmental institutions**

Ministers have constant needs to be well briefed and generally to seem on top of their responsibilities in order to impress the media and reassure the general public. Because of the complexity of modern political life and the level of media and public expectations, they could not adequately perform their various tasks without the constant help and support of their Private Offices (staffed by civil servants) and of their Departments in general. Indeed, because of the cross-cutting nature of many political problems, Ministers, both individually and collectively, will often need briefing and assistance from civil servants in several Departments and Agencies across Whitehall. Such work has, therefore, to be coordinated by either the Cabinet Office or the relevant lead Department which will take charge of Civil Service input into Ministerial policy and decision making.

In doing this vital work, civil servants are not usually expected to be highly original; rather there is a premium upon their ability to be accurate, up-to-date and wise in the material they provide – material which is often drawn either from the body of knowledge and information already held within central Government or from acknowledged and trusted experts to whom recourse can be had when necessary. Civil servants also provide information and advice against which Ministers and their Special Advisers can test the soundness or otherwise of their political ideas or their party commitments made in speeches, pamphlets and Manifestos.

In helping Ministers to get legislation through Parliament, civil servants are involved in some of the most intensive, but often rewarding, work that crosses their desks or populates their computers. With Government sponsored public Bills representing the dominant proportion of the legislation handled by Parliament every year, civil servants who work on Bill teams, or who contribute information and advice to such support groups, can find themselves working very long hours for weeks or even months on end. The burdens borne by those most closely involved are considerable and have seemingly not been much diminished by the introduction of timetabling for all Government Bills in the Commons. The House of Lords is, as yet, a different matter in that its determination to cling to self-regulation and the fact that the governing party does not have an overall majority in the Second Chamber mean that the burdens of briefing Ministers in the Lords are, if anything, greater than those involved in dealing with legislative scrutiny in the Commons.

Reflecting the emphasis upon interdepartmental working, senior civil servants spend much of their time representing the views and positions of their Departments or Agencies on committees and working groups within Whitehall. Sometimes they will be taking the initiative at a bureaucratic level; sometimes they will be representing their Ministers or Agency Chief Executives in gatherings designed to prepare the way for subsequent high-level decisions. At all times they need to be careful not to go beyond the bounds of their own responsibilities or to trespass into the essentially political spheres of their Ministers. This involves striking some tricky balances between the administrative and the political, but it is something which they are frequently expected to do. When involved in meetings or correspondence with stakeholders, who will probably be familiar with the key aspects of Government policy but who will not necessarily be allowed into every bureaucratic loop, civil servants are wise to err on the side of caution by not revealing any more than their interlocutors need to know in order to contribute to the policy-making process.

In rehearsing the main elements of civil service work, mention should also be made of the personal responsibilities of Permanent Secretaries and Chief

Executive Officers who act as the Accounting Officers of their Departments or Agencies respectively. In this capacity each of these very senior civil servants is responsible for the good management of the bureaucracies which they lead, and especially the public expenditure incurred for which they have to answer retrospectively and in detail to the Public Accounts Committee of the House of Commons. Such financial accountability is taken very seriously by all Accounting Officers, although it should be added that the severity of the 'punishment' used by the PAC (and the National Audit Office which supports it) whenever egregious errors have been made does not seem to be as impressive as the conventional folklore might lead people to believe. Furthermore, if any Accounting Officer really wishes to guard his back, he or she has only to insist upon an explicit written instruction from the relevant Secretary of State in order to be placed in the clear in the event of any PAC criticism.

Since 1997 the modern functions of civil servants, especially those in the Senior Civil Service, have become much more managerial and concerned with the *delivery* of public policy and of the objectives set by Ministers for the benefit of the British public. For example, Ministers may be committed to raising the standards of state education, improving the standards of health care in the NHS, improving the safety and reliability of public transport, raising the level of social security benefits or the efficiency of the tax system, improving levels of public safety against threats from criminals or terrorists and many other worthy objectives set by Ministers for the various public services. Civil servants will often have to achieve these goals in *partnership* with the private and voluntary sectors and will therefore have to be familiar with best practice beyond the boundaries of public administration.

This shift of emphasis in the balance of the work done by civil servants has been driven in large part by the creation of about 130 Executive Agencies which often operate on a highly focused basis to 'deliver' Departmental objectives in a particular area of policy or public service. For example the Department for Work and Pensions is responsible for staffing and managing the network of front-line offices known under the generic title of Job Centre Plus.

14.3 permanent values and changing conventions

Ever since the Northcote-Trevelyan Report in 1854, British civil servants have clung to some precious permanent values which have been reiterated by successive Cabinet Secretaries and Heads of the Home Civil Service. These include, but are not necessarily confined to, the following:

 • *Integrity* – in the sense of not succumbing to the temptation to be anything less than totally upright and correct in the conduct of their professional lives
 • *Impartiality* – in the sense of not taking sides politically, so that in the future they are able to serve Ministers of any political persuasion

- *Honesty* – in the sense of 'speaking truth unto power' and giving honest advice to Ministers without fear or favour
- *Objectivity* – in the sense of analysing problems and making considered recommendations to Ministers which are objectively based upon the best available information and evidence.

Against the background of these timeless principles, Ministerial expectations – and hence the conventions of civil service behaviour – have subtly changed from one decade to another and often from one Administration to another. For example, most civil servants before 1979 were involved in public administration at one level of sophistication or another, depending upon their rank and responsibilities in the various Departmental hierarchies. This began to change under Margaret Thatcher who deliberately set out to make the Civil Service smaller and more delivery orientated and who achieved her radical goals by privatising most of the activities previously performed by the industrial civil service (for example, the Royal Naval Dockyards) and in the late 1980s by introducing so-called Next Steps or Executive Agencies to do much of the service delivery work previously done by the same state employees within Departments. Her successor at 10 Downing Street, John Major, took this policy one stage further by requiring many civil servants who had direct contact with the public to heed the principles of his so-called Citizen's Charter which he introduced with a great fanfare in 1991. In essence, this was designed to ensure that civil servants at all levels spend more time and nervous energy focusing upon how they can deliver public services more effectively to the British people and less upon pandering to the sometimes idiosyncratic whims of Ministers involved in the making and presentation of policy.

This culture shift under two successive Conservative Administrations marked a significant development in the role of civil servants which, when originally laid down in the Northcote-Trevelyan Report, had been 'to advise, assist and, to some extent, influence those who are set over them (Ministers) from time to time.'[3] It also indicated a move away from the traditional Whitehall culture of the gifted generalist which had been lauded by Lord Bridges (Secretary to the Cabinet and Head of the Home Civil Service from 1938 to 1947) when he defined a good civil servant as someone 'who knows how and where to find reliable knowledge, can assess the expertise of others at its true worth, can spot the strong and weak points in any situation at short notice, and can advise upon how to handle a complex situation.'[4] Of course, these traditional skills of the British mandarin class are not to be derided, even in the very different circumstances of today, since it can be said that there is professional skill involved in public administration and the insight of generalists can often be a useful complement to the methodology of any number of trained specialists in 'new public management'.

Moreover, in the Civil Service reforms sponsored by the Wilson Labour Government from 1966 to 1970 and later by the Blair and Brown Labour Government from 1997, there has been a continuing subtext which has been the desire of Ministers to broaden the intake into the Civil Service and remove the barriers which had stood in the way of entry and promotion on merit (a

Northcote-Trevelyan principle) for traditionally excluded or under-represented groups, such as people of working-class origin, women, ethnic minorities and people with disabilities. Bearing in mind that John Major also felt fairly comfortable with this general objective, it could be said that this has been part of the overall democratisation of the British Civil Service, which has been taken a long way down the road by successive Governments of various political persuasions and which is not over yet.[5]

The necessary balance between continuity and change in the British Civil Service has been reinforced by subtly changing conventions of behaviour and practice which have been sufficiently flexible to allow a series of apparent contradictions to be resolved in a satisfactory way. For example, the convention of Ministerial accountability to Parliament for issues of both policy and administration in the various Departments and Agencies of central Government means that civil servants have to put the needs of Ministers at the top of the list (especially in a crisis), notwithstanding all the rhetoric and pious objectives embodied in the Citizen's Charter and subsequent similar initiatives. Equally, the convention that civil servants should always be mindful of their duty to conduct the business of government according to the highest standards of probity and equity is a non-negotiable part of their employment contracts and of the Civil Service Code.[6] The former element often involves them in exercises of damage limitation on behalf of the Ministers they serve, while the latter element is an important criterion when fending off charges of bias or maladministration. These considerations have tended to encourage a rather cautious, even defensive, bias in the role of civil servants when advising and supporting Ministers, a situation which does not sit very easily with the Blair Government's commitment to a more entrepreneurial and innovative approach in modernised policy making.

Another time-honoured convention in Whitehall, which might be better defined as an aspiration, is that the Government of the day should at all times have a coherent and defensible position on every issue of policy or turn of events with which it has to deal. In the complex and fast moving modern world, this is a very tall order, but it is a minimum requirement for satisfactory Cabinet Government which is still supposed to be based upon the principle of collective responsibility. This means that a great deal of Civil Service time and effort is spent upon producing agreed positions to which all the relevant players in Whitehall can agree. However, it is because of this that incoherence and even chaos can sometimes overtake the governmental machinery and lead to bureaucratic shambles and ultimately Ministerial resignations.[7]

14.4 modernisation and reform

The theme of modernisation has been integral to the New Labour project ever since Tony Blair became Leader of the party in 1994. Following the overwhelming Labour victory in 1997, both Tony Blair and Gordon Brown set about carrying the principles of modernisation into practice.

In 1998 Tony Blair asked the then Cabinet Secretary, Sir Richard Wilson, to conduct an internal review of the policy and administration in central Government. This led to the publication of a key text on government modernisation, namely the White Paper entitled *Modernising Government* which appeared in March 1999 a year after the equivalent text dealing with local government.[8] In his foreword to this foundation document Tony Blair maintained that 'modernisation must go further – it must engage with how government itself works … (it) is a vital part of our programme of renewal for Britain'.

The White Paper made five main commitments:

- Forward-looking and evidence-based policy making
- Responsive public services to meet the needs of citizens rather than to suit the convenience of public-service providers
- High-quality public services with ambitious targets and rigorous performance monitoring
- Information-age technology for joined-up government and better 'customer service'
- A Civil Service of integrity reflecting the diversity of the population and capable of effective delivery.

The mechanisms for delivering these various aspects of modernisation were to be:

- Massively increased public investment (not implemented until 1999–2000) in the priority areas of education, health, transport and law and order
- Radical reform of working practices and methods of delivery both in the Civil Service and in the public sector more broadly via Public Service Agreements, Delivery Agreements and other contractual arrangements, such as Delivery Partnerships with the private and voluntary sectors
- The widespread use of the latest information technology and the temporary employment of IT and management consultants.

In March 2000 the overall plan for Civil Service and public service modernisation was applied to each Department and Agency of central Government. Since the 2001 General Election the main emphasis has been upon raising the standards of performance and delivery in the public services. This engendered a blizzard of further initiatives for effective policy delivery and vastly extended the reach of e-government to all Departments (with varying degrees of success). At the same time there has been a sustained effort to transform the capabilities and performance of all civil servants by extending a programme of Professional Skills for Government (PSG) into every corner of central Government.

This modernisation agenda built upon the reforms introduced by both the Thatcher and the Major Administrations, but in many ways Labour Ministers have gone much further than their Conservative predecessors would have dared or wished to go. The strategic intention has been to mobilise the whole resources of the public sector, often in partnership with the private and voluntary sectors, to work effectively across institutional boundaries in order to deliver positive results for the users and beneficiaries of the public services and indeed for the nation as a whole, while continuing the familiar Treasury drive for greater efficiency and cost effectiveness.

The PSG agenda sees a continuing need for core skills and traditional values in the Civil Service, but insists that truly modern and effective civil servants will, in addition, be able to demonstrate:

‣ Experience of operational delivery of public services in many different settings
‣ Experience of working with or in the private and voluntary sectors
‣ In some cases, possession of valuable professional qualifications and expertise – for example, in accountancy, information technology or human resources
‣ An ability to develop modern styles of leadership appropriate to the team-work approach so necessary when dealing with cross-cutting issues.

On top of this agenda to raise the quality of modern civil servants, New Labour Ministers have also sought to encourage a range of desirable attitudes which would demonstrate the 'modernity' of all civil servants and indeed others who work in or for the public sector. This is being done by:

‣ The pursuit of ambitious goals to increase social diversity and inclusion in a Civil Service of over 520,000 people
‣ The development of entrepreneurial and innovative attitudes to solving some of the most intractable problems facing contemporary government
‣ The willingness to share rather than hoard bureaucratic power and Civil Service capacities, so that all those involved can contribute more successfully to good governance.

So ambitious is this change agenda for possibly the largest and most transparent organisation in Britain that, if it can be successfully implemented, it will underpin a degree of cultural transformation not seen for more than a century – excluding two periods of world war.

In the first term of the Blair Administration from 1997 to 2001, the appeal of 'modernisation' seemed to be virtually unanswerable with only a few hard core Old Labour figures and a small number of discredited Conservatives inclined to put up anything more than token resistance. Following the 2001 General Election, however, when the national turnout was only 59 per cent, the perception was that the voters had put Tony Blair on notice that they expected New Labour promises to be delivered or they might be inclined to withdraw their support for the whole adventure. By the time of the 2005 election, New Labour modernisation had become more controversial and there were growing signs of scepticism and opposition, especially from the front-line professions and public-sector trade unions whose members are directly involved in delivering public services. Some of these responses suggested that many public- sector employees were becoming increasingly cynical about the methods of modernisation and that some civil servants were not prepared to do much more than recite the rhetoric of modernisation when suffering from initiative fatigue and the colonisation of their territory by an army of private sector IT and management consultants.

Against this background there are a number of leading questions about the trajectory and likely effects of further modernisation which are of concern to those civil servants who retain a reputation for impartiality and objectivity:

- Is modernisation just a matter of words, slogans and management jargon or does it have real and enduring value for those who administer policy and deliver public services?
- Has modernisation involved excessive centralisation within central Government with too much power and interference from 10 Downing Street, the Treasury and the Cabinet Office or is this a necessary price to pay for real transformation throughout Whitehall?
- Is it realistic for modernised policy to become even more New Labour or has the time come for a degree of prudent consolidation in order to ensure that the revolution is sustained in the longer term?

The British Civil Service has seen many different Administrations rise and fall and many different big ideas come and go over the century and a half since the Northcote-Trevelyan Report in 1854. It is at least possible that modernisation in its Blairite form will fade away as other seemingly compelling doctrines have done before. If so, senior civil servants will want to reflect upon the intended and the unintended consequences of this policy cycle and note that circularity is as prevalent as linearity in the British system of government.

14.5 methods of supervision and control

Over the years politicians in office and those in opposition have developed various ways of supervising and controlling the Civil Service. Each of the methods has proved useful to one or other of the participants in the process, but none has proved sufficient. It has therefore proved necessary to use all of them in one combination or another in a continuing effort to ensure that the permanent Executive behaves properly and discharges its functions in ways which benefit the electorate.

Ministerial responsibility

The classic method of controlling the Civil Service is based upon the traditional doctrine of Ministerial responsibility. The idea is that civil servants work for Ministers and Ministers are responsible for what Government does, or fails to do, in a given area of policy. It is in the interests of Ministers, therefore, to supervise and control those who act on their behalf, since they will be held responsible by Parliament, the media and the public for what civil servants do in their name at least as much as what they say or do themselves.

This doctrine was quite effective in the nineteenth century when the scope of central Government was nothing like as large as it is today and in the first half of the twentieth century when there were not many professional and full-time politicians and the practice of Ministerial resignation was largely adhered to. However, with the vast scope of government today and with Ministers who are often not prepared to accept responsibility for things done in their name about which they may have know little, if indeed anything, the doctrine is honoured much more in the breach than the observance and civil servants tend to carry the can for their own failures.

Modern central Government and its Agencies have become so large and complex that Ministers, however dutiful and energetic, cannot possibly be aware of, let alone determine, everything which happens or fails to happen within their allotted spheres of responsibility. The best that sensible Ministers can do is to insist that their civil servants draw to their attention in a timely way – that is, at a stage when Ministerial intervention could make a difference – all the most important and politically sensitive issues which arise within their allotted spheres of responsibility. This means that civil servants who work closely with Ministers must be able to distinguish between issues which are politically sensitive and run-of-the-mill public administration. If such assumptions cannot safely be made, then the whole idea of Ministerial responsibility in a modern setting is fatally flawed and out of date.

The fundamental problem is that there are only 24 hours in a day and most Ministers have neither the time nor the inclination to supervise everything which happens or fails to happen within their spheres of 'responsibility' – especially now that there are so many Executive Agencies with CEOs who are supposed to take operational responsibility for the delivery of Government policy. The net result is that Ministers sometimes resign (or are sacked by the Prime Minister) when they have become an egregious embarrassment to their colleagues in the governing party, but very rarely on the grounds of policy failure and virtually never on the grounds of defective public administration.

hierarchical management of the bureaucracy

Partly because of the shortcomings of Ministerial responsibility, line management within the bureaucracy of central Government has become the orthodox method of supervising and controlling the work of the Civil Service in Britain. Once again this approach can be traced back to the Northcote-Trevelyan Report in the mid-nineteenth century with its emphasis upon selection on merit, professional conduct and high standards of bureaucratic integrity. It was also made clear to all who joined this professional Civil Service that Ministers were responsible for policy, while senior civil servants at the head of the various Departments of central Government were responsible for the correct and prudent management of their institutional fiefdoms. Indeed, in the last decade of the twentieth century, this line management became much more corporate at the most senior levels of the bureaucracy with the Head of the Home Civil Service chairing a Permanent Secretaries' Management Board in much the same way that the chairman of a holding company in the private sector might chair a supervisory group Board consisting of the CEOs of all the subsidiary companies.

In theory, this binary division between the responsibilities of Ministers and very senior civil servants seems to have lasted until the present day. It is operated on a hierarchical principle and, even though there are now fewer layers of management in central Government Departments and Agencies than there used to be years ago, the idea of upwards accountability to your line manager who is in his or her turn accountable to someone more senior and so on right to the top of the tree has survived all the fashions and vicissitudes of frequent bouts of Whitehall reform. On the other hand, the influence of 'modernisation' has made itself felt since 1997 with greater emphasis upon 'delivery' responsibilities and upon middle and even junior management in the hierarchy being held responsible for their own actions and contributions to the collective purposes.

In practice, the most senior civil servants and the Agency Chief Executives can be so preoccupied with their roles as leading policy advisers and implementers of their Ministers' wishes that they have little time or inclination to spend upon the detailed tasks of day-to-day management. These tasks therefore have to be delegated down the line to middle- and even junior-rank civil servants who may be in charge of directorates or sections or teams. There is also a good deal of self-management at the lower levels, which is almost certainly a good thing in structures which are supposed to be influenced by a professional ethos. In such circumstances modern civil servants can fairly claim that 'we are all managers now'.

business efficiency imported from the private sector

Another relatively modern method of controlling the Civil Service is based upon the principle of business efficiency imported from the private sector. Back in 1968, this idea was one of the main thrusts of the Fulton Report[9] commissioned by Harold Wilson and it has been promoted, to a greater or lesser extent, by British Governments ever since.

The central ideas in this approach include aiming for a target level of output with reduced levels of financial and other inputs; inviting different suppliers of goods or services to tender for contracts; using cost-benefit analysis in the process of decision making; and publicising standards of private sector best practice which the public sector should aspire to achieve.

It is fair to say that such techniques imported from the private sector have not always been easily transferable to the public sector where the goals, constraints and criteria of success or failure have tended to be rather broad and often highly political. In the private sector, the main goal is usually profit, the constraints are largely market driven, and the criteria of success or failure include the assessments made by investors, customers and competitors. In the public sector, on the other hand, the goals tend to be more open-ended and changeable, the constraints include considerations of equity between citizens and recognition of 'the public interest', and the criteria of success or failure are often determined by media reactions or the changing priorities of different Ministers.

Notwithstanding the problems inherent in applying business techniques and priorities to management of the public services, successive Governments since the early 1970s have sought to make progress in this direction. Indeed, the thrust of 'modernisation' under successive Blair Administrations since 1997 has taken much further in a 'business-like' direction some of the reforms introduced by previous Conservative Administrations. This has been done by emphasising the crucial importance of 'delivery' and the need to treat all users and beneficiaries of the public services as if they were customers in the private sector with an ability to choose between competing providers and, ultimately, to take their business elsewhere (with the support of public finance) if they are not happy with the service offered in the public sector.[10]

judicial review

Yet another method of controlling the Civil Service is that of judicial review by the courts and various quasi-judicial bodies, such as administrative tribunals. The attraction of this approach used to be that it provided standards for good administrative practice without being too legalistic. However, in recent years – and especially since the passage of the Human Rights Act 1998 – Ministers and civil servants have had to be particularly alert to what is known as 'the judge over your shoulder'[11] and the possibility of judicial review being triggered by aggrieved citizens or group interests taking cases to the High Court if they believe that Ministers or civil servants have committed sins of commission or omission in the actions they have taken or failed to take.

For a long time the courts were rather cautious about challenging Ministers (or civil servants acting on behalf of Ministers), especially when it could be shown that members of the Executive were acting in good faith in pursuit of what could be defined as 'the public interest'. This meant that most judicial intervention in the acts of the Executive was based upon the doctrine of *ultra vires* which had been developed to discourage Ministers and officials from going beyond the proper limits of the law as it stood at a particular time. Apart from that, only the so-called 'Wednesbury rule' – which measured any action by a member of the Executive against the principle that it should not exceed what a reasonable person would do in reasonable circumstances – constituted a significant barrier to unreasonable use of Executive discretion.

In the more legalistic atmosphere engendered by Britain's evolving membership of the European Union and the more litigious atmosphere engendered by the idea of citizen activism imported from the United States, the courts and some administrative tribunals – for example, employment tribunals or immigration tribunals – have become bolder in their willingness to scrutinise and review acts of the Executive. Furthermore, all public Bills put before the two Houses of Parliament have to be certified by the relevant Minister as compliant with the Human Rights Act 1998 and members of the senior judiciary take a keen interest in promoting Continental axioms of jurisprudence, such as proportionality, which further inhibit some forms of Executive discretion. Short of amending or repealing some of the primary legislation from which this judicial activism derives, it seems likely that civil servants will have to devote more time and attention to these constraints when giving advice to Ministers or seeking to deliver Government policy.

Before concluding this section, mention should also be made of the Parliamentary Commissioner for Administration (commonly known as the Ombudsman) who since 1967 has had statutory authority to investigate complaints of maladministration by central Government raised by constituents and submitted mainly by MPs on their behalf. Although the Ombudsman has no powers of quasi-judicial initiative or legal enforcement on their own account and can only recommend appropriate courses of action which may involve Departments and Agencies apologising or making good their mistakes, the office has been successful over the years in rectifying faulty procedures in Whitehall and occasionally persuading a Department at fault to make an ex gratia payment by way of compensation for those with clear and justifiable grievances. These powers of publicity and persuasion, backed by the House of Commons Select Committee on Public Administration, have proved to be useful additions to the various methods available for oversight and control of the Civil Service in Britain.

14.6 perennial issues and concerns

There are several perennial issues and concerns in the continuing debate about the evolution of the Civil Service in Britain. In a sense the debate is never likely to be definitively concluded, because the Civil Service is there to serve both Ministers and the general public, as well as to be the guardians of some timeless standards of conduct in public administration. For example, since the early 1990s there has been much talk of a possible Civil Service Act to give statutory backing to the Civil Service Code and to strengthen the backbone of all civil servants if and when they find themselves at odds with Ministers. Hitherto this initiative has not seemed to attract sufficient Ministerial priority to find an urgent place in the Queen's Speech and in any case it would need to attract solid all-party support. Yet the independent Civil Service Commissioners support the idea and its hour may come if there continues to be media and public concern about excessive or insidious party-political pressures upon civil servants.

The British Civil Service has both strengths and weaknesses which stem mainly from the requirements of Ministers and the nature of British Parliamentary Government. Since the position can be regarded from at least two contrasting angles, it is wise not to be dogmatic when making an assessment. Furthermore, there has nearly always been a shifting balance between continuity and change – with the modernisation and reform initiated by the Labour Government since 1997 being only the latest example of this.

One striking element of continuity is the intellectual and advisory ability of those who find their way into the Senior Civil Service. This reflects the high entry and selection standards and the continuing attractions of a Civil Service career for people of drive and ability. It is fed by annual intakes of 'fast-streamers' who are usually identified when they join the service and who tend to benefit from accelerated promotion throughout their careers thereafter. However, since the 1990s this privileged cadre has been swollen by somewhat older recruits who come into the civil service from the private and voluntary sectors and who also benefit from accelerated promotion. This is particularly true of those with specialist qualifications in information technology, accountancy, human resources and customer delivery who can demonstrate skills needed to blend with the more traditional attributes of what used to be known as 'the administrative class'. One result of these developments is that about one third of all the direct entrants into the Senior Civil Service (Grade 5 and above) now come from outside the Service.

Policy advice for Ministers and sound delivery of Ministerial objectives are still the core functions of the most talented civil servants from any quarter who rise to the top of the core bureaucracy of central Government. However, in an organisation of more than half a million employees, there are bound to be some crucial managerial functions which are the responsibility of the senior and middle management echelons, but which do not always appeal to the people who are supposed to discharge these functions. For example, there is a basic requirement for financial accountability which is policed by the Public Accounts Committee and the National Audit Office and which imposes clear fiduciary duties upon all civil servants, but especially Permanent Secretaries of Departments and Chief Executives of Agencies in their roles as Accounting Officers.

There is also a basic requirement for sound and reliable public administration which is supposed to cascade from one level to the next throughout the many layers of the bureaucratic hierarchy. This may seem somewhat tedious to many of the high- flyers who are excited by dealing with the requirements of public policy or the arts of managing the Parliamentary process. Yet, as far as Ministers are concerned, it is an absolutely vital requirement for any Government which wishes to avoid political embarrassment, waste or scandal – as can be seen in the woeful litany of accidents, incompetence and muddle which has beset the Home Office and several other Departments in successive Administrations led by Ministers of various political stripes. The essence of this requirement is still administrative competence – ensuring that an organisation is 'fit for purpose' – and, no matter how it is dressed up in corporate jargon as 'delivery' or 'customer focus' or 'efficiency and effectiveness', it is an unglamorous necessity for any well-run state bureaucracy.

a model employer and exemplary employees?

For the best part of four decades following the Fulton Report in 1968, the British Civil Service was criticised by people on the Left for being (at least in its higher echelons) too elitist and unrepresentative of the population as a whole. Since about the mid 1990s and especially since the arrival of a 'New Labour' Government in 1997, there have been conscious efforts made at the behest of Ministers to recruit more entrants into the fast stream from universities other than Oxford or Cambridge, more women rather than men, more people from ethnic minorities and more of those with physical disabilities. These efforts have begun to pay off with the result that the Civil Service is now more representative of the UK population as a whole and able to mount a credible claim to be something of a model employer capable of setting an example to other employers in the private and voluntary sectors.[12]

The present Government's diversity agenda for the Civil Service is one way in which Labour Ministers are able to demonstrate that things are being modernised and changed for the better in the smaller public sector which remains following the long years of privatisation under both Conservative and Labour Governments. Perhaps more critical to the nation's economic and social success, however, is the ambitious programme to enhance the professional skills and competences of all civil servants.[13] This amounts to nothing less than trying to entrench and reinforce a range of behavioural changes in the bureaucracy of central Government, including more commercial attitudes, more innovation, more leadership, more risk taking and more 'customer focus' in providing benefits and services for the British public.

To be precise, the programme of continuing professional development involves the gradual acquisition throughout the Civil Service of four different categories of skills and experience. The *first* is 'leadership' which presupposes that civil servants will be able to develop and demonstrate more self-confidence in their dealings with each other and their work for Ministers. The *second* is a huge bundle of 'core skills' which includes people management, financial management, project management, analytical skills, 'strategic thinking' (whatever that may be), communication skills and marketing. The *third* category is supposed to involve the acquisition of job-related professional skills in areas such as law, accountancy and information technology. The *fourth* encourages those who aspire to reach the very top of their career ladders to acquire some relevant experience in other adjacent fields of activity, including spells in the private or voluntary sectors and in supranational or subnational government.

It remains to be seen how swiftly and how extensively these changes become rooted in the soil of the Civil Service in Britain. If this sort of 'modernisation' is taken up by the Opposition parties, then it seems likely that it will be here to stay for a considerable period of time. After all, the context within which the Civil Service and the public services operate is changing swiftly and extensively and this includes some far-reaching changes in the public expectations to which elected politicians seek to respond.

loyalty to Ministers and the public interest

In the 2006 version of the Civil Service Code, civil servants are servants of the Crown and owe their loyalty to the Administrations in which they serve (which constitutionally form part of the Crown). This means loyalty to the UK Government of the day and to the devolved Administrations in both Scotland and Wales – and also in Northern Ireland when circumstances permit – subject only to the provisions of the Code. However, the proviso is important because the Code lays down a number of important principles which should govern the behaviour of civil servants and, if necessary, protect them from any unreasonable demands made by Ministers.

Civil servants therefore have a duty to conduct themselves with integrity, impartiality and honesty, and these values should inform all their dealings with Ministers and with the general public. In the course of discharging their responsibilities, they should recognise:

▸ The accountability of civil servants to Ministers
▸ The duty to discharge their functions reasonably and according to the law
▸ The duty to comply with the law and uphold the administration of justice and professional ethical standards.

Of the three core values to which civil servants are supposed to adhere, political impartiality is perhaps the hardest to uphold in view of the fact that Ministers in the Government of the day expect a significant degree of commitment and enthusiasm from those who serve them. Yet politicians in Opposition also expect civil servants to conduct themselves in ways which deserve and retain the confidence of others whom they may be required to serve in some future Administration of a very different political persuasion. This may pose real problems for senior civil servants who have close working relationships with Ministers in one particular party that has been in office continuously for a long time. It may even strengthen the case for importing more staff from outside the Civil Service to assist new Ministers in fulfilling their strategic objectives and delivering their radical policies.

In the event that a civil servant believes that he or she is being required to act in an illegal, improper or unethical way in breach of a constitutional convention or professional code or involving possible maladministration or in other ways inconsistent with the Code, he or she has the option of reporting the matter upwards in accordance with Departmental guidelines and, if necessary, of taking the matter higher to the independent Civil Service Commissioners.

Thus loyalty to Ministers and their policies cannot and should not be taken too far. On the other hand, civil servants have a duty not to frustrate the policies, decisions or actions of the Administration they serve and in the final analysis they should either carry out (proper) Ministerial instructions or resign from the Civil Service.

From all of this it would seem quite clear that in the vast generality of cases civil servants owe their loyalty and their energy to Ministers. Yet there is something called 'the public interest' which can creep into the equation and which may, on occasion, appear to be in conflict with what Ministers want to do. Certainly there are some centres of countervailing power in the British political system – such as the media and the Courts – which can often exercise the right to define 'the public interest' in ways which are at odds with Ministers in the Government of the day. In a free society with a pluralistic distribution of powers there are respectable arguments for challenges such as these. However, civil servants should not succumb to the temptation to join in criticism or resistance to Ministers, since the traditional convention is that it is Ministers who are entitled to define 'the public interest'. Civil servants, as subordinate members of Her Majesty's Government, should by all means feel free to put their point of view to Ministers very forcefully and in private; but, once decisions have been made, they should faithfully implement what their political masters have decided. On the rare occasions since the Second World War when civil servants have defied these conventions – as with the case of Clive Ponting in 1984 – the matter has ended in a sacking and/or a court case which has damaged both the whistle-blower and the Government of the day.[14]

A more problematic situation arises when, for one reason or another, there is a contradiction between what Ministers want and what might be described as 'Departmental policy'. This has happened on several occasions in the Foreign and Commonwealth Office where for more than four decades officials have evinced a bureaucratic bias in favour of European integration and in favour of the Arab interest in the Middle East, whereas incoming Ministers have often been 'Euro-sceptics' and reasonably well disposed towards the Israeli interest. It also happened in the Home Office where officials often held the line for a 'liberal' penal policy and a 'liberal' policy on asylum and immigration against a succession of rather more hard-line Home Secretaries (both Conservative and Labour). The fact that influential officials in these two Departments have seemed to win the argument on many occasions is testimony to the fact that relationships between Ministers and their closest officials can be more akin to partnerships than command-and-control structures and the fact that in modern central Government there is seldom any simple binary division between Ministers who decide and officials who deliver.

14.7 conclusion

On the basis of the evidence adduced in this chapter, it is reasonable to conclude that senior civil servants wield considerable power and influence in British central Government. In so far as this influence over both policy and delivery may have become greater since the advent of 'modernisation' in 1997, it may be one explanation why there has been a growing tendency when things go wrong for Ministers and the media to point the finger at civil servants and even to call for their resignation when serious failures of policy or process are revealed for all the world to see.

On the other hand, with the emergence of growing complexity in the public policy issues and managerial challenges with which senior civil servants have to deal, it is not surprising that the forces of energetic bureaucracy and representative democracy are more evenly balanced than they used to be and are therefore usually obliged to work together in delicate and shifting partnerships. Officials are still there to guide, assist and advise Ministers and then to play a leading role in the delivery of policy objectives, not to control or inhibit Ministerial behaviour. If the relationship between Ministers and civil servants works more or less as it is supposed to, there need be no problems caused by over-mighty officials or hyperactive politicians.

SUGGESTED QUESTIONS

1   Describe the structure of the Civil Service in Britain both in general and within a 'typical' Department.
2   What are the functions of the Civil Service?
3   Is the contemporary Civil Service 'fit for purpose'?

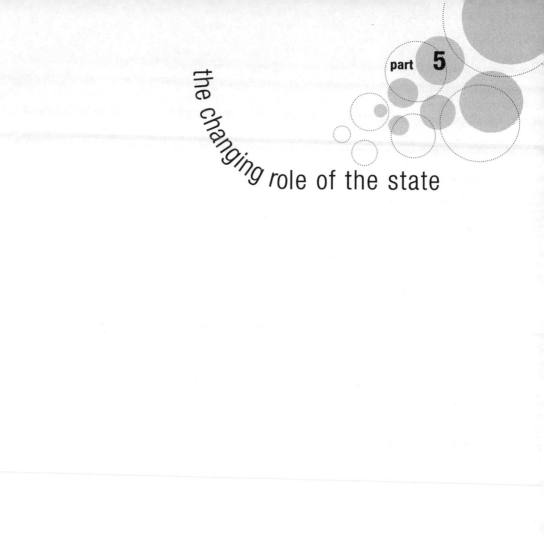

part **5**

the changing role of the state

from provider to enabler and regulator

chapter 15

15.1 background

Nation states first emerged as institutional structures designed to provide a framework for the enforcement of law and order at home and the provision of military power to protect the state from threats from abroad. The raising of taxation and the regulation of commerce were also core activities of the nation state. Over the centuries the character of nation states gradually changed to encompass social functions which included the provision of social security, education, basic pensions and health care. This had the effect of creating a sense of national solidarity which was often reinforced at times of war or other national emergencies.

In the United Kingdom, the imperatives of total mobilisation during the darkest days of the First World War in 1916 when conscription was introduced and women were drafted into the factories and farms to replace the men who left to fight for King and country, the experience of the Great Depression following the financial crash of 1929–30, and the total mobilisation of the Second World War – particularly in 1940–41 when Britain stood defiantly alone against the might of Nazi Germany – all combined to strengthen the sense of allegiance which the British people felt towards their nation and its national institutions. Consequently, when the post-war Labour Government began to implement a new, much wider definition of the role of the state and its agencies, most people welcomed this and the resulting creation of a more ambitious Welfare State, coupled with a much larger state industrial sector comprising a large number of state-owned enterprises whose purpose was, at least in part, to guarantee high levels of employment. These policies came to be accepted across a wide political spectrum and the ambitious definition of the state and its responsibilities which they implied formed the basis of the post-war consensus that lasted for a quarter of a century.

It was not until the oil crisis of 1973–74 that the United Kingdom and other advanced industrialised countries were shaken out of their previous complacency about the viability of such an extended state. From 1979 onwards three successive Conservative Administrations under Margaret Thatcher demonstrated a determination to open up the British economy to global influences via the abolition of exchange controls and to 'roll back the frontiers of the state' via an ambitious programme of privatisation (returning state-owned enterprises to the private sector). In the course of this turbulent period the post-war consensus about the extended role of the state was first punctured, then overturned and eventually re-established on a much more limited basis influenced by the theories of Friedrich Hayek and Milton Friedman. The new Thatcherite consensus, which was so painfully established in the 1980s, survived in somewhat attenuated form under the Administrations of John Major (1990–97) and, despite the arrival of a Labour Government in 1997, has survived in a recognisable form under three successive Blair Administrations. However, under what has been styled as 'New Labour', the state has been somewhat redefined in an enabling, purchasing and regulating role with a touch of redistribution engineered via the tax and social security system. In short, the British state could now be characterised as a partner and referee for the private and voluntary sectors.

15.2 shifting the balance from public to private

In Britain over many years public ownership had long been associated with the model of the public corporation. Yet there had been many varieties of public ownership which had been tried over the years. In the second half of the nineteenth century, the early Socialists advocated municipal ownership of key public utilities, such as gas, water and electricity. Over subsequent years municipal authorities also provided passenger transport, civic amenities such as parks and libaries, and other local services via direct labour departments.

Following the 1945 General Election when the Labour party secured an overwhelming victory, the focus of public ownership shifted to nationalisation which meant the ownership by the state on behalf of the people of 'the means of production, distribution and exchange' (in the words of the 1945 Labour Manifesto). The main purpose of this change was to give priority to national planning, economies of scale and distributional equity. The model of centrally controlled nationalised industries, including notably the National Health Service after 1948 which was more of a national service than a national industry, became the archetypal public sector institution until at least the early 1980s when an alternative policy of privatisation (involving selling the nationalised enterprises to the private sector) began to be implemented by successive Conservative Administrations under Margaret Thatcher and John Major.

Other forms of public ownership were attempted, however, during the four decades which separated the Attlee and Thatcher Administrations. These included administrative control by Whitehall Departments – for example, of the Post Office until 1969; financial control by state holding companies, such as the Industrial Reorganisation Corporation in the late 1960s or the National Enterprise Board in the late 1970s; and the establishment of state-owned financial institutions, such as the Giro Bank in 1969. Notwithstanding these variations, the dominant model continued to be exemplified in the public corporations. At their peak in 1982 such institutions employed about 7 per cent of all those in work at the time, created about 11 per cent of Gross Domestic Product and accounted for about 17 per cent of total fixed investment.[1] Such industries had come to dominate four vital sectors of the economy: energy, transport, steel and communications. They included long established institutions, such as British Rail and the National Coal Board, as well as some newer institutions, such as British Telecom and the British National Oil Corporation. In their heyday they were important suppliers and customers of the private sector and they had a profound effect upon the health of the British economy and the course of British politics.[2]

common characteristics

Public corporations had a number of common characteristics which set them apart from other industrial and commercial undertakings in Britain.[3]

- They were established by Acts of Parliament as statutory bodies responsible for the production of goods or the provision of services specified in legislation
- They were publicly owned in the sense that any securities which they issued carried no private risk and usually paid fixed rates of interest, although in some cases they paid public dividends to the Exchequer – for example, the Post Office did for many years
- They were subject to Government control via the indirect mechanisms of required rates of return on capital, external financial limits on investment and borrowing, and Ministerial appointments of their Chairmen and Board members
- In return for meeting these politically determined obligations, they enjoyed varying degrees of managerial autonomy, their employees were not civil servants (unlike in France or Germany, for example) and they enjoyed some limited financial freedoms from Treasury control, although increasingly less so as time went by.

essential problems

There were a number of essential problems which beset public corporations in Britain over the years. To a considerable extent these stemmed from the conflicting pressures and obligations which gave rise to their establishment in the first place.

1 The theory of public ownership assumed that the major issues of macro-economic policy could be kept separate from the day-to-day problems faced by senior management and that Ministers and Boards could play distinct and complementary roles. In practice, these were soon shown to be heroic

or naïve assumptions. This was partly because of the economic weight and political importance of public corporations and partly because the utopian Socialist ideals that had inspired their creation were only too often replaced by more practical attempts to preserve jobs and limit competition in vital sectors of the economy.

2 The problems of dealing with the public corporations were not made any easier by their diversity which was reflected in their widely differing economic fortunes. For example, at various stages during their public ownership, British Airways, British Gas, British Telecom and the Post Office each generated impressive profits which were then paid in large part to the Exchequer in the form of public dividends; whereas British Rail, British Coal, British Shipbuilders and London Transport each had economic difficulties and were seldom able to generate an overall profit for the nation. The former group provided examples of successful industries with effective management which were capable of producing good returns on their capital and labour employed, whereas the latter group provided examples of strife-torn industries with economically debilitating social and regional obligations.

3 The public corporations suffered over the years from the fact that their very existence was the subject of bitter and long-lasting political conflict both between and occasionally within the Labour and Conservative parties. In many respects they were treated as a political football to be kicked back and forth between two entrenched ideological positions on the Left and the Right of British politics. The hard Left of the Labour Party invariably pressed for an enlarged public sector and the nationalisation (or renationalisation) of key sectors of economic activity. The free-market wing of the Conservative Party consistently sought to reduce the size and weight of the public sector and, from the early 1980s in particular, to privatise as many public corporations as possible. Indeed, the extent of this determined drive to privatise the public sector is demonstrated by the fact that between 1979 and 1997 there were at least 50 significant acts of privatisation in Britain which reduced the remaining nationalised industries to under 2 per cent of GDP and an employment level of approximately 1 per cent of the total workforce.[4]

4 However, the central problem of the public corporations in Britain was the difficulty of establishing a satisfactory arm's length relationship between the Boards of the industries concerned and Ministers in the Government of the day. In so far as this was ever achieved, it involved reconciling managerial freedom for the Boards with the constant political temptation for Ministers to interfere with the managerial ground rules of the public sector. Traditionally, the public corporations had been charged in their founding statutes with twin duties: to break-even financially taking one year with another and to operate in the public interest. Needless to say, these duties were often incompatible and, when they were, it was usually the latter (as defined by Ministers) which prevailed. This might have been alright

if there had been a clear and lasting consensus between the two main political parties about what constituted 'the public interest' at any given time. Yet such a consensus never really existed, since there was an inherent conflict between the interests of the employees of public corporations who wished to maintain their jobs and improve their rewards, who were usually backed by Labour, and the interests of taxpayers and others in the wider community who wished to contain the amount of financial support for the public corporations and who were invariably backed by the Conservatives.

In short, experience over at least five decades in Britain demonstrated the great difficulties in maintaining a satisfactory arm's length relationship between public corporations and the Government of the day. All too often the former were required by the Treasury to reduce or defer their investment programmes for the sake of wider objectives of national macro-economic policy, notably Government determination to limit or reduce the level of public-sector borrowing. On other occasions they were obliged to subordinate their commercial judgement to the political priorities of Ministers. For example, there were occasions when British Coal wanted to close uneconomic pits, but the Government of the day insisted that these be kept open for social or political reasons. There were other occasions when British Steel was required to invest heavily in new plant and equipment at the behest of Ministers – notably by the Conservatives in 1972–73 – only to find, when the new plant came on stream, that the forecast expansion of the market did not materialise. Even the rhetorically non-interventionist Conservative Government in the early 1980s instructed the nationalised gas and electricity industries to raise their prices by more than their commercial judgement suggested was wise simply to increase the flow of revenue to the Exchequer. In all such cases it could be argued that the nation as a whole suffered the effects of policies which combined the worst of both worlds.

In the wake of a massive and sustained onslaught upon the public sector in Britain by the Conservatives during their long period of office from 1979 to 1997, the Labour party felt obliged to revise and eventually abandon its traditional policy favouring nationalisation and renationalisation. Thus at the 1994 Labour Party Conference Tony Blair, the new leader, declared his intention to rewrite the 1918 Labour party constitution and notably the party's long-standing commitment to public ownership of the means of production, distribution and exchange enshrined in Clause 4 of the constitution – a step which was taken by the party in the following year. During the 1997 General Election campaign Blair went further when he declared that 'where there is no overriding reason for preferring the public provision of goods and services, particularly where these services operate in a competitive market, then the presumption should be that economic activity is best left to the private sector with market forces being fully encouraged to operate'.[5] This statement foreshadowed the approach adopted by the Labour Government in office from 1997.

Indeed, it is worth noting that from 1997 the Labour Government was quite well disposed towards selective acts of privatisation. For example, in 1998 the

Government announced that it would sell a majority stake in the Air Traffic Control system and that it would examine the case for privatising all or part of the Royal Mint and the horse racing Tote. Moreover, the policy of Public Private Partnership embodied in the Private Finance Initiative (PFI) and other similar accounting devices has been pushed forward with enthusiasm in an attempt to attract private capital into the provision of public services and to take many public-sector assets and liabilities off the public-sector balance sheet. Between 1997 and 2006 about £50 billion worth of public–private deals were concluded including the Channel Tunnel Rail Link, a considerable number of new schools, hospitals and prisons, a range of road and rail infrastructure projects, a new National Insurance Records System and a supercomputer for managing NHS patient records and other clinical information.[6] In the 2006 budget, Gordon Brown announced a £26 billion expansion of PFI contracts across 20 public sector projects.

Thus it appeared that the long struggle over nationalisation and denationalisation had come to an end after about a century of fierce political controversy. It has been replaced by a more subtle debate about how to regulate and control the public services in the public interest.

15.3 the growth of the wider public sector

While the 'narrow' public sector has been shrunk by privatisation under successive Conservative and Labour Governments, the wider public sector has grown remorselessly in scope and complexity at least since the Second World War and arguably a good deal earlier. Various parts of this leviathan are covered in other chapters – see, for example, central Government in Chapters 12, 13 and 14 and devolved and local government in Chapters 16 and 17. This section is concerned with all public bodies of an autonomous or quasi-autonomous nature which operate at arm's length from Ministers and Departments, but which operate either as agencies to deliver certain aspects of Government policy or as regulatory bodies safeguarding the public interest. The various categories of institution covered by these broad definitions are shown diagrammatically in Figure 15.1.

executive agencies

When Executive Agencies in something like their current form were first approved at the highest political level by Margaret Thatcher in response to the Ibbs Report in 1988, they were supposed to be an organisational device to separate administration, or execution, from the making of public policy. Hence they were an attempt to rationalise a binary distinction which had long been in the minds of Whitehall mandarins who were usually enthused by the challenge of advising Ministers on policy, but rather bored by the chores of seeing that the policy upon which they had advised was executed in a cost-effective and successful way. In the early years of this experiment there were not many 'Next Steps Agencies' (as they were originally called) and they were certainly still on an invisible, but very real, umbilical cord attached to their sponsoring

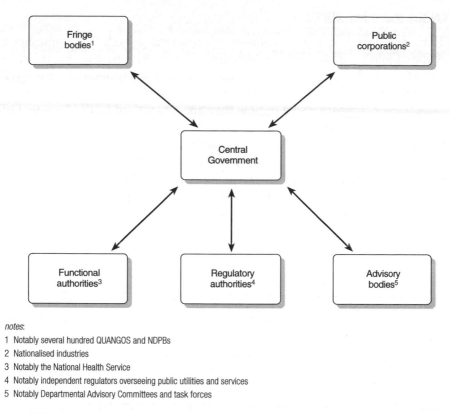

notes:
1 Notably several hundred QUANGOS and NDPBs
2 Nationalised industries
3 Notably the National Health Service
4 Notably independent regulators overseeing public utilities and services
5 Notably Departmental Advisory Committees and task forces

figure **15.1   the composition of the public sector**

Departments and reporting to the Permanent Secretary rather than directly to any Minister. Thus they could not in the early years really be described as part of the wider public sector.

As time has gone by, however, Executive Agencies (as they came to be known) have expanded considerably in number and in bureaucratic weight as both Ministers and Permanent Secretaries came to realise that it was in the public interest (and in their interests) to allocate clearer lines of executive responsibility to the Heads of Agencies and to recruit people from all sectors of society, especially the private sector, to perform the managerial tasks of delivering central-Government policy objectives. The result of this gradual process, which has only come fully to fruition under successive Labour Administrations since 1997, is that there are now more than 130 Executive Agencies, each with a considerable degree of managerial freedom to organise its methods of working in ways best designed to achieve the corporate objectives set for it by Ministers in its sponsoring Department and by the Government as a whole. Thus, although still technically the executive arms of central Government, Agencies have become increasingly capable of earning a real degree of institutional autonomy as long as they manage to achieve, or surpass, the delivery targets set for them by Ministers and by the Treasury in particular in Public Service Agreements.

There has been a significant, almost remorseless, growth in the number and scope of public-sector bodies which are not actually a part of central or local Government, but which are often satellites of Government at one level or another and which carry out specific tasks on behalf of Government. No matter what these bodies are called or how they are categorised by the Cabinet Office or by commentators, it is easy to recognise these institutions at first sight, because they or their predecessors have been around (and causing periodic concern) at least since the 1920s. They are best defined by the purposes given to them by Ministers and by the *modus operandi* they adopt when they are in existence. Their usual purposes are to manage and deliver public-policy objectives at arm's length from Ministers, Councillors and officials; and to do so in a low-key bureaucratic way designed to limit the political salience of their activities.

QUANGOs (Quasi-autonomous non-governmental organisations) have been causing concern in modern times at least since the late 1970s when Geoffrey Bowen identified 252 non-departmental public bodies (NDPBs) which were the same thing by another name.[7] At that time they included a wide range of executive or advisory institutions – for example, the British Library, the Equal Opportunities Commission, the Gaming Board, Trinity House, the Wales Tourist Board, the White Fish Authority and the Supplementary Benefits Appeals Tribunals. Political and media preoccupation with this bureaucratic jungle subsided after a while, but a decade later in the late 1980s Margaret Thatcher initiated another review of non-departmental public bodies and at the end of that exercise announced to Parliament that this murky administrative area would be regularly reviewed at least every five years.[8] She did not stay in office long enough after that to preside over another review, although she was right to be concerned about the matter because in the previous decade or so many more such organisations had been created, such as NHS Trusts, Further Education Colleges, Urban Development Corporations and Regional Development Agencies. All this proved was that this particular form of bureaucratic bindweed was capable of thriving under very different Governments.

In 1995 the then Leader of the Opposition, Tony Blair, pledged to 'sweep away the QUANGO state' should Labour be elected to power.[9] Although there were no precise figures for the number of QUANGOs or NDPBs then in existence, official figures produced after Labour came to office actually showed a decline in the numbers from 1128 in 1997 to 849 in 2003 when the calculation was made.[10] The suspicion must be that Ministers waited for the end of the QUANGO hunting season before announcing the results of their cull. As it was, successive Blair Administrations were fond of the concept of 'partnership working' between the public sector and the private and voluntary sectors as a convenient means of co-opting the energies and ambitions of people not in Government but prepared to work for Government, becoming involved in such things as Task Forces, Working Parties, Action Teams, Policy Reviews and the like. They proved to be a successful means of giving a patina of private-sector credibility to New Labour both before and after 1997 and of extending a new variety of political patronage to fashionable business people who often appeared to be flattered to be asked to advise or do things on behalf of the Government of the day. Figure 15.2 shows the extent of Ministerial patronage under this rubric.

If a serious attempt is made to analyse this hugely diverse aspect of British public administration, it is possible to discern a number of common characteristics in nearly all these organisations:

▸ They derive their existence from Ministerial decisions and can be answerable to Ministers for what they do or fail to do
▸ Their creation normally requires legislation by Parliament and most of them produce annual reports which can be debated by Parliament
▸ They are usually financed by Exchequer grants, but may in some cases be given power to raise statutory levies
▸ The Chairman and Boards are appointed by Ministers for fixed terms of office and can be reappointed at the end of such terms
▸ Their staff do not usually have the status of civil servants, but their pay and conditions are often comparable with those of civil servants
▸ Their annual accounts are audited commercially or by the National Audit Office.

In short, they represent an identifiable and increasingly significant species of public administration in Britain.

Ministers, officials, media commentators and academic observers have paid considerable attention to these public bodies over the years and have invariably identified a number of advantages and disadvantages in their existence for the body politic. It would be fair to say that the advantages usually seem more compelling to the supporters of the Government of the day, whereas the disadvantages usually seem more obvious to its opponents.

On the *positive* side, it can be argued that such public bodies:

▸ Permit certain activities of importance to the state to be conducted outside the strict limits of Government Departments, yet within the spheres of influence of Ministers and officials in Whitehall
▸ Permit such activities to be conducted free from direct or frequent oversight by Parliament and therefore insulated to some extent from party politics at Westminster
▸ Enable Parliament to pass what is often only framework legislation with the confidence that any problems of implementation which may arise can be solved in a low-key and practical manner
▸ Make it easier in some spheres to maintain a broad continuity of policy on a largely non-partisan basis when dealing with technical matters

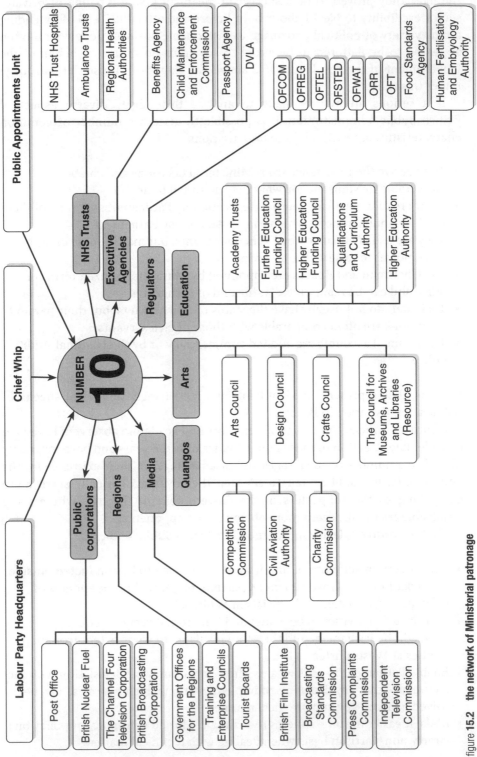

figure **15.2   the network of Ministerial patronage**

- Relieve civil servants of many administrative chores, thus enabling Departments of central Government to concentrate more on policy advice, financial control, management and delivery
- Provide Ministers with useful opportunities for dispensing political patronage and wider recognition for their prominent supporters.

On the negative side, it can be argued that such public bodies:

- Betoken a lack of clarity or agreement about how best to administer a complicated area of policy
- Signify a degree of institutional proliferation which has proved expensive to administer and difficult to supervise or control
- Provide too much scope for political patronage distributed by Ministers in the Government of the day
- Demonstrate not only a lack of clear accountability, but also a lack of effective democratic control and a parallel lack of financial control in certain important areas of policy and administration.

The conclusions which people reach about these anomalous and sometimes opaque bodies vary between approval, boredom and strong disapproval – depending upon whether the observer is in or out of Government at the time. Other people's QUANGOs tend to be seen as wasteful and unnecessary, whereas your own can usually be justified on apparently rational grounds. One thing, however, is clear and that is that the species in all its various manifestations is never likely to disappear as long as the public sector remains so large and so complicated in Britain.

Royal Commissions, Committees of Inquiry and other review bodies

There was a time several decades ago when the appointment of a Royal Commission or a Committee of Inquiry (under the Public Inquiries Act 1921) was quite a common response by the Executive to a large and intractable policy issue or a disastrous turn of events which needed both independent investigation and solid answers. These procedures seem to have gone out of fashion with Ministers since 1997, partly because they have a habit of being too long in the gestation (sometimes lasting 2 years or more), but mainly because the independence of such bodies means that Ministers can lose control of the process and the outcome. The last Prime Minister to see attractions in the inherent procrastination of such processes was Harold Wilson in the 1960s who had a scholar's fondness for thorough investigations and an old-style fondness for Fabian political tactics.

When Lord Benson and Lord Rothschild examined the record in this area for the period from 1954 to 1969, they identified 24 Royal Commissions and more than 600 Committees of Inquiry during that 15 year period.[11] Had they conducted their detailed examination 20 years later, they would have found fewer examples. Twenty years after that – during the current period – they would have found even fewer, because Ministerial preferences have switched to the practice of setting up carefully selected Task Forces and Review Groups with narrowly defined remits and often headed by congenial senior figures from outside central Government. Even in 2003–04 when the then Prime Minister, Tony Blair, was in dire political straits during the period of Western military intervention in Iraq, the two Inquiries which he reluctantly established to look into things and report to Parliament and the nation – the Inquiry under Lord Justice Hutton and the independent Review under Lord Butler – had terms of reference which were so carefully drawn up and investigators who were so exquisitely discreet that many critics of British policy on events in Iraq and the wider Middle East dismissed the results as a whitewash or a cover-up.

By contrast, Tony Blair's and Gordon Brown's fondness for setting up Task Forces and Review Groups under prominent business people soon became legendary, reaching more than three figures in Labour's first year of office alone. For Labour Ministers there were at least two purposes behind these developments: to burnish the Government's 'business friendly' image which had been so assiduously cultivated in Opposition and to co-opt influential business figures into the policy- and decision-making process of central Government.

departmental advisory committees

There is a myriad of advisory committees which assist Whitehall Departments in the course of every day policy making and policy implementation. Regular consultations with acknowledged experts and groups with well-established interests is nowadays a fundamental part of the process of central Government. This has long been the case under previous Administrations, but since the advent of New Labour in 1997 much greater emphasis has been put upon evidence-based policy making and other detailed consultations with those best placed to advise on implementation and enforcement, whether of primary or secondary legislation or of Ministerial decisions taken under the authority of established law.

Such systematic processes of consultation may often be on the basis of a consultative document which invites responses on certain aspects of a planned course of action within a specified period of time often geared to a subsequent legislative timetable. Yet they can also help to meet the needs of Whitehall Departments for timely information and advice, while satisfying the claims of sectional interest groups for regular access to central Government and influence on policy making or policy delivery. In more abstract terms, such procedures provide one more means by which any Government can seek to gain and retain the consent of the governed – at any rate those who are likely to be most directly affected by the consequences of a Ministerial decision or a broader strand of Government policy.

Such advisory committees are particularly well developed in the detailed preparation of secondary legislation and technical Statutory Instruments. Indeed, civil servants could not really do without such advice, because few of them possess the technical expertise which is required to bring about the effects desired by those who promoted the legislation in the first place. Many Acts of Parliament place statutory duties on Ministers to consult specified interests before taking action via secondary legislation. The Police Act 1964 and the Social Security Act 1975 are well-established examples of this phenomenon.

The process has been taken even further in recent years by the consultative requirements established within the European Commission in Brussels. The so-called 'Eurocrats' there have gradually developed the practice known as 'comitology' whereby vested interests and acknowledged experts from many corners of the European economy and from many aspects of European society sit with Commission officials on interdisciplinary and multinational committees of experts whose advice can be absolutely decisive in leading the Commission to formulate its draft Directives in one way rather than another. Of such technical advice is the body of European law created.

Special Purpose Authorities

Another category of public institution in Britain has been that of Special Purpose Authorities – most notably in the sectors of water and health. Until the privatisation of the water supply industry in the late 1980s, there were ten *Water Authorities* in England and Wales (with separate ones for Scotland and Northern Ireland) which were responsible in the public sector for about three-quarters of the water supply, water treatment and sewerage services in the United Kingdom. These Authorities had been established by Act of Parliament in 1974 with clear statutory duties to provide comprehensive water services within hydrologically defined geographical areas. Other water services in some parts of the country were provided by smaller private water companies which had been in existence in some cases since Victorian times.

An even better example of Special Purpose Authorities has been provided by *Health Authorities* in all their various nomenclatures and institutional incarnations. The original structure was determined by Aneurin Bevan and the post-war Labour Government and enshrined in the 1948 National Health Service Act. This was left essentially unchanged for a quarter of a century, but since the mid 1970s has been subjected to frequent bouts of reorganisation.

Traditionally, Health Authorities within the National Health Service (NHS) were responsible for the organisation, financing, regulation and delivery of health services to the British public on the understanding that health care would be provided to people according to clinical need and would be free to all patients at the point of delivery. A few minor exceptions to this principle were made in the case of spectacles and dentures in the early 1950s and Aneurin Bevan's original deal with the medical profession had allowed consultants to continue with some private practice while working principally for the NHS and had recognised the right of General Practitioners (GPs) to act as private contractors to the NHS.

These principles were substantially changed in the early 1990s following the 1990 Health Service Reform Act passed by Parliament at the behest of the Major Administration. Under this legislation a clear distinction was drawn – the so-called *purchaser–provider split* – between those who were responsible for regulating and purchasing the medical services required by patients (Health Authorities in various shapes and sizes) and those who were responsible for providing the services (GPs, NHS Trusts, private hospitals and various clinics and specialist facilities). Perhaps the most controversial aspect of these changes was the introduction of GP fund-holding practices where the doctors had the freedom to use their practice budgets to purchase health care for their patients from any provider, acute or primary, as they saw fit. This was fiercely resisted as inequitable by the Labour Opposition and many who worked in the NHS, yet in the fullness of time the Labour Government first elected in 1997 gradually came to accept this reform.

The most distinctive themes of Labour's approach to running the NHS from 2000 were, *first*, the doubling in real terms of the amount of taxpayers' money allocated to the NHS under a highly ambitious ten-year plan and, *second*, the emphasis upon partnership working and standard raising in every aspect of clinical practice. Prominent institutional examples of the latter theme have been the Health Services Commission with its responsibility for general oversight and the National Institute for Clinical Excellence with its role in advising on the use (or non-use) of particular new medicines.

Notwithstanding the huge increase in financial resources allocated to the NHS from 2000, there continued to be extensive controversy about the changing organisation and standards of delivery for health care in Britain. It has not been possible to reach reassuring consensus upon such a highly politicised area of public policy and disputes have raged in Parliament and the media about the suitability and cost-effectiveness of new drugs, infections acquired by patients in hospital, and financial deficits for some Health Trusts (a state of affairs supposedly proscribed in the relevant legislation). In truth, the NHS remains, in effect, one of the last great 'nationalised industries' in Britain: it is highly unionised, highly politicised and has long since become something of a sacred cow in British society. In such conditions it is very difficult for any Government to lead a rational debate and impose successful policies.

15.4 the role of the voluntary sector

The voluntary sector in Britain has become significant in its own right and significant as a contractor for services in the wider public sector. In 2003–4 the voluntary sector had an income of £26.3 billion, 38 per cent of which came from statutory sources – in other words, provided by Ministerial and official decision and courtesy of legislation sanctioned by Parliament.[12]

Within the voluntary sector the number of large charities with annual incomes of more than £1 million has more than doubled over the period 1995–2005, reflecting what has been described as the 'charitisation' of the public sector or, equally, the transformation of a large part of the voluntary sector into agencies of the public sector. This may be convenient for Ministers and civil servants, but it has meant a loss of some independence for charities and a growing sense of inhibition towards any public criticism of the Government of the day. The process of concentration within the voluntary sector and the emergence of some 14 'super charities' with annual incomes of over £100 million each have crowded out many of the smaller charities and made for an unhealthy mutual dependence between some of the charities which are household names and their sponsoring Departments in Whitehall. As has been said: 'these organisations (the super charities) are likely increasingly to shape public perception of the (voluntary) sector as a whole, while being responsible for an increasing proportion of the public services delivered by the sector.'[13]

The other major development which has gradually changed the nature and behaviour of the voluntary sector is the growth of *social enterprise* – the description usually given to the processes by which charities generate earned income through their trading activities which is now greater than the voluntary income they secure from public donations. Thus over time expert observers believe that the voluntary sector is coming to resemble the private sector in many respects, while simultaneously becoming more dependent upon resources from the public sector sanctioned by Ministers and civil servants in the form of various contracts for services. Such transfers from the statutory to the voluntary sector were estimated to be more than £10 billion in 2003–04, roughly £700 million more than income raised directly from the public revealing a gradual shift from voluntary fund-raising to lobbying of Government and, in the latter category, from grants to contracts.

15.5 oversight, control and regulation

No matter how far successive Governments have gone in moving away from accepting direct responsibility for the *provision* of public services, they still accept responsibility for enabling, financing and regulating what is delivered to the public. This is principally because Ministers tend to claim the credit when advances in quality and coverage are made, whereas the public and the media tend to attribute blame to the Government of the day when things go wrong or the public services under-perform. In spite of the huge extent of privatisation, contracting out and partnership delivery in the last few decades, there has been no escape from the need to have a *regulatory state* which can at least try to ensure broad equality of provision and probity of administration in all the public services for which Government and Parliament still accept some degree of responsibility. Indeed, the more distant and arm's length is the relationship between the elected Government and the providers of public services, the more essential it has become for Ministers to promote statutes which guarantee the role of independent regulators to oversee and improve the public services. This is the essential reason for the development of a modern regulatory state in Britain.

Ministerial oversight

Ministerial oversight has been the traditional method of controlling the public sector. It has really been a short-hand for supervision and periodic interference by Ministers and senior policy-making civil servants. As far as the public corporations were concerned, this usually took the form of frequent conversations between Ministers in the sponsoring Departments and Board members of the public corporations on significant issues of policy – for example, plans for large scale corporate investment, key pricing decisions, important pay negotiations and matters to do with the impact of corporate activity upon the wider political and social environment. In these relationships Ministers and Board members alike sought to preserve the fundamental distinction between day-to-day management decisions (usually matters for Boards) and long-term strategic decisions with a high political content (usually matters for Ministers and officials). Each side was sometimes tempted to blur or ignore this vital distinction and when this happened, significant problems often ensued.

When there was serious conflict between Ministers and Boards, it was often because the latter chose to interpret their statutory duties more narrowly and commercially than Ministers would have wished, which then faced Ministers with an invidious choice between doing nothing about an unpopular Board decision and so risking political and public criticism for their apparent inactivity, and intervening in a controversial Board decision and so perhaps jeopardising the commercial prospects of the public corporation. On the whole Ministers preferred to take the latter risk, which was really a reflection of the fact that Parliament and the general public had more impact upon Ministerial prospects than the Board of any public corporation.

Ministerial oversight of the core public sector, such as the institutions of the NHS or state schools, has proved more durable and much more intrusive. Since 1997 the Labour Government has staked much of its political reputation on getting tangible improvements in the performance of the core public sector – whether in health, education, law and order or transport – and this has necessitated frequent Ministerial interventions, target setting and new contractual arrangements under the auspices of Public Service Agreements and the like. Although Ministers do not have managerial responsibilities in these spheres of public-service delivery, they remain in ultimate political control of the policy, resources and structure, and the media and the public hold them to account for the results.

Parliamentary control

Parliamentary control is essentially the counterpart of Ministerial oversight, because elected MPs as well as members of the House of Lords tend to take a close political interest in the public services. Nowadays a considerable degree of accountability to Parliament is achieved via the mechanism of Select Committees which conduct detailed scrutiny of Government Departments, Agencies and the other institutions within the wider public sector which come within their orbit. However, perhaps one of the most effective ways of exercising public accountability is the straightforward practice of MPs writing to or going to see Ministers and Agency Chief Executives whenever they have good cause to do so on behalf of their constituents. Such representations can be supplemented in various higher-profile ways, such as pointed interventions in Parliament, larger scale lobbying and public demonstrations in which MPs and peers also get involved from time to time. Since ultimately all public sector bodies depend for their continued existence upon the support and approval of Parliament, MPs and peers have both the ability and the right to be quite demanding when they choose to be.

arm's length regulation

From time to time other regulatory mechanisms have been used in various attempts to exercise control over institutions in the public sector. For example, the Monopolies and Mergers Commission conducted efficiency audits of public corporations under powers provided in the 1980 Competition Act. Occasionally, Ministers have decided to establish a Royal Commission or a Committee of Inquiry to conduct a full scale and supposedly independent review of a public corporation or other institutions in the public sector. For example, in 1985 the Thatcher Administration established the Peacock Committee to look into the future financing of the BBC.[14]

However, the real growth of arm's length regulation has stemmed from the dynamics of privatisation under both Conservative and Labour Governments. In the absence of effective Ministerial control and with Parliament only marginally able to interfere in the activities of privatised public utilities, it has proved necessary to establish a wide range of independent regulatory bodies, such as OfCom, OfWat, OfGem and many others, to monitor the operations of privatised industries and to intervene from time to time to rectify egregious cases of market failure when there has been insufficient competition for the benefit of consumers. Paradoxically, the process of privatisation created a vacuum of political control in sensitive sectors which has had to be filled, in part at least, by the establishment of statutory regulators with a remit to safeguard the public interest.

It is an irony of privatisation that the transfer of responsibility for the production of vital goods and services from the public to the private sector has necessitated more elaborate and detailed forms of regulation than was the case when there was a large public sector under the political control of Ministers and Parliament. In other words, the market liberalisation implicit in the policy of privatisation has required a degree of re-regulation more explicit and more legalistic than ever before. Whereas in dealing with public corporations it was often necessary for Ministers to intervene in order to protect the interests of taxpayers against the commercial inadequacies of nationalised industries, it has often been necessary for the independent regulators to intervene to protect the interests of consumers against the abuse of market power by newly privatised undertakings.

Thus one of the general problems caused by the regulatory consequences of privatisation has been the difficulty in developing forms of regulation which are acceptable to the privatised undertakings and seen as fair by the general public. This has been a difficult balance to achieve, especially when the actions of the regulators have seemed arbitrary and even capricious. Yet one principle is clear: the more genuine competition there is in a privatised sector, the less need there is for elaborate and detailed regulation – with the possible exception of political intervention to protect the interests of the poorest and weakest in society who, by definition, are not likely to prosper in a market driven sector.

from trust to contract

The organisation and management of the public sector in Britain has changed almost out of all recognition since the mid 1980s. To begin with, the sector was dramatically reduced by the policy of privatisation under successive Governments, both Conservative and New Labour. Then Ministers and officials discovered that however radically you change the *ownership* of public corporations and other bodies in the wider public sector, you cannot so easily get rid of the *political responsibility* for what happens or fails to happen in the sector. Consequently, Ministers began to develop a contractual approach to the delivery of important public goods and services whereby various potential providers engage in a competitive bidding process to establish which of a number of organisations is best placed to provide public goods or services of high quality at an acceptable price to the Exchequer.

Thus during the period which straddled the Thatcher, Major and Blair Administrations, we have seen a move from command (via nationalised industries) to contract via legalistic arrangements in which the state in one of its many manifestations acts as an informed purchaser and regulator, but leaves the provision of public goods and services to those who successfully gain and retain public contracts. This policy change began fairly timidly with 'market testing' to see whether existing public-sector providers were efficient and competitive; it developed into arrangements such as 'compulsory competitive tendering' for non-core services in the NHS, the MOD and other public purchasers; and, for better or worse, it has reached maturity in the sort of arrangements now operating on the railways where the track is the responsibility of Network Rail and the trains are run by private operating companies which have successfully bid for a franchise that allows them to provide rail services for a contractually determined period of years.

What all these examples amount to is that the state and its agencies have largely withdrawn from their previous combined roles as purchasers, regulators and providers of public goods and services to the more limited roles of agenda setter, informed purchaser, partner for the private and voluntary sectors, and independent regulator. In the core public sector, however, (for example, health, education, law and order) such withdrawal of the state has not – at least as yet – been politically feasible, so New Labour Ministers have imposed the more hands-on mechanisms of targets, milestones and Public Service Agreements (already discussed earlier in this chapter). In short, since the late 1980s we have seen deliberate attempts by successive Governments to engineer purchaser-provider splits in the public sector and a strategic shift from trust to contract.

15.6 conclusion

Significant changes have taken place both within the British state and between the state and society since 1979. The wide range of changes has included privatisation, Executive Agencies, market testing, contracting out, performance evaluations, Citizen's Charters, Public Private Partnerships, private finance initiatives, delivery targets, new regulatory arrangements, audit commissions and a host of other initiatives too numerous to record in this summary paragraph.

The cumulative effect has been to reduce the role of the state and to change its focus from that of universal provider to that of enabler, purchaser and regulator. The result is that public services are no longer necessarily synonymous with the public sector. This is not to say that the public sector has withered away – far from it – but there is nowadays a much more varied and complex pattern of public services provision. The core public services are still largely delivered by the state and its agencies, but the tasks of the wider public sector are now increasingly performed by others in the voluntary and private sectors with the state (essentially government at every level) being the ultimate guarantor of public services and retaining ultimate accountability for the outcomes.

Against this changing background, it is unwise to be in any way dogmatic about the future of the public sector in Britain. However, the three main political parties seem to be converging upon a multiparty consensus and it is possible to discern a few signposts for the future.

Firstly, in the mixed economy of Britain today there are certain goods and services which are still more appropriately provided by the public sector if they are to be provided at all – such as loss making postal services, accident and emergency health care or guarantees of law and order on the streets.

Secondly, there will often be compelling arguments for the public sector to take charge of certain large and high-risk technology projects, such as the further development of civil nuclear power, which would otherwise not materialise if the economic and social risks were to be carried solely by the private sector. Yet even in these limiting cases, there will be a substantial role for private-sector firms which contract to supply or maintain such mega projects.

Thirdly, there is still a good deal of argument about how far it is desirable or possible to apply private-sector managerial techniques and accounting conventions to core activities within the public sector. Such questions have been posed in relation to market testing, compulsory competitive tendering and resource accounting for example. Such debate will doubtless continue, especially in the controversial sphere of Public Private Partnerships where agreement upon the transfer of risk is vital.

Fourthly, when public services are inherently more of a gift relationship than a commercial transaction – for example, in treating acute cases or chronic conditions in the NHS – such activities (in Britain at any rate) will almost certainly have to remain within the public sector. Such services are likely to remain largely free at the point of use and the time of need and therefore constitute classic examples of real 'public goods'. Nevertheless there will probably be continuing discussion about how much of these 'free goods' can be afforded at any time. Core public services and the modernising drive for a more commercial approach to their delivery have been difficult to reconcile in the past, but there is reason to suppose that this dilemma may be easier to deal with now that a durable cross-party consensus appears to have emerged.

SUGGESTED QUESTIONS

1   To what extent should we be concerned by the 'new magistracy' of unelected Government in Britain?
2   What issues of accountability have been raised by the policy of privatization and by the growth of the 'new magistracy'?
3   'The State in Britain has moved from being a provider to being an enabler and regulator.' To what extent is this a valid assertion?

chapter 16

devolved and regional government

The United Kingdom is a unitary, multinational state – what some describe as a 'union' state. This concept is reflected not only in some well-established ethnic, cultural and institutional differences between the four components of the UK, but also in the arrangements for devolved government which were introduced for Scotland, Wales and Northern Ireland by the first Blair Administration during the 1997–2001 Parliament. Yet political authority is ultimately centralised, since constituencies in all the component parts of the UK – England, Scotland, Wales and Northern Ireland – send representatives elected on a common franchise to the UK Parliament at Westminster and the whole country is governed by a political Administration drawn from the majority party in the House of Commons.

The approach to devolution in England has been very different, since the Labour Government has been opposed to the idea of creating an English Parliament and has never fully accepted the alternative of dividing England into a number of regional entities, each with its own identity reflected in an elected regional Assembly. Admittedly, an abortive attempt was made in 2004 to offer such a solution to the North East of England, but it was firmly rejected by the people of that region in a referendum and the idea has not been resuscitated since then either there or in any other region of England.

In considering this general topic, it is important to distinguish between *devolved government* which implies a directly elected Parliament or Assembly from which the political members of the Executive are drawn and *devolved or regional administration* which implies the existence of regional Offices and Agencies and the local administration of justice. The main focus of this chapter is upon the former – namely, the directly elected Scottish Parliament and the directly elected Assemblies in Wales and Northern Ireland. For completeness, and more briefly, we shall also cover the structures of government and democratic oversight in the regions of England.

In the 1960s and 1970s the governance of both Scotland and Wales came to the fore as an issue of political debate to an extent not seen in those parts of the UK for more than two centuries. In 1966 Plaid Cymru, the Welsh Nationalist party, won a seat at Westminster for the first time since its foundation in 1925. Similarly, the Scottish National party, established in 1928, won its first seat at Westminster in a by-election in 1967. In this climate of growing nationalist feeling a Royal Commission on the Constitution was established in 1969 initially under the chairmanship of Lord Crowther and subsequently under Lord Kilbrandon. It reported in 1973 with recommendations that rejected both separation for Scotland and Wales and federal arrangements for the whole United Kingdom. However, it approved the idea of devolution – a halfway house between the status quo and independence – including the establishment of a directly elected Scottish Assembly.

In the October 1974 General Election, when the Scottish National party received 30 per cent of the Scottish vote and 11 MPs, and Plaid Cymru received 11 per cent of the Welsh vote and 3 MPs, devolution became even more salient. This provoked the Labour Government, led first by Harold Wilson (1974–76) and then by James Callaghan (1976–79), to introduce legislation – which failed at the first attempt in 1975 but succeeded at the second attempt in 1978 – to provide for directly elected Assemblies for both nations. However, the legislation was subject to retrospective referenda in both those parts of the UK. In Wales only 12 per cent of the electorate voted in favour with 47 per cent voting against. In Scotland 33 per cent of the electorate voted in favour and 31 per cent against. Each case failed to pass the threshold of 40 per cent of those entitled to vote which had been stipulated in amendments sponsored by influential Labour backbenchers during the committee stage of the Bills. Consequently, the legislation was not implemented and neither Assembly was brought into being.

At the 1979 General Election the Conservative party came into office and wasted no time in securing the passage of two resolutions nullifying both the Scotland Act 1978 and the Wales Act 1978. From then on devolution was dormant as a political issue and did not come to the fore until the late 1980s when revived pressure from the Labour and Liberal Democrat parties north of the border and from UK-wide pressure groups, such as Charter 88, began to put constitutional change back on the political agenda. In Scotland the result of this party and non-party pressure was the creation of a Scottish Constitutional Convention in 1989 which, by 1992, succeeded in galvanising all those who supported devolution and in persuading the Labour party, by then under the leadership of John Smith, to incorporate a commitment to devolution into its policy platform.

Such developments were not supported by the Nationalist parties in Scotland and Wales – seeing them as moves to prevent their goal of independence – on the one hand or Unionists, such as the Conservative party – who saw the moves as a threat to the union – on the other. In the event this difference of opinion did not matter, because the Labour party won the 1997 General Election with a landslide majority and a clear mandate to introduce varying degrees of devolution for Scotland, Wales and Northern Ireland – subject only to the prior approval of the people in each of those parts of the UK in three separate referenda. As things turned out, each of these referenda produced a vote in favour of devolution – enthusiastically in Scotland and Northern Ireland, but grudgingly with only the narrowest of majorities in Wales. This enabled the new Labour Government to get the necessary legislation through Parliament in 1998 and to get the various devolved Assemblies established in 1999.

By the turn of the century it had become clear that what had been achieved was best described as a quasi-federal United Kingdom with asymmetrical devolution. The people of *Scotland* seemed pleased with its new Parliament and the opportunity to exercise a significant range of devolved legislative powers. The people of *Northern Ireland* seemed content with its more inhibited form of devolution, but the issues remained controversial in Unionist quarters and the difficulties of making devolution work on a power-sharing basis were recurrent and at times insuperable. The people of *Wales* remained divided on the issue and the opponents of the more dilute policy of administrative devolution were only gradually reconciled as the new Assembly built some credibility over the years.

As for the position in *England*, no one (except the Liberal Democrats) was talking seriously about devolution to regional legislative Assemblies, because even the proponents of such a scheme in the Labour party had recognised when the party was in Opposition that this commanded little or no support in the country. There was not any significant public demand for another tier of subnational government, even though there was a case for creating some suitable type of institution which would be able to oversee the activities and the public expenditure carried out by the Government Offices for the Regions which had been created by the Major Administration in the early 1990s.

Against this background, the Labour party in its 1997 General Election Manifesto held back from repeating its earlier pledge to create elected Regional Assemblies and committed itself instead to establishing nominated Regional Chambers to coordinate transport, planning, economic development, bids for EU funding and land use planning. However, it also declared that it would introduce legislation to allow the people of England, region by region, to decide by referenda whether or not they wanted devolved regional government. Only where clear popular consent had been established would any such arrangements be made, and then only where this would not mean adding a new tier of subnational government (namely, in those parts of the country where there was already a unitary system of local government) or increasing overall public expenditure.

16.2 structure and personnel

Since 1997 the Labour Government has created structures of devolved government in the United Kingdom which are distinguished by their asymmetry and deliberate lack of any unifying principle. This pragmatic approach was designed to do what was thought necessary to propitiate the nationalists in Scotland, Wales and Northern Ireland and to bring the exercise of political power closer to the people in the outlying parts of the UK, but without disturbing too much the governance of England or over-stimulating the appetite for self-governance and independence in the non-English parts of the United Kingdom. In other words, if ever there was an exercise in political expediency, this was it. Yet, for all the criticisms which can be made of the lack of thematic coherence in the policy, at the time of writing it seems to have worked to a greater or lesser extent in all the parts of the UK where there has been some public demand for it.

Scotland

The Scotland Act 1998 provided for a unicameral Scottish Parliament with 129 members (MSPs), of which 73 are constituency members elected by first past the post and 56 are party list members elected under the Additional Member System (AMS), a type of proportional representation in which seven candidates are chosen for each of the eight Scottish regions. Each elector therefore has two votes: one for a constituency MSP and one for a party list MSP. This system has ensured that even the Conservatives have won some 'list seats' at a time when the party has had virtually no MPs in Scotland.

The Scottish Parliament sits for a four-year term and the Scottish Executive is headed by a First Minister who needs to command sufficient support within the Parliament – from his own party and sometimes from a coalition partner as well – to form an Administration. In the first elections held in May 1999 no single party had an overall majority, so the Scottish Labour party – the largest single party – formed a coalition with the Scottish Liberal Democrats, sharing the posts in the 'Cabinet'. This coalition arrangement was also used following the second elections in 2003, because once again the Labour party on its own did not achieve an overall majority.

Because there are a range of 'reserved powers' (see p. 363) which can only be exercised by the UK Government at Westminster, there is still a Secretary of State for Scotland and a Scotland Office based in Whitehall and in Edinburgh. The person chosen for this role is still a member of the UK Cabinet and helps to ensure that Westminster interests are upheld in Scotland and, to a degree, that Scottish interests are represented in London. Many people regard this as a transitional situation and since 2003 it has been the case that the Secretary of State for Scotland has allocated the bulk of his time to being the UK Secretary of State for Transport as well.

Wales

The Government of Wales Act 1998 provided for an Assembly with 60 members (AMs), 40 of whom are directly elected by first past the post and 20 of whom are elected as list members under the Additional Member System (AMS), four from each of the five European Parliamentary constituencies in Wales. Once again each elector has two votes: one for a constituency AM and one for a party list AM. As in Scotland, the purpose of this mixed electoral system was to increase the chances that the composition of the Assembly would reflect party support amongst the Welsh electorate.

The Welsh Assembly began to function in 1999 following elections earlier that year. The initial First Minister was Alun Michael MP, a member of the then UK Government, who was chosen for the position by Tony Blair as UK Prime Minister and then endorsed by the Labour AMs in the Assembly. This sent the wrong signals to the Labour party in Wales and it was not long before the AMs reacted against such an English imposition and took an early opportunity to choose their own First Minister, Rhodri Morgan AM, in 2000. The First Minister chooses a 'Cabinet' from among colleagues in the Assembly and together form the Welsh Assembly Government.[1] Since the introduction of devolution the Welsh Labour party has formed the government, although has experienced minority, majority and coalition (with the Liberal Democrats) status.

There continues to be a Secretary of State for Wales (who since 2003 has also been Secretary of State for Northern Ireland) who sits in the UK Cabinet and divides his time between London and Cardiff. Unlike the situation for the Secretary of State in Scotland, the individual concerned can participate, although not vote, in Welsh Assembly debates – something which reflects the more dilute version of devolution so far enjoyed in Wales. Once again the theory is that, by having such a Minister in the British Cabinet, it is possible to represent the UK interest in Cardiff and the Welsh interest in London.

Northern Ireland

Under the terms of the 1998 Belfast Agreement (also known as the Good Friday Agreement), which was subsequently endorsed by the people of Northern Ireland in a referendum, a devolved Assembly was established at Stormont following elections held in June 1998. The Assembly comprises 108 members all of whom are elected by Single Transferable Vote (STV) with six members being elected from each of the 18 Westminster Parliamentary constituencies. Also created was a 12-member power-sharing Executive headed by a First Minister from the majority Unionist community and a Deputy First Minister from the minority Nationalist community. Proposals put to the Assembly by the Executive are decided by a system of weighted majority voting to ensure that no single section of the Northern Ireland community can dominate all the others, (as had happened for 50 years under the Unionists from partition in 1922 to the introduction of direct rule in 1972).

All the parties involved in the 'peace process' leading up to the 1998 Belfast Agreement had been careful to provide for an elaborate network of institutional bodies to buttress the precarious settlement so painfully arrived at. These included a North–South Ministerial Council as a forum to promote the common interests of the Governments in Dublin and Belfast; a British-Islands Council as a forum to promote the common interests of all the political components of the British Isles; and a British–Irish Inter-Governmental Conference as a forum in which the British and Irish Governments could promote their common interests in relation to Northern Ireland.

As a result of recurrent difficulties with the peace process, the Northern Ireland Executive and the Assembly to which it is accountable have been suspended on a number of occasions since 1998. At the time of writing these devolved institutions have been suspended by the British Government since October 2002 resulting in another period of direct rule from Whitehall and Westminster. In April 2006 the British and Irish Governments stipulated that the Assembly would be reconvened in May and then be given to the end of November – subsequently extended into 2007 – to establish another power-sharing Executive on terms fully compatible with the conditions laid down in the 1998 Belfast Agreement.

English regions

Since 1997 England has had a measure of regional government in each of its nine regions, but this has not involved the devolution of any legislative powers to elected regional Assemblies because none of these yet exist. Prior to the change of power at Westminster, the Major Administration had created a number of Government Offices for the regions which acted as outposts of central Government beyond London and regional coordinators of national policy. After 1997 Labour's only substantial regional initiative was to establish nine Regional Development Agencies to coordinate economic planning and promote inward investment as well as administer funding secured from EU and other sources.

In an attempt to introduce an element of public accountability the Government established a Regional Assembly in each of the English regions outside London consisting of up to 70 per cent of nominated local government members and at least 30 per cent of members nominated by regional stakeholders, such as industry and commerce, the trade unions, the National Health Service and voluntary organisations. In a subsequent White Paper in 2002 the Government outlined further proposals for these bodies to become directly elected. However, it was stipulated that such an Assembly could only be established if a majority of people in the region concerned voted for it in a regional referendum. The Government identified three 'pilot' regions where this idea might be taken a stage further – the North East, the North West, and Yorkshire and Humberside. However, the wind was taken completely out of the Government's sails when in November 2004 the people of the North East voted decisively (by 78 per cent to 22 per cent) against the idea and the policy was taken no further.

16.3 powers, functions and finance

Scotland

The approach to devolution taken in the Scotland Act 1998 was that all powers not specified in the schedule of devolved matters would be reserved to the UK Parliament at Westminster. The devolved powers gave the Scottish Parliament the right to pass primary legislation in the specified areas, which meant that Scottish law could be significantly different to British law in certain policy matters. The schedule of devolved policy areas is summarised in Figure 16.1.

More controversially, the Scottish Assembly was given some limited tax-varying powers, namely the power to vary the standard UK rate of income tax for taxpayers in Scotland by 3 pence in the Pound up or down. It was also given the freedom to vary spending on different items within the overall sum of public expenditure (£26.4 billion in 2005–06) assigned to Scotland under the Treasury formula.

Another distinguishing feature of Scottish devolution is to be found in the ways in which the Scottish Parliament has worked since 1999. Its business is controlled by a Bureau on which all the parties are represented; the legislative process works through a system of permanent committees which can initiate legislation in the devolved areas; the Scottish Executive is accountable to the Scottish Parliament and accessible to the Scottish people in a variety of informal ways and it oversees all the various public bodies which are responsible for the delivery of devolved functions and public services. European Directives are also scrutinised and implemented in Scotland via devolved legislative procedures.

- Agriculture
- Arts
- Countryside and environment
- Economic development and inward investment
- Education and training
- Fishing
- Food standards
- Forestry
- Health services
- Housing
- Law and order (police, civil law, criminal law)
- Local government
- National Heritage
- Social work services
- Sport
- Transport (most aspects).

figure **16.1** **Scotland: devolved policy areas**

- ▶ The United Kingdom constitution
- ▶ Foreign policy and international negotiations
- ▶ Defence and national security
- ▶ Protection of borders
- ▶ Immigration and nationality
- ▶ Macro-econmoic and monetary policy
- ▶ Employment legislation
- ▶ Social security benefits
- ▶ The regulation of professions (including doctors)
- ▶ Energy
- ▶ United Kingdom transport
- ▶ Abortion
- ▶ Human fertilisation and embryology
- ▶ Nuclear safety
- ▶ The licensing of cinemas.

figure **16.2** **Scotland: UK reserved policy areas**

The policy areas and matters which are reserved to Ministers in Whitehall and members of the Westminster Parliament are set out in Figure 16.2 and include foreign policy and defence, immigration and nationality, fiscal and monetary policy (with the exception of the marginal tax-varying power already mentioned), employment legislation and social security.

The Scotland Act 1998 confirmed the legislative supremacy of the Westminster Parliament and underlined this principle by stipulating that all devolved legislation passed by the Scottish Parliament would have to receive Royal Assent prior to becoming law. However, on the other hand, the so-called Sewell convention subsequently made it clear that the Westminster Parliament would not knowingly or deliberately legislate on any matter which was within the devolved legislative competence of the Scottish Parliament.[2]

Wales

Under the Government of Wales Act 1998 the Welsh Assembly did not have the power to pass primary legislation on devolved matters nor to vary the standard rate of income tax. However, it did have the power to pass secondary legislation on devolved matters and responsibility for a large part of the public expenditure assigned to Wales (£12.7 billion in 2005–06), much of which is spent by a wide range of Welsh Agencies and public bodies. The areas of power devolved to the Welsh Assembly include education and training, health, housing, local government and social services. See Figure 16.3.

All the other policy areas were reserved for Government in Whitehall and Parliament at Westminster – for example, foreign affairs, defence, fiscal and monetary policy, social security and broadcasting.

- Agriculture
- Ancient monuments and historic buildings
- Arts, culture, heritage and the Welsh language
- Economic development
- Education and training
- The environment
- Forestry
- Fisheries
- Food
- Health
- Highways, transport and roads
- Housing
- Industry
- Local government
- Planning (town and country)
- Social services
- Sport and recreation
- Tourism.

figure **16.3   Wales: devolved policy areas**

In July 2002 the Welsh Executive appointed a Commission under Lord Richard to consider whether the Assembly had sufficient powers to operate effectively and whether any other changes should be made to its methods of operation or its composition. In 2004 the Commission reported with recommendations that the Assembly should be replaced by two separate bodies – an Executive and a Legislature – and be given enhanced powers of primary legislation in devolved matters. Furthermore, in those circumstances, it recommended that the number of AMs be increased from 60 to 80.

In June 2005 the Labour Government in London responded to the Richard Commission Report with a White Paper entitled *Better Government for Wales*[3] and this was followed by legislation to give effect to the White Paper which became the Government of Wales Act 2006.[4]

Firstly, the Act brought about formal separation between the executive and legislative arms of the Assembly making the former more clearly accountable to the latter for the exercise of its powers and the use of its financial resources.

Secondly, the Act enhanced the legislative powers of the Assembly in three ways: by conferring wider powers on the Assembly to make subordinate legislation, by providing an Order in Council mechanism to allow Parliament at Westminster to confer enhanced legislative powers on the Assembly in relation to specific matters within devolved fields, and, with the backing of a positive vote in a Welsh referendum, by authorising the Assembly to make law on all the matters within its devolved fields of competence without further recourse to Parliament at Westminster.

Thirdly, the Act reformed the electoral arrangements of the Assembly by debarring candidates from standing both for a constituency and for a position on a party list, by providing for extraordinary elections in exceptional circumstances within the Assembly's normal four-year term, and by giving the Assembly a new power to arrange for public information campaigns to promote participation in its elections.

Northern Ireland

Under the Northern Ireland Act 1998 the Northern Ireland Assembly, when it has not been suspended, has exercised full executive and legislative authority over all devolved matters – such as education and training, environment, health and social services – and these are listed in Figure 16.4.

However, since 2002 devolved government has been suspended and, with the reversion to Direct Rule, legislation that would normally have been passed by the Assembly has been made by UK Orders in Council. When devolution in Northern Ireland was in operation (from 1999 to 2002), the Assembly was able to pass legislation relating to the devolved agenda in Northern Ireland, provided it was non-discriminatory, consistent with European law and the European Convention on Human Rights. Throughout this period of political volatility, the Secretary of State for Northern Ireland has remained accountable to the UK Parliament for the reserved powers which have remained within the jurisdiction of Westminster on such matters as security, policing , criminal justice, taxation, national insurance and international relations.

Provision for the financing of government and public services in Northern Ireland is achieved via the allocation of a block grant to the Province which, when devolution is in operation, the Northern Ireland Executive can distribute between the various devolved services as it sees fit (subject to UK-wide public entitlements) and for which it is democratically accountable to the Northern Ireland Assembly. For non-devolved responsibilities the money is raised and distributed in the normal way by the UK Exchequer and HM Treasury working in collaboration with the relevant delivery Departments in the British Government.

- Agriculture and rural development
- Culture, arts and leisure
- Economic development
- Education, training and employment
- Enterprise, trade and investment
- Environment
- Finance and personnel
- Health, social services and public safety
- Regional development
- Social development

figure **16.4 Northern Ireland: devolved policy areas**

The idea of regional administration in England takes on a practical manifestation in the shape of nine Government Offices for the Regions (GORs), nine non-elected Regional Development Agencies (RDAs) under the guidance of the GORs and nine Regional Assemblies to oversee each of the RDAs. What is missing from this jigsaw is any credible form of regional government answerable to democratically elected Regional Assemblies. The structure which has been created by successive Governments in London is essentially prefectorial with a facade of quasi-democratic oversight by nominees from local government and representatives of leading local stakeholders   The staff of the Government Offices, who are themselves managed and represented in Whitehall by a Regional Coordination Unit, monitor the RDAs and manage the spending programmes of various Government Departments involved in aspects of regional policy. In 2005–06 these amounted to total expenditure of £... billion. The Regional Development Agencies are run by Chief Executives and Boards drawn from the Civil Service and other stakeholders appointed by and to some extent answerable to the Department for Trade and Industry. In 2005–06 the RDAs spent in excess of £2 billion on the promotion of five statutory goals: economic development and regeneration, business efficiency and competitiveness, employment creation, skills up-grading and sustainable development.

The Regional Assemblies oversee and advise the RDAs whose officials are obliged to consult members of the Assemblies on a regular basis and to submit themselves to a process of annual scrutiny by the members of the Assemblies. The Assembly members have three core duties: to scrutinise the work of the RDAs and other public sector bodies active in the regions, to give voice to regional concerns and aspirations in Whitehall and in European institutions, and to engage in the formulation of Regional Spatial and Transport Strategies.

16.4 conclusion

The process of devolution, which has created a Parliament for Scotland, an Assembly for Wales, an Assembly for Northern Ireland (when the peace process has not required its suspension) and a regional tier of governance for England, has been little short of a constitutional transformation for the United Kingdom. More by default than by design, a new quasi-federal system of government, with a division of powers on geographical and historical lines, has come into being.

The various devolution Acts of the late 1990s and the early years of the twenty-first century left little to chance and Ministers demonstrated their determination to apply considerable amounts of glue to hold the United Kingdom together. For example, most of the big policy issues remain matters which are legally reserved to Whitehall and Westminster; a complicated paraphernalia of constitutional checks and balances (Memoranda of Understanding, Concordats, UK-wide Joint Ministerial Committees, constitutional conventions and other devices) was introduced to make it very difficult for the UK to break apart; and the officials serving the various devolved Administrations have been obliged to remain part of the UK Civil Service. These precautionary measures will almost certainly prevent such a deterioration in relations between the UK authorities and the devolved Administrations that it becomes necessary to refer a dispute to the ultimate arbitration of the judiciary.[5]

Devolution is really a matter of letting go the better to hold on to what you have long enjoyed. The real political risk to this strategy could arise if the English lost interest in 'defending the Union' and if at the same time the Nationalists succeeded in assuming power in Scotland and possibly Wales and Northern Ireland. This scenario is perhaps unlikely, but not impossible. It has to be put in the scales alongside the more idealistic arguments for devolution all round, such as the view expressed by the Constitution Unit that 'breaking the central monopoly on the design of public policy could bring overall benefits through the encouragement of competition, diversity and wider participation in the political process.'[6] This could still be one of the prizes of an adventurous policy.

SUGGESTED QUESTIONS

1   Explain the structure of devolved and regional government in the United Kingdom.
2   What functions and powers have been devolved in the United Kingdom and what remain the responsibility of the centre?
3   'The United Kingdom is a unitary state with all political authority ultimately centralised.' Discuss.

local government

Within the nations of the United Kingdom, the term 'local government' is a somewhat misleading one as it has been used to describe what has been and is largely the implementation and delivery of national policies under the guidance of locally elected Councillors.

When considering this subject it is important to distinguish at the outset between *local government*, which can be defined simply as directly elected Local Authorities (the term often used to describe the units of local government in the United Kingdom); and *local administration*, which includes the local offices of central Government and its Agencies (see Chapter 14) and the local administration of justice (see Chapter 18). The focus in this chapter is on directly elected local authorities – in other words, primary local government.

Local authorities do not have any real autonomy and are constitutionally subordinate to Parliament at Westminster (and, where applicable, to devolved Assemblies). What they can and cannot do is specified in Acts of Parliament (as interpreted by the Courts), which means that Parliament at Westminster can both create and abolish local-authority powers and, indeed, local authorities themselves. Consequently, local authorities are only allowed to do what is authorized by law; anything else is **ultra vires** (beyond their authority). If Councillors act 'ultra vires' they can be prosecuted and fined. In short, two features of local government in Britain are key – namely no guaranteed constitutional status or protection and no unambiguous power of general competence.

17.1 functions and powers

The functions and powers of local government in England and Wales are set out in the relevant statutes, notably the Local Government Acts of 1888, 1972, 1985, 1992, 2000 and 2003. Such legislation specified the powers which are to be exercised by the various levels of local government, and there is a clear understanding that all powers, which are not statutorily designated for local authorities, remain the preserve of either devolved Parliaments/Assemblies or ultimately central Government – assuming that Parliament has provided the necessary statutory powers in the first place. Indeed Parliament is able to create, modify or even abolish aspects of local government in the United Kingdom, as was witnessed in 1972 when the Northern Ireland Stormont Parliament was suspended and its powers transferred to Parliament at Westminster, or in 1984–85 when legislation was put through Parliament to abolish the Greater London Council (GLC) and the other Metropolitan County Councils, or in 1997–99 when legislation was passed to create a Scottish Parliament, a Welsh Assembly and a Greater London Authority (GLA).

statutory duties

Local authorities are given statutory duties in Acts of Parliament (or Acts approved by devolved Parliaments/Assemblies). Such legislation – be it Westminster legislation or legislation from a devolved Parliament/Assembly – sets out what the statutory duties shall be in each case. This means that local authorities have to perform certain functions which either the Westminster Parliament or devolved Parliament/Assembly has assigned to them and they carry out their duties in accordance with the terms of the legislation.

For example, the **1944 Education Act** stipulated that local Authorities should be responsible for providing public education for all children in their areas who are within the statutory age range for school education. Equally, the **1972 Chronically Sick and Disabled Persons Act** laid statutory duties on local authorities to provide care for all such people within their areas in the various ways prescribed in the legislation. Or again the **1977 Homeless Persons Act** imposed a statutory duty on local authorities to house the homeless, provided the latter satisfy certain prescribed conditions and have not made themselves deliberately homeless. Similarly, the **1992 Community Care Act** obliged all local Authorities to take the lead in organising suitable care and support for all those who need care in the community, including the chronically sick and those with physical or mental disability. More recently, the **1998 Crime and Disorder Act** formally provided a community safety role for local authorities; while the **2000 Freedom of Information Act** imposed a duty on public bodies to publish information and gave citizens a statutory right of access to information held by public bodies. However, statutes are sometimes vague, while Circulars from central Government are not binding. So even when performing statutory duties, there can be variations in the actual outcomes in local authorities. Consequently the professionals involved in the implementation of national standards can have an important effect upon what is or is not delivered.

discretionary powers

Local authorities are also given discretionary powers in Acts of Parliament (or in Acts from the devolved Parliament/Assemblies). Once again such legislation sets out in each case the areas and the extent to which such powers may be exercised. This means that local Authorities are endowed with discretionary powers to provide certain services, *if they wish to do so and assuming they can raise the necessary finance.*

For example, the **1969 Children and Young Persons Act** gave local authorities the discretionary powers to do all sorts of caring and compassionate things for young people in trouble, but failed to make available the extra money without which it proved difficult to implement large sections of the Act. More recently, the **2000 Local Government Act** gave local authorities the power to promote the economic, social or environmental well-being of their area and the ability to review and make new arrangements.

The **2003 Local Government Act** included a general power for Best Value Authorities (as defined in section 1 of the 1999 Local Government Act) in both England and Wales to charge for discretionary services.

During the period of public expenditure restraint imposed by the Conservative Government after 1979, many local authorities pressed for discretionary rather than mandatory powers whenever they were affected by new legislation, so that they might have a better chance of living within the tight financial limits set by central Government. Thus the discretionary powers, which used to be seen as a way of extending local provision of national services, came to be regarded by many local authorities as a way of saving money, since this allowed them to reduce or withdraw such services without incurring legislative or judicial penalties.

division of functions

There is certainly no sense that 'one size fits all' as far as local government is concerned. At the most local level there are more than 11,500 *Parish, Town or Community Councils*, entities that represent community views and have very restricted powers, providing what are referred to as 'low-level' local services – such as village halls, war memorials and playgrounds, as well as having some involvement in community transport initiatives, cultural projects and the use of crime prevention equipment. In addition, they must be notified of all planning applications and consulted about certain by-laws.

Putting Parish Councils to one side, the traditional structure of local government in England has been organized in two tiers, namely District Councils and County Councils:

At present, *County Councils* – of which there are 34 in England – have statutory responsibilities for transport, highways, police, fire service, Court administration, overspill housing, strategic planning, consumer protection, refuse disposal, education, public libraries and personal social services.

Non-Metropolitan *District Councils*, of which there are 238 in England, have statutory responsibilities for housing, local planning, environmental health, minor roads, licensing of public houses and places of entertainment, and the registration of births, marriages and deaths.

In the six metropolitan areas of England – Greater Manchester, Merseyside,

South Yorkshire, Tyne and Wear, West Midlands and West Yorkshire – there are 36 *Metropolitan District Councils* (sometimes referred to as Borough Councils or City Councils) though, since their abolition in 1986, there are no Metropolitan County Councils. The former have the same statutory responsibilities as the non-Metropolitan District Councils, with the addition of education, public libraries and personal social services. Before 1986 the upper- and lower-levels of Metropolitan local government used to share statutory responsibility for museums and art galleries, parks and open spaces, municipal swimming baths, regional airports and land acquired for development. However, as a result of the abolition of the Metropolitan Counties in 1986, these tasks were taken on by the Metropolitan Districts. Only police, fire services and public transport were transferred to statutory joint boards, while a few residual functions, such as land drainage, flood protection and some arts sponsorship, were transferred to other public bodies.[1]

In London, in addition to 32 *Borough Councils* and *the Corporation of the City of London*,[2] there is a *Greater London Authority* (GLA) consisting of a directly elected executive *Mayor* and a 25-member *Assembly*. Proposed by the Labour Government in 1998[3] and approved by the people of London in a referendum in May 1998,[4] the GLA assumed its responsibilities in 2000. The Mayor, who is scrutinized by and accountable to the Assembly, has responsibility for transport, planning, economic development and regeneration, the environment, policing, fire and emergency planning, health, and culture, media and sport. As such the mayor is accountable for an expenditure budget of £10.7 billion (2007–08).

In July 2006, following a consultation process launched the previous November, the Government announced an enhanced package of powers for the Greater London Authority (GLA). This included new lead roles for the Mayor on housing and adult skills; a strengthened role over planning; and additional strategic powers in a wide range of policy areas including waste, culture and sport, health, climate change and appointments to the boards of functional bodies. In addition, the package enhanced the ability of the London

Single-tier Unitary Authorities, introduced in 1995/96, took over all aspects of local government within their geographical area. There are currently 47 such authorities in England, 32 in Scotland, and 22 in Wales. In addition there are 26 single-tier District Councils in Northern Ireland.

Also of note has been the appearance of directly elected executive Mayors, an option which was formally introduced in the 2000 Local Government Act. By 2007 13 directly elected Mayors were in place.[5]

Under the pressure of successive phases of Westminster legislation passed at the behest of the Conservative Government in the 1980s and 1990s, elected local government was required to 'market test' many of its own services, to introduce compulsory competitive tendering (CCT), and to cede to Special Purpose Bodies many of the duties, powers and functions which it previously performed within a legislative framework set by statute.[6]

Consequently, there are a large number of 'Special Purpose Bodies' or *Quangos* involved in one way or another in the delivery of services at the local level.[7] This gradual erosion of the role of local government as a *provider*, as distinct from purchaser or regulator of local services, was commended by its proponents as a drive towards the creation of 'enabling' local authorities. Although in 1999 the Labour Government replaced CCT with a new duty for local Councils to ensure 'Best Value' in procuring local services for the public, this did not reduce the role of these Special Purpose Bodies.

The division of functions and the distribution of responsibilities between the different kinds of local authorities and the various levels of local government – as well as the vesting of functions in Special Purpose Bodies which by-pass local government altogether – is fiendishly complicated and has been subject to a number of changes over the years. The current arrangements are shown in Figure 17.1.

Local authority responsibility for major services in England

	Metropolitan areas		Shire areas			London area		
	Single purpose authorities	District councils	County councils or unitaries	District councils or unitaries	Single purpose authorities	City of London	London boroughs	GLA
Education		✔	✔			✔	✔	
Highways[a]		✔	✔			✔	✔	✔
Transport planning		✔	✔			✔	✔	✔
Passenger transport	✔		✔					✔
Social services		✔	✔			✔	✔	
Housing		✔		✔		✔	✔	
Libraries		✔	✔			✔	✔	
Leisure and recreation		✔		✔		✔	✔	
Environemntal health		✔		✔		✔	✔	
Waste collection		✔		✔		✔	✔	
Waste disposal[b]	✔	✔	✔			✔	✔	
Planning applications		✔		✔		✔	✔	
Strategic planning		✔	✔			✔	✔	✔
Police	✔				✔	✔		✔
Fire[c]	✔		✔		✔			✔
Local taxation		✔		✔		✔	✔	

(a) Transport for London (TfL) is the highways authority for about 5% of London roads.

(b) Waste disposal for some areas of London is carried out by separate waste disposal authorities. The GLA has strategic, but not operational, responsibility for municipal waste.

(c) Combined fire authorities are responsible for fire services in the shire areas affected by reorganisation from April 1998.

source: 'Local Government Finance Statistics England', No 16, Office of the Deputy Prime Minister, 28 November 2005.

figure **17.1** **Local government (England) functions and responsibilities**

17.2 structure

historical origins

The system of local government that exists in Britain today is deeply rooted in the past. Indeed, it is possible to trace its origins back at least to medieval times.[8] Important towns and cities were given powers of self-government by Royal Charter, the first such Charter being granted to Malmesbury in Wiltshire in 800, with many more being granted from the twelfth century onwards. In rural communities a limited form of local government began to develop based upon church parishes as a consequence of the introduction of the Poor Law at the beginning of the seventeenth century.[9] It was the Industrial Revolution that provided the impetus for more significant reform to deal with issues such as housing, sanitation and policing in the rapidly expanding urban areas. Corporate boroughs were created in 1835 and their powers enhanced later in the nineteenth century, while separate bodies were established to deal with matters such as education and highways. Nonetheless, the first comprehensive system of local Councils was not established until the latter part of the nineteenth century: In 1888 and 1889 elected County Councils were introduced in England, Scotland and Wales; and a lower tier of local government was introduced in England (excluding London) and Wales in 1894, in London in 1899 and Scotland in 1900.

twentieth-century developments

By the beginning of the twentieth century local government functioned on a predominantly two-tier structure, although the major towns and cities (excluding London) were distinct and self-governing entities. Broadly speaking this system remained unchanged until the 1960s and 1970s.

In 1965, as a result of the **1963 Greater London Act**, the government of London was reorganized. The London County Council was abolished and replaced by a much larger strategic authority, the Greater London Council (GLC), and 32 London Borough Councils. The Corporation (City) of London continued as a distinct, separate entity.

In 1966 a **Royal Commission on Local Government in England** was established under the chairmanship of Lord Redcliffe-Maud. The Report, published in 1969, recommended the creation of a broadly single-tier system in England, along with a higher tier of regional government.[10] The Labour Government published a *White Paper* on Local Government in England which supported most of the findings of the Royal Commission, particularly in respect of unitary local government.[11] However, following the change of Government as a result of the 1970 General Election, a new *White Paper* on Local Government in England was published in 1971 which rejected unitary local authorities and supported two-tier local government throughout England and Wales. As a result, the **1972 Local Government Act** (which came into effect in 1974) reduced the previous mosaic of about 1300 local authorities to six large Metropolitan Councils, 39 County Councils (for example, Devon, Kent, Norfolk), 36 Metropolitan District Councils, and 296 County District Councils. Thus, a total of 377 Local Authorities replaced the previous 1300 or so, and the interdependence of town and country became the guiding principle of the structure of local government in England.

In *Wales* local government was reorganized by the 1972 Act, which introduced eight County Councils and 37 District Councils on the same basis as in England. In *Scotland* – through the 1973 Local Government (Scotland) Act which came into effect in 1975 – a two-tier structure of nine Regional Councils and 53 District Councils was introduced everywhere except in the three island areas of Orkney, Shetland and the Western Isles. The division of functions between the two levels was in many ways similar to that introduced in England and Wales. In *Northern Ireland* the system of local government was determined by the 1972 Local Government (Northern Ireland) Act which came into force in 1973 and which created a single tier of local government in the shape of 26 District Councils.

Significant reforms took place under the Conservative Administrations of Margaret Thatcher (1979–90) and John Major (1990–97). The Greater London Council and the six Metropolitan County Councils were abolished by Acts of Parliament in 1984 and 1985 which came into effect in 1986. The functions of the Metropolitan County Councils were reallocated to the Borough and District Councils, statutory Joint Boards and various unelected bodies. The abolition of the upper-tier authorities was intended to remove a source of bitter conflict with central Government, to save money after incurring some transitional costs, and to provide a simpler and more accountable structure of local government in the large Metropolitan areas.

The **1992 Local Government Act** created a new Local Government Commission to review local-government structures and boundaries in England. Its task was to tour the country examining the structures of local government in the different localities. The intention was that its recommendations would lead to Parliamentary legislation for a wide variety of structural changes, or possibly no change at all, according to the strength and direction of local representations. In this process there was to be no single model of local government for England, although Ministerial guidance in Circulars indicated a general preference for the abolition of the Counties and the introduction of sizeable unitary authorities based on enlarged Districts. In the event the Commission recommended the retention of two-tier local government, but did suggest unitary authorities in some areas. As a result, 14 Unitary Authorities were introduced in time for the May 1995 Local Government Elections – for example, Bristol, the Isle of Wight, Middlesbrough and Hull – and these took up their responsibilities in April 1996.

In March 1993 a White Paper was published on the reorganisation of local government in *Wales* which proposed the creation of 21 Unitary Authorities. In fact 22 single-tier Authorities were created in time for elections in May 1995 and the resulting Councils took up their responsibilities in April 1996. Similarly, in July 1993, a White Paper proposed the reorganisation of local government in *Scotland*, recommending the creation of single-tier Councils. These proposals were given statutory effect in the 1994 Local Government (Scotland) Act which created 29 Unitary Councils together with the three Unitary Island Councils that already existed – a total of 32 Unitary Authorities with responsibility for the full range of local government services.

post-1997 developments

When the Labour party under Tony Blair entered office in 1997, it did so promising a more cooperative and collaborative relationship between central and local government. In July 1997 the Government published a Green Paper entitled **New Leadership for London** outlining its proposals for modernizing the government of London.[12] This was followed in March 1998 by the publication of a White Paper entitled **A Mayor and Assembly for London**[13] which proposed a new strategic authority for the city, to be called the Greater London Authority (GLA), made up of a directly elected Mayor and an Assembly, with new bodies responsible for transport and economic development and new independent authorities for police, fire and emergency planning. Following a London-wide referendum on the matter, which resulted in an affirmative vote, Parliament approved the passage of the **1999 Greater London Authority Act** establishing the Mayor and the GLA.

In July 1998 the Government published a White Paper entitled **Modern Local Government – in touch with the people** which outlined a programme for the reform and modernization of local government in England.[14] It focused on the creation of new political structures, improving local democracy, increasing local financial accountability, establishing a new ethical framework for Councillors and Council employees, and improving local services through 'Best Value'. Underpinning the approach was a dual emphasis upon democratic renewal and service improvement. In March 1999 another White Paper, **Local Leadership, Local Choice**, was put forward by the Government as the next step in local government modernization and in bringing about fundamental cultural change in local government.[15]

The Government sought to extend the concept of 'modernisation' to local government via initiatives, such as the 'Beacon Councils' which were recognized as examples of best practice in service delivery across local government and then rewarded with a greater degree of institutional autonomy for delivering services in the most effective ways to meet the requirements of their local communities. This initiative was supported by the use of performance indicators and performance plans whereby all Councils had to produce a plan that outlined what services they would deliver and how and when they would improve services. Another feature in this approach was the focus on Local Public Service Agreements whereby each local authority would negotiate directly with the relevant central Government Department on its targets, on its plans for electronic service delivery and new patterns of public service partnerships.

Under the **Local Government Act 2000** all local authorities were required to choose a new structure of political management, separating their executive and scrutiny functions, and to keep open the possibility of opting for directly elected executive Mayors in the event that people voted for it in a local referendum.

In December 2001 another White Paper was published – **Strong Local Leadership and Quality Public Services** – which set out proposals to reform Council services with an emphasis upon a new performance framework focusing upon outcomes rather than processes and enhancing local democracy and community leadership. In 2002 this approach resulted in the introduction of a Comprehensive Performance Assessment for each local authority designed to give an overall view of how each authority was performing and how well placed it was to deliver further improvements. The system was to be operated under the auspices of the Audit Commission.

In May 2006 a new Department for Communities and Local Government (DCLG) was established with responsibility for local government, housing, urban regeneration and planning, as well as a remit to promote community cohesion and equality. In preparation for another Local Government White Paper the Government outlined a shift from the 'top-down state' to the 'trusting state', from 'earned autonomy' to 'presumed autonomy', from a process-driven system to a people-driven one.[16] It remains to be seen what all this political rhetoric will mean in practice.

17.3 financial arrangements

Local government expenditure accounts for about a quarter of public spending in the United Kingdom and for 2007/08 expenditure by UK local authorities was estimated at £158 billion. The methods of financing local government have varied over the years, but local government revenue has traditionally come from three main sources: local taxes; grants from central Government and the devolved Administrations; and from rents, fees and charges.

local taxes

The form of local taxation to finance local government has varied over the years from **Domestic and Business Rates** before 1990 to the **Community Charge or Poll Tax** from 1990 to 1993 to the **Council Tax** since 1993. All of these taxes have been unpopular to a greater or lesser extent with various groups in the population, and any alternative, such as local income tax, would also attract criticism.

Rates are property taxes levied according to a complicated formula on domestic, commercial and industrial (but not agricultural) buildings and are assessed on the rateable value of the land or buildings concerned. In theory, they represent the rent at which the property could be let (if there were a market for such lettings) minus the notional cost of repairs, insurance and other maintenance expenses. When they existed, they were paid every year (normally in two or more instalments) and the abstruse calculations on which they were based were reviewed about every ten years by the Inland Revenue in periodic revaluations which took account of inflation and any improvements to the property over the intervening period. Before 1979 rates raised nearly half of the revenue needed to finance local government services. Although they were an unpopular form of taxation, it was never easy to identify a simpler or more cost-effective way of raising large sums of revenue from local sources.[17]

Nonetheless, the third Thatcher Administration (1987–2000) was determined to abolish the domestic rates, but not the business rates, and introduce a *Community Charge* or *Poll Tax* in their place. The initial attractions of the Poll Tax were that it had to be paid by everyone and that the cost of local government services would be borne, at least in part, by all those that used them. However, the tax was regressive in that it hit the poor proportionately more than the rich and entailed finding out who and where everyone was, an aspect of its operation which provoked thousands of people to disappear from the electoral register. It did not take long for the tax to provoke massive opposition, first in Scotland and then in the rest of Great Britain. There were riots in the streets of London and other major cities and Ministers eventually realized that it was a hopeless cause. It made the Conservative Government deeply unpopular and contributed to the downfall of Margaret Thatcher in November 1990.

When John Major became Prime Minister in succession to Margaret Thatcher in November 1990, he and his colleagues had little difficulty in persuading Parliament to abolish the Poll Tax and replace it with a *Council Tax*, which came into effect in April 1993.[18] This tax, which is levied on every residential household, is calculated largely on the basis of property values as reflected in broad valuation bands based on property prices in April 1991 and supposedly revalued every ten years. It also takes account of the number of people living in each dwelling by allowing a 25 per cent discount for those living alone. It was introduced at relatively low levels thanks to a considerable Exchequer subsidy paid for by increasing the standard rate of value added tax from 15 per cent to 17.5 per cent, and its early impact was also mitigated by transitional relief phased over a number of years. For commercial and industrial premises the Uniform Business Rate was retained, although efforts were made to ameliorate its impact upon industry and commerce by adjusting the transitional reliefs. Agricultural land remained unaffected.

grants from central Government or devolved Administrations

The bulk of the money needed for local government spending has traditionally come from a system of central Government grants. These have taken two main forms. *First*, there are specific grants in aid of particular local purposes – for example, 50 per cent of local police expenditure or specific housing subsidies for poorer tenants. *Second*, there are general grants to each local authority in order to increase its overall income, especially if it is located in a poorer part of the country.

The total amount of *Rate Support Grant* (RSG) is fixed every year by central Government after consultation with the local authority Associations and the Consultative Council on Local Government Finance. The RSG is composed of a *needs element* assessed for each local authority mainly on the basis of demographic factors, a *resources element* paid to those authorities where the rateable base is below the national average, and a *domestic element* designed to bring some relief to all Council Tax payers. The most notable characteristics of the system are a bias in favour of income redistribution from the richer to the poorer parts of the country and considerable power for central Government in its ability not only to limit the expenditure of individual local authorities, but also to switch or withhold grants from individual local authorities.

rents, fees and charges

A small proportion of local authority expenditure is financed from rents, fees and charges for local services. Examples would include charges levied for the use of leisure facilities and fees charged by libraries for late returns.

general observations

It seems that there is never any certainty and certainly not much continuity in the system of local government finance. Following yet another review of local government finance in England, which was published in 2004, the Government announced that the Council Tax was to be retained, but that an independent inquiry under Sir Michael Lyons, a former senior local government official, was to be set up to make another examination of the options for further reform. It issued its report in 2007.[19] A breakdown of local government income and expenditure is provided in Figure 17.2.

The financing of local government has been both complicated and controversial in Britain. From the early 1950s local authority spending grew steadily and usually at a faster rate than the economy as a whole. This growth was bearable in the 1950s and 1960s when the British economy was growing at about 3 per cent a year and there was general public and political support for constantly increasing public expenditure. However, following the 1976 financial crisis, when the then Labour Government had to turn to the International Monetary Fund (IMF) for assistance, successive Governments have felt it necessary to control all forms of public spending and local authority spending has been no exception to this rule.

The fact that local government spending is primarily financed by grants from central Government or the devolved Administrations, that in England and Wales the non-domestic rate is set nationally by central Government (in Scotland non-domestic rates are levied by local authorities), that central Government has the power to limit increases in local authority budgets and hence the level of Council Tax, all combine to ensure that central Government

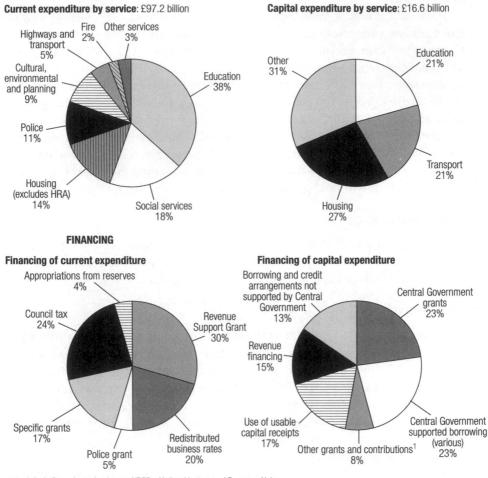

EXPENDITURE

Current expenditure by service: £97.2 billion

- Highways and transport 5%
- Fire 2%
- Other services 3%
- Cultural, environmental and planning 9%
- Police 11%
- Housing (excludes HRA) 14%
- Education 38%
- Social services 18%

Capital expenditure by service: £16.6 billion

- Other 31%
- Education 21%
- Transport 21%
- Housing 27%

FINANCING

Financing of current expenditure

- Appropriations from reserves 4%
- Council tax 24%
- Specific grants 17%
- Police grant 5%
- Redistributed business rates 20%
- Revenue Support Grant 30%

Financing of capital expenditure

- Borrowing and credit arrangements not supported by Central Government 13%
- Revenue financing 15%
- Use of usable capital receipts 17%
- Other grants and contributions[1] 8%
- Central Government grants 23%
- Central Government supported borrowing (various) 23%

note: 1. Including private developers, NDPBs, National Lottery and European Union
source: Office for National Statistics

figure **17.2**   **local government in England: expenditure and financing in 2005–06**

is very much in the driving seat as far as the financial arrangements for local government are concerned. However, this weakens local government and severely limits its real autonomy as a public service provider.

The financial problems of local government have also not been made any easier by the fact that so much of the new legislation initiated by central Government and approved by Parliament has had financial implications for local Authorities for which they have not always been sufficiently compensated by the Exchequer. Many statutory duties have been placed on local authorities over the years in fields such as housing, education, social services and community care, but without all the financial support from the centre which is required to guarantee the delivery of high-quality public services with only limited possibilities of raising extra finance from local sources.

The composition of local authorities in England and Wales can be summarised by saying that each Unitary Council has between 40 and 70 elected Councillors, each County Council has between 60 and 100 elected Councillors and each District Council has between 30 and 80 elected Councillors. In each case, Councillors are elected for fixed terms. At present those elected to the London Borough Councils, the Unitary Councils, the County Councils and some of the non-Metropolitan District Councils are elected every four years, whereas in some other non-Metropolitan District Councils and in the Metropolitan District Councils outside London one-third of the Councillors are elected every third year. For electoral purposes some of the Unitary Councils and all of the County Councils are divided into single-member constituencies, whereas the District and London Boroughs and some Unitary Councils are divided into wards, each represented by between one and three Councillors, depending on geographical area and population.

The Labour Government that came to power in 1997 declared that the traditional way in which Councils worked – namely, through a cumbersome committee system whereby decisions were taken in committees and subcommittees which were microcosms of the full Council – no longer worked satisfactorily and showed signs of inefficiency, opacity and weak local accountability.[20] It was, therefore, not surprising that for this reason the **Local Government Act** 2000 sought to reform local government political structures and offered local Councillors a choice of three or four different political structures, each of which was designed to separate those with a (front-bench) executive role from those with a (back-bench) scrutiny role. The three basic models ere:

- A directly elected executive Mayor with his or her appointed Cabinet drawn from among the elected Councilors
- A Council Leader with a Cabinet of senior colleagues who could be appointed by the Leader and/or elected by the Council
- A directly elected non-executive Mayor with a Council Manager appointed by the Council.

A fourth option was also possible in local authorities with a population of under 85,000 – namely, a model in which the full Council would have an enhanced policy-making role and all Councillors would act together.

In order to secure a directly elected Mayor, public endorsement would have to be obtained through a local referendum. The legislation also placed a duty on Councils to review their management arrangements and draw up a plan with a timetable for the introduction of one of the new models. By 2007 the following types of political arrangement had been made in England:

- Mayor and Cabinet (10 of these)
- Leader and Cabinet (316 of these)

- Mayor and Council Manager (1 of these)
- Other arrangements (59 of these).

In addition, all Councils now have either a single scrutiny committee to oversee the work of the entire Executive or several scrutiny committees for the various areas of local government responsibility – for example, education, social services or the environment. Such committees consist of Councillors who are not members of the Executive and who reflect the political balance of the local authority as a whole. At the same time regulatory committees continue to exist for the oversight of quasi-judicial decisions on matters such as local planning and licensing.

Councillors are not much more representative of the general public than are Members of Parliament. To be eligible for election, however, they must live or work in the local authority area concerned. There is not a great deal of statistical evidence about their make-up and socio-economic characteristics. [21]

In 1998 a census conducted by the Local Government Management Board showed that women, ethnic minorities and the young were seriously under-represented in the Councils of England and Wales; indeed about three-quarters were male and 97 per cent were white. The survey showed that the 'typical' Councillor was a 55-year-old white male with a degree or professional qualification who had held such a position for almost nine years and who was also a school governor or on the board of another public body.[22]

The picture has not changed much since then, as no more than 29 per cent of Councillors in England are female, as compared with 22 per cent in Scotland, Wales and Northern Ireland respectively.[23] Survey data also shows that 52 per cent of Councillors in England and Wales are in work and therefore carrying out Council duties in addition to their day jobs, while the remaining 48 per cent are either retired or not working. The average length of service for a Councillor in England and Wales is eight years.

Local authority officials are the other vital element in local government. In general, they assist Councillors in much the same way as civil servants assist Ministers, but there are some significant contrasts with the Civil Service, especially the fact that the key officials in local government are normally well-qualified professionals in the particular sphere of local government activity in which they are engaged. Thus Chief Education Officers and their senior colleagues are often former teachers, Directors of Social Services and their senior staff are often former social workers, and Chief Planning Officers and others within the Planning Department are often qualified planners, surveyors or architects. The key point is that Departments of local government are staffed by professionals and, as such, have a considerable influence on the policy of elected Councillors.

The main similarity between local government officials and civil servants in central Government is that both are expected to remain politically neutral and to carry out the policies of their political masters. In local government the principal effect of such political neutrality is that most policy decisions are heavily influenced by the technical and expert advice of the officials concerned. Of course, the actual decisions are taken by the Councillors, but there can be occasions when they appear to be acting as little more than political spokesmen for the officials. On the other hand, there has also been some concern expressed over the years that some local government officials appear to be uncomfortably 'political' in their motivation and their actions. A balanced conclusion would suggest that both propositions have some truth in them.

17.5 local–central relations

The relations between local and central Government have seldom been easy or unambiguously defined. In the nineteenth century there was a lengthy search for a system of local government which would be both efficient and democratic, although not necessarily for a relationship with central Government that was designed to be mutually beneficial. Throughout the twentieth century and on into the twenty first there have been notable occasions when the usual habits of cooperation between local and central Government have broken down and given rise to serious misunderstanding and conflict. In general, however, local authorities have sought faithfully to perform their statutory duties and have acted within the statutory constraints laid upon them by Parliament.[24]

constitutional relations

The constitutional relations between local and central Government have varied greatly over the centuries in Britain. Between 1688 and 1835 the effective independence of local government could hardly have been greater, since there was virtually no interference from central Government and only minimal control. However, following the 1835 Municipal Corporations Act, the powers and influence of central Government grew steadily and there has been an apparently remorseless tendency towards the centralisation of political power. This should not be thought particularly surprising in a unitary state, such as Britain, in which all the legal power and authority of local government has always derived from Acts of Parliament and in which local government has been able to rely only on local elections and local pride to buttress its sense of legitimacy in dealings with central Government.

Today the constitutional relationship between local and central Government is invariably described by Ministers as a partnership, but by Councillors in much less flattering terms and, occasionally, as a central dictatorship. Despite the fact that the pendulum swings back and forth over the years, it is not only cynics who conclude that, in both Whitehall and Westminster, not much more than lip-service is paid to the idea of real powers for local government.

It might have been more logical over the years to have developed clear-cut statements and constitutional rules about the division of powers and responsibilities between local and central Government, and then to have entrenched such arrangements in a new constitutional settlement. Yet the principle of Parliamentary supremacy did not permit such an outcome and it seems rather unlikely that it ever will, unless such a move is brought about by Britain's membership of the European Union. Consequently, the compromise which has been reached gives local government a clearly *subordinate* constitutional position, while allowing it a more *coordinate* relationship with central Government when dealing with a wide variety of practical issues.

administrative relations

The administrative relationship between local and central Government has not always been transparent and clear cut, something that was apparent from the 2000 report of the Phillips Inquiry into BSE and variant CJD in the United Kingdom.[25] This pointed out that *although the Department of the Environment was responsible for local government structure and funding, no single Government Department was responsible for central/local government relations overall. Each Department's contact with the authorities related to the service(s) with which it was concerned.*

The Labour Government that came to power in 1997 declared that it was in favour of 'joined-up government', by which it meant that central Government would respond to public interests and concerns in a coherent and seamless way rather than pursue policies and methods of public administration via vertical 'silos' or delivery mechanisms. Initially, it set out to do this via a monster Department for Transport, Local Government and the Regions (DTLR) which was successively under the leadership of a leading Blairite, Stephen Byers, and the Deputy Prime Minister, John Prescott. When this Department proved too unwieldy for the Ministers concerned, its many responsibilities were divided up and distributed among several different Departments. In 2005 the administrative relationship with local government was given more focus in a new Department for Communities and Local Government (DCLG) with responsibilities for local government, housing, urban regeneration and planning among other things. It seems that, whatever the Departmental architecture in Whitehall, there is no escape from the need for a lead Department to coordinate central–local relations in government and for a variety of other functional Departments, such as the Home Office or the Department for Transport, to deal with their counterparts in local government on a sectoral basis.

political relations

Political relations between local and central Government have not been easy in modern times, since they are often characterised by inherent conflict of interest and incompatible political objectives. This was especially true in the 1980s when an ideological Conservative Government under Margaret Thatcher had a long-running battle with many urban local authorities led by left-wing Labour politicians of a campaigning disposition. Of course, there is bound to be tension or worse in a relationship which depends on mutual understanding and cooperation between inherently unequal partners. Furthermore, the relationship is bound to become rather bitter when central Government seeks to impose tight financial constraints on local authorities and when many local authorities are run by politically motivated individuals with principles and objectives which are at odds with those of Ministers.

Since 1997 with the Labour party in Government at Westminster, the Conservatives and Liberal Democrats have made advances in local government elections at the expense of Labour. As a consequence of these developments, mutual suspicion and resentment has once again been in evidence between local and central Government, although Labour Ministers have made frequent attempts to alleviate such difficulties with modernized policies and procedures which have included the use of Comprehensive Performance Assessments (CPAs) designed to allow more real autonomy to cost effective and efficient local authorities.

In general, the partnership between local and central Government is bound to involve some sharing of decision-making powers – with central Government providing the financial and legislative framework through Parliament and local government providing many of the delivery mechanisms for public goods and services. Yet most people in local government would probably agree with N.P. Hepworth when he wrote that 'local government does not share in the decision making of central Government; it makes representations, but that is not the same thing'.[26] On the other hand, the partnership can seem quite real, in that many aspects of Government policy depend for their success on the active and willing cooperation of local government. For example, with local authorities accounting for a little more than one-quarter of total public spending, overall public expenditure control is dependent on local government cooperation. Similarly many of the statutory obligations placed on local government by Parliament are couched in broad terms of principle which leave the precise methods of implementation in the hands of local authorities – not to mention the discretionary powers whose use or non-use depends entirely on local government decisions. Furthermore, local authorities have tended to combine in order to maximise their influence on central Government. They do this through their representative bodies – for example, the Local Government Association (LGA) formed in April 1997 to promote the interests of English and Welsh local authorities and whose members include County Councils, Metropolitan District Councils, English Unitary Authorities, London Boroughs, shire District Councils and Welsh Unitary Authorities, as well as Fire Authorities, Police Authorities, National Park Authorities and Passenger Transport Authorities.

While the relationship between local and central Government is reasonably clear cut in constitutional terms, it has often been muddled in administrative terms and ambiguous, even hostile, in political terms. Nevertheless, neither level of government can afford to alienate the other, and neither can achieve all its objectives without the cooperation of the other. Local government now depends very heavily on central Government grants and money from the Uniform Business Rate whose level in any year is determined by central Government. On the other hand, central Government depends heavily on local government for the local administration of national services.

There are four principal ways in which central Government has sought to control local government: namely, legislative control, policy control, administrative control and financial control. Of these, financial control is the most important, but we shall consider each of them in turn.

legislative control

It is the legislative control in Acts of Parliament which establishes the nature and extent of the subordinate powers conferred on local government. As J.A.G. Griffith has explained, 'within the terms on which these powers are bestowed, local authorities are autonomous bodies and a Department [of central Government] which proposes to control the way in which or the extent to which local authorities exercise their powers must be able to point to statutory provisions authorising this intervention.[27] Thus legislative control provides legal safeguards for local government as well as a means of control for central Government.

One of the most widespread criticisms of central control of local authorities, however, has stemmed from the excessive frequency of new Westminster legislation designed to limit, if not remove, what little is left of local government's legal discretion. It has been calculated that at least 150 Acts of Parliament were put on the Statute Book in the years between 1979 and 1997 and more than 60 between 1997 and 2007 which, in one way or another, limited the powers of local authorities. This has done much to demoralise both Councillors and officials in local government.

Such legislative control can take various forms. In many cases the original legislation confers on Ministers the power to make detailed regulations which are binding on local government. For example, it is customary for Whitehall to produce Statutory Instruments which set out the building regulations and the planning regulations to be observed in carrying out local property or transport developments. In some cases local authorities are given power to make by-laws about public footpaths and other very local matters. Yet it is always made clear in the original Westminster legislation that these by-laws must be confirmed by the relevant Minister. Of course, legislative control involves two-way influence and communication, since the representative bodies of local government are extensively consulted in the preparation and the implementation of Westminster legislation which affects local Authorities.

policy control

Another form of central control is provided by the power and influence of Government policy. This can take various forms, depending on the priorities of the party in office and the legal basis of the relationship between local authorities and the various Departments of central Government. For example, the 1948 Children Act and the 1969 Children and Young Persons Act each stipulated that local authorities should exercise statutory functions in this area of policy under the guidance of the relevant Ministers, which has meant, in effect, the policy pursued by the Government of the day. Similarly the Secretary of State for Education has a supervisory and promotional role in relation to the organisation of schools and the supply of teachers in all the Local Education Authorities in England and Wales. This power derives from the 1944 Education Act, as amended by subsequent Education Acts, and it has been exercised by successive Ministers in accordance with their own education policies. Other examples of policy control by Ministers and their civil servants in Whitehall can be found in the spheres of housing and social services. Successive Conservative Governments in the 1980s and 1990s promoted policies of home ownership and home improvement, while since 1997 the Labour Government promoted affordable *home ownership schemes* in order to give greater choice and opportunity to first-time buyers, social tenants, key workers and people who rented privately. Another example would be the requirement laid down by Ministers in 2000 that all public services delivered by local government be made available electronically by 2005. In these ways the policy of the Government of the day has had a considerable influence on the actions and behaviour of local authorities.

As some of the most frequent delivery agents of Government policy, local authorities support, and occasionally challenge, what central Government wishes to do. For example, in the case of the Licensing Act 2003, which came into force in November 2005 and established a single integrated scheme for licensed premises, local Councils were given the responsibility for issuing licences to a wide variety of premises, such as pubs, nightclubs, off-licences and late-night takeaways, most of which had previously been licensed by Magistrates advised by the police. However, Ministers faced considerable criticism for failing to take into account the views and concerns of local authorities and failing adequately to support local authorities as they struggled within a tight deadline to implement a complex new regime that was not of their own choosing. This was a good example of the need for policy to be considered against the criteria of delivery and enforcement which are among the recurrent concerns of local government.

administrative control

Administrative control is another form of control which derives from central Government's responsibility for setting national standards and promoting the efficiency of local government. Ever since the nineteenth century it has been accepted that many functions of government in Britain should be national services locally administered. This has implied the need for administrative control via national standards drawn up by Whitehall civil servants and enforced in many cases by independent inspectorates. For example, Her Majesty's Chief Inspector of Schools at the head of the Office of Standards in Education (OFSTED) monitors educational quality and attainment in schools and regulates the work of other registered inspectors. In the case of the police, the payment of central Government grants to Police Authorities is conditional on satisfactory reports from Her Majesty's Inspectorate of Constabulary about the practices and performance of each of the 43 Constabularies in England and Wales.

The range and power of administrative controls exercised by central Government over local authorities have become increasingly formidable over the years. This is evidenced by initiatives, such as the award of 'Beacon Council' status to encourage best practice in service delivery across local government, the 'Best Value' approach to public procurement and service provision in local government, the use of Local Service Agreements whereby each local authority negotiates directly with the relevant central Government Department to identify agreed targets for service delivery, and by the introduction of Comprehensive Performance Assessments – operated under the auspices of the Audit Commission – to give an overall view of how each local authority is performing and whether it can do even better.

At the same time there is a constant need to deregulate in modern government simply to prevent the inexorable growth of red tape. This has been a continuing challenge in view of the tendency for government at all levels to impose its will upon the private, voluntary and public sectors alike. The spread of regulation of every kind is driven by at least three powerful engines. Firstly, there is the growth of primary legislation under all Administrations in response to interest group pressures, the campaigns of the media and the insistence of public opinion. Secondly, there is the tendency of bureaucrats at all levels of government to 'gold plate' the regulations which are introduced in order to close every loophole and attempt watertight solutions to every problem. Thirdly, there is the joint ambition of politicians in office and the public looking on to raise regulatory standards to meet continually rising public expectations. In this regulatory-merry go-round local government is both a perpetrator and a victim.

financial control

The most powerful form of central control over local government has always been the financial control exercised by the Treasury on behalf of central Government. This can be traced back at least to the 1929 Local Government Act in which the earlier system of assigned revenues was abolished and replaced with a system of specific grants, together with a block grant from central Government to each local authority. In 1948 this system of financial control was supplemented by a system of deficiency payments to those local authorities with rateable values below the average, and in 1958 the whole system was rationalised to enable a new block grant, the Rate Support Grant, to replace the wide variety of specific grants which had grown up over the years. At every stage from then until the present day financial support from central Government has been accompanied by financial control by central

Government. Little more than lip-service has been paid by central Government to the idea of encouraging real financial independence for local Authorities, because the Treasury has traditionally been determined not to relax its control over any significant category of public spending nor to relinquish the right to tax to subnational or supranational levels of government.

In summary, the financial control by central Government of local government has taken four main forms:

- Central Government's ability to set a spending limit for each Council via the Standard Spending Assessment
- Its ability to support local government current expenditure to the tune of 52 per cent on average basis via the Aggregate Exchequer Grant paid to each local authority according to its needs and its population
- Its ability to set the level of the Uniform Business Rate, which currently covers about 21 per cent of all local authority expenditure
- Its ability to control local authority capital expenditure via strict Treasury borrowing limits on local government which forbid the latter from spending more than 25 per cent of their receipts from the sale of Council housing and 50 per cent of their receipts from other asset sales in any one year.

A final point which relates to central Government financial controls over local government is that between 1979 and 1997 a total of more than £25 billion of annual expenditure was transferred from local authorities to special purpose bodies created by central Government. This transfer greatly reduced the amount of public spending over which elected Councillors had some influence and further enhanced the degree of central financial control from Whitehall. This general approach was continued under the post-1997 Labour Governments.

17.7 local government: agent or partner?

With common sense and goodwill on both sides it should be possible to achieve fruitful cooperation between local and central Government. There appear to be three basic conditions which need to be accepted for this to come to pass:

- That there are certain minimum nationwide standards for national services which are provided locally
- That local authorities are best placed to coordinate, if not necessarily provide, many of the public services which people expect
- That the relationship between local and central Government can only work satisfactorily on a basis of trust and mutual respect.

Unfortunately, the second and third of these conditions have proved difficult, if not impossible, to fulfil, especially during the period between 1979 and 1997 when the Conservative Government conducted something close to a vendetta against Labour- and Liberal Democrat-controlled local authorities and the politicians in local government were strongly opposed to many aspects of Conservative national policy. Since Labour came into office in 1997, it has pursued the broad theme of 'inclusion' and this has led Labour Ministers to be less overtly party-political than their Conservative predecessors in dealings with local government. Consequently, it has appeared that central–local relations have improved, although there are still misgivings among local Councillors and local officials about the extent of detailed interference from central Government.

greater local autonomy or further centralisation?

The relationship between local and central Government in Britain has to be considered in the light of broader arguments for greater local autonomy on the one hand or further centralisation on the other. To summarise each side of this important debate, it could be said that the arguments in favour of greater local autonomy include:

‣ The need to diminish the remoteness of Government from its citizens
‣ The desirability of enhancing democratic accountability at local level
‣ The opportunities which could be created for greater public participation
‣ The superior efficiency of small units in the delivery of public services
‣ The reduced financial burden on the Exchequer – as long as local government is given control over more of the revenue needed to finance local services.

On the other hand, the arguments in favour of further centralisation include:

‣ The public pressure for common national standards of service provision
‣ The fact that the attainment of national standards is most likely to be achieved by the imposition of national policy – as for example in school standards
‣ The existence of a Jacobin attitude among Ministers and civil servants which sees any real local autonomy as a threat to coherent national policy.

Bearing in mind that the United Kingdom is probably the most centralized democracy in the Western world, there is obviously a strong case for more countervailing local autonomy. As Professors Jones and Stewart have argued, greater autonomy should be encouraged 'not to let loose rampant and uncontrolled localism and the sharpening of geographical inequalities, but to maintain a more balanced array of pressures in public policy making'.[28] In other words, there is strength in diversity and value in variety, not least as a way of minimising the risk of replicating policy and delivery mistakes on a large scale.

The Labour Party fought the 1997 General Election declaring that there was a need for a new partnership between local and central Government. However, when it came to introduce its most significant piece of legislation on this matter – the Local Government Act 2000 – it was hard to conclude that central Government had abandoned the habit of excessive interference in the detail of local government and there was certainly no sign of willingness on the part of the Treasury to relinquish its control over local expenditure and local revenue. Perhaps the most hopeful development from local government's point of view was the encouragement that Ministers gave to those local authorities which were able to raise their game in service delivery and so earn a degree of greater autonomy. Moreover, if the regionalization of England had taken off, it seems very likely that local government – and especially the County Councils – would have been the losers.

17.8 conclusion

It should be clear from this chapter that the position of local government in the United Kingdom is neither immutable nor easy to describe. However, it can be assessed in terms of its efficiency, vitality, adaptability and capacity for genuine partnership with central Government. We conclude by touching upon each of these aspects in turn.

With regard to *efficiency*, it seems clear that the present division of responsibilities and functions is fairly defensible and does not put such a high premium on the interests of local democracy that the interests of efficiency are unduly compromised. For example, the emphasis on techniques of corporate management within local authorities and the discipline of tough financial limits set by central Government appear to have had a positive effect on the efficiency of local government – certainly that is what the advocates of this approach would argue. On the other hand, the morale of those in local government may have suffered in the relentless drive for efficiency savings.

With regard to *vitality*, the available evidence is somewhat contradictory. On the one hand, the normal turnout at local elections is seldom more than about 40 per cent of those entitled to vote, and at local by-elections it can fall below 30 per cent. This suggests rather scant public interest in the democratic processes of devolved and local government. On the other hand, even a cursory glance at the columns of the local press in any part of the country reveals considerable public interest in the actual decisions of local government. For example, Council Tax payers are very interested in seeing that value for money is secured in local authority spending, while beneficiary groups invariably support the expansion of existing services or the creation of new ones.

With regard to *adaptability*, the record over the years has been quite good. Throughout the 1980s and 1990s, when many social needs increased, the financial resources made available by central Government to local government were consistently squeezed, with the result that the Aggregate Exchequer Grant eventually covered less than half of the total local authority spending compared with nearly two-thirds during the 1970s. The response of local authorities was one of angry criticism, especially from those local authorities in inner-city areas where the social problems were often greatest and it was clear that local

Councillors of all parties resented the financial restrictions which were imposed by central Government. Since the financial year 1999–2000 public expenditure has been more generous, even for local government, and this has lubricated the central–local partnership. However, at the time of writing, the financial climate is once again less benign and the old problem of an inadequate resource base for local government may reappear.

As for the capacity of local government to maintain a *genuine partnership* with central Government, this has been affected by the diminishing extent to which local government has retained responsibility for providing local services. Successive Governments – Conservatives in the 1980s and 1990s and Labour since 1997 – have made determined attempts to encourage the contracting out of local services and to separate the idea of local government *provision* from local government *responsibility* – for example, in the field of Community Care. However, the main explanation for the rather lopsided partnership between local and central Government has been the failure of the former to secure any significant degree of financial autonomy. Indeed, with the switch from local business rates to the Uniform Business Rate and the threat of central Government financial capping, the extent of local government financial autonomy decreased still further. It is, therefore, hard to demonstrate that local government has anything like an equal partnership with central Government.

Even allowing for all its problems and shortcomings, local government in Britain has several points in its favour:

- The diversity of local government contributes to political pluralism
- The institutions of local government offer an important sphere of political activity to a considerable number of elected representatives
- The process of local government stimulates public interest in the local provision of national services
- The delivery of public services has been improved by the application of central Government targets under the general heading of 'modernisation'
- The devolved Administrations in Scotland, Wales and Northern Ireland have brought some valuable variety and public benefit, as well as local accountability, to many parts of the United Kingdom.

Such positive attributes should not be underestimated or ignored. Indeed, with 'the new localism' promoted by all the main parties, the revival of local government may be at hand.

SUGGESTED QUESTIONS

1 Explain the structure and role of local government in Britain today.
2 How is local government financed?
3 'Local government can do only what central Government wants it to do. As a result, local autonomy is a farce.' Is such a view justified?

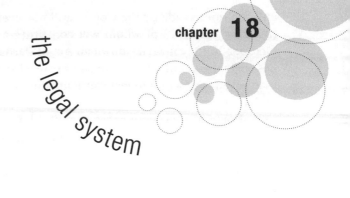

the legal system

There are four main aspects of the legal system in the United Kingdom.[1] All of them are significantly affected by the peculiar nature of the British constitution, which is partly unwritten, partly written but uncodified and which vests supreme legal authority in Parliament rather than in any Court. They are:

- The sphere of *criminal justice*, which involves the application of the criminal law to cases brought to Court by the prosecuting authorities and others
- The sphere of *civil justice*, which involves the application of the civil law to cases brought by various plaintiffs, including individuals, corporate bodies and the Law Officers of the Crown
- The process of *judicial appeal*, which allows those who are dissatisfied with the verdicts of lower Courts or Tribunals to seek redress or reversal of judgment in the higher Courts of Appeal
- The sphere of *administrative law*, which enables the Courts to review the actions of Ministers, local authorities and other public bodies.

A fifth aspect, namely the important sphere of *civil rights and duties*, which determines the complex legal relationship between citizens and the state, is considered in a separate chapter (Chapter 19). This chapter reviews each of these four main aspects. It does so against a contemporary backdrop which reveals further reform and a relationship between the judiciary and the Government which has become strained by the legal implications of 'the war against terror'.

For our purposes in this chapter, the most important single feature of the British constitution is *Parliamentary supremacy* which, in most circumstances, permits the Executive to dominate the political sphere through Parliament. There is no formal separation of powers; rather, the Executive and the Legislature are intertwined and together are able to override the Judiciary. This position is derived from the traditional idea dating from the seventeenth century that Parliament can do anything it wishes: it can make, amend or repeal any law, with the consequence that primary legislation passed by Parliament overrides any decisions made by the Courts and not even the highest Court in the land (the Law Lords, 12 of whom will constitute a separate Supreme Court from October 2009) can strike down an Act of Parliament as unconstitutional.[2] This has shaped and influenced much of the legal system in Britain and traditionally made even very senior judges cautious about explicitly challenging the authority of Parliament.

It should also be noted that common law and statute law are two distinct sources of law, and the power given to judges who use common law as a basis for judgment is of some constitutional significance. Judges are appointed from the ranks of legal professionals with experience in advocacy, there is an independent body of barristers or advocates and Court procedures are based for the most part on adversarial rather than inquisitorial proceedings.

18.1 criminal justice

machinery and procedure

The majority of criminal cases are disposed of in *Magistrates' Courts* and only a minority are tried in the higher Courts. Trial in a Magistrates' Court is summary (that is, without a jury) and takes place before a bench of two or more Justices of the Peace. Most cases are brought by the Crown Prosecution Service which prefers charges against defendants on the basis of police evidence and legal advice.

In the minority of cases which go to *Crown Courts* the procedure is one of trial by jury before a High Court Judge, a Circuit Judge or a Recorder (that is, a practising barrister or solicitor sitting in a judicial capacity). Most of the more serious cases are transferred automatically to the Crown Courts, although even in less serious cases the defendant can opt for trial by jury in a Crown Court rather than summary trial in a Magistrates' Court and many do so in the hope and expectation that they will stand a better chance of acquittal in front of a jury.

The most serious cases (for example, murder, rape or armed robbery) must be tried in the *High Court*. Other serious cases (for example, manslaughter or serious assault) are usually tried by a High Court Judge, but sometimes released to a Circuit Judge or a Recorder. Cases which involve lesser indictable offences or those in which the defendant has opted for trial by jury are usually tried by Circuit Judges or Recorders. In all these cases the most important role of the judge is directing the jury on matters of law.

Yet the passing of sentence on convicted defendants has become increasingly significant, at any rate in very serious cases, since judges have tended increasingly to make specific recommendations about the length of prison sentence which should be served, largely to pacify public opinion which has become increasingly vexed not only by what is widely regarded as insufficient or too lenient sentencing, but also by the practice of granting parole or remission of sentence sometimes when as little as a third or a half of a sentence has been

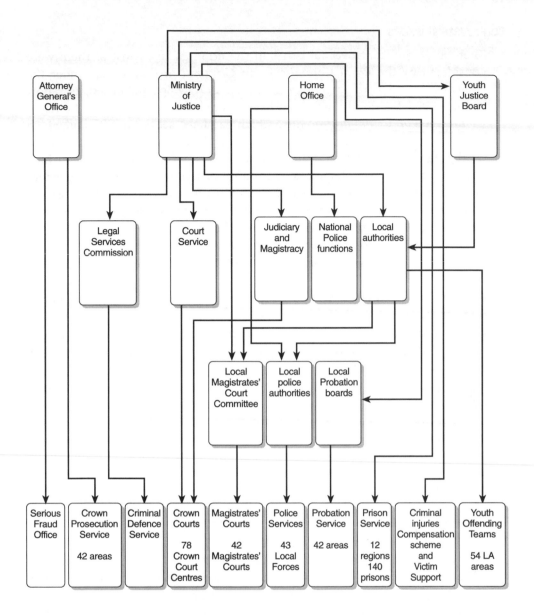

figure **18.1** **the structure of the Criminal Justice System**

served. It was for this reason that in the 1988 Criminal Justice Act the Attorney General was given the power to refer certain cases to the Court of Appeal if it was thought that the sentence imposed by a Crown Court Judge was unduly lenient. This power was extended by the Labour Government's 1998 Law and Disorder Act. As a result, the Attorney General intervened 75 times in 1995 and 122 times in 2005. See Figure 18.1 for a diagram of the system of criminal Courts.

There are many controversial issues in the criminal law. Most of them were considered by the *Royal Commission on Criminal Justice*, set up under the chairmanship of Lord Runciman in March 1991 which published its report in July 1993.[3] Previously there had been a similar investigation by the *Royal Commission on Criminal Procedure* which had been set up in 1977 and which reported in 1981.[4] Under the chairmanship of Sir Cyril Philips it had touched on the right of silence for criminal suspects, the exclusion of evidence which had been improperly obtained, the definition of arrestable offences, the extent of police powers to stop and search, the limits on detention in police custody, and the use of tape-recordings in interviews of criminal suspects. The result was the *1984 Police and Criminal Evidence Act*.

The Runciman Commission was established in the wake of a number of prominent miscarriages of justice, not least the case of the 'Birmingham Six' who had each served more than 16 years in prison for a terrorist crime they did not commit. The 1993 Report included a total of 352 recommendations on virtually every aspect of the criminal justice system, including a defendant's right to silence, the use of DNA profiles, the issue of confessions, continuous tape-recording in custody suites in police stations, police disciplinary action, greater supervision of police investigations, the training of police, lawyers and judges, the ending of a defendant's right in certain cases to opt for trial by jury, discounts on sentences to encourage defendants to plead guilty, the abolition (where possible) of pre-trial committal hearings, time limits on the preparation of cases, and the establishment of an independent body to carry out investigations into alleged miscarriages of justice. By way of response the Conservative Government of the time brought forward two pieces of legislation, both of which attracted considerable criticism from the judiciary, lawyers, the police, pressure groups and Opposition parties. Nevertheless the proposals became law in the shape of the *1994 Criminal Justice and Public Order Act and the1994 Police and Magistrates' Courts Act*.

The Labour Government which came into office in 1997 was determined – in Tony Blair's words – to be 'tough on crime and tough on the causes of crime' and pledged to tackle youth crime by introducing a new 'fast-track' system for persistent young offenders, by replacing repeat cautions with a single final warning, by streamlining the system of youth Courts, and by introducing Parental Responsibility Orders. In addition it promised to decentralise the work of the Crown Prosecution Service, to introduce stricter punishment for serious repeat offenders, to operate a 'zero tolerance' approach to tackle both anti-social behaviour (an approach which saw the introduction of Anti-Social Behaviour Orders), and to create a new offence of racial harassment and a new crime of racially motivated violence. Its proposals to these ends were enacted in the *1998 Crime and Disorder Act*. In the period from then until June 2006 more than 50 additional Bills to reform the criminal justice system – introducing more than 700 new criminal offences – were placed on the Statute Book.[5]

However, criminal justice continues to be an area of considerable controversy, not least because there are often tensions between the rather reactionary views and prejudices of the general public and much of the tabloid press on the one hand and the more enlightened, often pragmatic, views of judges, magistrates, police and the prison service on the other. At the same time although the level of overall crime fell from 1997 to 2007, the level of violent crime against the person continued to rise.

18.2 civil justice

machinery and procedure

Most civil cases are heard initially either in County Courts by Circuit Judges or in one of the three civil Divisions of the High Court by High Court Judges. Magistrates' Courts have original jurisdiction in some cases involving the summary recovery of certain kinds of debt and some domestic proceedings, such as separation and maintenance, guardianship or adoption.

In the *County Courts* the jurisdiction is both local and limited. Such Courts deal with actions founded on the law of contract and tort where the claim of the plaintiff does not exceed the sum of £20,000, equity cases up to a value of £30,000 which affect trusts, mortgages and the dissolution of partnerships – both figures set in 1995 – and actions concerning the recovery of land. They also deal with matters arising from social legislation, such as the adoption of children, the validity of hire purchase agreements, and disputes arising from the various Rent Acts. Since 1977, undefended divorce cases have been dealt with under a 'special procedure' at a Divorce County Court. The procedure is administrative – there are no formal hearings – while complaints of racial discrimination are heard in Tribunals specially designated for the purpose in which procedures are intended to be less formal than in Court. While both barristers and solicitors may appear on behalf of those who come before these Courts and Tribunals, the judge often has to hear the case on the basis of submissions made by members of the public.[6] In none of these cases is there call for a jury.

In the High Court, the *Queen's Bench Division* deals principally with actions founded on the law of contract and tort.[7] It also deals with actions on bills of exchange, insurance claims, shipping actions and some landlord and tenant actions. Only a small proportion of the actions actually come to Court and few are fought to a conclusion, since those involved are usually keen to avoid the high legal costs associated with fighting such cases. Either party may request a trial by jury in cases involving defamation of character, malicious prosecution, false imprisonment, fraud or seduction. The final decision as to whether or not a jury shall try such a case rests with the judge concerned. Another important function performed by this Division is the supervision of the lower Courts and Tribunals. This is done on an application for Judicial Review by issuing prerogative orders, such as *prohibition, mandamus* or *certiorari*, as well as an order of *habeas corpus*.[8] Whereas in former times these rights were available only to the Monarch, they can now be issued by the High Court upon application from an ordinary plaintiff.

The *Chancery Division* of the High Court, which was established in London in 1873, has effective jurisdiction over the estates of deceased persons, the execution of trusts, the dissolution of partnerships, disputes in private companies and the redemption or foreclosure of mortgages. In 1921 bankruptcy jurisdiction was added to its various responsibilities and breach of contract can be investigated here or in the Queen's Bench Division.

The *Family Division* of the High Court dates from 1971, when cases to do with wills and divorce were separated from those to do with shipwrecks with which they had been incongruously lumped since 1873 when the Probate, Divorce and Admiralty Division was established.[9] Today the Family Division deals with all domestic and matrimonial cases, guardianship and probate. Most of its work is concerned with divorce proceedings in an age when one in three of all marriages end this way.

Following more than 300 recommendations put forward in the watershed **1996 Woolf Report** into civil justice procedure, a number of fundamental reforms to improve and streamline the process of civil litigation – designed to reduce the cost, delay and complexity of what was involved – were introduced, the intention being to ensure that 'disputes should, wherever possible, be resolved without litigation' but that, where litigation was unavoidable, 'it should be conducted with a view to encouraging settlement at the earliest possible stage'.[10]

To many, the topic of the modernization of the procedures of civil justice may appear to be inordinately dull. Nonetheless, it is certainly relevant in a wider context as the issues involved have a direct impact upon both the quality and the accessibility of justice. As has been pointed out 'not only is it true that justice delayed can be justice denied; it is also true that obscure and costly judicial procedures have often deterred people from securing their human or property rights in court and thus prejudiced the principle of equality before the law'.[11]

controversial issues

The main controversial issues in the civil law are connected with the public image of the law and lawyers, and with the costs and delays in the processes of the law. We shall, therefore, look briefly at each of these issues in turn.

It is a widely held belief among the general public that the attitudes of lawyers and judges – indeed, the whole paraphernalia of the law – are distinctly old-fashioned and middle class. Indeed, ever since the notorious Taff Vale case in 1901,[12] many have believed that the judiciary has been biased against trade unions, and the development of judge-made case law over the years has not done much to dispel that belief. As Gavin Drewry pointed out in 1975, 'most of the really telling criticism of lawyers centres upon their failure to win the confidence of working-class people and their inability to achieve an image of independence from the Establishment'.[13] It is a view many would share today.

When hearing cases, judges are supposed to be strictly impartial. This means not only that they must not show any personal bias or prejudice, but also that they must exclude from their judgements any political or moral views which they may hold as individuals. Naturally, this is difficult for anyone to achieve, so there have been times when judges have appeared to be far from impartial in the eyes of those who come before them. There is at least circumstantial evidence for these misgivings.

Firstly, judges have tended to be drawn disproportionately from the ranks of the upper and middle classes; they are usually white, male[14] and tend to be quite elderly by the time that they reach the bench. As J.A.G. Griffith argued, 'they have by their education and training and the pursuit of their profession as barristers acquired a strikingly homogenous collection of attitudes, beliefs and principles which to them represents the public interest'.[15] However, during the 1990s the Conservative Government sought to open up the system of judicial appointments and from 1997 New Labour Ministers, such as Lord Irvine and Lord Falconer, made extensive efforts to modernise the judiciary and judicial appointments and some progress has been made by extending more equal opportunities for women, ethnic minorities and individuals with disabilities to join the ranks of the judiciary.[16]

Secondly, Griffith and others have argued that the judicial conception of the public interest has invariably been based upon the interests of the state, notably the preservation of law and order, the protection of property and the promotion of certain other political views traditionally associated with the Conservative Party. In so far as this may be so, it is almost inevitable that there are some people, especially among ethnic minority groups and other under-represented sections of the community, who believe that judges are inherently biased against them and their interests. Nonetheless, despite the clashes between the judiciary and the Labour Administrations since 1997, the practice of Judicial Review for decades past has failed to show any significant bias in favour of the Conservatives.

Thirdly, there has been a widely held view that the system of legal aid was unfair, ineffective and increasingly expensive. The system was characterized by three main weaknesses. Firstly, there was no satisfactory or systematic assessment of who needed what sort of legal advice. Secondly, there was a fragmentation of sources of legal help or advice. Thirdly, there was no assurance of consistent quality in the legal services available across the country. When Labour came to power in 1997 it was committed to replace the existing system with a new Community Legal Service (CLS), a move very much in-line with the leading themes of 'modernisation' – namely, joined-up public services and social inclusion. The **1999 Access to Justice Act** replaced the legal aid system in England and Wales with two new schemes administered by a new Legal Services Commission replacing the Legal Aid Board. The two new schemes are the Community Legal Service fund, replacing legal aid in civil and family cases, and the Criminal Defence Service. The idea in both cases was to secure legal services for the less well off through contracts with 'quality assured providers', an approach that has resulted in a new structure of non-departmental public bodies, funding arrangements and Public Private Partnerships at arm's length from government. Since 2007 the money available to the CLS Fund has been set by the Minister for Justice (in negotiation with the Treasury Ministers). The Commission is under a duty to spend its resources in ways which secure the best possible value for money.[17] Between 1997 and 2006 the cost of legal aid for criminal cases rose by 37 per cent which suggests either that legally aided cases have become more expensive or that more people have qualified for legal aid or a combination of the two. In 2006, following a review chaired by Lord Carter of Coles,[18] it was announced that a new market-based model was to be introduced in which all legal aid lawyers would move to fixed fees and have to tender for such work.

Fourthly, there is the deterrent effect of delays in the legal system. It is not just in Dickens's novels that characters sometimes die before their legal case is over. In Britain the problems of delay can be ascribed to the rising demand for litigation, the relative shortage of judges to hear cases, the time taken in amassing all the relevant evidence for use in Court, and the traditional commitment to an adversary procedure which involves the very time-consuming business of hearing and cross-examining witnesses testifying on oath. Some of the problems have been mitigated by improvements in the procedure of Small Claims Courts, which have served to speed up this particular kind of justice. Yet further progress could undoubtedly be made if more judges were appointed and if more use could be made of written evidence, at any rate in all those cases where the facts of the matter are not seriously contested by both sides.

Fifthly, some have argued that the very nature of the legal system and the middle-class image of the law deter many poor or inarticulate people from seeking the benefit of legal advice or legal services. To many people traditional legal procedures seem very off-putting, with all the wigs and processions and general mumbo-jumbo. Indeed, this is exactly why some of the procedures have been simplified and made more 'user-friendly' in recent years, notably in cases involving families and children, and why the Woolf reforms were so necessary.

18.3 judicial appeal

machinery and procedure

The process of judicial appeal in Britain can be applied equally to cases of criminal and civil law. Most of the *criminal appeals* are heard by the criminal Division of the Court of Appeal. This is presided over by the Lord Chief Justice or a Lord Justice of Appeal. Queen's Bench judges sit with Appeal Court judges and there are usually three judges on the bench for any hearing. When a case raises an issue of general public importance, a further appeal may be made to the Law Lords, but in criminal cases such appeals are rare.

Most of the *civil appeals* are heard by the Master of the Rolls and the Lord Justices of Appeal, although the Lord Chief Justice and a few other very senior legal figures may sit *ex officio* (by virtue of their offices) in exceptional circumstances. An odd number of judges (usually three) hear such appeals and decisions of the Court are taken by majority.

On important points of law with wider legal application there is the possibility of further appeal to the House of Lords. Such appeals are made to the *Appellate Committee*, which, until 2009 as a result of the changes brought about by the 2005 Constitutional Reform Act, is the final Court of Appeal and which can only be overruled by Parliament as a whole passing new legislation. The work of the Appellate Committee is done by the Law Lords, 12 Lords of Appeal in Ordinary.[19] The Appellate Committee is usually made up of five Law Lords and their judgments take the form of motions, with each judge expressing a judicial opinion on the matter in question. Prior to 1966 the House of Lords had always been bound by its previous judicial decisions; since 1966 it has been able to overrule them and depart from precedent if necessary.

Mention should also be made of the Judicial Committee of the Privy Council, which was established by statute in 1833. This is the court of final appeal for some UK overseas territories and Crown dependencies (for example, the Falkland Islands and Gibraltar), and for those Commonwealth countries that have retained a right of appeal to Her Majesty in Council or, in the case of Republics, to the Judicial Committee[20]. Five judges normally sit to hear Commonwealth appeals and three for other matters. The Judicial Committee deals with between 55 and 65 appeals a year. As a result of the devolution statutes of 1998 it is also the court of final appeal for determining serious issues of dispute arising from devolution, although the 2005 Constitution Reform Act transferred this jurisdiction to the new Supreme Court.

Since accession to the European Community in 1973 Britain has been subject to the jurisdiction of the *European Court of Justice* in all those areas of national life covered by European law. This has meant that in an increasingly significant area of legal competence the European Court has provided a final level of judicial appeal higher than the House of Lords/Supreme Court. Under Section 2 of the 1972 European Communities Act and subsequent legislation the Westminster Parliament is under a self-imposed legal duty at all times *not* to pass legislation which would conflict with any European legislation. Thus it can be said that in the areas of European competence, as defined by European Treaty obligations, European law takes precedence over national law and an appeal to the European Court of Justice trumps any appeal to a national Court. As a direct consequence of the *Factortame Ltd* judgment in 1990 (see Chapter 21), it is clear that if an Act of Parliament is inconsistent with European Law, the Courts in Britain have to refuse to give it effect.

In this context it is also worth noting the scope of the *European Court of Human Rights* which since 1966 has been available to UK citizens, but which stems from the European Convention signed by Britain in 1951. The Convention was incorporated into UK domestic law in the 1998 *Human Rights Act* and this made it an offence for any public body to act in a way incompatible with the Convention, gave previous decisions of the European Court of Human Rights precedence over domestic law and obliged British Courts to interpret legislation in a way compatible with the Convention.

controversial issues

The process of judicial appeal does not normally give rise to great political controversy, except on those occasions when issues of wider political importance are raised in particularly contentious cases. When this happens, judgments in the House of Lords/Supreme Court are final, except when they trigger the Government of the day to introduce fresh legislation to overturn or confirm the previous legal position; when the British legal system is in effect overruled by the European Court of Justice; when the courts declare legislation incompatible with the European Convention on Human Rights (they can neither strike down nor amend it); or, very occasionally, when an issue is considered for a second time as it was in the case of General Pinochet's possible extradition to Spain in 1998–99 for alleged crimes against humanity in Chile in the 1970s and 1980s.

Early examples of the first of these alternatives were provided by the 1906 Trade Disputes Act, which overturned the House of Lords' judgment in the 1901 Taff Vale case, and the 1913 Trade Union Act, which overturned the House of Lords' judgment in the 1910 Osborne case. A later well-known example was the 1965 War Damage Act, which overturned the 1965 House of Lords' judgment in the case of Burmah Oil. A notable example from the 1980s was the 1983 Transport Act, which took account of the 1982 House of Lords judgment in the case of *Bromley Borough Council v. the Greater London Council* on the politically contentious issue of passenger transport subsidies in Greater London. More recently, we have seen the case of the *2001 Anti-Terrorism, Crime and Security Act*, part of which provided for the indefinite detention without trial of any individuals suspected of terrorist activity who could not be deported if their security could not be guaranteed on return to their country of origin. Between 2001 and 2004, 17 individuals were detained as a consequence of this Act, prompting a series of legal challenges and resulting in a ruling by the Law Lords that the powers of detention conferred by the legislation were incompatible with the European Convention on Human Rights. The Government responded by revising the legislation. When matters of political importance have been involved, the Government of the day has felt obliged to introduce legislation either to overturn or to ratify the legal position as defined by the House of Lords.

Over the years there have been periods of judicial activism and creativity, and periods when the behaviour of the judiciary has been characterised by conservatism and a determination to defend the established legal order. On the whole, judicial conservatism has been the more prevalent. This is partly a reflection of the inherently conservative background and outlook of the judiciary in Britain, to which reference has already been made. Yet is also reflects the well-established constitutional attitude held by the judiciary over many years and most succinctly expressed by Lord Reid on several occasions. In 1961, in *Shaw v. the Director of Public Prosecutions*, he observed that 'where Parliament fears to tread, it is not for the Courts to rush in', and in 1972 he maintained that cases which raised political issues should be decided 'on the preponderance of existing authority'.[21]

In these matters much has depended on whether the judiciary construes the law passed by Parliament literally and narrowly or contextually and broadly. For example, Lord Denning in his many years as Master of the Rolls and Chairman of the Court of Appeal (1962–82) was usually inclined to interpret the law in a way which was well disposed towards whichever litigant he considered to be the underdog. Naturally, this did not endear him to those organisations which he deemed oppressive (for example, trade unions) or indeed to the Law Lords, who often had to review his judgments on further appeal. Much has also depended on the extent to which the judiciary has thought it proper or prudent to flex its muscles in defiance of the Government of the day. It has been said that on the whole Labour Governments have found themselves in conflict with the judiciary more often than their Conservative counterparts. However, in the 1980s the judiciary was something of a brake upon the radical intentions of the Thatcher Government, and in the early-to-mid 1990s the judges were some of the sharpest critics of the Major Government's proposals to reform the criminal justice system. Similarly, the judiciary has been a thorn in the side of the Labour Government particularly where anti-terror laws were concerned and especially in the period since 2001.[22] Indeed, it could be argued that such facts demonstrate the simple reality that there is always likely to be a conflict between the judiciary and any Government which tries to make radical changes or oversteps the limits of Ministerial discretion.

In the late 1980s and into the 1990s the most controversial legal issues arose from the clash of jurisdictions between British legal institutions and those of the European Union. In essence this meant a *political* struggle between, on the one hand, those politicians and others who wished to preserve the legal sovereignty of Britain's national Courts and, ultimately, of Parliament itself; and, on the other hand, those politicians, officials, interest groups and others who saw sectional and national advantage in Britain being prepared to pool its sovereignty with that of other member states in those policy areas covered by the European Treaties.

More recently, in the aftermath of the attack on the World Trade Centre in New York on 11 September 2001, the most controversial legal issues have arisen over the balance between civil liberties and security, with some people seeing 'draconian' legislation as an affront to civil liberties and others seeing a need to 'modify' freedoms in order to foil the intentions of terrorists. This is a matter to which we shall return in Chapter 19.

From a political point of view, it is administrative law which is probably the most important aspect of the legal system in Britain. H.W.R. Wade defined this area of the law as 'the body of general principles which govern the exercise of powers and duties by public authorities.'[23] Since the early twentieth century there has been a great expansion of Parliamentary legislation and hence a notable multiplication of administrative bodies created by statute. This has led to growing judicial and quasi-judicial intervention in the field of public administration. Members of the general public have felt the need to appeal to Tribunals and ultimately to the Courts on many points of administrative law. For its part the judiciary has attempted to compensate for the failure of Parliament adequately to protect citizens from the shortcomings or injustices which can be perpetrated by the public administration.

Tribunals

In the modern British political system a bewildering array of administrative Tribunals have been created by Acts of Parliament: Tribunals which decide disputed claims to benefits were established as a function of the Welfare State; Tribunals which adjudicate on claims of industrial injury, unfair dismissal and other employment disputes were related to the problems often associated with industrial relations; Tribunals which deal with housing disputes; Tribunals which deal with pensions or unemployment; Tribunals which deal with immigration; Tribunals which deal with the National Health Service; and this is by no means an exhaustive list. All exist in order to provide simpler, cheaper, quicker and more accessible forms of justice than are available in the Courts.

The Labour Government, which first came into office in 1997, was determined to modernize this particular aspect of administrative law. In 2000 Sir Andrew Leggatt was appointed to review the delivery of justice through Tribunals other than ordinary courts and to make recommendations designed to ensure that:

- There are fair, timely, proportionate and effective arrangements for handling such disputes
- The administrative and practical arrangements for supporting those procedures meet the requirements of the European Convention on Human Rights
- There are adequate arrangements for improving people's knowledge and understanding of their rights and responsibilities in relation to such disputes
- The arrangements for the funding and management of Tribunals and other bodies are efficient, effective and economical and pay due regard both to judicial independence and to Ministerial responsibility for the administration of public funds

- Performance standards for Tribunals are coherent, consistent and public and that effective measures for monitoring and enforcing such standards are established
- Tribunals constitute a coherent structure for the delivery of administrative justice.

Sir Andrew's Report was published in 2001.[24] It criticized the arrangements for supporting Tribunals and recommended that the best way to achieve independence and coherence was to have all Tribunals supported by a common administrative service independent of those bodies whose decisions the Tribunals were reviewing.

In 2003, the Government announced its response to the Report, in particular its intention to an independent Tribunals Service comprising a number of non-devolved central Government Tribunals. Further details of these proposals were set out in a White Paper published in 2004[25] which sought to set the reform of Tribunals in a wider context of reform. This resulted in the establishment in 2006 of the Tribunals Service, an executive Agency headed by a Chief Executive to provide common administrative support for the main Tribunal.[26]

Characteristics of Tribunals include:

- They are normally established by Act of Parliament
- Their decisions are quasi-judicial in the sense that they investigate the facts of the case and then apply certain legal principles in an impartial manner
- They are independent in the sense that their decisions are in no way subject to political or administrative interference
- Their membership varies, but they usually consist of a legally qualified chairman and lay members representing relevant interests
- They are assisted by clerks who are usually civil servants from the relevant Department
- Appeals against their decisions may lie with a Minister, a superior Tribunal, or a superior Court, (or there may in fact be no provision for appeal).

18.5 methods of oversight and control

by Ministers responsible to Parliament

The traditional view is that the public interest can best be safeguarded by Ministers responsible to Parliament. Yet this idea has been something of a constitutional fiction ever since its mythical properties were first revealed by Lord Hewart and Professor Robson in the middle of the twentieth century.[27] The criticism then, and even more so today, is that Ministers cannot possibly be well informed about, still less truly accountable for, everything which happens (or fails to happen) within all the various administrative Tribunals and quasi-judicial bodies for which they may be nominally responsible.

Equally, it has been recognized, that Parliamentary control of Ministers is vitiated by the growth of delegated legislation and the purity of judge-made law is threatened by the growth of quasi-judicial powers exercised by civil servants in the name of Ministers.

In general, Ministerial control has not been an adequate response to the problem of overseeing and reviewing this type of law. In effect, it has sought to deny the significance of the problem by assuming that public administration is bound to reflect the public interest as long as each Department is headed by a Minister responsible to Parliament. Such an idea is obviously defective now that the whole process of Government has become so large and complex. In circumstances in which few Ministers achieve control over their Departments and Parliament has even less effective control over Ministers, it is naïve to pretend that the principles of Ministerial control and Ministerial accountability to Parliament can provide a satisfactory answer.

by the Ombudsman

Another approach to solving the problem of administrative law has been the creation of an independent institution designed to limit serious abuses of administrative power and to deal firmly with any which arise. In Britain, as in some other countries, this has been achieved by the Parliamentary Commissioner for Administration, commonly known as the Ombudsman.[28] The institution was created by Act of Parliament in 1967 in a further attempt to ensure that the administrative procedures of central Government and its Agencies are correctly followed and that any allegations of maladministration are investigated and, if possible, rectified.

The Ombudsman, who is usually a former senior lawyer or senior civil servant, is appointed by the Crown on the advice of the Lord Chancellor. The constitutional status of the position is similar to that of a High Court judge, namely complete independence from Governnment. The Ombudsman can only be removed from office by the Crown after addresses by both Houses of Parliament; in other words, the incumbent is effectively unsackable during a five-year term of office. The staff of the Ombudsman is usually drawn from the ranks of the Civil Service; and his or her jurisdiction is confined to the Departments of central Government, the National Health Service and certain non-Departmental public bodies.[29]

The jurisdiction of the Ombudsman does not cover either the police or public corporations nor does it extend to international relations, Court proceedings, employment issues or the commercial transactions of central Government. Furthermore, there is no right to investigate cases where the complainant can have recourse to an Administrative Tribunal or a remedy in the Courts. Nor can complaints be investigated if made more than one year after the date when the complainant first had notice of the matter. In short, Parliament in 1967 did not exactly give the institution *carte blanche*, largely because at the outset it was seen by many MPs as an interloper in their territory.

Once the complaint has been officially received, it is for the Ombudsman to decide whether or not it properly falls within the jurisdiction of the office. In fact, fewer than half the complaints received fall within the Ombudsman's jurisdiction. If it does, all official documents, except Cabinet papers, have to be produced for inspection by the Ombudsman who has the same powers to compel disclosure as a High Court judge. When an investigation is complete, a Report is normally sent to the MP concerned, who then sends it on to the complainant. The Ombudsman has no executive powers, but the reports often suggest appropriate remedies upon which the Department concerned normally takes action. The remedies may include financial compensation from public funds, remission of taxation, administrative review of earlier decisions or revised administrative procedures. For example, in the 1989 Barlow Clowes case the Ombudsman recommended that the private investors who had lost all their money to two investment funds which were not properly supervised by the Department of Trade and Industry should receive substantial financial compensation for their losses. MPs work quite happily in partnership with the Ombudsman in joint efforts to secure redress for their constituents. In formal terms this relationship has been cemented by the work of the Public Administration Select Committee of the House of Commons which supervises the work of the Ombudsman and, where appropriate, takes evidence from Departments which are the subject of such investigations. This all helps to ensure that the recommendations are carried out.[30]

In 1999, as part of the Labour Government's 'modernisation' agenda, a review of the public sector Ombudsmen – the Parliamentary Ombudsman, the Health Service Ombudsman and the Local Government Ombudsmen – was set up and its findings were published in 2000. Following a further review and consultation exercise the Cabinet Office published a *Consultation Paper on the Reform of Public Sector Ombudsmen Services in England* in 2005.[31] Various reforms were outlined which were intended to enable the three main public sector Ombudsmen to work together more efficiently and provide complainants with a more effective and streamlined service.

by judicial review

Another way of dealing with injustices or abuses which are perpetrated by the public administration is judicial review. The basic leverage for the judiciary is provided by the doctrine of *ultra vires*, which holds that acts of public administration can be unlawful if they offend against the rules of natural justice or otherwise go beyond the bounds of statutory powers. It is this doctrine which enables the High Court to set aside administrative decisions which are plainly unreasonable. The issues involved are controversial, since the nub of the argument is usually the degree of discretionary power which can properly be exercised by a public body. The judiciary has the difficult responsibility of interpreting the meaning of statutes on the basis of what reasonable people would reasonably decide. This can be approached in a narrow and literal sense or a broad and contextual sense, and the outcome of such cases will often depend upon which of the two approaches is adopted.

When a complaint against the public administration is brought before the High Court, several legal remedies are available to the plaintiff. There are the traditional prerogative remedies which were originally vested in the Monarch, but which are now available to ordinary citizens. These are *certiorari* to quash an administrative decision already made; *prohibition* to prevent a public authority from considering a matter which it has no statutory right to consider; and *mandamus* to compel a public body to perform a public duty. Then there are the two non-prerogative remedies which are often more useful nowadays. These are an *injunction* to prohibit a public body from doing something and a *declaration* which is simply a statement by the Court clarifying the legal position, so that the powers and duties of a public body can be defined more precisely.[32]

Judicial review is impartial in the sense that it is not influenced by the position of the complainant or the power of the public body about which the complaint has been made. Yet there are weaknesses in such procedures. For example, the Courts can only intervene if a plaintiff starts legal proceedings; it can only deal with the case before it; it usually lacks the detailed expertise of the public administration which it seeks to control; it cannot oversee the way in which its remedial orders are carried out; and it proceeds so slowly and expensively that many would-be plaintiffs are deterred from going to law in the first place.

In conducting the process of judicial review, a judge tends to be guided essentially by the principles of natural justice. These are the right of the complainant to be heard before the relevant decision is taken and the absence of prejudice on the part of the Court or other public body charged with the duty of adjudication. Clearly, there is a difficult balance which has to be struck by the Courts between the interests of the plaintiff and those of the general public as represented by the decisions of public bodies. The balance has shifted back and forth over the years. Yet as Hartley and Griffith have pointed out, the Courts have tended to be guided 'more by policy than by precedent, more by what they think is fair and reasonable than by rigid rules.[33] Judicial review is therefore a more than usually political form of justice.

Since the mid 1960s the judiciary in Britain has been prepared to play a more active part in arguments of political principle. This has been evident especially in cases which bear upon the definition of individual rights, such as personal property, retention of office and access to employment, liberty and freedom of movement. Throughout, the judiciary has shown a growing willingness to use the process of judicial review to deal definitively with disputes which can arise in the sphere of public administration.[34] Although not all cases challenge the action of Ministers, and notwithstanding the fact that in those that do, not all result in the action of the Minister being struck out, the greater willingness of the Courts to play an active role in this respect has shifted the balance of power somewhat against the Government of the day no matter which party is in offie.

Court rulings against Government include:

- In 1976 the Courts struck down a direction by the Secretary of State for Education to Tameside Council to implement a scheme to convert a number of grammar schools to comprehensive schools
- In 1981 the High Court ruled that the Secretary of State for the Environment had acted improperly in refusing to listen to representations from various London Boroughs concerning his decision to reduce their rate support grant
- In 1990 the High Court overruled Government guidelines on the administration of the Social Fund introduced in 1988
- In 1994 the High Court found that the Foreign Secretary had acted illegally in authorising aid worth £234m for the Pergau Dam in Malaysia
- In 1995 the Law Lords ruled that the Home Secretary had abused his powers and flouted the will of Parliament when he introduced a cheaper, fixed rate Criminal Injuries Compensation Scheme
- In 1997 the Law Lords noted that the Home Secretary had acted illegally when he raised the term of imprisonment imposed on the two boys convicted of murdering James Bulger from ten years to 15 years
- In 2003 the courts ruled against the Government in their policy of restricting benefit payments to asylum seekers who had not registered immediately on arrival
- In 2004 the Law Lords ruled that the indefinite detention without trial of suspected foreign terrorists under the 2001 Anti-Terrorism, Crime and Security Act was a disproportionate response to the threat of terrorism and discriminatory if applied only to foreign nationals and, consequently, was unlawful
- In 2006 the High Court ruled against attempts by the Home Office to remove nine Afghan hijackers from Britain, granting them instead temporary leave to remain until is was safe for them to return
- In 2006 the High Court ruled that the Home Secretary did not have the power to make 'control orders' – a key part of the Government's policy to combat terrorism – and that, therefore, such orders had to be quashed.

Continental solutions

There are some who argue that Britain should look further afield to find the most effective ways of supervising and controlling public administration. Specifically, they maintain that the best solution would be to establish in Britain a new Administrative Division of the High Court (similar to that which exists in France) or a new Administrative Appeals Tribunal (along the lines of that which exists in Sweden). Such approaches have been advocated by those members of the judiciary who would like to see the process of judicial review extended into all corners of the public administration.

Such solutions would almost certainly be opposed by those who already harbour a deep suspicion of the judiciary and hence a strong unwillingness to allow them a more influential political role. Certainly many of those on the Left of British politics would oppose any extension of the powers and competence of the judiciary unless and until they could feel satisfied that the judiciary had ceased to be drawn from such a deeply conservative section of the population. At the same time many of those on the Right would resist it on the grounds that it is undesirable to import foreign judicial practices into Britain.

constitutional reform

Finally, some eminent legal figures have argued the case for comprehensive constitutional reform entailing a new Bill of Rights and the introduction of an entrenched and codified constitution which would be interpreted and protected by a newly established and completely independent Supreme Court.[35] Those who favour this way of dealing with the problems of administrative law have to contend with the traditional British response that civil rights and political liberties are most secure if founded upon the established custom and practice of common law. Of course, others would probably reply that the traditional approach has become ineffective in view of the scope and complexity of public administration.

Whatever the attractions of this idea, there could be considerable difficulties were such an approach to be adopted in Britain. Notwithstanding the fact that the European Convention on Human Rights has been enshrined into British law, and notwithstanding the fact that the passage of the 2005 Constitutional Reform Act established a new, independent Supreme Court, there would need to be nothing short of a new constitutional settlement. Such a settlement would introduce a formal, codified constitution which anyone could invoke in the event of a dispute with the public authorities. There would need to be public acceptance of a very different and more distinctive role for the senior members of the judiciary, and, above all, Members of Parliament would have to acknowledge that Parliament could no longer claim its traditional constitutional supremacy.

It is interesting to note that the 1998 Human Rights Act actually stipulated that the British Courts did *not* have the power to set aside Acts of the United Kingdom Parliament, but only to make a 'declaration of incompatability' and leave it to the Government acting through Parliament to resolve the contradiction. Among those who favour all-embracing changes, Nevil Johnson argued that 'the challenge is to construct a different relationship between law and politics and in so doing to give law ... a new and wider part in the regulation of the affairs of society.'[36] It remains uncertain whether politicians in all parties can accept the idea of playing second fiddle to judges in the determination of some of the really big legal and constitutional issues. At present this seems very doubtful.

18.6 conclusion

It remains to be seen whether the legal system in Britain will develop in a more creative and independent direction, or whether it will remain essentially obedient to the idea – however mythical – of Parliamentary supremacy. There are clearly major implications for the traditional doctrines of Ministerial responsibility and Parliamentary accountability if the judiciary does develop more independent and creative powers. Having said this, however, it is worth remembering the words of H.W.R. Wade, namely that 'if they [the judges] fly too high, Parliament may clip their wings'.[37] In other words, a change of this kind is unlikely to come about unless the Judiciary *and* the Legislature make common cause against the Executive and that is unrealistic in the British political system where the Executive and the Legislature are fused.

It is well to remember that there never has been a truly effective separation of powers in Britain. Such a triangular balance nearly came about in the eighteenth century, when central Government was at its weakest. Yet in more modern times the politicians in Government have definitively asserted their position and the judiciary has been careful not to step too far out of line with the Government of the day. This is because in the last resort the politicians in office can always use their whipped majority in the House of Commons to trump any judicial challenge.

Of course, relations between the Judiciary, the Executive and the Legislature may change in future in response to more demanding public attitudes or different constitutional arrangements. For example, the public may come to expect more from the Courts by way of judicial protection and redress against an over-mighty or unrepresentative Government. The incorporation into British law of certain fundamental constitutional principles enshrined in the European Convention on Human Rights and effected in the 1998 Human Rights Act may alter entrenched attitudes as time goes by. Equally, the supremacy of European law over British law, at least in the areas of expanding European competence, may hasten the day when the traditional doctrine of Parliamentary supremacy has to give way to judicial supremacy on Continental lines – but that remains to be seen.

SUGGESTED QUESTIONS

1   Describe the structure of both the criminal justice and the civil justice system in contemporary Britain.
2   How appropriate and effective are the arrangements for applying and reviewing administrative law in Britain?
3   What is the constitutional position of the courts in the United Kingdom? What does this mean in practice?

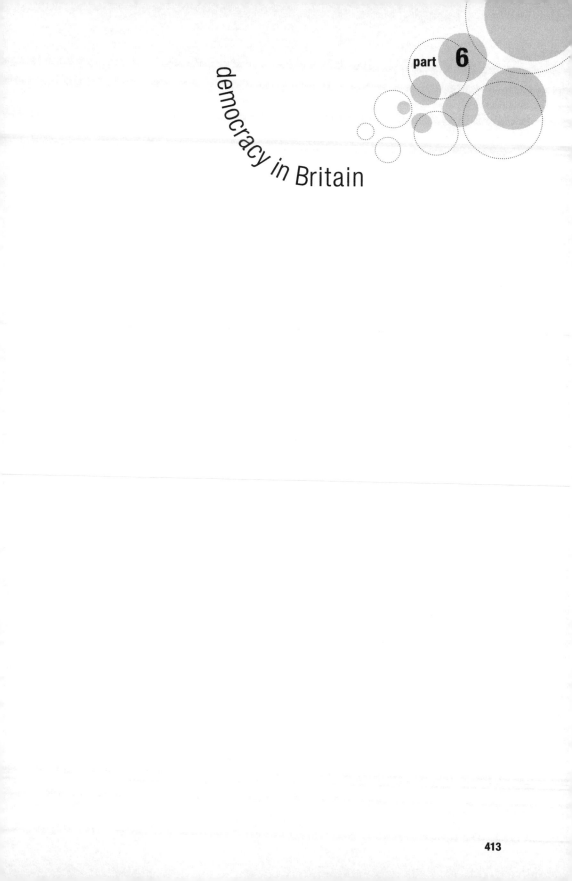

part **6**

democracy in Britain

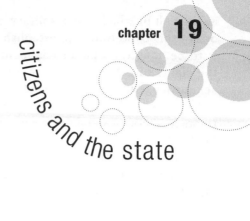

chapter **19**

citizens and the state

In the modern world the complex relationship between citizens and the state raises political and legal issues of great importance. Citizens expect to enjoy certain inalienable rights, including freedoms of both a positive and negative kind. There are the freedoms *to* do certain things, and the freedoms *from* having certain things done to you. Each category of freedom is equally valuable. Yet in every case the rights concerned have to be qualified or counterbalanced by certain rights of the state or its agencies to act on behalf of the community as a whole. It is against this backdrop – establishing and holding a balance between the rights of citizens and the interests of the state – that Governments, politicians, agencies of law enforcement and indeed the legal system in Britain have had to try to resolve some of the most difficult problems confronting contemporary society.

19.1 the British approach

The British approach arises from a belief that the traditional way of doing things – and the arrangements that result from such an approach – fully protect the rights, liberties and freedoms of the people. This 'traditional way' incorporates the twin pillars of Parliamentary Sovereignty and the Rule of Law, together with an acceptance that there is a political culture of liberty, fairness, moderation, pragmatism and common sense.

When dealing with the citizen and the state, *Magna Carta* (1215), the *1679 Habeas Corpus Act* and the *1689 Bill of Rights* are all important: Magna Carta because it marked a significant challenge to the idea of absolute rule and from which such concepts as natural justice and trial by jury are derived; the Habeas Corpus Act stipulated that people could not be arbitrarily imprisoned; and the Bill of Rights set out certain rights and liberties, such as rules against excessive bail or fines as well as the concept of cruel and unusual punishment, which British subjects have been able to claim ever since.

The philosopher **Thomas Hobbes** (1588–1679) believed that men in a state of nature, that is a state without civil government, are in a war of all against all in which life is solitary, poor, nasty, brutish and short. The way out of this condition is to establish the state to keep peace and order. This is to be done through a social contract by which individuals acknowledge the rights of others in the same way as they wish their own rights to be acknowledged.[1]

It was with the coming of the Enlightenment that the concept of human rights in a more general sense came to the fore. The English philosopher **John Locke** (1632–1704) was important in this regard with his argument for a social contract between the rulers and the ruled. He argued that if people gave up their natural freedoms, they should expect their ruler in return to protect their life, liberty and property.[2]

Despite the promotion of individual rights and equality as a basis for both the French and American Revolutions, it was in fact **Edmund Burke** (1729–97), a contemporary of Thomas Paine and the Founding Fathers of the United States, whose ideas had the greatest impact in Britain. Burke rejected abstract theory and experimental or doctrinaire constitutions, believing that the main question was 'whether you will choose to abide by profitable experience or mischievous theory; whether you choose to build upon imagination or fact'. He believed that a constitution must: 'Compensate ... reconcile . balance ... to unite into a consistent whole the various anomalies and contending principles that are found in the minds and affairs of men.'[3]

Emerging from this tradition, the constitutional theorist **A.V. Dicey** (1835–1922) argued that individual liberties were more effectively protected by Parliamentary sovereignty, an uncodified constitution and the common law than by Continental systems with their codified constitutions and entrenched rights. Inherent in the British system, he maintained, was the assumption that every subject was free to do that which was not forbidden in law – what are generally known as 'negative rights'. He declared that it was precisely because rights were not written down, but upheld by common law and judicial rulings, that it was very much more difficult for Governments to take away or reduce the liberties of the people.[4]

It is Dicey's arguments that remain the basis for the continuing adherence in Britain to the long-established belief in 'negative' rights as opposed to the model of entrenched 'positive' rights. Even when the first Blair Administration legislated to incorporate the **European Convention on Human Rights** into United Kingdom law it continued to attach importance to the traditional approach, arguing that: '*To make provision ... for the Courts to set aside Acts of Parliament would confer on the judiciary a general power over the decisions of Parliament which under our present constitutional arrangements they do not possess, and would be likely on occasions to draw the judiciary into serious conflict with Parliament*'.[5] In the same vein, when addressing the issue of legislative entrenchment, the Blair Government declared: '*[An] arrangement of this kind could not be reconciled with our own constitutional traditions, which allow any Act of Parliament to be amended or repealed by [a] subsequent Act of Parliament*'.[6]

For centuries the British have been subjects of a Monarch; subject to the laws that came from the Monarch and the supporting aristocracy. Gradually, however, with the development from a system of government in which the Monarch dominated to one in which the Monarch played little part, a constitutional monarchy evolved (see Chapter 9), so that by the Treaty of Maastricht in 1992 when British subjects legally became citizens, the relationship between the Monarch and the people was put on a more modern legal basis.

The broad concept of citizenship has also evolved over the years and notably during the twentieth century:

- From the end of the Second World War to the mid 1970s – essentially the period of the post-war consensus – there was broad agreement among the political elite that 'citizenship' encompassed civil, political and social rights which the state had a responsibility to provide and protect.
- The election of the Conservatives under Margaret Thatcher in 1979, and their subsequent re-election in 1983 and 1987, ushered in a radical change in both perspective and approach. What can be described as 'neo-liberal tendencies' came to the fore which ensured that much greater emphasis came to be placed upon 'market forces' and personal responsibilities. People were encouraged to take more personal responsibility for their own lives and not to look to the state for solutions.
- The subsequent Administrations under John Major (1990–97) were responsible for two developments which have a bearing on this subject. In 1991 John Major introduced what he called the **Citizens Charter** which was an attempt to improve standards in public service by treating people as citizens with rights rather than mere subjects who traditionally were supposed to be grateful for whatever service the state decided to provide. The approach undoubtedly popularised the concept of *citizenship* and introduced a new dimension to public accountability in the public sector – namely, *direct accountability* of public servants to the *users* of public services as much as to their traditional Ministerial masters.

  The second development at the time which bore upon the concept of citizenship as applied to the United Kingdom was the 1992 Maastricht Treaty which turned the European Community into the European Union. Part of this treaty had the effect of making every citizen of each member state a citizen of the European Union with rights to live, work and vote (in local and European elections) anywhere in the Union.
- At the European Union Summit in Nice in 2000 a **Charter of Fundamental Rights**[7] was agreed which set out a whole range of civil, political and social rights – covering everything from workers' social rights to bioethics and the protection of personal data – applicable to all EU citizens. The Charter was signed by all of the EU member states as a 'political declaration', meaning that it could be taken into account by national law Courts and the European

Court of Justice, but that it would not be legally binding. Subsequently, the Charter was incorporated into the draft EU Constitution of 2000 and it gave to citizens of the Union the right to take national Governments to the European Court, to petition the European Parliament and to appeal directly to a European Ombudsman.

▶ Since 1997 the Labour Government has been committed to 'modernising' citizenship, particularly with regard to constitutional reform and attempts to tackle social exclusion and promote individual responsibility. In taking this approach, the Government declared that: 'in promoting citizenship … we are building on an existing legal definition in a way that is fully consistent with our position as subjects of a constitutional Sovereign. There is no contradiction in promoting citizenship so that people uphold common values and understand how they can play their part in our society while upholding our status as subjects of H.M. the Queen'.[8]

▶ The 2002 *Nationality, Immigration and Asylum Act* introduced a formal ceremony for the induction of new British citizens incorporating not only an oath of allegiance to the Crown, but also a pledge to give loyalty to the United Kingdom and respect its rights and freedoms; to uphold its democratic values; to observe its laws faithfully; and to fulfil duties and obligations as a British citizen.[9]

▶ In 2002 'Citizenship' was introduced as a compulsory part of the national curriculum in secondary schools, the intention being to teach social and moral responsibility and to encourage community involvement and political literacy. In short, the idea of being a British subject has come to be seen by many as anachronistic, even patronising.

Because of the ancient origins and evolutionary development of the political system, it has been a slow and difficult process to graft a political culture based upon citizenship out of a more antiquated one based upon the deferential behaviour of subjects. Nevertheless, in the dynamic context provided by the European Union and by the considerable increase in net immigration, it has proved possible to begin doing just that.

19.3 freedoms and restraints

equality before the law

The principle that all citizens should be equal before the law is a worthy aspiration in Britain as in other countries, but in Britain's constitutional arrangements it is not enshrined in a codified constitution. From the mid 1960s Parliament has legislated against racial discrimination (1965, 1968 and 1976), religious discrimination (2003 and 2006), sexual discrimination (1975), discrimination of the disabled (1995 and 2005), discrimination on the grounds of age (2006), and discrimination on the grounds of sexuality (2006). Indeed, attempts have been made to eradicate such discrimination from all public behaviour, with public-sector institutions, such as the Civil Service, often required to set an example to the private sector. Many of the initiatives in these spheres have been taken by the Commission for Racial Equality, the Disability Rights Commission and the Equal Opportunities Commission – all of which were replaced, as a result of the **2006 Equality Act**, by the Commission for Equality and Human Rights (CEHR) whose task, from October 2007, was to promote equality and tackle discrimination in relation to gender, gender reassignment, disability, sexual orientation, religion or belief, age, race and promote human rights.

An important aspect of 'equality before the law' is the long-established common law concept of trial by jury. This has had to be qualified in the special circumstances of Northern Ireland where the so-called Diplock Courts operated without a jury from 1973 to 2007 because of the problems of intimidation. Attempts by the Labour Government to do without juries in trials which could expose jurors to intimidation or which involved the complexities of sophisticated fraud failed to gain the approval of Parliament.[10]

liberty, identity and property

Magna Carta in 1215 stipulated that 'no free man shall be taken or imprisoned or dispossessed or outlawed or in any way destroyed … unless by the lawful judgement of his peers or the law of the land'. This was an early expression of what became known as the 'rule of law' – in essence a belief that all are equal before the law and that no one can be punished without due process of law.

Although British citizens are free people, in certain circumstances they can lawfully be detained. For example, in 1940, when a German invasion appeared imminent, Parliament introduced Regulation 18B allowing individuals considered to be a danger to the state to be detained. Similarly, internment without trial was a policy in Northern Ireland from August 1971 to December 1975. More normally, an individual can be detained after arrest and pending trial on a criminal charge (assuming bail is refused by a Magistrates' Court), or when a local authority decides within its statutory rights to take a child into care. Nonetheless, any abrogation of personal liberty can raise considerable controversy.

Powers of arrest, which are normally exercised by the police (but are legally available to any citizen), are regulated by a variety of Acts – for example, the 1984 Police and Criminal Evidence Act, the 2002 Police Reform Act and the 2006 Terrorism Act. The 1998 Crime and Disorder Act introduced Anti-Social Behaviour Orders (known as ASBOs) and Acceptable Behaviour Contracts (ABCs), giving local Councils and the police powers to clamp down on low-level youth crime – such as abusive and intimidating language, drunken behaviour, excessive noise, graffiti and litter. ASBOs were applicable to any person over ten years of age, by complaint to the Magistrates' Courts by the local authority or the chief officer of police for the area. If made, such orders sought to prevent named persons from behaving in an anti-social manner and ran for a minimum of two years or 'until further order'. Breach of an ASBO constitutes a criminal offence, punishable by fine or imprisonment. This approach was taken further in the 2003 Anti-Social Behaviour Act.

Also relevant in this context is the 2003 Extradition Act which was introduced to speed up the transfer of suspected terrorists from one jurisdiction to another. Under this legislation the United States was able to secure the extradition of a UK citizen without having to provide any evidence. In 2006 this led to the extradition of three former NatWest executives wanted in connection with the collapse of Enron. Indeed, a large number of measures designed to combat terrorism have been introduced over recent years – for example, the 2000 Terrorism Act, the 2001 Anti-Terrorism Crime and Security Act, the 2005 Prevention of Terrorism Act and the 2006 Terrorism Act. These involve such matters as police powers to 'stop and search', 'Control Orders' (limiting the movement and communications of suspects) and 'detention without charge'. Consequently they have an important bearing upon personal liberty. Indeed, there has been a continuing debate about the conflicting demands of liberty and security. For example, Amnesty International argued that the 2001 legislation 'violated a wide range of human rights' and that provisions within the 2006 legislation 'undermine[d] ... the right to liberty, the prohibition of arbitrary detention, the rights to the presumption of innocence and fair trial'.[11] On the other hand, Charles Clarke, when Home Secretary, observed that: 'it is a fundamental civil liberty of people ... to be able to go to work on their transport system in the morning without being blown up'.[12]

The *2006 Identity Cards Act* paved the way for the introduction of a National Identity Card Scheme designed to provide all UK residents over 16 with a universal means of identification. The Act established a National Identity Register; provided powers to issue identity cards; ensured checks could be made against other databases; set out the information which would be held and the safeguards which would be in place; enabled public and private sector organisations to verify a person's identity by checking against the National Identity Register and, with the person's consent, to validate someone's identity before providing services; included powers which would allow access to specified public services only on the production of a valid identity card; and provided for it to become compulsory to register and be issued with a card, including penalties against failure to register. The Government announced that it expected to begin issuing Identity Cards from 2008/09.

As for property rights in Britain, these have never been regarded as absolute or sacrosanct. Parliament has legislated on many occasions to limit such rights when they have conflicted with what is deemed by Ministers to be in the public interest – for example in the spheres of public health, nationalisation or compulsory purchase. As a general rule, in modern times there has not been as much determination to safeguard economic or property rights as there has been to defend rights of personal liberty. This is in accordance with the European Convention on Human Rights which has a similar bias. However, it should be noted that some people considered that the employment legislation in the 1980s gave more weight to property rights than rights of personal liberty.

Wrongful interference with the rights of personal liberty and property can be countered by the use of various legal remedies. These include civil action for damages, prosecution for assault, exercise of the right of self-defence, use of the police complaints procedure, and even the invocation of *habeas corpus*.[13] Yet there are no final or definitive solutions to these problems, since the law governing these aspects of civil rights can be changed from time to time by Act of Parliament – for example, the 1998 Crime and Disorder Act, the 1994 Criminal Justice and Public Order Act, or the 1991 Child Support Act – and, in any case, all these issues have to be seen increasingly within a European context.

freedom of movement

Under the 1981 British Nationality Act all British citizens have the same legal rights and status, although this applies only to those with full British citizenship. The position of others resident in Britain is limited by the various legal provisions governing the control of immigration and asylum.

Under European law, all citizens of the member states have the right to take up residence in any part of the Union. In practice, this 'right' is not exercised by many people, although following the enlargement of the European Union in 2004 to include ten central and eastern European countries, it was estimated that as many as 500,000 people from Poland moved to the United Kingdom. This development led to some concern and calls for restrictions on the possible movement of people from Romania and Bulgaria once they become part of the European Union in 2007. However, overall figures suggested that only a comparatively small number of people from other member states of the Union have settled in Britain, and an even smaller number of British have moved to settle in other parts of the European Union.[14]

The provisions of the *2006 Immigration, Asylum and Nationality Act* sought to deny asylum to terrorists, improve the ability to deport those who were deemed to pose a serious risk to the UK's interests, and speed up the appeals process in deportation cases. It also introduced a points-based system for managed migration and restricted appeals for those refused entry to the UK for work or study; introduced a new civil penalties scheme for employers who knowingly used or exploited illegal workers; and sought to strengthen borders by providing for data sharing between the Immigration Service, Police and Customs.

freedom of expression

It has been argued that it is in the nature of the British State to seek to restrict freedom of expression.[15] In Britain there is no equivalent of the First Amendment to the United States Constitution which guarantees freedom of expression for all. British law on the other hand has tended to rely upon the principle that anything which is not prohibited is permitted. Yet the extent to which restrictions on free speech have been imposed in civil or criminal law has varied from time to time. For example, the law of defamation protects individuals from slander and libel or rather it provides a form of legal redress if the person concerned can afford to fight a case. Substantial damages may be awarded for injury to a person's reputation, and in some cases even the threat of such legal action can be sufficient to secure a retraction or to get a newspaper to publish a (usually inadequate) note of correction. In some cases those accused of defamation can plead absolute privilege typically by demonstrating fair and accurate reporting. The defence of 'fair comment' can also protect expressions of opinion on matters of public interest, even if someone thinks what has been said is defamatory.

In the criminal law there are the offences of sedition, blasphemy, obscenity and criminal libel which theoretically protect society from some of the excesses of free expression. Yet in practice actions are rare and of dubious utility, since it is difficult to get juries to convict on the basis of such ancient laws. Furthermore, as was seen in the much publicised instance of Salman Rushdie's *Satanic Verses*,[16] the law (in this case of blasphemy) does not always apply. In this case an alleged blasphemy against the prophet Mohammed fell outside the terms of the statute, which is concerned only with blasphemy in a Christian context.

Freedom of expression in the media has traditionally been controlled to some extent by a combination of self-regulation on the part of the more responsible media and the intervention of certain statutory bodies whose task it has been to maintain what are regarded as 'proper' standards. In the case of newspapers, the Press Complaints Commission has had an unimpressive record in preventing and an even less impressive record in punishing severe lapses of taste or decency, or unacceptable invasions of privacy. The same can be said of the Broadcasting Complaints Commission and more recently the Broadcasting Standards Commission. However, the BBC Trust (formally the Board of Governors), the Independent Television Commission (ITC) and the Radio Authority have some powers over the broadcasters in radio and television, but have taken few opportunities to use their powers, especially if urged to do so by the Government of the day. In the sensitive areas of sex and violence on television the Broadcasting Standards Council and, since April 1997, the Broadcasting Standards Commission has wielded its statutory powers with apparent enthusiasm.

In the world of cinema, video and DVD the British Board of Film Classification has the task of certifying films for public release and can prohibit exhibition on the grounds that it 'would offend against good taste or decency or would be likely to encourage or incite to crime or to lead to disorder or to be offensive to public feeling'. As far as advertising is concerned, standards of public taste and decency are monitored by the Advertising Standards Authority (a self-regulatory body created by the industry), but usually without much impact. In certain respects the media have become more unrestrained with the liberalisation of the airwaves in the 1990s and the increasingly intense competition between tabloid newspapers. It is also difficult, if not impossible, to regulate the world of cyberspace because there is no unified jurisdiction to rely upon.[17]

It should be noted that it is not unknown for governments to attempt to exert pressure on broadcasters in relation to particular programmes. For example, in 1985 the Conservative Government of the time leaned heavily on the BBC to withdraw the *Real Lives* programme which focused on a prominent member of the IRA. Similarly, in December 1987 the Government took out an injunction to prevent the broadcast of a Radio 4 series *My Country Right or Wrong*. Nonetheless, those who work in the media jealously guard their freedom and seek vigorously to resist such Government interference. This was evident in the strength of the media reaction to the *Real Lives* controversy and to similar Government attempts in 1988 to ensure that an ITV programme, Death on the Rock, was not broadcast because of its portrayal of an SAS killing of three IRA terrorists in Gibraltar. Government can, however, use the law to curtail freedom of expression, as happened between 1984 and 1994 when the media were not allowed to broadcast the actual voices of members of the IRA and Sinn Fein, even though their pictures could be shown on television and their words were spoken by actors.

In 2003 an argument broke out between the Government and the BBC over a report by a BBC journalist, Andrew Gilligan, on the Radio Four programme *Today* which claimed that the Government had 'sexed up' its dossier on the threat from Iraq in an attempt to make the case for going to war against Saddam Hussein. The dispute led to the establishment of the Hutton inquiry. The Hutton Report[18] was more critical of the BBC than the Government, which contributed to the resignation of both the Chairman and the Director General of the BBC.[19]

The **2006 Terrorism Act** made 'glorification' of terrorism an offence. This provoked a concerted campaign and a Commons rebellion to block attempts that would have made it illegal to make remarks capable of inciting religious hatred. Critics argued that, in its determination to tackle terrorism, the Government had lost sight of the obligation to protect free speech.

freedom of association, procession and protest

In modern times it has been difficult to strike a balance between the rights to meet, process and protest freely, and what are deemed to be necessary restraints in the interest of public order, since any attempt at balance is bound to involve constant adjustment and compromise between conflicting interests. In principle, such freedom is not extended to senior civil servants, the armed services, the police or registered charities. However, the Civil Service is heavily unionised at all levels and the police of lower ranks have powerful representation from the Police Federation. There is also a grey area covering registered charities and their ability apparently to circumvent some of the legal limitations of their charitable status. The provisions of the1986 Public Order Act and the 1994 Criminal Justice and Public Order Act curtailed what may lawfully be done on the streets and in public places by providing the police with stronger powers to avert public disorder. For example, the 1986 Act introduced a new offence of disorderly conduct to deal with some forms of modern hooliganism and the 1994 Act created new offences concerning various forms of trespass and ways of causing intentional alarm or distress which were designed to deal with racial violence and other forms of harassment. Provisions contained within the 2005 Serious Organized Crime Act outlawed unauthorized demonstrations within two miles of the Houses of Parliament. The first person convicted under this legislation was Maya Evans who had been involved in reading out in Whitehall the names of soldiers killed in Iraq.

Public and private meetings for any purpose are constrained not so much by the law as by the need to secure prior permission from the owners of suitable halls or open spaces. However, the 1994 Criminal Justice and Public Order Act contained powers to ban certain 'trespassory assemblies', while public meetings may not lawfully be held on the public highway and any such obstruction is an offence under the 1959 Highways Act. This has special relevance to the right to picket, which is supposed to be confined under the 1980 Employment Act to peaceful persuasion in contemplation or furtherance of a trade dispute by people attending either at their own place of work or that of so-called 'first customers' and 'first suppliers'.[20] Legal protection against disorderly conduct at a public meeting is still provided by the 1908 Public Meetings Act, as amended by the 1936 Public Order Act; although in modern conditions this has little practical bearing upon such problems.

In general, the preservation of public order in processions and public meetings depends on the police who can exercise considerable discretion. Among the powers available to Chief Officers of Police under the 1986 Public Order Act are the powers to specify routes for marches and demonstrations and to impose conditions on public meetings. The 1994 Criminal Justice and Public Order Act gave Chief Officers additional powers to apply to the relevant District Council for a ban on public meetings for up to four days within a specified area and for a ban of not more than three months on any category of public procession or occasionally on all public processions. In Northern Ireland the 1998 Public Processions (Northern Ireland) Act established a Parades Commission with responsibility to promote greater understanding by the general public of issues concerning public processions; to promote and facilitate mediation as a means of resolving disputes about public processions; to keep itself generally informed as to the conduct of public processions and protest meetings; and to make recommendations to the Secretary of State concerning the operation of the Act.

freedom of information and the right to privacy

The principles of secrecy and disclosure coexist rather uneasily in the British political system. Indeed, there is a real conflict of interest between the protective, sometimes punitive, role of the state in its efforts to safeguard 'national security' and the legitimate expectations of its subjects/citizens that they can or should be allowed to share in a more open and participatory form of politics. There is also a parallel conflict between the privacy interests of private individuals, who want confidential access to and safeguards for the security of official information about themselves, and the public interest of society as a whole which may occasionally require the sharing or disclosure of sensitive personal information at least on a 'need-to-know' basis within and sometimes beyond the institutions of government. The interests of state security were invoked to justify the passage of both the *1911 Official Secrets Act* and the *1989 Official Secrets Act*, the retention of the D notice system as well as a whole host of activities such as the interception of private communications by telephone-tapping and other techniques of electronic surveillance. These practices have taken place on the basis of rather tenuous legal authority, subject to no more than indirect control by Ministers (notably in a Cabinet Committee on the Intelligence Services chaired by the Prime Minister) and in Parliament by the Intelligence and Security Committee under the chairmanship of a senior Privy Councillor. Traditionally, security matters of this kind were kept under review by the Security Commission, a small supervisory body of Privy Councillors chaired by a Law Lord, which reported regularly to the Prime Minister and occasionally to Parliament; the whole process was shrouded in mystery. Since the early 1990s, however, a little more information has been made available about MI5 and MI6 and the Security Service has been put on a statutory footing.[21]

Against this background it is not surprising that there has been pressure for reform which would put more emphasis on the rights of ordinary citizens and less on the needs of national security. For a long time there was an active, all-party campaign for freedom of information throughout the sphere of Government and the public sector and this had some success at least in relation to local government and the release of environmental information. The problems of striking an appropriate balance between the needs of official secrecy on the one hand and the rights to information on the other have been considerable. Indeed, the difficulties have been exacerbated by the growing use of computers throughout the public sector and by the development of the Government Data Network and other forms of data sharing. Public concern about the possible misuse of personal information kept on official files led to the *1984 Data Protection Act*, which provided some safeguards against malpractice in relation to nearly all official information which is electronically processed and stored. However, with the prospect of the widespread use of identity cards by 2009–10 and the likelihood that different state agencies will be able to share information collected from the public, the problem of how to balance security and privacy could become more acute.

In 1994 a new Code of Practice came into effect obliging Government Departments to respond to 'reasonable' requests for information. The Code stipulated that information would be provided 'as soon as practicable', with a target of 20 working days for 'simple requests for information'. Where information could not be provided, Departments were obliged to provide an explanation. Breaches of the Code were to be monitored by the Parliamentary

Ombudsman. There were, however, a wide range of exemptions, including all 'policy advice' to Ministers unless the Government considered it 'relevant and important'; 'original documents', which Ministers only had to disclose in digest form; and information harmful to national security, defence or international relations. The *1998 Data Protection Act* extended the access rights for individuals to structured sets of manual records (such as card indexes and microfiches), but did not create a general 'right of access' by individuals to all their personal files.

Such initiatives did not defuse the pressures for real freedom of information, not least from groups such as the Campaign for Freedom of Information and Liberty. By the mid 1990s the Labour Party and the Liberal Democrats were pledged to introduce legislation providing for freedom of information and it was a pledge which the first Blair Administration acted upon in its first Parliament.

In December 1997 the Government published a White Paper entitled Your Right To Know[22] in which it proposed to give the public a statutory right of access to official records and information not only held by Government Departments, local authorities, organisations such as the National Health Service and bodies like the Atomic Energy Authority, but also the police, schools, colleges universities and a whole host of other Non-Departmental Public Bodies, committees and advisory bodies as well as privatised utilities. Certain bodies were excluded, such as the Intelligence Services; and a number of areas protected, such as national security, official advice to Ministers, personal privacy and commercial confidentiality. It was proposed that an Information Commissioner be appointed to adjudicate and enforce rights of access, and that a new criminal offence for willful or reckless destruction, alteration or withholding of information from the Commissioner be introduced. It was not until June 1999 that the Government published a draft Bill, one viewed with disappointment by many of the campaigners for freedom of information because it was seen as a retreat from many of the positions taken in the White Paper. A Freedom of Information Bill was eventually introduced at the end of 1999 and enacted as the **2000 Freedom of Information Act**.[23] This provided clear statutory rights for those requesting information together with an enforcement regime. Under the terms of the Act, any member of the public is able to apply for access to information held by a wide range of public authorities, including Parliament, Government Departments, local authorities, health trusts, doctors' surgeries and thousands of other organisations. The main features of the Act included:

- A general right of access to information held by public authorities in the course of carrying out their public functions, subject to certain conditions and exemptions
- A new office of **Information Commissioner** and a new **Information Tribunal**, with wide powers to enforce the right of access to information were created

- A duty was imposed on public authorities to adopt a scheme for the publication of information. The schemes, which had to be approved by the Commissioner, had to specify the classes of information an authority intended to publish, the manner of publication and whether the information was available to the public free of charge or on payment of a fee.[24]

The legislation was however criticised by some – and continues to be so – for the conditions and exemptions placed on the general right of access –(a formidably long list which was contained in Part II of the Act). The criticism was aimed at the fact that the Information Commissioner was only able *to require* public authorities to consider the public interest when exercising their discretion about disclosure as opposed to an ability to enforce release of official information on that ground, and because discretion remained with the public authorities concerned which were not obliged to give reasons for a refusal if these would involve the disclosure of exempt information.[25] In short, the Government was criticised for not apparently appreciating the important distinction between a genuine Freedom of Information Act creating statutory rights with the minimum of closely defined exemptions and a paternalistic measure to promote open government with Ministers deciding what the public need to know.

Additionally, however, there is the context of the right to privacy, and increasingly concerns have been expressed about the development of what has been termed 'a surveillance society'. A surveillance society is one where technology is extensively and routinely used to track and record the activities and movements of people. This includes systematic tracking and recording of travel and use of public services, automated use of CCTV, analysis of buying habits and financial transactions, and the work place monitoring of telephone calls, email and internet use. Such developments can often be in ways which are invisible – certainly not obvious – to members of the general public as they are watched and monitored. Research shows just how pervasive surveillance is and how it looks set to accelerate in the years to come.[26] Some see surveillance as a malign plot hatched by evil powers to control the population. A more realistic view is that the surveillance society has come about almost by accident. However, techniques such as automatic classification, social sorting and risk-based profiling can create real problems for individuals – social exclusion and discrimination – and can as a result have a very negative impact. These are issues that are not going to go away.

state security and emergency powers

Issues associated with state security have come particularly to the fore as a result of the terrorist attacks on the United States in September 2001. This preoccupation was brought home to people in the UK following the bombings in London on the underground train and bus networks in July 2005. Despite the fact that there were, according to some estimates, some 200 pieces of anti-terrorist legislation already on the Statute Book the British Government responded by bringing forward successive waves of legislation providing for extra powers to combat the threat. Critics responded by declaring that, in the name of counter-terrorism and public order, the Government was assaulting civil liberties and seriously limiting freedom in the name of greater security.

In most serious emergencies the police, fire and ambulance services can cope with any problems which arise. Yet there are some occasions when the military has to be called in to assist the civilian power or to deal with particularly serious threats to the life and well-being of the community. For the last few decades the most notable example has been the need to keep thousands of British troops in Northern Ireland in order to help the civil authorities preserve peace and public order. More recent examples have included the need to counter the action of terrorists by calling in the Special Air Service (SAS) and other special military units to assist the police and security services as happened at Heathrow Airport in April 2003 after intelligence reports suggested terrorists might be plotting a missile attack on a plane. The legal position on all such occasions is that military personnel have a duty to support the civil power when requested by the latter to do so. Since such emergencies usually involve sensitive and difficult issues of public safety, they require Ministerial decision and control at the highest level.

During peacetime a state of emergency may be declared under the authority of the 1920 and 1964 *Emergency Powers Acts*. These statutes permit the Government of the day to make use of wide-ranging powers designed to ensure the maintenance of essential services, subject to Parliamentary approval at least every seven days. During wartime even more far-reaching powers were available to the Government of the day in the shape of the 1914 and 1915 *Defence of the Realm Acts* and the 1939 and 1940 *Emergency Powers Acts*. These statutes, which were later repealed, gave the Government of the day almost unlimited powers, including detention without trial for indefinite periods and the seizure of private property without compensation. This legislation was subject to Parliamentary approval at least every 28 days.

In the case of special measures to deal with terrorism, Parliament passed some draconian statutes in 1973 and 1975 to deal with the threat in Northern Ireland from the IRA and other terrorist organisations, and in 1974 and 1976 to deal with terrorist offences anywhere in the United Kingdom. This legislation conferred very extensive powers upon the Government of the day, which enabled it to take almost any measures deemed necessary to counter such threats to national security, including detention without charge for up to seven days (subsequently reduced to three days with the endorsement of a Court in more recent legislation) and the power to exclude undesirable people from the country. In view of the political sensitivity of the terrorist threat from Northern Ireland over the years, the *Prevention of Terrorism (Temporary Provisions) Act* and the *Northern Ireland (Emergency Provisions) Act* have been re-enacted on many occasions and been put to Parliament for renewal on an annual basis.

More recently as part of the 'war against terror' a whole series of counter-terrorist measures have come into force, measures designed to reflect what the Government sees as the international nature of the terrorist threat:

The **2000 Terrorism Act** introduced new powers for police to hold terrorist suspects for up to seven days without charge and widened powers to ban international terrorist organizations. In addition, new offences were created of inciting terrorist acts, providing training for terrorist purposes and providing instruction or training in the use of firearms, explosives or chemical, biological or nuclear weapons.

The **2001 Anti-Terrorism Crime and Security Act** gave the Home Secretary powers to hold foreign terrorist suspects indefinitely without trial if they could not be deported for human rights' reasons and provided for suspects not to be given full details of the evidence against them in order to protect the position of the intelligence services.

The **2003 Criminal Justice Act** extended police powers to hold terrorist suspects for up to 14 days without charge.

The **2005 Prevention of Terrorism Act**, which was brought forward in light of a ruling by the Law Lords that detaining foreign terrorist suspects without charge was illegal, repealed those powers and, instead, introduced powers to impose 'Control Orders' which limited the movements and communications of suspects and which were extended to cover British and foreign nationals.

The **2006 Terrorism Act** made it a criminal offence to encourage or glorify terrorism; to disseminate terrorist publications, including via extremist bookshops and internet activity; to prepare or plan to commit a terrorist act, or to assist others to do so; and to give or receive terrorist training or attend a terrorist training camp. The legislation also sought to give the police powers to hold suspects for up to 90 days – a period that was reduced to 28 days following resistance in both Houses of Parliament.

When in 2006 the *Terrorism Act*, the *Immigration, Asylum and Nationality Act* and the *Identity Cards Act*, all came into force, the Home Secretary at the time, Charles Clarke, declared: 'There is a balance to be struck between the rights and freedoms of individuals and the security of all our citizens. This new legislation together will allow us to uphold our democratic right to freedom of speech and to free movement within the United Kingdom, as well as encouraging managed migration which will benefit the UK economy. At the same time, it will strengthen our ability to keep our borders secure, tackle illegal working and to go about our day to day business safely and secure in the knowledge that people are who they say they are'.[27] An alternative case was argued by Amnesty International, namely that provisions of the Terrorism Act 'undermine[d] the rights to freedom of expression and association, the right to liberty, the prohibition of arbitrary detention, the rights to the presumption of innocence and fair trial'.[28] These issues remain matters of lively public debate and, as yet, there is no durable political consensus for dealing with them.

the European and international dimension

Increasingly, these matters have to be seen in not only a European but an international dimension, because of the wide range of civil rights declared in European and international Conventions. The protection of civil rights is a matter of wide international concern. National governments have been prepared to make purposeful moves in this direction at least since the 1948 UN Declaration of Human Rights and the 1950 European Convention on Human Rights. The latter, which was ratified by the British Parliament in 1951, provides judicial procedures by which alleged infringements of civil rights in Britain may be examined at international level. The European Convention provides an overt constraint upon the legislative supremacy of Parliament in that successive British Governments have not wished to be found in breach of its provisions. However, the Convention was not originally incorporated within British national law on the somewhat complacent grounds that civil rights in Britain were adequately protected by British law and that such incorporation would be inconsistent with the traditional British claim to legal supremacy for Parliament at Westminster. Indeed, it was not until 1966 that the United Kingdom formally recognised the right of individual petition to the European Commission on Human Rights or the compulsory jurisdiction in Britain of the

Date	Issue	The Court ruled:
2005		That it was a disproportionate breach of human rights of prisoners to deny them the right to vote
2003		That the Royal Navy court martial system was an infringement of the right to a fair and independent trial
2002		That a transsexual born a man had a right to be recognised as a woman and allowed to marry
2001		That the Government had breached Article 2 (the right to life) in cases of 10 IRA men killed by the Security Authorities in Northern Ireland between 1982 and 1992
1999		That the ban on gays and lesbians serving in the armed forces to be illegal under the right to privacy and family life
1997		That the army court martial system was unfair and in breach of human rights
1996		That the Home Secretary should no longer have the power to detain child killers indefinitely
1995		That the shooting dead of three IRA bombers by the SAS in Gibraltar was a violation of their human rights
1990		Three sex offenders won a ruling forcing a review of the way life-sentence prisoners were released on lience and then recalled
1988		The convicted killer Jimmy Boyle won a claim that letters were unlawfully interfered with in jail
1985		Three women from Malawi, the Philippines and Sri Lanka successfully challenged immigration laws that denied their husbands automatic entry into Britain
1982		corporal punishment in state schools
1979		That it had been wrong to block publication in *The Sunday Times* of reports about children whose mothers had taken the thalidomide drug during pregnancy
1978		Against birching as a punishment in the Isle of Man
1975		That prisoners had the right to consut a lawyer, write to an Mp or newspaper, and to sue the Home Office without having to have permission of the Home Secretary

source: Adapted (and updated) from *The Guardian*, 11 September 2000 and The Times, *25 October 1997*.

figure **19.1   key British cases before the European Court of Human Rights**

European Court of Human Rights. Since then various proceedings under the Convention helped to bring about changes in British law and legal practice, for example the introduction of immigration appeal Tribunals, revised rules on access to lawyers for prisoners, press freedom and restrictions on the use of corporal punishment. In 1998 the Convention was finally incorporated into domestic law with the passage of the Human Rights Act. Figure 19.1 highlights a list of key British cases before the European Court of Human Rights.

It is also worth noting the European Union aspect of the matter. For example, the 1992 Maastricht Treaty created a range of positive citizens' rights and established a European 'Ombudsman' to which all citizens of the Union have the right to appeal if they feel in need of redress.[29]

19.4 the role of the police

For much of their contemporary history the police in Britain have been held in high regard and placed on a pedestal by public opinion as exemplifying an ideal model of behaviour and character. In short, the 'British Bobby' came to be seen as representing all that was 'right and proper' in British society. One survey in the early 1960s showed that no less than 83 per cent of those interviewed professed great respect for the police.[30] This level of public support had been the result principally of four particular features of policing in Britain:

First, with certain exceptions, such as the Diplomatic Protection Group and the police in Northern Ireland, the police did not normally carry firearms.[31]

Second, individual police forces were locally based and locally controlled. There was no 'national' police force, but rather 52 local police forces in the United Kingdom – 43 in England and Wales, eight in Scotland and one in Northern Ireland. Outside London each force was under the direction of a Chief Constable who, in turn, was responsible to a local Police Authority. In London, with the exception of the City of London, the Metropolitan Police Force was under the command of the Commissioner who, in turn, was responsible to the Home Secretary.

Third, there was a belief that there was only one category of police officer, whether uniformed or plain-clothed, rather than a range of special police forces answerable to different parts of Government as is the case in many other countries.

Fourth, there was the perception that the police were non-political, non-partisan and impartial. Indeed, it was to preserve this position that the police were kept at arm's length from direct Government control and there were a number of local forces rather than a single national force.

Since the late 1960s however, violence has become a more apparent feature of British society and the reputation of the police has increasingly been tarnished in the eyes of the media and the public. Between 1996 and 2005 the proportion of respondents who told the British Crime Survey that the police were doing a good or excellent job fell from 64 per cent to 49 per cent.[32] An opinion poll in mid 2005 found that only 58 per cent of people trusted the police to tell the truth.[33]

This movement of public opinion has been the cumulative consequence of some related developments, including police corruption and other scandals, changes in policing methods, police malpractice in certain areas, problems of police powers and accountability, and rising levels of crime. It has also reflected moves away from the four foundations of traditional policing.

First, *the issue of an increasingly armed police force.* Despite the fact that Britain has a long tradition of unarmed police officers, the number of operations and the range of circumstances in which the police carry guns have increased. In 2003 a pilot project allowing police officers in five forces to use Taser electric stun guns was introduced and in 2005 the Home Office announced that the experiment was to be extended. Police officers have been the target of gun crime and a number of deaths have occurred – such as that of WPC Sharon Beshenivsky who was shot and killed in November 2005 as she sought to deal with a raid in a travel agent's shop in Bradford. On the other hand, events such as the Stockwell Tube shooting by police of the Brazilian, Jean Charles de Menezes, in July 2005 and the Forest Gate shooting by police of Mohammed Abdul Kahar in June 2006 damaged public confidence in the police and added to concern about the development of an armed police force.

Second, *the concept of local police forces locally controlled.* This has been a traditional and popular concept. Nonetheless, early in 2006 the then Home Secretary, Charles Clarke, came forward with plans to merge a number of police forces, reducing the total in England and Wales from 43 to as few as 17 in a move that was said to be necessary to combat terrorism and organized crime. However, in the face of considerable public opposition the plans were dropped by the then Home Secretary, John Reid, in June 2006.

Third, *the aspiration that there should be only one category of police officer.* This too has changed as the police service has become more fragmented. The most recent example of this was the Serious Organised Crime Agency which was launched in 2006 and which brought together more than 4000 police, customs and immigration experts with new multiple powers to go after international drug traffickers, people traffickers and fraudsters. Long before that there had been firearms officers, diplomatic protection officers, Special Branch and a wide variety of other specialists including the British Transport Police, all of which reduced the cohesion of the police overall. In addition, and as a result of the Police Reform Act 2002, the role of Police Community Support Officer (PCSO) has developed, with PCSOs working alongside the police in a supporting role patrolling local areas, providing a visible presence and helping to reassure the public and dealing with incidents of nuisance and anti-social behaviour. In 2005 there were over 6700 CSOs (and an intention for there to be 16,000 in 2007).

Fourth, *the perception that the police are non-political*, non-partisan and impartial. This was something that was undermined during the political battles of the 1980s when the ideological content of British politics intensified and 'law and order' issues came to the fore. It was also something undermined by public perceptions – fuelled by the Stephen Lawrence case[34] – that the police were institutionally racist.[35]

With regard to *police corruption and other scandals*, public confidence in the police received a severe jolt in 1969 when *The Sunday Times* revealed the existence of institutionalised corruption in the Metropolitan Police, a situation made worse when it became apparent that members of the police force were covering up for each other. More revelations concerning corruption came to the fore, resulting in a massive internal police investigation known as 'Operation Countryman'. This was reported in 1978 and, although it failed to substantiate most of the allegations, the damage had clearly been done. The public perception was that there had been a police cover-up, whether or not there had been any substance to the allegations. Since then a number of cases have come to light in which innocent people were convicted on the basis of falsified or distorted testimony in which police officers were implicated. There were the notorious cases of the Guildford Four, the Birmingham Six, the Maguire family and the Tottenham Three. If these had been the only examples, they could perhaps have been explained away as special cases involving terrorism in the first three instances and the brutal murder of a police constable in the fourth. Yet there have been other cases involving serious police malpractice, for example in the West Midlands Serious Crime Squad in the 1980s and the case of Stefan Kiszko who spent 16 years in prison because irrefutable evidence, which showed that he could not possibly have committed the crime for which he had been sentenced, was withheld from the Court by the police. Add to this more recent evidence such as the Stockwell Tube and Forest Gate shootings, and the cumulative result has been to damage the image and standing of the police in the eyes of the media and large sections of the British public.

With regard to *changes in police methods*, the main factors have been the reorganisation of the foot patrol system into a motorised system in the late 1960s and the growing use of new police equipment. The unintended consequence of the first development was to make the police seem more remote and less reassuring to the law-abiding public. The consequence of the second development, which involved supplying the police with new equipment, such as helmets with visors, riot shields, long truncheons, CS gas, pepper sprays, tasers and the increasing use of firearms, has been to disturb and alienate many members of the general public. Such high-pressure policing may have been necessary in certain violent circumstances – for example, the direct action by the miners in 1984–85 or the Poll Tax Riots in the late 1980s or certain terrorist actions in 2005 and 2006 – but it has done little to reinforce the traditional British doctrine of policing by consent.

With regard to *police malpractice*, the police have increasingly been accused of bias in their dealings with certain minority groups, especially ethnic minorities. For many this view was substantiated by the failure of the police to bring the racist killers of Stephen Lawrence to justice. Allegations of police racism have grown, with the police being accused of taking a heavy-handed approach especially towards members of the Afro-Caribbean community.

One survey showed that Afro-Caribbeans were 50 per cent more likely to be stopped in their vehicles than white people and nearly four times more likely to be stopped on foot. Yet the rationale for this was that the incidents of unlawful behaviour, such as the carrying of knives and other offensive weapons, was most prevalent among these youngsters. More recently the anti-terror laws have been seen by many within the Muslim community as a form of religious and racial discrimination which soured the relationship between the police and this particular minority.

Similarly, the police have been accused of taking a provocative stance when dealing with public demonstrations and have been blamed by some extremist elements for outbreaks of violence on occasions, such as the Trafalgar Square Poll Tax riot of 1990 or the Hyde Park riot against what is now the 1994 Criminal Justice and Public Order Act in October 1994. In short, some have come to see police malpractice as widespread as evidenced by the 483 actions received against and the £1.9 million paid in Court and out-of-Court settlements to plaintiffs by the Metropolitan Police in 2005–06.

As for *the nature and extent of police powers and related questions concerning police accountability*, these have also become more salient since the 1980s and led to the establishment of the **Independent Police Complaints Commission**, an independent, national system for dealing with complaints against the police, following the 2002 Police Reform Act in 2004. Nonetheless, in the context of the post-9/11 and post-7/7 world, the adequacy of the powers of the police and the effectiveness of legal safeguards against police abuse have became highly topical and highly controversial issues, with civil liberties groups demanding additional safeguards and the 'law and order' lobby demanding greater police powers to combat the threats that exist.[36]

Lastly, there has been the rising level of crime and lawlessness. In the early years of the twentieth century the British police recorded fewer than 100,000 offences each year. This figure rose gradually to reach 500,000 by 1950. Since then recorded crime rates have risen dramatically, according to the British Crime Survey in 2004–05, the total number of crimes in England and Wales was around 10,850,000 and nearly 24 per cent of the population were the victim of some type of crime.[37] Despite the obvious difficulties associated with such statistics,[38] they have provided the focus for much of the debate. The perception of a significant proportion of the public is that little public benefit has been gained from the more than 50 items of law and order legislation, introducing more than 700 criminal offences, that have been passed by Parliament in the period 1997–2007, or from the 13,000 more police offices and from the 56 per cent increase in spending on the police between 2000–01 and 2007–08. Public confidence in the police has undoubtedly been eroded, a climate of cynicism and even paranoia in some sections of the public has been created, and a sense of anxiety bordering almost on hysteria has been fostered among politicians and public alike.

19.6 conclusion

One of the difficulties in reaching balanced and lasting conclusions about the role of the police in Britain is that many of the issues raise important questions to do with the relationship between the police and the public, especially in some inner-city areas where the relationship can be very strained between police officers and people from the ethnic minority communities.[39] Problems have arisen particularly in the area of police powers to stop and search people for offensive weapons, such as knives and other sharp instruments. There have also been intermittent complaints from suspects that they have not been able to consult a solicitor before being charged or that they have been 'fitted up' by the police with fabricated evidence and induced to make false confessions. Such problems are likely to persist as long as there are shortcomings in police practice, great media and public pressures upon the police to catch and charge someone for offences of a particularly heinous character, and a deep and lasting mistrust of all law-enforcement agencies among some disaffected individuals and groups in the population.

A more general problem is caused by the constant need to strike a fair and effective balance between the interests of the law-abiding majority, which wants the police and the Courts to maintain law and order in a strong, even draconian way, and those of certain vociferous minorities who are often more concerned with the protection of civil liberties and the maintenance of civil rights. Since it is always difficult to strike an appropriate balance between such strongly conflicting interests, the solution has typically involved attempts to balance increased powers for the police and the Courts with more effective legal safeguards for the law-abiding community.

Those who are strongly committed to the maintenance of law and order have invariably argued for changes in the criminal law – for example, the return of capital punishment – which they believe would enable the police and the Courts to deal more effectively with the current levels of crime and lawlessness. Indeed, very few people have argued for a more permissive attitude towards crime – except those who wish to decriminalise the purchase and use of soft drugs or legalise and regulate prostitution – or more lenient procedures for dealing with convicted criminals. However, growing concern has been expressed, not only by liberal-minded opinion-formers, about the large and growing number of people sent to prison in Britain[40] and about the smaller (but highly publicised) number of incidents of wrongful conviction.[41] Others have argued the need for improved procedures to deal with complaints against the police – arguments that continue to be made despite the establishment of the Independent Police Complaints Commission following the 2002 Police Reform Act in 2004.

There is a section of opinion which is disturbed by the occasional tendency for the police, the security services and the paramilitary units of the modern state to overstep the traditional bounds in a few highly publicised instances of brutality, excessive surveillance and democratically unacceptable uses of force. Examples cited include the actions of the South Yorkshire Police against miners at the Orgreave Coke Plant during the 1984–85 strike; the death in 1993 of Joyce Gardner, a Jamaican woman living in London, who collapsed during a struggle with police officers from the deportation squad; and some of the actions of the police during the protests by Animal Rights campaigners outside the Essex port of Brightlingsea in 1995.

Profound social factors underlie the issues which have generated controversy around the police. Since the late 1960s the social conditions which must underpin what can be termed 'policing by consent' have been eroded; economic and social inequality has increased; British society has become less homogeneous and less deferential than before. Consequently, as was pointed out by Lord Scarman in his Report into the 1981 Brixton disorders, it is no good blaming the police for rising crime and declining respect for the law. All sections of society must take responsibility for what has happened and act constructively together to deal with both the causes and the consequences of crime and public disorder.

Since the beginning of the 'war on terror' an increasing number of people have argued that civil liberties are under assault in Britain. Indeed, some observers have sought to draw attention to what they regard as an alarming tendency for British society to develop in an authoritarian direction wholly at variance with British liberal traditions. Certainly the basis of civil rights in Britain is to some extent precarious, since there is neither a codified constitution nor an entrenched Bill of Rights. Notwithstanding the incorporation into domestic law of the European Convention on Human Rights in the form of the *1998 Human Rights Act*, the Courts do not have the power to set aside primary legislation, but only to issue a Declaration of Incompatibility with the European Convention and then to wait for Parliament to rectify the situation if inclined to do so. We may soon witness more frequent clashes between the Sovereignty of Parliament and the rule of law and the battleground seems likely to be the relationship between the citizen and the state.

SUGGESTED QUESTIONS

1   To what extent can it be said that there has been a movement from 'subject' to 'citizen' in contemporary Britain?

2   What is the nature of the legal relationship between the state and its citizens in Britain today?

3   Can a 'balance' be struck between the security of the state and the rights of its citizens?

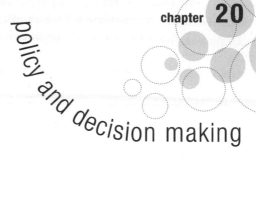

chapter **20**

policy and decision making

In this chapter we are concerned with the policy- and decision-making process. Most of the analysis will focus upon the Labour and Conservative parties – but account will also be taken of the Liberal Democrats, since their policy making has had an influence on the other parties in what is now a system of multiparty politics.

Policy may be defined as a deliberate course of action or inaction worked out by the leading figures in a political party with the help of others in order to define their political purposes and, to some extent, the methods by which they intend to achieve them.

Decision making may be defined as an act by a Minister or Ministers collectively (and sometimes by civil servants in the name of Ministers) to choose a particular course of action or inaction on a matter of public policy.

Both these definitions assume, for the sake of simplicity, that real political decisions are made *in Government* rather than in Opposition. Strictly speaking, this is true because the political power to do things – rather than the ability to criticise or support a particular aspect of policy or a particular decision – is available only to Ministers in the Government of the day. However, it must be conceded that large and consequential decisions are often made by senior political figures when their party is in Opposition with the clear intention of putting such decisions into effect if and when their party is able to form the Government.

The other general point which should be made at the outset is that, since Labour came to power in 1997, there have been some deliberate and significant changes in the way that policy is made and delivered by the party in Government – notably, the introduction of '*modern policy making*' by a self-consciously modernising Government.[1] Some of these changes have been essentially presentational and part of the so-called New Labour project designed to persuade the electorate that the Labour party had abandoned, once and for all, its historical tendency to pursue policies based upon a traditional Left-wing ideology and the advancement of trade union and public sector interests. Yet a good part of modern policy making has involved a new departure into evidence-based policy making which is intended to be rational, inclusive, sustainable, non-ideological and 'joined up' right across Government.

The effects of this new methodology have not been confined to the Labour party in office, but have extended to the attitudes and practices of the other parties. All parties seem to have learned how to manage and 'spin' the policy- and decision-making process to their own short-term advantage and decisions now owe at least as much to focus groups and mass media reactions as to organised discussion within the shrinking tribes of party activists and members. The process has also become much more porous in practice and presidential in style with many policy outcomes influenced by financial supporters, informal advisers and participants in the 'court politics' which has emerged around Tony Blair and, to a lesser extent, around the leaders of the other parties as well.

Since suffering what was interpreted as an electoral setback at the 2005 General Election, Tony Blair and his senior colleagues vowed to listen to their backbenchers more carefully and to take fuller account of all the various reservations and resentments which surfaced among the general public during the election campaign. Most of this criticism could be traced to three – overlapping – sources:

▸ Those in the Labour party who were never happy with the modernising policies of New Labour (for example, in relation to City Academies, foundation hospitals and Public Private Partnerships)
▸ Those in the media and the general public who disliked the 'presidentialism' of the Blair regime which has variously been criticised for being either too high-handed or too beholden to the latest influential group or individual to put pressure upon the Prime Minister
▸ Those in the party, the media and the general public who were opposed to British policy in relation to Iraq and Weapons of Mass Destruction (WMDs), opposed British participation in the war in Iraq and who felt that Tony Blair was too closely associated with US policy generally and with President Bush in particular.

The net effect of these conflicting pressures and assessments of modernised policy and decision making has been to tar nearly all national politicians with the same brush, although it is fair to say that the Liberal Democrats have so far emerged with a much lighter coating of media and public criticism than either the Labour or Conservative parties. The irony is that there seems to be no politically viable alternative to some version of 'modernisation', yet any loss of policy coherence or further diminution of trust in Government is often attributed to it by a gathering coalition of people ranging from critical academics, such as Peter Hennessy and Denis Kavanagh, to eminent former civil servants, such as Lord Butler and Sir Michael Quinlan.[2]

In many ways it is somewhat artificial to divide the policy- and decision-making process into a sequence of discrete stages, since in reality there is always a good deal more overlap and confusion than any schematic presentation of this kind would suggest. It is also somewhat arbitrary to draw a distinction between the traditional model which applied before 1997 and the modern model which has applied since Labour came to power in that year. Yet this distinction is meaningful, because both Tony Blair and Gordon Brown – and other senior Ministers – have been determined to approach these matters in a modern way and have had some real success in using 'modernisation' as a vehicle for attitudinal and procedural change in the Civil Service.

Figure 20.1 is a simplified, linear model of the way in which the policy- and decision-making process has worked since the middle of the twentieth century. Such a traditional model is still valid, but it no longer captures all the multidimensional realities of the modernised process, which we attempt to convey in the much more complicated diagram shown in Figure 20.2.

policy germination

Whether in the traditional or the modern model, the process begins with the stage of policy germination. Traditionally, this stage usually takes place when a party is in Opposition, although it also has to take place when a party is in Government if the party concerned has been in power for at least one term of office.

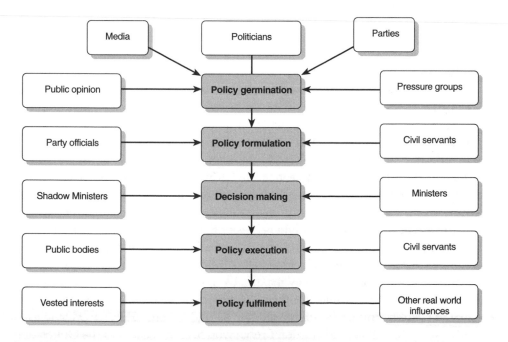

figure **20.1   the traditional policy- and decision-making process**

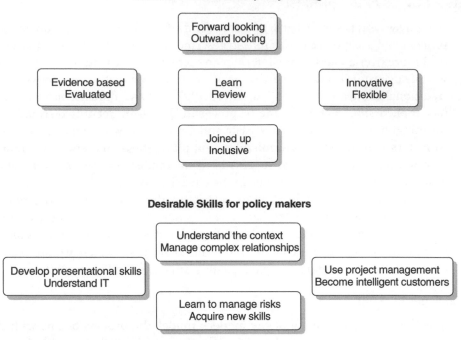

Features of modernised policy making

Forward looking
Outward looking

Evidence based
Evaluated

Learn
Review

Innovative
Flexible

Joined up
Inclusive

Desirable Skills for policy makers

Understand the context
Manage complex relationships

Develop presentational skills
Understand IT

Use project management
Become intelligent customers

Learn to manage risks
Acquire new skills

figure **20.2** **features of modernised policy making/desirable skills for policy makers**

In the *Labour Party*, policy used to germinate in a way which reflected the organisational and ideological traditions of the party in that political power and influence over policy were traditionally shared among the various components of the Labour Movement – the affiliated trade unions, constituency activists and members of Parliament. Thus ideas and pressure for the germination of policy came from a wide range of sources, including internal party pressure groups, friendly academics, Think Tanks and experts in mass communications. The role of the Parliamentary leadership was often to act as something of a brake on the wilder policy ideas which might emerge, especially at those times in the party's history when the Left was influential.

Following Labour's third electoral defeat in a row in 1987, all this began to change when the then party leader, Neil Kinnock, and his closest colleagues recognised the need for a thorough review of both the organisation and the policy process in the Labour Movement. In organisational terms, the conclusion drawn by the leadership was the absolute necessity to entrust the policy- and decision-making process into the hands of the party leader and a few trusted colleagues. In policy terms, Neil Kinnock came to the conclusion that only a revisionist and modernising approach to policy making would suffice if the party were to have a real chance of returning to office. These strategic conclusions were broadly shared by John Smith, who succeeded him as leader from 1992 to 1994, and even more so by Tony Blair and Gordon Brown who became Leader of the Opposition and Shadow Chancellor respectively following John Smith's untimely death.

Since 1994 the drive for modernisation has been the dominant theme of Labour policy and decision making. It began with the reform of Labour party structures, which had originated under John Smith with his moves towards One Member One Vote (OMOV). It developed further momentum in Opposition under Tony Blair with his reformulation in modern language of the classic Clause IV of the party constitution and his growing reliance upon modernising Think Tanks, such as the Institute for Public Policy Research (IPPR), focus groups and private opinion pollsters, such as Philip (now Lord) Gould. Since Labour came to power in 1997, the modernising theme has been carried forward by Tony Blair, Gordon Brown and a whole cohort of New Labour Ministers. The exercise, which has been variously described at different times as New Labour, Third Way or Stakeholder Democracy, has involved all parts of the Labour Movement in the work of the Labour Policy Forum, although it is fair to say that the influence of New Labour has waxed and waned since 1997, depending upon the changing political fortunes of the Prime Minister – first Tony Blair and subsequently Gordon Brown – in Parliament and the country at large.

It is equally important to realise that modernised policy and decision making under New Labour has involved far reaching reform of objectives, methods and rhetoric. The *objectives* of policy have been essentially to reassure and persuade the British people that Labour can be trusted not to revert to its old habits of tax and spend, not to intervene excessively in business or in the conduct of people's lives, and to govern for the many rather than the few by creating a fairer society characterised by equality of opportunity. The *methods* of policy making have involved persuading civil servants and everyone else with a stake in the process to develop certain core competences and professional skills designed to ensure that every policy proposal approximates as closely as possible to best practice – as is indicated by Figure 20.3.

The *rhetoric* used to communicate and explain New Labour policy has varied both in tone and in substance between Tony Blair and Gordon Brown, even though strenuous efforts have been made to keep both of them and their respective supporters 'on message' all the time.

One other problem with the germination stage of policy making under New Labour has been the growing tendency for political advisers based at 10 Downing Street or in the Cabinet Office to exploit their privileged and private access to the Prime Minister by proposing policy initiatives which may not have been adequately discussed with senior members of the Cabinet, let alone other relevant Ministers and officials down the line in Departments. In a Parliamentary democracy in which members of both Houses are sometimes among the last to learn about policy initiatives and in which relevant policy officials in Whitehall Departments or delivery Agencies may not be consulted in a timely and effective way, there is always the risk that informal advisers who have the Prime Minister's ear (such as – in the case of Tony Blair – Lords Levy, Birt and Turner) will be able to influence the political agenda in ways which produce policy incoherence and are not subject to enough timely and expert analysis before the Government goes public with an idea.

Features of 'best practice' policy making:
- Clearly defines outcomes and takes a long term view, taking into account the likely effect and impact of the policy in the future five to ten years and beyond
- Takes full account of the national, European and international situation;
- Takes a holistic view looking beyond institutional boundaries to the government's strategic objectives
- Is flexible and innovative, willing to question established ways of dealing with things and encourage new and creative ideas
- Uses the best available evidence from a wide range of sources
- Constantly reviews existing policy to ensure it is really dealing with problems it was designed to solve without having unintended detrimental effects elsewhere
- Is fair to all people directly or indirectly affected by it and takes account of its impact more generally
- Involves all key stakeholders at an early stage and throughout its development
- Learns from experience of what works and what does not work through systematic evaluation.

Themes:
- Vision
- Effectiveness
- Continuous improvement.

Core competencies:
- **Forward Looking** – Defining policy outcomes and taking a long-term view
- **Outward Looking** – Taking account of the national, European and international situation; learning from the experience of other countries; recognising regional variations
- **Innovative, Flexible** – Questioning established ways of dealing with things, encouraging new and creative ideas, identifying and managing risk
- **Joined Up** – Looking beyond institutional boundaries; setting cross-cutting objectives; defining and communicating joint working arrangements across departments; ensuring that implementation is part of the policy process
- **Inclusive** – Consulting those responsible for implementation and those affected by the policy; carrying out an impact assessment
- **Evidence based** – Basing policy decisions and advice upon the best available evidence from a wide range of sources; ensuring that evidence is available in an accessible and meaningful form.
- **Evaluated** – Systematic evaluation of the effectiveness of policy is built into the policy-making process
- **Reviews** – Existing/established policy is constantly reviewed to ensure it is really dealing with problems it was designed to solve
- **Lessons learned** – Learning from experience of what works and what does not work.

Source: 'Professional policy Making for the Twenty First Century', Cabinet Office Strategic Policy Team, 1999.

figure **20.3   policy making and 'best practice'**

In the *Conservative Party*, policy germination seems likely to follow a broadly similar course if the Conservative 'modernisers' gain the upper hand, since they believe there is political advantage for the party in emulating many, if not all, the practices of New Labour. Once again the distinctions between objectives, methods and rhetoric apply. Because of the underlying similarity of the challenges facing all three main parties, there has been a continuing tussle for the middle ground of public opinion and little appetite for establishing 'clear blue water' between them and their opponents. Of course, this may change in future, but for the time being we must base our analysis on current political realities.

To provide a simple explanation of practice in the Conservative Party, what usually happens at the germination stage is that the leadership identifies a problem or a set of problems arising from its previous experience in office or from the political imperatives of the current economic, social and political scene, and then works with its advisers on the development of new policy or the reconsideration of existing policy to address the situation. It then has to ascertain whether there are the necessary sources of information, analysis and advice within the party fold or among business people and others well disposed towards the party to enable it to embark upon the subsequent stages of policy making.

For example, during the 2001–05 Parliament, when all the main parties were engaged in something of a Dutch auction to decide which of them could extract the largest financial savings by cutting Civil Service numbers and other overheads of Government, Michael Howard appointed a City businessman, David James, to chair a committee designed to generate recommendations in this area of policy which was central to the political debate in the lead-up to the 2005 General Election. Equally, during the same period in Opposition Chris Woodhead, a former Chief Inspector of Schools, was appointed to advise party frontbenchers on education reform policy, while the search for expert opinion on the development of health policy relied upon intermittent contacts with the Conservative Medical Society and other experts in the relevant professions. In general, parties in Opposition are dependant upon help from sympathetic and expert outsiders who can be trusted to keep a confidence and who have both the time and the inclination to do such policy work.

When Margaret Thatcher was leader of the party (1975–90), the more ideological thrust of Conservative policy was influenced by Think Tanks, such as the Institute of Economic Affairs or the Centre for Policy Studies. Throughout the Thatcherite period such bodies helped to create an intellectual climate which made it easier than it had been for Right-wing and free-market policy ideas to germinate, although one should not underestimate the importance of Margaret Thatcher herself as an unusually strong-willed and ideologically driven politician.

Under John Major's leadership (1990–97), the influence of such Think Tanks diminished, while the influence of the Policy Unit at 10 Downing Street and of senior civil servants increased as the process of policy and decision making in Government became more short term and reactive to events. John Major usually listened closely to the Chief Whip – he had been an effective member of the Whips' Office himself at an earlier stage of his political career – and he was predisposed towards a more collegiate style of political leadership. However, his wish to lead a united crew through troubled waters (especially when dealing with the Euro-sceptics in the Cabinet and on the backbenches) was made much more difficult by a shrinking Parliamentary majority and his increasingly precarious authority in the party.

Under the leadership of William Hague (1997–2001) and Iain Duncan Smith (2001–04), when the party was back in Opposition, one of the key themes was the promise of wider and deeper involvement in the policy process for the dwindling party membership in the constituencies. This was to be achieved through a newly created Conservative Policy Forum and ballots of the entire party membership on big issues, such as whether Britain should adopt the Euro, or the final approval of the party Manifesto. This drive made some progress under William Hague, but not under Iain Duncan Smith who was forced out of office by the Parliamentary party and replaced with Michael Howard in another attempt to enhance the party's diminished credibility.

In the *Liberal Democrat Party* policy has been decided at the annual conference, although its Federal Policy Committee – a body of over 30 individuals, including the leader, president, representatives from the English, Scottish and Welsh parties, 4 elected by MPs, 1 elected by peers, 1 elected by MEPs, 3 elected by Councillors and 15 elected by conference, as well as a number of co-opted non-voting members – has drawn up the manifesto. It is a process that has been open to criticism as it has been possible to commit the party to specific and controversial policies on the basis of a brief, even desultory debate during a sparsely attended session of conference. Indeed, it was as a consequence of just such a process that other parties and the media were able to focus – during the 2005 election campaign - on suggestions that prisoners be given the vote, something that, although not included in the manifesto, had been adopted as policy by conference.

As a result, following the 2005 election, the then Liberal Democrat leader, Charles Kennedy, announced that the way that the party made policies was to be reviewed, not least of all with a view to making the whole process more flexible, as was the way in which the party conducted its business. Part of this approach saw the establishment of a commission – headed by a former Treasury civil servant with over 30 years experience – to look at the party's tax plans. The review was continued by Kennedy's successor, Sir Menzies Campbell.

The mechanisms described in each of the three main parties should be seen as simplified and idealised models of the policy germination stage. In practice, this stage of the process is often quite chaotic and incoherent, since it is often influenced by the media and developments in the real world which require pragmatic and short-term policy responses.

In the contemporary world, however, nation states and national Governments are not as autonomous as they may once have been and the germination of policy is increasingly influenced by European or global events to which Government and Opposition politicians alike feel the need to respond. For example, the determination of the Bush Administration soon after the al-Qaeda attack on the World Trade Center in New York on 11th September 2001 to react by going to war to prosecute regime change in Iraq, matched by the apparent determination of Tony Blair to keep the United Kingdom Government completely alongside its American counterpart, effectively distorted a good part of the policy and decision making in the United Kingdom for nearly the whole of the 2001–05 Parliament and distracted many British politicians from the domestic political agenda on which they would otherwise have been focused. Equally, the requirements of participation in the policy and decision making of the European Union, and its impact upon domestic politics and legislation in all the member states, mean that every British Prime Minister and many of his Ministerial colleagues have to devote up to 40 days a year to these aspects of Britain's overseas role and responsibilities.

At this malleable stage in the policy- and decision-making proces, the key questions are:

- Who defines the problems to be addressed?
- Who sets the priorities for the policy work to be undertaken?
- What are the political and ideological objectives of the most influential participants?

When a party is in Opposition, it is normally the party leader and a handful of his most trusted colleagues and advisers who determine the policy which germinates and how it comes about. When a party is in Government, a much wider range of considerations tend to apply and the cast-list of influential participants can include senior members of Governments, senior executives in multinational companies, influential global media figures and top bureaucrats or judges active in the EU institutions

policy formulation

The next stage in the process is that of policy formulation. By this we mean the translation into coherent policy proposals of the political ideas which have germinated in the ways already described. This is a stage which may take place more systematically when a party is in Opposition than when it is in Government, although it is difficult to generalise because much will depend upon the intellectual resources available to Opposition parties and much will depend upon the time reserved for this stage when Ministers are busy with the pressing problems of Government.

In the *Labour Party*, when it is in Opposition, the work of policy formulation is done by Party officials employed by the Party's Research Department. They work under the direction and control of the leading politicians in charge of the various policy groups which, in turn, are located within a formal structure of policy committees under the auspices of the National Executive Committee (NEC). Such officials do not disappear when the Party is in Government and their role in policy formulation remains significant.

In Government, Labour Ministers have more extensive resources of people to draw upon for the policy-formulation stage, since in the lengthy run-up to what are usually well-signposted General Elections, Ministers rely heavily upon a cohort of about 80 Special (Political) Advisers who are distributed in the Policy Unit at 10 Downing Street and in each of the Government Departments. Although formally civil servants during their tenure in Whitehall, these political appointees revert to being political activists once a General Election is called. Thus, because of their special status in Whitehall, they can legitimately engage in the party political work of policy formulation long before a General Election is called and so spare mainstream civil servants from any embarrassment which can be generated if and when Ministers ask them for 'factual' material to support the formulation of policy by the governing party.

In the Labour Party the structure of policy groups tends to be as elaborate when the party is in Government as when it is in Opposition, since the NEC provides the framework for the policy-making process at any rate in formal terms. Informally and in reality, however, the actual situation has tended to allow Labour leaders who are senior Ministers to impose their authority and, on most occasions, to get their way in the policy-making process. In such circumstances the main tensions at the formulation stage have tended to arise between different senior Ministers rather than between the Parliamentary party and the other parts of the Labour Movement, as happened when Labour was previously in office before 1979.

In the *Conservative Party*, policy formulation is usually the work of party officials and other auxiliaries who draft the papers in which policy proposals are contained. Of course, such people work under the careful direction and control of frontbenchers who chair the policy groups concerned and ultimately of the Party leader and his most senior colleagues. For many years in the past this work was invariably done by officials of the Conservative Research Department (CRD), a relatively small back-room organisation staffed mainly by young men and women with personal political ambitions. The role of the CRD was deliberately downgraded by Margaret Thatcher after her electoral victory in 1979 and in 1980 it was subsumed into Conservative Central Office. Since the Thatcher era the CRD seems to have staged something of a recovery under successive Tory leaders first in Government and then in Opposition, although in all the main parties the accent in recent times has been much more upon making policy positions subservient to Party image and to political marketing considerations than to the more cerebral criteria of yesteryear.

The structure of policy groups in the Conservative Party has tended to be less elaborate when the Party is in Government than when it is in Opposition. This is because there has been no real equivalent of Labour's National Executive Committee and because the Party leader and other senior figures in Parliament have retained almost complete control of the policy-formulation stage of the process. The various policy formulations are considered and reconsidered by the policy groups which will normally be made up of a fairly broad spectrum of interested Party opinion from both the Parliamentary Party and the Party in the country. Under the Party reforms introduced by William Hague the voluntary side of the Party was encouraged to play a more prominent part in the policy-making process via the newly established Conservative Policy Forum (CPF) and via regional policy meetings. Once policy proposals have been formulated and refined in this way, they are submitted to the Leader of the Party and his senior Parliamentary colleagues for the key decisions about inclusion or exclusion from the Party Manifesto. The whole membership of the Party is then asked to endorse the broad lines of the Party's appeal to the electorate.

In this scheme of things, which has become somewhat similar in both the Labour and Conservative parties, the emphasis has shifted over the years away from an elite model of policy making towards structures of self-conscious inclusion designed to ensure that the activists in the constituencies at least feel that they can play a fuller and more meaningful part in the whole process. In both parties this has been achieved by introducing the formal device of a Policy Forum, although the political and policy clout of the Labour version seems to be greater than its Conservative counterpart. In some ways this difference should come as no surprise, since it needs to be seen against the background of the parts previously played by the respective Party Conferences. The history of the Labour Conference was, until the New Labour reforms of the 1990s, essentially that of a rather messy _decision-making body_; whereas the history of the Conservative Conference was essentially that of an _advisory body_ with a heavy dose of social and theatrical purposes.

Under the influence of 'modernisation' the Labour Party in office has moved decisively away from its former model of ideologically driven policy making towards a much more inclusive model based upon _extensive and thorough consultation_ of every identifiable 'stakeholder' in the policy area concerned. This systematic approach is supposed to have a number of political benefits for Labour and general benefits for society at large:

- Less likelihood of overlooking a vital interest or policy angle
- Greater likelihood that the policy will prove acceptable to all who are directly affected
- Co-option of many vociferous minorities who might otherwise have obstructed or undermined the policy.

On the other hand, there are a number of drawbacks which should be mentioned:

- The policy which emerges can be so bland and unadventurous that it is unlikely to make a radical contribution towards solving an intractable problem
- It can produce politically correct proposals which may suit the vested interests and 'usual suspects' who are permanently in the loop of Whitehall consultations but largely exclude the concerns of the silent majority
- It represents a deliberate attempt by New Labour to take party politics out of policy making – a move which is either naïve or disingenuous, depending upon your point of view.

With regard to the _Liberal Democrats_, policy formulation has traditionally been the responsibility of Party officials and others who draft the papers in which policy proposals have been contained. These individuals have worked under the guidance, direction and control of the appropriate Party spokesperson who would chair the policy group concerned and ultimately of the Party leader and his most senior colleagues. As has been pointed out previously, following the 2005 election it was announced that the way that the Party has made policies was to be reviewed, not least of all with a view to making the whole process more flexible.

In general, it is backbench MPs who have had the fewest opportunities for real influence upon the formulation of Party policy. Even when they are invited to serve on policy groups or to attend Policy Forums, they retain a legitimate suspicion that they have been co-opted for placebo reasons and that the policy decisions which really matter remain in the hands of the Party leaders and their senior Cabinet or shadow Cabinet colleagues.

decision making

The next stage in the process is that of decision making. On all important and politically sensitive issues this is unavoidably the work of Party leaders and their most senior political colleagues.

In Opposition, the requirements and procedures are quite simple. Usually all that is necessary is that the Shadow Cabinet should meet to accept or reject the policy proposals which have germinated and been formulated in the ways already described. Of course, there are some issues which require lengthy discussion even at this stage and which cannot be resolved at a single business-like meeting. Yet in most cases, by the time that a policy formulation reaches this stage, the actual decisions can be taken quite quickly, not least because the leader of the Party and his close colleagues will have taken the trouble to prepare the ground by briefing or squaring any potential opponents.

In Government, this stage in the process is both more varied and more complex. Some Government decisions can be taken quite quickly by individual Ministers acting within their allotted spheres of responsibility. Some are taken by a group of Ministers within a particular Department. Yet nearly all important Government decisions affect a variety of Departmental interests and are therefore taken by a Cabinet Committee or by the Prime Minister in bilateral meetings with senior colleagues.

It is difficult to make any definitive and lasting generalisations about decision making at the apex of national Government, since the situation will vary from case to case and from Cabinet to Cabinet and from Prime Minister to Prime Minister. Tony Blair has come in for a good deal of criticism for the way in which he handled British decision making on the Iraq war, specifically for the way in which some key decisions were taken informally by groups of senior Ministers, top officials and members of the intelligence and military communities without the due process of a Cabinet Committee with its written record and official papers as a basis for discussion and decision. On the other hand, John Major was praised by his political colleagues for the way in which he consistently tried to involve even the most tiresome and disloyal Cabinet Ministers. In any case, it is less common nowadays than it used to be in previous decades for a Prime Minister to go out of his way to encourage full discussion of the big political issues around the complete Cabinet table, simply because a plenary meeting of that many is too large for such purposes and can only be used sensibly for ratifying decisions taken elsewhere in much smaller groups.

When a Cabinet Committee is charged with making decisions on a particular topic, the terms of reference are usually supplied to the senior Minister in the chair either by the Prime Minister or, occasionally, by the Cabinet as a whole. It is then for the person in the chair to hold as many meetings as necessary in order to reach decisions which can be recommended to Cabinet, often within an agreed timescale. If it is an ad hoc Committee, it only remains in existence for as long as necessary to reach its agreed recommendations. If it is a standing Committee, such as the Defence and Overseas Policy Committee or the Domestic Affairs Committee, then it is there as a permanent group of Ministers to whom tricky and often interdepartmental issues can be referred for resolution. In several different Administrations it has been conventional from time to time that any member of the Cabinet not on a particular Cabinet Committee should not challenge the decisions of the Committee in full Cabinet without prior leave from the Prime Minister or the colleague chairing the Committee. Indeed, the whole rationale of Cabinet Committees is that they should be able to take decisions on behalf of the Cabinet without normally having to submit such decisions to a further stage of discussion in full Cabinet. Only if they function in this way can they truly be said to save the time and energy of the Cabinet as a whole, particularly when it is noted that middle rank and junior Ministers are the workhorses of the Cabinet Committee system and so relieve their Secretaries of State of some of the burdens of joined-up government.

The fact that under three successive Blair Administrations regular weekly meetings of the Cabinet have usually been confined to about 45 minutes of brief discussion during which members of the Cabinet listen to brief reports from the Prime Minister, the Chancellor, the Leader of the House and other senior colleagues as necessary implies that the Cabinet is essentially a ratifying body for decisions actually taken elsewhere, whether in Cabinet Committees or in bilateral meetings between the Prime Minister and a senior colleague such as the Chancellor or the Home Secretary. Indeed, the traditional forms and procedures of Cabinet government seem to have been somewhat marginalised by the trend towards informal decision making or 'sofa politics' at 10 Downing Street or at Chequers, the Prime Minister's official country residence. In periods of 'presidential politics', such as we have seen under Tony Blair and also saw under Margaret Thatcher, big decisions are made in the name of the Cabinet but not by the Cabinet.

Yet it remains true that the convention of collective responsibility and the tradition of Cabinet government in Britain entitles any Cabinet Minister, if he or she is sufficiently determined, to pursue a particularly sensitive or important political issue in full Cabinet and to insist upon having it put on the agenda of a future meeting. It is also open to any Cabinet member at a meeting of the full Cabinet to intervene in any discussion led by the Prime Minister or one of his colleagues and express measured or even fierce doubts or disagreement. An extreme example of this happened in 1986 during the Westland Affair when Michael Heseltine, the then Secretary of State for Defence, stormed out of a meeting of the full Cabinet and resigned, plunging the Government – and particularly the position of the Prime Minister at the time (Margaret Thatcher) – into crisis. If Gordon Brown, as Chancellor of the Exchequer and the second most powerful figure in the Cabinet at the time, had chosen openly to register opposition to Tony Blair's policy of giving British military support to the American invasion of Iraq, then a similar crisis could have arisen.

One of the manifestations of 'creeping presidentialism' in British politics has been the tendency for successive Prime Ministers to rely more upon a coterie of formal and informal advisers than upon their Cabinet colleagues for help and support in the policy- and decision-making process. This was true of Winston Churchill, Harold Macmillan and Harold Wilson in the distant past; it was true of Margaret Thatcher in the recent past and it seems to have been true of Tony Blair since he became leader of the Labour party (and effectively Prime Minister in waiting) in 1994. Tony Blair's inner circle may have included senior Ministers from time to time and on specific issues, but the people to whom he has listened most closely have been those whose access and influence has depended upon their personal relationship with the Prime Minister – for example, Jonathon Powell (his Chief of Staff), Alastair Campbell (his former Director of Strategy and Communications), Philip Gould (his private pollster and organiser of focus groups) and Peter Mandelson (his former ideological mentor and long-standing political friend).

Notwithstanding all these personal aspects, three general points should be borne in mind. *Firstly*, and as highlighted in Chapter 12, there is an important distinction between the appearance of Prime Ministerial dominance in policy and decision making and the reality which makes it impossible practice for any Prime Minister to control all the levers of power all the time. Indeed, the power sharing between Tony Blair and Gordon Brown, which was implicit ever since 1994 but which has been increasingly explicit during Labour's period in office since 1997, is further recent evidence of this point.

Secondly, although the Cabinet has long since ceased to be a real decision-making body and even its Committees matter in this regard only occasionally, it does still provide the rubric, if no longer much legitimacy, for all the various decisions taken in its name and for that reason it has to be 'managed' by any successful Prime Minister. Consequently, a sensible Prime Minister will 'take the voices' around the Cabinet table before important decisions are reached, because it is clearly in his interest to carry his senior colleagues with him and to bind them into collective responsibility on the issues which really matter.

Thirdly, it should always be remembered that all Prime Ministers need a measure of good fortune during their time in office, because even if they are 'control freaks', they cannot actually determine the course of events, whatever their transient power and authority on the political stage. Democratic politics in contemporary Britain is invariably more reactive than proactive and to be the top politician, even in a nation with the fourth largest economy in the world, by no means guarantees that you will get your way on the most important issues – still less that you will be able to set the political agenda for a generation as Margaret Thatcher did and Tony Blair has aspired to do.

policy delivery

Policy delivery is the stage at which civil servants used to excel when policy execution was simply a matter of clearly communicating Ministerial decisions to those who needed to know about them. Since 1997, however, there has been a Blair-led drive for 'modern government' that includes everything from modernising the methodological approach to policy making to improving *the outcomes* of the process, which is another way of saying that policy objectives should be delivered to the satisfaction of the citizens who are the users and beneficiaries of the process. This emphasis upon outputs, outcomes and the experience of the general public can be traced back to John Major's initiative for a 'Citizen's Charter' in 1991, which was his 'big idea' designed to make the Civil Service and those who worked in the broader public sector more responsive to the needs and wishes of the general public, as well as mindful of the needs and wishes of the Ministers whom traditionally they had sought to serve.

The roots of policy delivery can be traced back to an earlier stage in the policy- and decision-making process. Once the main objectives of the various party policies have been set and a General Election campaign has begun, it is normal for policy-advising civil servants in all Government Departments and many executive Agencies to prepare a range of different position papers designed to assist any group of incoming Ministers to implement their policies, no matter which party wins an electoral mandate to form the Government. The advice is neither sanguine nor cautious, but merely intended to suggest the most effective ways of implementing the policies of the returning (or incoming) Government, while drawing attention to any practical problems which could arise in the course of delivery.

From then on the initiative is with Ministers and their Special Advisers. Their behaviour varies according to their personal drive and ambition, and the extent to which the party commitments in their own spheres of responsibility are given priority by the Prime Minister and the Cabinet as a whole. If a Minister is charged with the delivery of a policy which is given a high political priority (for example, under Labour, the introduction of identity cards or improvements in the quality and choice of schools) and if the commitment is clearly expressed in the Party Manifesto or other formal statements by the Party leadership, then it will usually be a matter of getting the agreement of the Legislative Programme Committee in order to secure a prime slot in the legislative programme for the first Session of Parliament. Equally, some political issues may be very salient, but may not require anything more than clear Ministerial decisions under the terms of existing legislation in order to put the Government's policies into effect – for example, the political imperative of securing cleaner hospitals so that patients do not suffer from MRSA or other hospital acquired infections.

On the other hand, if a Minister has to oversee the delivery of a policy which has been given a low political priority by his party in office (for example, long-term pension reform or fundamental changes in the working of the European Union), there will probably be little alternative to preparing the ground with internal Whitehall lobbying and Ministerial speeches or Green Papers in the hope of securing a slot for legislation in a subsequent Session of Parliament. In anticipation of such progress, a Minister may be able to improve his prospects by securing the interest and support of 10 Downing Street and the Treasury, stimulating positive interest in Parliament and the media, and mobilising the support of the relevant interest groups and even the general public. If all this can be done successfully, it will increase the chances of the Minister making his name with the new policy at a later stage in the Parliament.

Assuming that the appropriate Ministerial decisions have been taken in the Cabinet or one of its Committees, the long chain of policy delivery begins with the Cabinet Office which has to ensure that Ministers and officials in the lead Department for the policy area concerned are fully seized of their new task and aware of the timescale and the financial and legislative parameters within which they will have to operate. This stage will not come as a surprise to the lead Department, since its junior Ministers and officials are likely to have been fully engaged in the inter-Departmental and inter-Ministerial discussions which gave rise to the actual decision. On the other hand, a Ministerial decision on a smaller or more discreet matter may well be taken by Ministers in a single Department within their areas of responsibility and financial limits (for example measures to deal with indiscipline and disorder in schools), in which case only the relevant Department will be involved in the initial follow through at official level.

If the decision involves a matter of local government responsibility in England (such as local planning, housing or social services), it will be for the responsible Department to take forward the policy relayed by the Cabinet Office and so ensure that local authorities and the Regional Offices of central Government are fully cognisant of what is required of them. If the decisions concern Scotland or Wales, then different channels will be used (notably the territorial Offices of central Government) to try to ensure that the Ministerial decisions taken by the devolved Administrations in those parts of the UK are broadly compatible with what has been decided for England. As for Northern Ireland, when the devolved Assembly is suspended and the Province is under direct rule, delivery responsibility rests fairly and squarely upon the shoulders of officials in the Northern Ireland Office under the Ministerial oversight of the Secretary of State and his Ministerial colleagues. The complicated networks of inter-Departmental cooperation at official level complement and support direct communications between Ministers which take place in Cabinet Committees, bilateral meetings and on many other less formal occasions in Whitehall, Westminster and elsewhere.

As must be clear from the foregoing paragraphs, the *legislative process* is a key aspect of the delivery stage in policy and decision making. This is essentially because in Britain the Executive and the Legislature are fused, which means that a Government with a working majority in the House of Commons invariably gets its way if it chooses to achieve its policy objectives via the legislative route. If the legal advice available to Ministers is that a Ministerial decision requires legislation for its implementation, this becomes the responsibility of the Minister or Ministers from the lead Department who will have to pilot the legislation through both Houses of Parliament. The Department or Departments concerned have to work closely with the legislative draftsmen from the Office of Parliamentary Counsel who perform this specialised legal task for the whole of Government. The role of these experts in the delivery of policy can be of considerable significance, since the precise legal wording of Government Bills can sometimes be almost as critical as the fundamental principles which underlie the legislation – as the annual Finance Bill to implement the annual Budget frequently demonstrates.

If the execution of a Government decision requires new primary legislation, the process can normally be traced back to an important pre-legislative stage when, within the confidential confines of Whitehall, policy-advising civil servants explore the issues and problems that are likely to arise with knowledgeable and trustworthy outside experts. Thus the elements in a new Companies Bill would be explored with the Confederation of British Industry (CBI), senior members of the Commercial Bar, possibly some independent regulators, such as the Competition Commission or the Office of Fair Trading, and maybe a few authoritative academics.

Following such confidential discussions, there is usually a *formal consultative process* based upon a Government Green Paper or a draft Bill, which is the time when Ministers, officials and legislative draftsmen are prepared to reveal their policy intentions more widely in order to obtain expert comments and reactions from those – including Members of Parliament and members of the public – who may feel that they have something worthwhile to contribute. Nowadays all consultative documents are published on the relevant Departmental websites and there is customarily a period of at least three months in which anyone can respond. It is not unknown, however, for the results of this work to be rejected by the Legislative Programme Committee of the Cabinet (LPC) if the timetable for the proposed Government Bill is too tight or the legislative programme is too full or the necessary political benefits too problematic. By the time that a proposed Bill is deemed ready for inclusion in the Queen's Speech at the beginning of a Parliamentary Session, it is assumed that its content has been sufficiently discussed with all the relevant people to produce a satisfactory piece of legislation which will be effective and stand the test of time.

On the other hand, there have been a few occasions in the lifetime of all Governments when legislation has been introduced too swiftly on the basis of only minimal or perfunctory discussions even within Whitehall, let alone with the relevant agencies, public servants or others, including members of the judiciary, who are supposed to make it work. Examples of this phenomenon would include:

- The decision to abolish the Greater London Council and the other Metropolitan County Councils which was taken by Margaret Thatcher and a very small circle of Ministerial colleagues just before the 1983 General Election.
- The decision taken in 1997 by the Chancellor of the Exchequer, Gordon Brown, which then had to be defended by Harriet Harman as Social Security Secretary, to cut state benefits paid to single parents as part of the Government's 'welfare to work' policy.

• The decision taken in 2004 by the then Home Secretary, David Blunkett, under the Anti-Terrorism, Crime and Security Act 2001 to order the indefinite detention without trial of suspected foreign terrorists, which was declared by the Law Lords to be a disproportionate response to the terrorist threat and discriminatory if applied only to foreign nationals and which then had to be replaced by a new Prevention of Terrorism Bill authorising his successor, Charles Clarke, to make so-called Control Orders against anyone suspected of terrorist-related activity. The House of Commons passed this new Bill in just two days, but, in response to concerns expressed there and even more in the Lords, the Bill was further amended to introduce significantly tightened provisions for judicial review.

In many other instances, including, in most cases, the implementation in Britain of EU Directives affecting the entire European Union, the execution and delivery of a Ministerial decision may require only the introduction of Secondary Legislation, in other words Statutory Instruments issued under the authority of existing Acts of Parliament.

Once again such measures are usually preceded by detailed consultations within Whitehall with a wide range of relevant experts and interested groups. Such consultations are particularly necessary, since the procedures for formal Parliamentary scrutiny of Statutory Instruments in the Commons leave much to be desired, although it should be recognised that the Lords Committee on Delegated Legislation and Regulatory Reform does a much more thorough job.

Finally, it should be noted that many (indeed most) Ministerial and official decisions in Whitehall fall within the sphere of lawful administrative discretion derived from legislation which is already on the Statute Book. In these cases Ministers and civil servants act legitimately in an executive capacity and communicate their decisions or their policy directly to the persons or organisations concerned via Departmental circulars, ordinary letters or memoranda. In some cases, the decisions may entail the delegation of executive responsibilities to statutory bodies which already have lawful powers in specified areas, such as local authorities or the executive Agencies of central Government. In other cases, it is a matter of Departmental action carried out directly by civil servants acting on behalf of Ministers.

policy fulfilment

The final and most problematic stage in the process may be called policy fulfilment – in simple English, success. Experience over many years suggests that this has eluded many British Governments, regardless of the size of their majorities in the House of Commons. There can be many reasons for this rather bleak view: Governments have often tried to do too much, pursued often contradictory objectives, had to share power with other jurisdictional authorities and even some formidable non-governmental interests, found themselves constrained by anticipated or revealed public opinion, been pawns of the perversity and sensationalism of the media, and been obliged to work within the sometimes limiting framework of established social assumptions and other unforgiving realities of the modern world.

However, in order to be certain that a particular line of policy and decision making has been successful, it has become customary in recent times for the British and other Governments to use *the techniques of evaluation and post hoc review* to get an objective reading on how they are doing. These are techniques customarily employed in the corporate sector when senior management commission reports from management consultants, auditors or business school academics. Since 1997 they have been imported by New Labour into the sphere of British Government to give more reliable and rational assessments of the success or otherwise of initiatives and programmes introduced by Ministers and delivered by officials and others within the wider public sector.

The traditional way in which Ministers and others formed conclusions about the success or otherwise of central Government policies and programmes was simply to see whether, after four or five years, the British public was prepared to re-elect the party in office. If it did so, this was taken as a crude endorsement of what the Government had done during the previous Parliament. If it did not do so, this was taken as an indictment of the Government's record.

The modern way to arrive at such conclusions – especially when the electoral arithmetic enables the party in power to remain in office for several terms in succession – is to employ the techniques of policy evaluation. This is a complex area, since many different practices are categorised as 'evaluation'. The term includes everything from desk-top reviews of existing evidence to pilot projects and demonstration projects to quantitative economic appraisals to regulatory impact assessments to performance management mechanisms to soundings conducted with focus groups and much more. However, under New Labour there have been some common themes in all types of evaluation and these have included: evidence-based evaluation (to match evidence-based policy making), learning from experience and practice rather than abstract theory, regular review and testing of existing policies, the sharing of lessons with others, as much reliance upon 'soft' perceptions as 'hard' numerical evidence, and so on.

These techniques have begun to prove their value to a Government which has been elected on three consecutive occassions. The best interim assessment of this relatively new departure for British central Government would seem to be that honest and timely evaluations of both proposed policies and policies already in operation must make sense in a rational world, but that to avoid bias or error in such procedures there is a real need for independent evaluators whose professional prospects or future income do not depend upon those whose policies and programmes are being evaluated. The Holy Grail is probably rational, scientific and open-minded *self-evaluation* by all involved in the policy- and decision-making process and to do this as a systematic and regular procedure. Yet only time will tell whether this is an excessively idealistic prescription for the realm of British central Government.

It is one thing to try objectively to discover whether or not you are succeeding in Ministerial office. It is another to be able to resist the temptations to move the goalposts or tilt the table in your own favour. Yet it must be said that successive Governments have sought to do these things without explicitly admitting to doing so. Faced with the many real-world problems mentioned at the beginning of this section, successive Governments have sought to improve their chances of lasting success by using one or more of the following political techniques.

Firstly, there is *the technique of accommodation*. This is a standard political response whereby a Government seeks to neutralise threats to its policies and decisions by the simple expedient of accommodating some critical points of view and co-opting some critical opponents. It is a technique which is easier to implement if Ministers are studiously pragmatic and relatively non-ideological in traditional Left–Right terms. Thus New Labour, with its ability to triangulate opposition to its policies, has been quite effective in using this method to reject the policy extremes of Old Labour and unreconstructed Conservatism, while taking on board those in the mainstream of British politics who are willing to cooperate with what claims to be an inclusive political regime. It also involves making full use of the political patronage available to any modern Government in the shape of appointments to Task Forces, Review Groups, non-Departmental public bodies, QUANGOs and QUAGOs on which business people in particular seem very prepared to serve. Moreover, if the governing party manages to remain in office for several terms consecutively, it can gradually build a cross-party and non-party consensus which can turn previous critics or adversaries of Government policy into compliant or at least semi-pacified partners who are flattered by the attention they receive from Ministers and officials.

Yet in spite of the lure of a 'modernised' and business-like Government, there comes a time in the life of any long-serving Administration when it tends to inherit the consequences of its own earlier mistakes and then even its most pliant collaborators tend to lose faith in its approach. This happened in the late 1940s when the post-war consensus embodied in the Attlee Government began to be questioned and a growing section of the electorate began to hanker for policies which gave a higher priority to individual initiative and freedom. It could happen again if the policies of New Labour begin to try the patience of those in the media and corporate worlds who have contributed to its political hegemony.

A second technique is that of *manipulation*, or 'spin' as it has come to be known under New Labour. These are really no more than sinister and rather pejorative terms for the well-tried arts of political persuasion and they subsume the important skills of 'news management' – that is, attempting to influence the media and parts of public opinion in a direction favourable to the Government of the day. To do this, it is necessary to use the policies and decisions of Ministers to convey to the general public an impression of competence and caring, while retaining a sense of trust and reassurance at least among those parts of the electorate which are deemed to be 'biddable' in the auction of promises, semi-pledges and impressions which characterises every modern election campaign and most of the political activity between General Elections.

Such techniques have been used for years by successive parties in Government. The real difference under New Labour since 1997 is that 'spin' became a defining characteristic of New Labour's electoral appeal and of its ability to 'sell' its policies to voters who had been badly disappointed and disillusioned by the previous Conservative Government. However, when public opinion became more cynical and hostile towards New Labour in general and Tony Blair in particular during the 2001–05 Parliament, many in the media and the general public began to turn against the use of 'spin' which had once been admired, at least by the political class, as a sign of political skill and modernity.

A third technique is that of *public opinion mobilisation*. This is usually a matter of seeking the support of the silent majority in an attempt to redress the balance against the influence of vociferous or powerful minorities and individuals. It is worth noting in passing that in Britain the most influential individuals do not usually have to raise their voices to get their way, but tend to rely upon their discreet influence within the global power elite. This is exemplified by the likes of Rupert Murdoch, Sir Richard Sykes, Bill Gates, Lord May, Paul Dacre, Sir Martin Rees, Lord Broers and others typically located in the media, scientific or corporate worlds. As an exercise in political leadership, this technique is usually no easier than the others already mentioned. Indeed, it can often be more difficult in view of the problems involved in trying to hold public opinion to one particular line and then translating it, when necessary, into actual voting behaviour at an election or a referendum.

There are various ways in which this technique can be applied. These may involve the use of powerful rhetoric, the constant repetition of simple messages, symbolic gestures designed to strike a chord with a non-party-political public, visible alignment with well-known celebrities, such as Bob Geldoff on aid to Africa or Jamie Oliver on school catering, and the use of specially commissioned political advertising or private opinion polls. The common denominators in all these methods are the advantages which accrue to the party in power and the need to employ apparently non-political means to secure political ends in a society which seems quite hostile towards and alienated from the conventional political process. None of these methods on its own can decisively affect political outcomes, but all can be effective at the margin. Sensible politicians make use of more traditional methods as well.

Finally, there is the technique which may be called *political shock treatment*. This involves occasionally confronting the media and the public with the full implications of failing to support policies which Ministers say are absolutely vital in the national interest. In a sense this is the technique which was used by successive Thatcher Administrations in efforts to change management and trade union attitudes radically and permanently in the vital areas of industrial productivity and economic performance; and by Edward Heath in February 1974 in his declaration of a Three Day Week to deal with the energy crisis following the Yom Kippur War and the OPEC oil embargo. It is also a technique which has been used (and sometimes abused) by political leaders in times of war or clear and present danger to the national interest. One thinks of Winston

Churchill during the Battle of Britain in 1940, Anthony Eden at the time of the Suez Crisis in 1956, Margaret Thatcher when responding to the Argentinian invasion of the Falkland Islands in 1982, and Tony Blair in his very personal decision to send British troops to fight alongside the Americans in Iraq. Such political behaviour is not to be recommended in any but the most extreme or unusual circumstances.

20.2 strengths and weaknesses

There are both strengths and weaknesses in the policy- and decision-making process in Britain. It is neither one of the best nor one of the worst of its kind to be found in the liberal democracies of the world. It has some characteristics which are universal and some which are peculiar to Britain. In any event it ought to be assessed on its merits and within its own context.

strengths

The most obvious strength is the ability of the process to translate party-political commitments into Ministerial decisions or Government-sponsored legislation. This derives principally from the way in which the first-past-the-post electoral system is capable of turning a plurality of the votes cast for the winning party at a General Election into an overall majority of seats in the House of Commons. Thus it enables a narrow interpretation of the popular will to be transformed into executive or legislative action by the Government of the day, usually without encountering any insuperable obstacles in Whitehall or Westminster. This is sometimes referred to as 'the mandate theory' of British Government and it assumes that the achievement of two-fifths of the votes cast at a General Election (or less in some cases, as in 2005) entitles the winning party to implement the pledges in its election Manifesto, notwithstanding any strong reservations which may emerge in Parliament or the country at large. However, any Government may be vulnerable to a revolt among its own backbenchers – as was the case with the second Blair Administration on several occasions between 2001 and 2005, even though it enjoyed a majority of more than 160.[3]

Another strength of the process is its efficiency in turning Ministerial decisions into administrative action and public service delivery. This is a tribute largely to the professionalism of the Civil Service in the Departments and Agencies of Government. It means that the writ of Ministers usually runs quite effectively throughout the institutions of central Government, but less certainly through all the institutions of the wider public sector, such as public corporations, local authorities and Public Private Partnerships. In order to deal with any shortcomings in this 'command-and-control' system, Ministers and officials implementing policies under New Labour have relied extensively on Public Service Agreements and Service Delivery Agreements to enforce a contractual approach to the achievement of Ministerial objectives.

Yet another strength of the process is its ability to cope with abrupt and radical changes of policy, such as may be required when a different party with a different political agenda comes to power following a General Election or, more rarely, when the party in office does a U-turn in its own policy. Any governmental system which demonstrates this ability to deal with radical changes of direction so smoothly and completely has to be very robust, particularly when this is achieved without any large-scale change in the administrative personnel involved. By and large, British civil servants are able loyally to serve a Minister of any political persuasion who has been duly appointed by the Prime Minister of the day following a General Election or a major Ministerial reshuffle. However, not all the burdens of adjustment fall upon professionally impartial civil servants, since increasingly in recent years it has been accepted that incoming Ministers arrive in office with their own Special Advisers, of whom there were about 80 following the 2005 General Election and whose presence in Government shields normal civil servants from the risk of compromising their political impartiality.[4]

weaknesses

There are equally some notable weaknesses in the process which some observers consider to outweigh the strengths already noted. Since 1997 Labour Ministers have sought systematically to address most, if not all, the weaknesses associated with the traditional British approach to policy and decision making, although it can be argued that, in doing so, they have created other problems which also have to be addressed.

- Firstly, it can be argued that the robust flexibility of the process has permitted too many abrupt and often damaging discontinuities of policy,[5] although it cannot really be argued that the system has caused the volatility. Moreover, this criticism is relevant to the 1970s and 1980s when British politics were driven by polarised ideologies, whereas it is more difficult to pin the problem upon the post-Thatcherite consensus which has applied since 1997 when New Labour has tacitly accepted much of Margaret Thatcher's legacy.
- Paradoxically, another weakness may be said to be too much unimaginative continuity of thinking in Whitehall which may have limited the range of policy options put to Ministers by civil servants to a safe and politically correct agenda which seeks to include all the stakeholder interests, but therefore runs the risk of producing uninspiring, lowest–common-denominator solutions. Very often there is a need for a little ideological grit if the policy and decision making process is to produce a pearl.
- Another weakness of the process (which is not confined to Britain) is that media-led democratic politics encourages Ministers to pay too much attention to short-term political gains at the expense of sticking with sometimes unglamorous long-term policies which may not produce measurable results until long after a particular Minister has been promoted, sacked or moved sideways within the Administration or indeed when the Administration is no longer in office. While this is partly a function

of the four- or five-year electoral cycle in Britain, it is mainly because the ubiquitous media constantly fan public expectations that Governments can achieve instant results, but then go on to lambaste the politicians in office when they fail to achieve such unrealistic goals.

- Another weakness of the process has been described as 'Government overload'.[6] Essentially, this means that most Ministers and many civil servants with demanding responsibilities often have far too much to do in too little time. It is particularly true at the highest levels of Government and in the Private Offices of senior Ministers where a small minority of politicians and officials bear disproportionate burdens which can produce suboptimal performance. The obvious solution would seem to be for those Ministers and officials under most pressure to delegate or share more of their responsibilities with their colleagues. On the other hand, the radical solution may be for senior politicians to set themselves fewer and less complicated objectives and, when in office, learn sometimes to say 'No' to the media and the general public.

- A final weakness of the process could be said to be the limited scope for Parliamentary participation, notably by backbenchers on the Government side, and by the general public who may, admittedly, not be particularly interested in policy making. The reasons for this are essentially that policy making in Britain has been regarded by the political elite on the front benches and by the largely self-selected experts who advise them as a confidential preserve for those who are established participants in the policy-making community. Relevant and timely information and privileged access to these influential circles is the stuff of power in the British political system. Although there has been a marked tendency in nearly all parties since 1997 to become more transparent and inclusive, and despite initiatives such as petitions on the No. 10 website (designed to improve and facilitate engagement with the public), there is still a long way to go before British citizens can enjoy the citizens' initiatives of California or the cantonal referenda of Switzerland – which of course may not in themselves be either a panacea or produce better results.

20.3 current and potential improvements

This is not the place to rehearse in any detail the wide range of possible changes and improvements which have been proposed from time to time in order to improve the policy- and decision-making process in Britain. It is sufficient to mention here only a few of the more familiar steps which have been taken, or considered, over recent years in conscious attempts to address the problems.

modernised policy making

The seminal White Paper, *Modernising government*, which was published in March 1999 defined policy as 'the process by which governments translate their political vision into programmes and actions to deliver outcomes – desired changes in the real world'.[7] It argued that, because public expectations rise and people are more demanding about what Government and its Agencies can or should provide, policies must be constantly evaluated to see that they:

- Really deal with problems
- Are forward looking and evidence based
- Tackle causes rather than symptoms
- Are measured by results rather than activity
- Are flexible and innovative rather than closed and bureaucratic
- Promote compliance rather than avoidance or fraud
- Involve a continuous process of learning and improvement.

All of these principles for improvement seem eminently sensible and one might wonder why it was even necessary to emphasise them in 1999 during Labour's first term of office. The best explanation seems to be that Tony Blair, Gordon Brown and other senior Labour figures were determined to make a decisive break with the ideological approach to policy making beloved by 'Old Labour'. This White Paper and all the refinements which subsequently flowed from it were seen as the best way to convey a clear message to the governing party, the Civil Service and the general public that 'New Labour' was determined to do its policy and decision making differently in a rational and pragmatic way.

wider advice for Ministers

A wider range of advice for Ministers is another objective previously advocated in the 1970s and 1980s which has finally come to fruition under successive Blair Administrations since 1997. *Firstly*, there has been a conscious programme to bring into central Government a larger number of Special Advisers (typically at least two in each Department) to provide the party-political advice to senior Ministers which the Civil Service Code explicitly prevents mainstream civil servants from doing. However, since about half the 80 or so Special Advisers in Whitehall are now working for the Prime Minister in units attached to or within 10 Downing Street, these developments have also had the effect of centralising the policy-making capacity within the sphere of central Government itself. Nonetheless, policy making is very much a matter of using networks to advance or consolidate a particular point of view within central Government and in this context the informal network of Special Advisers is a particularly significant one.

Secondly, there have been determined efforts by Ministers and top managers in the Civil Service (the Permanent Secretaries and Agency Chief Executives) to recruit many more people from the private and voluntary sectors into the ranks of the Senior Civil Service. This process has gone on apace as part of the modernisation agenda of successive Blair Administrations with the result that about one third of new recruits into the Senior Civil Service now come from outside. Such people bring professional and technical skills – for example, project management, accountancy, human resources and IT – which traditionally have not been available in abundance in the ranks of those who have risen to the top of the Civil Service, so there has been a widening of the range of expertise, experience and advice available to Ministers.

Thirdly, Labour Ministers have made skilful and frequent use of Review Groups and Task Forces often chaired by senior figures from the private sector who have been lured into helping Government by the personal kudos of putting their names to prestigious 'independent reports' on many of the policy issues and intractable challenges which face the Administration. Examples of this phenomenon in recent years include Sir Peter Gershon from Marconi who made recommendations about public procurement, Sir Derek Wanless from NatWest who offered detailed analysis and recommendations about the future of the National Health Service, and Sir Philip Hampton from Sainsbury's who chaired the Better Regulation Task Force. All such initiatives promoted by senior Ministers are predicated upon the assumption that Government can learn from the experience of the private sector and they fit in well with Ministers' desires to portray themselves as 'business friendly' and in tune with the corporate sector.

strengthening the centre in Whitehall

For many years before Labour came to power in 1997, participants in and observers of British Government argued about whether there should be structural change in Whitehall to make the centre of central Government (10 Downing Street, the Treasury and the Cabinet Office) more powerful in relation to the various functional Departments and whether such centralisation would improve the coherence and effectiveness of the policy- and decision-making process. For example, Sir John Hoskyns, who headed Margaret Thatcher's Policy Unit at 10 Downing Street during her early years as Prime Minister, argued openly for the creation of a Prime Minister's Department (along the lines of the Executive Office of the American President). Later, Lord Hunt of Tanworth (Cabinet Secretary 1973–79) proposed the creation of a new central Department, whether located at 10 Downing Street or in a strengthened Cabinet Office, to provide enhanced political capacity and policy support for the Prime Minister of the day.[8]

In the event these suggestions were more or less adopted following Tony Blair's arrival at 10 Downing Street in May 1997, even though the changes made were never described in quite such explicit terms. The Policy Unit at 10 Downing Street was significantly expanded; Peter Mandelson was appointed as a coordinating Minister in the Cabinet Office and such a post has been maintained with various different remits and occupants ever since; and a Strategic Communications Unit was established under Alistair Campbell, the Prime Minister's Press Secretary who had worked closely with him in Opposition since 1994 and who (along with the new Chief of Staff, Jonathan Powell) was empowered by Order in Council in June 1997 to give instructions to civil servants. Subsequently, other manifestations of central capacity in 10 Downing Street or the Cabinet Office were created, such as the Strategy and

Innovation Unit, the Social Exclusion Unit and the Delivery Unit, all of them designed in one way or another to reinforce the central thrust and corporate thrust of the Government's programme.

Throughout the time that these centralising developments were taking place, Gordon Brown as Chancellor of the Exchequer was building up his own power base at the Treasury by exploiting the implicit power-sharing agreement that he had originally reached with Tony Blair at the time of the Labour leadership contest in 1994. He did this by micromanaging modernised policy not only in the Treasury's own sphere of the public finances, but also via a spider's web of Public Service Agreements and Service Delivery Agreements imposed upon every Department in Whitehall in an effort to improve the performance of central Government as a whole. The effects of this double-headed centralisation within Whitehall have been to create powerful competition between the only two really important figures in the Government since 1997 and simultaneously to downgrade the influence of the rest of the Cabinet to a low point seldom experienced before.

Under the aegis of these two dominant personalities there has been a dual shift of lasting significance in the policy- and decision-making process. Firstly, there has been an obvious tendency to present British central Government in increasingly presidential and personal terms, even if it has not always been obvious whether Tony Blair or Gordon Brown was playing the leading role. Secondly, there has been a marked shift from trust and hierarchy to targets and contracts as the way of getting the best out of the Whitehall machine. It may be that, sooner or later, the pendulum will swing back towards a more traditional form of Cabinet and Departmental Government.

increased support for the Opposition

Some people have argued for a long time that there should be increased support for the Opposition parties, so that they can be better informed and better placed both to challenge the Government of the day and to develop sensible policy ideas when they are not in office. To achieve this, it has been suggested that there should be created a small but capable Department of the Opposition to enable leading politicians not in office to scrutinise and challenge the Government of the day on a more equal basis and so contribute indirectly to the quality of policy and decision making. An implicit purpose of such a development might be to make Opposition parties more acutely aware of the realities and constraints of Government in the hope that this would reduce the risk that the policies of an incoming Government would reflect little more than the views and prejudices of unrepresentative political activists. It is also argued that this might raise the quality and sophistication of policy making in Opposition and make it less likely that policy arguments in Parliament will be dominated by voices in the governing party.

Another way of 'educating' the Opposition is to give Opposition parties much fuller and more frequent access to high-class official information and advice.

Traditionally, this happened to some extent with Privy Counsellors (former Cabinet Ministers and others of senior political rank) who are allowed to see restricted official information and advice on privileged terms. However, most of this material is now much more easily available to all politicians and, indeed, members of the public, thanks to the Freedom of Information Act 2000 – at any rate those provisions which govern the disclosure of factual information as opposed to official advice to Ministers.

Yet another way of achieving the objective of a more effective Opposition would be to provide all political parties with greater financial support from public funds – as happens in many Continental European countries – perhaps in proportion to the votes received by each party at the previous General Election. This would enable parties in Opposition to employ more of their own advisers and put at least their front-bench spokesmen on more equal terms with Ministers. Nevertheless, it would not guarantee a higher standard of Opposition policy and decision making, since that must ultimately depend upon the imagination, energy and talent of the leading politicians concerned.

a greater role for Parliament

Some people have been attracted by the idea that Parliament at Westminster should be given a greater role in the formative stages of the policy- and decision-making process. Such a change would add a creative role to the main aspects of Parliamentary activity which are those of scrutinising the acts of Government and mobilising democratic legitimacy for Government policy. To be successful, this would almost certainly require the further development of Select Committees in ways which would enable them to be more deeply involved in the formative stages of policy making. For example, it would mean Select Committees developing their present willingness to engage in pre-legislative scrutiny of draft Government Bills and perhaps being taken more into the confidence of Ministers and officials in advance of Government decisions. It might also be sensible to balance this with greater emphasis upon post-legislative evaluation and the systematic auditing of the effects of Ministerial decisions.

Such further enhancements of the role of backbenchers would benefit from the provision of expert and independent advice to ordinary MPs, perhaps via the expansion of existing capacities which already support backbenchers in their focus upon matters of financial and technological importance. Yet even with the benefit of such institutional reinforcement, there might be considerable resistance to going very far down such a road until there was a clearer separation between the roles of the Executive and the Legislature in Britain.

20.4 conclusion

A balanced view of the issues raised in this chapter might be that the policy- and decision-making process works rather well in Britain, but only if its performance is measured in terms of what Ministers and shadow Ministers want from the system and what policy-advising civil servants are used to providing. Beyond the twin citadels of Whitehall and Westminster, the process is not so satisfactory, as can be seen in the difficulties of achieving social inclusion and connecting with the general public.

Even the interest groups and other privileged bodies which are 'in the loop' and which engage frequently with officials and Ministers in the policy-making community cannot feel confident that they have more than occasional and marginal influence on the outcomes of policy making. This is because it is normally the most senior politicians and their trusted political advisers who conduct the discussions and monopolise the decisions. Notwithstanding the innovations which have come about under the general heading of 'modernisation', British policy making is still largely a matter of reacting to events which leaves little scope for proceeding from first principles.

To minimise the risk of further disappointments, the leading participants should try to explain more clearly the limitations of the policy- and decision-making process in a mixed economy and liberal democracy, such as Britain, which has to be globally competitive and politically astute if it is to thrive in contemporary world conditions. Britain may be fortunate to have a robust and mature political system, but there are no grounds for complacency when the policy problems remain so hard to solve.

SUGGESTED QUESTIONS

1   Describe the policy- and decision-making process in British central Government.
2   Where does real power lie in the policy- and decision-making process?
3   How can the policy- and decision-making process be improved in modern conditions which are so heavily influenced by external factors, such as the media and the markets?

chapter 21

Britain and the European Union

No textbook on the British political system can afford to ignore Britain's membership of the European Union and still be an accurate and complete reflection of contemporary political realities. The vast range of economic, social and political relationships that this involves, especially the legal and constitutional issues which it raises, are essential to a proper understanding of the subject material covered in this book.

Things have not been the same for Britain ever since it joined the European Community (as the European Union was then called) in January 1973. Indeed, a whole raft of significant changes have taken place and have had an impact. For example, the 1986 Single European Act opened the way for Britain's participation in the single European market, the 1992 Treaty of Maastricht set the course for Economic and Monetary Union and the 1997 Treaty of Amsterdam sought to improve the efficiency of the European institutions and extend the concept of European citizenship. Since then there has been an attempt at further institutional reform in the 2001 Treaty of Nice, an enlargement of the European Union from 15 to 27 member states in 2004–06, and an EU-wide political crisis precipitated by the failure in 2005 of both France and the Netherlands to ratify in national referenda the Treaty establishing a constitution for Europe.

The history of Europe over the more than 60 years since the end of the Second World War has been one of closer and closer political integration punctuated by political setbacks and crises in which Britain and France have played particularly prominent roles. Britain has been a reluctant and even semi-detached partner in the whole enterprise, whereas France has been a somewhat ambivalent leader of the whole project determined to safeguard French national interests, but also to bind Germany into peaceful political structures from which there would be no escape.

21.1 historical background[1]

Since 1975 Britain's membership of the European Union has not been seriously in doubt in the sense that British withdrawal is not considered to be a serious option by most people, notwithstanding the fact that the relatively small number of supporters and members of the UK Independence Party (UKIP) would favour just that. The initial enthusiasm among many people in all parties for Britain's membership of a European *Common Market* and later of the European *Single Market* has not been matched by a similar degree of British enthusiasm for 'an ever closer Union of the European peoples' (in the words of the preamble to the 1957 Treaty of Rome). This has been reflected in battles under the Thatcher, Major and Blair Governments to limit Britain's net contribution to the EC Budget and to limit the overall size of the Budget by radical reform of the Common Agricultural Policy. It has also been reflected in the continuing tendency for Britain to stand aside from some of the most radical departures into deeper political integration proposed by France, Germany and some other member states. For example, under the Major Administration (1990–97) Britain stood aside from those parts of the 1992 Maastricht Treaty which provided for phased progress towards Economic and Monetary Union and from a range of ambitious initiatives in the sphere of social policy – most notably the introduction into EC law of a Social Chapter designed to standardise social conditions in all member states.

At the same time successive British Governments have continued to champion the cause of enlarging the European Union and this helped to bring about the accession of Greece (1981), Spain and Portugal (1986), Austria, Sweden and Finland (1995), Poland, Hungary, the Czech Republic, Slovakia, Slovenia, Estonia, Lithuania, Latvia, (Greek) Cyprus and Malta (2004) and Romania and Bulgaria (2006). Turkey – having first applied in 1987 – is still hoping to qualify and be accepted for membership at some indeterminate point in the future. Other countries to the east and south of the EU also aspire to enter in the longer term (e.g. Croatia, Macedonia and the Ukraine, as well as Tunisia and Morocco), but following the rejection of the proposed European Constitution by the people of France and the Netherlands in national referenda in 2005, the 'European project' and specifically the prospects of further enlargement seem to have suffered a serious setback. The pro-integration political elites in countries such as Belgium, France, Germany, Italy and Spain give every appearance of believing that this crisis in the process of European integration will blow over and that a disgruntled European public will once more fall in love with the European ideal of ever closer integration. On the other hand, the British political class, encouraged by much of the British media, has become more Euro-sceptic and has begun to find allies in Denmark, Sweden, Holland and even France as well as from among the newer entrants to the Union whose Governments would prefer a more liberal and economically dynamic construction.

The European Union has reached an important crossroad in its political and economic development. Its future is now a matter of considerable controversy and relevant opinion on what to do next is divided both vertically and horizontally. *Vertically*, there are a variety of different national views on how far and how fast the process of integration should continue and how far and how fast the process of enlargement should continue. Those who favour still deeper and more ambitious integration (such as Belgium, Italy, Germany and Spain) are not necessarily champions of further territorial enlargement, while those who favour a pause or even a pulling back in the deterministic drive for deeper integration (such as Britain, Denmark, Sweden and Holland) tend to be better disposed to enlargement which they see as a desirable opportunity to dilute further integrationist tendencies. *Horizontally*, there are a variety of different views within each member state, depending upon where people stand in economic and social hierarchies, their age and lifetime experience, their political prejudices and the extent of their alienation from the ruling political, judicial, bureaucratic and business elites. Since the mid 1980s this has been described as a 'democratic deficit' in the European Union institutions according to which there is a perceived lack of accountability in the relationships between the decision makers and the peoples in each and every member state. Yet in fact the problem is larger and more serious than that, because the adverse public reaction in many member states is at least as much a reflection of public hostility towards national elites as it is a commentary upon the shortcomings of the European Union.

In this respect nothing much has changed since New Labour came to power in 1997, because in spite of some fairly positive political rhetoric on European Union issues, Tony Blair and his Ministerial colleagues demonstrated almost as much political caution towards the ideas and preferences of their Continental colleagues as did successive Conservative Administrations under Margaret Thatcher and John Major. For the minority of dedicated 'Europeans' in the United Kingdom, the Blair Administration has been a considerable disappointment: it declined to initiate procedures for possible adoption of the euro in Britain, it rowed back from some of its more positive statements in the sphere of European social policy, it fought hard to keep Britain's rebate in the financing of the EC Budget, and it sided with the Americans rather than with fellow Europeans on many issues of war and peace. In searching for reasons for this behaviour, one need look no further than the state of British public opinion on these issues which is influenced by the incessant anti-European propaganda emanating from much of the British media, not least from the Murdoch press.

21.2 legal and constitutional implications

Britain's membership of the European Union has profound legal and constitutional implications which have become increasingly apparent as the member states have continued to enhance the degree of integration with one another. Yet it is fair to say that the problems posed by the incursion of European law into British law should have been clear from the very beginning when Parliament debated Britain's entry into the European Community in 1971–72. The fact that many MPs and others may not have fully realised what they were letting themselves and subsequent generations in for owed a good deal to the fact that the then Conservative Government, in its understandable wish to secure Parliamentary approval for Britain's entry, was less than completely honest (or significantly underestimated) the longer term legal and constitutional implications of the European project.[2]

Section 2 (1) of the 1972 European Communities Act made provision for existing European law to take direct effect in the United Kingdom.[3] It provided for the European Treaties and European legislation under the Treaties to take direct effect in Britain. It also provided for all *future* European law to take effect and made it clear that European, rather than British, law would determine whether or not a particular provision was directly effective in Britain – i.e. would not require transposition into British law in order to be effective in Britain and be recognised by the Courts. Section 2 (2) of the Act made provision for the implementation of European law by means of subordinate British legislation at Westminster – i.e. Statutory Instruments. However, in Section 2 (1) it was made clear that such Statutory Instruments could not be used in four specific areas which would still require primary legislation in Britain, namely:

- The imposition of new or increased taxation
- The creation of new serious criminal offences
- Any retrospective legislation
- Subdelegated legislation.

Section 2 (4) determined that both past and future Acts of Parliament should be subordinate to European law in those areas where any conflict might arise. This was reinforced by Section 3 (1) which declared that any question about the effect of European law in Britain should be decided in accordance with the principles of any relevant ruling of the European Court of Justice (ECJ), the most notable of which is the supremacy of European law over national law in all the member states in areas covered by the Treaties. Thus all these interlocking and mutually reinforcing sections of the 1972 European Communities Act served to establish the supremacy of European law over national law, although it was an Act of Parliament at Westminster which made this possible in Britain and which, by implication, could be repealed by a subsequent Act of Parliament.

Over the years rulings of the European Court of Justice (ECJ) have had effects upon Britain and the British legal system in a variety of policy areas including, for example, fishing rights, compensation for civil litigants, anti-terrorism laws, state pension arrangements and employment rights. These are all examples of ECJ rulings which have gone against the British Government and have fed the suspicions of British Euro-sceptics. However, it is not just Britain which has been in the dock: France had to modify the protectionist measures which it had imposed upon British lamb exporters; Italy had to reduce the taxes which it imposed on luxury cars; and Spain had to change its rules on food additives which had damaged chewing gum exports from other member states. A balanced interpretation of the role of the ECJ should acknowledge that the Court seeks to protect (and advance) the European interest against all unlawful challenges from whichever quarter they come.

The most important features of the relationship between European law and national law in Britain are the direct effect of European law in British jurisdiction, the supremacy of European law over national law if and when the two are in conflict, and the procedures by which European law is enforced in Britain and other member states. We must be clear about the meaning and implications of these features, so we shall deal with each in turn. The *concept of direct effect* means that a provision of European law creates individual rights for citizens in Britain and the other member states which must be upheld by the national courts. This principle was clarified for the first time in the 1962 *Van Gend en Loos case*, when it was established that the European Court may legitimately determine that a provision of European law is directly effective in all the member states.[4] This principle may sound simple, but, as enunciated by the European Court ever since 1962, it has not accorded easily with the traditional view of such matters in Britain. The European Court's position was, and remains, that the EC institutions are 'endowed with sovereign rights, the exercise of which affects member states and their citizens' and that member states had 'limited their sovereign rights, albeit within limited fields' and that European law can confer rights on individuals 'which become part of their legal heritage'. At the time this was a bold interpretation by the European Court, which was based upon the *principle of conferral* that has informed all EC Treaties since the Paris Treaty in 1950. Yet it was distinct from the theoretical principle in British law which has always held that European legislation is applicable in Britain only because Parliament at Westminster delegated certain powers in the 1972 European Communities Act to allow the EC institutions to create law that can have direct effect in British jurisdictions – the *principle of delegation* which implies that what can be granted can also be repossessed.

The *supremacy of European law* means that any provision of EC Treaty law can always prevail over a provision of national law in any member state, irrespective of whether the former was made before the latter or *vice versa*. The 1977 *Simmenthal case* provided the judicial basis for this.[5] In this case the Italian authorities had argued that their national law should prevail, because it had been passed *after* the two relevant European directives, and alternatively that Italian national law should prevail at least until such time as its conflict with European law was declared unconstitutional by the Italian constitutional court. When the matter reached the European Court, it was held that the national court had a duty to give full effect to European law and not to apply any conflicting national provisions, even if these had been adopted after the European provisions. It also held that there was no question of waiting for national law to be set aside by a national court or a national legislature before finally accepting the supremacy of European law. The European Court ruling was necessarily limited by the Treaty provisions and it did not state that the conflicting national provisions were void, merely that they were 'inapplicable'. However, its ruling was of general application throughout the European

Community, since it applied to all national laws which 'encroach upon the field within which the Community exercises its legislative power'.

It is clear from this and other judgements of the European Court that European law prevails over national law in all cases covered by the Treaties, as long as the legal right contained in a given European instrument is successfully invoked against a member state by a litigant in the European Court or in a national court applying the principles of European law. Indeed, the 1973 *French merchant seamen case* had demonstrated that there is a positive obligation upon member states to repeal any national legislation which conflicts with European law, even if the latter is considered inapplicable by a national legal authority.[6] Experience has also shown that the powers of member states can be limited or removed even where the conflict with European law is only indirect or potential. For example, under Articles 113 and 238 of the 1957 Rome Treaty the member states have lost the power to enter into commercial or association agreements with third countries, since these powers are explicitly reserved to the European Commission acting on behalf of the European Union as a whole. Equally, the 1978 *Pigs Marketing Board case* demonstrated that under the Common Agricultural Policy (CAP), if the European Commission has introduced a common market regime for a given category of farm products, the member states are precluded from adopting any national measures which might undermine or create exceptions to it.[7] The most significant confirmation of this principle was the ruling in the 1991 *Factortame case* when the European Court ruled that the 1988 Merchant Shipping Act was in breach of European law, because it prevented Spanish-owned trawler companies from registering in Britain to take advantage of the British national fish catch quota under the terms of the Common Fisheries Policy. As a result of this ECJ decision, the British Government had to persuade the Westminster Parliament to repeal the offending portions of the Act.

The *enforcement procedures for European law* are the third important feature of the relationship between European law and national law. There are two ways in which European law can be enforced against national Governments in the member states. The first is through legal action taken by individuals or firms through the national courts seeking to apply the doctrine of direct effect. For example, when the Irish Government imposed restrictions on fishing in Irish waters which were contrary to the Common Fisheries Policy (CFP), a Dutch fisherman was able to invoke European law as a successful defence to the charge of illegal fishing.[8] Equally, when in 1977 the Ministry of Agriculture in Britain imposed a ban on the import of main crop potatoes, this was successfully challenged by a Dutch exporter as contrary to European law.[9] In both cases the European Court upheld the position of the plaintiff.

Another way in which European law can be enforced against national Governments is by direct legal proceedings against the member state concerned. This can be done under Article 88 of the 1951 Paris Treaty (ECSC), Articles 169–71 of the 1957 Rome Treaty (EEC) and Articles 141–3 of the Euratom Treaty. The procedure for doing this is divided into two stages. In the first stage, the European Commission either delivers a 'Decision' under the ECSC Treaty which is binding and conclusive (unless the member state concerned wishes to challenge it in proceedings before the European Court) or it merely delivers a 'reasoned opinion' under the EEC and Euratom Treaties which is not binding. This means that if a member state fails to comply, the European Commission can bring the matter before the European Court for definitive determination.

In the second stage, the proceedings in the European Court are not a review of the decision or reasoned opinion issued by the Commission, but rather a fresh consideration of the case to establish whether or not a violation of the Treaties has occurred. If the European Court finds that the allegations are proved, it will give judgement against the offending member state. Under the ECSC Treaty this has the effect of confirming the binding European Commission decision and it opens the way for the imposition of sanctions (probably a fine) against the offending state if that proves to be necessary. Under the EEC and Euratom Treaties, this takes the form of a declaration setting out how and why the offending member state has failed to fulfil its Treaty obligations. Although the European Court has no power to order a member state either to take or not to take a particular course of action and it cannot declare invalid any national legislation, the member state concerned is obliged by its Treaty obligations to terminate as soon as possible the violation found by the European Court.

Such enforcement procedures have been effective in most cases, even when a member state has indulged in deliberate delaying tactics. This is largely because in the leading *Pig producers case* in 1978, the European Court upheld the European Commission's application for an interim injunction to terminate a British subsidy scheme which had been designed by the British Government to help British pig producers compete against imports which were subsidised under the Common Agricultural Policy at European level. Together with a similar case at about the same time which was brought by the European Commission against Ireland for introducing fisheries conservation measures which were regarded as being contrary to European Treaty obligations (under the Common Fisheries Policy), this meant that the principle of using an interim injunction against an offending member state became established.[10]

Such legal developments are evidence of the political nature of European jurisprudence. When deciding whether to grant an interim injunction to the European Commission in an action against a member state, the European Court takes into account:

▸ The chances of the proceedings being successful
▸ The extent to which the matter is urgent
▸ Any evidence which there may be of the likelihood of irreparable damage being done to the European Union if no action were taken.

However, in those rare cases when a member state has *deliberately* sought to break European law and to defy the European Court, the issues have only been capable of resolution on a political basis, because it is on the *continuing will to cooperate* that the satisfactory functioning of the European Union finally depends.

principal problems for Britain

When Britain joined the European Community in 1973, it laid itself open to three principal legal and constitutional problems. The essential dilemma was vividly described by a senior judge who referred to the threat from 'the rising tide of Community law' and warned that 'we have to learn to become amphibious if we wish to keep our heads above water'.[11] In other words, as long as successive British Governments and Parliaments take the view that Britain's membership of the European Union is *on balance* beneficial to the interests of the country, the British are likely to tolerate the growing web of evolving European Community law. As this body of supranational law is extended by the Council of Ministers into more and more areas of economic and social activity (whether by unanimity or increasingly by qualified majority voting), the scope for autonomous action by Britain (or any other EU member state) will gradually diminish. Only significantly changed political and economic circumstances – such as the impact of further EU enlargement or of global economic competition from India, China and the Far East for example – are likely to slow down, halt or even reverse the secular trend in Europe. Even then, it is possible that the dominant response to such challenges could be a collective determination (among at least a core of member states) to go further and faster and deeper in an integrationist direction.

The first problem is that legal provision for Britain's membership of the European Community could not be made by means of a simple constitutional amendment – as happened in the case of Ireland, for example – but had to be made by the far more complicated and controversial method of passing an Act of Parliament, in this case the 1972 European Communities Act. The reason for this was, of course, the well rehearsed fact that Britain did not then have, and still does not have, a formal, written, codified constitution. We should therefore note the paradox that in Britain's case the legal means of providing for permanent membership of the European Community was the decidedly impermanent mechanism of an Act of Parliament which, by its very nature, can be amended or repealed at any time.

The second problem is that the British attitude towards international law is essentially dualist, which means that in Britain national and international law are regarded as being quite distinct. There never has been a general rule of law in Britain which allows treaties to take effect within the British legal system without the essential enabling mechanism of an Act of Parliament, although it should be noted that under the Royal Prerogative a British Government is free *to sign* a Treaty on behalf of the Executive acting in the name of the Crown. By contrast, in other European countries which have codified constitutions, such as France and Germany, international treaties signed by their Governments take precedence over national law and have direct effect in their national jurisdictions without any requirement for enabling legislation, as in Britain.

The third and most fundamental problem, which really underpins the first two, is the hallowed British constitutional principle of Parliamentary supremacy. This means that in the United Kingdom there is supposed to be no legal authority superior to Parliament and that any Parliament can amend or overturn the laws of its predecessors – in other words, no Parliament can bind its successors. *In theory*, this peculiarity of British constitutional arrangements means that Parliamentary supremacy and the doctrine of the primacy of European law in the areas covered by the European Treaties are fundamentally incompatible. *In practice*, the circle has been squared by another doctrine contained in Section 2 (1) of the 1972 European Communities Act which holds that Parliament evidently *intended* that all Acts of Parliament, whether before or after that Act, *should* be subordinate to European law in those areas of jurisdiction covered by the European Treaties and subsequently confirmed by rulings of the European Court.

On the face of it, this resolution of the problem seems to be inconsistent with the rule that no British Parliament can bind its successors and the possibility that a future British Parliament might pass an Act which defied European law and then persevere with that stance to the extent of repealing the 1972 European Communities Act and so destroying the legal basis upon which it had been obliged to adhere to European law. Such an acute constitutional dilemma could conceivably arise, but it is highly unlikely for two main reasons. *Firstly*, if a future British Parliament at Westminster were determined to pass a new law which flouted some important aspect of established European law, it would probably do so only in circumstances in which a British Government was actively considering British withdrawal from some or all of Britain's obligations to the European Union – a situation which is unlikely to materialise unless it were a condition precedent to a thoroughgoing renegotiation of the basis of Britain's relationship with the rest of the European Union. *Secondly*, as long as the Government of the day with the support of a reliable majority in the House of Commons continues to value British membership more than partial or complete withdrawal, then the situation will not arise. Indeed, Section 2 (4) of the 1972 European Communities Act makes it clear that Parliament at Westminster is presumed *not* to intend any future statute to conflict with, still less override, any provisions of European law, thus prejudging the intentions of any future Parliament. In other words, the legal basis of Britain's continuing membership of the European Union is essentially the *political* assumption that successive British Governments, backed by successive British Parliaments, will *choose* to remain in the European Union and be bound by European law in those areas of economic, social and political activity covered by the European Treaties.

Since the 1992 Treaty of Maastricht and on through the disputes over the 1997 Amsterdam Treaty, the 2001 Nice Treaty and the attempts to agree a Treaty establishing a Constitution for Europe since 2004, there has been deep and continuing disagreement in Britain and, to a growing extent, in the other member states of the European Union about the pace, scope and direction of European integration. Whereas in 1990–91 during the run-up to the Maastricht Treaty (which created the 'European Union' and provided for Economic and Monetary Union) only the Danish Government joined its British counterpart in expressing reservations about the European project; by 2004–05, in the wake of the Constitutional Convention, the roster of sceptics and those parts of political and public opinion with national(ist) reservations about developments in the European Union had grown to include large sections of public opinion in Sweden, the Netherlands and even France – not to mention some of the new member states in central and eastern Europe which had joined the EU in 2004. In particular, the rejection of the proposed Constitutional Treaty by the people of France and the Netherlands in the summer of 2005 was widely, if tacitly, assumed to have aborted this particular stage in the 'European project' and to bode ill for the prospect of future enlargements of the EU to include Croatia, Macedonia and Turkey.

The growing band of 'Euro-sceptics' in many member states is drawn from a number of different schools of thought and does not really constitute a single coherent critique of the most recent stages in European integration. Some are uncomfortable with the lingering federalism of many Europhiles, some are expressing their opposition to further enlargement of the EU which, they believe, will make it increasingly ungovernable and which may threaten their national economic interests, and some are simply taking an opportunity to express their sense of alienation from the bureaucratic and political elites who have been in control of the European project since its inception more than 50 years ago. On the other hand, what tends to unite the critics is the realisation that, in any important legal or constitutional dispute on these matters, it is ultimately the European Court which will arbitrate and they argue that its record over many years shows a clear institutional and jurisprudential bias in favour of defending the *acquis communautaire* (the body of already established European law) and advancing the interests of the other supranational institutions of the EU, notably the Commission and the Parliament. For these reasons they argue that cumulative European case law is likely to favour the cause of ever closer European integration and they warn that those who put their faith in doctrines of subsidiarity or repatriation as the best ways of limiting the ambitions of those who are still dedicated to the goal of 'an ever closer union' are likely to be bitterly disappointed.[12]

21.3 political and institutional impact

The political and institutional impact of Britain's membership of the European Union has already been significant and seems likely to become more significant in future. Ever since Britain's entry into the European Community in 1973, the country has been involved to an increasing extent in the expanding process of European integration. This process was well described by Sir Michael Butler, a former UK Permanent Representative at the EC institutions in Brussels, as 'primarily about solving detailed, complicated and usually technical problems by consensus in a political framework which makes it extremely difficult for the national Governments to do other than agree in the end.'[13] It is this apparent inevitability and irreversibility of European integration which has been both the secret of its success and the main cause for concern among those in Britain and other member states who wish to limit, or even reverse, the process. Certainly the historic drive towards 'an ever closer union among the peoples of Europe' seems to have posed greater political and institutional problems for Britain than for any of the other member states.

impact on Ministers

The impact of Britain's membership of the European Union has been felt first and foremost in the sphere of central Government. This is because Ministers in all British Governments since January 1973 have played an active part in the process of European policy and decision making. From the beginning this has involved Departmental Ministers representing Britain and defending British national interests in the Council of Ministers, whether the General Affairs Council composed of Foreign Ministers or the specific 'subject' Councils, such as Agriculture, Finance, Transport or the Environment, depending upon the particular policy area under discussion. Since 1974 it has also involved the Prime Minister of the day participating in what came to be known as 'the European Council' with the other Heads of Government and the President of the European Commission. Such 'summit meetings' are now held four times a year under the chairmanship of whichever member state holds the rotating Presidency of the European Union for the relevant six-month period. The essential purpose of these top-level meetings has been to provide renewed impetus and strategic direction for the development of the European Union and on a number of occasions this is what has been achieved.

The most obvious consequence for Ministers of all these meetings has been the growing amount of time which they have had to devote to them as the spheres of European competence have been extended by agreement into more areas of policy. For example, there was no mention of environmental policy in the 1957 Treaty of Rome, since at that time there was no general recognition of the importance of acting at European level to deal with environmental problems, whereas nowadays these matters are considered to be significant supranational concerns. Equally, the 1992 Treaty of Maastricht enshrined an agreement by all the member states (except Britain and Denmark which reserved their national positions) to proceed in stages towards economic and monetary union based upon a single European currency administered and safeguarded by an independent European Central Bank by 1999 at the latest – and this is broadly what happened.

The traditional method of decision making in the Council of Ministers has been to continue the discussion on difficult issues, such as the reform of the Common Agricultural Policy or the level of each country's net contribution to the EC Budget, until the combined effects of physical exhaustion and the

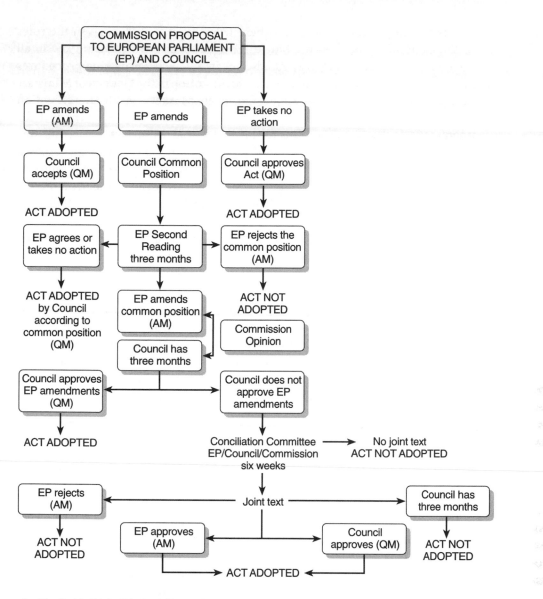

COMMISSION PROPOSAL TO EUROPEAN PARLIAMENT (EP) AND COUNCIL

EP amends (AM) → Council accepts (QM) → ACT ADOPTED

EP agrees or takes no action → ACT ADOPTED by Council according to common position (QM)

Council approves EP amendments (QM) → ACT ADOPTED

EP amends → Council Common Position → EP Second Reading three months → EP amends common position (AM) → Council has three months

EP takes no action → Council approves Act (QM) → ACT ADOPTED

EP rejects the common position (AM) → ACT NOT ADOPTED

Commission Opinion

Council does not approve EP amendments → Conciliation Committee EP/Council/Commission six weeks → No joint text ACT NOT ADOPTED

EP rejects (AM) → ACT NOT ADOPTED

Joint text

EP approves (AM) ↔ Council approves (QM) → ACT ADOPTED

Council has three months → ACT NOT ADOPTED

notes: AM = Absolute Majority of Members in European Parliament; QM = Qualified Majority Vote in the Council.

source: 'The European Union', delegation of the EC to the US, Washington DC, USA, October 1999.

figure 21.1   the EU policy- and decision-making process

spirit of Community compromise emerge and combine to make a European decision possible. This so-called 'Community method', which is usually based upon emerging consensus rather than explicit voting, has not only contributed to the number and duration of Ministerial meetings – and as a result the amount of time Ministers are obliged to devote to European business – but also imposed great strains upon Ministers themselves.

It is also important to note that there were significant changes in the rules of the game in 1986 when the Single European Act (SEA) became law in all the member states. This important advance in EC decision-making procedures involved the introduction of qualified majority voting in the Council of Ministers on all issues to do with the Single European Market – with the exception of taxation, immigration and employment rights which were reserved for unanimous decision making. This means that British Ministers – like Ministers from other member states – can find themselves outvoted when the Council of Ministers takes decisions by qualified majority, unless a blocking minority of votes can be assembled – a figure which has obviously changed as the EU itself has enlarged its membership from 12 at the time of the SEA in 1986 to 27 twenty years later.[14]

On the other hand, it is well to remember that qualified majority voting can, and often has, worked in Britain's favour, so the rules of the game can cut both ways. For example, it would have been much more difficult to make speedy progress with implementing the Single Market if the policy had remained subject to decision making by consensus or unanimity. Although there is nearly always considerable pressure to find a compromise even in the most intractable disputes in the Council of Ministers, national Governments sometimes find it quite convenient to be outvoted if they have significant problems with public opinion in their own countries, but nevertheless recognise privately that the decision taken is the right one in the interests of Europe as a whole.

impact on civil servants

The impact of the European Union upon civil servants has probably been even greater than the impact upon Ministers. This is because Britain's membership of the European Union has spawned vast networks of bureaucratic relationships between Whitehall and the various EC institutions in Brussels, Luxembourg, Strasbourg, Frankfurt and elsewhere – as well as a complicated skein of bilateral relations between London and the other member-state capitals. Within Whitehall itself it has been necessary for the Foreign Office and the Cabinet Office to coordinate the work of all the various Departments involved in the EC policy- and decision-making process. Those civil servants, who are involved in dealing with actual or potential issues of European policy, spend a good deal of their time commuting to and from Brussels for meetings with their Community counterparts from other national capitals and from the EC Commission. A significant number are stationed at the UK Permanent Representation in Brussels (UKREP for short) where they have an essential role to play in liaising with civil servants from the EC institutions and the other national delegations. They are also involved in preparing the British Government's position at meetings of the Council of Ministers and in assisting their sponsoring Departments in Whitehall. In this way they seek to carry forward the process of permanent discussions between the British Government, the European institutions and the Governments of the other member states.

In view of the growing volume of European legislation emanating from the EC institutions in Brussels, British civil servants in those Departments most deeply involved in European policy have had to spend an increasing amount of their time upon the negotiation and subsequent implementation of EC law. For example, the Department of the Environment, Food and Rural Affairs (DEFRA) spends probably three-quarters of its official time on business related to the working of the Common Agricultural Policy in Britain, while the Departments of Trade and Industry (DTI), the Department of Work and Pensions (DWP), the Home Office and the Treasury are among those busiest with European regulations and directives. In addition, a growing proportion of the issues considered by the Cabinet and its Committees has a European dimension of one kind or another, while Whitehall preparations for meetings of the European Council involves strenuous work for those in 10 Downing Street, the Cabinet Office, the Foreign Office and many other Departments. This is, of course, particularly so when the UK holds the rotating Presidency of the European Union for six months every so many years, as it did during the second half of 2005. It can therefore be argued that the administrative processes of the European Union have affected the British Civil Service more than any other component of the British political system. This bureaucratic characteristic is one of the reasons for the continuing 'democratic deficit' in the European Union which has contributed to the widespread sense of public disenchantment and alienation felt by so many people.

impact on Parliament

The impact on Parliament of Britain's membership of the European Union has been emphasised by the 'Euro-sceptics' and anti-Europeans as perhaps the most serious and adverse of all the negative consequences flowing from the original decision to enter the European Community taken by the Westminster Parliament in October 1971. This argument was put with great conviction during the tense debates on the European Communities Bill in 1972 and again in 1992–93 when the legislation to give effect to the Maastricht Treaty in Britain was fought by the Euro-sceptics every inch of the way. Yet the suspicion remains that the doom-laden forecast that Parliament at Westminster (and the Parliaments of the other member states) will one day be reduced to the status of county councils in a federal Europe has been exaggerated for propaganda effect.

Indeed, some political developments over the past decade or so have suggested a revived role for national Parliaments in the European Union. For example, the 1997 Treaty of Amsterdam encouraged national Parliaments to take a closer interest in European Union matters by introducing a minimum period of six weeks within which they are able to make their views known on draft proposals before the Council of Ministers. Another (largely British) proposal at that time was that a European Second Chamber, comprising members from each national Parliament, should be created to give stronger representation in EC policy and decision making to all the national Parliaments. More recently, the European constitutional Treaty published in 2004 contained a Protocol 'desiring to encourage greater involvement of national Parliaments in the activities of the European Union and to enhance their ability to express their views on draft European legislative acts as well as on other matters which may be of particular interest to them.'[15] It also provided for 'effective and regular inter-Parliamentary cooperation within the Union', so it can at least be said that the case has not gone by default.

When considering the prospects for Parliament at Westminster, it is as well to remember that Ministers in Britain have long been able to conclude Treaties without prior Parliamentary approval by exercising the powers of the Royal Prerogative. Thus the largely retrospective nature of Parliamentary control in Britain in relation to major developments in the European Union is essentially no different to the limited and retrospective power which MPs have over British Ministers acting within the national jurisdiction. Whereas Parliament at Westminster has long claimed to have supreme jurisdiction in the United Kingdom, since 1973 it has had to share jurisdiction with the European Parliament (and to some extent with the other national Parliaments) in the sphere of European legislation introduced under the European Treaties. In attempting such power-sharing, the Westminster Parliament has been able to develop a number of Parliamentary devices which have gone some way towards clawing back the ability to scrutinise European legislative proposals at the level of representative national institutions. For example, a total of more than 70 peers are involved in scrutinising EU policy, decisions and draft legislation in the House of Lords European Union Select Committee and its 7 Subcommittees. It is widely agreed in Brussels and elsewhere that the quality of this scrutiny is high and provides a model for other national legislatures in the EU to emulate.

Notwithstanding the valiant efforts of both Houses of Parliament to get to grips in a timely fashion with the large and growing legislative output of the European Union, there are a number of intractable problems of procedure which have been identified by expert observers and practitioners alike. *Firstly*, there is the sheer volume of European legislative proposals which is hard for both Houses to handle within the constraints of an already congested agenda. In the Commons, attempts have been made to address this problem via the European Scrutiny Committee which sifts all EU legislative proposals at the draft stage and draws attention to those which merit closer attention by the House as a whole. There are typically over 1000 documents a year which have to be dealt with by the Committee and of these about one-third are typically judged to be of sufficient importance to merit taking oral or written evidence and producing a detailed report for the benefit of the House. In doing its laborious work, the Committee is assisted by the so-called 'Scrutiny Reserve' which amounts to an understanding backed by successive Resolutions of the House in 1980 and 1990 that British Ministers will not normally agree to EC legislative proposals ahead of Parliamentary scrutiny at Westminster. These undertakings were subsequently reinforced by another Resolution of the House in November 1998. This took account of the development of the 'co-decision procedure' introduced in 1993 which had had the effect of increasing the legislative power sharing between the European Parliament and the Council of Ministers at the expense of national Parliaments. Thus, in spite of the best endeavours of Parliament at Westminster to keep abreast of and have some timely influence upon the spate of legislative proposals from Brussels, it has to be admitted that preserving the traditional role of Westminster in this burgeoning legislative arena has proved to be an uphill struggle.

About two-thirds of the EU documents considered by the European Scrutiny Committee in the Commons are typically found to be insignificant in political and legal terms and no further action in Parliament is recommended. However, the Committee can take one of three further actions on those documents which it considers to be significant: it can simply report on the issues raised; it can recommend that the matter be debated in one of three European Standing Committees (see below); or it can recommend that there be a debate on the floor of the House – which happens no more than about three times a year, provided the Government can find the Parliamentary time for such a debate. There are also three European Standing Committees with different subject remits.[16] They conduct their business with a mixed procedure beginning with up to one and a half hours of questions to the relevant Minister, then debating a motion (with the possibility of amendments) for up to one and a half hours, with an outer limit of two and a half hours for the entire proceedings. The Chairman of the committee reports the outcome of the proceedings to the House where a motion relating to the matters concerned is usually moved (without debate) a few days later. If a matter is recommended by the Scrutiny Committee for debate on the floor of the House and if the Government finds time for such a debate, it is for Ministers to decide the terms of the motion tabled for the occasion.

In the House of Lords, the work of the European Union Select Committee and its seven subcommittees complements the work of the Commons in that it produces briefer reports on fewer EC documents, but conducts detailed enquiries on particularly significant subject areas, such as EC fraud, foreign and security policy or the working of economic and monetary union. Its reports are either for information purposes or may involve recommendations for debate on the floor of the Upper House. Such reports are usually of high quality, reflecting the expertise and experience of those who serve on the committees, and frequently make an impact upon thinking in the EC institutions. The Lords committees may confer and cooperate with their Commons counterparts, but such possibilities are rarely exploited in formal terms.

Successive British Governments since 1973 have tended to regard both Houses of the British Parliament as natural allies in the process of continuous negotiations in Brussels, so the Prime Minister, the Foreign Secretary and other Ministers often take the opportunity to report back to Parliament at Westminster by making oral or written Ministerial statements on the outcome of the many EU meetings in which they participate. This means that lively discussion of significant EU matters is by no means confined to the work of specialist committees, but takes place on the floor of both Houses as well.

More recently, there was active discussion in the European Convention, which was later reflected in a Protocol of the Treaty establishing a Constitution for Europe, of the need for more cooperation between the national Parliaments of the 25 member states and between each of them and the European Parliament in continuing efforts to link the national and supranational dimensions of the European Union and to deal with the problems caused by the so-called 'democratic deficit' between EU decision makers and the European peoples. So far these worthy aspirations have not had much real effect. If anything, in Britain and other member states the underlying concerns have grown with the passage of time.

The second and more serious problem for Parliament at Westminster, which came to the fore at the time of the 1986 Single European Act and which has been more in evidence in successive EU Treaties ever since, is that the growing use of qualified majority voting in the Council of Ministers has reduced the scope for any member state Government to veto proposed decisions at European level. Any reduction in the effective power of member state Governments is effectively an equivalent reduction in the power of national Parliaments to which the Governments are accountable and this realisation has not exactly commended the EC institutions or their ways of doing business to Members of Parliament in Britain and many other member states. Consequently, there is a strong and growing sense in national Parliaments that the further development of the European Union is essentially a zero sum game in which every step intensifying the process of European integration is likely to weaken the relative power and influence of national institutions and notably national Parliaments. This may not be of great concern in some member states where traditionally the power and influence of Parliament has been weak, but it has exercised nearly all MPs and peers at Westminster, the 'Mother of Parliaments'.

Whereas Parliament at Westminster has had to struggle to keep its end up within the institutional structures of the European Union, the European Parliament has come to wield more power and influence in the European legislative process. Originally, the 1957 Treaty of Rome gave the European Parliament only a minor consultative role. Subsequent European Treaties, right the way through to the Treaty of Nice in 2001 and the Treaty establishing a European Constitution in 2004, have sought to extend the influence of the European Parliament via both the 'co-operation procedure' and the 'co-decision procedure' to the extent that the Parliament and the Council of Ministers now share the power of legislative decision making in many areas of policy. Once the Council of Ministers has reached a common position by qualified majority (or simply by consensus), the European Parliament has the power to reject this common position or propose amendments to it which, if then adopted by the European Commission (which made the original proposal for legislation), can only be amended by the Council of Ministers on a basis of unanimity. The general effect of this procedure has been to cause the European Commission to modify its original proposals in something like one-third of all cases when the European Parliament has used this aspect of its power.

impact upon the political system

It is clear that Britain's membership of the European Union has had a significant impact upon the British political system in a number of ways. This has been manifest in nearly all areas of political activity to a greater or lesser extent, although it has obviously been concentrated in the areas of EU legal competence, such as agriculture, competition policy and external trade.

It is fair to say that the European Union provides the economic, political and institutional context within which many important decisions are taken in Britain. Unless a future British Government backed by a future British Parliament (and by the British people in a future referendum) were to take Britain out of the European Union, Britain's membership of it (even if put onto a modified basis) is likely to play an increasingly important part in the lives and well-being of the British people.

Firstly, British political parties are increasingly affected by the need to conduct politics not just at the local and national levels, but also at a European level in the European Parliament and the various transnational political groupings of like-minded parties. For example, the Labour Party is part of the European Socialist Group, the Conservative Party is part of the European Peoples' Party and the Liberal Democrats are part of the Alliance of Liberals and Democrats for Europe. Even though European Parliamentary elections every five years tend to be fought on issues specific to each individual member state, there also seems to have been a gradual development of transnational political alignments as the level of political controversy has risen about what kind of Europe is most appropriate for the challenges of the twenty-first century.[17]

Secondly, the development of the European Union is having a powerful influence upon many interest and pressure groups in Britain and the other member states and increasingly upon the private sector in general. As more decisions of direct interest to the private sector are taken by the European institutions rather than exclusively by national Governments and Parliaments, political power has gradually levitated to the supranational level. For example, British farmers lobby the European Commission and the European Parliament via a transnational European organisation, COPA (Comite d'Organisations de Producteurs Agricoles), probably more energetically than they lobby DEFRA (Department of the Environment, Food and Rural Affairs) and the Westminster Parliament via the National Farmers' Union (NFU) and other national pressure groups. This is because they know the political power in their sector of the economy has shifted to the supranational level, although it should be added that many levers are still available at the national and subnational levels as co-financing and other methods catch on within the process of CAP reform. Similar conclusions have been drawn by corporations and individuals in

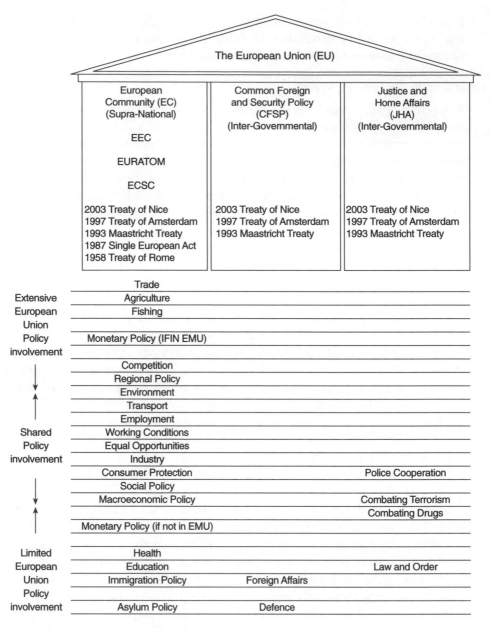

	European Community (EC) (Supra-National)	Common Foreign and Security Policy (CFSP) (Inter-Governmental)	Justice and Home Affairs (JHA) (Inter-Governmental)
	EEC		
	EURATOM		
	ECSC		
	2003 Treaty of Nice	2003 Treaty of Nice	2003 Treaty of Nice
	1997 Treaty of Amsterdam	1997 Treaty of Amsterdam	1997 Treaty of Amsterdam
	1993 Maastricht Treaty	1993 Maastricht Treaty	1993 Maastricht Treaty
	1987 Single European Act		
	1958 Treaty of Rome		

The European Union (EU)

Extensive European Union Policy involvement	Trade		
	Agriculture		
	Fishing		
	Monetary Policy (IFIN EMU)		
	Competition		
	Regional Policy		
	Environment		
	Transport		
	Employment		
Shared Policy involvement	Working Conditions		
	Equal Opportunities		
	Industry		
	Consumer Protection		Police Cooperation
	Social Policy		
	Macroeconomic Policy		Combating Terrorism
			Combating Drugs
	Monetary Policy (if not in EMU)		
Limited European Union Policy involvement	Health		
	Education		Law and Order
	Immigration Policy	Foreign Affairs	
	Asylum Policy	Defence	

figure **21.2** **areas and extent of European involvement and legal competence**

the manufacturing and service sectors wishing to take full advantage of the Single European Market with its common rules and obligations for the entire European Union. This has been particularly true in the vast financial services sector where Britain stands to gain disproportionately from significant market liberalisation.

Thirdly, the working of the European Union is having a growing impact upon devolved and local government in Britain and the other member states. Devolved and Local authorities are looking to European institutions for political and financial support. For example, the nationalist parties in Scotland, Wales and Northern Ireland see assistance and recognition at the European level as one of the best ways of developing economic and political counterweights to the influence of UK central Government and the UK Parliament at Westminster. In these circumstances it is not surprising that the Scottish National Party adopted the idea of 'an independent Scotland within a united Europe' as one of its more powerful slogans.[18] Equally, some of the poorest conurbations and geographical areas in the outlying regions of England – such as Merseyside, parts of Cornwall and the industrial North East – are very interested in benefiting from EU funds and have persistently lobbied the European Commission and the European Parliament for a fair share of the European transfer payments which are available.

Fourthly, it is becoming increasingly obvious that large parts of the media, and hence public opinion, in Britain are affected by Britain's membership of the European Union. Of course, the nature and extent of this influence fluctuates according to the turn of events. Sometimes there is great interest in European issues – as there was at the time of the French and Dutch referenda on the Constitutional Treaty in 2005. At other times European issues, which often tend to be rather bureaucratic and technical, have taken a back seat when the British people are faced with other more pressing concerns, such as terrorism or weakness in the housing market. Yet as the world has come to seem smaller and decisions taken at European level have begun to impinge more and more upon people's daily lives, it has become both necessary and natural for the British - and others – to take a closer interest in European affairs.

21.4 the dynamics of European integration

It is difficult to foresee how the European Union will develop in the years ahead and almost as difficult to predict how Britain and its political institutions will respond to the challenges involved. Yet some developments are discernible which seem likely to be among the driving forces of European integration over the coming years, while there are other developments in prospect which could be factors for disintegration.

main driving forces

The first and most obvious driving force in the European Union both now and in the future is the determination of firms and individuals in the private sector to take advantage of the economic and commercial opportunities offered by the increasingly unified European Single Market of more than 460 million people. In this sense it is the private sector which is likely to put the most pressure upon the Governments of member states and the European institutions to agree to further moves towards deeper integration. Prominent among these organisations with a strong vested interest in 'more Europe' are all the multinational companies based in third countries, such as the United States, Japan and, increasingly, China and India, which sometimes seem to have the clearest view of the advantages of economic integration in Europe. National organisations and public-sector bodies are, by comparison, often quite slow to respond to such economic opportunities and are usually content to validate, but sometimes try to obstruct, those developments in the global market place which enhance both the threats and the opportunities of greater competition.

The best examples of this drive for deeper private-sector integration are to be found in the activities of large companies, whether based in the EU jurisdiction or outside, which seek to advance their own corporate interests by putting pressure upon the Governments of member states and the EC institutions (notably the Commission) to reach binding agreements on a growing web of common rules, standards and obligations which will enable them to exploit the full potential of the European Single Market and the eurozone. Where the large companies lead, the medium and small companies are likely to follow as and when they find lucrative market niches to exploit. All companies, large and small, are pursuing their own corporate interests, but in doing so they are driving forward the whole process of European integration.

A *second* significant driving force is the power and influence of the transnational trade union confederations as they act effectively to advance the interests of organised labour at EU level. Powerful national trade unions, such as IG Metal in Germany or UNISON in Britain, forge alliances with their counterparts in other member states and exploit transnational representative bodies, such as the European TUC, in order to increase their influence upon the decisions of employers and bureaucrats alike. It seems that this approach to macro-economic management is likely to encounter a more friendly response in the 'core Europe' of France, Germany, Italy and the Benelux countries – the original 'six' (or 'old Europe') – than in Britain and some of the new member states where the Governments prefer a more liberal and less corporatist approach to economic policy. There are already areas of EC policy, such as the Working Time Directive or legislation on the employment rights of part-timers, which have been the subject of considerable controversy and disagreement at EU level, but which were eventually incorporated into the *acquis communautaire*. As the threat of global competition from lower cost economies in India, China and other parts of Asia grows apace, it will be important to see whether the vested interests of core Europe – principally 'the social partners' which are consulted so assiduously by the EC Commission and the Governments of these member states – can hold the line against the other member states and their more liberal corporate interests which argue that the economic ways of 'old Europe' are no longer successful in a highly competitive global economy.

A *third* main driving force will continue to be the power and influence of highly mobile finance and investment capital. We have already seen the emergence of London, Frankfurt and Paris as centres of financial activity in the European time zone, filling the temporal gap between Tokyo and New York in global financial trading. Such activity is likely to grow in future as and when agreement can be achieved on a supportive legislative framework applicable to the entire EU – something which, at the time of writing, has not been realised because of French-led opposition to the ways of Anglo-Saxon 'turbo-capitalism'.[19] When it does, the smart money is on London to retain a comparative advantage over its EU rivals because of the liquidity of its markets and the sophistication of its global networks. Yet there are no certainties in this area, not least because Britain is not yet in the eurozone and this could work against the City of London's financial ambitions.

A fourth driving force for the future development of Europe is the incremental development of EC law, which is likely to continue in spite of growing resistance to it in Britain and some of the other more sceptical member states. There is something remorseless about this factor in the European equation, since it is a reflection both of bureaucratic and political ambitions among the Europhiles and of the myriad of micro-economic developments and decisions taken in the private sector. Every time that the member states collectively decide at a European Council to make a leap, or even a few steps, forward, the result has been yet another EC Treaty containing new European commitments and obligations which tend to increase the scope of the EC institutions and diminish the autonomy of national Governments. Even though the European vanguard suffered a serious setback in 2005 when the French and the Dutch electorates rejected the proposed constitutional Treaty, the pro-European cause has demonstrated considerable resilience in the past and is likely to do so in the future. Indeed, because of the inherently pro-European predisposition of the judges on the European Court of Justice and of the Advocate General who guides their jurisprudence at the formative stages of a case, the ECJ (and the national courts which take their lead from it) are likely to come down in favour of protecting the *acquis communautaire* and interpreting any ambiguous sections in the EU Treaties in favour of the Community interest.

main divisive issues

Since the beginning of the drive towards European unity in the 1950s, there have been a number of divisive issues which have caused difficulties and sometimes crises for the member states of what is now the European Union. Yet whenever the member states have been plunged into crisis, they have usually emerged with their fundamental unity intact and sometimes even strengthened by the experience. This has been the pattern with each successive enlargement until perhaps 2004–06 when the membership of the EU grew from 15 to 27 member states. It is too soon to tell whether this enlargement, which has incorporated several ex-Communist states in central and eastern Europe, will push the whole EU in a more loosely knit and laissez-faire direction or whether the EU will effectively divide between a core vanguard group of member states led by France and Germany which presses for further and deeper integration and a more peripheral group led by Britain which presses for looser arrangements and greater freedom to pick and choose between different models of European integration.

The most fundamental divisive issue arises from the continuing debate about national sovereignty in Europe and around the world. There is fundamental disagreement about what the term means and the extent to which it can be or should be safeguarded. The concept has different meanings and elicits different reactions in the various member states and national traditions. Virtually everywhere in the western half of the Continent, except perhaps in Denmark and Holland and in some sections of French opinion, the idea of pooling national sovereignties in certain sectors of economic and social activity for the common good of Europe as a whole has not provoked much opposition from politicians and constitutional lawyers alike. This is partly because in many cases the nation states on the Continent have had chequered and even discredited histories, whereas in Britain the nation state still largely symbolises the pride of the British (more accurately the English) in their own nationality and the perceived success of the nation state; of *their* nation state. It is also because the so-called 'Community method' has held few fears for Governments and peoples on the Continent, since for several decades they have been committed to working pragmatically towards 'an ever closer union of European peoples' (in the words of the 1957 Treaty of Rome) and have become used to the habits and compromises of European integration; whereas successive British Governments and the British people have tended to be much more concerned about the prospect of an apparently remorseless and irreversible loss of national sovereignty every time the member states commit themselves to a new phase of European integration. For British 'Euro-sceptics', who have become more vociferous and more numerous in recent times, the implied erosion of Parliamentary supremacy and the perceived threat to national identity have been the most potent bogies.

With regard to the threat to the supremacy of Parliament in the United Kingdom, we have already noted the dislike expressed by Euro-sceptics and others towards the primacy of European law and its direct effect within the UK jurisdiction. However, at the time of the 1992 Treaty of Maastricht, Ministers in the Major Administration began to argue that the process of European integration and the primacy of European law had reached a high-water mark, since the 'architecture' of the Treaty included two *international* (as opposed to supranational) pillars (foreign and security policy, and home affairs cooperation) and since the doctrine of 'subsidiarity' opened the way for the repatriation of at least some EU competences to the national level of decision making. In the event the passage of time has falsified this British analysis and nearly all the EU institutions have joined the drive towards a more supranational destiny.

As for the perceived threat of the European Union to British or indeed other national identities, such misgivings and fears cannot easily be dismissed because of their subjective character, but they can be rationally challenged by those who observe that the French seem no less French, the Germans no less German or the Italians no less Italian as a consequence of their long involvement in the process of European integration. The problem for the British in this regard seems to be that their sense of national identity is disproportionately bound up with some defining moments in their national history, such as 1940–41 when Britain stood defiantly alone against Hitler's Germany, and with the symbolic importance of the 'Crown in Parliament'– the formal way to describe Britain's constitutional Monarchy and Parliamentary democracy and which are not readily compatible with the habits and assumptions of much Continental custom and practice.

The substantial aspect of the debate about national sovereignty concerns the allocation of political and institutional *competences* between the various levels of government. It raises theoretical questions about whether or not the member states have a *legal right* to act unilaterally in the spheres covered by the European Treaties and more practical questions about whether or not they have *the capacity* to act effectively in those same areas of policy – an issue which has become particularly controversial in the modern global economy. No one really denies that each member state retains the right to act in defiance of European law – at the risk of being disciplined by the European Court of Justice – and the ultimate right to adopt an 'empty-chair' policy or even to leave the European Union altogether.[20] Yet in contemporary circumstances these are somewhat theoretical rights which run counter to the basic rationale for EU membership that each member state is, on balance, better off and more able to fulfil its objectives by pooling some portions of national sovereignty than by attempting autonomous action which is unlikely to be effective.

While a growing part of political and public opinion in Britain has become sceptical about pro-European arguments, an arcane and rather obscure discussion has developed about the allocation of governmental functions in the EU member states and the most appropriate levels of government at which these should be exercised. This debate hinges upon the concept of *subsidiarity*, an idea advocated by Jacques Delors when President of the European Commission (1985–95) and subsequently supported by the British and German Governments in particular.[21] The essence of the doctrine is that no new functions should be exercised at the supranational level in the EU which could more appropriately and effectively be exercised at national or subnational level. Indeed, this principle was reaffirmed in Article 1-11 (3) of the 2004 Treaty establishing a Constitution for Europe and in the Second Protocol which sought to ensure that 'decisions are taken as closely as possible to the citizens of the Union.'[22] However, it has made little difference to the day-to-day working of the EU institutions, especially the European Court of Justice which is still the final arbiter on the distribution of competences between the various levels of government.

Assuming that national powers and functions continue to levitate upwards to the EU level and gravitate downwards to the institutions of devolved and subnational government, many political theorists and practitioners believe that the current 'democratic deficit' in the European Union could get worse at the national level, unless the member state Governments can find convincing ways in which to give a greater role in EC decision making to national Parliaments and open up the proceedings of the Council of Ministers to the media and public gaze. If such reforms are not achieved, there is a danger of growing disenchantment, even alienation, in public attitudes towards the European project and this could lead to widespread rejection of both the methods and the goals of the European Union.

21.5 conclusion

We have seen in this chapter how Britain excluded herself from full participation in the early stages of European integration after the Second World War and how the country paid an economic and political price for this self-imposed exclusion. However, since joining the European Community in 1973, Britain has played a part in nearly all European developments, even if she has frequently been ranged on the side of those trying to slow the pace and limit the scope of European integration.

When New Labour came to power in 1997, it was opposed to the concept of a federal European superstate, preferring instead a European Union of nation states choosing to cooperate to achieve various objectives together which they could not achieve alone. This meant a willingness to pursue measures leading to the full realisation of the European Single Market, pushing hard for further enlargement of the European Union to the East, pressing for reform of the Common Agricultural Policy and the Common Fisheries Policy, and urging greater openness and democracy in the EU institutions. To achieve these goals, Britain has been willing to accept some extensions of qualified majority voting in the Council of Ministers, while seeking to retain the national veto in the core areas of national interest – taxation, public expenditure, industrial relations, immigration, security, defence and Treaty changes. On issues of European social policy, the Blair Administration was prepared to make concessions in 1997 when it signed the Social Chapter of the 1992 Maastricht Treaty which the previous Conservative Government had refused to sign. On the issue of Economic and Monetary Union, it has been positive in principle about the idea of Britain joining the project, but cautious in practice by insisting that five economic tests be satisfied before any decision of Government and Parliament is put to the British people in a national referendum.[23]

The reasons for this balanced, but cautious approach to deeper British involvement in the European Union have been well rehearsed in this chapter. All that need be added at this stage is that many of the misgivings felt in Britain about British membership of an ever closer European Union stem from the semi-detached stance taken by successive British Governments in their dealings with the Continent of Europe over decades, even centuries of history and, more recently, from the tendency for successive British Prime Ministers from Churchill to Blair to feel more comfortable in a 'special relationship' with the United States rather than an integrated political structure with the other member states of the European Union. Whatever happens in British politics over the coming years, Britain is almost certain to remain in the European Union, although the precise nature of her relationship with it and with the other member states may evolve in uncertain ways.

1   What impact has membership of the European Union had on British politics?

2   How profound and far-reaching are the legal and constitutional implications of Britain's membership of the European Union?

3   What seem likely to be the main driving forces and divisive issues in the European Union in the future, and in what ways are these likely to affect the course of British politics?

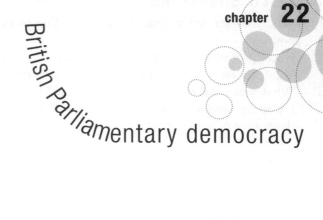

chapter 22

British Parliamentary democracy

British Parliamentary democracy has evolved over the centuries. From Simon de Montfort's Parliament in 1265 to the outbreak of the English Civil War in 1642, it was based upon the changing relations between the Monarch and the various Estates of the realm. By the time of the Bill of Rights in 1689 a more explicit constitutional contract had evolved between the Monarch's Government and the two Houses of Parliament. From then until the 1832 Reform Act Britain was essentially governed by the landed aristocracy. With successive extensions of the franchise from the 1867 Representation of the People Act to the 1969 Representation of the People Act, a recognisably modern democracy gradually emerged. The contemporary result of this long evolutionary process is that since the entry of the United Kingdom into the European Community in 1973, British politicians and people alike have lived in a Parliamentary democracy which is a constitutional monarchy within a partly supranational European Union.

22.1 essential characteristics

It can be said that there are a number of essential characteristics in British Parliamentary democracy. These have been widely recognised over many years and we shall take a closer look at each of these in turn.

a representative and accountable system

The first essential characteristic of British Parliamentary democracy is that it is a representative system which functions in a reasonably accountable way. By this we mean that MPs, who, within the limitations of their party affiliations, seek to represent all their constituents (and not simply the minority who voted for them), are regularly accountable to the electorate every four or five years at General Elections and, between elections, have to justify the positions they take on a weekly basis (when Parliament is sitting) to the media and the electorate. This has some advantages for the political system. It endows the Government of the day with a degree of democratic legitimacy, although a wise Government will not make extravagant claims in this regard or take its political authority for granted. It allows the electorate to deliver periodic verdicts upon the party in office and the competing attractions of the other parties. In the shape of the two Houses of Parliament it provides institutional channels of communication between the Government and the governed, although by no means the only channels in a pluralist political system in which the components of civil society are so significant. It can serve the useful purposes of magnifying or filtering the force of public opinion, depending upon the various issues which emerge and the assessments made by the various politicians of how best to handle the issues as they arise.

Notwithstanding these positive characteristics, the British form of Parliamentary democracy has not always been held in high repute. This is partly because the main political parties have too often been in the habit of raising their party-political conflicts above all other considerations. It is also because the nature of the political debate, as conveyed by the media, seems to be scarcely related, if at all, to the concerns and aspirations of the general public, but rather to a continuous form of party-political point scoring. The main result has been that public expectations have been seriously disappointed and large sections of public opinion (particularly among younger people) have felt alienated from the entire political process. In these circumstances it is not surprising that reformers in all parties and in none have argued for the one procedural change which might make a large and permanent difference to the British style of politics – namely, the introduction of some form of proportional representation for elections to Parliament at Westminster.

For as long as each of the two largest parties believe that they have more to lose than to gain from such a fundamental reform, things will continue much as they are. With the leading conventions of British politics still in place, it is argued that British representative democracy is essentially based upon an implicit contract between the Government and the people. Ministers accept that there are limits to the action they can properly and prudently take if they are to remain within the bounds of public tolerance and British constitutional convention. The British public accepts (often with deep reservations) that the party in office should be allowed considerable latitude in its attempts to fulfil its electoral mandate and, even more so, in its day-to-day government of the country.

The limits of public tolerance vary from time to time and from Government to Government. Much depends upon the extent to which Government policy runs counter to powerful opinion in vested interest groups and in the ever strident media. Much depends upon the perceived gravity of the situation with which Government has to deal on behalf of the whole community. Thus frantic efforts led by Ministers and other figures in authority to deal with imminent and ubiquitous threats from terrorists are not regarded by the general public with the same suspicion as the recurrent tendency of the main party political spokesmen to vie with one another over who can promise the most generous public spending on the NHS, education or public transport. Some issues will turn upon the likelihood of a policy reversal in the event that one of the Opposition parties wins power at the ensuing General Election. All in all, such limits are distinctly contingent and variable and cannot easily be determined in advance.

Those who are critical of the British political system argue that the power of the electorate is no more than indirect and intermittent, since it is usually confined to only a broad-brush choice between three or four parties, exercised only once every four or five years and unevenly distributed between marginal and so-called 'safe' constituencies. Yet even this assessment needs to be qualified in a number of significant ways.

Firstly, the ability to influence political decisions between General Elections is probably greater for those who are prepared to join political parties and pressure groups than for those who simply wait for a General Election every four or five years. Some may say this is perfectly fair, because it rewards participation by active citizens and penalises those who are too lazy or indifferent to stir themselves.

Secondly, the range of democratic choice at a General Election is usually rather limited and the outcome rather inequitable, since as a consequence of the *distribution* of party-political support in a first-past-the-post electoral system, it takes about 40,000 votes to elect a Labour MP, about 50,000 votes to elect a Conservative MP, but about 90,000 votes to elect a Liberal Democrat MP. Moreover, while voters may be lucky and get the Government that they want at national level, they are quite often unlucky and unable to get an MP who reflects their own party preferences at constituency level.

Thirdly, it may be added that the ignorance and apathy of many voters has led a large proportion of them not to vote at all at recent General Elections and, even more so, at local or European elections. This political apathy, amounting to alienation in some cases, produced a national turnout of just below 60 per cent in 2001 and just above 60 per cent in 2005, a disappointing level in each case which, if it were to become the norm, would further damage the respect in which elected politicians are held and the democratic legitimacy which they can command.

the vital role of political parties

The second essential characteristic of British Parliamentary democracy is the vital, but much criticised, role of political parties as the principal pool of talent from which Government and Opposition frontbenchers are chosen, the essential organisers of Parliamentary business through 'the usual channels' and the traditional forms of communication between the politicians and the electorate. In other words, for better or worse, British politics is party politics with all that this implies for partisanship and sometimes messy compromise in dealing with political issues both large and small.

In order to be clear about why the political parties still play such an important, if sometimes resented, role in British politics, it is worth bearing in mind that they simplify and organise the choices to be made by the electorate at every election – something which can be seen to have intrinsic value when contrasted with the uncertainties and even chaos associated with earlier models of 'independent' representation, for example in the eighteenth century when individual MPs could be 'bought' by the highest bidder. They also simplify and organise the conduct of Parliamentary business in both Houses of Parliament through the well-established networks of Government and Opposition, frontbenchers and backbenchers, Whips and their party flocks. Modern MPs and peers can be very busy people with a multiplicity of different commitments and claims upon their time. It is the Party Whips and business managers working through the 'usual channels' who enable Parliamentary politics to be conducted in a reasonably orderly and effective way. Without Party loyalties and Party discipline the system would break down and the Government of the day would be unable to govern the country in fulfilment of its election pledges and with a minimum of democratic legitimacy.

Of course, it is quite obvious that the political parties are by no means the only intermediaries in the British political system or even necessarily the most influential and this reality is perhaps reflected in the low and declining figures for paid-up membership in all the main parties. However, they still manage to channel the energies of political activists and to represent a wide variety of economic and social interests in Britain's pluralist and multicultural society. As long as the parties perform their representative tasks with a degree of effectiveness, those who have political interests to defend or causes to advance should feel it possible to do so within these familiar structures. As and when this ceases to be the case and the general reputation of the parties begins to languish in the minds of the media and the general public, there may be growing concern for the health of British Parliamentary democracy.

the complexity of modern government

The third essential characteristic of British Parliamentary democracy in its contemporary setting is the complexity of modern government. This is reflected in a number of obvious ways, such as the large and growing volume of Government-sponsored legislation and other instruments of regulation. It is also reflected in the myriad of groups and established interests which constantly seek to influence or capture the policy and decision making of every Government. In such circumstances it is difficult for national Government to hold the ring and define the national interest when faced with the need to reconcile so many conflicting and often mutually exclusive interests. It is even more difficult when any effective solution to a large political or economic problem may require agreed international action by a wide range of other national Governments and economic interests all of which have their own difficulties in balancing short-term selfish interests with the long-term interest of the global community.

For example, it is widely (but by no means universally) agreed that urgent action must be taken at an international level to curb the growth of carbon emissions and other greenhouse gases and so reduce the level of global warming. The British Government and many other national Governments signed the Kyoto Protocol in 1997 in order to help bring this about and at the time of writing a total of 141 countries have ratified the agreement which is officially known as the United Nations Framework Convention on Climate Change. Yet the range of conflicting economic and social interests which are affected by such a policy, both in Britain and worldwide, is so large that it is dubious whether much progress will be achieved before ecological disaster strikes. The problem is not so much in the scientific controversy, but in the realm of political will among those at the helm of some of the largest resource users in the world – such as the United States, India, China and Brazil.

Another contemporary example of almost bewildering complexity which faces national Governments and the agencies of law and order is the problem of global terrorism. This pathological condition takes many different forms in many different countries, but it is national Governments which tend to be held responsible by the media and the law-abiding public for dealing with it and for putting in place effective measures to safeguard the safety of their peoples. Their tasks are made more difficult by the porous and anonymous nature of modern society which provides terrorists and their sponsors with numerous loopholes through which they can slip in order to escape detection and capture. Yet ironically it is the very freedoms and human rights, which many of these same Governments have insisted upon enshrining in legislation and in their constitutions, that provide members of the independent judiciary, whether in Britain or other jurisdictions, with the opportunity and the obligation to strike down or amend some of the very measures which Governments introduce in their attempts to safeguard the security of their peoples.

In arriving at a balanced assessment of this aspect of the political system, one of the most appropriate questions to ask is how far any Government genuinely seeks to represent and defend the general interest and how far it demonstrates an ability to do so without simply equating the general interest with its own partisan view of the world. Too great an emphasis upon self-serving political objectives – such as Tony Blair's repeated insistence that Britain's experience of terrorist attacks in London had nothing to do with his willingness to approve Britain's participation in the American invasion and occupation of Iraq – lays any Government open to charges of self-serving duplicity. On the other hand, too much cynicism about the motives and ideas behind political decision making at any level of government exposes the general public to levels of ignorance and misunderstanding which can erode public trust in even the most reputable political system.

22.2 other significant features

British Parliamentary democracy has had some other significant features which need to be taken into consideration if we are to get a complete picture of it in modern conditions. Each of the following features has assumed importance at particular times, but all have shaped the British political system in varied and sometimes conflicting ways.

political polarisation and political consensus

The tendency towards political polarisation in Britain has deep historical roots in the eighteenth-century struggle between Whigs and Tories and the nineteenth-century struggle between the Liberals and the Conservatives. During most of the twentieth century it was the Conservative and Labour parties which slugged it out with each other, sometimes in a spirit of considerable class bitterness and recrimination. For example, in the 1970s and 1980s the two main parties became particularly polarised, partly as a function of internal dissatisfaction within each of the parties with the way in which their former leaders, Harold Wilson and Edward Heath, had followed what were perceived to be misguided or vacillating policies, but mainly because it had become clear by the mid 1970s that the post-war consensus had run its course. The result of these matching developments was that by the mid 1980s politics in Britain was more polarised than at any time since the 1930s.

This state of affairs was in marked contrast to the much more limited party-political differences between 1951 and 1970 when each of the main parties broadly accepted what came to be known as the post-war political consensus. Equally the period under John Major, Tony Blair and Gordon Brown from 1990 to the present day has been characterised by another kind of political consensus based upon post-Thatcherite economics coupled with a mild dose of New Labour social policy designed to equalise social opportunities while limiting any redistribution of income or wealth that would alienate the middle class.

In many ways it is rather surprising that, in a political system which is better known for its power-hoarding than its power-sharing, there should have been such long periods of relatively benign and non-controversial political consensus.[1] The explanation seems to be that many members of the British public feel distinctly uncomfortable with party-political conflict and tend to gravitate quite naturally towards passive acceptance of whatever form of political hegemony may apply at the time. Another explanation may be that during periods of power-sharing and political consensus the Liberals and, more recently, the Liberal Democrats have been able to act as a stabilising influence, at any rate in local and devolved government where they have been partners with Labour in relatively successful coalition Administrations.

A standard criticism of the British political system used to be that power can be abused whenever a single party in office at national level has behaved as virtually 'an elective dictatorship'.[2] This temptation has been there for many years, at least since the achievment of universal adult suffrage in 1928 and especially when the winning party at a General Election is able to collect around 60 per cent of the seats in the Commons on the basis of between 35 and 50 per cent of the votes cast. However, such an abuse of political power tended to be alleged only by the losing parties at any General Election and was not necessarily borne out by the passage of events. The reality has usually been that beyond the twin citadels of political power at the national level in Britain – Whitehall and Westminster – all Governments have had to share power and allow significant influence to a wide variety of private and voluntary, subnational and supranational interests if they are to govern successfully in the modern world.

institutional inertia

Institutional inertia is another significant feature of the British political system which tends to coexist with the political polarisation already described. Although a large number of institutional reforms have been made in Britain over many decades – for example, frequent reforms of local government, the introduction of devolution, successive waves of Civil Service reform and, most recently, the Blairite drive to 'modernise' both Government and Parliament – few of the changes have been an unqualified success and all have entailed considerable, often unforeseen, consequences. This has led those who are inherently sceptical about institutional change to insist that such initiatives often do more harm than good and are not necessarily a remedy for political problems which may be attitudinal or cultural in origin. They have also argued that the organisational upheaval which such changes can bring in their wake entails a level of extra cost and disruption which is inimical to the interests of good government.

On the other hand, there is a strong case which can be made for modernisation and reform, especially when the needs and expectations of the public are rising fast and the context within which public services are delivered is changing all the time. In simple terms, Governments, politicians and public institutions have to run to stand still and cannot safely assume that practices which worked well 10 or 20 years ago will serve as well today. The pace of technological change is one of the factors which brings this situation about – for example, the application to the public services of computerised networks intended to retain and reconcile diverse bits of information is revolutionising the ways in which Departments and Agencies of Government cooperate and the ways in which they interact with stakeholders and the users or beneficiaries of public services. As more state functions are privatised or put out to competitive tender, the influence of private-sector experience and methods of working upon the performance of public-sector tasks is another dynamic factor which can have far reaching effects upon the ways in which politicians and officials discharge their duties as laid down in legislation and regulations.

In the end nearly everything depends upon the perceived needs of the times, the policies favoured by the politicians in office and the balance of political forces in Parliament. Indeed, a dispassionate look at the performance of the Labour Government since 1997 bears out Lord Irvine's claim that 'principled pragmatism' has been the basis of many of Labour's institutional and constitutional reforms. Sometimes these reflected a sense of political urgency, as with the commitment to devolution for Scotland; sometimes they reflected a well-considered attempt to deal with widely acknowledged gaps or shortcomings in Britain's constitutional arrangements, as with the Political Parties, Elections and Referendums Act 2000. In any event, few fair-minded observers would say that Labour Ministers have allowed much institutional inertia to take hold since 1997.

shrinking national sovereignty

A growing theme in this and earlier editions of the book has been the diminished scope for effective action in the modern world by national Governments and, indeed, all national authorities. This amounts to shrinking national sovereignty and there are several good reasons for the diminished power and status of national institutions in Britain and other developed countries.

One reason is that in a modern pluralist society the successful implementation of policy often depends upon at least the tacit acquiescence, if not the active support, of those stakeholders and members of the public most directly affected by the policy. As examples, it is only necessary to reflect upon the successful campaign of opposition to the Poll Tax in the late 1980s and early 1990s or the cautionary influence of the Ulster Unionists in the long drawn out 'peace process' in Northern Ireland. Equally, New Labour Ministers since 1997 have been strongly committed to timely stakeholder consultations and have built this process systematically into the preparations for every Government Bill and every major Ministerial decision – so much so that its absence might be adversely commented upon by the High Court if a Ministerial decision were subjected to judicial review.

Another reason for the reduced power of national Governments is that many problems in the world today are not really susceptible to solutions imposed by politicians and civil servants through legislation or administrative action. Rather they require action to be taken by individuals, families and private organisations exercising free choices within the law. The cautionary tale of Conservative Government attempts to implement a social policy under the banner of 'Back to Basics' in 1993–94 served to illustrate the point, as did the more recent attempts by the Labour Government to bring about radical changes in the eating and drinking habits of the general population as a contribution to the campaign against obesity. In another sphere of activity, some transactions in the financial services sector are so opaque and sophisticated – for example, equity and bond derivatives or pension scheme investments in hedge funds – that officials and regulators find it hard to keep pace with the innovation in the private sector and even when they do, such activities may move 'off-shore' to preserve their market advantages.

The most significant reason why national Governments and national authorities are suffering from shrinking 'sovereignty' – a word perhaps most usefully defined as 'the capacity and exclusive right to determine what happens in your own territory or to citizens of your own nationality' – is that they do not operate easily on the levels required to match the most significant developments in the global economy. For example, organised crime, international terrorism, illegal migration, financial engineering, software development and fossil-fuel depletion are all areas of human activity which have tended to stay several steps ahead of the national Governments and regulatory bodies which seek to monitor tax and control them. In these circumstances the best that national authorities have been able to do has been to combine their jurisdictional power and influence through international organisations – such as Interpol, the World Health Organisation and the Bank for International Settlements – and occasionally to go one stage further by creating supranational organisations with supranational jurisdictions, such as the European Union, the World Trade Organization and the International Criminal Court.

The dilemma for any British Government, and indeed all other national authorities, is that if they persist in making claims to 'the capacity and exclusive right to determine' what happens in their territory and to their citizens, they are likely to disappoint their clientele and discredit themselves in the eyes of their electorates, because of their almost certain inability to deliver much of what they promise. On the other hand, if they give up many of their traditional rights and claims, their peoples may look elsewhere for satisfaction of their material needs, social aspirations and collective security.

22.3 lessons from the past and signposts to the future

At the beginning of the new century we can already discern some of the most significant trends and issues which are likely to influence the scope and nature of British politics for years to come. Among the most significant of these trends are likely to be:

- The spread of modernisation in all its forms
- The ambiguity of Britain's commitment to the EU
- The emergence of serious threats to democracy in a multicultural world.

The extent to which the British and other political systems manage to make sense of and handle these challenges will go a long way towards determining whether they can keep the principal hallmark of any sound democracy – the ability to gain and retain the consent of the people.

limited scope for setting the political agenda

It may seem to be a paradox that although successive Governments in Britain since 1945 have sought to make a significant mark upon British society and advance the well-being of the British people, there have been relatively few developments of lasting significance which have been brought about or even validated by politicians in office. In a short list one might well cite: the establishment of the National Health Service and the granting of independence to India in the late 1940s; the decolonisation of much of the British Empire and the beginnings of ethnic minority immigration in the 1950s and 1960s; the entry of Britain into the European Community and the erosion of the post-war political consensus in the 1970s; the abolition of exchange controls and the spread of privatisation in the 1980s; the departure of sterling from the European Exchange Rate Mechanism and the closer alignment of British and American interests in both financial and military matters in the 1990s; the application of 'modernisation' to Government and the impact of globalisation upon Britain's economy and society in the first decade of the twenty-first century. It is noteworthy that few of these developments are confined to Britain's domestic jurisdiction and that increasingly it is the impact of the rest of the world upon Britain rather than the impact of Britain upon the rest of the world which matters most.

The explanation for this situation is that any national Government has only limited means at its disposal with which to shape society and no guarantee that, even when it does so, its achievements will stand the test of time. Essentially, national Governments can act in one or more of the following ways: they can introduce new or amended policies by Ministerial decision; they can persuade their national Parliaments to change or amend the law; they can create, reform or abolish institutions; and they can modify or transform public attitudes by the use of rhetoric, argument, manipulation or political symbolism. Successive British Governments have used some or all of these methods in their quest for success.

In the 1950s and early 1960s British Governments attempted only fairly minor policy adjustments within a well-defined and broadly accepted political consensus which had been in place since the late 1940s. In the later 1960s and the 1970s successive Governments concentrated more upon trying to make necessary institutional changes – for example, in the legal status of trade unions – as a way of modernising Britain's under-performing economy. In the 1980s under Margaret Thatcher's leadership the British people were subjected to a programme of radical economic and social change comparable in its significance to the great radical Administrations of the past – notably, the Liberal Government of 1906 to 1916 and the Labour Government of 1945 to 1951. Great claims have been made for the positive impact of 'Thatcherism' and it is fair to say that its ideological legacy has been apparent to a greater or lesser extent ever since. Yet a sober verdict upon the Thatcher years (1979–90) would be that while a sizeable minority of the British people learned to seize their individual opportunities in an era of economic liberalism, the vast majority were either unwilling or unable to change their attitudes and their behaviour to take full advantage of what was offered to them by the Thatcherite revolution.

Nevertheless some of the main themes of Thatcherism survived under the subsequent Administrations led by John Major, Tony Blair and Gordon Brown. Indeed, Lord Tebbit (a member of Margaret Thatcher's praetorian guard) offered the opinion some years later that his leader's greatest political achievement had been to transform British politics to such an extent that it became safe for the voters to elect a Labour Government.[3] We can see evidence for this claim in the prudent macro-economic policy pursued by Chancellor Gordon Brown which eschewed any change in the symbolically important rates of income tax and gave operational independence to the Bank of England in the conduct of monetary policy. We can also see it in some rhetorical aspects of the whole 'New Labour project' articulated by Tony Blair who (in domestic policy at any rate) tried not to frighten the middle classes or incur the wrath of the Daily Mail and The Sun.

modernisation – an elastic and elusive theme

Much has already been written, in this volume and elsewhere, about the significance of modernisation in all its forms for the British Government and the British body politic. Yet such an elastic and elusive theme in the New Labour project has been important to the domestic credibility of the Labour Government. As a device of political rhetoric, it has helped to position successive Blair Administrations at the head of a progressive consensus stretching well beyond the Labour party, while avoiding the pitfalls of any association with the class warfare beloved of many Old Labour politicians. As an approach to policy and decision making, it has encouraged civil servants and others involved in public policy to approach their tasks in a joined-up and rational way using demonstrable evidence, pragmatic argument and rigorous evaluation. When applied to the delivery of public services, it has helped to justify a more commercial and business-like approach designed to treat all citizens more like customers than passive recipients of state-funded and state-organised entitlements or benefits.

Modernisation has also been the term applied by New Labour to its piecemeal reforms of both Houses of Parliament. In the *House of Commons*, the emphasis has been upon changing and shortening the hours of business during the Parliamentary week in order to enable MPs to spend more time with their families and in their constituencies, while assisting the Government business managers by timetabling all Government Bills and experimenting with the carry over of a few Bills from one session to the next. The general thrust has been to reduce opportunities for the traditional Opposition tactics of delay and obstruction, while ensuring that the Government gets its legislative business (at least in the Lower House) at a time of its choosing and, as far as possible, with the support of reasonably contented backbenchers on its own side.

In the *House of Lords* the cause of modernisation has been more difficult to impose because, in spite of the removal of all but 92 of the hereditary peers via the House of Lords Act 1999 and despite the fact that Labour has now become the largest single party in the House, there remain four serious obstacles in its path. The *first* is that in the 2001–05 Parliament, when these matters were debated and voted upon at Westminster, the House of Commons was not able to agree on any approach to the reform of the membership of the House of Lords. The *second* is that any reform has to be acceptable to the majority of members of the House of Lords itself and, as has often been observed, 'turkeys do not vote for an early Christmas'. The *third* is that there is disagreement between those reformers seeking to alter the composition but leave the powers and functions of the House as there are, and those who would alter both the composition and the powers and functions – while within that category there exist those who would seek to strengthen the powers of a reformed House and those who would seek to reduce the powers of a reformed House. The *fourth* is that any plan for workable and sustainable reform needs to tackle the challenges of the two Houses together rather than each House separately. Until solutions to these problems can be found, it seems unlikely that comprehensive and durable reform will be achieved or, if achieved, be effective.

Europe or America – which model for Britain?

One of the great strategic questions facing any British Government is whether it should be a major policy objective to get closer to our partners in the European Union or to the United States of America. On the one hand, there is the school of thought which suggests that it is from the Continent of Europe that most of the threats to these islands have come and therefore we in Britain are better off keeping our distance from any political or economic arrangements on the Continent rather than committing ourselves to closer alliance or deeper integration with any Continental Power, including the power block now represented by the European Union. This school of thought, which might be termed 'Churchillian' with its preference for the inherent unity of the English-speaking peoples, holds that the experience of the twentieth century demonstrates the wisdom and attractions for Britain of aligning its policy and interests with those of the United States, our strongest and most reliable ally in two world wars and in other times of trouble. It is a view of the world which has been strongly endorsed by Margaret Thatcher and other Atlanticist interests in Britain, including multinational business, the military and the security services.

On the other hand, there is the school of thought associated with the pro-European Movement in Britain which for years has been of the view that Britain's future lies at the heart of Europe as a full and constructive member of the European Union. This was a strong strand of opinion among those with personal memories of the Second World War and its aftermath, such as Sir Edward Heath and Lord (Roy) Jenkins, and others of later generations, such as John Smith and Robin Cook, who were convinced by the political arguments for European integration. Such people and their political disciples have deplored the increasing Euro-scepticism of many parts of the British media and a majority of British public opinion which for the past eight years or so has turned the leadership of the Conservative Party and a good part of the Labour Party against the idea of unqualified British participation in the European Union. The result is that nowadays there are fewer politically influential people both in Britain and in other member states who see great merit in totemic European projects, such as Economic and Monetary Union or a codified European constitution. It is, therefore, increasingly hard to counter the argument that an exclusively European destiny for Britain is in fact an outdated model for this country's future.

This leaves a rather trite, third alternative future for Britain as a 'bridge' between Europe and America – a metaphor which Tony Blair has been fond of using in some of his speeches and public statements, especially since Britain joined the United States in the invasion and occupation of Iraq.[4] In some ways this is the same idea as Winston Churchill's 'three circles' (of Europe, the Empire and Commonwealth, and the 'special relationship' with America) which he so strongly advocated in the late 1940s and early 1950s. In that sense it appears that many of the British political elite have made no progress in their geopolitical thinking for more than 50 years.

Of course, the debate about the relative attractions for the British people of Continental Europe and North America raises more than just issues of foreign policy. Fundamentally, it concerns the choice between two competing models of capitalism: the Anglo-American liberal market model and the Franco-German social market model. The former favours maximum privatisation and minimum state interference through politically inspired regulation. The latter is often reluctant to privatise large state utilities and prefers to run the economy on corporatist lines with the approval of the 'social partners'. The former is comfortable with individual success or failure, whereas the latter prefers to deal with collective interests and favours high levels of state-sponsored or state-financed social protection. Notwithstanding these differences on each side of the Atlantic, in Britain the pervasive influence of American-owned big business, cheap international travel and communications, and trans-Atlantic popular culture conveyed in something approximating to a common language has brought many younger people decisively into the North American camp – so much so that in terms of social behaviour and public attitudes Britain has appeared to some to resemble the fifty-first state of the United States.

threats to democracy in a multicultural world

In recent years it has become something of a commonplace to point out that one of the most significant aspects of globalisation has been to make nation states more porous to immigration both legal and illegal as thousands or even millions (globally) of people from poor or destitute countries move to seek new opportunities and a better life in Britain and other advanced post-industrial societies. This means that the national authorities in Britain and similar countries have had to work out how best to deal with the social problems which can arise from rapidly changing demography in their own national jurisdictions and especially in the large conurbations where newly arrived immigrants tend to congregate. This, in turn, highlights both the challenges and the opportunities of multiculturalism in all its various manifestations.

In Britain, where the immigrant population is still less than 10 per cent of the total, it is possible for older generations in the longer-established population to look back to a time in the fairly recent past when both the political class and the general public were relatively homogeneous and uniform in their national identity which could reasonably be characterised as white, Anglo-Saxon and protestant. However, it is also necessary to look forward to a time when multiculturalism becomes such a defining characteristic of our society that it produces competing local or universal loyalties which may undermine the sense of nationhood and shared national values that are essential if British Parliamentary democracy is to continue working satisfactorily.

Any attempt to deconstruct the idea of 'British Parliamentary democracy' in this context reveals that each of the three component terms is more problematic than it used to be. Notions of 'Britishness' are not as clear cut as they were when they connoted white, Anglo-Saxon and protestant in the years before large-scale immigration, both legal and illegal, began to change the demographic and cultural composition in the United Kingdom. Received ideas about Parliament as the unchallenged source of legal authority and democratic legitimacy in this country have had to be re-examined in the light of incursive European law and the decline of public respect for Parliamentarians which is manifest in relatively low turnout at General Elections. The traditional attachment to democracy as a superior form of government is no longer shared, if it ever was, by significant sections of public opinion in Britain, notably those who feel alienated from mainstream British political culture and those of the Islamic faith and some Christian fundamentalists who believe more in the rule of God than in the rule of the people. There is therefore due cause to be somewhat pessimistic about the outlook for British Parliamentary democracy, especially if the current attempts to defend the British way of life from terrorist attacks and Islamic suicide bombers have the unintended consequence of coarsening our democracy and abridging human rights.

Democracy in Britain and in other democratic countries has tended to require a self-conscious national people (*demos*) as its essential foundation and building material. It is, however, open to challenge by any transnational or universal movement, faith or religion which demands a superior loyalty from its members. In the current world order people are citizens of nation states or subjects of monarchs (or both in the case of Britain) and as such they are supposed to be loyal to their country (*patria*) and to abide by its laws and customs. If they are also true believers in a collective religion or sect, they can be expected to be loyal to their faith and to abide by its laws and customs. This is where questions of identity can raise problems in a multicultural society such as Britain today, because many people with multiple identities will have a hierarchy of possibly conflicting loyalties and may not necessarily put their political nationality and civic duties above their membership of a universal religion or even a cult. It is possible that for some people in Britain such conflicts of identity and personality will become so hard to resolve that sections of our multicultural society will begin to fragment with damaging consequences for the legitimacy of our national institutions and the cohesion of our national society.

the importance of consent

In the final analysis all these considerations emphasise the fundamental importance of public consent in any arrangements which have to be made to bind our national democracy together. Of course, in many cases little more than the tacit acquiescence of the general public will suffice. Yet for assured commitment and success active public consent is usually required and this implies meeting a number of important conditions:

- The involvement of a well-informed and representative Parliament in which all MPs and peers who are not in the Government have real opportunities to influence policy and to scrutinise and control the Executive
- Genuine and extensive involvement in the political process for the wide range of economic, social and cultural groups which make up the mosaic of contemporary British society
- A serious and responsible approach by all elements of the media to the reporting, discussion and interpretation of the political issues of the day with due attention being paid to the cultural sensitivities of minority elements in society.

Even if all these conditions are met, the achievement of good government can still be vitiated by a wide range of complicated and unexpected factors which can be grouped under the general heading of 'events', as Harold Macmillan once memorably pointed out.

Furthermore, if any British Government is to deal successfully with the most intractable problems of our time – for example, the scourge of terrorism, the emergence of global warming, or the financing of pension and other welfare arrangements for an ageing population – there will always be a premium upon responsible and far-sighted leadership from politicians and other opinion formers. In a world in which some things change very rapidly while other things seem to change hardly at all, such leadership will require both judgement and determination and the ability to change one's mind when the situation changes. Even on the optimistic assumption that people get the leaders they need rather than those they deserve, it will not be possible to avoid periodic disappointments and we should be psychologically prepared for those as well.

22.4 conclusion

It should be clear from this book that British Parliamentary democracy is neither easy to describe nor to explain. Moreover, it is not very easy to defend some of its more traditional manifestations. Although it has undergone frequent changes, in many ways it has remained recognisably the same. It is imbued with fascinating paradoxes and several contradictions. While the political system allows for and even encourages strong government, it is less good at legitimising the decisions actually taken or inspiring the trust and confidence of the people. This is because some of the most controversial decisions are not founded upon a sufficiently broad basis of public consent. Yet it also seems to derive from a tendency to will the ends but not necessarily the means and a failure to see the wood for the trees.

We have seen how the political mould set during and just after the Second World War was finally broken by Margaret Thatcher's brand of Conservatism in the early 1980s, just as in the world at large the long era of the Cold War was finally brought to an end by the collapse of Communism in the late 1980s. Since the late 1990s Westminster and Whitehall have been under the spell of New Labour whose Parliamentary hegemony has been based at successive General Elections upon something between 35 and 40 per cent of the votes cast and little more than one-quarter of those entitled to vote. The outlook now for our particular form of Parliamentary democracy is probably more problematic than it has been at any time since the 1970s when there was widespread discussion about whether Britain was governable. Yet we have weathered many storms in the past, so there is no decisive reason why we should not deal successfully with those of the present and the future.

SUGGESTED QUESTIONS

1   What is the essence of British Parliamentary democracy?
2   Is the British political system successful in gaining and retaining the consent of the people?
3   Can British Parliamentary democracy survive the challenges posed by globalisation?

Chapter 1

1. See D. Kavanagh, 'Political Culture in Great Britain: The Decline of the Civic Culture' in G. Almond, and S. Verba (eds), *The Civic Culture Revisited* (Boston: Little, Brown, 1980), pp. 136–62.
2. R. Butt, *A History of Parliament: The Middle Ages* (London: Constable, 1989), p. 2.
3. *Ibid.*, p. 60.
4. The Dunning Motion – a resolution by John Dunning in April 1780 and approved by 233 votes to 190. See: J. Brooke, *King George III* (London: Constable, 1992), pp. 201–18.
5. On 11 September 1997, on a turnout of 60.16 per cent, 74.29 per cent of the Scottish electorate voted in favour of there being a Scottish Parliament, and 63.48 per cent agreed that such a Parliament should have tax-varying powers.
6. For example, in 2005 voters of South Asian ethnicity accounted for 51.2 per cent of all voters in Birmingham Sparkbrook & Small Heath, and almost 40.0 per cent in Bethnal Green & Bow. See *General Election 2005*, House of Commons Library, Research Paper 05/33, 17 May 2005, p61.
7. For example, many more women now go out to work than in former times and in some households women are now the principal or sole earners.
8. In 1995 a report from the Joseph Rowntree foundation ('Inquiry into Income and Wealth', February 1995) chronicled the widening of the gap between rich and poor during the 1980s to the point where, by 1992–93, one in four people was living on income below half the national average. In 1996 a report entitled 'Poverty: The Facts' published by the Child Poverty Action Group claimed that poverty was widespread and had grown alarmingly since 1979, explaining that by 1992 24 per cent of the population (13.7 million) were on or below the level of income support – while in 1979 the proportion had been 14 per cent; and that by 1992–93 25 per cent of the population (14.1 million) were on incomes less than half the average after allowing for housing costs – in 1979 the proportion had been just 9 per cent. Having said this, however, a study by Alissa Goodman and Steven Webb for the Institute for Fiscal Studies, entitled 'For Richer, For Poorer; The Changing Distribution of Income in the United Kingdom, 1961–91' (IFS Commentary No. 42, June 1994), showed that the increase in income inequality during the 1980s dwarfed the fluctuations in inequality seen in previous decades. The income share of the poorest tenth of

the population fell back from 4.2 per cent in 1961 to 3 per cent in 1991 with most of this fall occurring during the 1980s. By contrast the share of the richest tenth of the population rose from 22 per cent to 25 per cent over the three decades. In 1999 an assessment by the New Policy Institute stated that although some key indicators of social exclusion were getting better, there was 'no general pattern of improvement' and that some inequalities may be getting worse. At the beginning of 2000 figures from the OECD showed that Britain had the worst record for deprivation in the West, with poverty affecting 20 per cent of the population. According to a report published in December 2006, despite significant reductions in the levels of both child poverty and pensioner poverty, poverty among working-age adults had not been reduced. (See G. Palmer, T. MacInnes and P. Kenway, *Monitoring Poverty and Social Exclusion 2006* (York: Joseph Rowntree Foundation, 2006). For further information see: http://poverty.org.uk.

9. See A. H. Birch, *The British System of Government*, 9th edn (London: Allen & Unwin, 1993).

10. See: N. Nugent *The Government and Politics of the European Union*, 6th edn (London: Palgrave, 2006) and D. Dinan, *Ever Closer Union*, (London: Palgrave, 2005).

11. For example, see: P. D. William, *British Foreign Policy under New Labour 1997– 2005* (London: Palgrave, 2005); A. Forster, and A. Blair, *The Making of Britain's European Foreign Policy* (London: Longman, 2002); and J. Redwood, *The Death of Britain?* (London: Macmillan, 1999).

Chapter 2

1. Thomas Paine for example declared that unless a constitution could be produced 'in visible form, there is none'.

2. House of Lords Select Committee on the Constitution, *Reviewing the Constitution: Terms of Reference and Method of Working, Session 2001–02*, First Report, HL Paper 11 (London: Stationery Office, 2001), p.9.

3. Namely, it had evolved gradually over a long period of time rather than being derived from a particular moment in history – a 'revolutionary' moment as in the case of France and the United States – or 'break' from the past as in the case of both (West) Germany and Japan after the Second World War and, more recently, both Afghanistan and Iraq.

4. Although the European Convention on Human Rights was finally incorporated into domestic UK law in 1998 with the passage of the Human Rights Act, the British courts were not given the power to set aside primary legislation on the grounds of incompatibility with the Act, only the right to bring such incompatibility to the attention of Parliament.

5. William Blackstone, who was professor of Common Law at Oxford University, published his famous *Commentaries upon the Laws of England between 1765 and 1769*. In that work he presented a clear and systematic description of English law in the mid-eighteenth century. Walter Bagehot was equally famous in the nineteenth century for his great work, *The English Constitution*, which was published in 1867. This set out what he saw as the principles of British Parliamentary democracy at that time. Sir Ivor Jennings, with his *Cabinet Government, Parliament and The*

British Constitution, was perhaps the best-known and most authoritative writer on British constitutional law and practice in the middle of the twentieth century.

6. See W. Bagehot, *The English Constitution* (London: Fontana, 1978) and A. V. Dicey, *The Law of the Constitution* (London: Macmillan, 1959).

7. See R. H. S. Crossman's Introduction to W. Bagehot, *The English Constitution,* p. 35.

8. See L. S. Amery, *Thoughts on the Constitution* (Oxford: OUP, 1947), and H. Morrison, *Government and Parliament* (Oxford: OUP, 1959).

9. L. S. Amery, *Thoughts on the Constitution,* p. 32.

10. See Q. Hailsham, *The Dilemma of Democracy* (London: Collins, 1978) for an exposition of this argument.

11. For a fuller discussion of this subject see D. E. Butler and A. Ranney (eds), *Referendums: A Comparative Study of Practice and Theory* (Washington, DC: American Enterprise Institute, 1978), V. Bogdanor, *The People and the Party System* (Cambridge: CUP, 1981), pp. 11–93 and C. H. de Vreese, (ed.), *Dynamics of Referendum Campaigns: An International Perspective,* (London: Palgrave, 2007).

12. In the event the vote in Scotland recorded 52 per cent of those who voted in favour and 48 per cent against, while the vote in Wales recorded a mere 20 per cent of those who voted in favour and 80 per cent against. This meant that in the Scottish case only 33 per cent of the qualified electorate voted 'Yes' and in the Welsh case only 12 per cent.

13. See: M. Sandford, and P. Hetherington, 'The Regions at the Crossroads: The Future for Sub-National Government in England' in A. Trench, (ed.), *The Dynamics of Devolution: The State of the Nations 2005* (London: The Constitution Unit, 2005), pp. 91–113.

14. See Chapter 21.

15. See Chapter 21.

16. Gordon Brown, cited in *The Guardian,* 29 January 2007.

17. George Osborne, Annual Olsen Memorial Lecture, 'Politics and the Media in the Internet Age', 14 November 2006.

18. Internet Access, Office for National Statistics, 23 August 2006, http://www.statistics.gov.uk/CCI.

19. For a fuller exposition of this argument see C. Graham and T. Prosser, *Waiving the Rules: The Constitution under Thatcherism* (Milton Keynes: Open University Press, 1988).

20. Charter 88 was launched in London as a non-party political movement on 29 November 1988. It took the view that fundamental liberties were insufficiently protected by the British constitution, since liberty in Britain was based not so much on a set of rules as a state of mind. It therefore called for a codified constitution, electoral reform, a new Bill of Rights, reform of the House of Lords, reform of the judiciary, and more equitable power sharing between central and local government. The other seven points recommended in Charter 88 were: the subjection of executive and prerogative power to the rule of law; the introduction of freedom of information and more open government; the creation of a democratically elected, non-hereditary House of Lords; control of the Executive by a democratically renewed Parliament; legal remedies against the abuse of power by central or local government; a more equitable distribution of power between the various levels of

Government; and a written and codified constitution anchored in the principle of universal citizenship.

21. See 'Blair: A Modern Tradegy. The Definitive Guide to the Tony Blair Era', *The Spectator* (supplement), 12 May 2007 and 'The Blair Years 1997–2007, *The Observer*, 8 April 2007.

22. See White Paper, *Modernising Government*, Cm 4310, (London: Stationery Office, 1999).

Chapter 3

1. See P. Norris and C. Wlezien (eds), *Britain Votes 2005*, (Oxford: University Press, 2005).

2. The figures stated here do not include the results from the constituency of South Staffordshire where the vote was postponed due to the death of the Liberal Democrat candidate. An election for this seat took place on Thursday 23 June.

3. The four Boundary Commissions – on each for England, Scotland, Wales and Northern Ireland – are advisory non-departmental public bodies required by the Parliamentary Constituencies 1986 Act, as amended, to keep Parliamentary constituencies under continuous review and periodically (every 8 to 12 years) to conduct a General Review of the number, boundaries and names of all Parliamentary constituencies, and make recommendations. See: http://www.statistics.gov.uk.

4. With the exception of Harlow, all the constituencies within Great Britain had declared by 2.00pm on the afternoon of Friday 6 May. The results from Northern Ireland were declared between 2.18pm and 9.41pm on Friday 6 May.

5. Mr Justice Richard Mawrey, cited in *The Times*, 5 April 2005.

6. According to a survey in *The Times* postal vote applications rose substantially in the following constituencies:
Cheadle: 485% to 8,226
Dorset South: 192% to 6,557
Thanet South: 219% to 1,129
Dorset Mid and North Poole: 318% to 4,306
Rugby and Kenilworth: 207% to 6,847
Norfolk North: 163% to 6,323
Weston-super-Mare: 240% to 6,323
Braintree: 333% to 10,000
Taunton: 282% to 11,700
Orpington: 246% to 6,429
See: BBC web news, 15 April 2005.

7. *Securing the Vote* (London: The Electoral Commission, 2005).

8. *Electoral Administration Act 2006*, ISBN 0 10 542206 1, (London: Stationery Office, 2006).

9. This is stipulated in the Representation of the People Act 1981 and was a direct result of the Bobby Sands case in Northern Ireland.

10. These figures are periodically reviewed and increased if needs be. Under the rules, separate, higher, limits apply in the case of Parliamentary by-elections. In 2005 the basis was £100,000.

11. In the 2005 General Election the average amount spent by candidates was just under £4,000. Almost 40 per cent of all candidates spent less than two-fifths of

their limit. Elected candidates spent on average more than unsuccessful candidates; more than half of elected candidates spent over four-fifths of their statutory limit. See *Election 2005: Campaign Spending* (London: The Electoral Commission, March 2006).

12. The official expenses – the cost – of the 2005 General Election was estimated to have been in excess of £60 million (quite apart from the annual cost of compiling the electoral register, which is estimated at more than £55 million in 2004–05), and are met by the Government out of the Consolidated Fund. This was a figure only slightly offset by the £692,500 received by the Treasury from lost deposits.

13. According to an analysis of campaign finance figures it was estimated that the 2004 US presidential and congressional elections cost a record $3.9 billion. The presidential race alone was said to cost an unprecedented $1.2 billion. *Report*, The Center for Responsive Politics, USA, October 2004. Also see: C. Berens, 'What Price Democracy', *Financial Management*, February 2005.

14. General Elections took place in: 1945, 1950, 1951, 1955, 1959, 1964, 1966, 1970, February 1974, October 1974, 1979, 1983, 1987, 1992, 1997, 2001 and 2005.

15. See *The Report of the Hansard Society Commission on Electoral Reform* (London: Hansard Society, 1976); *The Report on Electoral Reform* (Chair: Prof. Raymond Plant) (The Labour Party/Guardian Newspaper, 1991); and *The Report of the Independent Commission on the Voting System*, CM 4090-1 (London: Stationery Office, 1998) for fuller discussion of proportional representation.

16. *The Report of the Independent Commission on the Voting System*, CM 4090-1, (London: Stationery Office, 1998).

17. See *5 May 2005: Worst. Election. Ever* (London: Electoral Reform Society, 2005).

18. See *The Independent*, 1 July 2005. Within the first month of the launch of the campaign it had attracted more than 35,000 responses from readers.

19. See W. J. M. Mackenzie *Free Elections* (London: Allen & Unwin, 1958), pp. 69–71.

20. For further information on the effectiveness of the legislature see Chapter 11. Also see: Baldwin, N. D. J., (ed.), *Parliament in the 21st Century*, (London: Politico's/ Methuen, 2005).

21. See *The Tactics of Tactical Voting*, BBC news website 8 April 2005 and S. Ward, 'The Internet, E-Democracy and the Election: Virtually Irrelevant? in A. Geddes and J. Tonge (eds), *Britain Decides: The UK General Election 2005* (London: Palgrave, 2005), pp. 200–2.

22. Polling for 'Make Votes Count' conducted in 1998 showed that 72 per cent would support electoral reform. Even after hearing arguments for first-past-the-post, 57 per cent favoured reform. See S. Twigg, 'Votes for PR', *The Guardian*, 20 June 1998. YouGov/Daily Telegraph poll conducted immediately following the 2005 General Election asked about the fairness of the electoral system and just over half of respondents said they thought the present system was unfair, and that it should be changed. See: YouGov, 19 May 2005.

23. See S. Collins, 'Vote for Change Overwhelming', *New Zealand Herald*, 21 September 1992.

24. The statistics on turnout at General Elections depend very much on the accuracy of the Electoral Register. On average, it has been little more than 90 per cent accurate and even less so in inner city areas where the population is very mobile. In addition, it has been claimed that there has been an increase in the number of unregistered voters since the 1980s (not least of all as a direct result of individuals choosing

not to register in an attempt to avoid paying the poll tax in the period 1988–92). In September 1994 a Labour Party report ('The Missing Millions: Disenfranchised Citizens') claimed that 20 per cent of people in their early 20s, nearly 25 per cent of black people and 38 per cent of those relying on a private landlord to fill in registration forms, did not appear on the electoral register. Despite campaigns like 'Rock the Vote' and 'Operation Black Vote' aimed to attract the missing young and ethnic minority voters, by 1998 it was estimated that some two million voters were not on the register. (See: *The Independent*, 4 February 1998). Following the 2005 General Election an official report revealed that up to 3.7 million people eligible to vote were not registered. The report went on to reveal considerable variation among individuals of different ethnic backgrounds in this regard, with non-registration applying to 6 per cent of white people, 7 per cent of Asian people, 9 per cent of black Caribbean people and between 24 per cent and 37 per cent of black Africans, other black groups, Chinese people and those in other ethnic minority groupings. (See: Report, *Understanding Electoral Registration*, Electoral Commission, September 2005.)

25. *Worst. Election. Ever*, (London: Electoral Reform Society, 13 May, 2005), p.20.
26. See W. Rees-Mogg, 'The Primrose Path to PR', *The Times*, 26 March 1998.
27. See F. Mount, 'Say Hello to the Hell of PR Voting', *The Sunday Times*, 30 November 1997.
28. See P. Chapman, 'Voters get Cross with PR in New Zealand', *Electronic Telegraph*, No 930, 10 December 1997.
29. Quoted in E. Longford, *Victoria R. I.* (London: Weidenfeld & Nicolson, 1964), p. 518.

Chapter 4

1. See I. Crewe and K. Thomson, 'Party Loyalties: Dealignment or Realignment?', in G. Evans and P. Norris (eds), *Critical Elections: British Parties and Voters in Long-Term Perspective* (London: Sage, 1999).
2. See B. Sarlvik and I. Crewe, *Decade of Dealignment* (London: CUP, 1983).
3. Following the 2005 General Election an official report revealed that up to 3.7 million people eligible to vote were not registered. The report went on to reveal considerable variation among individuals of different ethnic backgrounds in this regard, with non-registration applying to 6 per cent of white people, 7 per cent of Asian people, 9 per cent of black Caribbean people and between 24 per cent and 37 per cent of black Africans, other black groups, Chinese people and those in other ethnic minority groupings. (See: Report, *Understanding Electoral Registration*, Electoral Commission, September 2005).
4. See: *An Audit of Political Engagement 4* (London: Hansard Society and the Electoral Commission, 2007); *An Audit of Political Engagement 3* (London: Hansard Society and the Electoral Commission, 2006); *An Audit of Political Engagement 2* (London: Hansard Society and the Electoral Commission, 2005); *An Audit of Political Engagement 1* (London: Hansard Society and the Electoral Commission, 2004). Also see: *Power To the People. The Report of Power: An Independent Inquiry into Britain's Democracy* (York: York Publishing Distribution, 2006).
5. P. Pulzer, *Political Representation and Elections in Britain* (London: Macmillan, 1967), p. 98.

6. For a fuller discussion of this subject see R. T. McKenzie and A. Silver, *Angels in Marble* (London: Heinemann, 1968) and J. H. Goldthorpe, *Social Mobility and Class Structure in Modern Britain* (Oxford: Clarendon Press, 1980).

7. See I. Crewe, 'A New Class of Politics', *Guardian*, 15 June 1987.

8. Guardian, 13 June 1983.

9. See: Mori poll, *The Sunday Times*, 12 April 1992 and Gallup Post Election Survey 10–11 April 1992.

10. See S. Saggar 'Racial Politics', in P. Norris and N. T. Gavin (eds), *Britain Votes 1997*, (Oxford: Oxford University Press, 1997), pp. 185–199.

11. Patrick Edwards, Director, Greater London Action for Racial Equality. Cited in *The Guardian*, 6 August 1994.

12. See: *Connections*, Commission for Racial Equality, August 1994.

13. For example see: A. H. Birch, *The British System of Government*, 8th edn (London: Allen & Unwin, 1990), pp. 78–82.

14. See: D. E. Butler and D. Stokes, *Political Change in Britain*, 2nd edn (London: Macmillan, 1974), pp. 48–66.

15. Nonetheless, the 2005 General Election result in the Blaenau Gwent constituency in Wales – where the independent Peter Law not only managed to overturn a Labour majority of 19,313 but construct a 9,121 majority of his own – showed that it is unwise for any party to take any constituency for granted.

16. See: J. Curtice and M. Steed, 'The Results Analysed', in D. Butler and D. Kavanagh (eds), *The British General Election of 1997* (London: Macmillan, 1997), pp. 299–300.

17. See *General Election 2005*, House of Commons Research paper 05/33, 17 May 2005.

18. See A. Heath et al, *How Britain Votes* (Oxford: Pergamon Press, 1985).

19. See, for example, D. Bell, *The End of Ideology*, revised edition (New York: Collier, 1962).

20. See P. Norris and C. Wlezien (eds), *Britain Votes 2005*, (Oxford: University Press, 2005), pp.146–61.

21. See B. Sarlvik and I. Crewe, *Decade of Dealignment*, pp. 247–344.

22. See B. Sarlvik and I. Crewe, *Decade of Dealignment*, p. 113.

23. *The Guardian*, 14 June 1983.

24. See D. Kavanagh, 'Spirals of Silence', *Guardian*, 21 April 1992.

25. *The Guardian*, 16 June 1987.

26. H. T. Himmelweit et al., *How Voters Decide* (London: Academic Press, 1981), p. 14.

27. See D. Butler and D. Kavanagh, *The British General Election of 1997* (London: Palgrave, 1997).

28. See A. Geddes and J. Tonge (eds), *Britain Decides: The UK General Election 2005* (London: Palgrave, 2005), pp. 261–78.

29. See P. Kellner, 'Why the Tories were Trounced', in P. Norris and N. T. Gavin, *Britain Votes 1997* (Oxford: Oxford University Press, 1997), pp. 108–22.

30. See T. Baldwin, 'A New Style of Campaign which Left too Many Voters Outside', in *The Times Guide to the House of Commons 2005* (Times Books, London, 2005).

31. *Ibid.*

32. See A. Heath et al., *How Britain Votes*, pp. 170–5.

33. J. Blondel, *Voters, Parties and Leaders* (London: Penguin, 1974), p. 86.

34. B. Sarlvik and I. Crewe, *Decade of Dealignment* (London: CUP, 1983), p. 66.

Chapter 5

1. E. Burke, 'Thoughts on the Cause of the Present Discontents' (1770), Works Vol. I. See G. H. Sabine, *A History of Political Theory*, 3rd edn (London: Harrap, 1968), p. 611. Also see I. Hampshire-Monk, *A History of Modern Political Thought: Major Political Thinkers from Hobbes to Marx*, (Oxford: Blackwell, 1992).
2. See R. T. McKenzie, *British Political Parties*, 2nd edn (London: Heinemann, 1963), p. 645.
3. See *Report of the Committee on Financial Aid to Political Parties*, Cmnd 6601 (London: HMSO, 1976).
4. See A. Seldon, *Major: A Political Life* (London: Weidenfeld & Nicolson, 1997), pp. 498–502, 610–11 and 713–16.
5. See: Committee on Standards in Public Life. *The Funding of Political Parties in the United Kingdom*, Fifth Report, Cm 4057, (London: Stationery Office, 1998).
6. White Paper, *The Funding of Political Parties in the United Kingdom*, Cm 4413, (London: Stationery Office, July 1999).
7. *The Registration of Political Parties Act 1998* (London: Stationery Office, 1998).
8. *The Political Parties, Elections and Referendums Act 2000*, (London: Stationery Office, 2000).
9. See Electoral Commission, http://www.electoralcommission.org.uk.
10. See P. Seyd, P. Whiteley and J. Parry, *Labour and Conservative Party Membership: Social Characteristics, Political Attitudes and Activities* (Aldershot: Dartmouth, 1996).
11. *Ibid.*
12. S. Beer, *Modern British Politics* (London: Faber, 1969), p. 135.
13. S. Beer, *Modern British Politics* (London: Faber, 1969), p. 247.
14. *Built to Last, Statement of Aims and Values*, (London: Conservative Party, 2006).
15. See H. Rumbelow, 'Plenty of Action on the Fringe but not Many Seats', in T. Hames, and V. Passmore (eds), *Guide to the House of Commons* (London: Times/Dod's, 2005) p. 52.
16. See M. Brown, 'Watch Out for the Others – They Could Stop David Cameron Winning a General Election', *The Independent*, 13 December 2006.
17. See P. Webb, 'The Continuing Advance of the Minor Parties', pp. 106–7 in P. Norris and C. Wlezien (eds), *Britain Votes 2005* (Oxford: University Press, 2005).

Chapter 6

1. Quoted in R. Rose, (ed.), *Studies in British Politics*, 3rd edn (London: Macmillan, 1976), p. 343.
2. G. C Moodie, and G. Studdert-Kennedy, *Opinions, Publics and Pressure Groups* (London: Allen & Unwin, 1970), p. 60.
3. S. E. Finer, *Anonymous Empire, revised edition* (London: Pall Mall, 1966), p. 3.
4. P. Shipley (ed.), *Directory of Pressure Groups and Representative Associations* (London: Wilton House, 1976), p. 3.
5. Membership figures provided by the Trades Union Congress, January 2006.
6. Membership figures are those provided by the groups concerned.
7. Quoted in R. Kimber and J. J. Richardson (eds), *Pressure Groups in Britain* (London: Dent, 1974), p. 280.

8. Corporatism is a term which has often been used pejoratively by those who believe that democratic representation should be territorially based on constituencies rather than functionally based on the various sectional interests in society. For our purposes here it is taken to mean the tendency in modern British politics for Government to deal directly with the 'social partners' (that is employers and trade unions) to the detriment perhaps of the elected Members of Parliament. See: R. K. Middlemass, *Politics in Industrial Society* (London: Deutsch, 1979), for a fuller discussion of this subject.

9. Syndicalism is a term which was used originally to describe the movement among industrial workers at the end of the nineteenth century (especially in France) of which the primary aim was the transfer of the means of production, distribution and exchange from capitalist owners to groups of workers at factory level. On the British experience of syndicalism see: B. Holton, *British Syndicalism, 1900–14* (London: Pluto Press, 1976).

10. Quoted in 'A Nation of Groupies', *The Economist*, 13 August 1994.

11. See J. Warner, 'The Clout of the Beerage', *The Independent*, 18 July 1989.

12. J. J. Richardson and A. G. Jordan, *Governing Under Pressure* (Oxford: Martin Robertson, 1979), p. 74.

13. See Butler, D. and Kitzinger, U., *The 1975 Referendum* (London: Macmillan, 1976), p. 285.

14. See H. Pelling, *A History of British Trade Unionism* (London: Macmillan, 1963) and H. Pelling, *A Short History of the Labour Party* (London: Palgrave, 2005), for an account of this relationship.

15. See 'Ecclestone: I Gave Blair £1M to Keep Taxes Down', *The Guardian*, 13 May 1998.

16. See M. Rush (ed.), *Parliament and Pressure Politics* (London: OUP, 1990).

17. See Chapter 20 for a fuller description of the policy and decision-making process in Britain.

Chapter 7

1. See: *Report of the Inquiry into the Circumstances Surrounding the Death of David Kelly* (The Hutton Report) (HC 247) (London: Stationery Office, 2004).

2. The Communications Market 2006 Report: http://www.ofcom.org.uk/research/cm/cm06/.

3. Among the most famous headlines over the past 25 years have been those which appeared in the Sun, such as 'Gotcha' at the time of the sinking of the Argentinian cruiser *Belgrano* during the 1982 Falklands conflict, and 'Up yours Delors' at the time of maximum conflict between Jacques Delors, President of the European Commission, and the British Conservative Government.

4. See: J. Curtice, 'Is the Sun Shining on Tony Blair? The Electoral Influence of Newspapers in Britain since 1992', *Harvard International Journal of Press and Politics* (Boston, Mass.: Harvard University Press, 1997).

5. Quoted in the Report of the Calcutt Committee on Privacy and Related Matters (London: HMSO, 1990).

6. *Report of the Committee on Privacy and Related Matters* (London: HMSO, 1990).

7. See: Press Complaints Commission, *Report Number 1, January–June 1991 and Report Number 2*, July–September 1991.

8. Lord McGregor, Press Complaints Commission statement, *The Times*, 9 June 1992.

9. David Calcutt, *Review of Press Self-Regulations* (London: HMSO, 1993).

10. *Privacy and Media Intrusion: The Government's Response* (London: HMSO, 1995).

11. *Human Rights Act 1998*, ISBN 0 10 544298 4 (London: Stationery Office, 1998). Also see: *A Guide to the Human Rights Act 1998: Third Edition*, DCA 51/06 (London: Department for Constitutional Affairs, 2006).

12. *Official Secrets Act 1989* (c. 6), ISBN 0105406880 (London: HMSO, 1989).

13. For example, in July 1987 Jeffrey Archer (as Lord Archer then was) was awarded £500,000 in damages against the *Star* which had libelled him with allegations about an assignation with a prostitute, and in December 1988 Elton John secured £1 million from the *Sun* in an out-of-court settlement for an alleged libel.

14. For a fuller discussion of the Lobby system see: J. Margach, *The Anatomy of Power* (London: Star, 1981), pp. 125–55.

15. See: *Broadcasting in the Nineties – Competition, Choice and Quality*, Cmnd 517 (London: HMSO, November 1988), para. 2.5.

16. A. Smith, *The Politics of Information* (London: Macmillan, 1978), p. 5.

17. This point was well made by John Birt and Peter Jay writing in *The Times* (28 February, 30 September and 1 October 1975).

18. See J. Trenaman and D. McQuail, *Television and the Political Image* (London: Methuen, 1961).

19. See M. Harrison on 'Broadcasting' in D. E. Butler and D. Kavanagh, *The British General Election of 1987* (London: Macmillan, 1988), p. 139.

20. See: D. E. Butler and D. Kavanagh, *The British General Election of 1992* (London: Macmillan, 1992), p. 253.

21. See H. A. Semetko, M. Scammell and P. Goddard, 'Television', in P. Norris and M. T. Gavin (eds), *Britain Votes 1997* (Oxford: Oxford University Press, 1997), pp. 101–7 and M. Harrison on 'Politics on the Air' in D. E. Butler and D. Kavanagh, *The British General Election of 1997* (London: Macmillan, 1997), pp 133–55.

22. See Glasgow Media Group, *Bad News* (London: Routledge & Kegan Paul, 1981), pp. 12–13.

23. See M. Harrison, 'TV News, Whose Bias?' (Hermitage, Berkshire: Policy Journals, 1985), and A. Hetherington, *News, Newspapers and Television* (London: Macmillan, 1985).

24. See A. Seldon, and D. Kavanagh (eds), *The Blair Effect 2001–5*, (Cambridge: Cambridge University Press, 2005) and A. Seldon (ed.), *The Blair Effect: The Blair Government 1997–2001* (London: Little, Brown and Company, 2001).

25. Reference to speech by Tony Blair on 12 June 2007 on the changing relationship between politics and the media.

26. Kenneth Baker, 'Towards an Information Economy'; speech to the British Association for the Advancement of Science, 7 September 1982.

27. A. Huxley, *Brave New World* (London: Penguin, 1932); G. Orwell *Nineteen Eighty Four* (London: Penguin, 1949).

28. *The Business*, 14 November 2005.

29. *Financial Times*, 14 June 1989.

30. See: Statement made by the Culture Secretary (Tessa Jowell), (London: House of Commons Hansard, 18 January 2007). Also see: White Paper, *A Public Service for All: The BBC in the Digital Age* (London: DCMS, 2006).

31. *Hansard*, 8 February 1989, col. 1011.
32. In spite of these Government decisions, Ministers in the Thatcher Administration seemed prepared to allow News International to be an exception to the general rule, since the company was permitted to establish Sky Television while retaining its ownership of 37 per cent of the national press in Britain.

Chapter 8

1. B. Parekh (ed.), *Bentham's Political Thought* (London: Croom Helm, 1973), p. 212.
2. Quoted in A. H. Birch, *Representative and Responsible Government* (London: Allen & Unwin, 1964), p. 172.
3. Cited in A. Andrews, *Quotations for Speakers and Writers* (London: Newnes Books, 1969), p. 376.
4. *Ibid.*
5. *Ibid.*
6. *Ibid.*
7. A. V. Dicey, *Introduction to the Study of the Law of the Constitution*, 10th edn (London: Macmillan, 1967), pp. 59, 60, 71–85.
8. A. V. Dicey, *Law and Opinion in England in The Nineteenth Century* (London: Macmillan, 1905), p. 10.
9. V. O. Key, *Public Opinion and American Democracy* (New York: Knopf, 1961), p. 14.
10. D. E. Butler, and D. Stokes, *Political Change in Britain*, 2nd edn (London: Macmillan, 1974), pp. 19–151.
11. In H. R. Penniman (ed.), *Britain at the Polls, 1979* (Washington, DC: American Enterprise Institute, 1981), p. 282.
12. See I. Bulmer-Thomas, *The Growth of the British Party System* (Vol. II) (London: John Baker, 1965), pp. 103–4.
13. See A. H. Home, *Macmillan* (Vol. II) (London: Macmillan, 1984), pp. 331–51.
14. See D. Butler and U. Kitzinger, *The 1975 Referendum* (London: Macmillan, 1976).
15. See House of Commons Library Research Paper, *Referendums on Regional Assemblies*, 04/57, 19 July 2004 and House of Commons Library Research Paper, *Referendums: Recent Developments*, 99/30, 16 March 1999.
16. See M. Thatcher, *The Downing Street Years* (London: HarperCollins, 1993), pp. 642–67.
17. See F. Teer and J. D. Spence, *Political Opinion Polls* (London: Hutchinson, 1973), p. 138.
18. See F. Abrams, 'Public Opinion on Fox-Hunting Being Ignored', *The Independent*, 4 April 1998.
19. *The Scarman Report* (London: HMSO, 1981).
20. *Faith in the City: A Call for Action by Church and State* (London: Church House, 1985).
21. *Cross-Channel Passenger and Freight Traffic Report* (London: HMSO, 1992).
22. See N. Hawkes, 'Advisers Seek Public's View on Cloning Human Tissue', *The Times*, 30 January 1998.
23. See A. Mitchell, 'The Parliamentary and Constituency Roles of an MP: The Backbencher's Lament', in N. D. J. Baldwin (ed.), *Parliament in the 21st Century*, (London: Politico's, 2005), p. 63.

24. Jack Straw writing in *The Times*, 8 April 1998.
25. For example, Margaret Thatcher and her ministerial colleagues deliberately postponed an all-out confrontation with Arthur Scargill and the National Union of Mineworkers until 1984, when all the relevant preparations for a long industrial dispute had been made by the Government and the electricity utilities.
26. Tony Blair, *The Jimmy Young Programme*, BBC Radio 2, 29 July 1997.
27. It was the fact that the Conservatives trailed a long way behind Labour in the opinion polls during the final 16 months of Margaret Thatcher's leadership which, more than anything else, was responsible for the Cabinet-led back-bench revolt which brought about her downfall in November 1990.
28. This was certainly evident during the Bermondsey by-election in 1983, the Greenwich by-election in 1987 and the Glasgow Govan by-election in 1988. See: C. Cook and J. Ramsden, (eds), *By-elections in British Politics*, (London: UCL Press, 1997) and P. Norris, *The Volatile Electorate: British By-elections since 1900* (London: Oxford University Press, 1990).
29. For a fuller discussion see: D. E. Butler and A. Ranney (eds), *Referendums: A Comparative Study of Practice and Theory* (Washington, DC: American Enterprise Institute, 1978).
30. F. O. Goman, *Edmund Burke: His Political Philosophy* (London: Allen & Unwin, 1973), pp. 55–6.
31. J. J. Rousseau, *The Social Contract* (New York: Harper, 1949), p. 85.
32. See: D. Kavanagh and P. Morris, *Consensus Politics from Attlee to Thatcher* (Oxford: Basil Blackwell, 1989).
33. Norman Tebbit, *The Times*, 7 October 1987.
34. See A. Sampson, *Who Runs This Place: The Anatomy of Britain in the 21st Century*, (London: John Murray, 2004), *The Essential Anatomy of Britain* (London: Hodder & Stoughton, 1992), and *The Changing Anatomy of Britain* (London: Hodder & Stoughton, 1982) for a vivid description of the Establishment in Britain.
35. V. O. Key, *Public Opinion and American Democracy*, p. 285.

Chapter 9

1. See F. Hardie, *The Political Influence of the British Monarchy 1868–1952* (London: Batsford, 1970), pp. 150–3, and W. I. Jennings, Cabinet Government (London: Cambridge University Press, 1951), pp. 40–2.
2. See S. Bradford, *George VI* (London: Weidenfield & Nicolson, 1989), pp. 310–12.
3. See J. Campbell, *Heath* (London: Jonathan Cape, 1993), pp. 616–18.
4. See F. Hardie, *The Political Influence of the British Monarchy 1868–1952*, p. 67.
5. The Parliaments elected in 1910 and in 1935 were each extended by all-party agreement, in the former case until 1918 and in the latter case until the 1945 election which took place soon after the agreed ending of the 1940 Coalition Government.
6. Elizabeth II, Silver Jubilee Address to Parliament, 4 May 1977. See B. Pimlott, *The Queen* (London: HarperCollins, 1996) pp. 446–7.
7. Some historians have argued that in 1831 the threat of the mob and in 1911 the threat of rebellion in Ireland also played a part in persuading the Conservative peers to give way to the Government of the day in the Commons.
8. For example, immediately after the 1983 General Election William Whitelaw and George Thomas were made hereditary peers on the recommendation of

Margaret Thatcher. The former was in recognition of William Whitelaw's long and distinguished service to the Conservative Party and the nation, culminating in his period as Deputy Leader of the party from 1975 to 1983 and to enable him to take over as Leader of the Lords. The latter was in recognition of George Thomas's distinguished period as Speaker of the House of Commons from 1975 to 1983. In each case the Queen complied with the Prime Minister's wishes, as is customary in such matters, although the element of controversy in restoring the principle of hereditary peerages was reduced by the fact that William Whitelaw had no male heir, only daughters who were not eligible to inherit the title, and George Thomas was a bachelor. More recent departures from the modern norm in favour of life peerages were the granting of an hereditary Earldom to Harold Macmillan – who had male heirs – in 1984, an hereditary Dukedom to Princes Andrew on the eve of his wedding in 1986 and an hereditary Earldom to Prince Edward at the time of his marriage in 1999.

9. Although there have been occasions in the past when the honours system was abused for political purposes – for example, by Lloyd George as Prime Minister when Maundy Gregory was active on his behalf in offering peerages in return for financial support.

10. Among those who have expressed concern about this are Tony Benn in *Arguments for Democracy* (London: Jonathan Cape, 1981), and P. Holland and M. Fallon in *Public Bodies and Ministerial Patronage* (London: CPC, 1978).

11. See F. F. Ridley and D. Wilson (eds), *The QUANGO Debate* (Oxford: University Press, 1995) pp. 128–144, 145–162 and 163–181.

12. See A. Tomkins, *The Constitution after Scott: Government Unwrapped* (Oxford: University Press, 1998).

13. See House of Lords Select Committee on the Constitution Report, *Waging War: Parliament's Role and Responsibility* (HL Paper 236-I and II), 27 July 2006.

14. W. Bagehot, *The English Constitution* (London: Fontana/Collins, 1963) p. 111.

15. A point made by Dr David Butler in correspondence with one of the authors.

16. See http://www.duchyofcornwall.org/managementandfinances-finances-analysis.

17. In 1998 *The Sunday Times* calculated the Queen's private fortune to be some £250 million, comprised of an investment portfolio of £70 million, property of £100 million and jewellery, art and racing interests worth £80 million. See 'Rich List 1998', *The Sunday Times*, 19 April 1998, p. 20. In 2001 *The Mail on Sunday* put the Queen's fortune at more than £1.1 billion. See 'The Royal Rich Report', *The Mail on Sunday*, 2001

18. *The Sunday Times*, 23 March 1969.

19. *Now*, 8 February 1980 (a weekly news magazine which later ceased publication).

20. *The Times*, 22 April 1984.

21. ICM Polls, *Guardian*, 9 January 1995.

22. MORI/*Independent on Sunday*, 18 February 1996.

23. See 'Who should be President of Britain?', *The Times*, 18 January 1992.

24. Hugo Young, 'The Saving of the Monarchy', *Guardian*, 8 September 1997.

25. See MORI poll, *The Times*, 24 December 1997.

26. Walter Bagehot, *Op. Cit.*, p.120.

Chapter 10

1. R. Butt, *A History of Parliament in the Middle Ages* (London: Constable, 1989), p. 1.
2. W. Bagehot, *The English Constitution* (Glasgow: Fontana/Collins, 1963), p. 128.
3. *Ibid.*, p. 149.
4. Quoted in R. Rhodes James (ed.), *Churchill Speaks* (Leicester: Windword, 1981), p. 178.
5. See R. Jenkins, *Mr Balfour's Poodle* (London: Collins, 1954).
6. The 1963 Peerage Act was the direct result of the efforts of Tony Benn, who had inherited the title of Viscount Stansgate, to get the law changed so that he and other hereditary peers could disclaim their titles and consequently no longer be disqualified from standing for election or re-election to the House of Commons. In 1998 ten individuals had disclaimed their titles – although two of these sat in the Lords as life peers.
7. For a full account see J. Morgan, *The House of Lords and the Labour Government 1964–70* (Oxford: Clarendon Press, 1975).
8. White Paper, *Modernising Parliament: Reforming the House of Lords*, Cm 4183 (London: Stationery Office, 1999).
9. Report of the Royal Commission on the Reform of the House of Lords (Chairman: Lord Wakeham), *A House for the Future*, Cm 4534 (London: Stationery office, 2000).
10. The Weatherill Amendment. See: The House of Lords Act 1999 and the 'Weatherill Amendment', Crossbench Peers Website, http://213.52.137.147/index.html.
11. See *Report on the Reform of the Second Chamber*, Cmnd 9038 (London: HMSO, 1918).
12. Report of the Royal Commission on the Reform of the House of Lords (Chairman: Lord Wakeham), *A House for the Future*, Cm 4534 (London: Stationery Office, 2000).
13. See E. Crewe, *Lords of Parliament* (Manchester: Manchester University Press, 2005), pp. 72–4.
14. See Public Bill Sessional Statistics for the 1987–92 and 1992–97 Sessions, Public Bill Office, House of Lords.
15. See Public Bill Sessional Statistics for the 1997–2001 Sessions, Public Bill Office, House of Lords.
16. See Public Bill Sessional Statistics for the 2001–2005 Sessions, Public Bill Office, House of Lords.
17. White Paper, *Modernising Parliament: Reforming the House of Lords*, Cm 4183 (London: Stationery Office, 1999).
18. Aside from its Chairman, the former Conservative Minister Lord Wakeham, the membership of the Royal Commission comprised: Ann Beynon, National Manager of BT Wales; Lord Butler of Brockwell, the former Cabinet Secretary; Baroness Dean, the former Trade Union leader; the Right Reverend Richard Harris, Bishop of Oxford; Lord Hurd, the former Conservative Northern Ireland, Home and Foreign Secretary; Gerald Kaufman, the senior Labour MP; Anthony King, Professor of Government at Essex University; Bill Morris, General Secretary of the Transport and General Workers Union; Kenneth Munro, Chairman of the Centre for Scottish Public Policy and a former European Commission representative in Scotland;

Dawn Oliver, Professor of Constitutional Law at University College London; and Sir Michael Wheeler-Booth, former Clerk of the Parliaments.

19. White Paper, *The House of Lords: Completing the Reform*, Cm 5291 (London: Stationery Office, 2001).

20. Report, the House of Commons Public Administration Select Committee, *The Second Chamber: Continuing the Reform*, 5th Report, Session 2001–02, 12 February 2002, HC 494-I/II.

21. See: P. Norton, 'House of Lords Reform: The View from the Parapets', *Representation*, Vol. 40 (3), 2004, pp. 185–99.

22. See: *Constitutional Reform: Next Steps for the House of Lords*, Department for Constitutional Affairs, CPR 14/03, April 2004.

23. White Paper, *House of Lords: Reform*, Cm 7027 (London: Stationery Office, 2007).

24. A. Tyrie, *Reforming the Lords: A Conservative Approach* (London: Conservative Policy Forum, 1998).

25. N. Kent, *Enhancing our Democracy: Reforming the House of Lords* (London: Tory Reform Group, 1998).

26. *The Report of the Constitutional Commission on Options for a New Second Chamber* (Chairman: Lord Mackay of Clashfern), 1999.

27. *Conservatives Call for a New Elected Senate*, Conservative Party Press Notice, 14 January 2002.

28. See: *Here We Stand: Proposals for Modernising Britain's Democracy*, Liberal Democrat Federal White Paper, No. 6, September 1993.

Chapter 11

1. W. I. Jennings, *Parliament*, 2nd edn (Cambridge: CUP, 1969), pp. 7–8.

2. L. S. Amery, *Thoughts on the Constitution* (Cambridge: CUP, 1947), p. 12.

3. When the Labour Party is in Opposition and, consequently, forms a Shadow Cabinet, 15 members of it are elected each year by their colleagues in the Parliamentary Party. In addition, five others sit *ex officio*, namely, the Leader, the Deputy Leader, the Chief Whip, the Chairman of the Parliamentary Party and the Leader of the Opposition in the Lords (who is formally co-opted by the Party Leader).

4. See: *General Election 2005*, House of Commons Research paper 05/33, 17 May 2005.

5. Historic examples would include Tony Benn, Michael Foot and Neil Kinnock from among the ranks of Labour MPs and both Winston Churchill, and Harold Macmillan among Conservative MPs.

6. See M. Rush, 'Parliament: Pay and Resources', in N. D. J. Baldwin (ed.), *Parliament in the 21st Century*, (London: Politico's, 2005), pp. 326-340.

7. See M. Rush, 'Parliament: Pay and Resources', in N. D. J. Baldwin (ed.), *Parliament in the 21st Century*, (London: Politico's, 2005), p. 334.

8. W. Bagehot, *The English Constitution* (London: Fontana, 1978), p. 170.

9. See M. Rush, *Parliament Today* (Manchester: Manchester University Press, 2005), pp. 243–53.

10. Constitutional measures – such as the Maastricht Bill or the legislation to set up the Scottish Parliament and the Welsh Assembly – have to be taken in a Committee of the whole House in the Chamber itself.

11. See: R. Rogers and R. Walters, *How Parliament Works*, 6th edn (London: Pearson/ Longman, 2006), pp. 344–78.
12. For example, the Foreign Affairs Select Committee published a very influential report on the misuse of ODA support for the Pergau Dam project in July 1994, the Social Security Select Committee had a good deal of influence on the reform of the Child Support Agency in 1993–94, and the Treasury and Civil Service Select Committees helped to shape the new Code for the Civil Service in November 1994–January 1996. Also see: House of Commons Liaison Committee Report, *Shifting the Balance: Select Committees and the Executive*, First Report, 1999–2000 Session, 2 March 2000.
13. See R. Kelly, H. Holden and K. Parry, *Pre-legislative Scrutiny*, Parliament and Constitution Centre, House of Commons Library, SN/PC/2822, 8 February 2007.
14. The different, but overlapping aspects of the Westland crisis were examined by no fewer than three Select Committees – Defence; Trade and Industry; and Treasury and Civil Service. See especially the Defence Select Committee Report entitled 'Westland plc, the Government's Decision Making', HC 519 (1985–86), for further details.
15. The 22nd edition of *Erskine May* was published in 1997 and was edited by Sir Donald Limon, then Clerk of the House of Commons, and W. R. McKay, then Clerk Assistant, later Clerk of the House of Commons. It is particularly useful as a work of reference on current procedure and practice in the Commons.
16. See First Report, Select Committee on Modernisation of the House of Commons, *The Legislative Process*, Session 1997–98, HC 190, 29 July 1997.

Chapter 12

1. H. Wilson, *The Governance of Britain* (London: Weidenfeld & Nicolson, 1976), p. 8.
2. Quoted in R. Blake, *The Office of Prime Minister* (Oxford: Oxford University Press, 1975), p. 50.
3. A. Eden, *Full Circle* (London: Cassell, 1960), p. 269.
4. An example would be under Prime Minister James Callaghan at the time of the financial crisis/IMF loan in 1976. See K. O. Morgan, *Callaghan: A Life* (Oxford: Oxford University Press, 1997), pp. 545–9.
5. See http://www.cabinetoffice.gov.uk/about_the_cabinet_office/.
6. For a full listing of Cabinet Committees see: http://www.cabinetoffice.gov.uk/ secretariats/committees/.
7. Walter Bagehot, *The English Constitution* (London: Fontana/Collins, 1975), p. 68.
8. J. P. Mackintosh, *The British Cabinet*, 3rd edn (London: Stevens, 1977), p. 414.
9. See Tony Benn's *Diaries – 76*, pp. 661–690; Denis Healey's Memoirs, *The Time of My Life*, pp. 426–35 and Kenneth O. Morgan's *Callaghan: A Life*, pp. 545–9 for more detailed accounts of this critical period in the life of the 1974–79 Labour Government.
10. See A. Rawnsley, *The Observer*, 26 April 1998.
11. See editorial, 'President Blair', *The Sunday Times*, 26 April 1998.
12. See *The Ministerial Code: A Code of Conduct and Guidance on Procedures for Ministers* (Cabinet Office, July 1997). For the more recent version, *The Ministerial Code: A Code of Ethics and Procedural Guidance for Ministers* (Cabinet Office, 2007),

see: http://www.cabinetoffice.gov.uk/propriety-and-ethics/ministers/ministerial-code/.

13. P. Riddell, *The Times*, 1 August 1997.
14. White Paper, *Modernising Government*, Cm 4310, (London: Stationery Office, 1999).
15. *Modernising Government: Action Plan* (London: Stationery Office, 1999).
16. *Wiring it up* (London: Performance and Innovation Unit, 2000).
17. See A. Seldon and D. Kavanagh (eds), *The Blair Effect 2001–05* (Cambridge: Cambridge University Press, 2005), pp.12–13.
18. See P. Mandelson and R. Liddle, *The Blair Revolution: Can New Labour Deliver?* (London: Faber & Faber, 1996), p.235.
19. See No 10 Downing Street website: http:/www.number–10.gov.uk.
20. In A. King, (ed.), *The British Prime Minister* (London: Macmillan, 1969), p. 198.
21. In A. King, (ed.), *The British Prime Minister*, 2nd edn (London: Macmillan, 1985), p. 216.
22. R. Blake, *The Office of Prime Minister* (Oxford: Oxford University Press, 1975), p. 51.

Chapter 13

1. See *Report of the Committee on the Machinery of Government*, Cd 9230 (London: HMSO, 1918).
2. The *Lord President of the Council* is formally responsible for the Privy Council Office and takes charge at the infrequent formal meetings of the Privy Council, while the only remaining formal task of the *Lord Privy Seal* is to arrange Royal Proclamations. The formal responsibilities of the *Chancellor of the Duchy of Lancaster* is for the general administration of the Duchy of Lancaster estates and revenues, but the real work is done by the professional staff concerned.
3. W. I. Jennings, *Cabinet Government*, 3rd edn (London: Cambridge University Press, 1959), p. 133.
4. See *Report of the Inquiry into the Export of Defence Equipment and Dual-Use Goods to Iraq and Related Prosecutions* (The Scott Report), (HC 115) (London: Stationery Office, 1996); *The Report of the Sierra Leone Arms Investigation* (The Legg Report), (1016) (London: Stationery Office, 1998); *Report of the Inquiry into the Circumstances Surrounding the Death of David Kelly* (The Hutton Report), (HC 247) (London: Stationery Office, 2004); *Review of Intelligence on Weapons of Mass Destruction. Report of a Committee of Privy Counsellors* (The Butler Report), (HC 898), (London: Stationery Office, 2004).
5. Cited in P. Kellner and N. Crowther-Hunt, *The Civil Servants* (London: Macdonald, 1980), pp. 215–16.
6. See R. Rose, 'Too much Reshuffling of the Cabinet Pack?', *IEA Inquiry No. 27* (London: IEA, 1991).
7. See I. F. Nicolson, *The Mystery of Crichel Down* (Oxford: Oxford University Press, 1986) and J. Griffith, 'Crichel Down, The Most Famous Farm in British Constitutional History', *Contemporary Record*, Vol. 1 (1), Spring 1987 pp. 35–40.
8. See J. Callaghan, *Time and Chance* (London: Collins, 1987), pp. 215–25.
9. See: Lord Carrington, *Reflect on Things Past* (London: Collins, 1988), pp. 348–72.

10. For an explanation of the Westland Helicopter Affair see: M Linklater and D. Leigh, *Not With Honour: The Inside Story of the Westland Scandal* (London: The Observer/Sphere Books, 1986).

11. See J. Prior, *A Balance of Power* (London: Hamish Hamilton, 1986), pp. 232–3, and W. Whitelaw, *The Whitelaw Memoirs* (London: Anrum Press, 1989), pp. 211–13.

12. Estelle Morris, Letter of Resignation, 23 October 2002. Cited in *The Times*, 24 October 2002.

13. See M. Thatcher, *The Downing Street Years* (London: HarperCollins, 1993), p. 403.

14. This was the case, for example, in 1981 when Keith Speed, the junior Navy Minister, was sacked for speaking out publicly against planned cuts in the Royal Navy budget, and in 1989 when Nicholas Ridley, then Environment Secretary, was sacked for speaking out against the Germans.

15. For example, when the Expenditure Select Committee sought to cross-examine Labour Ministers on public financial support for Chrysler UK in the 1970s, the then Prime Minister, James Callaghan, prevented any of his Cabinet colleagues from appearing before the Committee. Equally not all the key official witnesses were permitted by Margaret Thatcher, when Prime Minister, to testify before Select Committees in the wake of the 1986 Westland crisis. Select Committees have also been denied access to material. For example, during their 1995–96 investigation into whether the Conservative MP and BMARC Director Jonathan Aitken knew whether the company was selling naval cannon to Iraq, the DTI Select Committee was denied access to classified intelligence documents.

16. http://www.cabinetoffice.gov.uk/propriety-and-ethics/special-advisers/code.asp.

17. See 'Mullin Condemns Ministerial Musical Chairs', *The Guardian*, 21 May 2005'; and R. Rose, 'Too much Reshuffling of the Cabinet Pack?', *IEA Inquiry No. 27* (London: IEA, 1991).

18. As Harold Macmillan laconically observed in 1955 when moving – after only eight months – from the Foreign Office to the Treasury: 'After a few months learning geography I've got to learn arithmetic.' See N. Fisher, *Harold Macmillan* (London: Weidenfeld & Nicolson, 1982), p. 154.

19. In 2007 some 24 Ministers – excluding the Prime Minister – had a total of 54 special advisers.

20. Quoted in H. Parris, *Constitutional Bureaucracy* (London: Allen & Unwin, 1969), p. 114.

21. H. Morrison, *Government and Parliament* (London: Oxford University Press, 1959), p. 311.

Chapter 14

1. See *Report of the Tomlin Commission*, Cmnd 3909 (London: HMSO, 1931).

2. See *The Civil Service Yearbook*, 45th edn (available online at: http://www.civil-service.co.uk). For Departmental expenditure see: http://www.hm-treasury.gov.uk.

3. Quoted in the Fifth Report of the Treasury and Civil Service Select Committee, *The Role of the Civil Service*, Vol. I, HC 27-I, 1993–94 (London: HMSO, November 1994), para. 65.

4. E. Bridges, *Portrait of a Profession* (London: Cambridge University Press, 1950), p. 25.

5. See *Report of the Fulton Committee*, Cmnd 3628 (London: HMSO, 1968); B. Sedgemore, *The Secret Constitution* (London: Hodder & Stoughton, 1980), pp. 148–53; P. Kellner and N. Crowther-Hunt, *The Civil Servants* (London: Macdonald, 1980), pp. 121–3; and Report, *House of Lords Select Committee on the Public Service*, (HL Paper 55), (London: Stationery Office, 1998), pp. 32–4.

6. The Civil Service Code, 6 June 2006. See: http://www.civilservice.gov.uk/publications/civilservicecode.

7. See O. Gay and T. Powell, *Individual Ministerial Responsibility – Issues and Examples*, Parliament and Constitution Centre, House of Commons Library, Research Paper, 04/31, 5 April 2004.

8. White Paper, *Modernising Government*, Cm 4310, (London: Stationery Office, 1999).

9. *Report of the Fulton Committee*, Cmnd 3628 (London: HMSO, 1968).

10. See A. O. Hirschman, *Exit, Voice and Loyalty* (Cambridge, MA: Harvard University press, 1970).

11. See *The Judge Over Your Shoulder: Judicial Review of Administrative Decisions*, Treasury Solicitor's Department in conjunction with the Cabinet Office (MPO) Training Division, (1987).

12. See *Civil Service Commissioners' Report, 1993–94 and the 1997–98 Report of the House of Lords Select Committee on the Public Service*, pp. 93 and 97–8, for evidence of this trend.

13. For details of the Professional Skills for Government agenda (PSG), see: http://psg.civilservice.gov.uk.

14. For a fuller analysis of the 'public interest' defence used in the Courts, see: R. Thomas, 'The British Official Secrets Act, 1911–39 and the Ponting Case', in R. A. Chapman and M. Hunt (eds), *Open Government* (London: Routledge, 1989), pp. 95–122.

Chapter 15

1. See *National Income and Expenditure 1983*, Tables 1.10 and 10.3; and *Economic Trends*, February 1983, Appendix 1, Table 1.

2. For example, in 1982 public sector purchases from the private sector amounted to about £9000 million, while public sector sales to the private sector amounted to about £11,000 million.

3. These generalisations refer essentially to the nationalised industries and not to all public corporations, some of which – such as the BBC created by Royal Charter in 1926 – were established for very different purposes.

4. See *Information on Privatisation in the UK*, HM Treasury, February 1998.

5. Tony Blair, *Guardian*, 8 April 1997.

6. See D. Osler, *Labour Party Plc: New Labour as a Party of Business* (London: Mainstream Publishing, 2002).

7. G. Bowen, *Survey of Fringe Bodies* (London: Civil Service Department, 1978).

8. See L. Pliatzky, *Report on Non-Departmental Public Bodies*, Cmnd 7797 (London: HMSO, 1980).

9. J. MacLeavy and O. Gay., *The Quango Debate* (London: House of Commons Library, Research Paper 05/30, 11 April 2005), p. 26.

10. J. MacLeavy and O. Gay., *The Quango Debate* (London: House of Commons Library, Research Paper 05/30, 11 April 2005), p. 22.
11. Lord Benson and Lord Rothschild, 'Royal Commissions, a Memorial', *Public Administration*, Autumn 1982.
12. See *UK Voluntary Sector Almanac*, 2006.
13. UK Voluntary Sector Almanac, (London: NCVO, 2006).
14. See: *Report of the Committee on the Financing of the BBC*, Cmnd 9824 (London: HMSO, 1986).

Chapter 16

1. 'The Government of Wales Act 2006 established the Welsh Assembly Government as an entity separate from, but accountable to, the National Assembly.'
2. See: http://wales.gov.uk.
3. White Paper, *Better Governance for Wales*, (Cmrd. 6582), (London: Stationery Office, 2005).
4. *The Government of Wales Act 2006* (London: Stationery Office, 2006).
5. See: House of Lords Select Committee on the Constitution Report, *Devolution: Inter-Institutional Relations in the United Kingdom*, Session 2002–03, 2nd Report, HL Paper 28, 17 December 2002 (London: Stationery Office, 2002). Also see: *Memorandum of Understanding and Supplementary Agreements between the United Kingdom Government, Scottish Ministers and the Cabinet of the National Assembly for Wales*, Cm 4444, (London: Stationery Office, 1999).
6. The Constitution Unit.

Chapter 17

1. The functions transferred to the Borough and District Councils included: planning, highways and traffic management; waste regulation and disposal; housing; trading standards and related functions; support for the arts, sport and historic buildings; civil defence and emergencies; funding for Magistrates' Courts and the probation service; Coroners; school crossing patrols; building control; tourism and the licensing of places of entertainment; archives and libraries; recreation, parks and Green Belt land; safety of sports grounds; registration of common land and town or village greens; public rights of way and the registration of gypsy sites.
2. See: cityoflondon.gov.uk.
3. White Paper, *A Mayor and Assembly for London*, (Cm 3897), (London: Stationery Office, 1998).
4. See: House of Commons Library Research Paper Referendums: *Recent Developments*, 99/30, 16 March 1999.
5. See: *The Greater London Authority: The Government's Final Proposals for Additional Powers and Responsibilities for the Mayor and Assembly – A Policy Statement*, 06 LGSRU 04007/B (London: Department for Communities and Local Government, 13 July 2006).
6. See http://www.nlgn.org.uk/public/elected-mayors/mayoral-links/.
7. See S. Weir and W. Hall, *Ego Trip: Extra-governmental Organisation in the UK* (London: Charter 88 Trust, 1990).
8. See F. F. Ridley and D. Wilson (eds), *The Quango Debate*, (Oxford: Oxford University Press/Hansard Society, 1995).

9. See G. B. Adams, G. B., *Constitutional History of England*, 2nd edn, (London: Jonathon Case, 1941).
10. See Stevens, A., *Local Government* (London: Politico's, 2003), pp. 7–56.
11. *Report of the Royal Commission on Local Government in England*, (Cmnd 4040), (London: HMSO, 1969).
12. Green Paper, *New Leadership for London*, (Cm 3724), (London: Stationery Office, 1997).
13. White Paper, *A Mayor and Assembly for London*, (Cm 3897), (London: Stationery Office, 1998).
14. White Paper, *Modern Local Government: In Touch with the People*, (Cm 4014), (London: Stationery Office, 1998).
15. White Paper, *Local Leadership, Local Choice*, (Cm 4298), (London: Stationery Office, 1999).
16. Letter from Ruth Kelly, Secretary of State for Communities and Local Government, sent on 12 July 2006 in reply to the Prime Minister's remit letter of 9 May. See: http://www.communities.gov.uk.
17. See: *Local Government Finance* (the Layfield Report), Cmnd 6453 (London: HMSO, 1976); *The Labour Government's response to the Layfield Report*, Cmnd 6813 (London: HMSO, 1977); and *Alternatives to Domestic Rates*, Cmnd 8449 (London: HMSO, 1981), for a fuller discussion of these issues.
18. See: *A New Tax for Local Government*, Department of the Environment Consultation Paper, April 1991.
19. See: *Final Report, Lyons Inquiry into Local Government*, (Chairman: Sir Michael Lyons), (London: Stationery office, 2007). The report observed that the: 'Council tax is not "broken" but is seen as unfair' and made a number of short-term and medium-term recommendations to deal with the issues it had identified:
Key short-term recommendations:
• Automatic rebate for those entitled to Council Tax benefit
• Raise savings limit for pensioners to £50,000 '
• New powers for councils to charge for domestic waste and levy a supplementary business rate in consultation with business
• End capping of local authorities
• Improve transparency of tax system
• Provide incentives for local authorities to promote economic growth
Key medium-term recommendations:
• Revalue Council Tax
• New bands for most expensive and cheapest properties
• Consider reserving a fixed proportion of income tax for local government
• Give Councils power to levy a 'tourist tax'
• Improve incentives within the grant system.
In response the Government reaffirmed its commitment not to revalue Council Tax during the lifetime of the Parliament elected in 2005, declared that it would not be introducing a tourist tax, and stated that it would not be giving up its right to cap the spending of local authorities.
20. White Paper, *Local Leadership, Local Choice*, (Cm 4298), (London: Stationery Office, 1999), 1.10, p. 8.
21. See: *Report of the Maud Committee on Local Government Management*, (London: HMSO, 1967); *Report of the Committee of Inquiry into the System of Remuneration*

of Members of Local Authorities, Vol. 2 CMND 7010 (London: HMSO, 1977); *The Conduct of Local Authority Business*, (CMND 9797), (London: HMSO, 1986), paras 2.23–2.31; and K. Young and N. Rao, *Coming to Terms with Change? The Local Government Councillor in 1993*, (London: Joseph Rowntree Foundation, 1994). For more information on the socioeconomic profile of councillors over the years.

22. 'Local Government Management Board Census, March 1998' *The Guardian*, 20 March 1998.

23. For example see: National Census of Local Authority Councillors in England 2004 at: http://www.lga.gov.uk/Documents/Briefing/CensusofCllrEngland2004.pdf.

24. See K. B. Smellie, *History of Local Government* (London: Allen & Unwin, 1968), for a detailed historical account.

25. Report of the Inquiry into BSE and variant CJD in the United Kingdom, (Chair: Lord Phillips of Worth Matravers), House of Commons Papers 1999–00 887, (London: Stationery Office, October 2000).

26. N. P. Hepworth, *The Finance of Local Government*, 4th edn., (London: Allen & Unwin, 1978), p. 255.

27. J. A. G. Griffith, *Central Departments and Local Authorities*, (London: Allen & Unwin, 1966), p. 49.

28. *The Times*, 14 August 1981.

Chapter 18

1. There is no single legal system – either in terms of judicial organisation or body of law – which is applicable throughout the United Kingdom. Rather, there is one set of arrangements in England and Wales, one in Scotland, and one in Northern Ireland. In the detailed descriptions of civil and criminal courts and proceedings which follow, the focus is on the system as applicable to England and Wales. Nevertheless, these five points are essentially applicable throughout.

2. This concept has, however, at least been 'modified' in significant respects by Britain's membership of the European Union (See Chapter 21 for more on this) and through the incorporation of the European Convention on Human Rights into British law through the Human Rights Act 1998.

3. See *Report of the Royal Commission on Criminal Justice*, Cmnd 2263 (London: HMSO, 1993).

4. See *Report of the Royal Commission on Criminal Procedure*, Cmnd 8092 (London: HMSO, 1981).

5. See A. Travis, 'Fifty Bills Add 700 Offences as Jails Fill Up', *The Guardian*, 24 June 2006.

6. Solicitors are the branch of the legal profession chiefly concerned with advising clients and preparing their cases, while Barristers who have been 'called to the Bar' (qualified) are entitled to practise as advocates in superior Courts.

7. These are breaches of duty leading to liability for damages, but non-contractual in the case of tort.

8. *Prohibition* prevents a public authority from considering a matter which it has no statutory right to consider. *Mandamus* enables the High Court to compel a public body to perform a public duty which it is statutorily obliged to perform. *Certiorari* enables the High Court to quash an administrative decision already made by a public body. A writ of *habeas corpus* is supposed to prevent the police from

detaining without charge for more than 24 hours those suspected of non-serious offences, although in the case of suspected terrorists there is statutory provision for this time limit to be extended to three days inland and seven days at a port of entry.

9. The reason for this incongruous grouping was simply that all jurisdictions had a common basis in Roman law.

10. *Access to Justice – Final Report*, (The Rt. Hon. the Lord Woolf), (London: HMSO, 1996).

11. *Access to Justice – Final Report*, (The Rt. Hon. the Lord Woolf), (London: HMSO, 1996).

12. See K. Laybourn, *A History of British Trade Unionism c. 1770–1990* (Stroud: Alan Sutton, 1992), pp. 88–6.

13. G. Drewry, *Law, Justice and Politics* (London: Longman, 1975), p. 128.

14. The first – and at the time of writing the only – female Lord of Appeal in Ordinary (Lady Hale of Richmond) was appointed in 2004.

15. J. A. G. Griffith, *The Politics of the Judiciary* (London: Fontana, 1977), p. 193.

16. For example, an independent Judicial Appointments Commission was established by the Constitutional Reform Act in 2005 to select judicial office holders. See: http://www.judicialappointments.gov.uk.

17. Legal aid has, however, grown dramatically over the years. For the first 20 years of the scheme the total cost of aid did not exceed £10m a year. By 1980 the cost had risen to £100m and by 1990–91 it had reached £682 million. In 1997 the figure stood at £1.5 billion and by 2006 it stood at over £2 billion, a figure that was costing each tax payer nearly £100 per year.

18. See: *Legal Aid: A Market-based Approach to Reform*, (www.legalaidprocurementreview.gov.uk).

19. Formerly there was no restriction on the participation of lay peers in the judicial proceedings of the House of Lords. However, after the O'Connell case in 1844 (see: N. Gash, *Sir Robert Peel*, (London: Longman, 1972) pp. 424–5), in which their intervention would have had the effect of overturning the decision of the Law Lords (that is, the Lord Chancellor, the Lords of Appeal and such peers as held or had high judicial office in a superior Court), it became an established convention that they should not take part in the judicial office. The 1876 Appellate Jurisdiction Act provided for the appointment of two Lords of Appeal and declared that appeals to the Lords should not be heard unless at least three Law Lords were present. In 1948 the Lords authorised (on a temporary basis at first) the hearing of appeals by an Appellate Committee drawn from amongst the appointed Lords of Appeal (including the Lord Chancellor) and the other senior legal figures already mentioned. After a time this innovation became permanent, so that nearly all appeals to the House of Lords are now heard by the Law Lords sitting as either one or two Appellate Committees, depending on the number of cases to be heard. The 2005 Constitutional Reform Act reformed the post of Lord Chancellor, transferring the judicial functions of the position to that of President of the Courts of England and Wales (the Lord Chief Justice), and established a new, independent Supreme Court, separate from the House of Lords; it is scheduled to begin in October 2009.

20. These are Trinidad and Tobago, Singapore, Dominica, Kiribata, and The Gambia.

21. Both quoted in J. A. G. Griffith, *The Politics of the Judiciary*, p. 179 and p. 183. See also *Journal of the Society of Public Teachers of Law*, Vol. 12, 1972, 22.

22. See: 'The Battle for Civil Liberties', *The Independent*, 24 April 2006; 'The Judges v the Government: Wigging out', *The Economist*, 20 May 2006; and P. Riddell, 'Balancing Act of Rival Judges and Politicians Cannot Last', *The Times*, 16 June 2006.

23. H. W. R. Wade, *Administrative Law*, 4th edn, (Oxford: Clarendon Press, 1979), pp. 5–6.

24. Report of the Review of Tribunals, *Tribunals for Users – One System, One Service*, (Chair: Sir Andrew Leggatt), 2001. http://www.tribunals-review.org.uk/leggatthtm/leg-fw.htm.

25. White Paper, *Transforming Public Services: Complaints, Redress and Tribunals*, Cm 6243, (London: Stationery Office, 2004).

26. See: http://www.tribunals.gov.uk.

27. See Lord Hewart, *The New Despotism*, 2nd edn, (West Point: Greenwood, 1945), and W. Robson, *Justice and Administrative Law*, 3rd edn, (London: Stevens, 1951).

28. See: C. M. Clothier, *Ombudsman: Jurisdiction, Powers and Practise*, (Manchester: Manchester Statistical Society, 1981), for a description of the origins, development and role of the Ombudsman in Britain.

29. In addition there is, post-devolution, a *Public Service Ombudsman for Scotland* and a *Public Service Ombudsman for Wales*; there is also – of longer standing – a *Northern Ireland Ombudsman*. There is also a *Local Government Ombudsmen* in England whose job it is to investigate complaints made against local government bodies, as well as a *Judicial Appointments & Complaints Ombudsman* with responsibility to consider complaints from those who are dissatisfied with the handling of a complaint about a judge's conduct. There also exists a *Housing Ombudsman*; a *Financial Services Ombudsman* (there had been *six financial services Ombudsmen* – for banking, building societies, insurance, investments, pensions and personal investments – which were amalgamated in 1998–99 by the new super-regulator, the Financial Services Authority, into a single Ombudsman); and a *Prisons & Probations Ombudsman* (established in 1994 to investigate complaints from prisoners) as well as Ombudsmen for the Legal Services, Estate Agents, Telecommunication Services and Funeral Services.

30. Since its inception in 1967 the trend has been for steadily increasing numbers of complaints to be received by the Ombudsman. By the early 1990s this amounted to some 800–900 cases, of which approximately 200 were taken to full investigation. In 2005-06 the Parliamentary and Health Service Ombudsman accepted 3162 cases for investigation which, along with those already in progress carried forward from the previous year, gave a workload of 5482 cases. Reports were made on 3606 cases with 1849 cases carried into 2006–07. Of the complaints investigated in 2005–06, 37 per cent were upheld in full, 30 per cent were upheld in part, and 33 per cent were not upheld. Over 99 per cent of the recommendations that the Ombudsman made were complied with. See: http://www.ombudsman.org.uk/.

On the European front, under the terms of the Maastricht Treaty a European Ombudsman has been appointed to consider complaints of maladministration levelled against the institutions of the European Union. Between 1995 and 2005 the European Ombudsman handled more than 20,000 complaints. In 2005 a total of 3,920 complaints were received – 3705 from individuals and 215 from associations or companies – some 627 inquiries were dealt with (284 carried over from 2004) and a total of 312 were closed. See: http://www.euro-ombudsman.eu.int.

31. *Reform of Public Sector Ombudsmen Services in England*, Cabinet Office Consultation Paper, (London: Stationery Office, 2005).

32. An *injunction* and *declaration* are two of the legal remedies generally available to litigants and they are not confined to cases in which citizens seek to challenge public authorities.

33. T. C. Harley and J. A. G. Griffith, *Government and Law* (London: Weidenfeld & Nicolson, 1975), p. 230.

34. The number of applications for judicial review has risen sharply over the years: from 160 in 1974 to 2886 in 1993 to 4539 in 1998. For further information see: A. Horne and G. Berman, *Judicial Review: A Short Guide to Claims in the Administrative Court*, House of Commons Library Research Paper 06/44, 28 September 2006.

35. For example, see: Lord Scarman, *English Law, the New Dimension* (London: Stevens, 1974), and Lord Hailsham, *The Dilemma of Democracy* (London: Collins, 1978).

36. N. Johnson, *In Search of the Constitution* (London: Methuen, 1980), p. 149.

37. H. W. R. Wade, *Administrative Law*, p. 30.

Chapter 19

1. Thomas Hobbes, *Leviathan* (1651), (London: Collins/Fontana, 1972).

2. John Locke, *Two Treatises of Government* (1690), (Cambridge: Cambridge University Press, 1965).

3. P. J. Stanlis (ed.), *Edmund Burke: Selected Writings and Speeches*, (Edison, NJ: Transaction, 2006).

4. A. V. Dicey, *The Law of the Constitution* (1885), (London: Macmillan, 1959).

5. *Rights Brought Home: The Human Rights Bill*, (CM 3782), (London: Stationery Office, 1997), 2.13, p. 10.

6. *Rights Brought Home: The Human Rights Bill*, (CM 3782), (London: Stationery Office, 1997), 2.16, p. 11.

7. *The Draft Constitutional Treaty for the European Union*, Cm 5897, (London: Stationery Office, 2003), Part II pp. 33–41.

8. White Paper, *Secure Borders, Safe Haven. Integration with Diversity in Modern Britain*, Cm 5387, (London: Stationery Office, February 2002), 2.1, p. 29.

9. See: http://www.ind.homeoffice.gov.uk/applying/nationality/citizenshipceremonies/.

10. See: P. Thornton, 'Trial by Jury: Struggling to Survive?', *The Barrister*, Issue 27, 2006.

11. Amnesty International submission to MPs, November 2005. See: *The Independent*, 2 November 2005.

12. Charles Clarke (Home Secretary), address to the Civil Liberties Committee of the European Parliament. *The Daily Telegraph*, 14 July 2005.

13. This is the name given to a writ addressed to an individual who holds another in custody, directing them to produce the individual held and show cause for their detention. Where a writ is granted the individual held must be released at once. Failure to do so amounts to contempt of court. See note 9 for more information.

14. International migration statistics. See: http://www.statistics.gov.uk.

15. See: D. Beetham, L. Byrne, P. Ngan and S. Weir, *Democracy under Blair: A Democratic Audit of the United Kingdom*, 2nd edn, (London: Politico's, 2002) and

F. Klug, K. Starmer and S. Weir *The Three Pillars of Liberty: Political Rights and Freedoms in the UK*, (London: Routledge, 1996).

16. Salman Rushdie's book *Satanic Verses* was seen by some Muslims as blasphemous and, as a result, Ayatollah Khomeini of Iran issued a fatwa (a decree of death) against the author in February 1989. This was perceived, almost throughout the world, as an attack on the fundamental freedom of expression, religious tolerance and rule of law.

17. This problem has been addressed in attempts to reach agreement between the nations in both the European Union and the Council of Europe. However, no international broadcasting agreement is likely to be completely effective in an increasingly deregulated, global media market.

18. *Report of the Inquiry into the Circumstances Surrounding the Death of David Kelly*, (The Hutton Report), (HC 247) (London: Stationery Office, 2004).

19. See: S. Rodgers (ed.), *The Hutton Inquiry and its Impact*, (London: Politico's/ Guardian Books, 2004).

20. This restricted legal immunity from civil action in the Courts to the employees of the firm in dispute or the employees of a direct supplier or customer of the firm in dispute, thus theoretically limiting the scope for 'blacking' or sympathy strikes.

21. For example, see: *Review of Intelligence on Weapons of Mass Destruction*, Report of a Committee of Privy Counsellors (Chair: Lord Butler), HC 898, (London: Stationery Office, 2004), and *Intelligence and Security Committee Annual Reports* (eg: 2005-06, Cm 6864, London: Stationery Office, 2006).

22. White paper, *Your Right to Know: The Government's Proposals for a Freedom of Information Act*, Cm 3818, (London: Stationery Office, 1997).

23. The legislation came into force in January 2005, from May 2007 the responsible Department was the Ministry of Justice. See: http://www.justice.gov.uk/whatwedo/ freedomofinformation.htm.

24. Freedom of Information Act 2000, (ISBN 0 10 543600 3), (London: Stationery Office, 2000).

25. See *Freedom of Information Act 2000*, Part II, (ISBN 0 10 543600 3), (London: Stationery Office, 2000).

26. *A Report on the Surveillance Society for the Information Commissioner*, Surveillance Studies Network, September 2006.

27. Charles Clarke (Home Secretary), Royal Assent Statement, March 2006. See: http://press.homeoffice.gov.uk/Speeches/.

28. Amnesty International submission to MPs, November 2005. See: *The Independent*, 2 November 2005.

29. *Treaty on European Union*, Maastricht, 7 February 1992, Cmnd 1934 (London: HMSO, 1992).

30. See 'Report of the Royal Commission on the Police', Cmnd 1728 (London: HMSO, 1962).

31. Indeed, only 5.3 per cent of police personnel were trained in the use of firearms (and no untrained personnel were issued with a firearm). Between 1987 and 1997-98 police personnel fired a total of 57 shots, an average of fewer than six shots a year.

32. See British Crime Survey statistics at http://www.crimestatistics.org.uk.

33. Ipsos MORI 10 March 2005. See: http://www.ipsos-mori.com/polls/2005.

34. See D. Lawrence, *And Still I Rise: Seeking Justice for Stephen*, (London: Faber & Faber, 2007).
35. See: The Stephen Lawrence Inquiry Report, (Chair: Sir William Macpherson), Cm 4262 I/II, (London: Stationery Office, February 1999).
36. For example, see: *Human Rights: A Broken Promise*, (London: Amnesty International, 2006); 'Bonfire of the Liberties', *The Independent*, 4 May 2006; and H. Porter, 'Blair Laid Bare: The Article that may Get you Arrested', *The Independent*, 29 June 2006 on the one hand and Demos speech: 'Security, Freedom and the Protection of our values', John Reid, (Home Secretary), Wednesday 9 August 2006, (BBC web news, 9 August 2006) on the other.
37. British Crime Survey 2004–05. See: http://www.crimestatistics.org.uk.
38. Many offences are never reported to the police, and some of those that are do not get recorded. Indeed, it has been estimated (British Crime Survey 1993) that only about one in three offences are recorded in official statistics.
39. For example, a survey published at the end of 1992 showed that while 76 per cent of white respondents said that the police did a 'very good' or 'fairly good' job, this figure was 62 per cent among Asian respondents and 52 per cent among Afro-Caribbean respondents. See: *Public Satisfaction with Police Services*, Home Office Research and Planning Unit, Paper 73, December 1992. Also see: *Winning the Race: Policing Plural Communities*, (London: Home Office, 1998) and *Winning the Race – Revisited*, (London: Home Office, 2005) – both available at: http://www.police.homeoffice.gov.uk.
40. See *Prison Numbers Hit Record High*, BBC News website, 6 March 2002; Prison Reform Trust Study (http://www.prisonreformtrust.org.uk), April 2006; *Prisoners Held in Record Numbers*, BBC News website, 29 March 2007; and Institute for Public Policy Research Report (http://www.ippr.org.uk), April 2007.
41. See C. Walker and K. Starmer (eds), *Miscarriages of Justice*, (Oxford: Oxford University Press, 1999). Also see: http://www.innocent.org.uk, a website dedicated to documenting miscarriages of justice in Great Britain.

Chapter 20

1. See: *Modernising Government*, White Paper, Cm 4310, March 1999.
2. For example see: G. Lodge and B. Rogers, *Whitehall's Black Box*, (London: IPPR, 2006), and: W. G. Runciman (ed.), *Hutton and Butler: Lifting the Lid on the Workings of Power*, (Oxford: Oxford University Press, 2004).
3. See: P. Cowley, *The Rebels: How Blair Mislaid his Majority*, (London: Politico's, 2005).
4. See: 'Defining the Boundaries within the Executive: Ministers, Special Advisers and the Permanent Civil Service', Committee on Standards in Public Life, Ninth Report, Cm 5775, April 2003. Also see: 'Code of Conduct for Special Advisors', http://www.cabinetoffice.gov.uk/propriety_and_ethics/special_advisers/code.
5. For example, the 1970–74 Conservative Government of Edward Heath introduced a prices and incomes policy in 1972 despite having ruled out such an approach in its 1970 election manefesto.
6. See A. King, 'Overload: Problems of Governing in the 1970s', *Political Studies*, Vol. xxii, June–September 1975.
7. *Modernising Government*, White Paper, Cm 4310, March 1999.

8. Lord Hunt of Tanworth, 'Cabinet Strategy and Management', CIPFA/RIPA Conference, Eastborne, 9 June 1983. Cited in: P. Hennessey, *Cabinet*, (Oxford: Basil Blackwell, 1986), p. 191.

Chapter 21

1. For a detailed account of the background of British European policy prior to Britain joining in 1973 see: H. Young, *This Blessed Plot: Britain and Europe from Churchill to Blair* (London: Macmillan, 1998).

2. The key paragraphs in the 1971 White Paper *The United Kingdom and the European Communities*, Cmnd 4715 (London: HMSO, July 1971) stated: 'there is no question of any erosion of essential national sovereignty; what is proposed is a sharing and enlargement of individual national sovereignties in the general interest (para. 29) [and] at present the Communities' institutions are purely economic – but if the development of European policies in non-economic fields calls for new institutions, then as a member Britain will play a full and equal part in devising whatever additions to the institutional framework are required' (para. 30).

3. Section 2 (1) of the 1972 European Communities Act states: 'all such rights, powers, liabilities, obligations and restrictions from time to time created or arising by or under the Treaties, and all such remedies and procedures from time to time provided for by or under the Treaties, as in accordance with the Treaties are without further enactment to be given legal effect or used in the United Kingdom, shall be recognised and available in law, and be enforced, allowed and followed accordingly; and the expression "enforceable Community rights" and similar expressions shall be read as referring to one which this subsection applies.'

4. See Case 26/62 (1963) ECR1.

5. See Case 10/77 (1978) ECR 629.

6. See *Commission v. France*, Case 167/73 (1974) ECR 359.

7. See *Pigs Marketing Board v. Redmond*, Case 83/78 (1978) ECR 2347.

8. See *Minister for Fisheries v. Schoenenberg*, Case 88/77 (1978) ECR 473.

9. See *Major v. Department of Trade*, Case 118/78 (1979) ECR 1387.

10. See *Commission v. Ireland*, Case 61/77 (1978) ECR 417.

11. See *Shields v. E. Coomes* (Holdings) Ltd (1979), 1 All ER 456, 461-2.

12. For example, see: J. Redwood, *The Death of Britain*, (London: Macmillan, 1999).

13. See M. Butler, *Europe, More than a Continent*, (London: Heineman, 1986), p. 169.

14. Qualified majority voting was originally defined in Article 148(2) of the 1957 Rome Treaty. Under this procedure today the votes of each of the 27 member states are weighted as follows: Austria 10, Belgium 12, Bulgaria 10, Cyprus 4, Czech Republic 12, Denmark 7, Estonia 4, Finland 7, France 29, Germany 29, Greece 12, Hungary 12, Ireland 7, Italy 29, Latvia 4, Lithuania 7, Luxembourg 4, Malta 3, Netherlands 13, Poland 27, Portugal 12, Romania 14, Slovakia 7, Slovenia 4, Spain 27, Sweden 10, United Kingdom 29; a total of 345 votes. A Qualified Majority is reached if a majority of member states approve *and* if a minimum of votes – namely 73.9 per cent (255 out of the 345) – is cast in favour. In addition, a member state may ask for confirmation that the vote in favour represents at least 62 per cent of the total population of the Union.

15. See 'Protocol on the Role of National Parliaments in the European Union', *The Draft Constitutional Treaty for the European Union*, Cm 5897, (London: Stationery Office, August 2003), pp. 150–1.
16. http://www.parliament.uk/parliamentary-committees/european-scrutiny.cfm.
17. See A. Geddes, 'Political Parties and Party Politics', in I. Bache, *The Europeanization of British Politics*, (London: Palgrave, 2006).
18. In the devolution arrangements made for Scotland in the 1998 Scotland Act it was stipulated that although relations with the European Union would remain the responsibility of the Government of the United Kingdom, the Scottish Executive would be involved as closely as possible in United Kingdom decision-making on Europe. Indeed, Ministers of the Scottish Executive are expected to participate in relevant meetings of the Council of Ministers and the Scottish Parliament has the authority to scrutinise legislative proposals emanating from the European Union.
19. See E. N. Luttwak, *Turbo Capitalism: Winners and Losers in the Global Economy*, (USA: Texere Publishing, 1999).
20. Under the terms of a Protocol to the 1992 Treaty of Maastricht it was recognised that 'the United Kingdom shall not be obliged or committed to move to the third stage of Economic and Monetary Union without a separate decision to do so by its Government and Parliament'. The Conservative Government of the time also secured an 'opt-out' from the social Protocol attached to the Maastricht Treaty under which 11 out of the then 12 member states declared their intention to introduce binding measures to implement the provision of the 1989 Social Charter which the UK did not sign. However, the pre-existing Social Action Programme, based on earlier Treaty commitments, was not affected by the UK 'opt-out' and the UK continued to participate in negotiations on Commission proposals in this area of policy. Subsequently, the Labour Government elected in 1997 ended this Social Charter opt-out. The 1997 Treaty of Amsterdam recognised the overall flexibility of the European Union by introducing ground rules allowing some member states to go faster than others in particular areas of policy.
21. The doctrine of 'subsidarity' has its intellectual origin in a pronouncement by Pope Pius XI in 1931 in his *Rundschreiben uber die gesellschaftliche Ordnung* (Encyclical in Social order).
22. See 'Protocol on the Application of the Principles of Subsidiarity and Proportionality', *The Draft Constitutional Treaty for the European Union*, Cm 5897, (London: Stationery Office, August 2003), pp. 152–3.
23. See 'The Euro' section on HM Treasury website: http://www.hm-treasury.gov.uk/documents/international-issues/the-euro.

Chapter 22

1. See J. A. Schumpeter, *Capitalism, Socialism and Democracy*, 3rd edn (New York: Harper & Row, 1962), pp. 289–96.
2. See Q. Hailsham, *The Dilemma of Democracy*, (London: Collins, 1978), pp. 280–1.
3. See R. Subroto and J. Clarke (eds), *Margaret Thatcher's Revolution: How It Happened and What It Meant*, 2nd edn, (London: Continuum, 2006).
4. See Tony Blair speech at the Foreign Office Conference, 7 January 2003.

further reading

Chapter 1

Almond, G. A. and Verba, S. (eds), *The Civic Culture Revisited*, (Boston: Little, Brown, 1980).

Baldwin, N. D. J. (ed.), *Parliament in the 21st Century*, (London: Politico's, 2005).

Blundell, J. and Gosschalk, B., *Beyond Left and Right: The New Politics of Britain*, (London: Institute of Economic Affairs, 1997).

Brittan, S., *Left or Right: The Bogus Dilemma*, (London: Secker & Warburg, 1968).

Childs, D., *Britain Since 1945, 5th edn* (London: Routledge, 2001).

Clark, P., *Hope and Glory: Britain 1900–1990*, (London: Allen Lane, 1996).

Duffy, M., *England: The Making of the Myth from Stonehenge to Albert Square*, (London: Fourth Estate, 2002).

Forman, F. N., *Constitutional Change in the United Kingdom*, (London: Routledge, 2002).

Foster, C., *British Government in Crisis*, (Oxford: Hart Publishing, 2005).

Harrison, B., *The Transformation of British Politics 1860–1995*, (Oxford: University Press, 1996).

Marquand, D. and Seldon, A., *The Ideas that Shaped Post-War Britain*, (London: Fontana Press, 1996).

Marr, A., *A History of Modern Britain*, (London: Macmillan, 2007).

Marr, A., *The Day Britain Died*, (London: Profile Books, 2000).

Marr, A., *Ruling Britannia: The Failure and Future of British Democracy*, (London: Michael Joseph, 1995).

Marwick, A., *The Sixties. Cultural Revolution in Britain, France, Italy and the United States*, (Oxford: University Press, 1998).

McCormick, J., *Contemporary Britain*, 2nd Edn, (London: Palgrave, 2007).

Mills, D., *The Tribes of Britain: Who are We? And Where do We Come from?*, (London: Weidenfeld & Nicolson, 2005).

Morgan, K. O., *The People's Peace, British History 1945–89*, (Oxford: OUP, 1990).

Morrison, J., *Reforming Britain: New Labour, New Constitution?*, (London: Reuters/Pearson, 2001).

Paxman, J., *Friends in High Places: Who Runs Britain?*, (London: Michael Joseph, 1990).

Roberts, A., *A History of the English-Speaking Peoples Since 1900*, (London: Weidenfeld & Nicolson, 2006).

Robbins, K., *Great Britain: Identities, Institutions and the Idea of Britishness*, (London: Longman, 1998).

Sampson, A., *Who Runs This Place: The Anatomy of Britain in the 21st Century*, (London: John Murray, 2004).

Tiratsoo, N. (ed.), *From Blitz to Blair*, (London: Weidenfeld & Nicolson, 1997).

Weight, R., *Patriots: National Identity in Britain 1940–2000*, (London: Macmillan, 2002).

Welsh, F., *The Four Nations: A History of the United Kingdom*, (London: Harper Collins, 2002).

Websites

National Statistics Online   http://www.statistics.gov.uk

EU Statistics UK   http://www.eustatistics.gov.uk

Social Trends 2007   http://www.statistics.gov.uk/socialtrends37

    Census in England and Wales (2001)   http://www.statistics.gov.uk/census

    Census in Scotland (2001)   http://www.gro-scotland.gov.uk

    Census in Northern Ireland (2001)   http://www.nisra.gov.uk

Chapter 2

Alexander, R., *The Voice of the People. A Constitution for Tomorrow*, (London: Weidenfeld & Nicolson, 1997).

Baldwin, N. D. J., (ed.), *Parliament in the 21st Century*, (London: Politico's, 2005).

Barnett, A., *This Time. Our Constitutional Revolution*, (London: Vintage, 1997).

Benn, T., *Common Sense*, (London: Hutchinson, 1993).

Bogdanor, V., *Power and the People. A Guide to Constitutional Reform*, (London: Victor Gollancz, 1997).

Brazier, R., *Constitutional Reform*, (Oxford: Clarendon Press, 1991).

Forman, F. N., *Constitutional Change in the United Kingdom*, (London: Routledge, 2002).

Foster, C., *British Government in Crisis*, (Oxford: Hart publishing, 2005).

Graham, C. and Prosser, T., *Waiving the Rules: The Constitution under Thatcherism*, (Milton Keynes: Open University Press, 1988).

Hailsham, Q., *On the Constitution*, (London: HarperCollins, 1992).

Hazell, R., *Wave upon Wave: The Continuing Dynamism of Constitutional Reform* (London: The Constitution Unit, 2006).

Hazell, R. (ed.), *Constitutional Futures. A History of the Next Ten Years*, (London: The Constitution Unit, 1999).

Hennessy, P., *The Hidden Wiring: Unearthing the British Constitution* (London: Victor Gollancz, 1995).

House of Lords Select Committee on the Constitution, *Changing the Constitution: The Process of Constitutional Change*, 4th Report, Session 2001–02, HL Paper 69, 2002.

House of Lords Select Committee on the Constitution, *Reviewing the Constitution*, 1st Report, Session 2001–02, HL Paper 11, 2001.

Johnson, N., *In Search of the Constitution*, (London: Methuen, 1980).

Morrison, J., *Reforming Britain: New Labour, New Constitution?*, (London: Reuters/Pearson, 2001).

Norton, P., *The British Constitution in Flux*, (Oxford: Martin Robertson, 1982).

Wright, T., *Citizens and Subjects*, (London: Routledge, 1994).

Websites

Department for Constitutional Affairs   http://www.dca.gov.uk

House of Lords Select Committee on the Constitution   http://www.parliament.uk/parliamentary_committees/lords_constitution_committee

The Constitution Unit   http://www.ucl.ac.uk/constitution-unit

Chapter 3

Bogdanor, V., *What is Proportional Representation?*, (Oxford: Robertson, 1984).

Butler, D. and Kavanagh, D., *The British General Election of 2005*, (London: Palgrave, 2005).

Butler, D. and Kavanagh, D., *The British General Election of 2001*, (London: Palgrave, 2001).

Butler, D. and Kavanagh, D., *The British General Election of 1997*, (London: Palgrave, 1997).

Butler, D. and Kavanagh, D., *The British General Elections 1945–1992*, (London: Palgrave, 1999).

Constitution Unit, *Changed Voting Changed Politics: Lessons of Britain's Experience of PR since 1997*, Final Report of the Independent Commission to Review Britain's Experience of PR Voting Systems, (London: The Constitution Unit, 2004).

Constitution Unit, *Interim Report of the Independent Commission to Review Britain's Experience of PR Voting Systems*, (London: The Constitution Unit, 2003).

Denver, D., *Elections and Voters in Britain*, (London: Palgrave, 2006).

Electoral Commisssion, *Election 2005: Campaign Spending*, (London: The Electoral Commission, 2006).

Electoral Reform Society, *5 May 2005: Worst. Election. Ever.*, (London: Electoral Reform Society, 2005).

Electoral Reform Society, *Elections in the Twenty First Century: from Paper Ballot to E-voting*, Report of an independent Commission on Alternative Voting Methods, (London: Electoral Reform Society, 2001).

Evans, G. and Norris, P. (eds), *Critical Elections*, (London: Sage, 1999).

Finer, S. E. (ed.), *Adversary Politics and Electoral Reform*, (London: Anthony Wigram, 1975).

Geddes, A. and Tonge, J. (eds), *Britain Decides: The UK General Election 2005*, (London: Palgrave, 2005).

Hansard Society, *The Report of the Hansard Society Commission on Electoral Reform* (London: Hansard Society, 1976).

House of Commons, *General Election 2005*, House of Commons Research paper 05/33, 17 May 2005

Johnson, R., *From Votes to Seats: The Operation of the UK Electoral System since 1945*, (Manchester: Manchester University Press, 2001).

Norris, P. and Wlezien, C., (eds), *Britain Votes 2005*, (Oxford: University Press, 2005).

Norton, P., 'Does Britain Need Proportional Representation?', in R. Blackburn (ed.), *Constitutional Studies*, (London: Mansell, 1992).

Plant, R. *The Plant Report on Electoral Reform*, (The Labour Party/Guardian Newspaper, 1991).

The Report of the Independent Commission on the Voting System, (Chair: Lord Jenkins), CM 4090-1, (London: Stationery Office, 1998).

Websites

The Boundary Committee for England http://www.boundarycommittee.org.uk

BBC General Election 2005   http://www.bbc.co.uk/election05/

The Electoral Commission   http://www.electoralcommission.org.uk

The Electoral Reform Society   http://www.electoral-reform.org.uk/

Chapter 4

Butler, D. and Kavanagh, D., *The British General Election of 2005*, (London: Palgrave, 2005).

Butler, D. and Kavanagh, D., *The British General Election of 2001*, (London: Palgrave, 2001).

Butler, D. and Kavanagh, D., *The British General Elections 1945–1992*, (London: Palgrave, 1999).

Butler, D. and Kavanagh, D., *The British General Election of 1997*, (London: Palgrave, 1997).

Denver, D., *Elections and Voters in Britain*, (London: Palgrave, 2006).

Electoral Reform Society, *Elections in the Twenty First Century: from Paper Ballot to E-voting*, Report of an independent Commission on Alternative Voting Methods, (London: Electoral Reform Society, 2001).

Electoral Reform Society, *5 May 2005: Worst. Election. Ever.*, (London: Electoral Reform Society, 2005).

Electoral Reform Society, *Turning out or Turning off? An Analysis of Political Disengagement and what Can be Done about it*, (London: Electoral Reform Society, 2004).

Evans, G., (ed.), *The End of Class Politics? Class Voting in Comparative Context*, (Oxford: Oxford University Press, 1999).

Franklin, M., *The Decline of Class Voting in Britain*, (London: University Press, 1985).

Geddes, A. and Tonge, J. (eds), *Britain Decides: The UK General Election 2005*, (London: Palgrave, 2005).

Hansard Society, *An Audit of Political Engagement 4*, (London: Hansard Society and the Electoral Commission, 2007).

Hansard Society, *An Audit of Political Engagement 3*, (London: Hansard Society and the Electoral Commission, 2006).

Hansard Society, *An Audit of Political Engagement 2*, (London: Hansard Society and the Electoral Commission, 2005).

Hansard Society, *An Audit of Political Engagement 1*, (London: Hansard Society and the Electoral Commission, 2004).

Heath, A. et al., *Understanding Political Change: the British Voter 1964–1987*, (Oxford: Pergamon Press, 1991).

House of Commons, *General Election 2005*, House of Commons Research paper 05/33, 17 May 2005.

Johnson, R., *From Votes to Seats: The Operation of the UK Electoral System since 1945*, (Manchester: Manchester University press, 2001).

King, A. (ed.), *New Labour Triumphs: Britain at the Polls*, (Chatham, NJ: Chatham House, 1998).

Miller. W. L. et al., *How Voters Change*, (Oxford: Clarendon Press, 1990).

Norris, P. and Wlezien, C., (eds), *Britain Votes 2005*, (Oxford: University Press, 2005).

Power To the People. The Report of Power: An Independent Inquiry into Britain's Democracy, (York: York Publishing Distribution, 2006).

Robertson. D., *Class and the British Electorate*, (Oxford: Martin Robertson, 1983).

Sarlvik. B. and Crewe, I., *Decade of Dealignment*, (London: University Press, 1983).

Scarborough, E., *Political Ideology and Voting*, (Oxford: Clarendon Press, 1984).

Wring, D., Green, J., Mortimore, R. and Atkinson, S. (eds), *Political Communications: The General Election of 2005*, (London: Palgrave, 2007).

Websites

BBC General Election 2005   http://www.bbc.co.uk/election05/

The Boundary Committee for England   http://www.boundarycommittee.org.uk

Centre for Research into Elections and Social Trends   http://www.crest.ox.ac.uk

The Electoral Commission   http://www.electoralcommission.org.uk

The Electoral Reform Society   http://www.electoral-reform.org.uk/

The Power Inquiry   http://www.powerinquiry.org

Chapter 5

Ball, S. and Seldon, A., *Recovering Power: The Conservatives in Opposition Since 1867*, (London: Palgrave, 2005).

Blake, R., *The Conservative Party from Peel to Major*, (London: Heinemann, 1997).

Cook, C., *A Short History of the Liberal Party 1900–1997*, (London: Macmillan, 1998).

Davies, A. J., *To Build a New Jerusalem*, (London: Michael Joseph, 1992).

Driver, S., *New Labour: Politics after Thatcherism*, (London: Pluto, 1998).

Ewing, K., *The Funding of Political Parties in Britain*, (Cambridge: University Press, 1987).

The Funding of Political Parties in the United Kingdom, First Report of the House of Commons Constitutional Affairs Select Committee, HC163-I/II, (London: Stationery Office, 13 December 2007).

The Funding of Political Parties in the United Kingdom, Fifth Report of the Committee on Standards in Public Life CM 4057-1 (London: Stationery Office, 1998).

Gould, P., *The Unfinished Revolution: How the Modernisers saved the Labour Party*, (London: Little, Brown, 1998).

Ingle, S. *The British Party System*, 3rd edn (Oxford: Basil Blackwell, 2000).

Jenkins, S., *Thatcher & Sons: A Revolution in Three Acts*, (London: Allen Lane, 2006).

Lynch, P., *The End of Conservative Britain?*, (London: Palgrave, 2007).

Norton, P. (ed.), *The Conservative Party*, (London: Prentice Hall/Harvester Wheatsheaf, 1996).

Riddell, P., *The Thatcher Era and Its Legacy*, (Oxford: Basil Blackwell, 1991).

Seldon, A., (ed.), *The Blair Effect: The Blair Government 1997–2001*, (London: Little, Brown, 2001).

Seldon, A. (ed.), *UK Political Parties since 1945*, (Hemel Hempstead: Philip Allan, 1990).

Seldon, A. and Ball, S. (ed), *Conservative Century: The Conservative Party Since 1900*, (London: University Press, 1994).

Seldon, A., and Kavanagh, D., (eds), *The Blair Effect 2001–5*, (Cambridge: Cambridge University Press, 2005).

Seyd, P., Whiteley, P. and Parry, J., *Labour and Conservative Party Membership: Social Characteristics, Political Attitudes and Activities*, (Aldershot: Dartmouth, 1996).

Shaw, E., *The Labour Party Since 1979: Crisis and Transformation*, (London: Routledge, 1994).

Stevenson, J., *Third Party Politics Since 1945: Liberals, Alliance and Liberal Democrats*, (Oxford: Basil Blackwell, 1993).

Webb, P., *The Modern British Party System*, (London, Sage, 2000).

Websites

Conservative Party   http://www.conservative-party.org.uk/
Labour Party   http://www.labour.org.uk/
Liberal Democrats   http://www.libdems.org.uk/
Plaid Cymru   http://www.plaid-cymru.wales.com/
Scottish National Party   http://www.snp.org.uk/
Sinn Fein   http://www.irlnet.com/sinnfein/index.html
Social Democratic & Labour Party   http://www.sdlp.ie/sdlp/
Ulster Democratic Unionist Party   http://www.dup.org/
Ulster Unionists Party   http://www.uup.org/

Chapter 6

Baggott, R., *Pressure Groups Today*, (Manchester: University Press, 1995).

Brennan, T., *Pressure Groups and the Political System*, (London: Longman, 1985).

Byrne, P., *Social Movements in Britain*, (London: Routledge, 1997).

Coxall, B., *Pressure Groups in British Politics*, (London: Longman/Pearson, 2001).

Crouch C. and Dore, R. (eds), *Corporatism and Accountability: Organised Interests in British Public Life*, (Oxford: Clarendon Press, 1990).

Grant, W., *Pressure Groups and Politics*, (London: Macmillan, 2000).

Greenwood, J., *Representing Interests in the European Union*, (London: Macmillan, 1997).

Jordan, A. G. and Maloney, A., *Democracy and Interest Groups*, (London: Palgrave, 2007).

Jordan, A. G. and Richardson, J. J., *The Protest Business? Mobilizing Campaign Groups*, (Manchester: Manchester University Press, 1997).

Jordan, A. G. and Richardson, J. J., *Government and Pressure Groups in Britain*, London: OUP, 1987).

Lowe, O. and Goyder, J., *Environmental Groups in Politics*, (London: Allen & Unwin, 1983).

Marsh, D., *The New Politics of British Trade Unionism: Union Power and the Thatcher Legacy*, (London: Macmillan, 1992).

Middlemass, K., Power, *Competition and the State, Vol. 3: The End of the Post-War Era*, (London: Macmillan, 1991).

Miller, C., *Lobbying Government*, (Oxford: Basil Blackwell, 1987).

Nownes, A., *Total Lobbying: What lobbyists Want (and How They Try to Get It)*, (Cambridge: Cambridge University Press, 2006).

Rush, M. (ed.), *Parliament and Pressure Politics*, (London: OUP, 1990).

Simpson, D., *Pressure Groups*, (London: Hodder & Stoughton, 1999).

Smith, M., *Pressure Power and Policy*, (Hemel Hempstead: Harvester Wheatsheaf, 1993).

Weir, S. and Beetham, D., *Political Power and Democratic Control in Britain*, (London: Routledge, 1999).

Whiteley, P. and Winyard, S., *Pressure for the Poor: The Poverty Lobby and Policy Making*, (London: Methuen, 1987).

Wilson, D., *Pressure, the A to Z of Campaigning in Britain*, (London: Heinemann, 1984).

Websites

Amnesty International   http://www.amnesty.org

Confederation of British Industry   http://www.cbi.org.uk/

Electoral Reform Society   http://www.electoral-reform.org.uk/

European Movement   http://www.euromove.org.uk

European Policy Forum   http://www.epflpd.org.

Friends of the Earth   http://www.foe.co.uk/

Greenpeace   http://www.greenpeace.org.uk

Howard League for Penal reform   http://www.howardleague.org

Mind (National Association for Mental Health)   http://mind.org.uk

Shelter   http://shelter.org.uk

Trades Union Congress   http://www.tuc.org.uk/

Chapter 7

Aaronovitch, D. et al., *The Hutton Inquiry and its impact*, (London: Politico's/Guardian, 2004).

Crewe, I., Gosschalk, B. and Bartle, J. (eds), *Political Communications*, (London: Frank Cass, 1998).

Curran, J. and Seaton, J., *Power without Responsibility*, 3rd edn (London: Routledge, 1991).

Gavin, N., *Media, Money and Democracy: Press and Television in British Politics*, (London: Palgrave, 2007).

Gibson, R., Nixon, P. and Ward, S. (eds), *Net Gain? Political Parties and the Internet*, (London: Routledge, 2003).

Hansard Society, *Members Only Parliament in the Public Eye*, Report of the Hansard Society Commission on the Communication of Parliamentary Democracy, (Chair: Lord Puttnam), (London: Hansard Society, 2005).

Hansard Society, *Parliament in the Public Eye 2006: Coming into Focus?*, (London: Hansard Society, 2006).

Hargreaves, I., *Sharper Vision*, (London: Demos, 1994).

Harris, R., *Good and Faithful Servant*, (London: Faber, 1990).

Ingham B., *Kill the Messenger*, (London: Fontana, 1991).

Jones, N. *Sultans of Spin*, (London: Orion, 2000).

Jones, N., *Soundbites & Spin Doctors*, (London: Indigo, 1996).

Kuhn, R., *Politics and the Media in Britain*, (London: Palgrave, 2007).

Margolis, M. and Resnick, D., *Politics as Usual: The Cyberspace Revolution*, (Thousand Oaks, CA: Sage, 2000).

Marr, A., *Ruling Britannia*, (London: Michael Joseph, 1995).

Negrine, R., *Politics and the Mass Media in Britain*, 2nd edn (London: Routledge, 1995).

Riddell, P., 'Parliament and the Media', in Baldwin, N. D. J., (ed.), *Parliament in the 21st Century*, (London: Politico's, 2005), pp. 48–59.

Sampson, A., *Who Runs This Place: The Anatomy of Britain in the 21st Century*, (London: John Murray, 2004).

Seaton, J. and Pimlott, B., *The Media in British Politics*, (Aldershot: Gower, 1987).

Seymour-Ure, C., *The British Press and Broadcasting since 1945*, (Oxford: Blackwell, 1991).

Tunstall, J., *Newspaper Power: The New National Press in Britain*, (Oxford: Clarendon Press, 1996).

Watts, D., *Political Communication Today*, (Manchester: University Press, 1997).

Wring, D., Green, J., Mortimore, R. and Atkinson, S. (eds), *Political Communications: The General Election of 2005*, (London: Palgrave, 2007).

Websites

Advertising Standards Authority   http://www.asa.org.uk

BBC   www.bbc.co.uk

Broadcasting Standards Commission   http://www.bsc.org.uk

Channel Four   www.channel4.co.uk

Department for Culture, Media and Sport   http://www.culture.gsi.gov.uk

Independent Television Commission   http://www.itc.org.uk

ITV   www.itv.co.uk

Media UK   http://www.mediauk.com

Media watch UK (Formerly the National Viewers' and Listeners' Association)   http://mediawatchuk.org.uk

National Consumer Council   http://www.ncc.org.uk

Office of Communications (Ofcom)   http://www.ofcom.org.uk

Radio Authority   http://www.radioauthority.org.uk

The Daily Telegraph   www.telegraph.co.uk

The Financial Times   www.ft.com

The Guardian   www.guardian.co.uk

The Independent   www.independent.co.uk

The Times   www.thetimes.co.uk

Chapter 8

Butler, D. and Kavanagh, D., *The British General Election of 2005*, (London: Palgrave, 2005).

Broughton, D., *Public Opinion Polling and Politics in Britain*, (London: Prentice Hall/ Harvester Wheatsheaf, 1995).

Clemens, J., *Polls, Politics and Populism*, (London: Gower, 1983).

Cook, C. and Ramsden, J. (eds), *By-Elections in British Politics*, (London: University College Press, 1997).

Geddes, A. and Tonge, J. (eds.), *Britain Decides: The UK General Election 2005*, (London: Palgrave, 2005).

Jowell, R. et al., *British Social Attitudes*, (London: Gower, 1990).

Moon, N., *Opinion Polls: History, Theory and Practice*, (Manchester: Manchester University Press, 1999).

Norris, P. and Wlezien, C., (eds), *Britain Votes 2005*, (Oxford: University Press, 2005).

Ranney, A. (ed.), *The Referendum Device*, (Washington, DC: American Enterprise Institute, 1981).

Teer, F. and Spence, J. D., *Political Opinion Polls*, (London: Hutchinson, 1973).

Worcester, R. M., *British Public Opinion: A Guide to the History and Methodology of Political Opinion Polling*, (Oxford: Blackwell, 1991).

Worcester, R. M. and Harrop, M. (eds), *Political Communications*, (London: Allen & Unwin, 1982).

Wybrow, R. J., *Britain Speaks Out, 1937–87*, (London: Macmillan, 1989).

Websites

Communicate Research   http://www.communicateresearch.com

Gallup Poll   http://www.gallup.com

ICM Polls   http://www.icmresearch.co.uk

IPSOS-MORI   http://www.ipsos-mori.com

National Centre for Social Research   http://www.natcen.ac.uk

Populus   http://www.populuslimited.com

YouGov   http://www.yougov.com

Chapter 9

Bagehot, W., *The English Constitution*, (London: Fontana/Collins, 1963).

Barnett, A., *Power and the Throne: The Monarchy Debate*, (London: Vintage, 1994).

Bogdanor, V., *The Monarchy and the Constitution*, (London: OUP, 1995).

Borthwick, R., *Long to Reign Over Us? The Future of the Monarchy*, (London: John Stuart Mill Institute, 1994).

Borthwick, R., *The Monarchy*, (Barnstaple: Philip Charles Media, 1990).

Bradford, S., *Elizabeth*, (London: BCA, 1996).

Dimbleby, J., *The Prince of Wales*, (London: Little Brown, 1994).

Douglas-Home, C., (and Kelly, S.), *Dignified & Efficient: The British Monarchy in the Twentieth Century*, (Wiltshire: Claridge Press, 2000).

Flamin, R., *Sovereign*, (London: Bantam, 1991).

Forman, F. N., *Constitutional Change in the United Kingdom*, (London: Routledge, 2002).

Hall, P., *Royal Fortune: Tax, Money and the Monarchy*, (London: Bloomsbury, 1992).

Hardie, F., *The Political Influence of the British Monarchy 1868–1952*, (London: Batsford, 1970).

Holden, A., *The Tarnished Crown*, (London: Bantam, 1993).

Keay, D., *Elizabeth II: Portrait of a Monarch*, (London: Ebony Press, 1992).

Paxman, J., *On Royalty*, (London: Viking, 2006).

Pimlott, B., *The Queen*, (London: HarperCollins, 1996).

Taylor, A., 'Down with the Crown', British Anti-monarchism and Debates about Royalty since 1790, (London: Reaktion Books, 1999).

Ziegler, P., *Crown and People*, (London: Collins, 1978).

Website

The Queen   http://www.royal.gov.uk/

Chapter 10

Bagehot, W., *The English Constitution* (1867), (London: Fontana, 1978).

Baldwin, N. D. J. (ed.), *Parliament in the 21st Century*, (London: Politico's, 2005).

Baldwin, N. D. J. and Shell, D. (eds), *Second Chambers*, (London: Frank Cass, 2001).

Baldwin N. D. J., *The House of Lords*, (Barnstaple: Philip Charles Media, 1990).

Bromhead, P. A., *The House of Lords and Contemporary Politics*, (London: Routledge & Kegan Paul, 1958).

Clarke, K., Cook, R., Tyler, P., Wright, T. and Young, G., *Reforming the House of Lords: Breaking the Deadlock*, (London: Constitution Unit, 2005).

Constitution Unit, *Reform of the House of Lords*, (London: Constitution Unit, 1996).

Crewe, E., *Lords of Parliament: Manners, Rituals and Politics*, (Manchester: Manchester University Press, 2005).

Department for Constitutional Affairs, *Constitutional Reform: Next Steps for the House of Lords*, Department for Constitutional Affairs, CPR 14/03, April 2004.

Dickson, B. and Carmichael, P. (eds), *The House of Lords: Its Parliamentary and Judicial Roles*, (Oxford: Hart Publishing, 1999).

Forman, F. N., *Constitutional Change in the United Kingdom*, (London: Routledge, 2002).

Initial report of The Constitutional Commission to Consider Options for a New Second Chamber (Chair: Lord Mackay of Clashfern), (London: Constitutional Commission, September 1998).

Limon, D. and McKay, W. R., (eds), *Erskine May's Treatise on the Law, Privileges, Proceedings and Usage of Parliament*, 22nd edn(London: Butterworths, 1997).

Morgan, J. P., *The House of Lords and the Labour Government, 1964–70*, (Oxford: Clarendon Press, 1975).

Norton, P. (ed.), *Parliament in the 1980s*, (Oxford: Basil Blackwell, 1985).

Report of the Royal Commission on the Reform of the House of Lords, (Chairman: Lord Wakeham), *A House for the Future*, Cm 4534, (London: Stationery Office, 2000).

Rogers, R. and Walters, R., *How Parliament Works*, 6th edn (London: Pearson/Longman, 2006).

Russell, M. and Sciara, M., *The House of Lords in 2005: A More Representative and Assertive Chamber?*, (London: Constitution Unit, 2006).

Shell, D., *The House of Lords*, 2nd edn (Oxford: Philip Allan, 1992).

Shell, D. and Beamish, D. (eds), *The House of Lords at Work*, (Oxford: Clarendon Press, 1993).

Smith, E.A., *The House of Lords in British Politics and Society 1815–1911*, (London: Longman, 1992).

Wells, J., *The House of Lords*, (London: Hodder & Stoughton, 1997).

White Paper, *House of Lords: Reform*, Cm 7027, (London: Stationery Office, 2007).

White Paper, *The House of Lords: Completing the Reform*, Cm 5291, (London: Stationery Office, 2001).

White Paper, *Modernising Parliament: Reforming the House of Lords*, Cm 4183 (London: Stationery Office, 1999).

Website

Parliament   http://www.parliament.uk/lords

Chapter 11

Baldwin, N. D. J. (ed.), *Executive Leadership and Legislative Assemblies*, (London: Routledge, 2006).

Baldwin, N. D. J. (ed.), *Parliament in the 21st Century*, (London: Politico's, 2005).

Brazier, A., Flinders, M. and McHugh, D., *New Politics, New Parliament?*, (London: Hansard Society, 2005).

Brazier, A., (ed), *Parliament, Politics and Law Making*, (London: Hansard Society, 2004).

Cowley, P., *The Rebels: How Blair Mislaid his Majority*, (London: Politico's, 2005).

Cowley, P. (ed.), *Conscience and Parliament*, (London: Frank Cass, 1998).

Drewry, G. (ed.), *The New Select Committees*, rev. edn (Oxford: OUP, 1989).

Forman, F. N., *Constitutional Change in the United Kingdom*, (London: Routledge, 2002).

Gay, O. and Leopold, P. (eds), *Conduct Unbecoming: The Regulation of Parliamentary Behaviour*, (London: Politico's, 2004).

Giddings, P. (ed.), *The Future of Parliament*, (London: Palgrave, 2005).

House of Lords Select Committee on the Constitution Report, *Parliament and the Legislative Process*, (Volume I and Volume II), HL Papers, 173-I and 173-II (London: Stationery Office, 2004).

Kelly, R., Holden, H. and Parry, K., *Pre-legislative Scrutiny*, Parliament and Constitution Centre, House of Commons Library, SN/PC/2822, 8 February 2007.

Limon, D. and McKay, W. R. (eds), *Erskine May's Treaties on the Law, Privileges, Proceedings, and Usage of Parliament* 22nd edn (London: Butterworth, 1997).

Norton, P., *Parliament in British Politics*, (London: Palgrave, 2005).

Norton, P., *Does Parliament Matter?*, (London: Harvester Wheatsheaf, 1993).

Norton, P., *The Commons in Perspective*, (Oxford: Martin Robertson, 1981).

Renton, T., *Chief Whip: People, Power and Patronage in Westminster*, (London: Politico's, 2004).

Report of the Commission to Strengthen Parliament (Chairman: Lord Norton of Louth): *Strengthening Parliament*, (London: Conservative Party, 2000).

Report, Select Committee on Modernisation of the House of Commons, *The Legislative Process*, Session 1997-98, HC 190, 29 July 1997.

Riddell, P., *Parliament Under Pressure*, (London: Victor Gollancz, 1998).

Rogers, R. and Walters, R., *How Parliament Works*, 6th edn (London: Pearson/Longman, 2006).

Rush, M., *Parliament Today*, (Manchester: Manchester University Press, 2005).

Rush, M., *The Role of the Member of Parliament Since 1868*, (Oxford: Oxford University Press, 2001).

Winetrobe, B. K., *Shifting Control? Aspects of the Executive-parliamentary Relationship*, Research Paper 00/92, (London: House of Commons Library, 2000).

Website

Parliament   http://www.parliament.uk/commons
Revolts by MPs   http://www.revolts.co.uk

Chapter 12

Allen, G., *The Last Prime Minister: Being Honest About the UK Presidency*, (London: Graham Allen MP, 2001).

Baldwin, N. D. J. (ed.), *Parliament in the 21st Century*, (London: Politico's, 2005).

Barber, M., *Instruction to Deliver – Tony Blair, Public Services and Archeiving Targets*, (London: Politico's, 2007).

Benn, A., *Diaries*, Vols. I–IV (London: Hutchinson, 1987–90).

Blake, R., *The Office of Prime Minister*, (Oxford: Oxford University Press, 1975).

Burch, M. and Holliday, I., *The British Cabinet System*, (Hemel Hempstead: Prentice-Hall, 1996).

Callaghan, L. J., *Time and Chance*, (London: Collins, 1987).

Cowley, P., *The Rebels: How Blair Mislaid his Majority*, (London: Politico's, 2005).

Fawcett, P. and Gay, O., *The Centre of Government – No 10, the Cabinet Office and HM Treasury*, House of Commons Library Research Paper 05/92, 21 December 2005.

Foley, M., *The Rise of the British Presidency*, (Manchester: Manchester University Press, 1993).

Forman, F. N., *Constitutional Change in the United Kingdom*, (London: Routledge, 2002).

Hennessy, P., *The Prime Minister: The Office and its Holders since 1945*, (London: Allen Lane, 2000).

Hennessy, P., *Cabinet*, (Oxford: Blackwell, 1986).

Hogg, S. and Hill, J., *Too Close to Call: Power and Politics – John Major in No. 10* (London: Little Brown, 1995).

Howe, G., *Conflicts of Loyalty*, (London: Macmillan, 1994).

James, S., *British Cabinet Government*, (London: Routledge, 1992).

Kavanagh, D. and Seldon, A., *The Powers Behind the Prime Minister*, (London: HarperCollins, 1999).

Kavanagh, D., *Thatcherism and British Politics*, (Oxford: Oxford University Press, 1987).

Lawson, N., *The View from Number 11*, (London: Bantam Press, 1992).

Major, J., *John Major: the Autobiography*, (London: HarperCollins, 1999).

Morgan, K. O., *Callaghan: A Life*, (Oxford: Oxford University Press, 1977).

Naughtie, J., *The Accidental American: Tony Blair and the Presidency*, (London: Macmillan, 2004).

Quinlan, M., 'Blair Has Taken us towards an Elective Dictatorship', *The Guardian*, 22 October, 2004.

Renton, J., *Tony Blair: Prime Minister*, (London: little, Brown, 2001).

Riddell, P., *The Thatcher Era and Its Legacy*, (Oxford: Basil Blackwell, 1991).

Seldon, A. (ed.), *The Blair Effect: The Blair Government 1997–2001*, (London: Little, Brown, 2001).

Seldon, A., and Kavanagh, D., (eds), *The Blair Effect 2001–5*, (Cambridge: Cambridge University Press, 2005).

Seldon, A., *Major: A Political Life*, (London: Weidenfeld & Nicolson, 1997).

Shell, D. and Hodder-Williams, R. (eds), *Churchill to Major: The British Prime Ministership Since 1945*, (London: Hurst and Company, 1995).

Thatcher, M., *The Downing Street Years*, (London: HarperCollins, 1993).

Watkins, A., *The Road to Number 10: From Bonar Law to Tony Blair*, (London: Duckworth, 1998).

Young, H., *One of Us*, rev. edn (London: Pan Books, 1990).

Website

No 10 Downing Street   http:/www.number–10.gov.uk

Chapter 13

Baldwin, N. D. J. (ed.), *Parliament in the 21st Century*, (London: Politico's, 2005).

Bruce-Gardyne, J., *Ministers and Mandarins*, (London: Sidgwick & Jackson, 1986).

Committee on Standards in Public Life, *Defining the Boundaries within the Executive: Ministers, Special Advisers and the Permanent Civil Service*, Ninth Report, Cm 5775, (London: Stationery Office, 2003).

Drewry, G. and Butcher, T., *The Civil Service Today*, 2nd edn, (Oxford: Basil Blackwell, 1991).

Fawcett, P. and Gay, O., *The Centre of Government – No. 10, the Cabinet Office and HM Treasury*, House of Commons Library Research Paper 05/92, 21 December 2005.

Forman, F. N., *Constitutional Change in the United Kingdom*, (London: Routledge, 2002).

Gay, O. and Powell, T., *Individual Ministerial Responsibility – Issues and Examples*, Parliament and Constitution Centre, House of Commons Library, Research Paper, 04/31, 5 April 2004.

Hennessy, P., *Whitehall* 2nd edn (London: Fontana, 1990).

Hennessy, P., *Cabinet*, (Oxford: Basil Blackwell, 1986).

House of Commons Public Administration Select Committee Report, *Politics and Administration: Ministers and Civil Servants*, HC 122-1, (London: Stationery Office, 2007).

James, S., *British Cabinet Government*, (London: Routledge, 1992).

Kaufman, G., *How to be a Minister*, (London: Faber & Faber, 1997).

Kellner, P. and Crowther-Hunt, Lord, *The Civil Servants*, (London: Macdonald, 1980).

King, S., *Regulating the Behaviour of Ministers, Special Advisers and Civil Servants*, (London: Constitution Unit, 2003).

Lodge, G. and Rogers, B., *Whitehall's Black Box: Accountability and Performance in the Senior Civil Service*, (London: Institute of Public Policy Research, 2006).

Nairne, P., *The Civil Service: Ministers and Mandarins*, (Barnstaple: Philip Charles Media, 1990).

O'Donnell, G., *The Modern Civil Service*, (London: Guardian Public Services Summit speech, 2006).

Report of a Committee of Privy Counsellors (Chairman: Lord Butler of Brockwell), *Review of Intelligence on Weapons of Mass Destruction*, HC 898, (London: Stationery Office, 2004).

Rodgers, S. (ed.), *The Hutton Inquiry and its Impact*, (London: Politico's/Guardian Books, 2004).

Runciman, W. G. (ed.), *Hutton and Butler: Lifting the Lid on the Workings of Power*, (Oxford: Oxford University Press, 2004).

Thompson, B. and Ridley, F. F. (eds), *Under The Scott-Light*, (Oxford: Oxford University Press, 1997).

Wilson of Dinton, Lord, *Tomorrow's Government*, (London: Constitution Unit, 2006).

Young, H. and Sloman A., *But, Chancellor*, (London: BBC, 1984).

Young, H. and Sloman, A., *No Minister*, (London: BBC, 1982).

Websites

A–Z of UK Central Government   http://www.direct.gov.uk

Cabinet Office   http://www.cabinetoffice.gov.uk

Department for Constitutional Affairs   http://www.dca.gov.uk

Treasury   http://www.hmt.gov.uk

Chapter 14

A Draft Civil Service Bill: A Consultation Document, Cm 6373, (London: Stationery Office, 2004).

Barberis, P. (ed.), *The Whitehall Reader: The UK's Administrative Machine in Action*, (Buckingham: Open University Press, 1996).

Bruce-Gardyne, J., *Ministers and Mandarins*, (London: Sidgwick & Jackson, 1986).

Burnham, J. and Pyper, R., *Britain's Modernised Civil Service*, (London: Palgrave, 2007).

Committee on Standards in Public Life, *Defining the Boundaries within the Executive: Ministers, Special Advisers and the Permanent Civil Service*, Ninth Report, Cm 5775, (London: Stationery Office, 2003).

Dickie, J., *The New Mandarins*, (London: I. B. Tauris, 2004).

Dyness, M. and Walker, D., *The Times Guide to the New British State: The Government Machine in the 1990s*, (London: Times Books, 1995).

Fawcett, P. and Gay, O., *The Centre of Government – No 10, the Cabinet Office and HM Treasury*, House of Commons Library Research Paper 05/92, 21 December 2005.

Forman, F. N., *Constitutional Change in the United Kingdom*, (London: Routledge, 2002).

Giddings, P., *Parliamentary Accountability: A Study of Parliament and Executive Agencies*, (London: Macmillan, 1995).

Henderson, N., *Mandarin*, (London: Weidenfeld & Nicolson, 1994).

Hennessy, P., *Whitehall*, (London: Secker & Warburg, 1989).

House of Commons Public Administration Select Committee Report, *Politics and Administration: Ministers and Civil Servants*, HC 122-1, (London: Stationery Office, 2007).

House of Commons Treasury and Civil Service Select Committee Report, *The Role of the Civil Service*, HC 27 I-III (London: November 1994).

James, S., *British Government: A Reader in Policy Making*, (London: Routledge, 1997).

Lipsey, D., *The Secret Treasury*, (London: Viking, 2000).

Metcalfe, L. and Richards, S., *Improving Public Management*, (London: Sage, 1989).

O'Donnell, G., *The Modern Civil Service*, (London: Guardian Public Services Summit Speech, 2006)

Report of a Committee of Privy Counsellors (Chairman: Lord Butler of Brockwell), *Review of Intelligence on Weapons of Mass Destruction*, (HC 898, (London: Stationery Office, 2004).

Report of the Inquiry into the Export of Defence Equipment and Dual-Use Goods to Iraq and Related Prosecutions, vols 1–5 and index (HC Paper 115, 1996), (London: HMSO, 1996).

Report, House of Lords Select Committee, *Public Service, 1997–98* (HL Paper 55) (London: Stationery Office, 1998).

Report, Performance and Innovation Unit, *Wiring It Up: Whitehall's Management of Cross-Cutting Policies and Services*, (London: Stationery Office, 2000).

White Paper, *Modernising Government*, Cm 4310, (London: Stationery Office, 1999).

White Paper, *The Civil Service: Taking Forward Continuity and Change*, Cmnd 2748 (London: HMSO, 1995).

White Paper, *The Civil Service: Continuity and Change*, Cmnd 2627 (London: HMSO, 1994).

Williams, W., Washington, *Westminster and Whitehall*, (London: Cambridge University Press, 1988).

Websites

A–Z of UK Central Government   http://www.direct.gov.uk

Cabinet Office   http://www.cabinetoffice.gov.uk

The Civil Service   http://www.civil-service.co.uk

Department for Constitutional Affairs   http://www.dca.gov.uk

Treasury   http://www.hmt.gov.uk

Chapter 15

Asher, K., *The Politics of Privatisation*, (London: Macmillan Education, 1987).

Communities in Control, (London: acevo/smf, 2005).

Dynes, M. and Walker, D., *The New British State*, (London: Times Books, 1995).

Flynn, N., *Public Sector Management*, 3rd edn (London: Harvester Wheatsheaf, 1997).

Gay, O. and Macleavy, J., *The Quango Debate*, (London: House of Commons Library Research Paper 05/30, 2005).

House of Commons Public Administration Select Committee, *Government by Appointment: Opening Up the Patronage State*, Fourth Report, 2002–2003, HC 165-I, (London: Stationery Office, 2003).

Institute for Public Policy Research, *Building Better Partnerships*, final report of the Commission on Public Private Partnerships, (London: IPPR, June 2001).

Kay, J., *Privatisation in the UK 1979–1999* (2001), http://www.ukprivatisation.com/.

Littlechild, S., *Regulators, Competition and Transitional Price Controls*, (IEA, 2002).

Marquand, D., *Decline of the Public*, (Cambridge: Polity Press, 2004).

Mather, G., *Making Decisions in Britain*, (London: European Policy Forum, 2000).

Needham, C., *The Reform of Public Services Under New Labour*, (London: Palgrave, 2007).

Norton of Louth, Lord, *Who Regulates the Regulators?*, (Bath: Centre for the Study of Regulated Industries, 2004).

Parker, D., *The UK's Privatisation Experiment: the Passage of Time Permits a Sober Assessment*, CESifo Working Paper 1126, (2004).

Parker, D., 'Editorial: Lessons from Privatisation', *Economic Affairs*, (IEA, 2004).

Pirie, M., *Blueprint for a Revolution*, 2nd edn (London: Adam Smith Institute, 1993).

Pirie, M., *Privatisation – Theory, Practise and Choice*, (London: Wildwood, 1988).

Plummer, J., *The Governance Gap – QUANGOs and Accountability*, (London: Demos, 1994).

Prabhakar, R., *Rethinking Public Services*, (London: Palgrave, 2006).

Prosser, T., *Nationalised Industries and Public Control*, (Oxford: Blackwell, 1986).

Redwood, J., *Popular Capitalism*, (London: Routledge, 1988).

Report of the Agency Policy Review, *Better Government Services – Executive Agencies in the 21st Century*, Office of Public Service Reform, July 2002.

Research Paper, *The Quango Debate*, House of Commons Library, Research Paper 05/30, 11 April 2005, (London: House of Commons, 2005).

Ridley, F. F. and Wilson, D. (eds), *The Quango Debate*, (London: Oxford University Press, 1995).

Skelcher, C., Weir, S. and Wilson, L., *Advance of the Quango State*, (London: Local Government Information Unit, 2000).

Taylor, I., 'New Labour and the Enabling State', *Health & Social Care in the Community*, Vol. 8 (6), 2000, pp. 372–9

Tyrrall, D., 'The UK Railway Privatisation: Failing to Succeed?', *Economic Affairs*, IEA, 2004.

Velijanovsky, C. (ed.), *Regulators and the Market: An Assessment of the Growth of Regulation in the UK*, (London: Institute of Economic Affairs, 1991).

Veljanovsky, C., *Selling the State*, (London: Weidenfeld & Nicolson, 1987).

Weir, S. and Hallfield, W., *Ego Trip – Extra Governmental Organisations in the UK*, (London: Charter 88, 1994).

White Paper , *The Citizen's Charter*, Cmnd 1599 (London: HMSO, July 1991).

Websites

A–Z of UK Central Government   http://www.direct.gov.uk

Adam Smith Institute   http://www/asi.co.uk

Association of Chief Executives of Voluntary Organisations   http://www.acevo.org.uk

Cabinet Office   http://www.cabinetoffice.gov.uk

The Civil Service   http://www.civil-service.co.uk

Department for Constitutional Affairs   http://www.dca.gov.uk

Food Standards Agency   http://www.food.gov.uk

Institute for Public Policy Research   http://www.ippr.co.uk

Office of Communication   http://www.ofcom.org.uk

Office of Fair Trading   http://www.oft.gov.uk

Office of Gas and Electricity Markets   http://www.ofgem.gov.uk

Office of Rail Regulation   http://www.rail-reg.gov.uk

Office of Water Services   http://www.ofwat.gov.uk

Social Market Foundation   http://www.smf.co.uk

Treasury   http://www.hmt.gov.uk

Baldwin, N. D. J. (ed.), *Parliament in the 21st Century*, (London: Politico's, 2005).

The Belfast Agreement, (CM 3883), (London: Stationery Office, 1998).

Bogdanor, V., *Devolution in the United Kingdom*, (Oxford: Oxford University Press, 1999).

Bradbury, J., *Union and Devolution: Territorial Politics in the United Kingdom*, (London: Palgrave, 2007).

Bulmer, S., Burch, M., Carter, C., Hogwood, P. and Scott, A., *British Devolution and European Policy-Making: Transforming Britain into Multi-Level Governance*, (London: Palgrave Macmillan, 2002).

Coulson, A., *Devolving Power: The Case For Regional Government*, (Fabian Tract 537), (London: Fabian Society, January 1990).

Dixon, P., *Northern Ireland: The Politics of War and Peace*, (London: Palgrave, 2007).

Draft Regional Assemblies Bill (Cm 6285) and *Policy Statement*, (code 04 RDG 02392), (London: Stationery Office, 2004).

Elcock. H., *Remarking the Union: Devolution and British Politics in the 1990s*, (London: Frank Cass, 1998).

Forman, F. N., *Constitutional Change in the United Kingdom*, (London: Routledge, 2002).

Hassan, G. (ed.), *A Guide to the Scottish Parliament*, (Edinburgh: Centre for Scottish Public Policy, 1999).

Hazell, R. and Rawlings, R. (eds), *Devolution, Law Making and the Constitution*, (Exeter: Imprint Academic, 2005).

Hazell, R. (ed.), *The State of the Nations 2003: the Third Year of Devolution in the United Kingdom*, (London: Constitution Unit, 2003).

Hazell, R. (ed.), *The State and the Nations: the First Year of Devolution in the United Kingdom*, (London: Constitution Unit, 2000).

House of Lords Select Committee on the Constitution, *Devolution: Inter-Institutional Relations in the United Kingdom*, 2nd report, session 2002–03, HL Paper 28, (London: Stationery Office, 2002).

Memorandum of Understanding and Supplementary Agreements between the United Kingdom Government, Scottish Ministers and the Cabinet of the National Assembly for Wales, Cm 4444, (London: Stationery Office, 1999).

Sandford, M., *The New Governance of the English Regions*, (London: Palgrave, 2005).

Trench, A., *Old Wine in New Bottles? Relations between London and Cardiff after the Government of Wales Act 2006*, (London: Constitution Unit, 2007).

Trench, A. (ed.), *The Dynamics of Devolution: The State of the Nations 2005*, (London: Constitution Unit, 2005).

Trench, A. (ed.), *Has Devolution made a Difference? The State of the Nations 2004*, (London: Constitution Unit, 2004).

Trench, A. (ed.), *The State of the Nations 2001: the Second Year of Devolution in the United Kingdom*, (London: Constitution Unit, 2001).

White Paper, *Better Governance for Wales*, (Cmrd 6582), (London: Stationery Office, 2005).

White Paper, *Your Region, Your Choice: Revitalising the English Regions*, Cm 5511, (London: Stationery Office, 2002).

White Paper, *A Voice for Wales*, (Cm 3718), (London: Stationery Office, 1997).

White Paper, *Scotlands' Parliament*, (Cm 3658), (London: Stationery Office, 1997).

Wintrobe, B., *Realising the Vision: a Parliament with a Purpose. An Audit of the First Year of the Scottish Parliament*, (London: Constitution Unit, 2001).

Websites

Department for Communities & Local Government   http://www.communities.gov.uk
Department for Constitutional Affairs   http://www.dca.gov.uk
Government Offices for the English Regions   http://www.gos.gov.uk
HM Treasury   http://www. hm-treasury.gov.uk
Northern Ireland Assembly   http://www.niassembly.gov.uk
Northern Ireland Executive   http://www.northernireland.gov.uk
Northern Ireland Office   http://www.nio.gov.uk
Scottish Executive   http://www.scottishexecutive.org.uk
Scotland Office   http://www.scotland.gov.uk
Scottish Parliament   http://scottish.parliament.uk
Welsh Assembly   http://www.wales.gov.uk
Welsh Assembly Government   http://www.new.wales.gov.uk
Wales Office   http://www.walesoffice.gov.uk

Chapter 17

Alexander, A., *Local Government in the 1990s*, (Barnstaple: Phillip Charles Media, 1990).

Butcher, H. et al., *Local Government and Thatcherism*, (London: Routledge, 1990).

Butler, D., Adonis, A. and Travers, T., *Failure in the British Government: The Politics of the Poll Tax*, (Oxford: OUP, 1994).

Byrne, T., *Local Government in Britain*, 7th edn (London: Penguin Books, 2000).

Denters, B. and Rose, L. E., *Comparing Local Governance: Trends and Developments*, (London: Palgrave, 2005).

Forman, F. N., *Constitutional Change in the United Kingdom*, (London: Routledge, 2002).

Final Report, Lyons Inquiry into Local Government, (Chairman: Sir Michael Lyons), (London: Stationery office, 2007).

Prabhakar, R., *Rethinking Public Services*, (London: Palgrave, 2006).

Ridley, N., *The Local Right: Enabling not Providing* (Policy Study no. 92), (London: Centre for Policy Studies, 1988).

Sandford, M. and Maer, L., *Old Habits Die Hard? Overview and Scrutiny in English Local Authorities*, (London: Constitution Unit, 2004).

Stevens, A., *Local Government*, (London: Politico's, 2003).

Stewart, J., *Modernising British Local Government: An Assessment of Labour's Reform Programme*, (London: Palgrave, 2003).

Stoker, G., *Transforming Local Governance: From Thatcherism to New Labour*, (London: Palgrave, 2003).

Stoker, G. and Wilson, D., (eds), *British Local Government into the 21st Century*, (London: Palgrave, 2004).

White Paper, *Strong and Prosperous Communities – the Local Government White Paper*, (Cm 6939-I and 6939-II), (London: Stationery Office, 2006).

White Paper, *Local Leadership, Local Choice*, (Cm 4298), (London: Stationery Office, 1999).

White Paper, *A Mayor and Assembly for London*, (Cm 3897), (London: Stationery Office, 1998).

White Paper, *Modern Local Government: In Touch with the People*, (Cm 4014), (London: Stationery Office, 1998).

Wilson, D. and Game, C., *Local Government in the United Kingdom*, 4th edn (London: Palgrave, 2006).

Young, K. and Rao, N., *Coming to Terms with Change? The Local Government Councillor in 1993*, (London: Joseph Rowntree Foundation, 1994).

Websites

Convention of Scottish Local Authorities (CoSLA)   http://www.cosla.gov.uk

Department for Communities & Local Government   http://www.communities.gov.uk

Department for Constitutional Affairs   http://www.dca.gov.uk

Greater London Authority   http://www.london.gov.uk/gla

HM Treasury   http://www. hm-treasury.gov.uk

LGA European & International Unit   http://www.international.lga.gov.uk

LGA Net Gateway   http://www.lganet.gov.uk

Local Government Association (LGA)   http://www.lga.gov.uk

Local Government   http://www.local.gov.uk

London Assembly   http://www.london.gov.uk/assembly

London Mayor   http://www.london.gov.uk/mayor

The New Local Government Network (NLGN)   http://www.nlgn.org.uk

Northern Ireland Local Government Association (NILGA)   http://www.nilga.org

Welsh Local Government Association (WLGA)   http://www.wlga.gov.uk

Chapter 18

Auld, Lord Justice, *Review of the Criminal Courts*, (London: HMSO, 2001).

Clothier, C. M., *Ombudsman: Jurisdiction, Powers and Practise*, (Manchester: Manchester Statistical Society, 1981).

Croft, J., *Whitehall and the Human Rights Act 1998*, (London: Constitution Unit, 2000).

Davies, M., Croall, H. and Tyrer, J., *Criminal Justice: An Introduction to the Criminal Justice System in England and Wales*, (London: Longman, 2005).

Department for Constitutional Affairs, *A Guide to the Human Rights Act 1998: Third Edition*, DCA 51/06 (London: Department for Constitutional Affairs, 2006).

de Smith, S. and Brazier, R., *Constitutional and Administrative Law*, 6th edn (London: Penguin, 1990).

Dickson, B., *The Legal System of Northern Ireland*, 2nd edn (1989).

Griffith, J. A. G., *The Politics of the Judiciary*, 5th edn (London: Fontana, 1997).

Horne, A. and Berman, G., *Judicial Review: A Short Guide to Claims in the Administrative Court*, House of Commons Library Research Paper 06/44, 28 September 2006.

Human Rights Act 1998, ISBN 0 10 544298 4 (London: Stationery Office, 1998).

Jackson, R. M., et al., *The Machinery of Justice in England*, 8th edn (London: CUP, 1989).

Leggatt, Sir Andrew, *Review of Administrative Tribunals*, (London: HMSO, 2001).

Le Sueur, A. and Cornes, R., *What Do The Top Courts Do?*, (London: Constitution Unit, 2000).

Morris, T., *Crime and Criminal Justice since 1945*, (Oxford: Blackwell, 1989).

Newburn, T., *Crime and Criminal Justice Policy*, 2nd edn (London: Longman, 2003).

Rights Brought Home: The Human Rights Bill, (CM 3782), (London: Stationery Office, 1997).

Stainsby, P., *Tribunal Practise and Procedure*, (London: Law Society, 1988).

Treasury Solicitor's Department in conjunction with the Cabinet Office (MPO) Training Division, *The Judge Over Your Shoulder: Judicial Review of Administrative Decisions*, (1987).

Wade, H. W. R., *Administrative Law*, 6th edn (Oxford: Clarendon Press, 1988).

Walker D. M., *The Scottish Legal System*, 6th edn (1992).

White Paper, *Justice for All*, (Cm 5563), (London: Stationery Office, 2002).

White Paper, *Criminal Justice: The Way Ahead*, (London: Stationery Office, 2001).

White Paper, *Modernising Justice*, (Cm 4155), (London: HMSO, 1998).

Websites

Department for Constitutional Affairs http://www.dca.gov.uk

Home Office http://www.homeoffice.gov.uk

Justice http://www.justice.org.uk

Law Officer's Department http://www.attorneygeneral.gov.uk

Liberty www.liberty-human-rights.org.uk

Lord Chancellor's Department http://www.lcd.gov.uk

Minisrty of Justice http://www.justice.gov.uk

Chapter 19

Bradley, R., *Public Expectations and Perceptions of Policing*, Police Research Series Paper 96 (London: Home Office Research, Development and Statistics Directorate, 1998).

Clothier, C. M., *Ombudsman: Jurisdiction, Powers and Practise* (Manchester: Manchester Statistical Society, 1981).

Crick, B., *Essays on Citizenship*, (London: Continuum, 2000).

Faulks, K., *Citizenship in Modern Britain*, (Edinburgh: Edinburgh University Press, 1998).

Forman, F. N., *Constitutional Change in the United Kingdom*, (London: Routledge, 2002).

Heater, D., *Citizenship in Britain: A History*, (Edinburgh: Edinburgh University Press, 2006).

Ingleton, R., *Arming the British Police*, (London: Frank Cass, 1997).

National Policing Plan 2005–08, *Safer, Stronger Communities*, (Home Office, 2004).

Pattie, C., Seyd, P. and Whiteley, P., *Citizenship in Britain: Values, Participation and Democracy*, (Cambridge: Cambridge University Press, 2004).

Reiner, R., *The Politics of the Police*, 2nd edn (London: Harvester Wheatsheaf, 1992).

Rights Brought Home: The Human Rights Bill, (CM 3782), (London: Stationery Office, 1997).

Robertson, G., *Street's Freedom: The Individual and the Law*, 6th edn (London: Penguin, 1989).

Report of the Inquiry into Police Responsibilities and Rewards, (Vols I and II), CM2280-T/CM 2280-II, 30 June 1993.

Stoker, G., *Why Politics Matters: Making Democracy Work*, (London: Palgrave, 2006).

White Paper, *Building Communities, Beating Crime – A Better Police Service for the 21st century*, (Cm 6360), (London: Stationery office, 2004).

White Paper, *Respect and Responsibility – Taking a Stand Against Anti-Social Behaviour*, (Cm 5778), (London: Stationery office, 2003).

White Paper, *Policing a New Century: a Blueprint for Reform*, (Cm 5326), (London: Stationery Office, 2001).

White Paper, *Police Reform*, (Cmnd 2281), (London: HMSO, 1993).

Wright, A., *Citizens and Subjects*, (London: Routledge, 1994).

Websites

Amnesty International   http://www.amnesty.org.uk

Department for Constitutional Affairs   http://www.dca.gov.uk

Home Office   http://www.homeoffice.gov.uk

Justice   http://www.justice.org.uk

Law Officer's Department   http://www.attorneygeneral.gov.uk

Liberty   www.liberty-human-rights.org.uk

Lord Chancellor's Department   http://www.lcd.gov.uk

Ministry of Justice   http://www.justice.gov.uk

Chapter 20

Barber, M., *Instruction to Deliver – Tony Blair, Public Services and Achieving Targets*, (London: Politico's, 2007).

Bulmer, S., Burch, M., Carter, C., Hogwood, P. and Scott, A., *British Devolution and European Policy-Making: Transforming Britain into Multi-Level Governance*, (London: Palgrave Macmillan, 2002).

Butler, D. et al., *Failure in British Government*, (London: Oxford University Press, 1994).

Dickie, J., *The New Mandarins: How British Foreign Policy Works*, (London: I. B. Tauris, 2004).

Dorey, P., *Policy Making in Britain*, (London: Sage, 2005).

Dynes, M. and Walker, D., *The Times Guide to the New British State: The Government Machine in the 1990s*, (London, Times Books, 1995).

Fawcett, P. and Gay, O., *The Centre of Government – No 10, the Cabinet Office and HM Treasury*, House of Commons Library Research Paper 05/92, 21 December 2005.

Forster, A. and Blair, A., *The Making of Britain's European Foreign Policy*, (London: Longman, 2002).

Healey, D., *The Time of my Life*, (London: Michael Joseph, 1989).

Hennessy, P., *Whitehall*, (London: Secker & Warburg, 1989).

Hill, M., *The Public Policy Process*, 4th edn (London: Longman, 2004).

James, S., *British Government: A Reader in Policy Making*, (London: Routledge, 1997).

Kaufman, G., *How To Be A Minister*, (London: Faber & Faber, 1997).

Lawson, N., *The View from Number 11*, (London: Bantam Press, 1992).

Meyer, C., *DC Confidential*, (London: Weidenfeld & Nicolson, 2005).

Runciman, W. G. (ed.), *Hutton and Butler: Lifting the Lid on the Workings of Power*, (Oxford: Oxford University Press, 2004).

Sanders, D., *Losing an Empire, Finding a Role – British Foreign Policy since 1945* (London: Macmillan, 1990).

Savage, S. P. et al., *Public Policy in Britain* (London: Macmillan, 1994).

Thompson, B. and Ridley, F. F. (eds), *Under The Scott-Light* (Oxford: Oxford University Press, 1997).

Van Zwanenberg, P. and Millstone, E., *BSE: Risk, Science, and Governance*, (Oxford: Oxford University Press, 2005).

Websites

A-Z of UK Central Government   http://www.direct.gov.uk
Cabinet Office   http://www.cabinetoffice.gov.uk
The Civil Service   http://www.civil-service.co.uk
Department for Constitutional Affairs   http://www.dca.gov.uk
No 10 Downing Street   http:/www.number–10.gov.uk
Treasury   http://www.hmt.gov.uk

Chapter 21

A Constitutional Treaty for the EU, Cm 5934, (London: Stationery Office, 2003).

Bache, I. and Jordan, A. (eds), *The Europeanization of British Politics*, (London: Palgrave, 2006).

Barnes, I. and Barnes, P. M., *The Enlarged European Union*, (London: Longman, 1995).

Bulmer, S., Burch, M., Carter, C., Hogwood, P. and Scott, A., *British Devolution and European Policy-Making: Transforming Britain into Multi-Level Governance*, (London: Palgrave Macmillan, 2002).

Business, Britain and Europe: The First 25 Years, (London: Anderson Consulting, 1998).

Cameron, F., *The Foreign and Security Policy of the European Union: Past, Present and Future*, (Sheffield: Sheffield Academic Press, 1999).

Cowles, M. G. and Dinan, D. (eds), *Developments in the European Union 2*, (London: Palgrave, 2004).

Dinan, D., *Ever Closer Union*, (London: Palgrave, 2005).

Forman, F. N., *Constitutional Change in the United Kingdom*, (London: Routledge, 2002).

Forster, A. and Blair, A., *The Making of Britain's European Foreign Policy*, (London: Longman, 2002).

George, S., *An Awkward Partner, Britain in the European Community*, 2nd edn (Oxford: Oxford University Press, 1994).

Hartley, T. C., *The Foundations of European Community Law*, 2nd edn (Oxford: Clarendon Press, 1988).

Hix, S., *The Political System of the European Union*, 2nd edn (London: Palgrave, 2005).

Holland, M., *European Integration – from Community to Union*, (London: Pinter, 1993).

Leonard, D., *Guide to the European Union*, 5th edn (London: The Economist/Profile Books, 1997).

Lost in Translation? Responding to the Challenges of European Law, Report by the Comptroller and Auditor General, HC 26 Session 2005–06, (London: National Audit Office, 26 May 2005).

May, A., *Britain and Europe since 1945*, (London: Longman, 1999).

Mc Cormick, J., *Understanding the European Union*, 3rd edn (London: Palgrave, 2005).

Miller, V., *The Extension of Qualified Majority Voting from the Treaty of Rome to the European Constitution*, House of Commons Library Research Paper 04/54, 7 July 2004.

Monar, J. and Wessels, W. (eds), *The European Union after the Treaty of Amsterdam*, (London: Continuum, 2001).

Neville Brown, L. and Jacobs, F. G., *The Court of Justice of the European Communities*, 3rd edn (London: Sweet & Maxwell, 1989).

Nugent, N., *The Government and Politics of the European Union*, 6th edn (London: Palgrave, 2006).

Pinder, J., *European Community, the Building of a Union*, 2nd edn (London: Oxford University Press, 1995).

Prospects for the EU in 2005, Cm 6450, (London: Stationery Office, 2005).

Reid, T. R., *The United States of Europe*, (New York: Penguin, 2004).

Siedentop, L., *Democracy in Europe*, (London: Allen Lane, 2000).

The Draft Constitutional Treaty for the European Union, Cm 5897, (London: Stationery Office, 2003).

The European Constitution in Perspective, (Stroud: British Management Data Foundation, 2004).

The Maastricht Treaty in Perspective: Consolidated Treaty on European Union, 3rd edn (Stroud: British Management Data Foundation, 1996).

The Treaty of Amsterdam in Perspective: Consolidated Treaty on European Union, (Stroud: British Management Data Foundation, 1998).

The Treaty of Nice in Perspective: Consolidated Treaty on European Union, (Stroud: British Management Data Foundation, 2001).

Treaty on European Union, Maastricht, 7 February 1992, Cmnd 1934 (London: HMSO, 1992).

Urwin, D. W., *The Community of Europe*, 2nd edn (London: Longman, 1997).

Young, H., *This Blessed Plot: Britain and Europe from Churchill to Blair*, (London: Macmillan, 1998).

Websites

European Central Bank   http://www.eub.int/
European Commission   http://www.cec.cu/
European Commission's Representative in the UK   http://www.cec.org.uk
European Council   http://www.ue.eu.int
European Court of Justice   http://www.curia.eu.int
European Movement   http://www.euromove.org.uk
European Parliament   http://www.europarl@eu.int
European Union   http://www.europa.eu.int
Eurosceptics   http://www.euro.sceptic.org/
Foreign and Commonwealth Office   http://www.flo.gov.uk
NATO   http://www.nato.int

Barker, R., *Political Legitimacy and the State*, (Oxford: Clarendon Press, 1980).

Barnett, A., *This Time: Our Constitutional Revolution*, (London: Vintage, 1997).

Beetham, D. et al., *Democracy under Blair: A Democratic Audit of the United Kingdom*, (London: Politico's, 2002).

Beetham, D., *The Legitimation of Power*, (London: Macmillan, 1991).

Blair, T., *The Third Way: New Politics for the New Century*, (London: Fabian Society, 1998).

Blundell, J. and Gosschalk, B., *Beyond Left and Right: The New Politics of Britain* (London: Institute of Economic Affairs, 1997).

Brittan, S., *The Role and Limits of Government*, (London: Temple Smith, 1983).

Dahrendorf, R., *Life Chances*, (London: Weidenfeld & Nicolson, 1979).

Foster, C., *British Government in Crisis*, (Oxford: Hart Publishing, 2005).

Giddens, A., 'After the Left's Paralysis', *New Statesman*, 1 May 1998, pp. 18–21.

Gould, P., *The Unfinished Revolution: How the Modernisers Saved the Labour Party*, (London: Little, Brown, 1998).

Hailsham, Q., *The Dilemma of Democracy* (London: Collins, 1978).

Hirsch, F., *Social Limits to Growth* (London: Routledge & Kegan Paul, 1977).

Jenkins, S., *Thatcher & Sons*, (London: Allen Lane, 2006).

Leadbeater, C., *Civic Spirit: The Big Idea For A New Political Era*, (London: Demos, 1997).

Luard, E., *The Globalisation of Politics*, (London: Macmillan, 1990).

Marquand, D., *Decline of the Public*, (Cambridge: Polity, 2004).

Marquand, D., *The Unprincipled Society*, (London: Fontana Press, 1988).

Marr, A., *Ruling Britannia: The Failure and Future of British Democracy*, (London: Michael Joseph, 1995).

Miliband, R., *Capitalist Democracy in Britain*, (London: Oxford University Press, 1984).

Schumpeter, J. A., *Capitalism, Socialism and Democracy*, 3rd edn (New York: Harper & Row, 1962).

Wright, T., *Who Wins Dares: New Labour – New Politics*, (London: Fabian Society, 1997).

Websites

Demos   http://www.demos.co.uk

Institute of Economic Affairs   http://www.iea.org.uk

Institute for Public Policy Research   http://www. ippr.org.uk

index